# Broadcast Writing

## PRINCIPLES

## AND PRACTICE

## McGraw-Hill Series in Mass Communication

**Consulting Editor**
**Barry L. Sherman**

Anderson: *Communication Research: Issues and Methods*

Carroll and Davis: *Electronic Media Programming: Strategies and Decision Making*

Dominick: *The Dynamics of Mass Communication*

Dominick, Sherman, and Copeland: *Broadcasting/Cable and Beyond: An Introduction to Modern Electronic Media*

Dordick: *Understanding Modern Telecommunications*

Hickman: *Television Directing*

Holsinger and Dilts: *Media Law*

Richardson: *Corporate and Organizational Video*

Sherman: *Telecommunications Management: The Broadcast and Cable Industries*

Walters: *Broadcast Writing: Principles and Practice*

Whetmore: *American Electric: Introduction to Telecommunications and Electronic Media*

Wilson: *Mass Media/Mass Culture: An Introduction*

Wurtzel and Acker: *Television Production*

# SECOND EDITION

# Broadcast Writing

## PRINCIPLES

## AND PRACTICE

Roger L. Walters

*California State University, Sacramento*

*McGraw-Hill, Inc.*
New York   St. Louis   San Francisco   Auckland   Bogotá   Caracas
Lisbon   London   Madrid   Mexico City   Milan   Montreal
New Delhi   San Juan   Singapore   Sydney   Tokyo   Toronto

# BROADCAST WRITING: PRINCIPLES AND PRACTICE

 This book is printed on recycled, acid-free paper containing a minimum of 50% total recycled fiber with 10% postconsumer de-inked fiber.

1 2 3 4 5 6 7 8 9 0   DOH   DOH   9 0 9 8 7 6 5 4 3

ISBN 0-07-068031-0

This book was set in Cheltenham by CRWaldman Graphic Communications.
The editors were Hilary Jackson, Fran Marino, and Tom Holton;
the designer was Robin Hoffmann;
the production supervisor was Kathryn Porzio.
The photo editor was Elyse Rieder.
R. R. Donnelley & Sons Company was printer and binder.

**Photo credits**

*Figure 8.1:* Left, Ed Carlin/Picture Cube; right, Horst Schafer/Peter Arnold.

*Figure 8.2:* Top left, Joel Gordon; top right, John Maher/Stock, Boston; below, Elizabeth Hamlin/Stock, Boston.

*Figure 8.3:* Left, Joel Gordon; right, McGraw-Hill photo by The Photo Works.

*Figures 8.4, 8.5, 8.6:* McGraw-Hill photos by The Photo Works.

*Figure 8.7:* Above, Alan Carey/Image Works; below, Frank Siteman/Picture Cube.

*Figures 8.8, 8.9, 8.15:* McGraw-Hill photos by The Photo Works.

*Photos on pp. 378, 379, 386:* Elyse Rieder.

**Library of Congress Cataloging-in-Publication Data**

Walters, Roger L.
    Broadcast writing: principles and practice / Roger L. Walters.—2nd ed.
        p.   cm.—(McGraw-Hill series in mass communication)
    Includes bibliographical references and index.
    ISBN 0-07-068031-0
    1. Broadcasting—Authorship.      I. Title.      II. Series.
PN1990.9.A88W3          1994
808′.066791—dc20                                              93-32501

**R**oger L. Walters is Professor Emeritus of Broadcasting at California State University, Sacramento, where he has been a member of the faculty since 1960. From 1960 to 1973 he was director of the university's instructional television center, responsible for producing a wide range of telecourses and mediated instructional modules for both resident students and community viewers. From 1973 to 1992 he was a full-time member of the Communication Studies Department. He originated and taught courses in broadcast writing, programming, management and mass communications, and managed the student internship program.

Prior to coming to CSU, Sacramento, Mr. Walters taught at Idaho State College. He has BA and MA degrees from Stanford University, and has done additional graduate work at Ohio State University and the University of Southern California.

One of Mr. Walters' long-standing interests has been public radio. He helped establish two stations. The first, licensed to CSU, Sacramento, was begun as a student laboratory; it is now KXPR, with a classical music and news format. The second, KZYX, Philo, California, went on the air in 1989. It serves Mendocino County, California, with a broad range of community and national programming. Mr. Walters was president of the KZYX board from 1983 to 1989.

Mr. Walters is a member of the Broadcast Education Association, the International Radio and Television Society and the Radio-Television News Directors Association. He is currently producing a series of audio cassette travel programs and is writing a book on careers in mass communications.

# CONTENTS

# P R E F A C E

At the beginning of the preface for the first edition of this text I stated my belief that writing is a craft that can be learned, but not taught, at least in a traditional sense. I said that texts and instructors can guide, point out pitfalls, suggest things to consider, and establish criteria for evaluation, but learning to write would come only through practice, whether in course assignments or on the job. I find it tremendously satisfying to see that this approach was so accepted by both students and instructors that there can be this second edition.

I further suggested that this text, along with comments and critiques from instructors, supervisors and colleagues, could help you in several ways. First, it sets forth criteria for good writing that you can use to evaluate your own work. It gives examples of structure, style and content from actual broadcasts. Second, it relates the writer's role both to the sponsors of broadcasts and to the interests of the users of broadcasts, the audiences. Third, and perhaps most important, the text describes principles and practices that are followed in the industry and provides reasons why those principles are important and those practices are followed.

As I embarked on the task of revision for this second edition I was faced with answering two important questions. First, have the principles of broadcast writing presented in the first edition stood the test of time? In recent years the broadcast/cable industry has gone through some substantial and rapid changes. Would my assertions of fundamental principles stand up against these changing practices? I think that most have withstood the test and I'm confident that the ideas presented here can be used successfully both by today's students and those who will follow.

Second, what examples would need to be replaced or modified to keep the book in sync with the times? It's a very risky proposition to include examples based on current TV series because individual series quickly disappear and even recently aired programs may never have been seen by today's students. Similarly, references to industry practices should be current, but sometimes old practices come around again, and sometimes current activities turn out to be only a passing fad. Many of the examples used in the first edition have been replaced, and at various places I have risked some speculation or vision about the future, but my vision can be as flawed as the next person's. There is a great deal of disagreement, even among professionals, as to where the industry is headed and what kinds of programs will be successful in the future.

In the spring of 1993 I attended two major conventions and accompanying trade shows that each year redefine the broadcast industry—those of the National Association of Television Program Executives (NATPE) and of the National Association of Broadcasters (NAB). This year the operative buzzword at both conventions was *multi.*

At NATPE the word was *multichannel.* We heard over and over again in conference sessions and in casual conversation how the industry was preparing for the coming 500-channel TV environment. In television's early years viewers had a choice of perhaps three or up to seven or eight over-the-air channels. Now many homes have (with cable) more than fifty or sixty choices. The next step, using digital compression and other technological changes, will expand the number of available channels into the hundreds.

At NAB the *multi* word was *multimedia,* in reference to the merging of traditional audio-video media with computer hardware and software. We saw demonstrations of video animation, for example, done entirely within a computer, not using a traditional camera at all.

I left those meetings wondering, first, to what extent these new directions for media would actually come to pass. In the past not every new means of program delivery or form of technology displayed at the conventions has come into widespread use. These two new directions, I decided, were already well established, although it will be some time before their implications reach throughout the industry.

Second, I wondered what the multichannel and multimedia environment would mean for my readers—the future writers, directors and producers of radio, TV and cable programs. Certainly expansion in the number of channels will have a major impact on programmers and executives at large media corporations. The amount of programming necessary to fill the new channels probably will mean programming on demand and increased repetition of old programs. However, it likely will also expand the opportunities for writers, as new programs will also be needed to fill the channels.

## FEATURES OF THE TEXT

Several features set this text apart from others in the field. The first and most obvious is its emphasis on principles. Throughout I have argued that the characteristics of the broadcast media as delivery systems and of audience behavior, taken together, establish broad principles writers must understand and apply if they are to be successful.

I believe these principles are not tied to any one program type or style of copy. That is, there is not one set of principles for dramatic writing and a different set for documentaries, or for news, or for talk programs. Certain principles may be more important, or more obvious perhaps, in writing certain types of copy, and each program type does have its own strengths and weaknesses, but most of the principles of good writing can be applied to most program types.

Writers also must understand how their jobs are shaped by the business of broadcasting, by the demands of sponsors and the requirements of programmers and managers. I will digress frequently from the specifics of writing to place that task in the larger contexts of programming and advertising.

Similarly, writers need a clear understanding of how programs and announcements are perceived and used by audiences. Broadcast communication is incomplete and ineffective if it doesn't reach, satisfy and even persuade audiences. Writers must know how to use the tools that accomplish those results.

Although this is not a production text, and it does not attempt to provide detailed instruction on the use of the facilities of broadcasting such as microphones, cameras, recorders, I have tried to show how the writer's task is affected by the production process. For example, the form in which copy is written is affected by whether a program is aired live or prerecorded.

Another feature presented even more strongly in this edition than in the first is its emphasis on the preparation for writing. One must understand the purpose behind the writing and carefully conduct whatever type of research and analysis is needed to understand that purpose in order to be a successful writer.

Exercises are provided at the end of each chapter. If you are using this book as a text, a selection of these may be assigned by your instructor. If not, I urge you to attempt some of them anyway. Again, practice is the only way you can learn to write.

Some of these exercises are intended to guide you through the process of research and decision making that takes place before actual script writing can begin. In the industry, professionals often make these judgments without conscious thought, but for beginners these exercises will help "talk you through" to the point where writing begins. Other exercises mirror, as much as possible, the actual tasks writers face within the industry. They are broadly described, to allow opportunity for you to seek creative solutions.

A list of key terms and concepts appears at the beginning of each chapter. These lists provide a good self-test. If you can define and explain the significance of these items, you will know that you have a good understanding of that chapter's contents.

A "Further Reading" section is included at the end of each chapter. Bibliographies are a traditional part of most texts, but I have approached these suggested readings in a nontraditional manner. If, as is my assumption, you aspire to a career in broadcasting that includes writing, you will need to build a substantial personal library, for both inspiration and reference. The inspiration will be needed when you are faced with a writing task to which you just can't at the moment find a good approach. You can turn to other writers and see how they approached similar situations. References, of course, are for checking—on style, grammar, layout, and so on.

Use these lists as an aid in building your library. Collecting all the texts listed would be both difficult, as some are out of print, and expensive, but you are urged to consider these suggestions as you start a collection for your personal library.

Additional exercises, suggested classroom activities, a bibliography of teaching resources, examination questions, model course outlines, and some suggestions on evaluating student work are contained in the *Instructor's Manual*.

## PLAN OF THE BOOK

The book is organized into five parts and seventeen chapters. This plan does not differ substantially from that of the first edition, although some topics have been regrouped in the revised chapters.

Part 1 consists of two introductory chapters. Chapter 1, "Creative Preparation," presents to the student some concerns about broadcast writing as a career. It also provides an overview of the writer's place within the industry, particularly as part of the creative team that originates the programs and announcements that make up broadcasting's content. This chapter also introduces the importance of preparation, of understanding clearly what the task is before beginning to write—a theme that will be revisited throughout the text.

Chapter 2, "Broadcast Communication," reviews the communication process as it applies to the broadcast media and draws some important distinctions between print media, spoken communication and broadcasting as their messages are received by audiences.

Part 2—"Principles"—contains six chapters. Chapter 3 is a discussion of aural style, an in-depth examination of the principles of writing that is to be heard by audiences through the broadcast media, in contrast to messages that are delivered via print or in person. Chapter 4 considers the relationship between writing and production. Chapter 5 covers matters related to script mechanics—script layout and other topics such as punctuation and using abbreviations.

The organizing of programs and their content to attract and hold audience attention is the topic of Chapter 6, "Program Structure." The final two chapters in this part examine in detail the ways in which writers manage the two senses—hearing and sight—in scripts and in program production. Chapter 7, "Handling Sound," reviews the uses of sound effects, music, and voice when used for its sound value. Chapter 8, "Handling Visuals," presents basic principles of visual grammar.

Part 3 discusses industry practices in two chapters. In Chapter 9, "Sponsors and Their Purposes: Persuasion," we consider, for example, who pays for broadcasting, and what these sponsors expect in return for their investment. Then we look at the process from a different perspective; Chapter 10 reviews audiences and their expectations, including the importance of satisfying audience gratifications.

Six of the major forms of radio and television programs are each presented in Part 4. Each chapter provides a broad, practical introduction to the form—sufficient for beginning writers to get started. Following the traditional categories of persuasion, information and entertainment, the first chapter, Chapter 11, "Commercials and Other Announcements" covers the major forms of persuasive content. Three chapters are devoted to different forms of broadcast material that are primarily informational: Chapter 12 reviews the basics of writing news; talk, interview and discussion programs are discussed in Chapter 13; and documentary programs are considered in Chapter 14. Another type of content that is usually informational in nature, but often not broadcast, is covered in Chapter 15, "Corporate and Instructional Programs."

Dramatic programs are discussed in Chapter 16. Although drama is not the only form of entertainment programming, it is probably the most important form and one that requires substantial skill and practice from a writer.

The final part, Part 5, consists of Chapter 17, "Legal and Ethical Considerations for the Broadcast Writer." While ethical issues are mentioned briefly in several of the earlier chapters, this summary provides a more substantial basis for discussion and review of these topics.

The arrangement of these parts permits this text to be used in a variety of sequences. If you are using this book as a text for an organized course, your instructor may choose to introduce both the principles of good writing and the forms of writing at any one of a number of entry points.

If you are not reading this book as an assigned text, you are of course free to approach it as you choose. I suggest you skim through the chapters of Parts 1 and 2 first, so you have some sense of what is included there—how the various principles relate to each other and to the practical tasks of preparing copy. Then, as you attempt to write for any particular form, you can refer back to those principles you find most important to your task.

## NEW TO THE SECOND EDITION

- The discussion of career opportunities and description of the nature of the broadcast writing experience has been moved from the final chapter to the first one. These is also an expanded discussion of the preparation for writing and research in the opening chapter.

- The impact of new production and distribution technology on writers has been revised in Chapter 4.

- In Chapter 6, new programs have been used as examples of how program structure may be analyzed.

- A new section on "Writing to Pictures" has been added to Chapter 8.

- Chapter 12, "News," has been extensively revised including a new section on "The Building Blocks of TV News."

- Several new forms of corporate writing are discussed and new examples shown in Chapter 15.

- An expanded section on writing dialogue for dramatic programs has been included in Chapter 16.

- The final chapter has been revised to include a new section on legal questions that affect writers, including discussions of the First Amendment, obscenity and indecency, libel, commercial speech and copyright. The section on ethical concerns has also been expanded to include questions relating to ethics and news, ethics and advertising, and ethics and entertainment programs.

## ACKNOWLEDGMENTS

My own career as broadcaster and educator has been influenced by three professors with whom I was fortunate to study. All three were outstanding teachers, who inspired the desire to learn in their students. They are Stanley Donner, with whom I studied at Stanford University, Harrison Summers at Ohio State University, and Kenneth Harwood, then at the University of Southern California.

Dr. Summers' ability to outline complex topics is directly reflected in several of these chapters. The organization of Chapter 6 on program structure and the concepts of sponsorship in Chapter 9 and audience gratifications in Chapter 10 are based on materials originally presented in his courses, although newer information has been added. I am also indebted to Professor Jay Blumler for his pioneering work on audience gratifications.

Some of the ideas in Chapter 3, "Aural Style," and Chapter 7, "Handling Sound," were originally presented by Albert Crews in his book *Professional Radio Writing*. Although that book dates from the 1940s and has long been out of print, much of what Crews said about writing for the ear is still relevant, and I've attempted to show its continued value to broadcast writing. Kent Lacin, a former colleague and creative visual producer, provided much of the organization of Chapter 8, "Handling Visuals."

A number of professional broadcasters have contributed their own work or collected examples from colleagues. Their contributions are greatly appreciated. The writers of individual scripts are credited wherever those scripts appear in the text, but others contributed who are not individually credited. They include Russ Heimrich, KXPR, and Kent Hunt, KXOA, both from Sacramento, who supplied radio news copy. Television news, documentary, commentary and editorials came from Steve Haskins and Joyce Mitchell, KOVR; Cal Bolwinkle, KTXL-40; Dick Cable, KXTV; and from KCRA-TV, all Sacramento stations.

The sample of TV dramatic copy from "Silk Stalkings" was written by Stephen J. Cannell and supplied by Stuart Tenzer.

Commercial scripts and storyboards were contributed by Jonathan Jacobs, Hal Riney and Partners, San Francisco; Gerard Wilson, Take 2 Productions, Glen Ellen, CA; Brian Burch, Mering and Associates, Sacramento; Walt Shaw, KRAK, Sacramento; Carolyn Zelle, Borders, Perrin and Norrander, Portland, OR; and Ann Joyce, Foote, Cone and Belding, San Francisco.

Examples of corporate and instructional scripts were supplied by Mark Krigbaum, Eclipse Productions, Walnut Creek, CA; John King, King Accelerated Schools, San Diego; and Elizabeth Fuller, 3M Corporation, St. Paul.

The manuscript for the second edition was reviewed by colleagues from several universities. Their comments were very helpful in identifying areas for revision. I gratefully acknowledge the assistance of Mark J. Banks, Slippery Rock University; Ajit Daniel, Winona State University; Terry Kauffman, North Carolina State University; George Mastroianni, California State University at Fullerton; David Ponting, Syracuse University; John Rosenbaum, Ithaca College; Richard Settle, University of North Carolina at Chapel Hill; and Max Utsler, University of Kansas. Joyce Mitchell, KOVR, Sacramento and California State University at Sacramento and Edward Fink, California State University at Fullerton also contributed.

The staff at McGraw-Hill has been wonderfully supportive. Roth Wilkofsky encouraged me to write the first edition while he was with Random House. After the merger of the Random House and McGraw-Hill College Divisions, Roth continued his strong support, as have Hilary Jackson and Fran Marino.

## LOOKING AHEAD

The multichannel environment and the multimedia marriage of video and audio equipment with computers are already well underway, and although the new technology will not immediately displace the traditional forms of production and program distribution, you will need to understand the capabilities of and learn to use these new tools. Individually you may not soon feel the effects of these changes, but some time during your career as a broadcast writer these and other changes as yet unforeseen will affect your craft.

*Roger L. Walters*

# Getting Ready to Write

**W**riting, in any style and for any medium, if it is to be successful, must strike a balance between creativity and effective communication. On one side of the balance there is the writer's desire to be original. On the other is the requirement that to communicate, a message must say something to someone. Lots of original material is produced that never has an opportunity to communicate; its message never reaches an audience. It may be that the author cannot find an appropriate medium or adequate financial support for the creative effort. Many book manuscripts are never published. Similarly, many TV program ideas are never produced, and others that are produced as pilots never make it as series. The demands and restrictions of the communications industries select and shape creative ideas for presentation.

The central purpose of this text is to help you learn to be a creative writer, but within the confines imposed by the radio and television media and the industry that supports those media.

These first two chapters are introductory. They establish the writer's position and role in broadcast communication. In Chapter 1 we consider the process from a personal perspective. How does a writer work? What is the writer's position as part of the creative team that produces programs and announcements? Copywriting is an essential part, but only a part, of a broader creative effort, and so we look at the tasks that writers perform and the expectations placed upon them within the industry. And we establish the importance of the preparation and research that take place before actual writing begins. That will be a recurring theme throughout this text.

In Chapter 2 we take a more theoretical approach. If you have had other courses in communication or journalism that used communication models, the basis of this chapter should be familiar. But of course the division into these two chapters is an arbitrary one. The process which begins with ideas and ends with completed productions is a single process. There are many individual steps along the way, and those steps are different for different types of programs and different styles of production. But the goal is always the same—successful communication of ideas to audiences. You can be successful at that task as a writer only if you understand how your contributions fit within the larger process of communicating to listeners and viewers.

# Creative Preparation

The creation of a successful broadcast program or commercial announcement is a substantial task, usually involving a number of people and a series of preparatory stages. Although these stages are not discrete—the process is continuous—for purposes of our discussion we can divide the task into four steps: research, writing, production and postproduction. For some types of programs these four steps are sequential; for other types they are collapsed so not all four are recognizable; and for others some aspects of all four, and especially writing and production, progress simultaneously.

The first two steps, research and writing, are often combined and called *preproduction*. Although we won't use that term often, throughout this text we do consider research and writing as two inseparable tasks. We will frequently emphasize the importance of sufficient and appropriate research in preparation for writing. We will not stress production and postproduction, but we will consider these parts of the process briefly in Chapter 4, as they do affect the form and complexity of the written materials used to create various types of programs.

When you finish this chapter, you will be able to:

- recognize the general nature of most broadcast writing activity as being (1) part-time, combined with other professional tasks, (2) team-oriented, and (3) filled with various types of pressure,

- understand the close relationship between broadcast writing and other production activities,

- understand the importance of preproduction research, of gathering accurate, complete data related to the task before beginning to write,

- follow a systematic, sequential process for incorporating research into writing and production,

- recognize "point of view" in a story or program script, and select "points of view" or "concepts" for your own scripts, and

- recognize and use these important terms and concepts:

account executive                                                    preproduction

concept formation: point of view, treatment        pressure

determining objectives                                              research

identification of needs


## THE DIVERSITY OF BROADCAST WRITING

Let's speculate on the reasons why you are interested in learning how to write for broadcast. Perhaps you want a career as a writer in the electronic media—as a writer of documentaries for public television, a writer-reporter for a major market TV station, a writer of daytime serial dramas, or a writer-salesperson for a radio station in your hometown.

Or you want to be a documentary *producer* or a news *anchor*, or to produce video programs for a major national corporation. Or your school requires a writing course as part of your media major, or, at least, an instructor at your university suggested you take a writing course as part of your preparation.

Or perhaps you have already finished a degree in another field but have always wanted to "try your hand" at writing TV dramas, or you work in public service and have been asked to prepare a media campaign for your agency.

We could never list all the possible reasons why you find yourself with this text in your hands, but those are a few including perhaps the most common. From just these very few examples—TV news reporter or anchor, corporate video producer, radio writer/advertising salesperson, public service agency producer, documentary writer or producer, writer for soap operas or sitcoms—and from your own observations, you know the broadcast industry encompasses a tremendous range of activities and occupations.

Given that range, it would be impossible to generalize accurately about the working situations that exist in all stations, agencies, production companies and networks. But there are some aspects of the job that are nearly universally true, and they are worth your consideration:

1. Writing is most often a part-time activity, which may be combined with any number of other tasks to make up the total job responsibilities of the individual.

2. The writer usually works as part of a team and is most often an employee. To be successful, you will have to adjust your own creativity to the goals of others and recognize the authority of supervisors.

3. The job comes with pressure built in—pressure to be creative and orig-

inal, but even more important, pressure to be on time. There is also the pressure, shared by all individuals in the industry, to be successful—to make a profit, if that's what is called for. And there will be pressure on you as an individual from those newer, younger talents who think they can do a better job than you and who are anxious to have the chance to prove it.

## Writing as a Part-Time Occupation

Most broadcast writers, especially those just starting their careers, spend part of their time writing and part of their time doing something else. It's quite likely, in fact, that the "something else" will be the primary reason why you have been hired and the writing comes along only as a secondary responsibility.

There are many combinations of writing and "something else" jobs, and the proportion of time spent in each different activity will vary considerably even within these combinations. Here are just a few examples.

### The Salesperson-Writer

In smaller markets, smaller stations and in radio the person who sells advertising time will also write much of the commercial copy for those clients that have been persuaded to buy time on the station. The small businesses that advertise in these markets and on these stations often can't afford advertising agencies with specialist writers. They depend on the station's personnel to prepare their ads for them, and the station provides this service as a necessary part of the process of attracting advertisers.

Another type of salesperson-writer can now be found working in independent instructional media production companies. This person will have been hired to seek out contracts from business, government and educational agencies for the production of mediated instructional and public information presentations. As part of the process of obtaining a contract, he or she may be called upon to prepare and present a script treatment to the prospective client. Then, after a contract has been signed, a final script will be completed, either by the salesperson or by another writer.

### The Account Executive-Writer

In advertising agencies the title "account executive" is used to describe the individual who is in charge of a client's account. In large agencies the account executive's role is largely conceptual and "creative" in a broad sense; specialists will actually write the copy. In a small agency, one person not only will be the account executive for several different accounts but probably will write the commercials for each of those clients.

### The Researcher-Writer

Almost all broadcast writing requires some form of research, whether the script be for a dramatic program, a news story, a commercial or whatever. Some types of programs require that an extensive, organized research effort be undertaken prior to writing the script. Research is especially important in developing instructional, informative and documentary programs, where the subject matter is likely to be complex and difficult to present understandably to an audience. In those situations, the writer must take the time to be sure that he or she understands the concepts correctly and that they are placed in the proper order, with appropriate emphasis. Both library research and interviews with experts may be needed before the script can be written.

Formal research may also be necessary before a writer can prepare the questions to be asked in an interview or panel discussion program. The persons assigned this task will discuss the topic with the expert guests who will be appearing on the program and then organize their material into a series of questions that can be asked by the program's host. Student interns and beginning employees are frequently asked to do this form of research.

### The Reporter-Writer

Most radio and TV reporters write their own copy, even those who work for large television stations and at the networks. They do so for two reasons. First, the reporter who has been on a story will be more familiar with the content and therefore is in the best position to be able to organize the story to present that content clearly and accurately to the audience. Second, reporters like to write the copy so that it fits their own personal style of delivery.

Larger stations do employ writing specialists to assist reporters, to rewrite copy coming in from outside sources, and to provide the script for news anchors. Although some anchors do write their own copy, most often the anchor's portion of a newscast will be prepared by an assistant in the news department.

### The Producer-Writer

Whether or not these roles are combined is largely a function of the size, scale, and budget of the production. In radio, and in corporate audio/visual production, producer's and writer's roles are frequently combined. The individual will function first as a producer, developing the concept of the program from the initial ideas of the client. Then he or she writes the script through however many drafts are needed. Finally, as producer again, he or she supervises actual production from the script.

In larger-scale productions the producer will maintain overall responsibility for the production, but will be able to hire (or have on staff) writing specialists.

### *The Publicist-Writer*

The job of a station's promotion department is that of "selling" the station itself, and promoting its programs and personalities. In order to accomplish that task, the station will use both its own airtime and cross-media promotion—that is, advertising its programs on other stations (TV on radio, and vice versa) and in newspapers. Staff members in the promotion department usually write these promotional ads as part of their jobs.

### *The Instructor-Writer*

This combination of roles is found in the preparation of corporate and other instructional materials. Frequently these are low-budget programs, and there are no funds to hire a separate writer or researcher. So the instructor, who is the content expert, is also given the task of preparing the script. Some instructors are able to translate their understanding of content into very good scripts; others never quite master the peculiarities of writing for broadcast, and their programs suffer as a result.

In these examples we've tried to suggest only a few of the situations and combinations in which broadcast writers work. This list could be almost endless, for every situation is unique in some respect. Note, however, this obvious lesson for the person who is starting out and who wants a job as a writer in broadcasting: Become adept at some other skills as well. Learn to be a reporter, or learn public relations and promotion, or sales, because probably you will need at least one of these other skills in addition to your ability to write in order to get that first job.

We do not mean to suggest that all broadcast writing jobs are part-time; there are full-time positions that are exclusively or at least largely devoted to writing. These are more likely to be found in larger markets, at larger stations, at larger agencies handling bigger accounts, and at the radio and television networks, where there is greater opportunity for specialization. These openings are not entry-level positions, but are filled by writers who have learned their craft in combination jobs like those described above.

## The Writer as Part of a Team

With few exceptions the creation of broadcast programs is a group effort. The writer works as part of a team. Of course, as noted in the previous section, in many situations one person may merely take off his or her hat as, say, salesperson, and put on another hat—that of writer. But only in very small operations does one individual have responsibility for all the creative effort.

The writer's place in the creative team is usually somewhere in the middle of the process. At the beginning are situations like these:

- A salesperson for a local radio or TV station will return from a visit to a client with the idea for a new commercial campaign; then the writer will turn that idea into a producible commercial.

- The assignment editor for the news department of a local TV station will select a story and give that story as an assignment to a reporter-writer to research, write and report for the evening news.

- A writer will develop the plot for a sitcom episode, but that plot must be based on existing characters and adhere to given locations and on-going situations.

After the writer has completed the script, it is unlikely (unless the writer is also the producer) that he or she will follow the script through to completed production, especially at larger stations and agencies. Creative control over a TV commercial shot on location will be in the hands of a director. The writer's script or storyboard will be followed in general, but decisions on details and the resolution of complications in the production will be made by the director. Similarly, the sequences in a drama will be modified first by the director and actors, then again in the editing process. Writers are sometimes frustrated because they see their creative efforts modified in ways they had not intended.

Recognize, too, that the broadcast writer is usually an employee or representative. He or she may work for a station or an advertising agency or a corporate media production department, or in any of the other situations we have described. Writers who are both employees and parts of a creative team must learn to subject their individuality to the client's goals, to the realities of the commercial marketplace and to the control of supervisors.

There are some exceptions. Opportunities exist for freelance writers, especially in two areas. Some drama programs accept freelance submissions, and a substantial number of corporate/instructional presentations are written by freelancers, who work under contract with the corporate clients or the independent production houses that produce for those clients. But just like employees, successful freelancers must understand the restrictions of the series for which they write and the requirements of clients.

At several places in the chapters that follow, we will take time out from the direct discussion of writing principles to consider relationships between the business of broadcasting—sales, programming, management—and the creative process. We will talk about advertising as the vehicle through which the costs of production are paid and profits generated. We will also consider sponsors' purposes, target audiences and audience gratifications. We believe that a writer must understand how programming and audience decisions establish the parameters within which a script is written.

## Pressure

Recognize at the outset that in broadcasting there are deadlines—daily, even hourly, in some cases. Broadcasting runs on time. Live broadcasts go on the air at the time they are scheduled, to the second. Prerecorded programs must be of exact length. Usually there will be a fixed schedule of days or hours set aside for production, and a preestablished budget. Extra time for rehearsal, production, or editing means extra money, a commodity sponsors are reluctant to part with.

The implication for the writer is that the script must be ready on time. At some point there no longer is any more time for additional research or for another rewrite to polish the dialogue or narration. When airtime or the scheduled production time arrives, the script must be there. Without the writer's contribution—a script—other people cannot do their jobs. The news announcer won't be able to read the news, or the entire cast and crew assembled to record a dramatic program will be idled.

Another aspect of pressure is the constant demand to be original. Not only must the script be written to meet a deadline, it is expected to be a good script—to follow the principles of good broadcast writing and to be different, distinctive, even unique. For commercial copy, it's also a good thing for the script to be successful—that is, to accomplish the advertiser's purpose of selling the product!

Not all scripts meet this criterion of originality. A lot of broadcast writing is ordinary, banal, crass. The industry is regularly criticized for turning out mediocre writing and programming. But when the tremendous quantity of material that has to be written every hour and every day is considered, the lack of consistent creativity may at least be understood. Even the best writers can't write truly creative, distinctive scripts every time. But knowledge of that fact doesn't reduce the pressure from producers, sponsors and audiences, who expect the writer to create a masterpiece for every broadcast.

Yet another form of pressure is the general pressure felt throughout the industry to be successful—to draw audiences, to sell advertising, to make a profit. Writers participate in this pressure because it is their copy that is expected to accomplish the goals that mean success.

Finally, there are more people seeking careers in broadcasting than there are jobs in the industry. There are new, young talents seeking the job you just won not so long ago. If you falter, if you grow tired or lackadaisical, someone will be there to push you out. Broadcasting is competitive at all levels. Some would say, even, that it is cutthroat.

# RESEARCH

We've already warned you that we will consider not only writing but the preparation for writing. In nearly every chapter there is some discussion of questions that must be answered before writing and production can hope to proceed to a successful presentation. Getting answers to those questions involves research. We use that term in a very broad sense, to identify a range of activities that differ depending on the specific circumstances surrounding the announcement or program being prepared. In the chapters of Part 4 that describe writing techniques for various genres, we consider the approaches to research that are unique to each of those kinds of programs. Here we deal with some concerns that affect preparation tasks in general.

In the introduction to his book *Designing the Effective Message*, Donald Wood describes communication as a cycle consisting of seven processes (Figure 1.1). The cycle begins with identification of a communication need, but by arranging the seven steps in circular fashion, Wood points out that once the cycle has been completed, with feedback and evaluation of a completed production, the process is ready to begin again with identification of a new need. Wood describes the first steps in this cycle—those that lead up to writing—this way:

**Figure 1.1.** Communication processes. (From Donald N. Wood, *Designing the Effective Message: Critical Thinking and Communication*, p. 9. Copyright 1989 by Kendall/Hunt Publishing Company. Used with permission.)

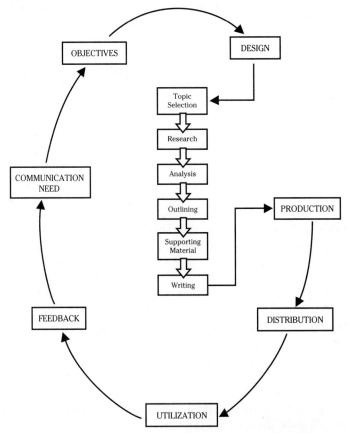

*Identification of Needs.* The first step in any communication act is to understand the reason for the communication. This involves looking at the situation both from the viewpoint of the sender (What societal or corporate needs do you . . . recognize that you want to address?) and the receiver's perspective (What needs does the receiver want answered by a media message—entertainment, information?)

*Determining Objectives.* Second, you must formulate objectives which you hope your communication will achieve. . . . Often [this statement] will be simply a reworking of your needs analysis—a specification of precise objectives based upon your analysis of the need or problem.

*Design and Writing.* We have divided this process into six . . . steps: selection of a precise topic, research, topic analysis, outlining, supporting material, and writing.[1]

The detailed examination of those six topics constitutes the bulk of Wood's text. We call your attention to this book for two reasons. First, its detailed examination of these topics can be extremely helpful, especially if you've had little previous experience with such tasks as topic selection or outlining. These are steps of preparation and analysis which are common to many types of communication activities, and you may have encountered them in other courses and other contexts. But if you have not, then we suggest you use Wood's text to help with those matters.

Second, we want to reinforce the statements we made at the beginning of this text and of this section: Writing does not take place all by itself but within a certain set of circumstances. Before you begin to write, there are always decisions to be made and data to be gathered. Throughout this text we approach prewriting decisions using different terminology from that used by Wood, and the words we use to describe the process will change from one program type to another, as the writers and producers use different terms to describe their tasks. But our goals are the same—to be sure you have collected the right data and analyzed it appropriately and thereby given yourself the best chance of writing successful copy.

## Data Gathering

Gathering data, as we conceive the task, includes the preliminary steps of determining needs and objectives, as well as other forms of research. Naturally, the amount and complexity of the information you need to gather depend in part on the kind of program that you are working on, and as promised, we will look at the specific forms of research needed for most program types in the chapters of Part 4. Gathering data also depends on your own background. If you, as the writer, are already familiar with the needs of the client for whom you are writing a commercial, or if you have been following an ongoing news story, then obviously it will take you less time and effort to prepare than if the assignment is totally new to you. Manager of broadcast stations who interview applicants for new positions regularly ask questions about current events and issues. Applicants who can demonstrate that they keep up with events and issues in the world and in their community are more likely to be chosen for the positions.

For that reason, and because it cuts the amount of time necessary to do research, your first assignment in preparing to be a broadcast writer is to become more familiar with the world around you and with the industry in which you plan to work. At least, read a daily newspaper and a weekly news-magazine, read a major broadcast industry trade magazine, and watch and listen to a variety of radio and television news programs and formats, including public broadcasting.

Another form of broad preparation is that which you are currently undertaking: your college education in general and courses in communication, journalism, writing, advertising or marketing in particular, depending on your more specific interests.

### Library Research

More specifically, data gathering for particular assignments will likely involve both library research and interviewing. Assume for the moment that you are a television reporter-writer. You have been assigned to prepare a series of investigative reports on a topic currently important in your community. Library research enables you to delve into the background of that story. Although library research often is slower than interviewing, it can be more thorough. It also avoids the danger of an interview giving you the opinion of only one person, which can be very dangerous indeed if the topic of your assignment is controversial. You avoid that problem, of course, by the breadth of your library research and by conducting several different interviews. Also, you need library research in order to prepare properly for interviews. You can't know if you are asking the correct or best questions of a source until you have made yourself generally familiar with the topic.

**Figure 1.2.** Reprinted with special permission of North America Syndicate.

The use of the term "library," however, does not necessarily mean going to a major public or university library, as you are used to doing for academic assignments. Many stations maintain their own files of previous stories, which may be used for background on your assignment and perhaps even worked into the story. Newspaper morgues may be useful. They contain far more stories, and in more detail, than station files. Many forms of data—financial, historical, biographical, geographical—can now be brought up "on-line" using computer-based services. In a professional setting, you should quickly discover what on-line services are available to you and learn how to access them.

Our example above involves a news story and news writer-reporter, but other forms of content may also require research using library or print sources.

### Interviewing

A second major means of gathering information is through interviews. Interviewing individuals who are experts in a field, or who have particular knowledge of an event, is often the most efficient use of your time, provided you can reach the appropriate persons.

Before continuing, it may be helpful to note that interviews are used for three purposes in broadcasting. First, as we have just described, they're efficient ways to gather information. Second, if you are interviewing to get information for a news story, then you have the opportunity to collect actualities that can be part of the story. Use the interviewee's actual voice in the story to add variety and credibility to the story. Third, interviews (and "conversations," which are nearly the same but don't adhere as strictly to a question-answer format) are a program form. In Chapter 13, we consider interviews and other talk-type programs in detail, including how best to prepare questions for talk-show guests.

Often a pre-interview will be done with a person who is later going to be a guest on an interview or discussion program. This conversation is used to assist in preparing a sequence of questions to be used later on the program itself. A writer who is preparing a commercial may be able to get a better sense of the product to be advertised by talking directly with the client. These interviews are nothing more than commonsense ways to gather information needed before you begin to write a piece.

While library research and interviewing are the most important forms of data gathering, other forms of research may be required on occasion. In our chapter on corporate/instructional programs, we describe how a program was developed to teach safety to a group of warehouse employees. The format for the program, using the structure of a game show, was decided upon only after research showed that the target audience was very attracted to broadcast TV game shows.

## Concept Formation

Careful and thoughtful attention to the prewriting questions will bring you to the actual task of writing copy with a pretty good idea of how to proceed, but there is one last decision you will need to make before writing most types of copy. And that is to select some organizing approach for the copy. Writers who deal with factual programs—news, talk shows, and so forth—must take the data gathered from their research and determine a perspective which best assembles those data for presentation to an audience. Practitioners in the industry use a number of different terms, some slang, to describe this task. News producers, for example, will ask what is the *point of view*, the *peg*, the *hook*, the *slant*, the *angle*, to be used for a story? We use *point of view* to describe this preparation step, as that term is the most commonly understood, at least for factual programs.

This step is somewhat different for writers of fiction. They are able to create their scripts totally from original ideas, rather than having to organize existing material. They use different descriptors; this beginning step is called the *concept*. It describes the idea from which the plot is developed, including the major characters, and what happens to them during the course of the drama. Concept is followed by a more detailed *treatment*. We consider these more fully in Chapter 16. Documentary producers tend to use this terminology—concept and treatment—even though documentary is not a fictional form.

What, really, are we talking about? Here are just a few examples. For news writers, how are the facts and sequence of a story best organized to make the best sense to an audience? Consider these situations. (Other examples of how points of view are developed are found in several of the chapters of Part 4.)

- You are employed by a TV station in an area that has just been devastated by a hurricane. For the next several days, obviously, almost all the local news stories will relate to that major event. Two levels of decision making are involved. First, what stories to cover from among the hundreds of possibilities—problems of providing emergency supplies, the role of the Red Cross, dealing with insurance companies, locating lost relatives, and on and on. Second, for each story, what organizing scheme—point of view—to take. The lost relative story might focus on one family trying to locate one person, the role of some agency that is assisting, or some other perspective or combination.

- Last night the city council accepted a draft report from the planning department, proposing major rezoning of previously agricultural land north of the city center. You've got the story for today's evening news. One approach might be just to review the major conclusions of the report and summarize any comments by council members. But more useful and interesting points of view can be developed. Your point of view will be dictated, in part, by the amount of airtime you are given for the story and by the amount of time you have to prepare. One might be able to look at the implications of this particular decision on community development. Does it open the door for new housing, or industrial development, or something else? Or what are the implications of the loss of agricultural land and possible future losses as well? Or look at the story from the position of various groups that may stand to benefit (or lose) from the decision. Or what is the impact on city services—water, sewer, etc.—the infrastructure of the community? Or tax implications? Or if this particular decision doesn't have an obvious impact on the community, perhaps it's still a good opportunity to review the process of zoning and rezoning, how various community groups are or are not involved in that process, etc.

- It's early April, and you're doing a series tied to income taxes. This particular story in the series is to be on individual retirement accounts (IRAs). The story might be covered as a straight informative piece, listing the various types of investment plans that can be used in an IRA account, the rates of interest currently offered and the risks involved. Interviews with bankers, brokers and other experts would make up most of the story. But a more interesting story might result if it were approached from the point of view of the consumer. Choose two or three widely different "clients"—a young, single career woman, a couple nearing retirement, a manual laborer who works by the job. Ask several different experts to plan IRAs for these people, then focus in the story on the similarities or differences in the proposals made by each expert for each different situation.

A similar exercise in determining a point of view is undertaken in selecting the topic and guest or guests for an interview, discussion or talk show. If the program includes interviews, what kind of interviews?

- Arrangements have been made for a well-known motion picture actress to appear on your program for an interview. This is not just any movie star; this celebrity has spoken out strongly on issues of world hunger and taken a leading role in distributing food in areas of famine. At least three quite different interviews are possible. One would emphasize the star's activities on behalf of world hunger; another would feature the star's film career, possibly promoting a just released film; the third would focus on the star's personal life. Each interview has a quite different point of view. (In Chapter 10 we consider the different gratifications involved and consequently the different audiences that are attracted when point-of-view decisions such as these are made.)

Similar decisions regarding point of view also face the writers and producers of discussion programs. What types of topics will be selected? What kinds of guests? Will there be studio audiences to ask questions? Will calls be accepted from viewers or listeners?

Finally, for the purposes of this discussion, what a point of view is not. It is not a statement of opinion, as we often use the phrase. It is not an editorial statement, nor is it a commentary upon an issue. It does not take a position on a topic. Opinion statements, editorials and commentaries have a place in broadcasting. We'll discuss them in later chapters. But here we are trying to emphasize only that a news story, discussion topic, documentary or nearly any program must be organized in some logical, reasonable fashion that its audience can follow. Note that in organizing and writing a story, you can cover a wide range of information and combine it a number of different ways, but you should be able to explain the entire story with one succinct statement of point of view. It's the broadcast equivalent of preparing topic statements for the speeches you delivered in your introductory public speaking course!

## CONCLUSION

You can have a successful and rewarding career writing for the electronic media: (1) successful in that you can see scripts that you have written turned into programs and announcements that appear on the air and have some impact on audiences and (2) rewarding in that you can get paid to write those scripts. You probably won't begin with immediate success, however. It takes time and practice to get to positions where your writing will be accepted by your supervisors or clients. We believe that the principles of good writing presented in this book will help you with that preparation.

Creativity counts for a great deal, but it alone will not take you to the top. Hard work and an understanding of how writing fits within the overall operation of the industry are also important. For that reason, three brief parts of this book deal with the writer's place within the industry. This part, including this chapter and the next, sets the stage. In Part 3, Chapters 9 and 10 look at the economic basis of broadcasting and how writers must accommodate the requirements of those who pay for broadcasting. Chapter 17, the final chapter, reviews some legal and ethical concerns.

Good luck helps as well. We wish you an abundant supply!

**Exercise**

1. The idea of point of view can be examined by comparing the approaches taken to a breaking news story by competing news departments, either local or network. (This exercise may best be handled as a group project or class assignment, and as part of the broader comparison of newscasts listed as an exercise in Chapter 12.) Record competing newscasts (that is, broadcasts airing at the same or approximately same time), and where

the same story is covered by different stations or networks contrast the approaches used. Some of the difference may be the result of one station's having allocated more resources to cover the story, but often the difference can be recognized as simply a different point of view. Consider whether one point of view does a better job of presenting the story, or whether there is one point of view that you prefer, and if so, why?

**Note**

1. Donald N. Wood, *Designing the Effective Message: Critical Thinking and Communication* (Dubuque, IA: Kendall-Hunt, 1989), p. 5. Reprinted by permission.

**Further Reading**

In the preface we made a statement about additional sources and readings that applies to this section of each chapter. We assume you are reading this book because you have an interest in broadcast writing as a career, or at least part of a career. To be successful in that endeavor, you need to have in your personal library both reference books and specialized texts. The references in these sections at the end of each chapter will help you build such a library, and the comments may help you select from among the books suggested.

The text used in this chapter to review the creative process is a good place to start:

Wood, Donald N. *Designing the Effective Message: Critical Thinking and Communication.* Dubuque, IA: Kendall-Hunt, 1989.

Along the same lines, our friend and colleague at CSU, Sacramento, Patrick Marsh, wrote this more detailed exposition of the design of communications messages for various media:

Marsh, Patrick O. *Messages That Work: A Guide to Communications Design.* Englewood Cliffs, NJ: Educational Technology, 1983.

You will need ready access to general reference works—a good dictionary, a thesaurus and an almanac as a minimum. You should also consider having available a specialized communications dictionary, such as

Diamant, Lincoln. *The Broadcast Communications Dictionary*, 3rd edition. Westport, CT: Greenwood, 1989.

Ensign, Lynne N., and Robyn E. Knapton. *The Complete Dictionary of Television and Film.* Lanham, MD: Madison Books UPA, 1985.

McDonald, James R. *The Broadcaster's Dictionary.* Denver: Wind River, 1987.

Weiner, Richard. *Webster's New World Dictionary of Media and Communications.* New York: Prentice-Hall, 1990.

Further useful compilations of suggestions to prepare you to be more effective in writing for any medium may be found in

Blakey, Ellen Sue. *Learning to Edit: A Workbook for Writers and Editors.* Dubuque, IA: Eddie Bowers, 1988.

Stott, Bill. *Write to the Point.* New York: Columbia University Press, 1991.

Yates, Edward D. *The Writing Craft*, 2nd ed. Raleigh, NC: Contemporary, 1985.

Consider also these titles that deal with gathering and organizing information:

Kessler, Lauren, and Duncan McDonald. *The Search: Information Gathering for the Mass Media.* Belmont, CA: Wadsworth, 1992.

Ward, Jean, and Kathleen A. Hansen. *Search Strategies in Mass Communication.* White Plains, NY: Longman, 1987.

In addition to these references, other titles that add to the topics discussed in this chapter are those on style and language suggested in Chapter 3, and those on interviewing in Chapter 13.

# CHAPTER 2

# Broadcast Communication

**W**riting for the electronic media is unlike other forms of writing you have done. The audiences for radio, TV and cable process the messages that they receive via these media quite differently from the way they receive and process messages from personal communication or from printed sources. Those differences in the reception of messages require writers to employ a different style.

When you finish this chapter, you will be able to:

- identify key components of the communication process,

- understand how those components uniquely relate to the electronic media—radio, television and cable,

- compare and contrast the process of communication when that communication is by print, by conversation or by electronic media,

- understand how those differences affect writing for the electronic media, and

- recognize and use these key terms and concepts:

| | |
|---|---|
| broadcasting | message |
| channel | origination/source |
| DBS | purpose |
| effect | ratings |
| feedback: direct and delayed | receiver/audience |

## COMPONENTS OF THE COMMUNICATION PROCESS

Researchers have developed various models to explain the process of communication. Among the commonly accepted components of many such models are these seven: (1) the *origination*, or source, of the communication,

(2) the communication itself, or *message*, (3) the *channel* through which the message is communicated, (4) the *receiver*, or audience, for the message, (5) the *purpose* of the message, (6) the *effect* of the message on its receivers, and (7) what mechanism, if any, is available for *feedback*—communication from the receivers back to the source.

You may be generally familiar with these terms and concepts from other courses or texts. Here we consider the special meaning that each takes on in broadcasting, with particular attention to its importance for writers and writing. We also consider the relationships that exist between a message (content) and its audience in three common situations: print, a public speech and broadcast. By contrasting these three, we can see how broadcasting's unique characteristics demand a special style of writing in order for messages to be effective.

## Origination

In most of the forms of communication with which we are familiar, messages are originated by individuals. Certainly that is true of our most common form of communication, interpersonal conversation. In contrast, broadcast messages are invariably team efforts. Further in contrast, two very different activities are involved as co-equal parts of broadcast origination. The first may be characterized as *creative origination*. It includes the work of writers, directors, producers, and all the other creative people who plan and produce the programs and announcements that make up the schedules of radio and television stations and cable systems.

The second part of origination involves the people and agencies who pay for the materials that are aired. There would be no outlet for any creative effort if there were no one willing to pay, in some form, for the costs of production and distribution. Within this category of originator, we can include advertising agencies and their clients, and the managers and programmers of stations, networks, and cable systems, among others. Later we will introduce the term *sponsorship* as the appropriate label to distinguish between this aspect of broadcast origination and the creative side.

## Message

The bulk of this text is devoted to the discussion of both the content and form of messages as they are developed by writers and others on the creative team, and because of that fact, we need say little more about them at this point. Note that for some programs a writer has full creative freedom—to take an idea and develop it into a plot, with characters, locations, scenes, and so on. In other situations a writer will not be doing original, creative work but will be rewriting material that originally appeared in some other form. For example, the content of a news program may be supplied to a station by a news service or information on an advertiser's campaign may be provided by the client or the station's salesperson. In those situations the writer's job will be to reorganize the content and rewrite it into an appropriate package—a program script or an announcement.

## Channel

Traditionally we think of radio and television as the channels of electronic communication. In recent years, however, these two have been both supplemented and challenged by several additional systems that deliver programs to audiences. Most important among these additional methods of delivery is cable. But the significance of, for example, home VCRs and the potential of direct satellite-to-home channels should not be overlooked.

VCRs make it possible for individuals to record programs to play back at more convenient times. With a VCR, you can select programs aired any time during the day or night, and view them when you want. You can also fast-forward through the commercials, a practice that very much disturbs advertisers. VCRs are also used extensively to distribute feature motion pictures and original programming directly to audiences, bypassing TV stations completely.

Direct satellite-to-home distribution (known as DBS, for direct broadcast satellite) is as yet only experimental, but it too bypasses traditional TV stations. (We are not considering here those who have satellite dishes and pick up directly from the satellite those programs intended to be redistributed by stations or cable systems.) If DBS programming does become widespread, it will not need traditional networks or stations to reach audiences. Those outlets then may have to reconsider what programs they can provide to remain in competition for audiences.

In its legal definition the term *broadcasting* is not accurate when used to describe all these delivery systems. Broadcasting is properly defined to include only over-the-air transmission of signals intended for general public use. Delivery of programming to homes via cable is therefore not truly broadcasting. We'll continue, however, to use the term broadcasting even though we intend to include cable and other delivery systems as parts of this discussion, because major portions of the industry still use broadcasting as an all-inclusive term. We'll also use *electronic media*, a term which is often used interchangeably with broadcasting but which at least anticipates cable, satellite, microwave, and fiber optic delivery systems.

As a writer, you should recognize that writing for cable and the other newer media differs somewhat from writing for traditional broadcast radio and television. One difference that has become very apparent in recent years, especially with the tremendous proliferation of cable channels, is that formerly large, diverse audiences are being divided into smaller, more narrowly defined groups. Often you will be expected to target both program scripts and advertising copy to these specialized audiences.

Note, too, that in broadcasting the concepts of origination, message and channel tend to overlap. A broadcast station, for example, operates a transmitter which sends its programs through the air to its audience. That transmission represents its use of a communication channel. The station will also be the originator of much of the program content which appears on the channel. And the station will be identified in the minds of listeners or viewers primarily by the content of the messages or programs it presents.

Your understanding of broadcasting will be improved by keeping clear in your mind the distinction between stations, networks, and other agencies as originators, and many of the same organizations when they serve only as channels to distribute messages originated by others.

## Receivers

In broadcasting the general communications term *receivers* may be translated to mean *audiences*. Although, as we have just noted, the absolute size of the audiences for individual programs declines as the number of choices increases, still the largest audiences are those for prime-time programs distributed by the major TV networks. And drawing large audiences is still the most important determiner of success in the business. Later, especially in Chapter 10, we discuss in detail a number of concepts related to audience size and to the composition and behavior of audiences, including audience targeting. Successful programs and ads are carefully targeted to specific audiences, and we will frequently emphasize how important it is that writers are clear on that concept.

## Purpose

Purpose is directly tied to origination. It is the originator's purpose with which we are concerned. Throughout this book, we will emphasize that the writer's job is performed in relation to goals and purposes set by other members of the origination teams—producers, managers, advertisers, corporate sponsors and others. In order to be a successful writer, and we will define success as the writing of copy that accomplishes the purpose intended by the originator, you must be able to identify clearly who the originators are for each piece of copy written and then understand precisely what they want to accomplish.

From time to time we will also refer to three fundamental purposes of communication. Long ago Aristotle postulated that all communication could be categorized as having either persuasion, information or entertainment as its purpose. We won't contradict Aristotle, but in Chapter 9 we advance the proposition that although information and entertainment are indeed used to attract and hold the attention of audiences, the overriding purpose behind all broadcast content is persuasion in some form.

Point of view, a concept that we introduced in Chapter 1 and will revisit several times in Part 4, is also related to this idea of purpose. A news story might be presented from any of several possible points of view or an interview with a celebrity conducted with any of several possible purposes, and we chose the examples in Chapter 1 to emphasize that alternative points of view or concepts can exist in almost any creative effort. When an approach is chosen, it must be one that will further the process of communicating; it must inform, entertain or persuade; and it must further the originator's purpose. Its effectiveness depends on the impact that the program or announcement has upon its audience.

## Effect

Effect and purpose are closely related, particularly as we apply the communication model to commercial broadcasting. The commercial system would quickly collapse if there were no effect on audiences after exposure to messages—if, for example, no products were sold as a result of advertising.

We will look at this part of the process from a slightly different perspective, however. Rather than examining the effects broadcast media have on audiences, we will look at the reasons why audiences choose to be exposed to programs—that is, what gratifications they get from their media experiences. We believe this approach, which is unique in a writing text, is much more useful for the writer who will be charged with the task of attracting and holding the attention of audiences with his or her scripts.

## Feedback

For the most part, once a message has been produced and broadcast, the only choice left to the audience is that of tuning in and listening, or tuning out—take it or leave it. The familiar radio and television channels provide no opportunity for immediate feedback from the receivers to the originators of messages, and therefore no opportunity to modify that communication while it is in progress.

There are some exceptions. Call-in programs are now quite common on radio, and some television talk programs (*Oprah* and *Donahue*, among others) use this technique as well. These programs encourage telephone callers to talk with a host, possibly also with a guest expert, and even react with a studio audience. Other types of interactive programming have been tried. Some early experiments with two-way cable systems that permitted audience members to respond to questions were unsuccessful. More recently, interactive games have gained a small following and home shopping channels have been very successful. Other forms are now appearing; nevertheless, opportunities for audience members to have an immediate influence on the content of programs remain exceptions.

Delayed feedback, on the other hand, is a powerful force in the selection and content of almost all programming. Delayed feedback takes the form of *ratings*—the estimates, based on samples of TV viewers or radio listeners, of how many people were watching or listening to particular programs. Television programming at the network level and in major local markets is measured by automatic meters that provide overnight results to stations, networks and advertisers. In smaller TV markets diary measurements are taken several times a year. Radio audience measurements are taken either by phone interviews or diaries and are conducted on an almost continuous basis except in the smallest markets.

Programs that do not deliver an adequate share of viewers or listeners (in the view of programmers or advertisers) will be removed from the air to be replaced by others which, it is hoped, will do a better job of attracting audiences. While broadcasters and critics alike deplore the "tyranny" of the ratings, no better system has been devised for determining the preferences of audiences or of managing the economy of broadcasting.

## CONTRASTS: PRINT, SPEECH, BROADCAST

Let's contrast some of these components of communication as they apply to three common situations: to an individual (receiver) reading a newspaper or other printed medium, to a public speech delivered by an orator to an audience in an auditorium and to a broadcast program.

### Print Messages

The actual materials prepared for presentation through print are sequences of symbols we have come to recognize as letters, words, sentences and paragraphs. These symbols are seen by the eyes and then given meaning in the brain of the reader. In order for the reader to interpret the symbols, he or she must know how to read. It is also necessary to know the particular language—the symbol code—in which the message is written, to know the meanings of the individual words, and to understand the significance of the sequence in which they are placed.

Once the printed communication has been prepared, its content and its style are fixed and cannot be changed, either by the writer/source or by the recipient/audience.

But while the content of the printed message has been frozen by its author, all other aspects of the reader's interaction with that message are under the reader's control. (We ignore here some rare occasions when readers must read under time restrictions, as in examinations.) The speed with which the material is read, the order in which various sections are read, the length of time spent reading and the amount of material read before stopping are all controlled by the reader. If that person wishes to reread a sentence, paragraph or chapter which is not clear, or which he or she simply enjoys reading again, he or she may do so. If certain words are not familiar, the reader may stop and look them up in a dictionary. When the reader loses interests or finds something more important to do, he or she may stop and start again when it is convenient to do so.

This ability of the recipient of the message to control its reception and processing is an important difference between print and broadcast communication.

## Oral Messages

The largest share of oral communication takes place in informal situations in which there is considerable dialogue among the two to several people present at the time. We will concentrate on the characteristics of the more formal public speech, where there are clearly defined roles for both speaker and audience. In this situation, the speaker usually has a prepared presentation. The content and sequence are already worked out. The talk may even have been written out word for word and rehearsed for timing, inflection and style. But until the actual moment of presentation, until the actual voicing of the words, changes can still be made—either on purpose, if the speaker sees reason to modify the text, or inadvertently, by forgetting or stumbling over words.

One reason why the speaker may want to make last-minute changes is that he or she senses something in the audience—boredom, restlessness, hostility, applause—which prompts a change in content or sequence. Even though there may be no verbal communication from the audience to the speaker, there is feedback in nonverbal form. Having the audience and the source present at the same place and time permits the audience to become a modifier of the message.

The spoken message is received by the members of the audience through their ears, then relayed to their brains for interpretation, a quite different process from that used in reading. In addition, the message is delivered using a specific style, with pacing, speed and inflection all determined by the speaker. Finally, the speaker accompanies the words with nonverbal forms of communication such as gestures, facial expressions, and movements which are visible to the audience and which supplement the verbal message.

## Broadcast Messages

Broadcast shares some of the characteristics of both print and spoken messages, and has some characteristics of its own.

Like print, the messages transmitted to audiences are predetermined by the source. But in this case it is not just message content and structure that are fixed by the writers and producers; so are all aspects of delivery to its audience. The sequence, speed, pacing and emphasis with which the message is delivered are also under the control of the producers. In this respect, broadcast differs markedly from print.

Like oral communication, the words of broadcasting are presented in spoken form. But unlike oral communication, there usually is no two-way channel, no mechanism for feedback from recipient to source.

From this discussion, we can summarize the characteristics of broadcasting under four headings. Individually, each heading shares some characteristics of the process of communication with other media and activities, and there are exceptions. We'll note those exceptions here and then discuss their implications in later chapters. In large part, however, these characteristics, when taken together, set the electronic media apart from other media and determine a unique style of writing.

1. The words used, and the sequence in which they are presented, are only heard, not seen.

2. The words and sequences are presented to the audience only once. There is no provision for the listener to get a repetition of the message.

3. There is usually no mechanism for immediate feedback and therefore no opportunity for the source to modify the message during its delivery in response to feedback.

4. Although broadcast audiences may be large in total, that large, aggregate audience is made up of many small groups or individuals at each receiving location.

### Words Heard, Not Seen

It's sometimes difficult for beginning writers to remember that the scripts they write are not seen by the audiences that are the receivers of broadcast messages. Most of us are accustomed to putting our words down on paper and then having the intended audience read them from that paper. For broadcast, however, when a script is used, in whatever form, its words are transformed from written to spoken copy by the actions of announcers and actors, by the use of sound effects and music, and for television, by the insertion of pictorial material. The script is only a transition stage in the process of communication; it is not seen by the audience.

There are a few situations in television where words are actually printed on the screen. Brand names and logos for products may be shown as visual reinforcement in a commercial. Printed "crawls" giving program information or a news headline may be displayed across the bottom or top of the screen during a program, without spoken accompaniment, to avoid interrupting a program. Some TV channels display stock market quotations, news, weather, or teletext information. We've also noticed a trend in commercials, possibly only a passing fad, to add questions or other phrases as written text, and move those phrases through the spot with other video material, pictures of an automobile, for example, in the background. This approach provides a form of visual variety to catch and hold audience attention.

Some recent commercials have carried this idea to an extreme. They present the entire verbal message as words printed on the screen. One such campaign, for Aetna insurance, provided short statements as text printed on the screen, with a sound track consisting of related sound effects. In one ad in the series, the text described Aetna's support for pre- and neonatal care; the sound track was babies crying.

But these are still exceptions. Usually, the visual display of words is only a reinforcement of the spoken text. The important point is that nearly all the verbal content of broadcast communication is received and interpreted through the audience's ears.

In order to become more conscious of the characteristics of this form of communication, the beginning writer should form the habit of reading copy aloud. When reading silently we tend to skip through the problems associated with poor broadcast style. Read aloud the draft of a piece of copy and it will make stylistic problems more obvious.

### One-Time Presentation

Recall the difference between this characteristic and that of print. Print material may be read whenever an individual reader is ready, in whatever sequence of items that person chooses, and with whatever rereading or analysis he or she chooses. The reader controls the reception of the message and the speed and order in which its content is processed by the eye and brain.

In contrast, the originator of the broadcast message determines both the sequence of ideas and their rate of presentation. If the listener is unable to follow that sequence or keep up with that speed, for whatever reason, he or she will turn off the program or be turned off by it.

Again, there are exceptions. Some forms of repetition exist. Cable News Network recycles its news stories throughout the day. Records are repeated on music radio stations, sometimes quite often, as are the music videos on MTV. Commercials are frequently rerun. Another exception is the use of home recording devices; when these are used to capture programs for later viewing, then the opportunity exists for repeated exposure at the discretion of the listener or viewer. But except in this last circumstance there is no opportunity to change the speed of the presentation or to manipulate the order in which the content is presented within the program, and the repetitive broadcast of musical selections and commercials is a random event.

Therefore, in most cases, broadcast requires especially careful attention to the sequence and pacing of materials, for the recipient's only choice is to accept the message as presented, or lose that content, possibly forever.

# BLOOM COUNTY                    by Berke Breathed

**Figure 2.1.** Reproduced by permission of the Washington Post Company. © 1983, Washington Post Writers Group.

## *Limited Feedback*

We've already discussed the problem of limited feedback as it affects broadcast communication. Immediate feedback that can be used to modify program or commercial content is still the exceptional circumstance, rather than the rule. But, as we noted earlier in the chapter, the industry is adapting to accommodate more instances of direct feedback, including telephone talk shows and messages delivered via interactive cable systems where audiences can respond. It is also now quite common for national programs and commercials to be pretested on sample audiences. If the test audiences do not react positively to a commercial message or to the pilot program for a new dramatic series, that commercial or program can be modified before final production and presentation to the mass audience, or dropped before large costs are incurred.

Corporate-mediated communications—sales and training videos and other forms of instructional media—are more and more being written and produced using some form of interactivity between the program and the viewer-student. We consider this form of exception in Chapter 15.

## *A Big Audience—of Individuals*

The business of broadcasting is profitable only because it is possible to reach large numbers of people, often numbering many millions, at one time and with one origination. But unlike other mass audiences, the broadcast audience is in many different locations, each isolated from the others. At best there will be only a small group of people, perhaps a family, receiving the program in one location.

In order to communicate effectively with broadcast audiences, the writer must remember to talk to them as individuals, casually and conversationally, not with the styles of oratory used for mass audiences assembled in a single location.

## CONCLUSION

In the two chapters of this introductory part, we've drawn a deliberately artificial distinction between the "creative" process of writing and writing as a "communication" activity. We've forced this distinction to try to make an important point. Over the years this author has seen too many examples of student writing that were highly creative and original but that were impossible to understand. They failed to communicate. They did not touch an audience. They did not serve the purposes of a client who would have been paying for their production and broadcast if the classroom assignment had been a real-world task. We hope that by highlighting the conflict between these two perspectives, you will understand how difficult it is, but how necessary, to find a balance between originality and effective communication.

As you begin to write for television or radio, whether your assignments are those given by an instructor or by a supervisor on the job, keep in mind the context of your task, as provided by these chapters. Refer also to the two chapters of Part 3 of this text, which amplify the relationships between originators and their purposes and audiences and their expectations.

But now, you want to write. The chapters ahead present broad principles of good writing for the electronic media. If you understand and practice these techniques in preparing your assignments, you can be an effective writer.

**Exercise**

1. What are the likely changes in the electronic media industries that will affect the employment of writers and the nature of their jobs in years to come? This is a wide-ranging question that does not have simple answers, nor is there likely to be agreement on the answers among either students or professionals. You can begin, however, by using the brief descriptions of typical types of writing opportunities in the industry presented in Chapter 1. Then investigate likely changes in the nature of the industry— many more cable channels, fragmentation of advertising revenue, and so on. Use articles and commentaries in current periodicals for this research, and interviews with professionals from your market.

**Further Reading**

There are three different categories of books that would be appropriate additional readings for the topics in this chapter. First are books that deal with communication theory and models of the communication process. We've listed several. Some of them were originally published quite a few years ago, but they are still useful "classics" in the field.

Berlo, David K. *The Process of Communication.* New York: Holt, Rinehart and Winston, 1960.

Blake, Reed H., and Edwin O. Haroldsen. *A Taxonomy of Concepts in Communication.* Mamaroneck, NY: Hastings House, 1975.

De Fleur, Melvin L., and Sandra Ball-Rokeach. *Theories of Mass Communication*, 5th ed. White Plains, NY: Longman, 1989.

Severin, Werner J., and James W. Tankard. *Communication Theories: Origins, Methods, Uses in the Mass Media*, 3rd ed. White Plains, NY: Longman, 1992.

Siebert, Fred S., Theodore Peterson and Wilbur Schramm. *Four Theories of the Press.* Urbana: University of Illinois Press, 1956. (A reprint of this original edition is available.)

Stamm, Keith R., and John E. Bowes. *The Mass Communication Process: A Behavioral and Social Perspective.* Dubuque, IA: Kendall-Hunt, 1990.

The second category is introductory or survey texts in mass communications. Most of these titles will include chapters on communication theory and models, but their primary focus is on the history, development and operation of the various media industries, and possibly on critical evaluation of those industries and on careers. Since an introductory course in mass communication is taught in many colleges and universities, you may already have a text in this category. There are many titles; these are the ones we think are best organized:

Agee, Warren K., Phillip H. Ault, and Edwin Emery. *Introduction to Mass Communications*, 10th ed. New York: HarperCollins, 1990.

Black, Jay, and Jennings Bryant, *Introduction to Mass Communication*, 3rd ed. Dubuque, IA: Brown and Benchmark, 1992.

Dominick, Joseph R. *The Dynamics of Mass Communication*, 3rd ed. New York: McGraw-Hill, 1990.

The final category differs only slightly from the second. These are texts that discuss the background and operation of the electronic media, omitting print, and usually also omitting sections on communication theory and models. The discussion of the electronic media industries—broadcast, cable, and so on—is therefore expanded. Despite the fact that some sections of these texts become dated quickly as the business and programming practices of the industries change rapidly, one of these works should be in your library for background reference to topics introduced in this chapter and elsewhere throughout this book. Although there are not as many titles in this area as in the previous one, there are several. These are representative:

Dominick, Joseph, Barry L. Sherman, and Gary Copeland. *Broadcasting/Cable and Beyond.* New York: McGraw-Hill, 1990.

Head, Sydney W., and Christopher H. Sterling. *Broadcasting in America: A Survey of Electronic Media*, 6th ed. Boston: Houghton Mifflin, 1990.

Whetmore, Edward Jay. *American Electric: Introduction to Telecommunications and Electronic Media.* New York: McGraw-Hill, 1992.

For recent events, read professional periodicals. Both of these weekly newsmagazines provide special subscription incentives for students:

*Broadcasting & Cable*, Cahners Publishing Co., 475 Park Avenue South, New York, NY 10016.

*Electronic Media*, Crain Communications, Inc., 740 Rush Street, Chicago, IL 60611.

# Principles

In organizing the content of this book, we have taken the position that there are principles of writing for broadcast—for radio, television, cable and other electronic media—that are peculiar to those delivery systems and to the way audiences receive information and use their content. We believe that the characteristics of the media and of audience behavior, taken together, dictate the approaches writers must take in order to be successful in communicating their ideas.

These principles, we believe, are *not* tied to one particular type of program or style of copy. That is, there is not one set of principles for writing dramatic programs and a different set for documentaries, or news, or interviews. To be sure, certain principles may be more important, or perhaps more obvious, in writing certain types of copy, and each type of program does have its own strengths and weaknesses from a writer's point of view. But we will argue, vigorously if necessary, that most of the principles of good broadcast writing we set forth in the chapters of this section can be applied to most of the program types described in the chapters of Part 4, as well as to other types too specialized to be covered in this text.

We would find it repetitious if, for example, we were to introduce the topic of program structure in the chapter on news, then again in the one on drama, then yet again in discussing documentaries. We will consider it in each of those chapters, but with attention to the unique structural problems of each genre. Similarly, matters of aural style and of the uses of sound and visuals need not be repeated in each of the genre chapters.

Here, then, are the matters we consider sufficiently important and sufficiently universal to be classified as principles of broadcast writing.

# Aural Style

I n the latter sections of Chapter 2 we referred numerous times to the unique nature of the style of writing that is most effective for broadcast or electronic media. The term which best describes this style is *aural* style—that is, pertaining to the ear and the sense of hearing. For communication to be successful, it has to be received and understood by its audience. An important part of that reception and understanding depends on the message's being *heard* correctly. Even with visual media, television and cable, a large portion of most programs' content is presented to the audience through their sense of hearing.

When you finish this chapter, you will be able to

- list a series of characteristics that define good broadcast writing style,

- recognize those characteristics in well-written copy and their lack in poorly written copy,

- write (and rewrite) radio and television copy that exhibits good aural style, especially avoiding redundancies, doublespeak and clichés, and

- recognize and use these important terms and concepts:

| | |
|---|---|
| active voice | inflection |
| aural style | onomatopoeia |
| cliché | pauses |
| delay | redundancy |
| doublespeak | repetition |
| feedback | transition words |
| homophones | |

# CLARITY

Our review of the process of broadcast communication has shown that if the receivers/audiences of the messages do not understand the communication, they have little opportunity to express that lack of understanding back to the source/originators. The message is fixed; it's delivered at a predetermined speed; and there's seldom any feedback that might be able to change the content or form of the message.

Therefore, for most messages it is crucially important that the writer and other persons involved in the production of programs and announcements strive consciously to make every message clear. The listener cannot review the content, reread the message, go to the dictionary to review unfamiliar words or respond by voice or other physical signs that he or she does not understand. The message must be clear immediately upon presentation.

We'd like to say that anything that might interfere with understanding the message must be sacrificed to clarity, and that this principle applies on all occasions. But there are exceptions. Some commercials and music videos flash visual images so rapidly that the viewer cannot really comprehend each individual picture. In the preceding chapter we mentioned commercials that mix printed text and sound effects in unusual juxtaposition. In these instances, writers and producers have deliberately chosen to replace clarity with ambiguity, to leave the viewer with a feeling, an emotion, rather than with a rational, informative message.

Such techniques do provide variety and may be effective in attracting audience attention, but they are risky. In later chapters we discuss the importance of accomplishing the goal set forth by a program's or a commercial's sponsor. These techniques may interfere with reaching that goal. So, in general, and certainly for informative content, clarity remains a prime consideration.

For example, a commercial may be constructed humorously, but the humor must support the persuasive message of the advertisement; it cannot mask it. A news story must present its information, which consists of events, names, dates, statistics, expert opinion and so on, in a sequence that places new facts into the already understood fabric of the story. New names, for example, cannot be introduced without explanation of their relationship to the other persons already involved in the story.

Clarity, of course, is clarity to the listener. We can discuss clarity only as it pertains to the ear and mind of the listener, and not in relation to the words written by the writer. As a writer, you may believe that what you have written is clear and will be understood by the people in the audience. But it may not be. How can you be sure that what you have written will be clear?

You cannot be absolutely certain, but you can increase the odds in your favor by observing these two fundamental rules:

1. Know as much as possible about the audience you intend to reach with your message. We will discuss target audiences in Chapter 10. The point

very simply is that certain types of people are more strongly attracted to certain types of content and styles of presentation than others. We will also consider in Chapter 10 how writers can adjust scripts to meet the interests of particular groups.

2. Write using an aural style—that is, using sentence and paragraph structures, grammatical constructions and vocabulary which help listeners to follow and to process the content of the message. For the remainder of this chapter, we will concentrate on these principles of aural style for ensuring clarity.

## CHARACTERISTICS OF AURAL STYLE

The single most distinguishing characteristic of the broadcast writing style, in contrast to that used for print, is that it is more informal and sounds more spontaneous. Our perceiving sense, the ear, cannot easily process the more complex, abstract and formal style found in most printed content. That style requires more effort and attention than broadcast audience members are able, willing or accustomed to giving. Instead, prepare copy that sounds as much like spontaneous speech as possible. These characteristics contribute to that impression and to clarity:

1. Use *language correctly*.

2. Use a more *restricted vocabulary* than is usually found in print copy.

3. Use *descriptive, connotative, forceful words*.

4. Use the *active voice*.

5. Use *contractions*.

6. Use *personal pronouns* extensively.

7. Use *simple sentences*.

8. Make frequent use of *transition words and vocal cues*.

9. Maintain a *moderate pace* that is within the listener's ability to comprehend.

10. Avoid *negative constructions*.

11. Avoid the use of *homophones*.

12. Avoid *redundancies, doublespeak* and *clichés*.

Strictly speaking, this list contains more than just characteristics of style. We have included some matters related to grammar, syntax and vocabulary as well. All are important considerations when preparing copy that will communicate clearly and effectively to one's intended audience. And most are good guidelines to follow for writing in general, using any medium.

Further discussion and examples can be found in general style manuals. If you enjoy the intricacies and idiosyncracies of the English language, we have included a list of books that discuss the uses and misuses of language in the Further Reading section at the end of this chapter. All the books are informative and interesting. Some are also very funny.

## Correct Language

It should not be necessary to remind writers that words should be used correctly and that grammar should be correct in all forms of writing, including broadcast, but the fact is that much too frequently words and grammar are not correct, and when they are misused, the listener will be confused.

Accuracy and precision in your choice of words are one mark of good writing. If only one word has the precise meaning you wish to convey *and if you believe your audience is familiar with that word*, then use it. On the other hand, if that word is *not* likely to be understood by your audience, you will have to rewrite to convey your meaning in a different way. Many common words are misused by students who simply have not had enough practice using vocabulary precisely.

Similarly, the structure of sentences and paragraphs needs to follow the rules of grammar. Listeners to a radio or TV newscast will be lost if what they hear are thoughts that are not expressed in commonly understood sequences. Consider these misplaced modifiers, for example:

```
National League President Bill White said Monday he will
decide Tuesday on a schedule of makeup games postponed
because of the riots in Los Angeles between the Los Ange-
les Dodgers and Montreal Expos.

Teenager dies defending gift of gold earrings from
muggers.
```

Some slips will happen no matter how careful you try to be; the above came from professional newspaper writers. But as you write, review all your copy carefully with the specific intent of identifying and correcting vocabulary and grammatical mistakes. Having, and using, a good dictionary and thesaurus will help you develop precision. These books should be the first two items in your personal library. The serious writer will also keep handy one or more style manuals or other specialized books on language. Several such manuals are listed in the Further Reading list.

## Restricted Vocabulary

The literary style can and usually does employ a much larger vocabulary than the aural style. The average person's reading vocabulary is about three times larger than his or her speaking vocabulary. A reader may recognize or be able to figure out the meaning of many words that would be lost completely if presented aurally. A reader can also look up strange words, which is a recourse not available to the listener.

The prime consideration in the choice of vocabulary is that the words used must contribute to clarity. The vocabulary should not confuse listeners. For confusion, even if it is only momentary, will cause the listener to miss a following portion of the message. The result is that he or she will be unable or unwilling to catch up to the communication and will tune out, either mentally or physically, by leaving the room, changing the channel, or turning the receiver off altogether. Therefore, the writer must choose words that will be readily recognized by listeners. That, in turn, means using a limited vocabulary for most broadcast writing, particularly if you are writing copy directed at a very broad audience, such as that for a prime-time television program. In order to reach as many of these people as possible without their turning away from the content of a program, the writer must use a straightforward, restricted vocabulary.

The structure of English is such that the setting in which a word is placed frequently gives clues to its meaning, or at least the overall sense of a message can be determined with reasonable accuracy even without knowing the meaning of every word in the statement. But the writer should not rely on this characteristic. Instead, avoid the use of "big words," when shorter, more common words will convey the same thought.

An important corollary to that principle is to avoid general, vague, abstract terms in favor of the particular word or phrase that most precisely and accurately fits the idea. The American grandmaster of style, William Strunk, insisted that

> If those who have studied the art of writing are in accord on any one point it is on this: the surest way to arouse and hold the attention of the reader is by being specific, definite, and concrete.

POOR:     A period of unfavorable weather set in.
BETTER:   It rained every day for a week.

POOR:     He showed satisfaction as he took possession of his well-earned reward.
BETTER:   He grinned as he pocketed the coin.[1]

Strunk was referring to print, but the instruction is even more important for broadcast, as the writer must work within the very precise time limits of an inflexible program schedule and the scheduled time for a story is measured in terms of seconds, not minutes.

As you become more experienced, you'll develop your own sense of words that are too abstract to make good, conversational copy. Remember,

| **Box 3.1  Words to Avoid** | | | |

| *Avoid these terms* | *Use these synonyms* | *Avoid these terms* | *Use these synonyms* |
| --- | --- | --- | --- |
| indignation | anger | summon | call |
| transmit | send | beverage | drink |
| remark | say | physician | doctor |
| exhibit | show | attorney | lawyer |
| require | need | passed away | died |
| lacerations | cuts | terminate | end |
| deceased | dead | commence | begin |
| attempt | try | endeavor | try |
| precipitation | rain, snow | utilize | use |
| energy | gas, electricity | edifice | building |
| livestock | pigs, cows, sheep | assemblage | crowd |
| cooking utensils | pots and pans | consequently | so |
| garment | coat | transpire | happen |
| educational institution | school | venture | try |
| petroleum | oil | cognizant | aware |
| sufficient | enough | youth | teenager |
| residence | home | abrasion | scrape |
| contribute | give | intoxicated | drunk |
| interrogate | question | visage | face |
| witness | see | indisposed | ill, sick |
| purchase | buy | | |

too, that the vocabulary you use should be matched to the audience. A more educated audience will understand, and expect to hear, a larger vocabulary and more precise words. But to give you some sense of what we mean, see Box 3.1 for some "big words" and for each a generally better understood, more concrete replacement.[2]

## Descriptive, Connotative, Forceful Words

A writer sensitive to words makes use of those that have high connotative value. Suggestive words will awaken associations in the mind of the listener and stir the imagination. They add color, warmth and life to a script:

> To say "His mind quickly comprehended a problem" would convey the meaning intended, but it would be more effective to say "His mind flashed to the heart of the problem." The word "flashed" carries with it a definite connotation and a sharp visual image which not only tells the listener what happened, but also gives him the feeling of its happening. . . . It is better to say that the wind "whined and clawed at

the corner of the house" than to say that the wind "was blowing." If a word can tell not only what was done but how it was done, so much the better.[3]

The use of descriptive words is particularly important in writing radio copy, where there is no visual accompaniment to the sound. Well-chosen descriptive words and phrases help the listener build a mental picture of the setting of a dramatic scene, or of an event.

Here are two brief passages of radio copy that use descriptive words effectively to build mental images. The first is an excerpt from one of Edward R. Murrow's accounts of the German bombing of London in World War II:

> Up toward London we could see billows of smoke fanning out above the river and, over our heads, the British fighters climbing almost straight up, trying to intercept the bombers before they got away. It went on for two hours, and then the all-clear. We went down to a nearby pub for dinner. Children were already organizing a hunt for bits of shrapnel. Under some bushes beside the road there was a baker's cart. Two boys, sobbing, were trying to get a quivering bay mare back between the shafts. The lady who ran the pub told us that these raids were bad for the chickens, the dogs and the horses. A toothless old man of nearly seventy came in and asked for a pint of milk and bitters, confided that he had always, all his life, gone to bed at eight o'clock and found now that three pints of beer made him drowsy-like so he could sleep through any air raid.
>
> Before eight the sirens sounded again. We went back to the haystack near the airdrome. The fires up the river had turned the moon blood-red. The smoke had drifted down until it formed a canopy over the Thames. The guns were working all around us, the bursts looking like fireflies in a Southern summer night. The Germans were sending in two or three planes at a time—sometimes only one—in relays. They would pass overhead. The guns and lights would follow them, and in about five minutes we could hear the hollow grunt of the bombs. Huge pear-shaped bursts of flame would rise up into the smoke and disappear. . . . It was like a shuttle service, the way the German planes came up the Thames, the fires acting as a flare path. Often they were above the smoke. The searchlights bored into that black roof but couldn't penetrate it. They looked like long pillars supporting a black canopy. Suddenly all the lights dashed off and a blackness fell right to the ground. It grew cold. We covered ourselves with hay. . . .

*Source:* Edward R. Murrow as quoted in Edward Bliss, Jr., and John M. Patterson, *Writing News for Broadcast*, 2nd ed. rev. (New York: Columbia University Press, 1978), pp. 20–21. © 1978, Columbia University Press. Reprinted by permission of the publisher.

This second example is the narrative introduction to a radio play:

```
SOUND:    FOGHORN IN THE DISTANCE—AT NATURAL INTERVALS IN BACK OF—

RAY:      Have you heard the voice of the fog? As the cold white

          loneliness creeps in, shrouding a desolate shoreline, blotting

          the stars, bringing stillness to the night and hushing the

          wind and muffling the sad wash of the sea; until there's no

          motion, no sound, no reality left; nothing but you and the fog

          and -- after a while -- a strained tense listening for the

          voice to speak. No. No, it's not the wailing cry of a lost

          gull overhead, nor the foghorn's weary dirge far away, not

          even the dim thudding beat of your heart. It's -- no, forgive

          me, please. Perhaps it's only to me that the fog's voice

          speaks. (TURN AWAY FADE)
```

*Source:* Dave Drummond, *Voice of the Fog*, an original radio play.

Short, forceful words are generally better than less emphatic ones:

POOR:     He has passed away.
BETTER:   He is dead.

POOR:     I demand that you surrender that volume.
BETTER:   Give me the book.

POOR:     Assist me to arise.
BETTER:   Help me up.

POOR:     I hold you in high esteem.
BETTER:   I like you.[4]

Aural style is also marked by words with high sound-effect value. The writer should make use of *onomatopoeia*, which is the use of words whose sounds suggest their sense. The words *tinkle*, *roar*, *crunch*, *crush*, *lull* and *soothe* are onomatopoeic words. Like any other technique, onomatopoeia can be overused or badly used; used with discrimination, it is an effective way to add color to narrative.

## Active Voice

In ordinary conversation we most often use the active grammatical voice. Since our goal is to make broadcast copy sound conversational, then the active voice is also appropriate for most broadcast copy. Its contrast is, of course, the passive voice. The very words chosen to describe these two linguistic styles—active voice and passive voice—give a clue to their use. The active voice is more dynamic, more forceful; it makes a commercial or news story seem more alive. The passive voice is just that, passive, and it usually requires more words.

A verb is active if the subject performs the action:

```
Police captured the sniper.

The chairmen of General Motors and Toyota signed an his-
toric agreement today.
```

A verb is passive if the subject receives the action:

```
The sniper was captured by police.

An historic agreement was signed today by the chairmen of
General Motors and Toyota.
```

Usually, passive voice slows down a story and weakens its impact. On the other hand, its occasional use can add variety to the structure of a story. It may also be the best way to make a point if the receiver of an action is more important than the doer.

```
Governor John Smith was seriously injured today when
struck by a sign carried by a picketer. The governor was
speaking from the steps of the Capitol to a group of peo-
ple protesting the recent state gas tax increase.
```

For the above example, passive construction conveys more information in a better sequence than: "A picketer's sign struck and severely injured Governor John Smith. . . ."

## Contractions

Normal conversation uses contractions frequently and naturally. Where you would be likely to use contractions in conversation, you should use them in broadcast copy. It simply sounds more natural, more spontaneous and more informal to say *didn't* instead of *did not*, or *we'll* instead of *we will*.

```
Come on down to the Saving Center this weekend. You'll
find a carload of bargains....

Interest rates may go lower than they are now, but they're
not going through the floor....

It's going to be a gorgeous weekend in the Pacific
Northwest....
```

One occasion when you should not use a contraction is when you want emphasis. The contrast between the normal use of the contraction and the deliberate choice not to use it stands out in the copy and provides the emphasis wanted.

```
The coalition claims that registering handguns will not
reduce crime, but will create another costly bureaucracy.
```

In this example, *will not* emphasizes the negative more than *won't*. It also provides a better contrast with *will* in the second clause.

## Personal Pronouns

A conversation is a conversation only if it involves two parties. In broadcast, those two parties are the individual listeners in the audience and the voice from the other end of the line—the announcer. The use of first- and second-person pronouns makes the copy sound more personal, more informal and more conversational than if the writer used just nouns or third-person pronouns:

```
If you're having trouble finding that special gift this
Christmas, I have some suggestions....

We're going to be in for cold weather....

Our utility bills will be increased drastically if the
plan is approved....

Most of us take it for granted that the sun will come up
every morning....
```

Of course, any stylistic device can be overused, and certain types of content adapt more easily to the use of pronouns than do others, but as a general rule the attention of each individual listener will be caught more easily by a story that seems to involve that listener. The use of *you* and *we* and similar pronouns accomplishes that involvement.

However, be sure that the pronoun references are clear. A confusing antecedent in broadcast copy will throw the listener off and cause him or her to miss subsequent information. Errors similar to these appear frequently in the inexperienced writer's copy:

```
My children had too many clothes, so I gave them away.
```
[The children?]

```
The American people have elected a number of poor presi-
dents, but Congress has generally kept them from ruining
the country.
```
[The people, or the presidents?]

## Simple Sentences

The sentences we speak are simpler than those we write, so to approximate conversational speech the writer generally should use simple constructions. It is possible to be grammatically correct and at the same time be much too complex for the listener to be able to follow a story.

One problem of particular difficulty for many beginning writers is the proper placement of modifiers within a sentence. If modifiers are placed incorrectly, the listener can easily become confused. Do not, for example, begin sentences with lengthy modifying phrases or clauses. The listener hears the modifiers first, without any reference to the main idea they are supposed to modify. Try reading these examples aloud, and you should be able to see the problem.

```
Now 68, silver-haired, and, with Muhammad Ali, the most
identifiable of retired athletes, Joe DiMaggio is solic-
ited regularly by writers and publishing houses to do a
book....
```

The listener cannot know who is being talked about until fifteen words into the sentence. His age, hair color, and comparison with Ali have nothing to do with the main thrust of the sentence. Begin with "Joe DiMaggio is solicited regularly. . . ."

```
After practicing for 18 months on common barnyard pigs,
Dr. Richard Ward, director of the liver transplant pro-
gram, says that he and his team of surgeons, technicians,
and nurses are ready when the first well-matched patient
and donor can be identified....
```

Again, we can't relate the "After practicing . . . on . . . pigs" to anything until after we understand that the story has to do with preparations for liver transplants. Start with the important facts; then show how the pigs tie in.

Having been a former pro football player and an athlete
since my Little League days, I consider the healthy human
body a gift from God and feel people should treat it right
-- by eating the right foods and exercising regularly....

Often the best way to eliminate the opening dependent clause is just to
reverse the main thought. Begin the sentence with the main clause: "I consider . . . exercising regularly. My feelings come from the fact that I have been
an athlete since my Little League days and a former pro football player."

Confronted by the possibility of lawsuits for false arrest
or slander, store owners have staffed their stores with
more visible security agents rather than undercover
agents....

In this case, the sentence is not overly long or complex. It can be im-·
proved easily simply by adding: "Because they have been confronted by."

Lengthy interjections in the middle of a sentence, between the subject
and the verb, also cause confusion. In general, subordinate clauses and mid-
sentence interjections should be moved to the end of the sentence. Even
better in many cases is to write them as separate sentences, as in these
examples:

**Poor:**   The annual Pig Bowl game, which pits the Bacon Bombers
from the Sacramento County Sheriff's Department against
the Razorbacks from the City Police for the benefit
of nine local charities, will be played this year on
January 21.

**Better:**  The annual Pig Bowl game will be played this year on January 21. As usual the two teams will come from Sacramento
law enforcement agencies -- the Bacon Bombers from the
Sheriff's Department and the Razorbacks from the City Police. Nine local charities will benefit from the proceeds.

**Poor:**   A computer system for fingerprints, which the San Francisco Police Department fought for years to acquire,
brought about the arrest yesterday of a suspect in the
fatal shooting of a Parkside District woman six years ago.

**Better:**  A new computer system for fingerprints caught its first
suspect in San Francisco yesterday. The computer identified the fingerprints of a man who has been arrested for
the fatal shooting six years ago of a Parkside District
woman. Police had fought for years to acquire the complex
computer matching system.

Another form of complexity that is difficult for the listener's ear is a long string of nouns used as adjectives. Avoid this kind of word sequence:

```
A black American beauty pageant contestant was accused....
```

Generally a straightforward subject-verb-object sequence is best, but avoid constant repetition of the same pattern of sentence construction. A story with sentences of uniform brief length and with sentences phrased in precisely the same subject-verb pattern will have a "singsong" effect and rapidly bore the listener. The ear is easily distracted; it is difficult to hold its attention without changes of pace and variation.

Thus far, we've insisted that you use grammar correctly and that you use simple but complete sentences. There are occasions, however, when you can legitimately use sentence fragments. We have been emphasizing "conversational" style, and we frequently speak using partial sentences, omitting, usually, the verb in a sentence. News "headlines" often are fragments. A series of items expressed in parallel phrases may be better handled as fragments, avoiding the clutter of a repetitive verb. But be sparing of this technique, and use it only if the meaning of your statement is still clearly communicated.

## Transition Words and Vocal Cues

Writing intended for the eye makes frequent use of punctuation marks, which are visual cues to indicate structure and emphasis. We paragraph copy to mark each stage in the development of a sequence of thought, and we punctuate within sentences to clarify sentence construction. We use italics and boldface type to make certain words and ideas stand out from others.

To accomplish the same thing in aural copy, the listener is led through the structure of the material by three types of cues: transition words, vocal inflections and pauses.

One group of cue or transition words relates to time sequence. It includes such words as *now, next, still, just, then, when,* and *finally.* Also *yesterday, today, tomorrow, last week* and so on. These words would be particularly helpful in constructing a news story in which a clear chronology of events is needed in order to understand the story:

```
ANNCR:    In San Francisco three hostages are still being held in a

          downtown office building by an unidentified gunman. They have

          been there since three P.M. yesterday, when an attempted

          holdup went awry. Police have reconstructed the events this

          way. Just shortly before three P.M. two men entered the

                          MORE MORE MORE
```

Crocker Bank office at Fifth and Oak. They walked up to a teller's window and demanded that money be placed in a paper sack which they held out. In the process of taking the sack from the robbers, the teller was able to trip a silent alarm, and when the men attempted to leave the bank, they found guards blocking their exit. At that time, one man pulled a gun and ordered three bank customers into an elevator, which they then took up to the top floor of the eighteen-story building. The second would-be robber evidently slipped away during the elevator ride, but one man and the hostages are still holed up in an unused office on the top floor. Negotiations between police and the gunman have been taking place, but no results have been announced.

Other transition words indicate cause and effect or similar relation-ships—such words as *because, for, thereby,* and *since.* Another group helps set up contrasts within a story: *however, on the other hand, but.* And there are the standard connectors: *and, also, too, in addition.* Be careful of these, however, as many beginning writers use connectors to make compound and complex sentences where two separate simple sentences would be better.

Changes in the vocal inflections used by announcers and actors also pro-vide aural cues to listeners. They are particularly helpful in emphasizing cer-tain words or phrases within a body of copy. The writer can indicate in the script where inflection is wanted by the use of standard punctuation symbols and by underlining to indicate emphasis. The actual inflection, however, has to be provided by the "voice" of the copy—the announcer or actor.

In the preceding sentence, for example, the use of quotation marks around the word *voice* would indicate to an announcer that the word should be given some special inflection which aurally sets it apart from the rest of the sentence. Here are two examples of how differences in emphasis can change the meaning of copy. First, try reading this famous line aloud with the different inflections noted:

- <u>Where</u> have all the flowers gone?

- Where <u>have</u> all the flowers gone?

- Where have <u>all</u> the flowers gone?

- Where have all the <u>flowers</u> gone?

- Where have all the flowers <u>gone</u>?

Now read the following line, in which the changes in emphasis substantially affect the meaning and therefore the audience's ability to understand the writer's intent:

```
The president insisted that the American forces would be
used for peacekeeping purposes only.
```

Emphasis on *president*—as opposed to some other official who might have made the same statement; emphasizes credibility of source.

Emphasis on *insisted*—makes his action the key to the sentence.

Emphasis on *American*—someone else's forces might be used differently, but not the American forces.

Emphasis on *peacekeeping*—as opposed to, possibly, war making.

Emphasis on *only*—no other activity is proposed.

Finally, broadcast copy makes frequent use of pauses, to allow time for the listener to process the preceding information before continuing with new information. Remember, in print the reader sets his or her own pace, but that cannot be done in broadcast. The writer of broadcast copy, then, will make frequent use of the punctuation marks that indicate pauses to the announcer or actors. Commas, dashes, and ellipses will appear more frequently in broadcast copy than in print and more frequently than is called for by the strict rules of grammar. You'll see these uses in scripts throughout this text.

## Moderate Pace

Because the broadcast program is presented in a fixed sequence and at a predetermined rate, pacing is crucial. Writers and producers must use considerable care to see that materials proceed at a pace that can be handled by the members of the audience. Too many ideas, presented too rapidly, and the information will become a jumble to the listener. Too slow, and the presentation becomes boring; the listener is ready for new material before it arrives.

The problem of too much density—too much information for the time available—can be solved in part by reducing the content, including only the most important facts within a news story, for instance, and limiting the number of persuasive concepts in a commercial. The problem can also be eased by spacing out those ideas which are presented so that the listener's ear and mind can process each idea before being hit with the next one. Transition words and pauses, already discussed, help with pacing. Two additional techniques are repetition and delay.

Repetition doesn't necessarily mean that the same words and phrases are repeated, but that a single idea is reinforced by alternative phrasings.

Reread the bank holdup story in the immediately preceding section. Notice the several times that the major ideas of the story—the robbery and the hostage taking—are mentioned throughout the story.

Delay is used to provide a buffer, a breathing space between stories or ideas. It gives the listener time to reflect, briefly, on the preceding information and then to focus attention on the upcoming story. News headlines provide warning and delay, as do some forms of news leads. Another common delay is the conversation between two news anchors prior to the presentation of the next story. This example provides transition, warning and delay:

| 2 SHOT ON 1: | STAN: In other capitol news, it looks like there's been a break in the deadlock over the state budget. |
|---|---|
| | MARY: That's right, Stan. State employees, who have been without paychecks for over two weeks now/because of the budget stalemate, may finally get paid. Today's meeting between Democratic leaders of the legislature and the governor seems to have cleared the remaining obstacles. Frank Jones has the story. |
| VOT—#1, Cut #2 @ 3:25 | Today's meeting between Assembly Speaker... |

Delay is also used to warn the listener that important information is about to be delivered. In a dramatic program, when a new character enters the scene with exciting information, she may say:

Wow! Have I got some news! You know that old bridge down on Simpson Creek, Well, it collapsed last night and ...

The first statement, "Wow! Have I got some news!" is the delay. It says to the listener: Pay attention!

Delays are important to space out material and to recapture the attention of listeners who may have tuned out mentally on one piece of material, so that they are tuned back in for the next story or commercial.

But the pacing of a message or the spacing out of the ideas does not mean that broadcast writing can be loose or sloppy. We have mentioned that simple sentence constructions are more conversational. The same is true for shorter sentences; they more closely approach normal speech. Brevity itself is not the issue, however. What is important, especially in broadcast news and commercials where time is measured in seconds, is that the words and sentences used all contribute to the message. William Strunk and E. B. White put it this way:

> A sentence should contain no unnecessary words, a paragraph no unnecessary sentences. . . . This requires not that the writer make all . . . sentences short . . . but that every word tell.[5]

## Negative Constructions

In general, negative statements are an obstacle to clarity. They are harder for audiences to comprehend. They are less descriptive and provide less information.

**Poor:** The baby ape was not breast-fed by its mother.

With Jupiter's dense gravity, you could not throw a ball very far.

Schubert's first published work was not well received by the general public.

I don't know that I am certain my father did not want to show his feelings.

The first three of these constructions are vague: They provide little information. The fourth, with its multiple negatives, is confusing as well. When the mind receives negative information, it wants and tries to convert that information into positive form; the mind wants to know what is, not just what is not.

**Better:** The baby ape was fed a prepared formula rather than its mother's breast milk.

With Jupiter's dense gravity, you could throw a ball only three or four feet, no more.

Schubert's first published work was received hesitantly by the general public.

I wonder if my father really wanted to hide his emotions.[6]

On the other hand, *not* is appropriate as a means of expressing denial, or as a contrast:

```
The state will not have a budget today. Although the Con-
stitution requires that the budget be completed by July
first each year, legislators will not finish their delib-
erations today—nor does it look like they will reach
agreement anytime soon.
```

But there is a danger, especially in news stories of this kind, that listeners will miss the negative word because of some distraction, and then will misinterpret the story. Repetition helps. Three negatives are used in the story above to guard against misunderstanding.

## Homophones

Homophones are words that sound alike but have different meanings. They are particularly difficult to work with in broadcast copy because the writer will clearly understand the meaning intended and not even recognize that a particular word has homophonous equivalents. The context and the (usually) different spelling of the other words with which a word might be confused lead the writer to believe that the meaning of the word is perfectly clear. But for a listener that may not be.

In this chapter we have already used part of one homophonous pair— *aural*, which is easily confused with *oral*. In print they are easily distinguished because they are spelled differently, but when heard aloud, they sound so alike that most listeners would be unable to distinguish between them. (For this pair, meanings are also often confused, as persons fail to distinguish between spoken, or oral, language and heard, or aural, language.)

Try reading the following bit of copy aloud. How might a listener react to this sports item?

```
The scorekeeper gave two too many runs to the home team.
Without that error the Sox would have lost two to one.
```

You can't avoid homophones entirely. Some words are so obviously the best to use in a given sentence that you'll never notice they sound like something else. But if you practice reading your copy aloud, you'll catch many of the potential problems, and when you run into a confusing homophone, rewrite.

We've been collecting lists of homophones we've seen in broadcast copy (see Box 3.2). These are not all pronounced exactly alike but are close enough that listeners usually can't tell them apart. They may help you become more aware of this problem. (Note, too, that many of these words are also misused grammatically. Quite a few college students still have trouble with *their, they're,* and *there*, for example.)

| | | |
|---|---|---|
| **Box 3.2 Common Homophones** | | |
| accept and except | heir, air and err | serial and cereal |
| advice and advise | its and it's | sex and sect |
| affect and effect | levy and levee | sight and site |
| aisle and isle | liar and lyre | stationary and stationery |
| alluded and eluded | palate, pallet, and palette | straight and strait |
| already and all ready | passed and past | symbol and cymbal |
| are, our, and hour | pier and peer | tee and tea |
| bail and bale | pour and pore | than and then |
| bore and boar | pray and prey | there, their, and they're |
| break and brake | presents and presence | use, ewes, and yews |
| capital and capitol | principal and principle | wait and weight |
| chord and cord | profit and prophet | wear and where |
| council and counsel | rain, rein, and reign | weather and whether |
| heel and heal | roomer and rumor | wholly and holy |

## Redundancies, Doublespeak and Clichés

Under this heading we have collected three problems that infect the English language and do it considerable harm. None are unique problems to broadcasting, but all are areas in which you as a professional writer can exercise some control over language abuse.

Among the authors who have spoken most forcefully, and at the same time entertainingly, about the correct use of language is Edwin Newman, who had a distinguished career as reporter and commentator for NBC News. In his book *A Civil Tongue* he writes:

> A civil tongue . . . means to me a language that is not bogged down in jargon, not puffed up with false dignity, not studded with trick phrases that have lost their meaning. It is not falsely exciting, is not patronizing, does not conceal the smallness and triteness of ideas by clothing them in language ever more grandiose, does not seek out increasingly complicated constructions, does not weigh us down with the gelatinous verbiage of Washington and the social sciences. It treats errors in spelling and usage with a decent tolerance but does not take them lightly. It does not consider "We're there because that's where it's at" the height of cleverness. It is not merely a stream of sound that disk jockeys produce, in which what is said does not matter so long as it is said without pause. It is direct, specific, concrete, vigorous, colorful, subtle, and imaginative when it should be, and as lucid and eloquent as we are able to make it. It is something to revel in and enjoy.

Unfortunately, it is also only a dream, for an ironic thing is happening in the United States. As we demand more and more personal openness from those in public life—unwisely, it seems to me—our language becomes more and more covered, obscure, turgid, ponderous, and overblown.[7]

We share Newman's concern, and by calling your attention to offenses against English with the examples in this section, we hope to enlist you in the fight to reclaim the clarity and precision of our language.

### Redundancies

Redundancies clutter copy, thereby reducing clarity. Not only does this verbiage clutter the narration and confuse the listener, it takes valuable time away, especially when appearing in a news story that is timed in seconds.
Here's how Edwin Newman writes of redundancies:

> We no longer have rules and prospects and news but ground rules, future prospects, and newsworthy happenings. Airlines tell us to read the instructions in the seat pocket in front of us not for our safety but for our personal safety. Companies do not grow; they enjoy positive growth. The Encinitas Union School District in California announces that it will provide equal employment opportunity not merely through affirmative action but through positive affirmative action. Do new cameras obviate special lighting? They obviate the need for special lighting. Is the horse Rogue's Gambit, subject of a story in the *Washington Post*, one of a kind? No, it is uniquely one of a kind. Does Nelson Rockefeller complain of a misrepresentation by Ronald Reagan? No, he complains of a factual misrepresentation, which cancels itself. Was a woman raped? No, she had a rape experience. Shall we face reality? We can do better. We can face reality as it is. Pillows renovated, a shop proclaims, like new. No trespassing, signs say, without permission.[8]

Eliminating surplus words does not contradict the principles stated earlier of providing repetition for emphasis and clarity, and of spacing ideas within copy so that listeners will not become lost in too much material presented too rapidly. Redundancies do not provide new information, nor do they remind the listener of facts or names that might have been lost over the progress of a story, nor do they reinforce a persuasive idea. They do not even provide stylistic parallelism. They just clutter.

### Doublespeak

Doublespeak has become the special interest of author William Lutz, who opens his book, titled simply *Doublespeak*, this way:

There are no potholes in the streets of Tucson, Arizona, just "pavement deficiencies." The Reagan Administration didn't propose any new taxes, just "revenue enhancement" through new "user's fees." Those aren't bums on the street, just "non-goal oriented members of society." There are no more poor people, just "fiscal underachievers." There was no robbery of an automatic teller machine, just an "unauthorized withdrawal." The patient didn't die because of medical malpractice, it was just a "diagnostic misadventure of a high magnitude." The U.S. Army doesn't kill the enemy anymore, it just "services the target." And the doublespeak goes on.

Doublespeak is language that pretends to communicate but really doesn't. It is language that makes the bad seem good, the negative appear positive, the unpleasant appear attractive or at least tolerable. Doublespeak is language that avoids or shifts responsibility, language that is at variance with its real or purported meaning. It is language that conceals or prevents thought; rather than extending thought, doublespeak limits it.

Doublespeak is not a matter of subjects and verbs agreeing; it is a matter of words and facts agreeing. Basic to doublespeak is incongruity, the incongruity between what is said or left unsaid, and what really is. It is the incongruity between the word and the referent, between seem and be, between the essential function of language—communication—and what doublespeak does—mislead, distort, deceive, inflate, circumvent, obfuscate.

*How to Spot Doublespeak.* How can you spot doublespeak? Most of the time you will recognize doublespeak when you see or hear it. But, if you have any doubts, you can identify doublespeak just by answering these questions: Who is saying what to whom, under what conditions and circumstances, with what intent, and with what results? Answering these questions will usually help you identify as doublespeak language that appears to be legitimate or that at first glance doesn't even appear to be doublespeak.[9]

As a writer you should take some pride in not creating doublespeak, but your greatest challenge will be to avoid repeating and transmitting doublespeak language created by others who do not want to provide clear statements and answers for your audiences. Often you will need to press an interviewee or a news source to be clear, when clarity may not be his or her intent.

### Clichés

The Random House Dictionary defines a *cliché* as

a trite, stereotyped expression; a sentence or phrase, usually expressing a popular or common thought or idea, that has lost originality, ingenuity, and impact by long overuse, as *sadder but wiser* or *strong as an ox.*[10]

That definition sums it up (to use one of our own). Although we hate to point fingers (yet another), in broadcasting perhaps the worst offenders are sportswriters and reporters. How many times have you heard:

```
He gives one hundred and ten percent in every game.

I expect the team to pull together and turn it around.

Hers is a real Cinderella story.

Pitching is the name of the game.
```
(Or substitute *hitting*, or *hustle*, or *pride*.)

```
Is your team hungry enough to win the pennant, Coach?
```

Perhaps we shouldn't pick on sportswriters too much. Clichés can be found in other types of material as well, anyplace where a writer just gets tired and loses the spark (whoops!) of originality:

```
The more things change, the more they stay the same.

Hard evidence...

Political football...

Like greased lightning...
```

While the use of clichés in news copy and interviewing indicates lazy writing, there is a place for the deliberate use of clichés to assist in the development of characters in a drama. We learn about characters, in large part, from how they speak and the words they use. Choosing appropriate clichés is an excellent shorthand way to give the audience a feel for a character.

## SPECIAL CONSIDERATIONS FOR VISUAL MEDIA

We have been emphasizing those basic characteristics relating to the preparation, transmittal and reception of broadcast content which are common to both radio and television. There is no hard copy for the recipient to process; the words are only heard; there is no opportunity for repetition; and there is no chance for feedback from recipient to source. These character-

**Figure 3.1.**
Reprinted with
special permission
of King Features
Syndicate.

istics dictate the basic style and structure of scripts for both audio only and audiovisual media.

But there are some situations in which the addition of the visual sense calls for modifications to aural style. The addition of sight means that often the TV writer can leave out descriptive material. For example, in a radio interview it may be important that the audience have a physical description of the interviewee—age, stature and so on. The writer or announcer must provide this. In television, the viewer can immediately perceive the physical characteristics of the person on the screen. In preparing a radio drama, the writer must describe the setting of each scene—not always in great detail because the imagination of the listener can fill in much of the scene, but with enough detail to support the plot. In television, the location of the scene can be seen—a signpost tells the name of the town being approached; a stove, pots, table and so on indicate that another scene is in a kitchen.

Color, if important in the radio description, must be explained—written into the narrative. Generally, color is not important and the script should be written in such a way as to avoid it, but if the advertiser wants to mention the "bright blue box" of a product, you'll have to write "bright blue box." In television, the color is there on the screen for the viewer to see, and "bright blue box" in the copy is used only if the writer wants to provide additional emphasis.

Finally, if you examine the two transmission channels of television separately—that is, the sound and the picture—you will find that in many cases the sound track is independent and would carry a coherent message even if there were no picture to accompany it. Often it is possible for audience members to obtain information through the aural channel while doing other tasks that require their vision be focused elsewhere. It is not even necessary to be in the same room with the television set to get information from the sound channel.

On the other hand, despite the claim that one picture is worth a thousand words and despite the very graphic images that can be displayed on TV, seldom does a picture, suddenly appearing on the screen, by itself give a complete message. Further, the viewer's full attention is required to obtain and process visual information.

This analysis of audience behavior in relation to the two channels is in no way intended to place the visual channel in a secondary position; there are many examples of the powerful impact of appropriate visual images. Almost any sporting event is more exciting to see than just to hear described; a travel program on radio pales in contrast to the visual beauty of some remote location; visual demonstration of a technique provides for better learning of how to do that task than do just words; and so on. But the point is that seldom can the picture stand alone. We are accustomed to hearing television as much as seeing it. A sound track that follows good aural style is as important to television as it is to radio.

## RESPONDING TO CRITICISM

Critics frequently have faulted broadcast writers for using an overly simplistic style. They have argued that the dramatic scripts for prime-time television programs, which aim to reach the largest possible audiences, use language and plot structures which are insulting to the intelligence of many people. To some extent, that criticism is justified. Some writers, and some authors of writing texts, have carried the instruction "keep it simple" to extremes.

The principles of aural style given here, however, still apply in general. Clarity is still the primary objective. If the purpose of a particular program is to reach a very large audience, the writing of that program—the plot, the language, the sentence construction and so on—must be kept sufficiently simple so that the large number and very diverse groups of people in the audience can follow and understand, and stay tuned.

Another critical argument is made about television's role as primarily an entertainment medium. These critics suggest that television has abdicated a responsibility to treat important issues in any significant fashion. Again, there is some truth to the criticism. Given the characteristics of the broadcasting process, it is difficult to present in-depth analyses of complex issues. In the electronic media, materials must be presented in a sequential fashion, and once organized into a sequence they cannot be rearranged, recalled, or examined at any length by members of the audience. These limitations do provide real constraints on the complexity of material that can be presented through these media and processed by their audiences. And one must admit that in practice the time and money necessary to prepare scripts based on complex and controversial material usually have not been provided. For the most part, the content of programs is kept to a level where audiences can listen or view with enjoyment and without effort.

But for the writer or the student who finds broadcast writing to be unchallenging, or a prostituting of his or her creative talent, there is hope. There are producers and writers in the industry who believe that the limitations of "aural style" simply provide a greater challenge to the creative use of the media and that the use of both pictorial information in motion and a creative sound track can in fact provide a better explanation of complex concepts than can print, and that therefore in-depth explanations of important and complex issues can be treated by television.

And there is a definite trend toward audience fragmentation—more channels, and narrower, more specific audiences. In these cases, writers will be permitted to use a larger vocabulary, more specialized language and more complex ideas—so long as the target audience for the program can process the information. Maybe we can modify the basic principle just a bit to reflect the trend away from large, undifferentiated audiences. We'll say that writers should use a style and vocabulary appropriate for the audience to which the content is targeted.

## CONCLUSION

Broadcasting is different from other forms of audio or audiovisual communication. The words used to communicate are only heard, not seen. The recipient's processing of the message is through the ear—the aural channel. These words are received at a speed and in a sequence which is predetermined by the source of the message, and they are presented only once. The recipient cannot control the process of reception except to tune away from the message.

These unique characteristics of broadcasting describe a situation in which the messages prepared by the writer must be immediately clear to the recipient audience. Clarity is enhanced by using the techniques of aural style in writing broadcast scripts. The beginning writer will need to practice these techniques consciously until they become automatic.

**Exercises**

1. From print sources—newspapers, magazines, books, trade journals—locate five complex sentences that use long opening modifying clauses. Copy these sentences and then rewrite them for aural style, simplifying and eliminating unnecessary, confusing material.

2. Look for examples of vague, abstract language; government documents are prime sources in which to find obscure, confusing statements. Rewrite for aural style.

3. Choose a major news story from a current newspaper, and rewrite it as a 90-second *radio* news story. Observe these cautions:

   a. Choose a timely story that contains enough important facts or statements for you to fill the time without padding.

   b. Your story should have a lead sentence, and the body of the story should present the information in a logical sequence. But if you have not yet covered the organization of news copy (Chapter 12), don't worry; that topic will be taken up later.

   c. Concentrate on the principles of aural style—all those things that make broadcast writing different from writing for print media.

**Notes**

1. William Strunk, Jr., and E. B. White, *The Elements of Style*, 3rd ed. (New York: Macmillan, 1979), p. 21.
2. Adapted from K. Tim Wulfemeyer, *Beginning Broadcast Newswriting* (Ames: The Iowa State University Press, 1976), pp. 8–9, and Mitchell Stephens, *Broadcast News: Radio Journalism and an Introduction to Television* (New York: Holt, Rinehart and Winston, 1980), pp. 20–21, 26.
3. Albert Crews. *Professional Radio Writing* (Boston: Houghton Mifflin, 1946), pp. 51–52.
4. Ibid., p. 51.
5. Strunk and White, *The Elements of Style*, 3rd ed., p. 23.
6. Gerald J. DeMartin, "Keep Your Script from Being Tied Up in 'Nots,' " *E&ITV*, August 1982, p. 65. Copyright 1982 C. S. Tepfer Publishing Company, Inc. Reprinted by permission.
7. Reprinted with the permission of Macmillan Publishing Company from *A Civil Tongue* by Edwin H. Newman, p. 6. Copyright © 1975, 1976, by Edwin Newman. Originally published by the Bobbs-Merrill Company, Inc.
8. Ibid., p. 160.
9. Excerpt from *Doublespeak*, by William Lutz. Copyright © 1989 by Blonde Bear, Inc. Reprinted by permission of HarperCollins Publishers, Inc.
10. *The Random House Dictionary of the English Language, Unabridged Edition* (New York: Random House, 1969), p. 276.

**Further Reading**

In this list we've included titles that relate directly to style, to the correct or appropriate uses of language, and to commentaries on language. The first item is one of the most widely accepted works on style and layout. It should be in every writer's library, even though little of its content applies directly to broadcast.

*Chicago Manual of Style*, 13th ed. Chicago: University of Chicago Press, 1982.

Two small volumes that over time have become standard and highly recommended works on the use of language are

Flesch, Rudolf. *The Art of Readable Writing*, rev. ed. New York: Macmillan, 1986.

Strunk, William, Jr., and E. B. White. *The Elements of Style*, 3rd ed. New York: Macmillan, 1979.

We recommend these also for your basic library, especially the Strunk and White book. Dr. Flesch has also written this useful companion volume:

Flesch, Rudolf, and A. H. Lass. *A New Guide to Better Writing*. New York: Warner, 1989.

Other helpful general reviews of style include

Blakey, Ellen Sue. *Learning to Edit: A Workbook for Writers and Editors*. Dubuque, IA: Eddie Bowers, 1988.

Bremner, John. *Words, Words, Words: A Dictionary for Writers and Others Who Care about Words*. New York: Columbia University Press, 1980.

Provost, Gary. *Make Your Words Work*. Cincinnati: Writer's Digest, 1990.

Stott, Bill. *Write to the Point*. New York: Columbia University Press, 1991.

Williams, Joseph M. *Style: Toward Clarity and Grace*. Chicago: University of Chicago Press, 1990.

More specifically for broadcast journalism, these references are recommended:

Hood, James R., and Brad Kalbfeld (eds.) *The Associated Press Broadcast News Handbook*. New York: Associated Press, 1982. (Revised edition under preparation, 1993)

Kessler, Lauren, and Duncan McDonald. *When Words Collide: A Journalist's Guide to Grammar and Style*, 3rd ed. Belmont, CA: Wadsworth, 1992.

MacDonald, R. H. *A Broadcast News Manual of Style*. White Plains, NY: Longman, 1987.

*United Press International Stylebook: A Handbook for Writers, Editors and News Directors*, 3rd ed. Chicago: National Textbook, 1992.

In this chapter we quoted from two authors who have written extensively and entertainingly about the English language. You should find these titles both useful and enjoyable:

Lutz, William. *Doublespeak*. New York: HarperCollins, 1990.

Newman, Edwin. *A Civil Tongue*. New York: Macmillan, 1976.

————. *I Must Say: Edwin Newman on English, the News, and Other Matters*. New York: Warner, 1989.

————. *Strictly Speaking*. New York: Macmillan, 1974.

Another author who enjoys the idiosyncracies of the English language is Richard Lederer. Here are three very funny short books of his:

Lederer, Richard. *Anguished English*. Charleston, SC: Wyrick, 1987.

————. *Crazy English*. New York: Pocket Books, 1989.

————. *Get Thee to a Punnery*. Charleston, SC: Wyrick, 1988.

# CHAPTER 4

# Writing and Production

**B**roadcast writing is a means to an end—the end being the completed and hopefully errorless presentation of a program or announcement. The members of the audience who listen to or watch that program do not see the written script. It is used only by the preparers of the program—by directors, announcers, actors and control room personnel. Its function is to enable them to put the final program together as quickly, easily and inexpensively as possible.

In this chapter we examine relationships between writing and production, for it is the form of production more than any other single factor that determines the layout, complexity and detail needed in the written plans for producing programs and announcements.

When you finish this chapter, you will be able to

- recognize how production factors affect the form and detail of scripts,

- identify audio and video equipment used to produce programs,

- understand how writing and production interact in program preparation, and

- recognize and use these important terms and concepts:

| | |
|---|---|
| ad lib | production variables |
| ENG and EFP | script: copy, semi-script, shot sheet, fact sheet |
| live-to-tape | transducer |

Since different types of programs are produced differently, they require different forms of written preparation. Not surprisingly, therefore, different words are used to describe the product of the process of research and writing. At the beginning of this chapter we used the word *script*. Another term often used is *copy*, as in news copy or commercial copy; sometimes you'll even see "script copy," a redundancy. The possibility for confusion exists, however, because some people use *copy* to refer only to announcements. Texts that teach *copywriting* are usually limited to teaching how to prepare commercials and public service announcements (PSAs). Also, the term scriptwriting is used by some to refer only to dramatic programs. A *scriptwriting* text will teach principles of dramatic program construction. When used this way, *script* implies a word-for-word (and, for television, a shot-by-shot) production plan.

Most of the time, however, you can use either term to describe the written text and directions for any type of program. We'll use both script and copy as general terms to describe the written preparation for programs and announcements.

Other terms are used to describe the written preparation for programs that do not use detailed scripts. An interview program, for example, may use a *semi-script*, which consists of a scripted opening and closing but only a series of written questions (no answers) to guide the interviewer through the body of the show. A TV documentary is often assembled from *shot sheets*, lists of each recorded camera shot, including the length of the shot, its basic visual content, and, if an interview, the essence of the comment made by the interviewee in that shot. Radio commercials, too, if they are to be delivered live by an announcer, may be read ad lib from just a *fact sheet.**

## PRODUCTION FACTORS AFFECTING SCRIPTING

Several factors affect the type and complexity of the written copy needed to produce a broadcast program. Obviously the type of program is one factor. A dramatic program is certainly going to have different requirements from a quiz show, a disc jockey program, or a news broadcast. But those factors that most directly affect the writer are connected to the method of production used. We've identified five such factors, which we shall call *production variables*:

1. What portion of the program will be delivered *ad lib*, that is improvised, without preparation—none, some, all?

2. Is the program to be aired live, or will it be prerecorded or a combination of both?

---

* Yet another term that this author has used since his days in radio is *continuity*. Radio writers and producers have long used that word in a broad sense, to describe the full range of written materials used to prepare programs, including but not limited to word-for-word scripts. But television and film people use continuity to describe something quite different—the visual consistency in a drama from shot to shot within a scene. To avoid confusion, we'll not use that word.

3. If prerecorded, how much editing, if any, will be done before broadcast?

4. How quickly must the program be prepared for broadcast?

5. How many people are going to be involved in the preparation of the broadcast?

All these factors work together to determine how much written copy can be prepared and will be needed in a given circumstance.

A very powerful example of how these variables interact can be found in the television news coverage of the opening days of the Persian Gulf war, the first war ever to be seen and heard live in American homes. Many of the stories sent back by field reporters were ad lib and live, when there was no time to jot down on paper even the briefest of notes before going on the air with an eyewitness description of incoming missiles and with video that was also spontaneous. Other stories were live but with some preparation—an arranged interview or a sequence of thoughts. Still others included a preshot and edited video sequence, with a written audio narration to fit the visuals.

Throughout the coverage, immediacy was an important concern. Some stories could not be delayed. Others were delayed briefly, while more important events elsewhere were covered. After the first few days, only the most important stories were not delayed, as the networks settled back into their normal programming schedule.

In the confusion and tension of those days, we saw situations where a reporter in Saudi Arabia, live on screen, was urging his crew to set up quickly, so that he could present his story. At other times, the network anchor asked his producers, live on screen, where they were going next. Under normal circumstances, such behavior would be considered very poor practice and the fault of not having a script to which all key production personnel and talent could refer.

In the early days of broadcast, both for radio and later for television, when recording was inefficient and of poor quality, most programs, including dramas, were aired live. Now, with the high quality and small size of origination and recording equipment, many combinations of ad lib or scripted, live or recorded and edited or not edited may be found. Most major network dramatic series are prerecorded and heavily edited, using single-camera field production techniques. Some situation comedies, however, although recorded, are shot in a studio using multiple cameras and long sequences—approximating live techniques. True live broadcasts include sports events, the anchor portions of TV newscasts and increasing numbers of stories reported live from remote locations via remote microwave or satellite feeds, C-Span coverage of Congress, radio call-in programs, and many other types.

Some programs are produced *live-to-tape*, which means that they are pretaped only for convenience. For example, a local TV public affairs program that airs in the early morning might be taped the preceding afternoon with guests who would would be unavailable at the early morning hour for a live broadcast. As far as the production is concerned, however, the program is handled as a live show, with no (or very few) retakes and as little editing as possible.

We can conclude by saying that if only one person is involved in the complete process from creative idea to on-the-air, such as a radio disc jockey or a one-person radio news operation, then a full script probably will not be prepared. But whenever precision and accuracy are needed and whenever there are groups of people involved in the production of the program, some form of written guideline will be required. And live programs, which are also unedited of course, require careful scripting (and, if possible, rehearsal) to minimize the possibility of foul-ups.

# AUDIO PRODUCTION

Both radio and television producers and writers must be concerned with sound production. For radio, the only sense which connects listeners to a program is a continuous flow of sound. Listeners expect to hear something at all times; an interruption of only a few seconds will bring the listener to the set—to see if the power has failed, or if program transmission has been interrupted. Listeners will quickly tune to another channel or turn off the set and probably not tune back.

In television, brief moments without sound can be tolerated, and some commercial writers seeking novel approaches have experimented with pictures without sound for an entire (but brief) spot. But here, too, audiences expect sound and will attempt to adjust the set if it disappears for long.

The sounds available to the writer-producer of any program are voices, music and sound effects. We devote Chapter 7 to an in-depth look at all three. Sounds may be presented live—that is, created at the moment of production or broadcast—or they may be prerecorded, edited and mixed with other sounds to form a composite track. The convenience of various recording formats makes many alternatives possible.

## Audio Facilities

The equipment used to produce and manipulate broadcast sounds can be grouped into three categories: (1) microphones, which pick up sounds; (2) storage devices, consisting of records, tapes and their associated recording and playback equipment; and (3) mixing and control consoles. You will find these in great variety at every station and production facility.

### *Microphones*

The initial capturing of any sound is done through a microphone, which is the *transducer* that converts sound energy to electrical pulses that then can be transmitted, stored on tape or disk, and/or mixed with other signals representing other sounds.

In simple production, a single microphone may be used to collect all the sounds which can be picked up at one location. But frequently better control of the relative intensities of multiple sounds can be gained if multiple microphones are used. At a football game, if each announcer has his or her own microphone for narration, and additional microphones are used to pick up crowd sounds, bands, and so on, you should be better able to balance voices with background noise and avoid having the announcers drowned out by the yelling when a touchdown is scored.

Similarly, multiple microphones recording the various instruments in an orchestra permit the control room operator to adjust each level to get the desired balance. Frequently each microphone will be recorded on a separate track, without mixing. When that is done, any number of trial mixes can be made in order to get the best final composite.

Multiple microphones (at least two) must be used to provide stereo recordings and broadcasts, where the final two tracks differ somewhat from each other, in order to provide the binaural effect. Until recently, broadcast stereo was possible only on FM radio stations (although of course it has been available on tape and disc recordings). Now AM stations and television are rapidly converting to stereo sound as well. Most of the production necessary to achieve stereo will be handled by technicians, but writers should be concerned with ways that stereo audio can enhance their scripts.

### Recording-Storage Devices

In this category are the substantial varieties of equipment that record sound and play it back. For many years the primary playback devices were turntables that handled, first, 78 rpm recordings, then LPs and 45 rpm discs. These turntables will still be needed for years to come to play back these older types of recordings, but they are being rapidly replaced by digital compact discs (CDs) and their playback units, which although initially more expensive, have fine fidelity and are very easy to use when cued up by electronic controls.

For many purposes, however, tape machines are the recording and playback mechanisms of first choice. Tape is more useful than discs because of the ease of recording and the speed and convenience with which recorded material may be edited and played back. Other advantages are the portability of equipment and low costs for both recorders and tape.

Three types of machines are likely to be found in a broadcast station, each with certain advantages and limitations. Reel-to-reel tape machines can handle long periods of uninterrupted recording or playback and often operate at higher tape speeds, thereby permitting greater fidelity. They can be purchased in configurations that accommodate simultaneous recording of multiple tracks. They are also most easily used for editing—that is, if one is physically editing with a blade and splicing tape.

Cassette units (like those you probably have at home) are small, and easy to use and carry. They have decent recording response for voices, but are not so good for full-fidelity music recording because of slow tape speed and narrow recording track. The tapes cannot be edited easily except by rerecording the content onto another machine.

Cartridge units are most commonly used for short recordings, such as individual commercials, short audio actualities to be inserted into a news story or individual musical selections. A cartridge can be quickly inserted into its player, will cue automatically, play and return to its starting position so that it is ready to play again. Carts can be changed quickly in their players, so two players in a control room can support an almost continuous sequence of different audio inserts.

Some production facilities are replacing cartridge units with digital disc units. These machines look and operate very much like personal computers. The same short pieces of material—commercials, actualities, and so on—are stored on the disc, and can be recalled very quickly for broadcast.

In the next chapter, one of our examples of a radio news script, Figure 5.3, shows an inserted actuality. Many stories will contain more than one. Depending upon the equipment available at the station, these audio inserts will be transferred from the tape on which the original recording was made onto one or more carts. Some stations place each actuality on a separate cart; others will put them on a single cart with brief pauses between or alternate cuts between two cart machines.

### Consoles

An audio *console* is the primary control device for the various sound inputs which might be used in presenting a program. First, it permits its operator to select one or more sources from among the various microphones, turntables, tape recorders, or remote lines that may be connected to it. Second, it allows the volume level of those sources to be controlled. Third, it permits multiple sources to be mixed together, and at appropriate levels. Finally, its output can be sent to various locations—for example, to a transmitter for broadcast, to a tape recorder for storage or fed down a cable from its location to a console at another location.

For a writer, it will be very helpful to know the limitations of consoles in those studios or remote locations where you may be producing programs. For example, you cannot write a dramatic program requiring more microphones than the console can handle.

## VIDEO PRODUCTION

Television audiences expect some video information on their screens at all times. Only a brief fade to black and back up to picture is allowed when changing scenes. The images that can be used to make up television programs are practically limitless, but it is useful, for discussion at least, to classify them in a few broad categories.

1. Talent—persons seen on screen. Talent is often subdivided into two categories: (1) performers, who appear as themselves, including newspeople, talk show hosts and guests, and so on, and (2) actors, who portray someone else in either a fictional or nonfictional story. We'll break the categories slightly differently, into four, but the point we want to make is simply that much of the time in a program there will be people on screen, and what they do and how they appear doing it is something that writers and producers must consider.

   a. Persons who are talking directly to the audience, such as news reporters, commercial announcers, lecturers or narrators. This category of images is often called "talking heads." Talking heads are inexpensive visuals; it costs less to point a camera at a reporter than it does to tape on location, even if it is less interesting. Also, it's faster.

   b. Persons talking to each other, as in a panel discussion program or interview. Critics see this use of the medium as only slightly better than talking heads. Again the same counterarguments apply—it's faster and less costly than location shooting.

   c. Persons performing—musicians, dancers, contestants in a quiz program. In these cases the visual content does provide attraction for audiences, but that attraction will vary tremendously depending upon the type of performance. A ballet performance is strong visually because of its movement; a symphony is not.

   d. Persons engaged in dramatic action, with accompanying dialogue, action, and so on. Here both the content and the action provide attraction for audiences.

2. Demonstration. The demonstration of activities, processes, and events is an obvious strength of television. The writers of commercials are aware of this strength; many effective commercials use demonstration in some way. Similarly, effective corporate and instructional programs make frequent use of demonstrations. Demonstrations may or may not use people. A role-playing segment in a training tape, for example, may use persons as actors in a dramatic sketch, but the purpose of the entire sketch may be to demonstrate, say, the appropriate behavior in an office.

3. Scenics. We'll use this term very broadly to categorize a range of images in which persons and demonstrations are not the primary focus. Many programs contain scenics—for example, to set the location of a dramatic program. Travelogues have a high proportion of scenic shots. News stories use them as well, on location at the scene of a news event, to show the audience what has happened and where.

4. Graphics. Also sometimes called visuals, but that term is somewhat misleading as all TV images are visuals. Graphics include all the various devices used in programs and announcements—program titles (even when they contain other visual content as well), charts and graphs, credits to performers and production personnel, the lower-screen identifications of guests and of actuality sources, the background pictures inserted behind a news anchor and so on. Also included in this category is the tremendous range of special effects that can be created using sophisticated computerized video equipment. Graphics may appear on the screen by themselves or as part of a composite image containing other pictorial elements.

The point we want to make here, with this very simplistic categorization, is that a picture must be on the screen at all times. Sometimes writers who are not used to writing for television become so involved in the sound of their scripts that they forget the corresponding obligation to identify some picture for each moment of broadcast as well. Using these broad categories can help remind you of basic choices to meet that requirement, at least until you develop a more sophisticated visual sense.

## Video Facilities

Video production equipment includes cameras, tape recorders and consoles as the major items. As with audio, these devices come with a wide range of capabilities.

### *Cameras*

The television camera (or film camera, for either can be used to collect visual images, and it is only a technical matter to convert film images for TV) is the *visual transducer*. It converts picture information into a sequence of electrical pulses in a similar though more complex manner than that in which microphones convert sound. These pulses may then be transmitted, stored, mixed with other sources or some combination thereof. Chapter 8 discusses the effects upon audiences when images are sequenced in various ways. The final sections of that chapter particularly consider the effects of sequence and transition from one picture source to another.

### *Tape Recorders*

Not many years ago a television tape recorder took up the space of a large desk plus that of several equipment racks. It recorded on 2-inch-wide tape at a speed of 15 inches per second. Reels of tape weighed 20 pounds or more. Editing was possible only with a blade, splicing tape, special solvents to "read" the patterns of magnetic particles on the tape and magnifying glasses. It was such a complex task that it was usually avoided.

Contrast that with the size and weight of present-day equipment. A combination camera-recorder all in one unit can easily be carried by a reporter for electronic news gathering. Editing, too, is all electronic and controlled by a form of computer. Video edits, and the insertion of titles and other graphics, are quickly and easily done. This ability to bring edited video to the screen rapidly and simply has dramatically enhanced the possibilities for television reporters, producers, and writers.

Reduced cost has also had an effect, making it possible for many people to purchase cameras and recorders for home use. Not only has professional production been changed, we now have network programs like *America's Funniest Home Videos* and *I Witness Video* which are made up of video material supplied by amateurs, and we have dramatic news actualities also recorded by amateurs, like the video of the police beating of Rodney King.

### Consoles

The video control consoles at a TV station are sophisticated devices with which operators select inputs, adjust levels and create all kinds of special effects. They are used both in master control, where programs are broadcast, and in editing suites, to assemble programs from various sources onto a master tape. The console may be used to select a sequence of visuals from various inputs with appropriate transitions, such as wipes, cuts and fades between shots. Or it may be used to provide two or more simultaneous visual images, such as the inserted picture behind a news anchor or a split screen showing both ends of a telephone conversation. Consoles can produce literally hundreds of different effects, especially when combined with sophisticated computer graphics units. For the writer, these capabilities add a new, dynamic dimension to visualization. The electronic manipulation of pictures may enhance and augment otherwise static images through new forms of motion or with new transitions. Writers need to know in general what the capabilities of a particular console are, but the actual creation of these complicated images is best left to specialists.

### Other Equipment

We've briefly mentioned the use of satellites, microwave remote units and computers. Their importance in changing the face of television production cannot be overemphasized. The first two have been particularly important in news production. Stations and networks are now able to get video back to their newsrooms very rapidly and to increase the number of "live shots" in their newscasts. Satellite distribution and sharing of news stories also allow stations to select stories from a wider variety of choices than previously available.

Computers facilitate the manipulation of images in ways not previously possible. Some critics complain that this manipulation is primarily glitz, intended only to capture audience attention and awe. But computers may also be used in production to prepare sophisticated graphics—charts and maps—and move those in such a way to communicate abstract ideas with more visual appeal and relevance.

One result of miniaturization and automatic controls on cameras, recorders and editing equipment has been to take much production out of studios to remote locations. *Electronic news gathering* (ENG) and *electronic field production* (EFP) use only a single camera and a video recorder. "Raw" video footage is recorded using an episodic, shot-by-shot production technique. Then those images are sequenced and edited into a final production, which might be a brief news story or a full program.

For writers, this approach means that it is easier to add visual variety to production. It also requires changes in writing technique. Instead of a pre-written script, narration to accompany a news story, for example, will be written parallel with the selection of shots from the raw tape that are being edited onto the story tape. During the editing process shot sheets and other forms of notes to keep track of the visuals are more important to the preparation of these productions than would be a traditional script, which couldn't be written in advance anyway.

Perhaps the best way to understand how ENG, EFP and tape editing have changed the requirements for scripting is to note that for live and live-to-tape production, scripts (in some form) must be completed *prior* to production, to aid the cast and crew in a successful presentation. In contrast, for many types of ENG and EFP productions, scripting will proceed *during* the production and editing process.

We don't mean to suggest that ENG and EFP have replaced studio production. There are advantages to studios as well, among them cost and control over such matters as lighting, sound and weather. We do suggest that the type of production will in many cases affect the form of written copy required.

## CONCLUSION

The written preparation, in whatever form it is put on paper, must facilitate completion of the production. The circumstances of the production, in turn, dictate the form the copy will take and the amount of detail required.

We have emphasized how production has changed over time, especially in the miniaturization and automation of equipment. We've also pointed to the effect on production created by the merging of traditional types of production equipment with computer controls. These changes apply to both audio and video equipment, but they are much more obvious in video, where ENG and EFP production techniques are now used on a scale not previously possible. In turn, this single-camera production has drastically changed the role of the writer and the forms of broadcast scripting.

Miniaturization, automation and the greatly reduced costs of small cameras and recorders have also increased the use of these items by amateurs, and we noted the most famous example of such use—the videotaping by an amateur of Rodney King's beating by Los Angeles police. TV stations now solicit and broadcast amateur videos to be included in their newscasts. That policy affects the professional writers on staff, who are expected to prepare narration to accompany the video, when neither the writer nor the narrator was at the scene to collect information firsthand. In later chapters we consider some of the implications for television news departments of the increased use of these amateur videos in news production and at some of the ethical questions raised by such use.

You will be a better writer if you are also familiar with production. At many smaller stations your job likely will involve some combination of writing and production. But you need not have had courses or practice in audio or video production in order to learn the basic principles of writing we present in this book.

**Exercise**

If you have had or are taking courses in radio or television production, you will have had opportunity to observe and to work with production equipment. If not, we suggest that you arrange to visit a radio and television station, or separate production facilities. Observe how the various pieces of equipment are used to get sound and picture onto the air. Note what types of scripts are used in the productions you observe.

**Further Reading**

A very wide selection of books and periodicals is available that discuss both audio and video production. Some are quite general, others consider very specific aspects of production. Some of the more specific titles are included in the references for other chapters. Here is a representative sample of basic texts under three categories. For audio/radio production:

Alten, Stanley R. *Audio in Media*, 3rd ed. Belmont, CA: Wadsworth, 1990.

Keith, Michael C. *Radio Production: The Art and Science*. Stoneham, MA: Focal, 1990.

Oringel, Robert S. *Audio Control Handbook*, 6th ed. Stoneham, MA: Focal, 1989.

Reese, David F., and Lynne S. Gross. *Radio Production Worktext: Studio and Equipment*. Stoneham, MA: Focal, 1989.

Thom, Randy. *AudioCraft: An Introduction to the Tools and Techniques of Audio Production*, 2nd ed. Washington, DC: National Federation of Community Broadcasters, 1989.

For video production:

Anderson, Gary H. *Video Editing and Post-Production: A Professional Guide*, 2nd ed. White Plains, NY: Knowledge Industry, 1988.

Arthur, Mavis, and James Caruso. *Video Editing and Post Production*. New York: Prentice-Hall, 1992.

Burrows, Thomas D., Donald N. Wood and Lynne S. Gross. *Television Production: Disciplines and Techniques*, 5th ed. Dubuque, IA: Brown and Benchmark, 1992.

Compesi, Ron, and Ronald E. Sherriffs. *Small Format Television Production*, 2nd ed. Needham Heights, MA: Allyn & Bacon, 1990.

Merrill, Joan. *Camcorder Video: Shooting and Editing Techniques.* New York: Prentice-Hall, 1991.

Millerson, Gerald. *The Technique of Television Production*, 12th ed. Stoneham, MA: Focal, 1990.

Schihl, Robert J. *Single Camera Video Production: From Concept to Edited Master.* Stoneham, MA: Focal, 1989.

Schneider, Arthur. *Electronic Post-Production and Videotape Editing.* Stoneham, MA: Focal, 1989.

Shook, Frederick. *Television Field Production and Reporting.* White Plains, NY: Longman, 1988.

Utz, Peter. *Today's Video: Equipment, Setup, and Production*, 2nd ed. New York: Prentice-Hall, 1992.

Verna, Tony, and William Bode. *Live TV: An Inside Look at Directing and Producing.* Stoneham, MA: Focal, 1987.

Yoakam, Richard D., and Charles F. Cremer. *ENG: Television News and New Technology*, 2nd ed. New York: Random House, 1989.

Zaza, Tony. *Audio Design: Sound Recording Techniques for Film and Video.* New York: Prentice-Hall, 1991.

Zettl, Herbert. *Television Production Handbook*, 5th ed. Belmont, CA: Wadsworth, 1992.

Although announcing was not discussed specifically in this chapter, for our purposes it can be considered an aspect of production. Here are some texts that can help you improve your skills if you are going to be on the air:

Cronauer, Adrian. *How to Read Copy.* Chicago: Bonus, 1990.

O'Donnell, Lewis B., Carl Hausman, and Philip Benoit. *Announcing: Broadcast Communicating Today*, 2nd ed. Belmont, CA: Wadsworth, 1992.

Utterback, Ann S., *Broadcast Voice Handbook.* Chicago: Bonus, 1990.

These periodicals are also useful sources for production information:

*In View*, Midwest Communications Corp., 920 Broadway, New York, NY 10010.

*Videography*, P.S.N. Publications, 2 Park Avenue, Suite 1820, New York, NY 10016.

*Video Systems*, Intertec Publishing Corporation, 9800 Metcalf, Overland Park, KS 66212-2215.

# Script Mechanics

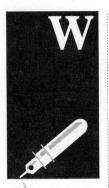

**W**e can describe a broadcast script as a blueprint, or perhaps as a road map. To make it possible for the production staff to prepare a program or announcement as efficiently as possible, all the materials that go into the script—the lines to be spoken and the instructions to cast and crew—must be clear, accurate, unambiguous, complete and presented in a standardized form that all the program's "preparers" can follow.

But as we showed in the preceding chapter, the precise form that the written copy will take depends on both the type of program and the form of production. Some programs require very detailed scripts; others can be successfully produced from a few quickly typed notes. In this chapter we follow Chapter 4's review of the relationship between production and writing and see how several common types of copy are prepared.

When you finish this chapter, you will be able to

- use correct layout form to prepare scripts for radio and television, including
    basic radio layout,
    radio news layout,
    television "live" split-page layout,
    television news layout,
    screenplay layout,
    the storyboard,

- use punctuation, numerals and abbreviations appropriately within scripts, and

- recognize and use these important terms and concepts:

| | |
|---|---|
| actualities | layout form/format |
| BIZ | LIVE—SOT |
| ellipses | master-scene layout |
| FONT/CHYRON/SUPER | MORE MORE MORE |

| | |
|---|---|
| off-camera/voice-over: VO | slug |
| on-camera: ON CAM, O.C. | SOUND/SFX |
| outcue | split-page layout |
| package | storyboard/photoboard |

Until recently, the layout of scripts had to be done entirely by typewriter. It was often a very tedious task to put all the script elements in the proper places on the page and to follow the generally accepted rules for spacings, columns, and so on. Even standard word processing programs do not accommodate some of the page layout required by various types of copy. They can be very frustrating when you try to use them to lay out a script. Now, computer programs are available that assist with many of the mechanics of script preparation. Some of these programs are intended to be used in connection with word processing software; they add formatting features to an existing file. Others combine word processing with special formatting features.

Many stations and agencies have these aids and freelance professional writers use them as well. Computerized television news management programs, for example, allow writers to "capture" stories from the news wire services, to track all the stories in progress during the day, to keep a running time on the newscast as the stories are being assembled, to prepare teleprompter copy, to control cameras, and, after the broadcast, to store the cast in the station's archives. Script formatting and editing functions are just a minor part of these programs.

Similarly, preparing a script for a television drama, which requires that scene descriptions, instructions to performers and spoken lines all be arranged on the page with different margins and spacings, is much simpler when specially designed software is used.

These programs tend to be expensive, however; their costs can be justified for commercial operations (or university writing labs) that produce lots of scripts, but they are not usually within the financial means of students or beginning writers. Nevertheless, you should be aware of the existence of these programs, for if you choose a career in writing for the electronic media you will most certainly use software to prepare your copy. Finally, although software can assist writers with many of their routine tasks—editing, layout, spelling, thesaurus, even grammar—and some of the programs claim to walk you through the process for writing salable drama series, none really can provide a creative spark.

## LAYOUT FORMS FOR SCRIPTS

We have a preference for using the term *layout form* to describe the arrangement on the typewritten page of the various elements that go into a script. Another word that is frequently used to describe the same thing is *format*, but in broadcasting *format* has several different meanings. A program producer or director uses it to refer to the structural sequence of events within a program. And in radio *format* is used to describe the image or sound of a station—for example, a station may have a "Top 40" format, or a "country" format. To avoid confusion with the other meanings, we prefer to call this topic *layout form*, but frequently we will defer to standard practice and use the word *format* as well.

In this chapter we will discuss six approaches to layout, which cover the major types of copy and program content:

1. Basic radio layout, used for most radio programs that require scripts, except news.

2. Radio news layout, a simplified version of radio scripting, which provides for the easy insertion of news actualities.

3. Television split-page layout, used for most live programming. Our examples show it used for announcements.

4. Television news layout, a modification of the split-page form. Many variations are used to accommodate the different ways in which visual material may be gathered and inserted into a story.

5. Television single-camera layout, for programs that are prerecorded and then edited on a shot-by-shot basis.

6. The storyboard, a visual layout used extensively for television commercials and in preparing slide-tape presentations.

By the way, if we have given you the impression that there are absolutely fixed rules for the layout of each broadcast script, that is not the case. As we've already discussed, different types of broadcast programs have different requirements, and those in turn result in differences in layout. Even a small change in the way a program is prepared often will lead to changes in scripting requirements. Many supervisors have their own rules—the way they want it done in their newsroom or their advertising agency. And if you are using scriptwriting software, each different program forces its own rules, and each is different from its competitors. When you get a job that requires writing scripts, do it the way your boss (or your instructor) wants it done. In the meantime, use the guidelines presented in this chapter, which reflect the large body of common practice generally accepted throughout the industry.

## Basic Rules for Scripting

Here are a few universal considerations:

1. All copy is typed or prepared using a computer keyboard and printer.

Keep copy neat, without strikeovers or deletions. Minor corrections may be added in pencil, if necessary, but there is always the danger that penciled changes will lead to misread copy. You cannot be sure that other people can read your writing or even that you will be able to at any given moment, so don't take chances.

2. Use standard 8½- by 11-inch paper. Scripts for talent, which will be read in front of live microphones, should be on a paper that does not rattle when handled. Many television news departments use specially prepared forms with the columns for audio and video already defined and padded to automatically provide multiple copies for the anchors, teleprompter, director, and producer.

3. Use only one side of the paper.

4. Most scripts will require multiple copies. Make sure sufficient copies are available for all who will need one.

5. There is no universally accepted standard for the headings to be placed on a script, or for other preliminary material that may be required. Stations, networks and advertising agencies all use forms that suit their own needs. Among the materials that appear in the heading are series title, program title, number of the program in the series, writer's, director's, and producer's names, length of program, date and time of broadcast, cast list, music list. This material may be at the top of the first page of the script or, if it is lengthy, on a separate title page. If a separate title page is used, only a brief identifying title need appear on subsequent pages.

## Basic Radio Layout

From the 1920s through the 1940s, radio was the dominant medium of home entertainment with the broadcast of many elaborate productions. Most programs were produced live and required very detailed scripts. Much more informal programming appears on most radio stations today. A single announcer or disc jockey often broadcasts for long periods without any formal script. All he or she needs is a music library, a collection of prerecorded tape cartridges containing commercials, and a microphone. The prerecording of commercial announcements can even be done by a creative producer with only a fact sheet about the product, a library of music themes and sound effects, and a fully equipped production booth.

Still, for many programs and announcements, writers must assemble on paper all the various elements that make up a complete script. Partly because of radio's long history, a quite standardized layout form has evolved. Here are two examples of this basic radio layout. The first is an excerpt from a radio drama (Figure 5.1); the second, a commercial (Figure 5.2). The commercial is also dramatic in form, and rather complex, requiring the integration of several voices with music and sound effects. Note especially how these effects—music and sound—are integrated into the scripts and how stage directions, stylistic instructions and characterization are separated from the spoken copy.

Follow these guidelines when preparing "standard" radio copy:

1. *Page layout:* Allow about a 1-inch left margin; then leave a column that will be used to identify the source of each sound. A colon may or may not follow these items. Then leave a few spaces and begin the copy block.

2. *Spacing:* All radio copy is double-spaced.

3. *Page numbering:* If the copy is more than one page long, number all pages at the top in sequence. Often the number is repeated, for example, 6-6-6-6-6, making it easier to identify pages and reassemble the script quickly should the pages become disarranged.

4. *Line numbering:* In complex scripts involving several characters and/or music and sound cues, the lines are numbered. The numbering aids in making corrections during rehearsals. For simple scripts, line numbering is usually omitted. Line numbers usually appear at the far left of the page, as shown in the "Gold Don't Rust" excerpt (Figure 5.1). Sometimes they are placed between the "sound source" column and the copy block this way:

```
ANNCR:     1 The holiday season is in full bloom at

           2 Crystal Florist. Color your Christmas

           3 with the traditional beauty of poinsettias.

           4 Crystal Florist has a stunning selection

           5 for you to choose from....
```

When used, line numbers are usually repeated on each page, as shown in "Gold Don't Rust," but sometimes lines are continuously numbered throughout an entire script.

5. *Source of sound:* This column at the left of the page is used to indicate the type of sound which is to appear at that point in the script and its source—that is, some identification of the VOICE delivering the line, or of MUSIC, or SOUND. If only a single voice is being used, it is frequently designated as ANNCR (for announcer) or NARR (for narrator).

Multiple voices may be identified by the names of the characters in the drama (BUBBA, ANGEL, ACE, etc.) or if the role is too small to have a name, as MALE VOICE, FEMALE VOICE, VOICE #1, VOICE #2, and so on. However, be careful in your identifications. If you use VOICE #1 and VOICE #2 as anonymous voices in one scene of a play and then want two different voices (persons) for small parts in a later scene, use VOICE #3 and VOICE #4. If you use the identifications VOICE #1 and VOICE #2 again, the actors playing the roles might use the same vocal characterization as in the earlier scene; the audience will believe the new characters to be the same as those heard in the first scene and will become confused.

6. *Music cues:* If the cue is for MUSIC, that single word is all that is needed in the sound source column; the description of the music appears in the copy block, as in these examples:

<u>MUSIC:</u>      <u>LATIN THEME ON SOLO GUITAR, UP FOR 5 SECONDS</u>

          <u>AND FADE UNDER</u>

<u>MUSIC:</u>      <u>STINGER</u>

<u>MUSIC:</u>      <u>JINGLE BELLS INSTRUMENTAL IN BG THROUGHOUT</u>

          <u>FOLLOWING</u>

Note that the full cue is written in all CAPITAL letters and underlined. Unless the length of the cue is obvious, some indication should be given as to how long the cue is to last and how it is to be removed.

7. *Sound cues:* Similarly, the word SOUND (some prefer SFX, for sound effects) will designate a sound cue. Its description will appear in the copy block. Sound cues are also typed in all CAPITAL letters and underlined.

<u>SOUND:</u>      <u>FOOTSTEPS ON PORCH, OPEN SCREEN DOOR, DOOR</u>

          <u>SLAMS</u>

<u>SFX:</u>       <u>FIRE SIREN. INTRODUCE LOW BEHIND FOLLOWING,</u>

          <u>BUILD INTENSITY TO (X), THEN SLOWLY FADE OUT</u>

As with music cues, indicate the length of the cue and, if necessary, how it is to be removed. In the second example above, an (X) will be inserted in the copy block to mark the point at which the siren should reach its greatest volume. This shorthand method avoids writing another full in-
(text continues on page 81)

GOLD DON'T RUST

1 SOUND:     STREET SOUND AMBIENCE THROUGHOUT

2           CAR PULLS UP, IDLES. WE HEAR RADIO MUSIC WHICH CUTS OFF

3           WHEN MOTOR IS TURNED OFF. CAR DOOR OPENS. DOG BARKING IN

4           BACKGROUND.

5 BUBBA:     (ON) That ain't Angel Luna polishing all those hubcaps

6           there, is it?

7 ANGEL:     (FADE ON) Que pasa, little Bubba? I ain't seen you in a

8           year, man, I figured you were dead or something.

9 SOUND:     CAR DOOR SLAMS.

10 BUBBA:    Not yet, Angel. My Uncle Ace around here somewhere?

11 ANGEL:    Where's he always, man? He's over there in his Cadillac

12          with a cooler full o'beer, staring off into space. While I

13          do all the work.

14 BUBBA:    He's got you on hubcap patrol, huh?

15 ANGEL:    Si...whatcha think? Is that beauty or is that beauty?

16 BUBBA:    I cain't even look, Angel...almost went blind when I drove

17          up.

18 ANGEL:    There must be three hundred of 'em...spinners, baby moon

19          ...looks like those giant pictures of a bee's eyeball,

20          don't it?

21 BUBBA:    Sure does. Hey, listen, I got to see the old man.

22 ANGEL:    There he is.

23 ACE:      (OFF) Hey, will ya look who's here!

24 SOUND:    FOOTSTEPS ON GRAVEL, THROUGH JUNK. DOG BARKING CLOSER NOW.

25 BUBBA:    Don't jump up, Uncle Ace...I'd hate you to get a hernia on

26          my account.

27 ACE:      (FADE ON) Get in, Bubba. It's real good to see you. Help me

28          drink some of this beer. Baby! Shut up over there!

**Figure 5.1.** Courtesy of the writer, Dan Paul Frizzelle.

```
 1  SOUND:     DOG QUIETS DOWN

 2  BUBBA:     How's the junk business treatin' you these days?

 3  ACE:       Oh, good and bad, you know...your wrecked car just ain't a

 4             quality item anymore.

 5  BUBBA:     I didn't know it ever was.

 6  ACE:       Oh yeah...but everything is made outa plastic nowadays

 7             ...one good wreck they just kinda disintegrate right there

 8             in the road. Cain't get many good parts off 'em.

 9  BUBBA:     You don't look real hungry.

10  ACE:       I get by...I just jack up the prices on the parts I sell

11             high enough to make a profit. (BUBBA REACTS) I'm just doing

12             my bit to keep inflation up there in the big numbers.

13  BUBBA:     You ever thought about a different line of work?

14  ACE:       Hell, Bubba, I was in a different line of work about ever'

15             two years most of my life...I just ended up here 'cause I

16             got tired of everything else.

17  BUBBA:     Seems like it'd get old, workin' in a junkyard.

18  ACE:       Aw...I don't do no work here. That's what I pay old Angel

19             for...Somethin' needs doin' I just tell Angel and he takes

20             care of it. He's been makin' quittin' noises lately but I

21             don't think he's gonna.

22  BUBBA:     He might, ya know.

23  ACE:       I ain't gonna worry a lot 'til he does it...then I'll have

24             my heart attack. Til then it's a real fine thing havin'

25             your own junkyard...you can pitch an empty beer can just

26             about anywhere you want and nobody says a damn thing.

27  SOUND:     EMPTY BEER CAN CLATTERS ON GROUND

28  ACE:       Reach me 'nother beer outta that cooler will ya?

29  BUBBA:     Sure thing.
```

**Figure 5.1.** (continued)

| | |
|---|---|
| ANNCR: | Perry Boys' Smorgy Presents another "Perry Tale" |
| SFX: | MUSIC BOX |
| ANNCR: | Once upon a time...there lived an old woman and her son, Jack...a promising horticulturalist. |
| MOTHER: | OK son, once more...what did you do with the cow??? |
| JACK: | (ENTHUSIASTIC) I traded her for a few magic beans...I'm gonna plant them in this pot...climb to the top of the beanstalk...and steal the hen that lays the golden eggs... |
| MOTHER: | I think I'll go lie down for a while... |
| ANNCR: | But Jack did plant the beans and a giant beanstalk grew into the sky... |
| SFX: | CRASHING WOOD |
| MOTHER: | OK, Mr. Green Thumb, who's gonna fix the hole in the roof??? |
| JACK: | Later, Mom...I'm gonna climb to the top... |
| SFX: | STRENUOUS CLIMBING |
| JACK: | Wow...a castle... |
| SFX: | GIANT FOOTSTEPS |
| JACK: | And...Uh-Oh... |
| GIANT: | (ECHO) Fee - Fi - Fo - Feel...I've found me a little meal... |
| JACK: | Please, Mr. Giant...I'm so scrawny...You'd still be hungry...Let me go and I'll tell you all about Perry Boys' Smorgy...with over 40 delicious things to eat...all better tasting than me. |
| GIANT: | Sounds good...race ya down the beanstalk. |
| SFX: | BREAKING SOUND |
| GIANT: | Yeeeeoww! |
| JACK: | (YELLING DOWN—ECHO)...You win... |
| ANNCR: | You'll always win when you eat at Perry Boys' Smorgy Restaurants...$4.99 for lunch and $7.99 for dinner...in Santa Cruz, Salinas...and Monterey at 2066 Fremont Boulevard. |

**Figure 5.2.** Courtesy of the writer, Frank LaRosa.

struction at that point to the person handling the effects. Several sound cues are shown in the "Gold Don't Rust" and Perry Boys scripts (Figures 5.1 and 5.2).

8. *Copy block:* In the body of the script, the material to be spoken is typed in normal copy style (upper- and lowercase). Everything that is not spoken on the air is typed in ALL CAPITAL LETTERS. In addition to sound and music cues, discussed above, this instruction also applies to directions to the performers; these directions are typed in CAPITALS and also set off by parentheses.

```
JOE:            (SLEEPILY) Well, I guess I had to get up

                anyway...



WOMAN #2:       ...If you need me, I'll be down at the

                beauty parlor. (TURN AWAY FADE)
```

9. *Use of MORE:* If the lines of one character continue from one page to the next, the warning cue MORE MORE MORE is placed at the bottom of the page. This warning prevents the actor from assuming that a speech is completed, pausing while the page is turned, and then finding that the speech continues, because by that time the continuity and smoothness of delivery will have been broken. If another character has the first line on the following page, this cue is not used.

10. *Dividing words:* Never divide a word across a page. Try not to divide a sentence across a page, or to divide a word between lines.

## Radio News Layout

Radio news broadcasts can use more informal scripts, particularly if they are both written and voiced by the same person. We have reproduced two sample scripts. They are from stations that have different needs and therefore use different approaches to scripting. Figure 5.3 is a story from a public radio station (KXPR). Figure 5.4 is a news summary from a commercial station (KXOA-FM) that is largely a one-person operation. It uses a very relaxed form and even ungrammatical style. If you work for a station, follow its guidelines; otherwise, use these general rules:

1. Some sort of *slug* is used to head the story. At a minimum the slug should include a one-word title (two words at most), the date and time of broadcast and the writer's name, as:

```
STORMS

11/10

7:30 am

Doyle
```

Time of broadcast is particularly important for continuing stories and if the station has several newscasts during the day. Different versions— each updated with whatever new information has become available— may be scattered around the newsroom; the announcer needs to know that he or she has the most recent one.

2. Usually there is no need for a sound source column, because often only one person will read the entire newscast. If more than one person is used as a reader, their names can be penciled in the margins next to the stories they will each read.

3. Some complication is added when the actual voices of people featured in the story are inserted in the form of prerecorded *actualities*. The recorded quote must be identified so that production people can insert the recording at the proper spot in the story. Station practices vary; our two stations use different styles, but three items usually appear: (1) some identification of the tape cartridge on which the recorded cut is stored. Many stations identify carts by the name of the person whose voice is on the cart; (2) the time (length) of the excerpt; and (3) the outcue, that is, the last few words of the actuality, as:

```
CART:    GARCIA

TIME:     :46

OUT:     to sand bags.
```

The outcue is particularly important so that the announcer will know precisely when to resume the narration. It avoids the awkwardness of "dead air" that would otherwise result if the announcer had to wait until being sure the recorded cut was finished. The word END or ENDS is sometimes used instead of OUT.

4. We prefer to see the copy block typed using the normal pattern of lower- and uppercase letters we recognize from print. But many newsrooms prefer scripts to be typed in all capital letters. Their preference may be the result of years of experience with copy sent over the Associated Press (AP) and United Press International (UPI) teletype wires, which transmit in all caps.

Catholics                              Quinn                              Milne

910131

Local/UPI

:15


A group of Roman Catholics pleaded "not guilty" yesterday in Sacramento
to disrupting Governor Wilson's inaugural church service and demanded
jury trials. The 11 people arrested on January 6th at Sacramento's
Cathedral of the Blessed Sacrament are angry with Bishop Francis Quinn
of the Sacramento Diocese for allowing a service honoring a pro-choice
governor to be held in a Catholic church. They have since mounted a
letter-writing campaign to the Pope requesting the Bishop's ouster.
Bishop Quinn defends the group's right to protest...but he acknowledges
that civil law prohibits disturbing church services.

> Cart: Catholics
>
> Time: :15
>
> Out: achieve those goals

Seven of the 11 people arrested want a jury trial and three others are
letting their lawyers handle it. An 11th man is hoping to get the
charges dropped. He says he was an innocent bystander...not a protester.
The trials are set to begin in March.

                                                      Rec Date 1/30

                                                      Tot Time 1:00

**Figure 5.3.** Courtesy of KXPR-FM, Sacramento, CA.

GOOOOD MORNING...IT'S 8:30 AND _____ DEGREEZ. THIS IS THE K108 EARLY
MORNING NEWS. I'M KEN HUNT.

_____

   IT'S ALMOST LIKE A MILITARY BASE TODAY IN WASHINGTON, D.C. SECURITY
IS THAT TIGHT AROUND THE CAPITOL PRIOR TO TONIGHT'S PRESIDENTIAL STATE
OF THE UNION SPEECH. JUST ABOUT ALL OF THE FEDERAL GOVERNMENT WILL BE IN
THE AUDIENCE:
Q: HARMLESS EQUIPMENT 22
   LOUISE SKIAVONEY REPORTING FOR K108.

_____

   SACRAMENTO CONGRESSMAN VIC FAZIO WILL BE THERE TONIGHT...WHEN
PRESIDENT BUSH TALKS TO THE CONGRESS ABOUT THE GULF WAR.
Q: CHAMBER 13
   FAZIO SAYS EVEN HIS CAR IS SEARCHED BY BOMB SNIFFING DOGS WHEN HE
DRIVES TO THE CAPITOL.

_____

   U.S. MILITARY COMMANDERS IN SAUDI SAY THEY KNOW NOTHING ABOUT IRAQI
REPORTS THAT A FOREIGN PILOT HAS BEEN KILLED BY ALLIED BOMBING RUNS OVER
BAGHDAD. THE PENTAGON LISTS SEVEN AMERICANS AS P-O-WS.

_____

   THE PENTAGON IS RELEASING MORE PICTURES OF SUCCESSFUL MISSIONS
AGAINST IRAQI MISSLES. JERRY BOLANDER HAS HAD A LOOK.
Q: THE GULF 17
   THERE IS SOME GOOD NEWS ABOUT THE OIL SLICK IN THE PERSIAN GULF. NAVY
REAR ADMIRAL DAVID FROST...
Q: SLOWED DOWN 11

                              MORE MORE MORE

**Figure 5.4.** Courtesy of KXOA-FM, Sacramento, CA.

THE SAUDIS ESTIMATE THERE'S ABOUT 460 MILLION GALLONS OF CRUDE OIL IN
GULF WATERS...THREE TIMES MORE THAN ANY PREVIOUS OIL SPILL IN HISTORY.

————

ON THE HOMEFRONT....

WE'VE TOLD YOU ABOUT THE OVERWHELMING DEMAND FOR AMERICAN FLAGS IN
SACRAMENTO SINCE THE WAR BEGAN. BUT, AS WE HEAR FROM K108s JOE
STRENG...THAT'S NOT STOPPING ONE LOCAL FROM SHOWING SUPPORT FOR U.S.
TROOPS IN THE DESERT.

Q: POSTAGE 28

————

THE GULF WAR...ALSO ON THE LIPS OF POP—ROCK AND RAP STARS.

Q: AWARDS 19

AMERICAN MUSIC AWARDS LAST NIGHT IN LOS ANGELES...EASTBAY RAPPER MC
HAMMER WALKED OFF WITH AN ARMLOAD OF HONORS.

————

KINGS WON LAST NIGHT...DID SO WITH SEVERAL MILITARY FAMILIES FROM
BEALE AIR FORCE BASE IN ATTENDANCE.

————

MORE SUNNY SKIES AHEAD TODAY....

THE DETAILS COMING UP NEXT....AT 8:33....WE'RE K108FM.

**Figure 5.4.** (continued)

5. Words that are unfamiliar and may be difficult to pronounce should have
   a pronunciation key. A simplified phonetic spelling is inserted in parentheses immediately following the word:

   ANNCR:    Iran's President says he's willing to meet

             with the U-S. Hashemi Rafsanjani (Hah-shay'-

             mee Rahf-sahn-jahn'-ee) also said today...

ANNCR:     Winter's not over yet...at least as far as

           Punxsutawney (Punk-suh-taw-nee) Phil is

           concerned. The famous forecasting groundhog

           came out today...

Both AP and UPI provide brief lists of phonetic symbols. Box 5.1 is the AP list.

Here is how these guidelines appear in our two examples. The KXPR story slug contains the one-word identifier CATHOLICS; the writer MILNE; and the date, inserted by the software and in a rather awkward form—year, month, day—910131. The person quoted in the actuality is named in the slug: QUINN. Also included in the heading material are the sources of the story, LOCAL & UPI, and the length of the actuality, 15 (seconds). The actuality itself is identified by the slug name CATHOLICS (a practice which works if there is only one actuality per story); the time of the actuality (again), 15; and the outcue ACHIEVE THOSE GOALS. Other information, at the bottom of the page, is the date of recording the story, in this case one day before it was aired (1/30), and the total time of the story, 1:00.

The KXOA-FM (K108) summary is quite informal. Actualities are shown by a single line,

Q: HARMLESS EQUIPMENT 22

which gives both length and outcue. The lead line serves as a slug for the entire summary.

---

**Box 5.1  Associated Press List of Phonetic Symbols**

*Vowel Sounds*
a—bat, apple
ah—father, arm
aw—raw, board
ay—fate, ace
e, eh—bed
ee—feel, tea
i, ih—pin, middle
y, eye—ice, time, guide
oh—go, oval
oo—food, two

ow—scout, crowd
oy—boy, join
u—curl, foot
uh—puff
yoo—fume, few

*Consonants*
g—got, beg
j—job, gem
k—keep, cap
ch—chair, butcher

sh—shut, fashion
zh—vision, mirage
th—thin, path
kh—guttural "k"

*Source:* The Associated Press, *AP Broadcast News Handbook* (New York: The Associated Press, 1982), p. 230. Reprinted by permission.

## Television Split-Page Layout

Two quite different layout forms are used in television. One evolved from radio. It has a split-page arrangement, and is used for most multicamera production, including news, some commercials and other simpler programs. The other form, which comes from the motion picture industry, is used for single-camera productions, including dramas, in which individual shots are prerecorded on film or videotape and then edited into the final production. That form is described in the next section.

The split-page form allows the production crew and performers to deal simultaneously with both visual and sound elements. The two columns are headed AUDIO and VIDEO, but in practice some visual elements appear along with the spoken copy in the AUDIO column. The VIDEO column is used primarily by the director for camera cues and instructions to the technical crew. Usually VIDEO is placed on the left side of the page.

Follow these guidelines for split-page television layouts:

1. Divide your script into two parts: AUDIO and VIDEO. Instructions for things that are heard go under AUDIO; those for things that are seen go under VIDEO. One exception: Stage directions to performers generally appear on the AUDIO side, because the performers seldom pay attention to the VIDEO instructions and concentrate on the side of the page that contains their lines.

2. The basic layout is double-spaced, and audio copy is double-spaced. Video instructions, however, are single-spaced if the lines form part of the same instruction. Adjust spacing between the two columns so that audio and video are kept parallel—that is, the video instructions should come at the same point on the page as the audio they accompany. Spread out the copy whenever it begins to look cluttered. Don't try to save paper.

3. AUDIO may be handled several ways. If there is a complex sound track with numerous cues, follow the radio approach, because each source will need to be identified. Use a separate "sound source" column as in the Richter ad, Figure 5.5, or a variation, like the API script, Figure 5.6. If the audio is very simple, only a single narrator, for example, and there are no sound or music cues, the "sound source" column can be omitted.

   As with radio copy, anything that is spoken should be in upper- and lowercase. Anything that is *not* to be spoken should be written in ALL CAPITAL LETTERS, such as music cues, stage directions, and stylistic instructions.

4. Directions to actors or narrators within a speech should be placed at the point where they apply. Use parentheses around the direction, and type

in ALL CAPS. Such directions include stage business, instructions on how a line is to be delivered, the desired mood, and so on.

Also indicate in parentheses if the lines are to be delivered as a *voice-over*—that is, when the announcer or actor will *not* be seen speaking the lines, but will be voicing the copy over other visual material. Either of the following is acceptable:

```
NARRATOR (V.O.):
NARRATOR (OFF CAMERA):
```

The opposite situation, when the announcer or actor is to be seen on camera, is shown in the Amtrak spot, Figure 5.7, and is labeled ON CAMERA, or O.C.

Identify directions for the actions by talent and stage business with the word *BIZ*. Place this identification on a line by itself, in ALL CAPS AND UNDERLINED.

```
ANNCR:
                              BIZ
              CROSSES FROM FIREPLACE TO TABLE:
              PICKS UP BOTTLE AND GLASS; POURS.


              When I first tasted this new...
```

Identify other audio sources (music and sound effects) using the same layout as for radio.

5. On the VIDEO side we have used ALL CAPITAL LETTERS for all the directions, with one exception. That is for titles and other graphics when they are to be shown on the screen. Not all stations follow this guideline; some use normal copy style in the VIDEO column.

6. Titles and captions to be displayed on the screen are "flagged" by any of several words. Some stations use FONT, others CHYRON (the brand name of the character generator used at many stations). Still others use SUPER (short for superimposition, a now old-fashioned method for inserting graphics). Following that "flag" word, write out the font information exactly as you want it to appear on the screen. Place that information at the spot in the script at which it is to appear. Most stations establish by standard practice how many seconds a font will appear on the screen, so it is not usually necessary to write FONT OUT, but if you want the font to be on screen longer than normal, you will need to show that.

```
CHYRON:        Joe Jones
               County Supervisor

TOP FONT:      Recorded earlier

DIAGONAL
SUPER:         SPECIAL REPORT
```

7. A number of common abbreviations are used, especially in video termi-nology, to save space and make reading easier and faster for crew mem-bers. If you are not already familiar with video production terminology, you will be after you read this text. We will use many of the basic pro-duction terms in various chapters. In the meantime, use those terms and abbreviations you understand, but most important, use descriptions that will be understood by those who have to interpret your script for the TV screen.

Here are three examples—all announcements. There is some variation in the details of the layout because of the different production requirements for each script.

The Richter ad (Figure 5.5) uses simple, inexpensive production tech-niques. Two sequences—those that show the candidate talking—were shot on videotape. The other visual material is 35 mm slides. The audio employs two voices—the candidate and an announcer.

The Amtrak commercial, Figure 5.6, uses a simple production technique, but it depends heavily on the establishment of a mood. Therefore, there is an extensive description at the beginning of the setting and of the appearance required of the announcer.

The Animal Protection Institute announcement, Figure 5.7, uses a wom-an's voice and a sound effect to add interest, variety and realism to the nar-ration. Although it is written using the split-page form, it obviously requires a good deal of preproduction. The two video scenes—in the baby's room and in the forest—would be shot on film or videotape and edited. The wom-an's voice and the sound of the footsteps also would be preproduced on audio tape. Then video, sound, and narration would be mixed to produce the completed spot.

BERNIE RICHTER
TV Spot #1 "River"

| VIDEO | AUDIO |
|---|---|
| MEDIUM SHOT—BERNIE ON LEVEE (RIVER IN BACKGROUND) | BERNIE: I'm Bernie Richter...I think Butte County is a special kind of place...our farming is productive and our towns are prosperous... |
| DISSOLVE TO SHOTS OF: FARMER ON TRACTOR IN FIELD DOWNTOWN SHOPPERS CHILD EATING ICE CREAM TUBERS FAMILY ON BICYCLES FARM FAMILY AT DINNER STUDENTS ON CAMPUS WITH BOOKS | But most importantly, our people make this the greatest place in the world to live and raise a family.... They're hard-working, energetic, bill-paying people who deserve the best in the way of county government.... |
| CLOSEUP—BERNIE | Yet, there are some who would change our whole lifestyle to fit some misguided ideas... |
| SLIDE: RICHTER FAMILY | I think we've worked too hard to let that happen... Butte County is special... |
| SUPER: Paid by Citizens for Richter PO Box 1867 Chico, CA 95927 | ANNCR: Let's keep it that way.... Re-elect Supervisor Richter |

**Figure 5.5.** Courtesy of the writer, Frank LaRosa, and of Bernie Richter.

```
AMTRAK #1
WRITER: TAGHOLM
```

| SHOT No. | VIDEO | AUDIO |
|---|---|---|
| 1 | WS OF VACANT TRAIN STATION WHILE CAMERA BOOMS DOWN TO EYE LEVEL. THROUGHOUT THE BOOM A SINGLE FIGURE WALKS TOWARD THE CAMERA FROM SOME DISTANCE. THIS MAN IS THE ANNOUNCER. (THERE IS THE NATURAL SOUND OF THE MAN'S FOOTSTEPS HAVING AN ECHO QUALITY) | |
| 2 | CU MAN AS HE WALKS HEAD ON TOWARDS CAMERA. AS HE WALKS THE CAMERA TRUCKS BACK TO KEEP HIM FROM COMING TOO CLOSE AND TO GIVE A FEELING OF MOVEMENT. AS THE CAMERA TRUCKS BACK VARIOUS PARTS OF THE TRAIN STATION COME INTO FOCUS IN THE BACKGROUND. THE MAN IS SOMEWHAT ELDERLY.<br><br>THERE IS LITTLE DOUBT THAT HE ONCE WORKED FOR THE RAILROADS. HE IS DRESSED CASUALLY, BUT DOES NOT WEAR OVERALLS OR ANYTHING OPENLY TRITE. | MAN: (ON CAMERA)<br>Ya know, there was a time when this railroad station was full of people. People going places, places all over the country. Any more you're lucky if you can find a single soul in this entire room. Why I remember when hundreds even thousands of people would leave from here in just one day. That was when traveling by train was popular and the train was about the best way to get anywhere for a lot of folks.<br><br>In fact, for many they were the only thing available. You could |

                                    MORE MORE MORE

**Figure 5.6.** Courtesy of the writer, Bernard Tagholm.

SHOT
No.                          <u>VIDEO</u>                                                <u>AUDIO</u>

|  |  |  |
|---|---|---|
|  | CAMERA TRUCK STOPS & THE MAN TURNS TO STEP OUT THROUGH DOORS TO THE VACANT LOADING AREA. | get a ticket over there at the window for anywhere in the good ol' US and it didn't cost an arm and a leg. Oh there was some fuss'n around with baggage and all but before long you were rock'n to sleep over the clikity clack of the rails. |
|  | CUT |  |
| 3 | OUTSIDE, MAN APPROACHES CAMERA. | Yep, those were the days...don't reckon they'll ever come back. But the trains are back and they're better than ever. Trouble is nobody rides them. Guess they just don't know what they're missing. |
|  | CUT |  |
| 4 | WS MAN GETS ON TRAIN AS IT PULLS OUT SUPER: AMTRAK LOGO | <u>ANNOUNCER</u> (OFF CAMERA): <u>(NATURAL SOUND OF TRAIN UNDER)</u> Next time you travel, take the train and let the good times roll. |
|  |  | END |

**Figure 5.6.** (continued)

ANIMAL PROTECTION INSTITUTE

| VIDEO | AUDIO |
|---|---|
| FADE IN L.S. OF ROOM DARK WITH SHADOWS. BABY'S CRIB IN FOREGROUND. BACK OF ROCKING ROCKER IN FRONT OF FIREPLACE IN BG. DOLLY IN SLOWLY FOR M. CU OF BACK OF ROCKER | WOMAN'S VOICE, SINGING<br><br>Bye baby bunting<br>Daddy's gone a-hunting<br>to catch a baby rabbit's<br>skin to wrap my baby bunting in. |
| DISSOLVE. FOREST SCENE. SNOWING, SNOW ON GROUND AND ON TREES. L.S. OF UNBROKEN PATH THROUGH TREES. CAMERA WALKS ALONG PATH. AT TIMES BRANCHES BRUSH PAST SCREEN | LIVE SOUND. CRUNCH OF FOOTSTEPS.<br><br>NARR: (VOICE OVER) This lullaby would not give a baby sweet dreams to sleep with if she knew how daddy hunts for baby rabbit fur.<br>Animals are trapped for their fur. |
| TRAPPED ANIMAL BECOMES VISIBLE IN THE DISTANCE. IT IS CENTRAL FOCUS OF CAMERA<br><br>TILTED L.S. OF TRAP WITH RABBIT. TILTED M. CU OF TRAPPED RABBIT. TILTED CU. OF TRAP AND RABBIT. CU OF TRAPPED RABBIT'S FOOT | Every year thirty million animals, including fox, mink and raccoon are trapped in the United States. When the steel-jaw trap snaps shut, the animal faces a slow, agonizing death. Death from starvation, thirst, freezing or fear. (END FOOTSTEPS) |
| LAP DISSOLVE. CU OF RABBIT'S FACE. PAN UP TO THE TIP OF AN EAR | The lullaby is not beautiful. If it sends a chill down your back, don't throw on a fur coat to warm yourself. Please write to the Animal Protection Institute of America for information on how this cruel method<br>MORE MORE MORE |

**Figure 5.7.** Reprinted by permission of Animal Protection Institute, Sacramento, CA.

| <u>VIDEO</u> | <u>AUDIO</u> |
|---|---|
| | of trapping can be stopped. End the use of steel-jaw traps. Wrap your baby in your arms to keep her warm. |
| DISSOLVE. BABY RABBITS SLEEPING NEXT TO MOTHER RABBIT. | |
| SUPER: A.P.I., BOX 220505, SACRAMENTO, CALIF. | |
| CONTRIBUTIONS ARE TAX DEDUCTIBLE. | |
| FADE OUT. | |

**Figure 5.7.** (continued)

## Television News Layout

To prepare television news copy, use the basic split-page form and follow the guidelines given in the preceding section, with some modifications. Note, too, that many stations now have sophisticated computerized news management systems in place, and the details of script layout will be dictated by that software. Our example, from KOVR, Sacramento, is the lead story from a local evening newscast, Figure 5.8. The story is in three parts. The first part contains the lead-in delivered by both anchors from the studio. The story begins with the anchors live on-camera, then shifts to taped footage (ENG) while the female anchor (JENN) continues voice-over (VO). Next, the male anchor (DAN) continues the narration, a still-store map is shown, and then DAN is again seen (ON CAM).

The second part is the *package*. The video for the package was selected and assembled from material taped at the scene of the fire. It is narrated by the reporter who covered the story at the scene, Noel Nordquist. Normally, the details of the package do not appear in script form. The reporter, cameraperson, editor and whoever else helps assemble the package work from shot sheets and notes. The final script just makes reference to the package— length, outcue, source (which videotape machine will be used to play it back), and so on. But KOVR puts a rough outline of packages, including the outcues of actualities, into its computer for storage, and we've reproduced that here.

The final part is the anchor tag. Using this example, note these guidelines for preparing copy:

1. The slug will be similar to that used for radio: (1) a one- or two-word identifier for the story, (2) date (and possibly time), and (3) writer's name; also, page numbers if the story exceeds a single page, and possibly the length of the story (although that is more important on the rundown sheet used by the staff to organize and time the entire program).

2. The AUDIO column will contain the copy to be read by anchors or other reporters on the set. The narrow column is set up that way for easy reading off of the prompting device in the studio. Each anchor's lines are identified. The cut away to the package (PKG) is marked.

3. The VIDEO column will contain a wide range of instructions to the crew, depending on the types of inserts that may be used in the story. For this story there are:

| | |
|---|---|
| 2-SHOT | Live studio camera shot of both anchors |
| JENN & BOX | The female anchor with a graphics display in a box behind her |
| TAKE ENG/VO | Show the preedited videotape with anchor continuing to narrate over the silent tape (voice-over) |
| take ss/map | Video to be a map, preprepared and inserted into the "still-store," a storage bank for still pictures |
| DAN ON CAM | Back to live shot of the male anchor |
| TAKE ENG SOT FULL | Both video (ENG) and audio sound-on-tape (SOT) from the package |

4. It's important to indicate exactly when any changes take place in the sources of both audio and video material and where those sources are—studio, remote live location, a package, or wherever. Different types of TV news stories are covered in more detail in Chapter 12.

```
Slug:TANKER FIRE            V#1  U:BURKE
NN        02-14-91: 8:47:29A Q:11
```

| VIDEO | AUDIO |
|---|---|
| 2-SHOT | ((DAN))<br><br>THERE'S AN UNEASY PEACE IN A CARMICHAEL NEIGHBORHOOD TONIGHT.<br><br>RESIDENTS STILL RECOVERING FROM A LONG NIGHT OF CHAOS.<br><br>GOOD EVENING, I'M DAN GRAY.<br>((JENN))<br><br>AND I'M JENNIFER WHITNEY. |
| JENN & BOX | OUR TOP STORY...<br><br>500 CARMICHAEL RESIDENTS BACK IN THEIR HOMES TONIGHT.<br><br>BUT NOT BEFORE A HUGE FIRE RACED THROUGH THEIR NEIGHBORHOOD, FORCING THEM INTO THE STREETS IN THE MIDDLE OF THE NIGHT. |
| TAKE ENG/VO | THE FIRE BEGAN AT ABOUT THREE THIS MORNING WHEN A TANKER TRUCK CARRYING EIGHTY-FOUR HUNDRED GALLONS OF GASOLINE CRASHED ON FAIR OAKS BOULEVARD.<br><br>FUEL FROM THE TANKER POURED INTO A DRAINAGE DITCH AND THEN INTO STORM PIPES...ALL OF WHICH WENT UP IN FLAMES WHEN AN UNKNOWN SPARK SET IT OFF.<br><br>THE FIRE SPREAD THROUGH A CARMICHAEL |

```
                      MORE MORE MORE
```

**Figure 5.8.** Courtesy of KOVR, Sacramento, CA.

| VIDEO | AUDIO |
|---|---|
| | NEIGHBORHOOD, DESTROYING FOUR HOMES AND A HALF DOZEN CARS. |
| | THE DRIVER OF THE TRUCK MANAGED TO ESCAPE BEFORE IT EXPLODED. |
| | HIS INJURIES WERE MINOR. |
| | THERE WERE ONLY TWO OTHER INJURIES, BOTH MINOR. |
| | ##### |
| | ((DAN)) |
| | BUT HUNDREDS WERE WOKEN UP IN THE MIDDLE OF THE NIGHT AND SENT AWAY FROM THE HOMES. |
| take ss/map | FIREFIGHTERS EVACUATED A MILE SQUARE AREA, FROM FAIR OAKS TO GARFIELD TO EL CAMINO. |
| | THE CRASH OCCURRED IN THE MIDDLE OF ALL THIS ON A PARTICULARLY BAD CURVE OF FAIR OAKS BOULEVARD. |
| | RESIDENTS WERE ONLY ALLOWED TO RETURN TO THEIR HOMES THIS AFTERNOON. |
| DAN ON CAM | NOEL NORDQUIST WAS ON THE SCENE AS THE EVACUATED RESIDENTS STRAGGLED BACK INTO THEIR NEIGHBORHOOD AFTER THE ORDEAL. |
| TAKE ENG SOT FULL | ((PKG)) |
| | THE TRUCK'S CRASH WOKE MOST PEOPLE. |
| | THE SIRENS WOKE EVERYONE ELSE. |
| | AND FROM WAKE UP CALL TO ESCAPE...SECONDS. |
| BONNIE MILLER | 14:16 IT WAS AN INCREDIBLE SCENE TO WATCH AT |

**Figure 5.8.** (continued)

| VIDEO | AUDIO |
|-------|-------|

3:15...EVERYONE RUNNING OUT THE DOOR IN PAJAMAS
AND RUNNING."

14:56 WHEN YOU SAW ALL THE SMOKE.... I THOUGHT
THE IRAQI'S WERE BOMBING US."

THE FIRE'S PATH SEEMED ALMOST ARBITRARY...JUST
FORTY FEET WAS THE DIFFERENCE BETWEEN HAVING A
HOME AND LOSING EVERYTHING.

20:29 (TAPE 2) "EVERYTHING WENT WE HAD TO GET
OUT IN MINUTES."

CHARLES DETTINGER'S HOME IS A TOTAL LOSS.

(CLUNK RED WAGON)

SO IS MARGERY GLOOR'S.

(OLD LADY GETTING A HUG TAPE 3) NAT: 1:25:29 "I
WAS SCREAMING DOWN THE STREET."

BUT MOST PEOPLE WERE ALMOST GIDDY UPON FINDING
THEY STILL HAD HOMES TO RETURN TO.

TAPE 1 1:15)) "I LITERALLY LEFT BAREFOOT.... MY
HOUSE IS STILL STANDING."

STANDUP: 12:02 "THOUGH FIREFIGHTERS HAVE HAD
FANS VENTILATING THE AREA ALL AFTERNOON, YOU CAN
STILL REALLY SMELL THE GASOLINE. THEY SAY IT'S NOT
A DANGER ANYMORE, BUT THE ENVIRONMENTAL PROTECTION
DEPARTMENT WILL COME OUT TOMORROW TO DETERMINE
ENVIRONMENTAL DAMAGE."

MOST OF THE 84-THOUSAND GALLONS OF GAS WERE
SOPPED UP BY BOOMS AND VACUUMS, BUT THE EPA WILL
STILL LOOK FOR ANY GROUNDWATER CONTAMINATION.

AND THOUGH THE CLEANUP'S ALMOST DONE AND LIVES
ARE RETURNING BACK TO NORMAL, THERE'S STILL THE

**Figure 5.8.** (continued)

MORE MORE MORE

| <u>VIDEO</u> | <u>AUDIO</u> |
|---|---|
| | QUESTION OF THE FAIR OAKS CURVE--SCENE OF 15 ACCIDENTS IN THE LAST YEAR. |
| | BITE: "1:33:07 "I WANNA MOVE ESPECIALLY AFTER LAST NIGHT...BLOW UP BEHIND US." |
| | HIGHWAY OFFICIALS SAY THE ONLY WAY TO FIX THE CURVE, WOULD BE TO TAKE OUT SOME OF THE HOMES AND REDO THE ROAD COMPLETELY. |
| | IN CARMICHAEL NN KOVR 13 NEWS (((DAN))) |
| | DRUG AND ALCOHOL TESTS ADMINISTERED TO THE TANKER DRIVER IN THE FIELD INDICATE HE WAS NOT UNDER THE INFLUENCE. |
| | HE TOLD THE C.H.P. HE WAS REACHING FOR THE TRUCK RADIO WHEN HE LOST CONTROL ON THE FAIR OAKS CURVE. |

**Figure 5.8.** (continued)

## Television Single-Camera Layout

The script form used in the motion picture industry has quite naturally found a second home in television. Many of the dramatic programs on television are produced by the same studios and crews that produce feature motion pictures. And both feature films and television dramatic programs (except some situation comedies produced entirely in a studio) are originated as a series of separate camera shots. Each scene is set up and shot individually and not usually in the same order in which the scenes will be shown in the final program. After all scenes have been recorded on film or tape, they are edited into the final presentation.

This episodic, start-and-stop type of production is used for other types of production as well as for drama—corporate videos, location shooting of news and documentary stories, even commercials. When it is used, the script follows a different layout form from that used for multicamera production. Our example, Figure 5.9, is taken from the script of "Silk Stalkings," written by Stephen J. Cannell and produced by Cannell Entertainment. These pages are the concluding scenes from Act 2 of the four-act, hour-long drama. Stephen Cannell is recognized in the industry as a prolific and effective writer

40      EXT. ROXANNE DOCKWEILER'S HOUSE - DAY                          40

The use of the word "house" is an affectation.  What this
is is a concrete fortress designed in the twenties by
Senator Dockweiler.  There are enough European doodads
stolen from the great castles of Europe to qualify this
house as an historical monument.  Three acres and a mega
yacht go with the package.  Peter drives up the open drive
in a police black and white, stops and gets out...  walks
up to the front door, rings the bell which SOUNDS like the
noon tolling of Big Ben.  After a beat, the door opens and a
very old, very starched English butler is standing there.
His name is FREDERICK.

                          FREDERICK
                 Yes?


                          PETER
                 Frederick... Don't tell me you've
                 forgotten me...

                          FREDERICK
                 How could one forget you, Mr.
                 Lorenzo?  It was the first time
                 in my life I was forced to testify
                 against an employer.

                          PETER
                      (leans in)
                 Between you and me, I thought you
                 lied magnificently on the stand.

                          FREDERICK
                 A compliment I will cherish, sir.

                          PETER
                 Is Miss Dockweiler in?

                          FREDERICK
                 She's not receiving guests,
                 Sergeant.  She is having her
                 portrait done this afternoon.

                          PETER
                 Don't make me go for my badge,
                 Frederick.  I always tear my pants
                 getting it out.

                          FREDERICK
                 In which case, why don't you come
                 in?  Madame is in the sun room.

Frederick slowly and sadly steps aside as Peter moves into
the entry hall.

**Figure 5.9.** From ''Silk Stalkings'' by Stephen J. Cannell. © 1991 Cannell Entertainment,
Inc. Reprinted by permission.

41    INT. ENTRY HALL                                           41

      It is as we would expect... magnificent and perhaps slightly
      over-decorated.  The rich down here have so much money, it's
      hard to know when to stop adding accessories.  Frederick
      leads Peter to:

42    THE SUN ROOM - DAY                                        42

      This is really more of a garden room looking out on the
      magnificent property... mutton bar windows everywhere.
      Interesting as the room is, ROXANNE DOCKWEILER is even more
      interesting.  The portrait she is having done is boudoir
      photography.  She is about forty years old, maybe a shade
      older, but like Cher, she has been busting her ass to keep
      everything in place and she has succeeded...  long, dark
      hair, satin brown skin.  She's in a teddy and high-heels
      with a feather boa around her shoulders.  She is showing
      all that the law will allow.  The photographer is enjoying
      himself.  His name is EARL.

                          FREDERICK
                Sergeant Lorenzo, ma'am...

      She smiles and looks past Earl for a beat.

                          ROXANNE
                Earl, that will be fine for a
                minute.  Why don't you take five?

      Earl looks at Peter who shrugs.  The photographer moves out
      through the open door into the garden.  Frederick
      disappears.

                          PETER
                When I get my portrait done, I
                usually wear my blue pinstripe.
                I think I've been missing
                something...

      She gets off the high stool she's been posing on and moves
      to Peter, making no attempt to cover up.

                          ROXANNE
                Why Sergeant Lorenzo... can I
                offer you something?... maybe some
                coke?
                     (a grin)
                The soft drink, I mean.  I've
                certainly learned my lesson.

                          PETER
                I'm gonna need <u>something</u> if you
                keep standing like that...

                                           CONTINUED

**Figure 5.9.** (continued)

42    CONTINUED                                              42

>                    ROXANNE
>          I'm doing this for my new
>          boyfriend, Alex.  It's for his
>          birthday.  This is the tamest of
>          the three shots.  The nudes come
>          next.

>                    PETER
>          Need a steady hand on the flash?

She smiles at him for a long beat.

>                    ROXANNE
>          Didn't we play this scene in one
>          of those little green rooms you
>          have down at your office?  As I
>          recall, you weren't interested
>          then...

>                    PETER
>          I was on duty then.  I try not
>          to lay suspects... my one
>          concession to professional ethics.

>                    ROXANNE
>          I was doing my best.  You just
>          wouldn't come across.  I think
>          now the moment may have passed.

>                    PETER
>          Yeah, especially with Alex on the
>          scene.  By the way, what pool is
>          he working at?  I could swing by
>          and congratulate him.

>                    ROXANNE
>          Actually, he's in the four
>          hundred.  Alex Vanderlane.  You
>          may know him...  He races yachts.

>                    PETER
>               (shakes his head)
>          I only race taxicabs, buses and
>          an occasional freight train.

She smiles at him.

>                    ROXANNE
>          See how much fun we can have when
>          you aren't arresting me?
>          Although, I have to admit, I did
>          enjoy the little diversion with
>          the handcuffs.

                                        CONTINUED

**Figure 5.9.** (continued)

42    CONTINUED    (2)                                      42

                            PETER
              That's why they give 'em to us.

                            ROXANNE
              And what are you after this
              afternoon, Sergeant?

                            PETER
                   (a beat)
              Roxanne, I sense in you a
              mischievous spirit...

                            ROXANNE
                   (a devilish smile)
              Really?  And I thought I had it
              covered so nicely.

                            PETER
              You get a kick outta shocking that
              crowd you run with... This
              portrait will probably end up on
              your Christmas card...

                            ROXANNE
              What a splashy idea.

                            PETER
              I need to get into the Abbott
              compound... or get close to the
              Abbott clan.  I know you run in
              that school.  I thought maybe
              you'd like to see me do my trapeze
              act way up there... no net, lotsa
              clowns laughing...

         She looks at him for a beat and smiles.

                            ROXANNE
              You after Chief Justice Spencer
              Abbott... his ne'er do well
              middle-aged dropout son,
              William... or Little Willie, the
              rapist...?

                            PETER
              I'm never after people, Roxanne.
              I'm after justice.  That's what
              makes me such a special civil
              servant.

                            ROXANNE
              How could I have missed that?
                   (MORE)

                                      CONTINUED

**Figure 5.9.** (continued)

42      CONTINUED  (3)                                               42

                              ROXANNE (Cont'd)
                                (smiles)
                    Well, it would be sort of
                    scandalous for me to take you to
                    the Abbotts' Wednesday night pool
                    party... the cop who busted me.
                    That would get the ducks quacking.

                              PETER
                    Sounds interesting.

                              ROXANNE
                    I usually go stag, but in your
                    case, I'll make an exception.
                    Make it eight, tomorrow night.
                    I'll bring the prophylactics.
                    You bring the handcuffs...

                              PETER
                    One question...

                              ROXANNE
                    Go ahead.

                              PETER
                    What the hell are we gonna do with
                    Alex?

          Off her mischievous smile:

                                                      CUT TO


43      INT. ELECTRONICS COMPANY - DAY                               43

          A man with his back to Rita is going through the files.
          He turns with a slip of paper in his hand, moves to Rita.
          He is a German merchant named KLAUS REINAGER.

                              KLAUS
                    Ahh, here it is.  I sell dis to
                    Butch Lonigan.  His address is
                    on dat, dere.

                              RITA
                    Butch Lonigan.  He used to be on
                    the force.

                              KLAUS
                    Yah.  Private detective now.
                    Don't pay nobody for nothing.
                    Still owes me.  I call him, no
                    answer.  Dis guy got no friend,
                    no credit.
                              (MORE)

                                            CONTINUED

**Figure 5.9.** (continued)

43      CONTINUED                                                        43

                                    KLAUS (Cont'd)
                        You see him, tell him, to the
                        collection company I already turn
                        this over.

                                    RITA
                        Thanks.

        She turns and moves out of the building.

                                                    CUT TO


44      EXT. PALM BEACH - OLD TENEMENT AREA - DAY                        44

        This doesn't look anything like the swank condo district.
        This is the neighborhood for their gardeners and maids.
        Rita is moving into one of the buildings.


45      INT. TENEMENT BUILDING - STAIRWAY - RITA                         45

        looks at the address in her hand, gets to a door and finds
        it locked.  She KNOCKS, looks right and left, then takes
        out a lock pick and works quickly on the door.  She opens
        it, checks the hall and enters.


46      INT. ROOM - DAY - RITA                                           46

        enters to a horrible stench.  She grabs a handkerchief out
        of her purse and puts it up to her nose.  She moves slowly
        through the room to the bathroom.


47      INT. BATHROOM                                                    47

        Lying in the tub is Butch Lonigan.  Wrists cut, suicide note
        on the toilet... He's "punta de basta" -- long gone.


48      ANGLE - RITA                                                     48

        She goes to the note and looks at it without touching it.
        It reads:


49      INSERT - NOTE                                                    49

                        I got nothing left to live for.
                        Give my car to Linda Reed on the
                        first floor.
                                    Butch

**Figure 5.9.** (continued)

105

```
  #44000                        36.                          8/20/91

50    ANGLE - RITA                                                    50

      She looks at the dead detective, shakes her head and we:

                                                    FADE OUT

                              END ACT TWO
```

**Figure 5.9.** (continued)

and his studio has produced a number of series for both network release and syndication including *The A-Team*, *Riptide*, *Wise Guy*, and *Renegade*. "Silk Stalkings" is the pilot episode for a series with the same name. It takes place in Palm Beach, Florida, and features two attractive, sophisticated, smart homicide detectives, Rita Lee Lance and Peter Lorenzo. It's typical of Cannell's style.

Using this example as a guide, note these characteristics, which conform to more or less standard practice for scripting single-camera productions.

1. Several preliminary pages will precede the actual script action and dialogue, although we have not reproduced them here. These will include a title page with series title, episode title, writer and producer's names, copyright information and dates of various revisions. Other pages will describe the characters, wardrobe, settings, props and graphics needed. This information should not be included in the actual script, where it would clutter the layout. The amount of detail needed will vary with the program; for a continuing series much of this information will already be known to the crew members and need not be repeated with each script.

2. Number all pages. If the script will undergo revision, date the revised pages. For professional productions the new pages added at each revision are printed on a different color paper, so cast and crew can quickly identify where the most recent changes have been made.

3. Each scene, or camera shot, is handled individually. We say scene *or* camera shot, for there are two different approaches to teleplay writing. The more common approach is called the *master-scene* script. In this approach the writer describes the action in each scene and writes the dialogue, but individual camera shots within the scene will be selected by the director on location. The other approach, called a *shot-by-shot* script, provides a separate description of the dramatic action for each camera shot. Often master-scene scripts are revised into shot-by-shot scripts by the production's director. "Silk Stalkings" is written as a master-scene script.

4. Each scene is numbered consecutively at both the left and right margins. Often a scene or scenes appearing in an early draft will be omitted in the

final script, possibly because the cost or complexity of its production is too high, or more likely, to cut the length of the program if it is too long. When scenes are omitted, the scene numbers are left in, along with the word OMITTED. It would be much more complicated, and confusing to cast and crew, if scenes were renumbered after each revision.

5. Scene descriptions, stage directions, and camera directions, if they are given by the writer, are typed across the page within the scene numbers. LOCATION OF THE SCENE, indication of NIGHT or DAY, and CAMERA DIRECTIONS are typed in CAPITALS. Scene descriptions, mood, characters, actions, sound and music effects are typed in lowercase. Single spacing is used within each paragraph of description. Some of the descriptions used in "Silk Stalkings" are more descriptive than usual. Stephen Cannell not only writes dialogue and action in his distinctive style, his scene descriptions are also unique.

6. Dialogue is typed within a narrower column (about 3 inches) centered on the page. The name of the character who speaks is centered (in CAPS) just above his or her lines. The lines themselves are typed in upper- and lowercase, single-spaced. Directions on how the lines are to be spoken are placed between the character's name and the lines, in a column slightly narrower than the lines themselves, and set off by parentheses.

7. Double spacing is used to separate one scene from the next; also to set off methods of transition between two scenes (such as DISSOLVE, or CUT TO). It is also used to separate the lines of two characters, or lines from various types of directions. Paper is cheap, and the script may be more easily followed by performers and crew if it is not jammed up. When in doubt, space it out!

Several books provide detailed instructions for this form of script layout. If you plan to write dramatic programs, or other forms that use single-camera shooting, you should invest in one or more of these volumes. Full information on how to order them is given in the Further Reading section of this chapter.

## The Storyboard

The *storyboard* is a specialized form of audiovisual copy. For many years its primary function was to present, in draft form, the concepts for television commercials. A storyboard was prepared, for example, by an advertising agency to show a commercial idea to a client for approval. Then, if revisions were needed, they could be made much more quickly and cheaply at the storyboard stage, before the final script was written and actual production began. Storyboards were also used for corporate production, and for the development of sound-slide presentations. Often, if a good storyboard had been laid out and the production was not complicated, no further script would be needed.

While all of these uses remain, the merger of storyboarding with sophisticated computer software programs has led in recent years to a much expanded use for this form of scripting. Various forms of visuals can be "captured" from clip art, or photographs, or drawn and colored on a computer. Then these images can be manipulated into various special effects or animated. The images can be sequenced into a real-time presentation with sound, without ever leaving the computer. It's not television production any more; this form of message development is increasingly called multi-image or multimedia production. And the creative structure doesn't take the form of a traditional script. Script, storyboard and completed production are all one. Now, for example, we may see TV commercials on the air that are really just storyboards—drawn cartoon characters given animation and voices by a software program.

To prepare storyboards, follow these suggestions.

1. The number of cells (individual drawings, also called frames) in the storyboard will vary, depending on the complexity of the content. Usually a new drawing will be used for each important visual change—each new camera shot, or new character, or the addition of printed material or of the product logo. If the camera shot uses extensive camera movement, show the first camera position, and then the final position; in a zoom from wide shot to close-up draw both the wide opening and the final close-up.

2. Boards may be prepared as individual drawings, then pasted up on large poster board sheets, or by using pads of forms that are available commercially. Just make sure individual cells are large enough to accommodate the detail necessary in each picture without crowding.

3. The sound portion of the script, in written, script form, should parallel the picture cells.

4. Descriptive information—instructions about camera angles, camera movement and transitions between camera shots, such as cuts, dissolves, and wipes—will also accompany the picture cells. See the section in Chapter 8 for further discussion of visual transitions.

Our example (Figure 5.10) is titled "Delivery." It was prepared by Hal Riney and Partners agency for Stroh's beer. The spot was produced in both 30- and 60-second versions. This is the longer version. The action is complex, and so 32 cells were drawn, more than usual.

In other places in this text, especially in Chapter 11, we have reproduced additional storyboards and *photoboards*, which are similar to storyboards except that they are prepared from photos of the actual commercial after it is completed and usually contain fewer cells as they are used only for reference and promotion by the agency.

Storyboards are also used to prepare slide-tape presentations. The same basic guidelines apply except that for slide-tape the layout on the page is usually a two-column vertical arrangement. The sequence of drawing cells runs down on side of the page and the audio track—narration, dialogue, music, sound—down the other. The resulting layout looks very much like a split-page TV script except that the video column is drawings.

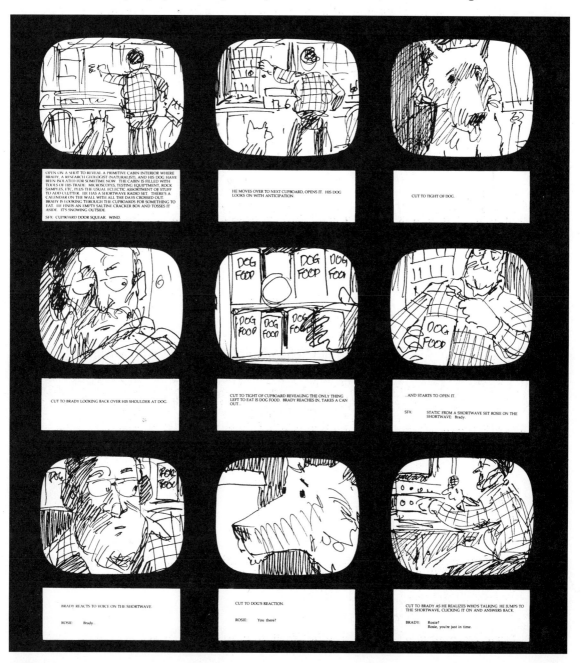

**Figure 5.10.** Courtesy of Hal Riney & Partners, Inc., San Francisco, CA.

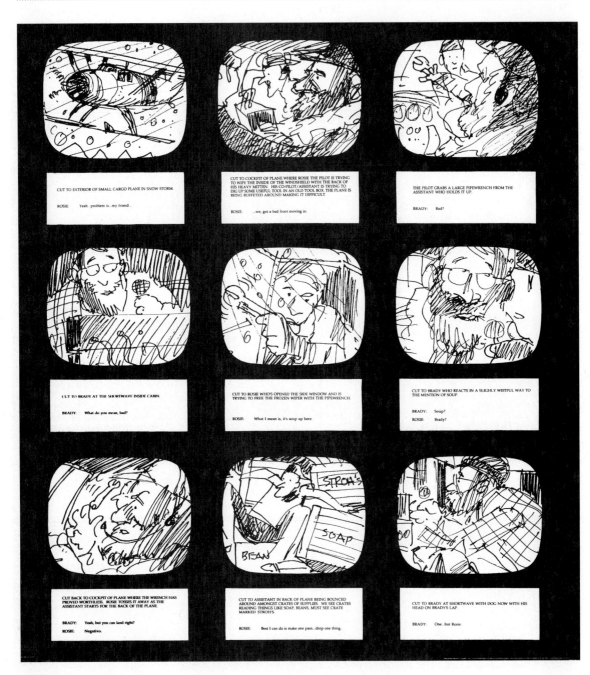

CUT TO EXTERIOR OF SMALL CARGO PLANE IN SNOW STORM.

ROSIE:        Yeah. .problem is...my friend...

CUT TO COCKPIT OF PLANE WHERE ROSIE THE PILOT IS TRYING TO WIPE THE INSIDE OF THE WINDSHIELD WITH THE BACK OF HIS HEAVY MITTEN.  HIS CO-PILOT/ASSISTANT IS TRYING TO DIG UP SOME USEFUL TOOL IN AN OLD TOOL BOX. THE PLANE IS BEING BUFFETED AROUND MAKING IT DIFFICULT.

ROSIE:        ...we, got a bad front moving in.

THE PILOT GRABS A LARGE PIPEWRENCH FROM THE ASSISTANT WHO HOLDS IT UP.

BRADY:        Bad?

CUT TO BRADY AT THE SHORTWAVE INSIDE CABIN.

BRADY:        What do you mean, bad?

CUT TO ROSIE WHO'S OPENED THE SIDE WINDOW AND IS TRYING TO FREE THE FROZEN WIPER WITH THE PIPEWRENCH.

ROSIE:        What I mean is, it's soup up here.

CUT TO BRADY WHO REACTS IN A SLIGHTLY WISTFUL WAY TO THE MENTION OF SOUP.

BRADY:        Soup?
ROSIE:        Brady?

CUT BACK TO COCKPIT OF PLANE WHERE THE WRENCH HAS PROVED WORTHLESS.  ROSIE TOSSES IT AWAY AS THE ASSISTANT STARTS FOR THE BACK OF THE PLANE.

BRADY:        Yeah, but you can land right?
ROSIE:        Negativo.

CUT TO ASSISTANT IN BACK OF PLANE BEING BOUNCED AROUND AMONGST CRATES OF SUPPLIES.  WE SEE CRATES READING THINGS LIKE SOAP, BEANS, MUST SEE CRATE MARKED STROH'S.

ROSIE:        Best I can do is make one pass...drop one thing.

CUT TO BRADY AT SHORTWAVE WITH DOG NOW WITH HIS HEAD ON BRADY'S LAP.

BRADY:        One...but Rosie.

**Figure 5.10.** (continued)

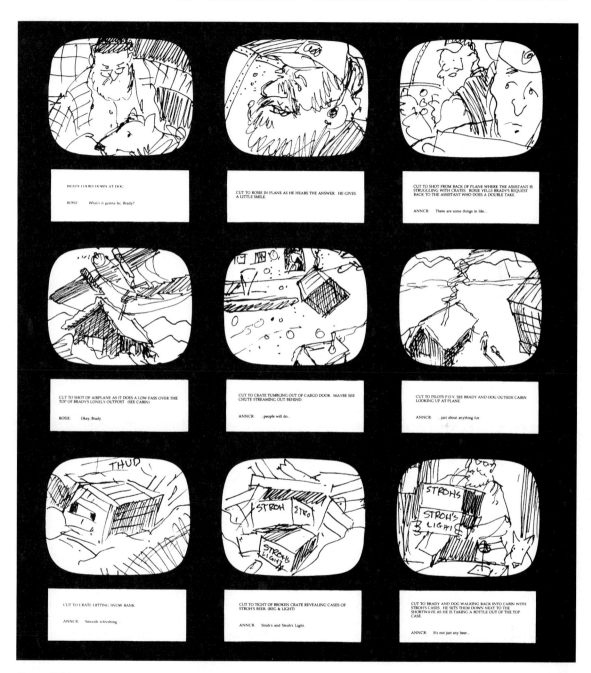

**Figure 5.10.** (continued)

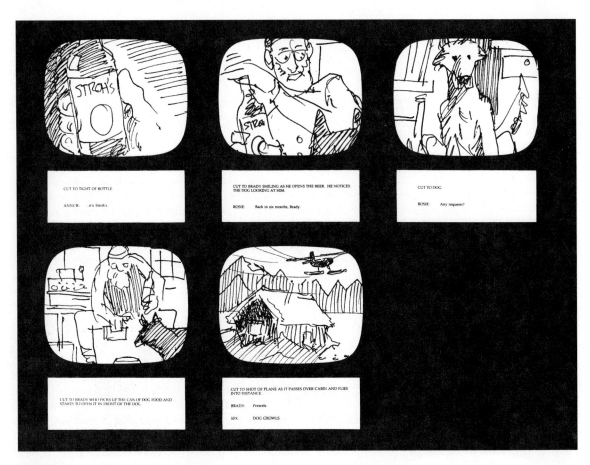

**Figure 5.10.** (continued)

## OTHER CONSIDERATIONS

Several other aspects of script mechanics can cause difficulties for both writers and other members of the production team—namely, how to handle punctuation, numbers, and abbreviations. Recall our admonition that the writer should prepare the script to be as clear as possible and to be quickly understood by talent and production personnel. Our guidelines regarding these mechanics are designed with that goal in mind.

### Punctuation

In broadcast copy, punctuation is intended only to help the reader of the copy deliver its meaning to the listener or viewer with maximum clarity. Most basic rules of punctuation still apply, but the single most important rule is that punctuation marks should be used to help the oral reader of the copy deliver that copy clearly, without stumbling and without ambiguity. Careful punctuation is particularly important if the reader will be working without rehearsal and therefore without any chance to mark the copy to suit his or her own style.

Punctuation marks in oral copy, then, generally serve one of two functions—to indicate *pauses* or to indicate *emphasis*.

### Indicating Pauses

The comma, the period, the dash, the ellipsis, and occasionally the semicolon are the punctuation marks used to indicate pauses in broadcast copy.

The comma is used more frequently in broadcast writing than in writing for print. It is used whenever a small pause is needed to establish the meaning of the copy, and not just where required by grammatical rules, such as setting off items in a series, separating dependent clauses, and so on.

The period is used in broadcast copy, as it is in print, to denote the end of a thought, the end of a sentence.

The dash (—) and the ellipsis (. . .) represent somewhat longer, more obvious pauses than does the comma. The use of these two varies somewhat with the preference of the writer or style manual being followed.

The *United Press International Broadcast Stylebook* says: Use an ellipsis to indicate a pause . . . a dash to indicate a longer pause—. This author prefers to use dashes within a sentence—denoting a pause only slightly more important than a comma—and to use ellipses to indicate longer pauses, especially those denoting hesitation or indecision, or at the end of an incomplete speech, or when one person's speech is to be interrupted by another. (Note how ellipses are used in the Perry Boys radio ad earlier in the chapter.)

The semicolon can be used as it is in print and to further set off series of phrases that already contain commas, but most writers prefer to use the dash in places where a semicolon might be grammatically correct.

### Indicating Emphasis

The most common punctuation marks used to provide emphasis in print material are the exclamation point and the question mark. The problem with the use of these two marks in broadcast copy is that they come at the end of the sentence. If the reader has not been able to read through the copy in advance, he or she may not realize until well into the sentence that special emphasis was intended by the writer. The outcome, which you probably have heard on radio or television at one time or another, is that a question may be read as if it were a statement; then the reader will discover the line was intended to be a question, fumble, pause, consider rereading the line, become confused, and sound unsure on the air.

Rather than relying on the exclamation mark and the question mark, it is better to <u>underline</u> those words or phrases that are to receive special emphasis and to reword questions so that they sound like questions from the very beginning of the sentence. Go ahead and include the marks at the end of the sentence, for they are grammatically correct there, but don't depend on the punctuation mark alone to show your intent.

Recall the two examples used in Chapter 3 to discuss the importance of correctly placed emphasis: "Where have all the flowers gone?" and "The president insisted that the American forces would be used for peace-keeping purposes only." Underlining is necessary in each of those examples to be sure the person who is reading the copy aloud provides the emphasis intended by the writer.

Be careful that you do not overdo exclamations or words and phrases to be emphasized. Many beginning writers are so concerned that the emphasis be in the right place that they underline words in every sentence of the copy. In most cases, the normal structure of the copy indicates to any experienced reader where the emphasis should be placed, and no extra marking is necessary.

### Useless Punctuation

Several punctuation marks have little or no value in spoken copy. One of these is the colon, a mark used to separate material. In spoken copy the separation is probably better done by a dash, which is much easier to see. Avoid colons.

Another mark that has no value in spoken copy is parentheses, used in printed copy to set off "interjected explanatory or qualifying remarks." In print the parentheses tell the reader that the material may be of some interest, but that it can be skipped without harm to the main sequence of ideas. In spoken copy, the material must either be delivered aloud or left out. It can't be partially set aside. So if the writer wants an idea to be spoken, it should be written into the text of the copy. If the idea is not to be used, delete it.

Parentheses are used, however, to separate nonspoken material, such as directions to a performer, from spoken copy, as we have shown in several examples.

Quotation marks are another punctuation symbol that presents a considerable challenge to the writer and the oral reader of broadcast copy. It is a very awkward punctuation mark to use, since again the listeners cannot see the words that have been set off by the marks. And the reader of the copy may not be certain of the method he or she should use to set the word or phrase in quotations apart from the rest of the copy. How should a news announcer handle the quotations in the following story excerpt, for example?

Treasury Secretary Lloyd Bentsen has spoken the magic words that make many tax experts and political visionaries glow: "consumption tax." When Bentsen told NBC's *Meet the Press* on Sunday that "some consumption tax is going to take place," he vindicated not only Jerry Brown, who advocated such a tax during the presidential campaign, but also a small army of economists who have labored in obscurity at the Treasury Department and various think tanks attempting to devise the perfect tax system.

"We have to do things to cut back on consumption and encourage investment for the creation of jobs in our country," Bentsen said. "We need a broad-based consumption tax to slay the deficit dragon and provide the wherewithal for doing something on the savings and investment side of the economy," said Mark Bloomfield, president of the American Council on Capital Formation in Washington. The odds for a consumption tax are clearly increasing, Bloomfield said. "It won't happen unless the president is willing to do it," he said, "but it's now on the table."

The most accurate reading would be to voice the marks—to say "quote" and "unquote" each time quoted material appears. That would make part of this story sound like this:

```
ANNCR:      ...quote, we have to do things to cut back
            on consumption and encourage investment for
            the creation of jobs in our country, unquote,
            Bentsen said. Quote, we need a broad-based con-
            sumption tax to slay the deficit dragon and
            provide the wherewithal for doing something on
            the savings and investment side of the economy,
            unquote, said Mark Bloomfield....
```

But these words are jarring to the ear; they are abrupt and they interrupt the flow of the story, especially for short quotes. Rather than clarifying, they may well confuse the listener. Even more stiff are the phrases "and I quote" and "end of quote."

Often, however, the sense of the story can be accurately transmitted without having to formally identify quoted material. One approach would be for the announcer simply to change the tone of delivery—in effect reading through the quotation marks. Another common way around the problem is not to quote at all; instead, use a paraphrase. Usually the exact words of a source are not as important as transmitting the sense of the story clearly to the audience. A paraphrase, which conveys the meaning but without the necessity to set apart the precise words of the source, becomes the preferred approach.

However, if a direct quote seems important or necessary, then alert the announcer and the listeners to the quotation in a manner similar to this example from the *United Press International Broadcast Stylebook:*

The senator attacks what he calls—needless and irresponsible use of federal powers. He says he believes this is our most serious problem. Then he adds—in these words—The tentacles of the state are closing around the individual.[1]

Quotation marks can be used to suggest emphasis on individual words or brief phrases. Like underlining, they call to the announcer's attention that the material in quotes should be given special emphasis or inflection to set it apart from the rest of the copy. The first quoted phrase in the story excerpt above, "consumption tax," is given that treatment. Here is another example:

```
Americans have a "thing" about labels, it seems. In the
1960s we labeled people with unusual lifestyles as "hip-
pies" and "beatniks."...
```

As with underlining, don't overdo this form of emphasis, and make sure the announcer understands that the quotation marks are in the script only to call his or her attention to the designated words, and not to identify a quotation.

## Writing Numerals

One matter of mechanics on which there is much difference of opinion is the proper way to present numerals in copy. Some style manuals say that all numbers should be written out, so that the announcer will not have to make a mental translation from numerals to words that may result in hesitation or error. But most writers feel that writing out all numbers as words is terribly cumbersome and suggest that complex combinations be written as numerals. The overriding considerations are that the writing should be clear and in a conversational style. In the absence of a specific guideline from your instructor, station or agency, here are our suggestions for writing numbers:

1. Write out all numbers from one through twenty: seven, ten, sixteen.

2. From 21 through 999 use numerals, unless there is a specific reason to use words: 47, 583.

3. Write out hundred, thousand, million, billion: thirteen hundred (which sounds better than one thousand three hundred), five billion, 69 million.

4. For large numbers, use a combination system that provides the greatest clarity: 4,329,733 would be four million, 329 thousand, 733. Other examples: one thousand, 49; five thousand, three; one thousand, three hundred, 22 (or, thirteen hundred, 22); three thousand, fourteen; eight million, three hundred thousand.

5. Write out fractions; one-third, five-eighths, six and one-half.

Note these problem areas in dealing with numbers:

1. The number 1954 may be read as one thousand, nine hundred, fifty-four, but the year 1954 is commonly read nineteen, fifty-four.

2. A business establishment with its address at 3850 Elm Street may want the number read as thirty-eight fifty. If that's the way they want it, write it that way.

3. A phone number—333-8800—can be read several ways. The client may prefer three, thirty-three, eighty-eight hundred. Or he or she may wish each digit to be read individually. The preferred method then would be to write it out in words: three-three-three-eight-eight-zero-zero. Some stylists, however, use digits with hyphens between: 3-3-3-8-8-0-0.

4. Rounded-off numbers, especially in the case of large numbers, are usually better than a long series of numerals. "A budget deficit of about four and a half million dollars" is more easily understood by the listener than "a budget deficit of four million, 433 thousand, 692 dollars," and most of the time the precise amount is not that important in the story.

## Writing Abbreviations

Do not use abbreviations in script copy, with the following exceptions:

1. These very common abbreviations may be used: Mr., Mrs., Ms., St. (when used for saint): Mr. George Brown, Mrs. Louise Smith, Ms. Penelope Jones, St. Louis.

2. Well-known acronyms may be given as initials. They are probably more easily recognized by their initials than by the full name anyway; A-M, P-M, U-N, Y-M-C-A. (The *United Press International Broadcast Stylebook* recommends using hyphens rather than periods between the letters in acronyms; we have followed that practice here.)

   Some acronyms are commonly pronounced as names. These do not take hyphens: OPEC, NATO, UNESCO.

3. Do not abbreviate fort, mount, names of cities, countries, states, or address identifications: *Fort* Hood, *Texas*; *Mount* Vernon, *New York*; the *United Kingdom*; *New Zealand*; *East Elm Street*; Sepulveda *Boulevard*; Orange *Avenue*.

4. Do not abbreviate days of the week or months of the year: Wednesday, September.

5. Do not abbreviate junior or senior after a person's name; company, corporation, or incorporated; or titles of officials: *Professor* James Edwards, *Junior*; the Xerox *Corporation*.

# CONCLUSION

The preparation of material for broadcast via television and radio almost always is a group activity that involves some combination of writers, actors, or other presenters, directors, equipment operators, and other personnel. In order for each of these people to contribute to the production, in order for rehearsals to be completed efficiently, and in order for materials to be presented without error, there must be an accurate blueprint for the program. That blueprint is the script. Errors that appear on the air usually can be traced to an incomplete, illegible, or inaccurate script, or to a person who did not have a script, did not follow a script, or did not make necessary corrections or notations on a script.

Regardless of what specifics are used, the goal remains the same. The copy and the instructions you write must make it possible for the presenters of the script to deliver the content easily and without error. The most important instructions to accomplish that goal are these: Be neat. Be accurate. Be consistent.

**Exercises**

1. In the remaining chapters of this book there are exercises to write particular styles or types of copy—radio commercials, TV news, drama, documentary, slide-tape instructional presentations, and so on. The most appropriate exercise for this chapter is to write those scripts using a format that meets the guidelines presented here.

2. Select a news story from your local newspaper. Rewrite it in the following versions, paying particular attention to aural style (Chapter 3) and layout.

   a. As a 45-second story for radio, single announcer.

   b. As a 60-second story for radio, with one actuality approximately 15 seconds long.

   c. As a 30-second story for TV, no visuals, single announcer.

   d. As a 60-second story for TV, but with visuals. Assume your camera crew was able to get whatever visuals were important.

   e. Same as (d), but including one actuality from a participant in the story.

3. Similarly, choose newspaper stories with these characteristics and rewrite as indicated. Again, consider primarily aural style and layout.

   a. A financial story with a lot of statistical detail. Rewrite for radio. Write the numbers to ensure clarity.

   b. A story that depends heavily on the descriptive accounts of witnesses or participants. Rewrite for television, with particular attention to the handling of quotations.

c. Rewrite and *punctuate* any story you find to be particularly complex and confusing in its printed version.

**Note**

1. *United Press International Broadcast Stylebook* (New York: UPI, 1979), p. 14.

**Further Reading**

Many of the books listed for other chapters contain sections on layout and mechanics and of course have examples that can be followed. Several of the style manuals listed for Chapter 3 are also helpful for layout, especially the Associated Press and United Press International manuals, for news.

For the layout of screenplays, the Writers Guild of America publishes a short but useful guide:

Coopersmith, Jerome. *Professional Writer's Teleplay/Screenplay Format*, rev. ed. New York: Writers Guild of America, East, Inc., 1983. [Available directly from the Guild, 555 W. 57th Street, New York, NY 10019. Write or phone 212-767-7800 for current prices and ordering information. Price is around $4.50.]

A much more detailed treatment of script layouts for screenplays and other filmed or taped drama programs is provided in these two volumes:

Cole, Hillis R., Jr., and Judith H. Haag. *The Complete Guide to Standard Script Formats—Part I: The Screenplay*. North Hollywood, CA: CMC, 1989.
Haag, Judith H. *The Complete Guide to Standard Script Formats—Part II: Taped Formats for Television*. North Hollywood, CA: CMC, 1988.

The authors of these two volumes distinguish between "filmed" one-camera production (covered in volume 1) and "taped" multiple-camera production used in sitcom and variety show production (in volume 2). Both texts are very useful, but they are not available through regular book outlets. Address inquiries to the publisher: CMC Publishing, 11642 Otsego Street, North Hollywood, CA 91601, or to Script City, 8033 Sunset Blvd., Suite 1500, Hollywood, CA 90046.

Another reference is

Lee, Robert, and Robert Misiorowski, *Script Models: A Handbook for the Media Writer*. Mamaroneck, NY: Hastings House, 1978.

# Program Structure

**P**eople usually watch television or listen to radio as a matter of choice. Except in unusual circumstances, viewing or listening is not a forced activity; it takes place because each individual person decides to watch or to listen.

From that premise, three corollaries can be stated:

1. Viewing and listening are in competition with many other possible activities in which each individual might engage at any particular time.

2. Each program is in competition with all other programs being presented at the same time.

3. If the program does not provide something of interest to each individual viewer or listener, that individual will turn to some other activity.

Successful programs will have some combination of both content and structure that will capture and hold the interest of audience members. In this chapter we look at those principles that pertain to structure—how to organize program materials to attract and hold audience attention.

When you finish this chapter, you will be able to

- recognize principles of good program structure in existing programs,

- evaluate the structure of programs,

- use structural principles in preparing your own scripts and program formats,

- understand the different functions performed by program openings and closings and meet those requirements in your own scripts, and

- recognize and use these important terms and concepts:

| | |
|---|---|
| attention span | climax |
| bumper | cold open |

| | |
|---|---|
| epilogue | prologue |
| gimmick | setup piece |
| pace | signature |
| pad | teaser |
| program element | unity |
| program identification | variety |

In this chapter we use episodes from three long-running TV series as detailed examples of structural principles. But you will be able to understand structural concepts best and use them most effectively if you use the principles presented in this chapter to make your own analyses and evaluations of programs you choose. Then, when writing scripts, consciously include these principles of program structure in your work.

## ATTENTION

Because there are many activities competing for a viewer's or listener's attention, that task—attracting and then holding attention—is the central principle of program structure.

The producers of *Nightline* are acutely aware of this challenge, and their task has been described this way:

> What is it that draws millions of sleepy viewers every night? . . . Just after Ted Koppel's opening, there is that pregnant moment when each viewer decides whether to stay with *Nightline*. "We spend a disproportionate amount of our time trying to figure out how to make the potential viewer *want* to watch *Nightline*," Koppel says. . . . "The first few seconds of our show are critical; either we grab the viewer then, or he goes away. Our opening minute—that's our headline."
>
> "The subjects we choose," Koppel says, "are not necessarily topics viewers think they want to see. We spend time on what they *should* watch and on making them want to watch it. We have a problem other news shows don't have: We are on late at night. People can watch entertainment as an alternative, or they may just decide to go to bed."[1]

Some years ago the way that audiences selected programs led to the formulation of an interesting proposal known as the "least objectionable program" theory. This viewpoint suggests that habitual viewers of television are prepared to watch something at a particular time and, in the absence of a program with positive appeal, will choose the program that is least objectionable.[2]

We doubt that this theory really ever worked very well. It certainly doesn't apply now, since most viewers have a choice of many different over-the-air and cable programs. If the program being presented does not provide some positive attraction for an individual, then that person will find some way to dissociate himself or herself from the program. He or she may ignore the program and turn to other activities in the same room, leave the room, change the channel, or turn the set off altogether. The outcome of all these behaviors, in which the message from the TV or radio is no longer being received, is negative, at least from the point of view of the program's producers and sponsors. They want the audience to stay tuned and to pay attention to the program and its commercial content.

## Intensity of Attention

Even when an individual has a program turned on, the intensity of his or her attention will vary. If the program contains content the individual perceives as being important, that person's attention will be focused on the program, and other activities competing for attention will be excluded. At the other extreme, if the content is uninteresting or unimportant, the individual will place attention elsewhere, and the broadcast program simply becomes background noise.

Between the two extremes is a whole range of other behaviors, including those of the person who watches the program most of the time but picks up a paper or magazine or starts a conversation whenever low-interest material appears; or the person who divides attention between the program and routine tasks such as knitting or ironing; or the person who habitually turns on the set and then goes about other activities around the house, to be drawn back to the receiver only if there is a major change in the content of the program—such as the sudden breaking into the program with a news bulletin.

## Attention Span

Not only does the intensity of a person's attention vary, but so does the length or span of attention. No person is able to give undivided attention to any one stimulus for very long; competing stimuli will draw off attention after a period of time. Some means must be provided in the program to recapture that attention, and to draw it back to the television or radio set.

The length of attention span will vary in relation to several factors: the extent to which the content of the program is of interest or value to that individual, the number of competing stimuli in the environment, and the ease

# ZIGGY™

**Figure 6.1.** Copyright 1983 Ziggy and Friends, Inc. Dist. by Universal Press Syndicate. Reprinted with permission. All rights reserved.

with which the materials can be processed by the individual. Complex, difficult material will mean a shortened attention span. And attention will vary by demographic characteristics as well—children as a rule have shorter attention spans than adults.

In general, after a minute or so of attention to one idea or element in a program, an individual's attention tends to diminish. That person can continue to focus on the sound coming from the radio or the picture from the television screen only by exerting some degree of effort. And the longer the same kind of material appears, the greater the effort becomes.

As a rule, audience members do not want to exert much effort to follow a television or radio program. We have become conditioned to look upon these media primarily as sources of entertainment. Therefore, the expenditure of mental effort, of "working" to pay attention to the program when the limit of attention has been reached, is at odds with the idea of relaxing, enjoying, and being entertained by the program. We will not and do not force ourselves to pay attention. It must be the program, and not the viewer or listener, that provides the impetus to return one's attention to the screen.

## PROGRAM ELEMENTS

To deal with this problem of holding attention, radio and television programs must—at very frequent intervals—give the listener something new to hear or to watch. Some sort of change is needed in some aspect of the program which will be sufficient to reattract the attention of the viewer or listener.

Each time there is such a change, some new element of program content has been introduced. We will use that term—*program element*—to describe segments of a program separated by some definite type of change. The program element will become our basic building block for analyzing and constructing broadcast programs.

The content of a half-hour television program, for example, may be made up of twenty to thirty, or even more, program elements. If too few elements are used to construct a program, each element, or some of them, will be long, and the limit of audience members' attention span will be reached before a new element is introduced. The program will seem slow and boring. If, on the other hand, a great many elements are used in a program, the program will be perceived as having a rapid pace, perhaps even too rapid for the comfort of the audience.

### Types of Program Elements

A number of different types of changes are possible in any program; new elements may be constructed in a wide variety of ways. The following list is suggestive of some of the more obvious ways in which changes can take place and new elements can be introduced. We are likely to think of these changes in relation to television, since that is where we find more structured programs. But the concept is equally valid for all types of radio programming as well.

- By making a change in the scene, or the setting before the cameras or microphones

- By changing the type of material presented, from talk to music, music to dance, action to talk, and so on

- By starting a new musical number after completing an earlier one

- By making a definite change in the topic or subject matter of a talk program—introducing a new idea

- By using a different method of presenting material, as in changing from a one-person talk to a two-person dialogue or to an interview

- By bringing a new, important character into a dramatic scene or taking one away, thereby creating a change in the relationships of characters in the drama

- By changing the mood, or tempo, or a scene; for example, from calm conversation to excitement and action

These descriptions represent the separation points of one element from another. The elements themselves may be further explained by these descriptions of types that commonly appear in broadcast programs.

### A Scene in a Dramatic Show

Any segment in which there is no change in main characters, in place, in time, or in subject discussed or amount of action is a single element. The same characters are involved and subject matter, mood, and action remain the same. If another major character enters the scene, there is invariably a change in emphasis and frequently in subject matter as well, and therefore the start of a new element. Change also would take place and a new element be introduced if during the scene one character sings a song, or if after a long "all talk" segment, there is a quick change to violent physical action.

### A Musical Number by a Vocalist or an Orchestra

Any self-contained musical selection of reasonable length would be a program element. If a longer number, begun by an orchestra, is followed by a substantial vocal section, you might be justified in separating them into two elements. Similarly, if the selection is begun by the orchestra or vocalist but contains a dance routine in the middle and the camera focuses on the dancers, even though the vocalist continues to sing, the focus of attention changes, and a new element has been started.

### A Commercial or Public Service Announcement

Obviously, the insertion of an announcement into a program marks a change from the type of material both preceding and following. Commercials and PSAs usually are not integrated into the content of programs, and from the audience's point of view they frequently are seen as interruptions. But in considering program structure, they must be considered along with the other elements that make up the total program. (By the way, each announcement is considered a single element, regardless of the number of changes which may appear within it.)

### A Major Item in a News Broadcast

It's difficult here to differentiate major and minor items; arbitrarily any news item of about 30 seconds or longer can probably be considered a separate element. Several short items presented by the same anchorperson probably represent only a single element.

### A Round of Questions in a Game Show

The description of a round will differ, depending on the structure of the game, but usually it will involve a series of similar questions to one contestant, or the responses of several contestants to one question. In *Family Feud*, for example, the starter "toss-up" question/response is one element, the continuation of that question line with one family is a second, and if they miss, the completion of the group of questions is yet a third.

Remember that the key to the identification of elements is change *that will recapture attention.* A lot of minor changes take place within all types of programs which are too brief or too inconsequential to be used to separate elements. For example, applause or laughter following a segment of entertainment material should not be classified as a separate element, but as part of the element it follows. A very short introduction of an entertainer or a musical number is combined with the element it introduces. Bridge music in a dramatic program and entrance music are too short to be elements.

Note that program elements in television are not the same as camera shots. Elements are portions of the content of a program; if the same essential materials remain "on stage" in a television show, changing the angle of the shot by shifting from one camera to another does not produce a new element, but having a variety of camera shots within an element may prolong the viewer's span of attention. Often several camera shots will appear within a single element, but what makes a new element as we have defined it is the change in the content being treated, not just in the technique of presentation.

Most well-structured programs will have elements usually between 40 seconds to 2 minutes in length, but there is no set length. In most programs not many elements will be shorter than 15 to 20 seconds. In TV, the possibility of having varying camera shots within an element makes it possible to have somewhat longer elements than normally would be used in radio.

## Using Program Elements

The concept of elements provides a useful and universal way to analyze the sequence and relationship of the various individual pieces that together make up a broadcast program. It should be understood, however, that this is not a precision tool. Two people analyzing the same program are not likely to agree completely on the number of elements in the program, nor on the precise points at which changes occur between elements. But it takes only a little practice to become familiar with the concept and to be able to identify the major types and locations of change within a program.

Here we show in a standardized format the element analyses for three television programs. We have chosen different types and lengths of programs to give some sense of the universality of this technique. The approach can be used to analyze any made-for-TV program, or at least any program in which attention span might be a problem, and that means everything but very short materials. After these analyses we will continue an examination of the principles of program structure, and then return to the examples to see how well they meet the criteria for a well-structured program. Much more important, however, than reading these analyses is for you to analyze current programs using the same method—locating the points that represent the refocusing of audience attention through changing program elements, counting the number of elements in a program, and timing each element. (An analysis form you can use for this practice is included in the exercises at the end of this chapter.)

Even doing an analysis of existing programs represents only an intermediate stage in your progress toward writing scripts organized to ensure maximum audience attention. Regardless of what type of program you may be called upon to write, be it news, documentary, drama, a game show, or a religious or political program, you will have to consider how you are going to maintain and recapture audience attention. Using the principle of program elements, and recognizing how these elements are provided in various types of existing programs, will help you to determine the most appropriate ways to structure your own scripts to hold audience attention.

The layout form used for our sample programs describes both the content and structure of the program. The five columns used for the first analysis, *Roseanne*, provide

1. A count of the number of elements in the program

2. A description of the content of each element

3. A word or two which identifies what in the program caused the change from one element to the next

4. The starting time of each element given in minutes and seconds from the beginning of the program

5. The length of each element

### Roseanne

The situation comedy series *Roseanne* should be familiar to most readers. It has had a very successful run in prime time, and will undoubtedly be seen for many years to come as an off-network syndicated series.

| Element # | Content/Description | Type of Change | Start Time | Length |
|-----------|---------------------|----------------|-----------|--------|
| 1 | Cold open: Roseanne & Dan's porch, sounds of screaming; Kathy (neighbor) comes to investigate, enters and walks through house nervously | | 0:00 | 2:00 |
| | | mood | | |

| Element # | Content/Description | Type of Change | Start Time | Length |
|---|---|---|---|---|
| 2 | Discovers Dan's "corpse" on sofa; screams | | 2:00 | 0:10 |
| | | character | | |
| 3 | Roseanne enters with knife in hand, "blood" on dress; she scares Kathy with talk of "killing" | | 2:10 | 0:45 |
| | | character | | |
| 4 | Dan gets up, scares Kathy again; all 3 in scene | | 2:55 | 0:20 |
| | | character | | |
| 5 | Dan & Roseanne yell "Happy Halloween"; Kathy exits; Roseanne & Dan tag | | 3:15 | 0:10 |
| | | material | | |
| 6 | Signature open; credits | | 3:25 | 1:10 |
| | | material | | |
| 7 | Commercial: Maybelline Great Lash Mascara | | 4:35 | 0:30 |
| | | material | | |
| 8 | Commercial: Jack in the Box | | 5:05 | 0:30 |
| | | material | | |
| 9 | Roseanne & Dan discuss trick played on Kathy | | 5:35 | 0:25 |
| | | character | | |
| 10 | Becky (daughter) enters; Roseanne, Dan & Becky discuss her Halloween plans | | 6:00 | 0:30 |
| | | character | | |
| 11 | Darlene (another daughter) enters, similar conversation | | 6:30 | 0:15 |
| | | character | | |
| 12 | D.J. (son) enters in Alfalfa costume; conversation with Roseanne, also with Dan & Darlene (who leaves) | | 6:45 | 0:50 |
| | | characters | | |
| 13 | D.J. leaves, Jackie (Roseanne's sister) enters, Dan leaves; Roseanne & Jackie discuss Jackie's not having a date for lodge Halloween party | | 7:35 | 1:50 |
| | | character | | |
| 14 | D.J. enters again in new costume, then leaves; Roseanne & Jackie tag | | 9:25 | 0:15 |
| | | location, time | | |

| Element # | Content/Description | Type of Change | Start Time | Length |
|---|---|---|---|---|
| 15 | New scene: exterior of lodge, then pan interior to show costume party in progress | | 9:40 | 0:15 |
| | | characters | | |
| 16 | Jackie meets Jessie, both dressed in same costume | | 9:55 | 0:45 |
| | | character | | |
| 17 | New character in costume enters to tell Jackie that Arnie (ex-boyfriend) has arrived | | 10:40 | 0:25 |
| | | character, location | | |
| 18 | Arnie & Jackie move to different room for brief conversation | | 11:05 | 0:20 |
| | | character | | |
| 19 | Host (MC) introduces the entertainment act for the party | | 11:25 | 0:45 |
| | | characters | | |
| 20 | Roseanne & Dan (as ventriloquist & dummy) are the act | | 12:10 | 1:25 |
| | | time | | |
| 21 | Afterward, Roseanne & Dan discuss act with other guests | | 13:35 | 0:35 |
| | | characters, topic | | |
| 22 | Kathy and husband Jerry enter; Roseanne is sure Kathy plans to get even for prank | | 14:10 | 0:30 |
| | | material | | |
| 23 | Commercial: Dristan Nasal Spray | | 14:40 | 0:30 |
| | | material | | |
| 24 | Commercial: Chef Boyardee | | 15:10 | 0:15 |
| | | material | | |
| 25 | Commercial: Hyundai Elantra | | 15:25 | 0:30 |
| | | material | | |
| 26 | Commercial: Dannon Yogurt | | 15:55 | 0:30 |
| | | material | | |
| 27 | Commercial: Triples Cereal | | 16:25 | 0:15 |
| | | material | | |
| 28 | Promotion: Homefront | | 16:40 | 0:15 |
| | | material | | |
| 29 | Local station news break | | 16:55 | 0:15 |
| | | material | | |

| Element # | Content/Description | Type of Change | Start Time | Length |
|---|---|---|---|---|
| 30 | Return to lodge party; Dan and MC talk about the new arrivals | | 17:10 | 0:35 |
| | | characters | | |
| 31 | Dan & Roseanne discuss her concern that Kathy plans to get even | | 17:45 | 0:30 |
| | | characters | | |
| 32 | Dan leaves, Jackie enters; Roseanne & Jackie discuss man in moose costume that Jackie is interested in | | 18:15 | 0:35 |
| | | time, characters | | |
| 33 | Exterior shot for time lapse, followed by Jackie & man in moose costume (Booker) | | 18:50 | 0:55 |
| | | characters | | |
| 34 | Dan and Jerry (Kathy's husband) discuss earlier prank | | 19:45 | 0:10 |
| | | characters | | |
| 35 | Back to Jackie & Booker (now unmasked) on their relationship | | 19:55 | 0:45 |
| | | characters | | |
| 36 | Kathy comes through scene, followed by Roseanne & Dan | | 20:40 | 0:25 |
| | | characters | | |
| 37 | Roseanne & Kathy confrontation, continues until Kathy walks out | | 21:05 | 1:05 |
| | | time, characters, location | | |
| 38 | Exterior shot of house; Dan & Roseanne at home after party | | 22:10 | 0:30 |
| | | mood | | |
| 39 | Dan & Roseanne discover snakes in bed | | 22:40 | 0:10 |
| | | characters | | |
| 40 | Kids enter, admit snakes are their prank | | 22:50 | 0:45 |
| | | characters | | |
| 41 | Kids leave, Roseanne & Dan tag | | 23:35 | 0:30 |
| | | material | | |
| 42 | Commercial: Red Lobster | | 24:05 | 0:15 |
| | | material | | |
| 43 | Commercial: Ford Trucks | | 24:20 | 0:30 |
| | | material | | |

| Element # | Content/Description | Type of Change | Start Time | Length |
|---|---|---|---|---|
| 44 | Commercial: Walt Disney Home Video | | 24:50 | 0:15 |
| | | material | | |
| 45 | PSA: Drug Free America | | 25:05 | 0:15 |
| | | material | | |
| 46 | Promotion: False Arrest | | 25:20 | 0:30 |
| | | material | | |
| 47 | Dan & Jerry setting up prank on porch | | 25:50 | 0:30 |
| | | character | | |
| 48 | Roseanne discovers prank (as they expected and while they watch), believes Kathy set it up | | 26:20 | 0:30 |
| | | characters | | |
| 49 | Dan & Jerry in bushes, tag | | 27:50 | 0:10 |
| | | material | | |
| 50 | Closing credits | | 28:00 | 1:00 |
| | END | | 29:00 | |

### This Week with David Brinkley

We chose *This Week with David Brinkley* for contrast with prime-time entertainment programs, and because in another chapter we want to consider the problem of attracting and maintaining audience attention in public affairs and informational programs, for which we'll use this analysis as an example. *This Week with David Brinkley* has long been a fixture in ABC's Sunday morning schedule. As we will see later, it is about as well structured as any public affairs program on the air.

| Element # | Content/Description | Type of Change | Start Time | Length |
|---|---|---|---|---|
| 1 | Introduction; Brinkley sets topic (changes in Soviet Union and implications for U.S.) & identifies guests to appear on program; program title | | 0:00 | 1:00 |
| | | material | | |
| 2 | Brinkley w/brief news story (Gainesville murder suspect caught) | | 1:00 | 0:30 |
| | | material | | |
| 3 | Billboard for advertisers | | 1:30 | 0:15 |
| | | material | | |
| 4 | Commercial—ADM Corp. | | 1:45 | 1:00 |
| | | material | | |

| Element # | Content/Description | Type of Change | Start Time | Length |
|---|---|---|---|---|
| 5 | Brinkley—historical background on topic; introduce news report | | 2:45 | 0:45 |
| | | presentation | | |
| 6 | Jack Smith—the "setup" piece; highly edited summary of recent news in U.S.S.R. & U.S. related to topic | | 3:30 | 5:15 |
| | | material | | |
| 7 | Brinkley—teaser; names upcoming guests | | 8:45 | 0:30 |
| | | material | | |
| 8 | Commercial—Merrill Lynch | | 9:15 | 0:30 |
| | | material | | |
| 9 | Commercial—GE light bulbs | | 9:45 | 0:30 |
| | | material | | |
| 10 | Commercial—Canon copiers | | 10:15 | 0:30 |
| | | material | | |
| 11 | Promo—ABC News | | 10:45 | 0:20 |
| | | material | | |
| 12 | Brinkley—introduce guest #1 (James Billington, Librarian of Congress) & interviewers (George Will & Sam Donaldson); interview | | 11:05 | 8:25 |
| | | material | | |
| 13 | Brinkley—tease for next guests | | 19:30 | 0:15 |
| | | material | | |
| 14 | Commercial—GE | | 19:45 | 0:60 |
| | | material | | |
| 15 | Promo—ABC | | 20:45 | 0:20 |
| | | material | | |
| 16 | Local station break | | 21:05 | 0:30 |
| | | material | | |
| 17 | Brinkley—introduce guest #2 (Igor Malashenko, U.S.S.R. Communist Party Central Committee, via satellite); interview w/same panel | | 21:35 | 6:00 |
| | | material | | |
| 18 | Brinkley—tease next guests | | 27:35 | 0:15 |
| | | material | | |
| 19 | Commercial—ADM Corp. | | 27:50 | 0:60 |
| | | material | | |
| 20 | ABC promo—Twin Peaks | | 28:50 | 0:20 |
| | | material | | |

| Element # | Content/Description | Type of Change | Start Time | Length |
|---|---|---|---|---|
| 21 | Brinkley—introduce guests #3 & #4 (Senators Bill Bradley and Pat Moynihan), interviewed together by same panel | | 29:10 | 10:30 |
| | | material | | |
| 22 | Brinkley—tease discussion coming | | 39:40 | 0:10 |
| | | material | | |
| 23 | Commercial—Merrill Lynch | | 39:50 | 0:30 |
| | | material | | |
| 24 | Commercial—GE dishwasher | | 40:20 | 0:30 |
| | | material | | |
| 25 | Commercial—Allstate Ins. | | 40:50 | 0:30 |
| | | material | | |
| 26 | Commercial—MCI long distance | | 41:20 | 0:30 |
| | | material | | |
| 27 | Promo—ABC PrimeTime Live | | 41:50 | 0:15 |
| | | material | | |
| 28 | Discussion—Brinkley, Will, Donaldson, Cokie Roberts; topic #1, appointment of Bob Strauss as new ambassador to U.S.S.R. | | 42:05 | 5:45 |
| | | topic | | |
| 29 | Topic #2, request by KQED-TV, San Francisco, to televise a California execution; good idea? | | 47:50 | 2:15 |
| | | topic | | |
| 30 | Topic #3, implications of news report that U.S. children can't do math; what solutions? | | 50:05 | 3:35 |
| | | material | | |
| 31 | Brinkley—tease closing item | | 53:40 | 0:10 |
| | | material | | |
| 32 | Commercial—GE | | 53:50 | 1:00 |
| | | material | | |
| 33 | Commercial—Merrill Lynch | | 54:50 | 0:30 |
| | | material | | |
| 34 | Brinkley—commentary; problems in Los Angeles with residents saving too much water during drought | | 55:20 | 0:40 |
| | | material | | |
| 35 | Closing commercial billboard | | 56:00 | 0:30 |
| | | material | | |
| 36 | Closing credits<br>END | | 56:30<br>57:30 | 1:00 |

### *Entertainment Tonight*

This program is a five-day-a-week syndicated series that most stations carry in the prime-time-access slot between local news and prime-time entertainment programming. The analysis follows the same layout form as before, except that we have eliminated the "Type of Change" column. In this program, almost every change is in the content or material. Many changes also involve alternating narration by the two anchor announcers, Mary Hart and John Tesh (noted in the analysis by their initials). Other shorthand notations we have used are S/B (to denote sound bites from one or more persons involved in the story) and O/C (on camera) to indicate when either or both anchors are actually seen on the screen. Other presentational techniques are discussed later in this chapter.

| Element # | Content/Description | Start Time | Length |
|---|---|---|---|
| 1 | Quick cold open, S/B Kim Alley; JT teases opening story | 0:00 | 0:30 |
| 2 | Brief title open (graphics behind, MH & JT O/C intros); lead into... | 0:30 | 0:25 |
| 3 | "Inside Story"—Donald Trump's new love interest, Kim Alley; rehash of background material; JT narrates with S/Bs & file shots | 0:55 | 2:20 |
| 4 | "Inside the Headlines"—a real-life parallel to Nightmare on Elm Street; phone interview with convicted rapist who calls himself Freddy Kruger; brief S/Bs with "experts" on pros and cons of glorifying a repulsive screen character; MH narrates with photos, clips from film, S/Bs | 3:15 | 2:30 |
| 5 | Tease tomorrow's "Inside Story" on TV stars taking their shirts off; S/B w/Neil Patrick Harris | 5:45 | 0:20 |
| 6 | Tease upcoming stories | 6:05 | 0:20 |
| 7 | Commercial: Energizer Batteries | 6:25 | 0:15 |
| 8 | Commercial: Red Lobster Restaurants | 6:40 | 0:15 |
| 9 | Commercial: Nestlé Raisinets | 6:55 | 0:30 |
| 10 | "Inside Pix"—graphic w/music | 7:25 | 0:05 |
| 11 | Commercial: Jackson Ford/Mercury | 7:30 | 0:30 |
| 12 | Commercial: Taco Bell | 8:00 | 0:30 |
| 13 | "Inside Television"—on new Farrah Fawcett documentary Prisoner of Wedlock; review of her earlier roles including last season's Good Sports, clips, S/Bs; MH narrates | 8:30 | 1:45 |
| 14 | "Inside Television"—TV movie premiere of Murder in New Hampshire, based on Pamela Smart murder story; | 10:15 | 2:40 |

| Element # | Content/Description | Start Time | Length |
|---|---|---|---|
| | clips & interviews with cast and victim's family; JT narrates | | |
| 15 | "Inside Television"—new TV series <u>Sibs</u>; interviews with cast (Marsha Mason & Alex Rocco), clips; MH narrates | 12:55 | 1:40 |
| 16 | "Coming Attractions"—promos for three new TV programs and record album using clips & S/Bs; JT narrates: (1) <u>Homefront</u>, | 14:35 | 0:40 |
| 17 | (2) <u>Perry Mason</u>, | 15:15 | 0:25 |
| 18 | (3) <u>White Lie</u>, | 15:40 | 0:15 |
| 19 | (4) Harry Connick record album | 15:55 | 0:15 |
| 20 | MH tease for coming stories | 16:10 | 0:10 |
| 21 | Commercial: GMC Sierra Trucks | 16:20 | 0:30 |
| 22 | KCRA News Promo—tomorrow's "Special Assignment" story, including clip from story | 16:50 | 1:00 |
| 23 | PSA: Recruiting New Teachers | 17:50 | 1:00 |
| 24 | "Inside Movies"—<u>Ramblin' Rose</u>; clips & interviews with featured performers; JT narrates | 18:50 | 1:10 |
| 25 | "ET Newsreel"—four stories; clips & S/Bs; MH narrates: (1) new inductees into TV Academy Hall of Fame | 20:00 | 0:40 |
| 26 | (2) benefit for the homeless based on <u>City Slickers</u> home video release; Billy Crystal S/B | 20:40 | 0:45 |
| 27 | (3) winner of GE "Name the Dog" contest | 21:25 | 0:15 |
| 28 | (4) Mickey Dolenz concert benefit for cancer research | 21:40 | 0:20 |
| 29 | JT O/C with graphics behind, series of: (1) <u>Conversations with Burt Reynolds</u> | 22:00 | 0:15 |
| 30 | (2) Eddie Murphy's new movie contract | 22:15 | 0:15 |
| 31 | (3) upcoming rock concert in Moscow | 22:30 | 0:20 |
| 32 | Bumper | 22:50 | 0:05 |
| 33 | Commercial: <u>Paradise</u> (film) | 22:55 | 0:30 |
| 34 | KCRA news promo | 23:25 | 0:30 |
| 35 | PSA: Arbor Day Foundation | 23:55 | 1:00 |
| 36 | PSA: Old Sacramento Boats on the Boardwalk | 24:55 | 0:30 |
| 37 | Credit for production assistance on program: Mastercard (graphic) | 25:25 | 0:10 |
| 38 | "Birthdays"—stills, JT narrates | 25:35 | 0:20 |
| 39 | Tease tomorrow's "Inside Edition" story; JT & MH O/C, lead into... | 25:55 | 0:20 |
| 40 | <u>Prince</u> music video behind closing credits | 26:15 | 1:00 |
| | END | 27:15 | |

These examples will give you an idea of how to approach the analysis of an existing program—that is, what information to observe and a useful form in which to collect that information. We'll return to these examples, and use these analyses in an evaluation of program structure, after we have presented some additional principles.

## THREE-PART STRUCTURE

Some types of program elements are self-contained—individual announcements, for example, and news feature stories which may be written and produced in such a way that they can be inserted randomly in a magazine-type program. But most of the time individual program elements do not stand alone. They are just as the name implies—elements or portions of programs. They must be organized and sequenced in various ways to meet the structural requirements of longer programs.

Almost all TV programs and a substantial number of radio programs are of predetermined, fixed length and have an identifiable three-part structure. They have an opening, a body or central part which contains the bulk of the content, and a closing. Each of these parts has a contribution to make to the overall structural strength of the progam, and to maintaining audience interest in it.*

## PROGRAM OPENINGS

### Functions of Program Openings

The opening of a broadcast program should accomplish two purposes: It should attract the attention of potential audience members, and it should identify the program and the series, if it is part of a series. The program opening may also be expected to accomplish some additional useful, but not critical or universal, purposes. It may set a mood or explain the nature of the program, or provide for the insertion of commercials or other types of announcements.

---

* One major category of exception we are not considering here is music radio stations. These stations play their particular style or format of music more or less continuously. Their programming does not have a formal structure.

Note also that under the system of programming used by most U.S. broadcasting stations, programs usually are separated by a "station break," a period of time (from 30 seconds or so up to a couple of minutes) which is used to provide station identification and to insert additional announcements into the station's schedule. The IDs and announcements that appear in these breaks are not part of the structure of programs as such.

### Attracting Attention

We've already discussed in some detail the importance of attracting audience attention. This is a particularly important consideration at the beginning of a program. For the person who is already watching television or listening to the radio, the end of one program and the beginning of another represent a break in that individual's commitment—an opportunity to change easily to another activity or another station. The person just tuning in will quickly determine if the program is one that is worth time and attention.

If the program is one episode of a continuing series which is very popular, then some audience members will make their commitment based in part on past pleasant experiences with the program. These individuals may be willing to wait a little longer before making a decision to change activity. The opening for *All in the Family* did not have strong attention-getting material; nevertheless, the program was a popular series for a number of years. But even in this situation, the writer cannot afford to have an opening that is too casual or too slow.

### Providing Identification

At the beginning of a time period audiences who have tuned to reach a particular program want to be assured that they have reached the program they were looking for. Other individuals, who may be tuning randomly just to see what they can find, will also want to know what program they have reached. Programs therefore provide identification to the audience through such standard materials as program and series titles and the names of featured performers and guest artists.

### Setting a Mood

In addition to the two primary requirements, a program opening may also be used to establish overall tone or mood. A lighthearted situation comedy should have a lively, friendly, humorous opening. Upbeat marching band music sets the mood for *Coach*; the young star of *Blossom* is seen dancing around to a snappy tune. A police drama that features a lot of on-location, exterior activity should set that tone in the opening with fast-moving action sequences and quick-cut camera action.

### Providing Explanations

Series that are familiar to the audience will not require much in the way of explanation, but new series and one-time special programs will usually require at least some brief description of the premise or purpose of the program.

Situation comedies are often based on some contrived or supernatural "gimmick." Openings for these programs require some explanation of that gimmick. One of the first program series to use this approach, *The Beverly*

*Hillbillies*, placed a family of country bumpkins into a mansion in Beverly Hills. The plots were based on their coping with the strange new environment. Audiences needed to know how they came to be in that situation, and so "the story" of the show was written into the opening portion of each program.

An explanation is needed for the witch who can perform magical feats by twitching her nose, in *Bewitched*, or the genie who can transport people by a similar action in *I Dream of Jeannie*. Similar explanations were required in *The Ghost and Mrs. Muir*, *Alf*, and *Mork and Mindy*. To explain to the viewers how a fully qualified and practicing medical doctor can be only in his teens, the creators of *Doogie Howser, M.D.* use a catchy tune combined with a series of newspaper clippings that tout the main character's brilliance. *Quantum Leap* is another series with a gimmick that requires an explanation.

Other forms of explanation needed in program openings are the "rules" that govern the actions of contestants in game or audience participation programs and descriptions of the topic and its importance for public affairs programs.

### Providing Place for Announcements

You are already aware of the need to place commercial announcements within the structure of most programs. When commercial breaks are required in a program, some of those breaks will appear in the opening. Their placement must be considered along with the other elements and requirements of the opening.

How these various purposes are best accomplished depends a great deal on the type of program being presented and on which of these purposes is considered by the producers and writers as being most important. Will commercials need to be inserted? How much explanation will be necessary? How easily will the audience be able to identify the program?

## Provide a Strong Start

At first glance it may seem that this instruction, to provide a strong start, is the same as the requirement to attract attention at the beginning of the program. Although they are related, they are not the same. An element included in the program opening and specifically designed to attract attention is only one of the types of material which may be included in that opening. Providing a strong start, on the other hand, considers all of the materials which are included in the opening portion of a program.

### Minimize Low-Interest Material

Some of the elements which go into the opening are likely to be low in audience interest. Their presence in the opening, although necessary, is in conflict with the requirement to attract audience attention. It becomes a challenge to the writer's creativity to include low-interest elements in such a way that their negative or weakening impact is minimized and the overall opening is kept as strong as possible, given the various elements that must be accommodated.

For example, audiences frequently view the placement of commercials in a program as an interruption of the entertainment, since they are not integrated into the program content. On the other hand, the advertiser who has paid to have an announcement inserted in the program does not see the commercial as unimportant. That advertiser wants the best possible placement for the ad and wants all the audience members to be paying attention when the announcement comes on.

The writer, in order to balance these conflicting views, must provide strong attention-getting materials to "hook" the audience before presenting announcements at the beginning of a program. If too many announcements appear in the opening moments of a program, or if they appear too early in the opening, before strong attention-getting materials have been presented, their presence will have a seriously negative effect.

### Avoid Lengthy Explanations

A well-constructed game show has very simple rules that can be explained very quickly, or that don't have to be explained at all for the audience to enjoy the program. The producers and writers of a public affairs program, as noted by Ted Koppel earlier, will have to point out quickly the importance of that material to the audience.

In new programs—the first program of a new series, or a one-time special—explanations and identifications may be more necessary than in a continuing series. Names of the cast may not be known, and a "gimmick" will have to be explained in more detail on the first broadcast. In those situations the writer is faced with the important and difficult task of incorporating the necessary explanations and identifications without becoming too detailed, and while maintaining audience attention. In all too many new or one-time programs, this problem has not been recognized by the writer and is not satisfactorily solved. The audience's reaction is one of impatience, waiting for the program to get going. They will not wait long.

### Limit Credits

Credits too may be low-interest materials. The problem of presenting credits in television may be contrasted with that of the motion picture. Traditionally movie credits are given at the beginning of the film (although even that has changed and now most credits are presented at the end). But in the theater the audience has paid an admission price to see the film and is not likely to leave and forfeit that price just because of a few minutes of low-interest credits at the beginning of the film. They would likely stay tuned to a pay-per-view movie for the same reason but not to "free" TV. There they will seek alternatives if the credits badly weaken the opening.

One effective technique for television drama is to show the credits graphically over the opening scenes of the drama, which are written without dialogue but establish the program's location and begin the action. This way there are no spoken words to conflict with the credits in the viewer's perception.

## Types of Openings

The creative challenge to satisfy the requirements set down for a program opening, and to do so while attracting and holding attention, has resulted in two basic types of openings and then many variations and combinations which have developed from them.

### The Signature Opening

This form of opening started in the early days of radio, when tuning into a program was a rather complicated task. There were no receivers with push-button tuning. People had to scan the dial to find the correct frequency position for the stations that carried their favorite programs. It was therefore important that programs have readily identifiable openings—a pattern of music, sound effects and/or voices that was the same for each broadcast in the series and that the audience could quickly and easily identify. This standardized opening is known as a *program signature*.

Among the well-known program signatures of network radio programs were a theme from "The William Tell Overture" used on *The Lone Ranger*; a montage of marching feet, whistles, sirens, clanging doors, and machine-gun fire, intended to be representative of crime and of prison, used on *Gangbusters*.

Even when radio tuning became much easier, program signatures continued and the form is now used in television as well. Well-known television programs using standardized signature openings include *M\*A\*S\*H*, *Star Trek*, *Happy Days* and *Barney Miller*.

In addition to providing identification, one other function easily accomplished with a signature is that of mood setting. In early radio, a very well known mood-setting signature was the sound effect of the squeaky door opening and the eerie, echoing voice of the narrator on *Inner Sanctum*. Most well-constructed signature openings in television also contribute to the mood of the show, or at least match the tone of the program in both style and approach.

The signature also can be an effective and efficient way to provide explanations, especially in dramatic programs where there is a gimmick to be explained. The program series given as examples in our earlier discussion of gimmicks—*The Beverly Hillbillies*, *Bewitched*, *I Dream of Jeannie* and *Doogie Howser, M.D.*—all use signature openings.

The most serious deficiency of a signature opening is that it does not satisfy the other major requirement of a program opening; its very familiarity weakens the signature as an attention-getting device. Since the audience may have seen or heard the signature many times previously, attention is not particularly drawn by that material.

### *The Cold Opening*

This type of opening originated on dramatic programs, but is now used with other types of content as well. With this opening, the program begins immediately with content material. The content starts "cold" without identification and may continue for up to several minutes before being interrupted by any other type of material. If material of high dramatic value—conflict, action—is chosen for the cold open, then the audience's attention will be strongly attracted.

Variations of the cold opening exist. One form, which was the first to be used extensively in television but is seldom seen anymore, takes a "chunk" of high-interest material out of the body of the program and opens with that material. That same "chunk" is then shown again in the program in its proper location. The value of this type of cold open is that the material can be taken from near the climax of the program, where the intensity of the material and audience interest would be high. The section lifted out also will involve the main stars in the program.

Both major purposes are accomplished. High-interest material is presented at the beginning of the program, and the program is identified for regular members of its audience through its performers. This opening sequence may last for a minute or so and then be followed by a more formal identification—titles, performer credits, and other opening materials, including announcements. The plot of the drama begins after all opening elements are completed.

A weakness of this form of opening is that it "gives away" some of the climax and lessens the impact of the material when it is shown the second time in its proper place in the plot. Probably for that reason, this approach is no longer used very frequently.

Another type of cold open also begins the program with content material, but in this case the content is in its proper sequence—the introductory section is the beginning of the plot. Then identification of the program is given, and commercials or other materials are presented. Finally, after the other opening elements are completed, the plot resumes from the point at which it had been interrupted.

Other types of programs may also use this type of opening. A talk-interview program may begin "cold" with conversation between host and guest, or a news program may open with headlines or one major story before the program is identified and other opening elements presented.

This form of opening does not give away any plot secrets, and if properly constructed can strongly attract and hold audience attention. But there are also some problems that need to be recognized and overcome in order to use this approach successfully. Traditionally, the opening of a dramatic plot includes material that sets the locale of the drama, introduces the characters and introduces the conflict. Often this expository material, though necessary, does not contain high-interest content. If used as an opening it would be slow and weak, without much attention-getting force.

If we reverse the situation, another problem emerges. Providing dramatic, high-interest, important material early will attract attention, but if important material is included too early in the cold open, late tuners will miss that content and will be behind in trying to understand the plot as it unfolds.

Finally, if the cold open does not contain the main characters—that is, those who are the readily recognizable stars of the series—audience members will have no way to identify the program and to confirm whether they have tuned to the right channel. They may tune away, or go searching for a TV log to see if perhaps the program they were expecting to see has been preempted, or changed to another time, or whatever. They have no clue that this is in fact the program they tuned in to see.

The solution to these three possible problems—taking advantage of the strong attention-getting characteristic of a cold open while at the same time starting the program at a logical beginning, accommodating late tuners, and identifying the program—requires a delicate balancing act on the part of the writer. So a well-constructed cold opening will:

- Contain high-interest material, even if that material is not directly related to the main content which will be developed later,

- Not include important facts or events too early which might be missed by late tuners,

- Have some easily recognizable element appear early, either the appearance of the featured performer or performers in the series, or the keying in of titles over program action, or something similar.

### Combination Openings

Because of the problems just mentioned that affect either signature or cold opens, very few current series use either type in a pure form. Most programs now use a combination of techniques, and creative writers are constantly developing new variations. One form of combination opening uses a sequence of quick scenes lifted from various places in the body of the program and formed into an audio-video montage intercut with the program title and identifications of the feature performers. Another variation is a montage from scenes lifted from preceding episodes, if the program is one with a continuing plot line, like *L.A. Law*, *Knots Landing* and most "soap opera" dramas.

*The Simpsons* opening animation changes slightly each episode, as Bart writes something different on the blackboard. *Cheers* opens with "cold" material, a brief comic bit between some of the regular cast members, who are easily identified. But the bit has no relationship to the primary plot, which is introduced after a signature title-credit sequence. *Seinfeld* opens with a brief stand-up routine, poking fun at the upcoming story. The result of these techniques is a form of signature. It's a standardized pattern that audience members can identify very quickly but with enough variation from program to program to provide interest in the opening itself.

*Law and Order* uses a very brief standardized signature to open, just enough to identify the series. That is followed by a lengthy opening plot sequence, sometimes called a *prologue*, in which the crime of the week is committed. Then comes a longer identification, cast credits, opening commercials and a return to the plot. All these combinations do a good job of meeting the requirements for program openings.

## THE BODY OF THE PROGRAM

In the main portion of the program it is necessary, first, to maintain or reattract audience attention, to provide changes of sufficient intensity and frequency to keep the audience tuned and interested in the program. Second, in most programs it will also be necessary to organize the content so that there are breaks for the insertion of announcements.

The type of content being presented dictates the structure and method of presentation. Dramatic programs are by definition different from news broadcasts, talk shows, musical variety programs, and so on. But the writer of a successful program will need to consider several structural requirements independent of the type of content. It is the writer's job to be sure the program provides unity, variety, good pacing, and a climax.

### Unity

This requirement refers to those characteristics in a program which make the audience feel the program "hangs together"—that it is a single, logical unit into which no extraneous elements have been introduced. A program that consists of elements apparently thrown together at random, without rhyme or reason, leaves the listener bewildered and uncomfortable, because it will require effort to follow the idea of the program.

Unity does not mean that only a single kind of material can be used—a musical program should not be made up entirely of vocal solos by a single entertainer. But the music used, no matter of what type or by what means it is presented, must harmonize with the general spirit of "mood" of the program. To use extreme examples, you wouldn't insert a rock and roll piece into a program of symphony music, nor would you put a prayer into the middle of a comedy monologue.

Unity in a program may be ensured or heightened by

1. Dealing with a single idea in the program. If it is a news program, it should deal with current news; if it is a forum, it should be a discussion of one topic.

2. Using a "theme" or "situation" that runs throughout the program. In a variety program, every episode or "act" might be related in some way to a program theme—in one program the theme might be based around a holiday, or a location, or some occupation or hobby.

3. Using a central "featured personality"—with the entire program revolving around that featured person or persons. This is one of the most common approaches to unity. The performer may be a featured entertainer, a master of ceremonies, the anchor in a news broadcast, or the "lead" in a dramatic program—but that person or persons has the duty of carrying the show.

4. Eliminating materials that obviously do not belong—scenes in dramatic programs which do not advance the plot and which seem to be dragged in; materials which do not fit the "mood" of the program, such as comedy routines in a serious program.

5. Making effective use of transitions. In a variety program, each "act" should be introduced. In a forum, a change in the subtopic discussed should be clearly identified by the moderator, so the listener knows that the material which follows is not intended to apply to the previous subtopic.

6. Handling middle commercial announcements in such a way that they provide the least possible interruption and listener annoyance.

In most programs, the most serious violations of unity result from the indiscriminate insertion of commercial announcements. Commercials are necessary in most programs, but they *can* be handled in a sensible manner. They can be inserted at natural breaks in program continuity—at the conclusion of the performance of an "act" in a variety show, or following the completion of a section devoted to some one type of news in a news broadcast, or at the end of a complete scene in a dramatic program. Dramatic programs written for the commercial broadcast media, if well written, will be structured into "acts" that provide logical breaks to accommodate commercial inserts. In contrast, a motion picture originally produced for theatrical release, where it is shown without interruption, will seem choppy when shown on television because the commercial breaks seem to be—and are—especially disruptive.

Commercials can be separated from program content by some type of *bumper*—a visual or aural midprogram signature, a gong ringing, a strain of music, a "freeze frame" of the last shot in the content, or some similar transition. Even "and now, a word from our sponsor," which is pretty crude, is better than nothing.

Another aspect of unity that is important in a program series is series unity. The viewer has a right to expect that all programs in a series will be similar. If he or she enjoyed the first broadcast, the expectation is that subsequent programs in the series will provide the same enjoyment. Any program in the series should be of the same general pattern as any other program of that series. Series unity is provided by consistent use of the same general kind of content, by the use in each broadcast of the same featured personalities, by the use of the same general sort of locale, and by the use of essentially the same format.

## Variety

The idea of *variety* has already been introduced under a different name—change—in the discussion of program elements. On first examination, the requirements for variety and for unity may seem to be at odds, but a well-structured program will have variety within a unified theme or approach. Some of the methods that may be used to provide variety include these:

### Variety in Kinds of Materials

Many different kinds of materials can be used in a broadcast program. In music alone, there is new wave, disco, country, folk, religious, jazz, Latin, and several styles of rock, just for starters. A variety program may offer comedy in the form of sketches and monologues, dance routines, musical numbers, and so on.

Daytime soap operas have long used multiple plots, unfolding simultaneously. But for many years the writers and producers of prime-time dramatic series used a form in which a single story line was presented and resolved in each separate episode. Gradually various prime-time series began to borrow the daytime structure. Several parallel plots would progress through each episode, with some plots resolved in that broadcast and others carried over to future episodes. *Love Boat*, *Fantasy Island* and *Hill Street Blues* used this approach, as does *L.A. Law*. Other series using this technique are *Civil Wars*, *Homefront* and *Beverly Hills 90210*. The presence of several plots does not violate the principle of unity so long as the various plots are connected in some fashion—using interlocking character relationships or the same locale—and so long as all the plots move forward toward eventual climax and resolution.

### Variety in Methods of Presentation

A musical number might be presented as a vocal solo, as a number by a trio, quartet, or other small vocal group, as a vocal solo with backing by a large chorus, as an instrumental solo, as a presentation by a small instrumental group, or as a full orchestra performance. Talk materials might be presented as "straight" talk by a single speaker, as dialogue between two speakers, as regular narration by two speakers alternating, as a question-and-answer segment, by a single speaker in the form of reading a section of a letter or part of a book, and so on.

A farm broadcaster may talk in general about farming and farm problems, but one portion of the program may be spent discussing market trends, another reading market forecasts from the U.S. Department of Agriculture, and another in discussing the need for spraying fruit trees—there are a lot of different subjects included under the general heading of "farming and farm problems."

The announcer can use actualities—the actual voices of farmers or agricultural experts—either live in the studio, by phone, or in pretaped segments. A secondary personality may be used on the program to permit back-and-forth talk, to present certain items in a semi-comedy "heckling" role, or to represent the "typical listener" and interrupt with questions.

### Variety in Types of Performers

This form is well illustrated by the types of characters ordinarily found in a dramatic program. Usually there will be a male lead and a corresponding female lead; possibly a comedy type who is a friend of the hero's; sometimes a juvenile character—a teenage boy or girl; occasionally a younger child; frequently one or two older people. In a well-structured play, hardly ever are there two important characters who are of the same sex and of approximately the same age unless variety is provided by making the characters quite different in other respects.

In a talk or discussion program, variety might be introduced by having both male and female and older and younger people appearing. But more important would be to have people with differing points of view regarding the topic. A discussion program in which all the participants agree is going to lose audience interest very quickly.

### Other Forms of Variety

Some additional ways of achieving variety include these:

1. The use of "feature spots"—material deliberately different in content and/or method of presentation from the surrounding materials in the program.

2. The use of music or sound effects for background, transition, or punctuation.

3. The use of different types of "stunts" for participants to perform and a variety of types of people as participants. For a quiz program, the subject

matter of the questions can be changed. Prizes are usually given in audience participation shows; here too there is opportunity for the introduction of variety and novelty.

4. The use of "characters" or entertainers who look different or who wear costumes of different types. Change also can be introduced in settings or backgrounds and by the use of lighting effects.

5. The use of "visuals"—slides, films, rear projection, charts or diagrams included in the set or with the format of the program. These graphic devices are frequently used in news and talk programs to provide visual variety.

## Pace

In every type of entertainment, pace is a requirement. *Pace* is not a synonym for speed; it refers primarily to an impression, the impression of "going somewhere" and not "dragging." In part, the effect of good pace comes from the avoidance of materials that themselves move slowly. In part too, the effect comes from avoiding the stretching out of materials. Otherwise listeners get the impression that the program lacked enough material to fill the time—and that interferes with listener attention and interest.

The impression of pace is provided by:

1. Seeing that participants do not include speakers who are needlessly and intolerably slow in their speech patterns—or if such speakers must be used, that they are held to short appearances.

2. Making use of entertainers or speakers who are vigorous and lively in their manner of speaking—obviously allowing for the use of some other types to satisfy requirements of variety.

3. Eliminating or shortening any materials or types of materials that tend to slow up the program—long explanations, or overlong, very slow musical numbers, or long talk scenes—exposition with no action—in a drama.

We have emphasized the *impression* or the *sense* of good pace provided in a well-structured program. But the most effective way to determine whether or not a program has good pace is to check on the number and consequently the length of the elements that make up the program. If the elements are regularly long, pace is necessarily slow and the program suffers. Even if just a few of the elements are unusually long, the listener will have the impression of the program being "draggy." You have undoubtedly seen programs that seemed slow. If you had numbered and timed the program elements, you would have found comparatively longer and fewer program elements than in a program in which each element is ended, and replaced by another, before the listener has a chance to get tired of the material in that element.

At the other extreme, a structural technique that was at one time popular but has now receded is that of consistently rapid pacing within a comedy-variety program. The technique was pioneered by *Laugh-In*. It incorporated a series of quick comedy bits using different cast members individually or in small groups, resulting in complete change of attention and new program elements every 30 seconds or so. The syndicated country-comedy show *Hee-Haw* still uses some of this approach.

## Climax

The requirement for climax is most easily recognized in dramatic programs. Throughout the body of the program, as the plot situations develop, the problems facing the central characters become more and more complex and reach what seem to be an unsolvable peak. The moment of greatest tension is the climax. It is followed quickly by the solution and the end of the program.

But this sense of building to climax, of raising audience interest to higher levels as the program progresses, is not and should not be limited to dramatic programs. In a variety or musical program, it can be the big closing production number in which all the featured performers and guests appear, along with the dancers, orchestra, and so on. It can also be accomplished by holding back some of the important guest performers until near the end of the program. In a quiz program or game show, it may be the awarding of the biggest prize at the end of the show. In an interview program, some of the more important questions to be asked of the interviewee may be held back and developed near the end of the program, in order to provide some strong material at the close which the audience perceives as climax and remembers after the program is over.

In addition to the use of tension or "bigness," climax may be achieved through emotional stimulation. A featured musical performer might, for example, appear alone and perform a song that has strong emotional associations for the audience. Some years ago the Tennessee Ernie Ford television program did just that, using a religious hymn as its final number each week. For the target audience, the emotional appeal of that powerfully and simply sung hymn provided a strong climax for which they waited each week with real anticipation.

News broadcasts would seem to be an exception to the climax rule. These broadcasts do place the most important news stories at the beginning of the newscast. Audiences cannot be expected to wait through an entire broadcast to find out the major stories. But frequently news programs will close with a human interest story, one that has strong emotional pull and that does provide a form of climax.

In addition to the "final" climax in a program, longer programs and programs which have breaks for identification and/or commercial insertions will need to have subclimaxes—one to precede each break in the continuity and to heighten audience interest enough to bridge the gap until the program is resumed.

This requirement for climax refers to the organization of the content materials in the program. But the content closing and the program closing are not usually the same, as we will see.

# PROGRAM CLOSINGS

In a dramatic program, the content close comes with the climax and the denouement, which is the final resolution of the plot. However, several minutes of other materials—credits, commercials—may still have to be presented before the program can end. In other types of programs, the time between the end of the content and the closing of the program may be somewhat shorter, but in all programs there are materials that come after the content of the show has been completed.

## Functions of Program Closings

A program closing has several important functions. The particular ones required will vary with the type of program and some of them are similar to those performed by openings.

### *Providing Identification*

Most of the members of the audience will have watched a program from its beginning and will know what program they have tuned to, but some late tuners may not know the name of the program. They should be given at least a brief identification somewhere in the close.

For that purpose, some programs use a closing signature, frequently the same signature used in the opening, or a shortened version of it, or the same sound track. Here, as in the opening, the familiar signature aids in identification and is also useful in providing a sense of finality to the program.

Closing credits are another type of identification. Usually the credits for the major performers are given in the opening, but those for production personnel and secondary performers are most often at the end. Audiences don't find this listing particularly interesting, but the contract for the broadcast of the program usually requires that these people be given credits, even if the listing is low-interest material.

When the movie *Superman* was first shown on television, it was split into two parts and shown on two successive nights. The contract stipulated that the full credits be shown on both nights—*eleven minutes of credits each time!* Certainly there was very little audience left at the end of that time to watch the following commercials and programs. But imagine how much worse the problem would have been in maintaining audience attention if those credits had been required at the beginning rather than at the end.

### Providing Place for Announcements

The closing for most programs must also contain positions to place announcements—commercials or PSAs—just as there is a need for such positions in the program opening and the body. However, the problem of holding audience attention, so that audience members can be exposed to those messages, must be approached slightly differently in the closing. In the opening and the body, if the attention-getting material has been effective and if the program is well structured and written, the audience will stay through commercials to watch the remaining content. In the closing, after the content of the program has been presented and completed, the plot climax has been reached and resolved, the major news stories have been given, or the major guests have appeared, it is much more difficult to keep the audience's attention for the closing commercials.

One device commonly used for this purpose is the *epilogue*. The epilogue in a dramatic program follows the closing commercials with some final bit of conversation among the major characters. It may be the denouement, or an explanation, such as how the detective figured out the murder, or a final laugh. If the epilogue for each episode of a series is well written, each week the audience will stay tuned through the closing commercials to see what "twist" the writer has put in for this episode.

Epilogues can appear in programs other than dramatic shows. In a news broadcast, the final "human interest" story may be held until after closing commercials for the same reason.

### Promoting Subsequent Programs

Frequently there will be material in the closing of a program used to attract the attention of the audience to a subsequent program. This material is called a *teaser*, and it can take several forms. It may be used to "tease" the audience into watching the next program of the same series, the next day or the next week, whenever that program series next appears. The producers and writers who decide to include this form of tease assume the people watching will then have a sufficiently strong mental image to remember and will tune in to the next broadcast.

A teaser may also be used to hold the audience over for the immediately following program. People are prone to stay with a channel or station anyway. However, this audience flow, which is an important strategy of programmers, may be strengthened by a teaser for the program to follow.

Or the programmers may use the teaser to promote some other program in the schedule appearing later in the day, or even on a subsequent day. This teaser may be for a new program that needs additional promotion, or a special, one-time program, or a program that has been reassigned to a new day or time, or one that is doing poorly in the ratings and the programmers feel needs a boost.

For television, if the tease is for the next program in the same series, it will probably take the form of some brief scenes lifted from that episode, very much like the montage of scenes used in many openings. But most often the teaser in television is an audio-only message—essentially a radio promotion delivered by an announcer over the visual closing credits. Seldom do audience members actually read the closing credits, and those few seconds can be used effectively, at least in the opinion of the producers, for a teaser.

### Providing a Sense of Closure

This function is that of "rounding out" or providing to the audience a feeling that the program has concluded. For most programs, again especially those that have been prerecorded and pretimed, there is no question as to when the program is over. Even live programs such as news broadcasts end with a closing statement by the anchor and a closing credit. But occasionally a program that has been badly timed and poorly prepared, or that has had to be put together at the last moment, will just end without the sense of finality it should have. If you have been in the audience for such a program, you can recall the momentary sense of frustration and bewilderment you felt when the program suddenly disappeared.

## Adjustments for Timing

One function of a program closing that merits special attention is timing. Broadcast programs, with rare exceptions, have precise time requirements. They must end exactly at the time scheduled, and can be neither short nor long. Most programs are prerecorded, and the final timing is done in the editing process before the programs are broadcast. Live programs, however, must contain provisions for timing adjustments.

Major adjustments will be made during the body of the show. A game show may not reach its final round in time for the contest to be completed in one episode, so the contestants will be asked to come back and complete the contest on the next program. In a news broadcast, the director will have preselected one story to be dropped if the program begins to run long.

Final, short, "fine-timing" adjustments will be made in the closing. The materials that will be used or dropped in the closing to make the final adjustments are known as the *pad*. These are items that can be expanded or contracted, run more slowly or faster, or omitted. On television, the closing credits are frequently used as the pad. They may be "rolled" across the screen at a faster or slower rate, as needed. For radio, a common pad is the theme music used for a signature, which may be played for varying lengths of time.

The following is a typical timing pad for a local live public affairs program. It uses only the moderator's voice to provide the necessary adjustments to get the program out on time:

MODERATOR:      Thank you, Martha and Joe.

1. Today's guests on "Community Viewpoint" have been Martha Jones, founder of the Concerned Parents' Patrol and Joe Smith, Community Services Director for the Sheriff's Office of Sacramento County. (0:15)

2. On our next program we will have as our guests Bill Wright, area representative of the California Taxpayers' Association, and Ken Irwin, County Supervisor from the Fourth District of Sacramento County. (0:15)

3. They will discuss recent changes in the state property tax laws and their effect on county taxpayers and on county revenues. (0:10)

4. Please join us next week at this same time for a lively discussion of a topic which is important to every householder in our community. (0:10)

5. I'm Mary Hammer, thank you for being with us on Community Viewpoint. (0:05)

6. This program is a presentation of the Community Services Department of KXXX (0:05)

MUSIC:          SIGNATURE UP TO CLOSE.

There are six separate segments in this close, not counting the signature theme. The six individually range in length from 5 to 15 seconds. They can be put together in varying combinations, depending on the time to be filled. Any 5-second length from 5 to 60 seconds can be accommodated by using an appropriate combination of segments.

| Use #5 | for a :05 second pad |
|--------|----------------------|
| #5, 6  | :10                  |
| #4, 5  | :15                  |

| #1, 5 (or #4, 5, 6) | :20 |
| #1, 5, 6 | :25 |
| #1, 4, 5 | :30 |
| #1, 2, 5 | :35 |
| #1, 2, 5, 6 | :40 |
| #1, 2, 3, 5 | :45 |
| #1, 2, 3, 4 | :50 |
| #1, 2, 3, 4, 5 | :55 |
| #1, 2, 3, 4, 5, 6 | :60 |

The closing elements of a program, then, should be chosen and arranged in such a way as to accommodate as many of these purposes as may be required and at the same time to close the program as quickly as possible after the climax has been reached. As we have noted, audience interest drops quickly after the resolution of the plot or the presentation of some form of climax. If the audience is going to be held for the following program, the closing materials must continue to hold attention, or at least be brief enough that anticipation of the upcoming program will provide the lure.

## ANALYSIS OF PROGRAM STRUCTURE

Having now established criteria for the evaluation of program structure, we can return to the three programs for which analyses were prepared, and see how well they measure up structurally. However, as we said earlier, it's a more meaningful exercise if you apply these criteria to programs you personally see and analyze.

### *Roseanne*

On all criteria this episode of *Roseanne* was well structured. For all practical purposes the program opens *cold*, with four elements that contain a good deal of mystery and uncertainty, followed by "Happy Halloween," which quickly resolves the miniplot of the opening. The first material on the screen is a very brief title, just the single word "Roseanne" for only a couple of seconds. That title acts as a safety valve, in case any viewers might be in doubt about the program to follow. After the opening plot, the program's signature is rather ordinary, but it does provide title identification and introduce the main performers, showing them around the kitchen table, playing cards—a sequence that won't clash with any plot being developed. The signature does not come until 3:25 into the program. Opening commercials follow the signature; they don't appear until 4:35, and there are only two ads in this group of commercials, totaling just 1 minute. Overall, the criterion of a *strong start* is well satisfied.

*Unity* is built around the central characters, Roseanne and Dan—one or both appear in nearly every element—and the Halloween theme. The primary plot involves the prank played in the opening on Kathy and Roseanne's certainty that Kathy will try to get even (despite her assurances that she intends no retribution). In the end, Dan resolves the plot by designing a prank and making it look like Kathy did it, so that Roseanne's anxiety will be relieved. Two very secondary developments are Dan and Roseanne's concern that their children no longer enjoy Halloween—resolved when they discover it is the children who pulled the prank of the snakes in the bed—and Jackie's problems with boyfriends.

As in most sitcoms, *variety* is accomplished mostly through changes in characters entering and leaving scenes. Three locations are used—Dan and Roseanne's porch (used in both the opening and epilogue), interiors in Dan and Roseanne's house, and the lodge. Since different rooms are used in the house, and several "areas" within the lodge, there is the appearance of considerable location variety as well. Variety can be further examined by a check of the total number of element changes. There is a total of 50 elements, or 49 changes. Even when commercials and opening and closing credits are subtracted (16 elements), there are 36 elements within approximately 22 minutes of program content.

The check of the number of elements also reveals the rapid *pace* of the program. The longest element (2:00) is the very first one, but it develops slowly on purpose, to heighten the sense of mystery as Kathy slowly walks through the house to locate the source of the mysterious screams. No other element lasts more than 1:50; most are 40 seconds or less. Note the placement of element 34, which is between two scenes with Jackie and Booker. Elements 33 and 35 could have been combined, but that would make one element lasting 1:40. A long, slowing element is avoided by inserting element 34 between those two.

*Climax* is held off until the final elements in the epilogue. Often the climax and resolution of a plot will come just before the closing commercials, and there is little left to say or do in the epilogue. Here, when Roseanne finds out that the "snakes in the bed" prank is not Kathy's doing, her anxiety returns—holding us through the closing commercials. Then Dan's prank in the epilogue resolves the episode.

### *This Week with David Brinkley*

In general, the structural criteria we have established are much more difficult to meet in public affairs programs than in entertainment programming or even in straight news reporting. The lack of a strong, easy-to-follow structure may be one reason why these programs do not draw large audiences. On the other hand, the more highly educated audiences that do watch these programs are more attuned to content than structure. They are more willing to stay through longer program segments and denser material if they find the subject matter interesting and important.

Nevertheless, structure should be considered, and the producers of *This Week with David Brinkley* obviously have done that. The program opens with Brinkley's introduction of the topic and the names and titles of the guests who will appear, followed by a very brief title identification. Brinkley then reads a brief (unrelated) news story which gives the program an added sense of immediacy. A billboard identifies the program's advertisers; that's followed by one commercial. This structure is a form of cold open. The low-interest commercial material is not presented until after the topic has been introduced and the news item read, and the commercial material (elements 3 and 4) takes only 1:15.

*Unity* is present at two levels. First, the program regularly and obviously deals with issues of national or international importance, even when more than one topic is discussed (as in the segment in the latter portion of the program, elements 28 through 30). Second, the bulk of the program is devoted to a single topic, identified by Brinkley in his opening and further introduced in the *setup piece* (element 6). In this program it was changes taking place in the structure of the Soviet government and economy.

*Variety* is one of the more difficult criteria to meet in public affairs programs, and too much variety in a program of this type can lead to a disjointed presentation in which issues are not given sufficient time to be fully examined. A simpler but poorer structure (often seen in local public affairs programs) would have a panel of guests sitting in a studio and carrying on a continuous discussion for the full length of the program—essentially one long program element with no changes to reattract audience attention. Here the main topic is divided into four major segments—the "setup piece" and separate interviews with guests 1, 2, and 3 and 4 together. Other topics are then introduced in the closing discussion and Brinkley's final commentary.

The setup piece (so described in the program itself by Sam Donaldson) provides background to the topic. It is constructed as a news summary, with a good deal of location footage and several sound bites, so even though it lasts over 5 minutes, it contains considerable internal variety, which we did not attempt to pull out as separate elements. The interview elements are also long, but they are aided by having several different persons (Brinkley, Will, Donaldson) asking questions of each guest. In the 10:30 interview with senators Bradley and Moynihan, there are two interviewees as well as the three interviewers.

Certainly the *pace* is not comparable to that of a comedy program. But as indicated above, the target audience for this type of program does not expect that kind of pace and would, in fact, be disturbed if the careful examination of important topics were to be replaced by rapid changes in guests or topics.

Earlier we noted that news programs are not structured to provide *climax* in the traditional sense, but will often provide a human interest story at the closing to give some sense of meeting this requirement. Public affairs programs are similar to news in this respect. Sometimes major questions can be sequenced to come near the end of an interview, thereby giving some sense of building to climax, but in live programs that's a difficult task. In this program the task of holding the audience to the end is given to Brinkley's closing piece—usually a wry commentary on an offbeat news story. In this broadcast, citizens of Los Angeles had done such a good job of saving water during the California drought that the water district was losing money. The district would have to raise rates to compensate for its losses, and citizens would now be penalized for doing what had been asked of them.

The closing commercials come before that commentary. Audiences familiar with the program will stay through those commercials for the commentary (epilogue). After the commentary there is only a brief closing billboard and closing credits.

## *Entertainment Tonight*

We did an analysis of *ET* for the first edition of this text and, at that time, noted how its focus on entertainment news and features provided a good bridge between news and entertainment programming. The structure of the program hasn't changed very much, but we found that the content has. There is more emphasis on "celebrity scandal" and on promoting upcoming TV programs, movies and concerts and less emphasis on newsworthy events taking place in the entertainment industry or affecting entertainment personalities. This change in the content and materials selected for the program is not really a matter for our attention in this chapter, but it does have an effect on the gratifications presented to the target audience, a topic we consider in Chapter 10. The program now aims to compete more directly with *Inside Edition, Hard Copy* and similar "reality" shows that are often scheduled in the same time slot between local news and the beginning of prime time.

The *opening* is very short. A cold start, including a sound bite which briefly shows the glamorous model now involved with Donald Trump, teases the opening story. The program identification is accomplished by graphics appearing behind the two hosts, as they identify themselves, and Tesh introduces the lead story. The total open is just under 1 minute, and the program identification takes less than 30 seconds. Opening commercials, the weak material, don't come until almost 6½ minutes into the program.

*Unity* is accomplished by the selection of material to be included, although, as noted above, some stories seem to have been selected because of their ties to celebrities and to social scandal, or to the promotion of upcoming events and programs, rather than for immediate news value. Nevertheless, all stories do relate in some way to the entertainment industry. The hosts also contribute to unity; all stories are narrated at least in part by either Hart or Tesh.

In any news program *variety* is easy to achieve and is dictated by the stories that develop and have immediacy on any given day. *Entertainment Tonight* further distinguishes different types of stories by using computer graphics and titles to label stories: "Inside Story" for the lead story, "Inside the Headlines," "Inside Television," "Coming Attractions," "ET Newsreel," "Birthdays."

*Pace* is very fast. Only three elements run longer than 2 minutes, and those are broken up by very fast camera cuts and frequent, brief sound bites. In fact stories throughout the program contain many quick, often one-line sound bites from participants in the story—celebrities if possible.

No *climax* is evident. The closing commercials are ahead of two final stories, but those stories—the list of celebrity birthdays and a tease for the lead story on the next day's program—are not strong elements. The closing credits are run over a part of a recently released music video, which may help hold part of the audience.

In these examples, and throughout most of this chapter, we have been emphasizing television program structure. But these concepts are equally applicable to radio. Most radio programming provides frequent change, even if that change is just from one record to the next. Unity and variety are also present. Unity is known by the terms *sound, image*, or *format*, referring to that general type of music (or talk) which provides the consistent sound of that station. Variety is the changes—of music recordings, or of voices and other material—within that format. Climax is not present on most radio stations, because programs of specific length are not provided. Audiences flow in and out throughout the day. But whenever there are programs of determinate length, all the structural requirements for opening, body, and closing should be considered.

## CONCLUSION

In this chapter we have shown how the behavior of audiences and the structure of programs are related. Programs must be structured to take into account the various levels of attention and the limited attention span of audiences. Only if audiences find the content of a program extremely interesting or important will they expend the effort to continue to watch or listen to a poorly structured program.

One universal tool that can be used to analyze existing programs and as a building block for writing new programs is the *program element*—a segment of a program separated from preceding or following segments by change of sufficient strength to reattract audience attention. All programs are made up of program elements of different kinds and lengths. Well-structured programs will have frequent new elements.

Generally programs have a three-part structure consisting of an opening, body, and closing. All three parts have important functions to perform within the program. The opening should attract attention to the program and identify it for its audience. It may also be used to set a mood, to provide explanations, and to provide a place for announcements to be inserted. Whatever functions are expected of the opening, the elements should be arranged so that the program gets off to the strongest start possible.

The structure of the body will depend in large part on the type of content being presented, but all programs should be organized to provide unity, variety, good pace, and a sense of climax, regardless of the specific content.

The closing may provide further identification, including credits. It may also be expected to provide a place for announcements, promote subsequent programs, and give a sense of closure to the show. Particularly important for live programs is the requirement to bring the program to a close on time.

If a program has been structured well, that structure will add to the inherent interest of the content and the two together—structure and content—will make the program attractive to its target audience and successful in accomplishing its purpose.

## Exercises

1. Complete an element analysis of a television program, using the layout form reproduced in part on page 159. The program may be any "made for TV" program—don't use sporting events, feature movies or other material not produced for TV. You may view a program of any length (30 minutes or more), but whatever length you choose, *analyze the entire program.*

   In the first column, number the elements. The total number of elements contained in a program provides some indication of pace.

   In the second column, give a brief description of the *content* of the element—an automobile chase scene, a conversation between which major characters, a song and dance routine by the program host. In a few words describe *what* is happening, *who* is doing it, and possibly *where* it is taking place. If the element is a commercial, what is the product?

   The next column is deliberately set off one-half space to emphasize that it represents change *between* elements. In it you should indicate the type of *change* that takes place between the preceding and following elements. If element 1 is a title sequence and element 2 is a commercial, the change between them is in the type of content or *material.* Other changes might be in *character*—a major character enters or leaves a dramatic scene; in *time*—a lapse between scenes; or *location*—change of location between scenes; or combinations of these. Other types of changes are possible—name and describe them briefly in this space.

   The column labeled "Start" is for the start time of each element *from the beginning of the program.* The first element of the program starts at

ELEMENT ANALYSIS                          Name _____

Program _____       Length _____

Station _____  Date/Day _____  Hour _____

| Description of Material | Type of Change | Start | Length |
|---|---|---|---|
| 1. _____ | _____ | _____ | _____ |
| 2. _____ | _____ | _____ | _____ |
| 3. _____ | _____ | _____ | _____ |
| 4. _____ | _____ | _____ | _____ |
| 5. _____ | _____ | _____ | _____ |

0:00. To calculate the start time of an element, add the length of the preceding element to its own start time. The start time for element 4 would be the start time of element 3 plus the length of element 3.

The column labeled "Length" is for the *length* of each element. You should try to be accurate to within about 5 seconds for each element.

Use the *Roseanne*, *This Week with David Brinkley* and *Entertainment Tonight* examples as models.

2. Using the element analysis from exercise 1, analyze that program for its structural strengths and weaknesses. Describe specifically what was done to satisfy each criterion and *evaluate* what was structurally good or bad on each point.

   a. The program opening
      _____ Attention getting?
      _____ Identification?
      _____ Strong start?
      _____ Place for announcements?
      _____ Other goals in the opening (e.g., mood setting)?

   b. The body of the program
      _____ Unity?
      _____ Variety?
      _____ Pace?
      _____ Climax?

    c. The program closing

        \_\_\_\_\_ Identification?

        \_\_\_\_\_ Place for announcements?

        \_\_\_\_\_ Sense of finality?

        \_\_\_\_\_ Other?

    d. What is your overall evaluation of the program's structure? What specific structural changes would you make to strengthen the program?

**Notes**

1. John Ehrlichman, "Why We Stay Up Late for Ted Koppel," *Parade*, September 27, 1987, p. 18.
2. The least-objectionable-program theory was originally presented in Pat Paul Klein, "The Men Who Run TV Aren't All That Stupid," *New York*, January 25, 1971, pp. 20–29.

# Handling Sound

**T**he broadcast writer deals with two uses of sound—with the meaning language conveys and with sound as such. In most of the other chapters of this book we are concerned with language and meaning. In this chapter we examine the second use of sound, which includes music, all the varied sound effects (to use the term in its technical application) and voices when used for their sound value.

Our examples come mostly from radio. Since that medium relies exclusively on sound for communication of its ideas, we can find clearer examples there without having to consider video simultaneously. But sound is used in television (and other audiovisual media) for all the same purposes and in the same ways it is used in radio.

We consider first the basic characteristics of sound. Then we examine techniques for using each of the three components of sound—sound effects, music and voices—to strengthen the structure of programs and announcements.

When you finish this chapter, you will be able to

- recognize the characteristics of sound and their application to audio copy,

- understand the use of sound effects and music in audio scripts,

- understand how voices are chosen and used for their sound value,

- use sound effects, music and voices effectively in your own scripts, and

- recognize and use these important terms and concepts:

| | |
|---|---|
| acoustical setting | juxtaposition (of sounds) |
| dialogue | montage |
| distance | music bed |
| fades: in, out, under, cross | on-mike and off-mike |

| | |
|---|---|
| narration and split narration | rhythm |
| natural sound | segue |
| pitch | volume |
| quality (of sound)/timbre | |

Some sounds appear in programs naturally. They are the inevitable and uncontrollable "natural" background sounds in a location news story, for example. We consider natural sound briefly in this chapter and elsewhere, but our primary interest is in the effective, appropriate use of created sounds. As the scriptwriter, it is your responsibility to describe what sounds are to be used and how they are to be used to achieve the desired effect. The actual music, sound effects and voices are created by actors, announcers and technicians on location, in a studio or in a control room. Usually, the scriptwriter will not be involved in the actual production; thus, to ensure that the result is what you envision, you have to write careful, detailed descriptions in the copy.

## CHARACTERISTICS OF SOUND

We are concerned here not only with the actual characteristics of sound but also with the perceptions sounds generate in the ears of the listeners. The writer needs to understand the psychological effects the various characteristics of sound produce in listeners, so our comments will be directed toward that end rather than to the physics of sound.

The characteristics we will examine are: (1) pitch, (2) quality, (3) volume, (4) distance, (5) acoustical setting, (6) rhythm and (7) juxtaposition. Although we describe each characteristic individually, in practice they cannot be separated and will be difficult to illustrate independently.

### Pitch

This is the term commonly used to describe the frequency of a sound, or the wavelength of the vibration of an object. Examine a piano keyboard. The long strings at the left end of the keyboard have a longer wavelength and a lower frequency or pitch than the shorter strings at the other end.

In general, low pitches are more pleasing to the ear; sounds become more disturbing and irritating as they get closer to the upper end of the range of human hearing. Pitch may be exciting, disturbing, or merely irritating as it goes upward, depending on the other characteristics of sound that accompany it.

The writer can use several methods to control pitch, depending on the kind of program and the specific circumstances of the script:

1. Choose music that will use a predominance of instruments in the desired pitch range. A bright, cheery pastoral musical bridge might be written this way:

MUSIC: FLUTE SOLO

or

MUSIC: LIGHT, AIRY

The music to *Peter and the Wolf*, in which each character in the story is represented by an instrument with a different pitch and quality, is a perfect example of using music to help define character.

2. Describe the voice of the person who should be chosen to read the lines. Assume we have a leprechaun as a character in a commercial. We don't know what leprechauns sound like, but the character could have a high-pitched, almost falsetto voice. This vocal pitch might be found naturally, but more likely it would be artificially assumed by the actor playing the role, or filtered electronically to give it an unnatural pitch range.

3. Write a stage direction to indicate how the line is to be read:

ANNCR:     (LOW, QUIET) One of the good things in life
           is being able to afford the luxury....

JIM:       (FRANTIC, TENSE, HIGH-PITCHED) My God, Pete,
           we aren't going to make it! We'll crash....

These directions indicate to the person voicing the copy what tone and especially what pitch are required to convey an intended message.

4. Write in a sound effect in which a particular pitch will predominate:

SOUND: HIGH-PITCHED WHINE OF JET ENGINE IN BG

This effect will help create tension in the scene. It would be appropriate behind dialogue in which two characters argue.

5. Choose words for the script that will help control pitch. You might write:

ANNCR:     Tonight, in the quiet the evening, when
           long shadows fill the corner of the room and
           memories drift in like the smoke of an autumn
           mist....

Notice how the word choice makes it easy to use a low pitch. The words *long, corners, room, smoke, autumn* all use vowel and consonant combinations that encourage low pitches. It would be hard to read the copy in a tight, high-pitched voice; the word choice discourages it. By way of contrast, suppose the announcer were given this to read:

```
ANNCR:      Settle back in your chair. Fill up your pipe.
            Put out the lamp. Look at the fire dance in
            the grate.
```

This piece of copy is an attempt to capture a mood of reminiscence, but it certainly does not encourage low pitch. The choice of vowels and consonants makes low, smooth reading difficult. Even though the ideas may be appropriate, the word choice is wrong if the writer wishes low pitches to predominate. The words *settle, back, look, dance*, and *grate* all have short vowels followed by consonants that cut them off sharply and discourage the use of low pitches. By choosing music, voices, and effects that have appropriate pitch ranges, the writer can manipulate and control this aspect of sound within a script.

## Quality

Also called timbre, this characteristic, described in terms of the physics of sound, represents the complexity of the wave form. A pure tone or frequency is an unpleasant sound if heard for very long. Most sounds are complex wave forms created by the interaction of several frequencies all present at the same time. For example, the presence of overtones, which are multiples of a fundamental pitch, distinguish a musical note played on a violin from the same note played on a clarinet.

The actual measurement of these complex wave forms can be done only by special instruments, but we recognize different timbres or qualities when we hear them and we use descriptive terms to indicate different qualities. We may talk about the *harsh* whine of a saw, and the *mellow* sound of a French horn; the *strident* call of a blue jay and the *soft* whisper of a breeze; the *brassy* fanfare from a trumpet and the *liquid* voice of a flute. We may describe the sound of an orchestra as *full*, or the simulated voice of a robot as *mechanical*.

The writer controls the quality of sound by the same methods used to control pitch. Since we tend to describe the quality of sound in terms that indicate its effect on us, the writer need only indicate the quality desired in any given spot, using standard descriptive words:

MUSIC: TO SIMULATE A BABBLING BROOK

SOUND: DISSONANT AUTO HORNS IN A TRAFFIC JAM

Consider again for a moment one of the problems posed in the discussion of pitch, the choice of words. In the two examples above, there is a marked difference in the quality of the sounds, quite aside from pitch and the ideas expressed. The words *long, room*, and *autumn* all use a long vowel in conjunction with a consonant that can also be prolonged. This helps create a soft, pleasant quality of sound. In the other example, *settle, pipe, look*, and *grate* all contain short sounds. The combination of vowels and consonants sounds abrupt. These are crisp, unmusical words, and the whole passage is affected by their quality.

## Volume

Audience reactions to various volume levels tend to be similar to those for pitch. Low volume tends to be soothing, comforting, and reassuring. As volume increases, sounds become more disturbing and more irritating until they reach the level of actual pain.

The writer controls volume through directions written in the script and through the selection of the music or sound effects to be used. Some music has to be loud to be right, and so do some sounds. There is no such thing as the quiet sound of an iron foundry or assembly line. The volume of the announcer's or actor's voice can be controlled by directions in the script. In the absence of directions to the contrary, such as LOUDLY or IN A WHISPER, script continuity is spoken at a normal speaking level.

One of the conventions established in the early days of radio drama was that background sound effects used to identify a location be introduced at normal volume, and then the volume be reduced behind the voices of the actors in the scene. Sometimes the sound was even removed after it had been established, even though in "reality" it would have remained in the location.

Suppose you are writing a scene that takes place in an automobile. By the very nature of the scene, if the car is running we should expect to hear the motor. To establish the scene, the sound of the car would be introduced at a normal volume. Then, as the scene progresses, it can be gradually reduced in volume until it is at a lower background level. It is still there enough to maintain awareness of the locale, but it is considerably faded down in volume and does not interfere with or distract the audience from the action. This process parallels what happens in real life when the human ear is exposed to continuous sound. The ear tends to get used to sounds, even fairly loud ones, and ceases to hear them in the foreground of attention. In conformity with this psychological fact, a good writer, having introduced a sound to indicate a continuing background effect, will submerge it gradually after the locale has been accepted.

The radio drama series *Dragnet*, when it was first broadcast, broke with that tradition. A unique characteristic of *Dragnet* was that background sound in a scene continued at a level more closely approximating the real situation. If the scene was in a factory and the actors would have to shout to be heard, then the script called for them to shout. Because it modified the convention, *Dragnet* became known as the first "realistic" radio drama. Now, the "realistic" use of sound is common practice in both radio and television. However, high-level sound should not continue unmodified throughout a scene. It can be very annoying if the audience is forced to fight the sound in order to hear dialogue.

Sound volume is also important to the aural perception of distance, which we consider next.

## Distance

In television, the positions of the various persons in a scene can be seen, so there should be no problem for the audience in that regard. But for radio, the relative positions of actors in a scene, and movement taking place within that scene, must be established in terms of perceived distance—the perception being in the ear of the listener.

One of the conventions of radio/audio writing is that the listener is always perceived to be with the microphone. This position is known as *on-mike*. If, for example, two voices are carrying on a conversation and both are at full, normal volume, then both are perceived to be in the same location and the listener, mentally, places him or herself as an observer at the same location.

If, instead, the writer wants to place some distance between the two persons (voices) and tell the audience that one of these voices is some distance from the scene (and the listener), that actor will be backed away from the microphone, and the script designation will read *off-mike*. If both voices are off-mike, the listener will perceive both actors to be at a distance from the location established as the center of action. Other effects can be accomplished by having the source of the sound, say, an actor, *fade* from on to off, or vice versa.

The normal position for any sound is on-mike. Unless the writer specifies a sound as off-mike, or fading, performers and technicians will assume all sounds are to be presented on-mike and at normal volume. Here are three brief examples employing both on- and off-mike dialogue.

SOUND:      GUNSHOTS IN DISTANCE; IMMEDIATELY FOLLOWED BY RICOCHET SOUND OF

BULLETS OFF ROCKS IN FOREGROUND

ONE:      Well, it looks like they found where we are, boys. We may be

pinned down here for some time.

TWO:     I don't know about you, but I don't want to sit here like a
         clay pigeon in a shooting gallery. There's got to be a back
         way out of this rockpile.

THREE:   Well, why don't you just go find it then, and we'll try to
         keep as hidden as possible.

TWO:     Ok, I will, (FADE) but you keep that posse occupied while I'm
         climbing around out there, y'hear.

SOUND:   MORE SHOTS—OCCASIONALLY THROUGH THE FOLLOWING:

THREE:   I didn't want to give him much encouragement, but I really do
         hope he can find a way out back there.

ONE:     Yep, me too. And I hope that if he finds a way he tells us
         about it.

THREE:   You don't suppose he'd just take off by himself, do you?

ONE:     Stranger things have been known to happen, y'know.

THREE:   Well, I'll be...I never thought...(SHOUTS) Hey, Pete. Are you
         still there? Have you found a way out? (PAUSE) He doesn't
         answer...Maybe you're right...Why that dirty, sneaky, no
         account...

ONE:     I wasn't sure about that guy from the very beginning. Well,
         now it looks like we're going to have...

TWO:     (OFF-MIKE SHOUTING) Hey, there is a way out, but you've really
         got to crawl to keep from being seen.


       In this example actor 2 leaves the scene during his second line as noted by the (FADE) in that line. The scene (center of activity) remains with voices 1 and 3. At the end, voice 2 is heard again shouting from off-scene (OFF-MIKE).


JOHN:    (PANTING—OUT OF BREATH) I've got to stop for a minute, Tim.
         I'm just exhausted.

TIM:        (A LITTLE BREATHLESS) Ok, I'm kinda tired, too, but we can't
            stop long. We've got to get out of this river bottom before
            dark comes.

JOHN:       I know, but I don't know if we're going the right way. Maybe we
            ought to split up and look for a trail.

TIM:        I don't want to, but maybe you're right, John. Why don't you
            try that canyon over there, and I'll go down stream some more.

JOHN:       OK, (FADE) I'm on my way. Keep yelling so we can find each
            other.

TIM:        (OFF-MIKE, FADING) I will, you just watch your step...don't
            fall and hurt...

JOHN:       (OFF-MIKE) Yeah, and the same thing goes for you...

> This time the scene is established with both John and Tim present; both
> are on-mike. Then they both leave the scene (each FADES) in different direc-
> tions, which has to be and is explained in their dialogue. Momentarily the
> listener is left at the scene they left, but the scene must now end, as there is
> no activity which can take place at the original location with no voices pres-
> ent. (If this were television, the sound description would be the same; viewers
> would see the actors leave as well as hear their fading lines, but the viewers
> could be left looking at the empty campsite without sound for a brief time.)

NANCY:      Is there anything in that trunk that will give us a clue to
            Mrs. Jones' disappearance, Mike?

MIKE:       It doesn't look like it, Nancy. Nothing in here but old
            clothes.

RAY:        But we've got to keep looking. Something up here in this attic
            really scared Mr. Hoffer when he came up here yesterday, and
            there hasn't been a chance for anybody to take anything away
            since.

NANCY:      Well, you fellows keep looking in here. I'm going to go look
            in that room over there. (FADE) It looks appropriately
            spooky—all full of cobwebs and all.

RAY:      I just wish we had some clue as to what we were looking for.

MIKE:     I know, but Nancy's right, Mrs. Jones wouldn't just get up and leave town without telling anyone. Something's wrong. (SHOUTS) Anything in there, Nancy?

NANCY:   (SHOUTS OFF-MIKE) No, I can hardly see anything. The window's so dirty that...wait a minute, maybe there is something. Hey, come here. I've found the answer.

SOUND:   HURRIED FOOTSTEPS

NANCY:   (ON-MIKE) This is it, fellows. This is what we've been looking for.

RAY:      You're right, Nancy. You've solved the mystery.

In this example, Nancy leaves the first location to go into another room; the scene stays for a time with Mike and Ray in the first location. Nancy is heard (SHOUTS OFF-MIKE) from the distant location, and then the scene shifts as Mike and Ray (and the listener) follow Nancy to the second room.

Two-channel stereo sound adds another dimension to the spatial relationship; it makes possible left-right shifts in the positions of characters as well as close–far away. In example 2 above, where John and Tim start in opposite directions, they would begin in the center (both channels); then Tim's microphone would be panned to the left channel as he fades, and John's microphone would be panned to the right channel. The use of stereo would give a clear indication to the audience that the characters were going in different directions.

As we noted, for television the viewer has no problem with perception; spatial relationships are easily seen. But the control of aural distance in television is the same as for radio; it should match the visual distance. For example, the voice of a character who is seen at a great distance should be faint and far away. If he calls to another actor from that distance, he will have to shout to be heard. That sound should have a distinct, forced quality. Similarly, the voice of a character leaving a scene should fade.

## Acoustical Setting

This characteristic refers to the changes or alterations made to a sound by the surroundings in which that sound is emitted. It might also be viewed as one means by which the quality of sound is changed, because the different spaces that enclose a sound affect its quality. A given sound will have one quality in the open air and quite another at the bottom of a well. In the first case, where there is no surrounding enclosure, the original sound is unaltered; in the other, where a very solid, close enclosure surrounds the sound, an echoing, boomy quality is given the sound by its reverberation within the enclosure. The yell "Help! Save me!" would sound much different in the two situations. The writer should be sure that the appropriate acoustical setting for the script has been written in.

Acoustical relationships are very important in the establishment of location in a radio broadcast because the listener cannot "see" the location of a scene, except as that scene is built up as a mental image in the listener's mind by the sounds presented in the script. Suppose you are writing a script and wish to establish the fact that the scene is taking place in a large, empty cathedral. The acoustical quality of that location can be approximated by adding a considerable amount of echo to the lines spoken by the characters in the script. The audience would assume from the echo that the scene was taking place in some fairly large, hard-walled enclosure. A simple statement in the script would be enough to let the audience know that it was a church.

Another example: A radio commercial calls for the announcer to be in the client's store during a sale, with large, excited crowds milling around in the background. The commercial will be prerecorded. There are no large crowds available at the moment, and better control (at less cost) can be obtained by working in the studio anyway. The writer calls for a sound effect:

```
SOUND:     CROWD NOISE IN BACKGROUND

ANNCR:     (SLIGHTLY OFF-MIKE: LOUD, WITH ENTHUSIASM). Good afternoon,

           this is Joe Jones, and I'm here at the biggest sale ever at

           Smith Brothers Furniture. The crowds are trememdous.
```

A little experimentation in the control room will find the proper balance between the recorded sound effect and the announcer's voice and provide the acoustical setting required. This same principle is applied to any scene where there would be an abnormal acoustical condition. The acoustic setting cannot just be suggested in the dialogue; it must be specified by the writer, with directions or production notes in the script.

## Rhythm

We are accustomed to thinking of rhythm as patterns of sounds or of music. Almost all music has some sort of rhythmic pattern, or beat. And many sound effects contain repetitive, rhythmic elements. In general we know that long, slow, steady patterns are reassuring; short, staccato, or irregular patterns are disturbing, upsetting, and exciting. The beat of jungle drums is a cliché with which everyone should be familiar. Other patterns of rhythm and sound quality are used to suggest space travel, electronic communication, factories, computers, and so on.

Another aspect of rhythm we don't frequently recognize is vocal rhythm—distinctive patterns of speech. Some announcers and newscasters have individual patterns that are highly distinctive, such as Paul Harvey, Christopher Glenn, Charles Osgood, Diane Sawyer and Ted Koppel. Most announcers and actors are adaptable enough that if a particular rhythm—slow and smooth, or rushed and breathless—is wanted, they can provide it.

Finally, the writer controls rhythm with the kind of words and sentences he or she writes. The style of the copy can control the rhythmic flow of the language to a greater extent than it can either pitch or quality, because the natural rhythm of the lines is completely under the control of the writer. Turn back again to the two brief examples used to demonstrate low-pitched words and notice how rhythm works. The first example flows smoothly. Each phrase can be read easily and smoothly, as a unit, and all the phrases flow together naturally with very little interruption in thought. The second example, on the other hand, is jerky. It stops and starts abruptly with each phrase. There is no smooth connection between phrases. Each comes to a full stop. They are written as commands, which encourages staccato reading. If the object was to create a piece of smooth, soothing copy, that would be impossible with the rhythm of the second example.

## Juxtaposition

By the *juxtaposition* of sound, we mean having several sounds introduced simultaneously, relying upon the ear's ability to determine the distance of each from the listener and from the other sounds and to distinguish differences in the quality, direction, volume, and pitch of the sounds.

The radio writer can use one sound juxtaposed against another to help tell a story and establish a scene. Suppose you are writing a scene at a football game. You may have an actor simulate an announcer working directly at the microphone. Behind this you might place in the script shouts of a crowd, some of them at fairly close range. Still farther away you might call for a band playing. The three sounds, occurring in juxtaposition to one another, would be sufficient to create a complete scene. The audience, hearing those simultaneous sounds and perceiving distance relationships among them, would recognize the situation. The writer would be using juxtaposition to help establish the locale.

As with the perception of distances, the juxtaposition of sounds is made more obvious by stereophonic broadcasting (or by other forms of audio presentation that feature more than one independent sound track). The human hearing system, which is a binaural system, readily perceives even small differences between two sound tracks being received simultaneously, and the brain translates those differences into perceptions of different positions and distances.

In the following example, several of the characteristics of sound are used simultaneously to develop a sense of excitement and tension in the scene.

| | |
|---|---|
| SOUND: | PLANES APPROACHING AND LANDING...GETS LOUDER AS THEY ARE LANDING. |
| BING: | See, Joyce—they top over there. |
| JOYCE: | I see. When does Wallie's plane come in? |
| BING: | His is in the next three to—Holy!— |
| JOYCE: | What's wrong? |
| BING: | Nan, you were right. Something must have happened. |
| NAN: | I told you I saw something fall off when they were way up. |
| JOYCE: | (GETTING EXCITED AND NERVOUS) What is it? What's wrong? |
| BING: | I don't know—but his landing gear has come off. |
| NAN: | What can he do? |
| BING: | Bail out. He can't bring that plane in. |
| JOYCE: | Oh no, Nan—I... |
| NAN: | Hold on, Joyce, don't let yourself go. |
| SOUND: | PLANE SOUNDS LOUDER |
| BING: | Why he's crazy—he's going to try to do it anyway. |
| NAN: | He can't land that way, can he? |
| BING: | (TENSE) It's a crackup for sure! Why doesn't he bail out? |
| JOYCE: | Oh, Nan, I can't stand this!—Wallie—please don't try to land. |
| BING: | He's bringing her in now. There's a chance in a million that he can do it. |
| NAN: | He's slowing down. |
| SOUND: | MOTOR CUTS |
| BING: | He has to. |
| JOYCE: | (FRANTICALLY) He's getting so low— |
| BING: | He's going to try to slide it in—a pancake! |
| NAN: | Bing, he's going to... |
| SOUND: | LONG SCREECH OF SLIDING PLANE...THEN SUDDEN QUIET |
| BING: | (PAUSE—RELEASES OF HELD BREATH) He did it. |

*Source:* Adapted from Albert Crews, *Professional Radio Writing* (Boston: Houghton Mifflin, 1946), pp. 64–65.

To begin with, there was a natural aid in the sound effect. The noise of a plane coming in to land increases in volume, which is in itself exciting. The pitch also increases as the plane comes closer. Both pitch and volume come to a crescendo as the plane skids to a stop on the runway. The actors' voices will build the tempo, volume, and pitch of the scene just as the sound builds. In fact, the increasing sound forces them to shout over it. Their tension also increases as the crisis comes to a peak. Notice how short and jerky the speeches are, how many of them are incomplete sentences. Toward the end they are little more than fragments, mounting in emotional intensity to match the scene. At the end, the sudden silence after the plane skids to a stop will be all the more effective after the climax of sound. One simple line releases the tension of the scene. All the basic factors of pitch, volume, quality, and rhythm go into the building of this climactic scene.[1]

These seven characteristics of sound—pitch, quality, volume, distance, acoustical setting, rhythm and juxtaposition—are universal. They apply to sound effects, to music, and to the voice when it is used as a sound instrument.

## SOUND EFFECTS

A *sound effect* may be defined as any sound occurring in a program that is not classifiable as speech or music. In an audience participation program, the laughter elicited from the audience is a sound effect. The cheering of a crowd picked up by the broadcasting of a football game is also a sound effect. Sound effects are not restricted to the dramatic programs with which they are most often associated.

Sound effects may be considered in two categories. In a realistic or non-dramatic program, managing the sound pattern consists chiefly of deciding which of the natural sounds actually being produced at the locale are desirable and should be picked up. For example, suppose the writer is designing an audience participation game show. Should the microphone be arranged so that the sounds made by the audience in the studio will be picked up? What sounds created by the mechanics of the program should be heard or enhanced? These are decisions the writers and producers of the program must make, though there is no problem in creating the sound. The sound is inherent in the situation; the only question is whether it should be picked up and broadcast or eliminated by technical means.

The second category are sound effects introduced by the writer to help create an illusion. These effects are employed mostly in dramatic programs or in dramatic vignettes in commercials. They must be artificially produced to simulate the sounds they represent.

## Uses of Sound

There are a number of different ways in which sound can be used to strengthen the structure of a program:

1. Establish a locale

2. Create a mood

3. Project action and support climax

4. Establish time

5. Indicate entrances and exits

6. Serve as a transition device between scenes

7. Contribute to a montage effect

Some of these are exclusively dramatic uses of sound, but most of them have equal application to nondramatic programs and may be either realistic or created sounds. Frequently a sound effect or group of effects will serve several of these uses simultaneously, so it is difficult to provide examples that illustrate just a single use.

### Establish a Locale

When a speech is to be broadcast from a banquet hall, the pickup of the rustle of the audience, the clatter of dishes, and the clink of glassware will help to establish the locale in which the speech is going to take place. If establishing that locale is important and the production director feels the audience should get the flavor of the meeting, arrangements are made to pick up some of these sounds just to help set the scene. In a dramatic program, if a similar locale were called for in the script, a similar pattern of sound would be produced artificially to establish that location in the play.

### Create a Mood

During the broadcast of national political conventions, pickups are frequently broadcast direct from the floor. The shouting, the talk on the floor, the confusion, the bands playing—all these are let into broadcast microphones and sent out over the air to give the audience the general mood, the atmosphere, the "feel" of the convention.

In a dramatic program too, the writer may wish to create a mood. Perhaps the scene is to take place along the waterfront on a dark, foggy night. An actor in the preceding scene can preview the scene with a line of dialogue; then a combination of sound effects both establishes the scene and creates a mood. Finally, dialogue confirms and completes the new locale.

BILL:       OK, now listen. We've got to get that stuff off the boat

            tonight. I'll meet you down at the dock at 10:30. You be there

            (FADE) and bring the big truck.

SOUND:      FOGHORN IN DISTANCE: SEAGULL CRIES: OCEAN WAVES, CONTINUES BEHIND

FRED:       (LOUD WHISPER) Hey Bill?—Where are you? (PAUSE) Bill?

BILL:       (OFF-MIKE) Over here. (FADING ON) Did you bring the truck?

FRED:       Yeah. It's on the other side of the dock.

### Project Action and Support Climax

Perhaps the most striking recent example of this use of sound comes not from radio but from television. The producers of the telecasts of the World League of American Football games have arranged for viewers to hear the radio conversations between coaches and their quarterbacks and the play calling of the quarterbacks. For a viewer, it's not the content of those messages that's interesting ("26 Spread Left," or similar nomenclature for the plays). Rather, eavesdropping on these sounds provides an opportunity to be that much more involved in the action, to participate through sound, even though TV is a visual medium.

Football also provides a good example of the buildup of climax through sound. A good broadcaster will let us hear the cheers of the crowd, which burst forth spontaneously as the ball is carried over the goal line. This natural sound effect creates the climax of the touchdown better than anything the announcer might say.

In a dramatic program, where pickup of sound from an actual event is not possible, appropriate sound effects will be added to provide realism to the script. Even the "impossible" events of purely imaginary stories—for example, Superman's flight through the air—can be projected by sounds which simulate an impression of what the real sounds might be.

### Establish Time

This use of sound effects should be familiar to everyone. In dramatic programs the use of striking clocks and crowing roosters has become so much of a convention that it is almost cliché.

Sound is also used to reinforce the passing of time. During the 20 seconds the contestant has in which to answer the question and win the big prize, a ticking clock (or another effect that simulates the rhythm of a clock) adds intensity to the passage of time.

### Indicate Entrances and Exits

This use too is very familiar to audiences. In dramatic programs, the dialogue usually indicates when an actor enters or leaves a scene and that dialogue may be supported by fades—a fade-in when the character enters the scene and a fade-out as the character leaves. But the use of sound reinforces those transitions; it makes them much more positive. If an actor leaves the scene angrily or hastily, he slams the door behind him. The impending appearance of a new character is signaled by a car driving up, a car door slamming, steps on the porch, a squeaky screen door opening, and finally, the actor's speech.

### Transition

Although music is a much more common transition device, especially in drama, sound effects can be used to accomplish the same purpose. The picking up of the bell and buzzer between rounds of a prize fight makes a transition from one scene to the next.The use of applause between numbers in a variety show is a conventional effect familiar to every listener.

### Montage

In a montage, a number of disconnected scenes are blended together by a unifying device. Music is sometimes used, but often some sound effect serves as the fusing agent that welds these successive fragmentary scenes together to produce an impressionistic effect. For example, suppose you want to tell the audience that revolt is breaking out all over the country. The device of a high-pitched radio code key might be used as a sound effect to knit the scenes together; between those quick, staccato dots and dashes might be heard the voices of various announcers with one or two lines each, giving us a fact here, a situation there, something breaking out somewhere else. All these reports, coming in quick succession with the sound tying them together, constitute the montage effect.

Properly used, sound effects add believability and realism to a scene and contribute important structural strength. There are, however, unforeseen pitfalls for the novice, and before leaving the subject we should add a few cautions.

## Unneeded Sound

Beginning writers have a tendency to overwrite sound effects. In an attempt to set up a realistic situation, the novice may write sound effects into a script that are meaningless in the scene. If the drama calls for a mob scene, the writer should realize that the scratching of a pencil as a reporter takes notes would be inaudible in the noise and confusion. Obviously, then, a quiet action sound should not be delivered in the midst of high-volume sounds that would drown it.

A scene taking place in a kitchen, with dialogue between two women, can be begun this way:

```
MARY:     Have another cup of coffee, Ruth?

RUTH:     Well, just a little; I really have to get back

          home.

MARY:     Please don't rush—I want to talk to you.
```

No sound effects are used to establish the scene. Various "kitchen" sounds—a whistling teakettle, dishes, pouring coffee—could have been added, but the few words of dialogue set the scene quite adequately and much more efficiently. Effects are frequently needed for all the reasons we have discussed, but they should never be included in a script just for the sake of having them there. A sound effect has no value unless it accomplishes a dramatic or an expositional purpose.

## Identifying Sound

In television, sound effects usually are reinforced for viewers by their being able to see the source of the sound. A repetitive click-click sound can easily be associated with a view of a train traveling down a track. In radio, the listener has only his or her ears to identify the effect, and unless there are clues or hints from the surrounding dialogue or narration, most effects can't be identified readily by listeners. Only a few sound effects are "self-identifying." This small group includes train whistles, fire sirens, door bells, telephones ringing and foghorns. But most sounds require some sort of support in the script, either in advance of the sound or immediately following its introduction.

Suppose the script calls for two people to be engaged in spirited conversation, and suddenly one of them slaps the other. If that sound effect is given without any warning, the listeners will not recognize what has happened. They will hear the sound, but will not be able to interpret it. On the other hand, if the lines clearly indicate that the two are quarreling and that physical violence is imminent, the audience will be prepared for the sound and will be able to identify it. Do not use a sound to project physical action unless the intention to act or the possibility of action has already been hinted at in the dialogue.

In a preceding section we described the use of sound to set a scene on a waterfront on a dark night. The sounds used to establish that scene—

foghorn, waves lapping at pilings on a pier—can be recognized and accepted by the listener because the final lines of dialogue in the preceding scene anticipated the location—on the waterfront.

Similarly, the rattling of a pan on a stove or the whistling of a teakettle will be recognizable if it has been established that the scene is in a kitchen; various clankings and motor noises will be accepted as factory sounds if that location has been previously established. The sound of galloping horses needs to have been established by previously indicating that horses are part of the scene.

## Writing Sound Cues

In Chapter 5 we showed the correct way to lay out sound cues within a script, but a few additional comments should be said about the writing of these cues. Each cue should describe as exactly as possible the effect desired. A cue saying only "footsteps" is not enough. The program producer needs to know what kind of footsteps—hurried or slow or walking at a normal pace; walking on what kind of surface and in what kind of shoes; footsteps of a man or a woman, of one person or many. "The closing of a door" does not tell enough to the production personnel who will have to execute the instructions in the script. Different kinds of doors have different sound qualities. Do you want the closing of a closet door, a screen door, a car door, or a bank vault door? Be specific.

In television, questions often arise about what to do with the normal sounds picked up in shooting on location. When that video is returned to the station and edited into a package, are those sounds, of a parade, for example, to be heard at full level, kept in the background while a voice narrates the video, or blocked out altogether? The package is likely to be made up of very brief video shots, many lasting only a few seconds, so if the natural sound were carried for each shot, there would be a discontinuous and possibly disconcerting sequence. One solution is to record one long section of background sound from the location, to get a cohesive and continuous bed, and place the various video cuts into it. If the volume level for that bed is kept low in the background and the reporter narrates over the various shots, listeners won't realize that the sound and pictures do not match precisely.

Many news producers instruct their crews to include natural sound whenever possible, believing that its presence adds authenticity and life to the story. In their newsrooms a script notation would be needed only if the sound were to be eliminated from a package. In other operations, the reverse may be true. The production crew will assume that the sound is to be suppressed and replaced by narration or music unless the script indicates otherwise. In the absence of a station policy, your script should be clear. If you want natural sound in a story, use the phrase: NATURAL SOUND (or NATURAL SOUND BEHIND NARRATION).

# MUSIC AS SOUND

Music has several possible uses within broadcast programs:

1. To act as a signature

2. To establish a mood or background

3. To serve as a transition device between scenes or between sections of a program

4. To serve as a sound effect

Keep in mind that here we are considering only the uses of music as sound. A great deal of programming consists of music, especially in radio. But we are not concerned here with music as a content form, only with its uses to strengthen or support the structure of other types of program content.

## Musical Signatures

Although signatures for radio or television programs can be constructed from sound effects and/or voices, writers almost always use some music. That music should be easily identifiable, distinctive enough to be remembered, and immediately associated with the program it introduces. Its instrumentation and arrangement should set the mood for the program to follow.

Beginning writers often start their scripts by simply writing "theme music" and letting it go at that. If the writer is to be a composer in sound, he or she cannot dismiss so important a part of the total sound of the program by simply indicating "theme." (Of course, once a theme has been established for a program, the use of "theme" is sufficient to describe to the production staff where that music is to be used in the script. But for assignments or for new programs, the writer must describe the music to be used.)

Decide on the effect you want from the music, then describe it accurately, including the length of the cue:

```
MUSIC:    FAST TEMPO MARIACHI BAND UP FOR 8 SEC, THEN FADE UNDER AND OUT
ANNCR:    Welcome to Down Mexico Way. Today's program features the Latin
          stylings of...
```

## Mood Setting and Background

One common use of music for background is to provide a music "bed" behind a commercial announcement. Usually this is done when the announcement is straight narration read by an announcer. A music bed can be useful when it really contributes to the ad, by adding emotional strength or setting a mood for the spot. Martial music behind an ad for a big weekend sale would add excitement; a dreamy, romantic tune would provide a mood appropriate to an ad for perfume. Christmas music, of course, contributes to the mood of that holiday season.

Some radio stations put a "bed" behind practically every commercial, under the assumption that the announcement will be less jarring to an audience if it is backed by music. But that can have a negative result; if the bed sounds too much like the regular content of the station, the audience may not pay attention to the commercial. It will seem to fade into the background, just like the musical content of the station.

Music may also be used in radio and in television as a background for other types of broadcast material. Some dramatic programs are almost completely scored for music, which supports most of the dialogue and narration in addition to providing transitions. Background music occupies a secondary level of attention behind the primary action. It is used to underline and highlight the emotional content of whatever is being broadcast over it and also, in many cases, to induce emotional reactions in the audience. This use of music demands very skillful planning and execution, but when it is handled well, it is extremely effective.

This interweaving of music with drama is obviously expensive and is generally available only to the networks, but it is perhaps the most challenging and exciting use of music in broadcasting.

## Musical Transitions

Transition music is usually used for two simultaneous purposes. First, it may separate scenes or other portions of a broadcast, or tie off the end of a scene. Second, it may resolve the mood or emotional key of a scene it follows and set the mood for the scene it precedes. Here are two examples:

BILL:      ...you can go ahead and try to get a divorce if you want, but
           I assure it won't be easy!

MUSIC:     ORGAN STINGER, 4 SECS, SEGUE TO SOFT ROMANTIC THEME ON GUITAR, FADE
           OUT BEHIND

TOM:       Was he angry?

BETTY:     Oh, Tom, he was furious. He won't let me go without a terrible
           battle....

```
BILL:        ...you can go ahead and try to get a divorce if you want, but

             I assure you it won't be easy!

MUSIC:       ORGAN STINGER, 4 SECS, THEN CROSS-FADE TO RINGING OF TELEPHONE

             (3 RINGS)

TOM:         Hello.

BETTY:       (ON FILTER) Tom?

TOM:         Yes...Betty? Is that you? How did it go?
```

The transition function is not limited to dramatic programs. It is a standard technique for any program where a division point is wanted—between two sections of a game show, between two acts of a variety program, and so on. Because of the high cost of having a live orchestra, recorded music is used for most transitions, and is added to the program during postproduction editing, but live musical transitions are still provided by the studio orchestra on *The Tonight Show.*

If you are not familiar with a range of musical styles, it will take some time to get a feel for the uses of music in broadcast. But time spent familiarizing yourself with different types of music will be worth the effort in becoming more creative and more effective in your writing. One crutch available to writers in many stations and advertising agencies is a recorded library of production music.

## Music as Sound Effect

Music is seldom used as a realistic sound effect, except when a dramatic scene calls for an orchestra playing in the background or something of the sort. Then, technically, the music would be fulfilling the function of sound. But in a nonrealistic program, music is quite often used as a sound effect. Suppose you are writing a children's program with a pseudoscientific script in which a comic inventor is getting ready to take off on a rocket trip to outer space. The launching of the rocket and the takeoff into the stratosphere could be done as a realistic sound effect. Those effects are available. But to maintain the mood of the show, the effect might very well be assigned to music, so that the audience, instead of feeling it was actually hearing the sound of a rocket ship taking off, would experience musically an impression of the same thing.

As with the writing of sound effects cues, music cues should indicate the nature of the music as precisely as possible to the production personnel who will assemble the final sound track. Indicate the artist and selection if recorded music is to be used, or at least the style and instrumentation desired. Also show in the script how long the music cue is to last, whether it fades behind dialogue or narration and when it is to be removed.

The most common terms used to manipulate music and sound cues are not difficult to understand:

| | |
|---|---|
| UP (or FULL) | At full (normal) volume |
| FADE-IN | Turn the mixer pot for the sound in the control room from zero up to normal volume |
| FADE-OUT | The reverse, from normal or whatever the present setting is down to zero |
| FADE-DOWN | Lower the volume, but not out completely; often used like FADE-UNDER |
| FADE-UNDER | When other material is to be given prominence |
| CROSS-FADE | Two different sounds or musical passages are manipulated simultaneously, one being faded in, the other out |
| SEGUE | One effect or passage is immediately followed by another, without any change in volume |

## VOICES AS SOUND

Voices can contribute to the overall sound of a program in ways quite different from their use to convey the meanings of words and sentences. They can contribute to the structural strength of a program, particularly to variety. Variations in vocal delivery can aid in providing clarity to the content, make it easier for audiences to follow a sequence of ideas and events, and provide the changes that help to maintain audience attention.

In the sections that follow we will examine several ways in which voices can be used to strengthen a program.

### Single-Voice Narration

The structural requirement to provide frequent change and variety (discussed in the preceding chapter) is difficult to achieve when the only sound track is that of a single voice reading a piece of copy. In television the boredom and monotony of the single voice can be partially overcome by changing the visual image, and a single narration is sustainable if sufficient visual variety is presented. In radio there is no visual help, and radio producers will go to considerable effort to avoid long talks.

On the other hand, for short materials, such as individual commercial announcements or individual news stories, a single voice often is used. It's less expensive to hire only one announcer rather than two or more, and there will be less time and money spent in production and editing. The cheapest form of commercial, and probably the only form many small businesses can afford, is straight announcer copy. In these cases, and in other small-scale productions such as locally produced and unsponsored public affairs programs, or the narration in small budget corporate/instructional presentations, the cost of talent can be an important limitation. Another answer is that it provides greater efficiency. The amount of information that can be presented in a given length of time is greater using a single voice, so it is a more efficient way to impart information when only a limited amount of time is available.

But regardless of the savings in cost or the greater efficiency, if a lack of variety in a script causes the attention of the audience to be lost, then the communication has been ineffective. The writer should work to provide vocal variety in a script whenever it seems that attention will be hard to maintain by other means, using techniques that employ multiple and different-sounding voices.

## Split Narration

We are not considering at this point talk programs that involve more than one person in conversation, such as interviews, panel discussions, phone-in programs, or studio audience participation. Those programs are structured from the outset to use multiple voices and automatically provide vocal variety. Rather, we are suggesting means by which multiple voices can be introduced for the specific purpose of providing a deliberate alternative to single-voice narration.

One technique is simply to split the narration between two voices. The approach is more effective and less obvious if some logical reason can be found for the split. The technique was used effectively in the early TV series *Winston Churchill: The Valiant Years*. Gary Merrill was the narrator. Churchill's own words, taken from his speeches and writings, provided the contrast, and were delivered by Richard Burton.

Another well-known series using two-voice narration is *The Cousteau Odyssey*. A narrator is used for the main commentary, but that is broken up by frequent use of Cousteau's own voice, explaining his thoughts and opinions on the subject, or amplifying the main narration, as in Figure 7.1.

The Cousteau program actually uses two different narrative techniques. At the beginning of the example, both the narrator and Cousteau are heard off-camera, narrating while the audience watches some marine activity. Later in the excerpt Cousteau is seen on-camera, in conversation with Barnes, in lip-sync sound. He then becomes part of the action, which is a different vocal technique.

The PBS documentary series *The Civil War* used a similar approach—not exactly dual narration, but the narration was broken up by other voices that read excerpts from the soldiers' letters, or by experts.

THE COUSTEAU SOCIETY

CALYPSO

Page 2

THE   COUSTEAU   ODYSSEY

THE WARM-BLOODED SEA:    Mammals of the Deep

| VIDEO | AUDIO |
|---|---|
| | ACT I |
| | COUSTEAU |
| ROCKET ASCENDS | Infinity beckons humanity.  We who hunger for companionship reach to distant planets, searching for liquid water, the cosmic sign of life. |
| MOON SURFACE/ MOON SURAFACE CU | Our expeditions end in dryness, desolation, dust. |
| EARTH RISING WATER PLANET | Obsessed with lifelessness in space, we have disinherited ourselves from life on earth. |
| SLOW MOTION WAVE | There _is_ a water planet. |
| EPISODE TITLE | THE WARM-BLOODED SEA Mammals of the Deep |
| | NARRATOR |
| CELL-LIKE MATTER IN WATER | The sea, indeed, is the womb of life.  Here the first cell took shape, with DNA, and its genetic codes, implanted like a seed within.  Creatures adapted to meet the menace of their environment. And eon after eon, they endowed their improvements to the future. |

**Figure 7.1.** Copyright 1984 by the Cousteau Society, Inc., a nonprofit, membership-supported organization located at 870 Greenbrier Circle, Suite 402, Chesapeake, VA 23320. Annual dues are $20 for an Individual Membership and $28 for a Family Membership.

THE COUSTEAU SOCIETY

C.αLVPSO

Page 5

THE   COUSTEAU   ODYSSEY

THE WARM-BLOODED SEA:   Mammals of the Deep

| VIDEO | AUDIO |
|---|---|
| | McCLOUD (SYNC)<br>Fossil whales  are known  from at least 45 million years ago.<br><br>COUSTEAU (SYNC)<br>Forty-five million years!  And is that about the time when those, some mammals came back to the, to the ocean?<br><br>BARNES (SYNC)<br>Yeah.<br><br>COUSTEAU (SYNC)<br>Or is it still further back?<br><br>McCLOUD (SYNC)<br>Well, it was at least at that time, perhaps a little older, when they came in the sea.<br><br>BARNES (SYNC)<br>This   ...   this is what the lower jaw of one of the earliest whales ever found looks like.<br><br>COUSTEAU (SYNC)<br>Where's your shark tooth?  To me these teeth look a little like shark teeth.  Triangular... |
| CHRIS BARNES HANDS<br>JYC SHARK TOOTH | |

**Figure 7.1.** (continued)

T H E   C O U S T E A U   O D Y S S E Y

THE WARM-BLOODED SEA:   Mammals of the Deep

| VIDEO | AUDIO |
|---|---|
| | (Sound of motor boat in the clear) |
| JYC AND CHRIS BARNES ON MOTORBOAT | Ancient bones have just been found in Southern California.  Cousteau visits the remote site with the son of  paleontologist Lawrence Barnes, who is directing a dig for the Los Angeles County Natural History Museum. |
| | COUSTEAU |
| JYC AND CB WALK AMONG DIGGERS; C/U BONES IN SAND | These hills were once submerged in primal sea. The bones here are scattered pieces to a prehistoric puzzle.  After millions of years spent adapting to land, some mammals returned to water.  No one knows why.  Motivations are not buried in clay; only broken skeletons, fragmented answers. |
| | (Sound of hammer in the clear) |
| | BARNES (SYNC) |
| BARNES POINTS OUT PARTS OF SKULL | We've got the skull here, and the front end of the skull is up here, the brain case back here.  The blow holes are between these...and the lower jaw lies to the side. |
| | COUSTEAU (SYNC) |
| KNEELING NEXT TO SKULL | How far back, uh, were fossils of whales found? |

**Figure 7.1.** (continued)

THE   COUSTEAU   ODYSSEY

THE WARM-BLOODED SEA:   Mammals of the Deep

| VIDEO | AUDIO |
|---|---|
| | COUSTEAU |
| GORGONIA, SHELL CRAB, NAUTILUS, OCTOPUS | The miracle of life defies the universal law of degradation, continually becoming ever more intricate.  This phenomenon inspired the French philosopher, Teilhard de Chardin, to envision three infinities.  There is the infinitely big, of course, and the infinitely small.  To them, Teilhard added the infinitely complex:  life itself. |
| | NARRATOR |
| TUNA | Landmarks of time:  nerves, jaws, vertebrates. Finally the cold sea embraced the model of cold blood --the shark. |
| SHARK TURNS | |
| IGUANA CLIMBS TO ROCK | After billions of years in its liquid cradle, life came to land.  Creatures now developed a new trait to help them master the onerous pull of terrestrial gravity. |
| BIRD-RHINO-LION | Warm blood.  With high central temperatures the body's inner combustion engine could be even more powerful.  The mammal appeared, quivering with energy, endurance, and formidable strength. |

**Figure 7.1.** (continued)

Another easily recognized use of dual narration is in sports announcing, where one announcer is designated as the "play-by-play" voice and the other as the "color" voice. Radio morning shows often use two or more personalities to read news, portray comic characters and deliver commercials.

In a commercial the same approach—dividing up the copy for more than one voice—is frequently used. The simplest way is to split the copy, but the use of more than one voice also permits the message to be presented in more attention-getting ways. In this example, Voice 1, an announcer, and Voice 2, representing the client, engage in a bit of banter. Voice 3 delivers the commercial pitch.

VOICE #1    Introducing the new, exciting miracle Linville Brothers....

VOICE #2    No, no, please stop. We're not new. We've been around for
            years, and hey, we don't create miracles, just honest
            business...

VOICE #1    OhhhhhKay, how about, if you really want to improve your
            social life get a front end alignment from Linville Brothers
            and a great set of tires at the same time...

VOICE #2    Oh please, we don't promise anything we can't deliver,
            (FADE) Great social life, Geez.

VOICE #1    How's this...if you want to keep pace with your neighbors...

VOICE #2    Come on, most of our business comes from referrals from
            friends and neighbors.

VOICE #3    If all you want is honest price and honest work for your
            tire and front end needs, Call Linville Brothers at
            929-63-82. We're on El Camino between I-80 and Ethan Way.
            We'll work while you wait. Be sure to check our specially
            priced clearance items. Just call us at 929-6382. Linville
            Brothers will give you the best work at the best price we
            can. You can ride on your reputation, we do.

VOICE #2    Ahhhhhhhh, that's more like it...

*Source:* Courtesy of KRAK Radio, Sacramento, CA.

## Drama and Narration

Some programs make effective use of a mixture of narration and dramatic dialogue. The combination can be mixed in varying proportions from mostly narration to mostly drama. Radio dramas usually require at least a brief narrative introduction at the beginning of the plot, to establish the locale and premise of the story. Those are very difficult things to present to an audience quickly at the beginning of a story by using dramatic exposition alone. The introduction to "Red Death" is an example of this use. Narration may also be used to provide a bridge between scenes and possibly a wrap-up at the conclusion of the story.

```
                              RED DEATH

MUSIC:        DESCRIPTIVE, FADING TO BACKGROUND UNDER

NARR:         The year 1915. The red soil of Georgia yields its rich

              rows of cotton. The hills of the Carolinas are lush and

              green, and the land is peaceful and good. The Gulf Coast

              is a blue curve against the high surf; and the rich sun

              slants through the canebrakes of the valley of the

              Mississippi. But stalking the Carolina hills, striding

              sure-footed across the copper earth of Georgia, through

              the black-belt to the banks of the great river and beyond,

              is Death—a red, ravaging phantom—choosing his victims

              without mercy, without design. No man sees him; no man

              knows the times of his coming, but all see where he has

              been, and all wonder and fear. For the cropper's hoe will

              fall to the earth, and the man bends double with the agony

              inside him, his face scarlet with the marks where the

              phantom has touched him—the raw, red mark of the Red

              Death—a mark shaped like a butterfly moth—and the sign of

              a man's doom is branded upon him—the moth-mark—the

              mockery of the Death that is red and moves invisibly among

              the poor folk, the cabin folk, of the hills and fields of

              America's Southland.
```

| MUSIC | UP TO A QUICK ENDING |
|---|---|
| VOICE: | 1915. Five thousand lie sick unto death of pellagra, the disease of the Red Death. |
| MUSIC: | UP FULL...FADE INTO |
| SOUND: | DOG HOWL IN DISTANCE |
| DR. HORNE: | Well Granny, I guess there's nothing I can do now. |
| GRANNY: | Dead. Sam's dead. They're all gone now. All my boys. |
| DR. HORNE: | I did all I could. I'm sorry, Granny. |
| GRANNY: | Cotton's going to rot this year—same as down to the Bennett's last month when Red Death took the old man away. What'll I do? |
| DR. HORNE: | Granny, things are going to be different now, maybe. The government's going to help us get rid of this plague. They say there's a big scientist coming down here. |
| GRANNY: | Humph! Government! What they know about Red Death any how? |

*Source:* Ruth Barth, "Red Death," in A. H. Lass, Earle L. McGill, Donald Axelrod, eds., *Plays from Radio* (Cambridge, MA: Houghton Mifflin, 1948), pp. 195–196. Reprinted by permission of E. I. duPont de Nemours & Co.

Narration is less needed, and less used, in television, because characters, locations and actions are introduced visually, and the dramatic action can proceed immediately and simultaneously with those introductions. Nevertheless, some TV shows use narration simply as a structural device. *Spencer for Hire*, *The Wonder Years* and *Love and War* are examples. *The Wonder Years* uses an unusual technique. The drama is presented as if it were all in the past. The adult voice of the lead character begins by narrating (in the present) and reminiscing about his past; the drama then takes us into the past. Periodically the adult voice returns to comment on the action or bridge to another scene. In *Love and War* the main characters occasionally talk directly to the audience.

An inexpensive and effective device for radio, but one that is no longer used very frequently, is to write a script that is largely narration but which is broken up by dramatic inserts. In the opening scenes of "Tabu" narration plays a prominent part in advancing the plot, but the narrator, Ray, also becomes an actor and interacts with other characters in a series of scenes which are held together by the narration.

<u>TABU</u>

MUSIC:      <u>THEME IN AND DOWN IN BACKGROUND</u>

ANNCR:      And now, an original radio play written and directed by Dave Drummond—with Ray Lewis as its narrator. Tabu!

MUSIC:      <u>UP TO A BUTTON AND OUT</u>

RAY:      How it is on the Tongans right now I just wouldn't know. No more of that South Seas stuff for me. I've got a cigar store on Fillmore Street and I'm doing all right—if making a living is doing all right. As for the Tongans, themselves, I'm not going back. Never heard of them? You haven't missed much. Just a handful of islands a long way from here. The friendly Islands is what it says on the charts but I think somebody was kidding. The trouble is, you see, the Tongans are too close to Malayanasia—to the Marquesas. And that's where the cannibals live—or did in my time. Nice chaps. With a taste for long pig, meaning somebody like you or like me. Boiled or roasted or raw. They're not fussy that way. Not good neighbors. But that's how it was when I took my bride out to Waka-Nui, that was the first mistake. The second mistake was taking young Watson along to help run the trading post. That was the worst mistake. I sent for him a week after we got there. (TURN AWAY FADE)

SOUND:      <u>FOOTSTEPS FADE IN TO MIKE ON WHARF AND STOP AT MIKE</u>

WATSON:      (SHORT FADE IN)....One of the boys came to my hut and said you wanted me, down here at the wharf.

RAY:      Yes.

WATSON:      Yes sir?

RAY:      I'm taking the schooner out, I'll be gone two months. I'm leaving this place in your charge.

```
WATSON:      Yes sir.

RAY:         You won't have any problems or trouble. Take care of the
             place and...of my wife.

WATSON:      Ruby?

RAY:         ...Ruby?

WATSON:      I meant...your wife.

RAY:         Yes, my wife.

WATSON:      She's not going with you?

RAY:         She's down with a touch of fever. I'm leaving her here.

WATSON:      ...Oh.

RAY:         Just keep one thing in mind...I'll be back!

MUSIC:       DANGER

Ray:         That was the third mistake. But I learn the hard way. Two
             weeks later, knocking around in strange waters, I put the
             schooner on a reef that didn't show on the charts and
             knocked a hole in her hull. Made it to shore all right in
             one of the boats and the natives there didn't like my looks.
             They knocked a hole in my head. That and fever and a lot of
             hard luck made a lot of time go past. It was a year before I
             saw my island again and when I put foot on Waka-Nui the
             place was deserted, the trading post looted, my bungalow
             burned down. No one left on the island but a Kanaka boy who
             thought I was a ghost because they'd heard I was dead. All
             he would say was: Him fella long time go. Long go! And he
             pointed toward the west—toward the Marquesas—where the
             cannibals were.
```

*Source:* Dave Drummond, *Tabu,* an original radio play.

A similar mixture of dramatic dialogue and narration can be used in a commercial. One common approach is to use the dialogue to set the scene, attract attention and possibly establish a problem. The announcer-narrator then delivers the "pitch" for the product. Variations are endless; here is one:

| ANNCR: | PERRY BOYS' Smorgy presents another "Perry Tale" |
|---|---|
| MUSIC: | HARP |
| ANNCR: | Once upon a time...there lived a boy and a girl named Jack and Jewel...Jack loved Jewel... |
| JACK: | I love you Jewel... |
| ANNCR: | And Jewel loved Jack... |
| JEWEL: | I love you Jack... |
| ANNCR: | Jack wanted so much to take Jewel to dinner...But alas, couldn't afford it...even now, he moonlighted counting sheep, Baaa Baaa, at the Mother Goose Amusement Park and Window Shade Company. One night...as Jack dreamily counted his sheep, there appeared his perry godfather...dressed in a chicken suit... |
| GODFATHER: | My other things are at the cleaners... |
| JACK: | What ho... |
| ANNCR: | Said Jack... |
| GODFATHER: | Ho, nuthin, you turkey... |
| ANNCR: | Said the godfather... |
| GODFATHER: | What have you already in your poke??? |
| JACK: | A pig. |
| ANNCR: | Said Jack, Oink...Oink... |
| JACK: | And only twenty dollars... |
| GODFATHER: | That is more than enough for dinner for you and Jewel at Perry Boys' Smorgy...they have over 40 good things to eat...and beer and wine are only a dollar... |
| JACK: | And we'll live happily ever after, right??? |
| GODFATHER: | Jack...you're a real Jewel! |
| SOUND: | HARP |

ANNCR:              `You'll live happily ever after...when you eat at Perry`

                           `Boys' Smorgy restaurants...$4.99 for lunch and $8.99 for`

                           `dinner...in Santa Cruz...Salinas...and Monterey at 2066`

                           `Fremont Blvd.`

*Source:* Courtesy of the author, Frank LaRosa.

## Actualities and Anchors

Two techniques used by news writers and producers to relieve the monotony of single narration within the newscast are the actuality and the anchor.

If the information in a news story comes from an authoritative source, the actual voice of that source can be used. The expert's voice is obtained by the reporter, in person or by phone, in the form of an interview. The complete interview is likely to be far longer than the small section which is finally chosen, edited and inserted into the story.*

The other technique is the use of news anchors. Most television stations use this approach, as do those radio stations that specialize in large blocks of news. In contrast to a single-person newscast, the anchor serves primarily to lead into and out of stories reported, on tape, by other reporters and other voices. To add even more vocal variety, most stations now use dual anchors on major newcasts.

## Different Voices

In the preceding section we have been making one critical assumption. We have assumed that the use of more than one voice provides variety *because the two or more voices sound different.* It would be of no value to the audience to have multiple voices if the listener couldn't tell them apart. Two voices that are similar in pitch, quality, or other vocal characteristics may actually make it more difficult for the audience members to follow, as they may have to concentrate on differentiating the voices rather than on the content of the program. The various voices must sound sufficiently different for the audience to be able to distinguish easily between them.

In a dramatic program, for example, the characters portrayed in a scene will usually be quite different—male and female, young and old, and possibly

---

* There is some disagreement in the industry on the terms used to describe this practice. Some persons use *actuality* to describe only real events recorded on location, such as at a fire, or a parade; for them, interviews recorded over the phone or in a studio are not actualities. Others use either the term *actuality* or *sound bite* to describe all inserts into a narrative newscast.

from ethnic groups with distinctive vocal patterns. Some dramatic scenes, however, will call for characters who are very similar—three Caucasian male teenagers, for example. In television, the characters would be chosen to be physically, visually different; in a radio drama, where only sound will distinguish among the characters, the vocal pattern and voice quality of each character must be easily distinguished by the audience.

Different vocal patterns not only help to set each voice in a scene apart from the others, but also aid in delineating character. When a script employing these variations is translated into sound, there is added to the meaning of the language the particular sound of each speaker. Contrast, for example, these two passages, which indicate two quite different characters, even though the speakers are really saying the same thing.

```
"Perhaps you'd better tell me. I'll find out under any
circumstance. You can save time for both of us by telling
me now what Mr. Davis did with those papers."
```

```
"C'mon, kid, spill it. It won't do you any good to dummy
up. I got my sources. Y'better give now before I get sore.
Where'd Douglas put them papers?"
```

The flavor of individual speech can be achieved by word choice, by distinctive sentence rhythms and by a characteristic sentence length. Staccato speech is full of short, quick vowels and short words that incorporate them. Slow, deliberate speech uses longer words, more sonorous, open vowel sounds, and longer sentences and sentence rhythms.

Distinctive speech patterns most often are the result of national, regional, or ethnic background. Recognizably different vocal characteristics exist in different countries and areas of the world, in different regions of the country, and among different ethnic groups. If the geographic, ethnic, or social background of the speaker is important to the development of the script, and if that background includes a speech pattern—pronunciation, intonation, or syntax—which is distinctive, then the writer must indicate that fact in the script.

For the writer, scripting to indicate a foreign origin of the speaker can be a difficult, laborious job. One simple technique that can be quite effective, however, is to use in English the grammatical structure of the foreign language to be suggested. Then allow the actor who is creating the part to make whatever dialect and pronunciation patterns are needed. For example, the expression of the same idea by different speakers might be indicated in a script as follows:

```
FRENCH:      "Is that not so, M'sieur?"
GERMAN:      "That is true, no?"
AMERICAN:    "Isn't that right?"
```

These three renderings, each idiomatically different but all in English, manage to give some flavor of the different background languages by means of word choice and word order alone. Here is another, similar situation:

```
ANNCR:         At ABW Foreign Auto Parts our clientele is very

               international.

SWEDE:         I need some valves for my Volvo.

BRITISH:       Old Chap, I need a muffler for the M.G.

ITALIAN:       I want-a-plugs for my Peugeot.

SOUTHERN:      I need one of them things that fits on the whatchamijigger

               for my Toyota Land Cruiser.

ANNCR:         Foreign auto parts--that's our business. Make sure that

               only original quality foreign parts are used on your

               car....
```
*Source:* Courtesy of KRAK, Sacramento, CA.

Regional and ethnic patterns can be handled similarly. In this country, there is a wide sectional variation in the English of ordinary speech. Some of these regional differences are actual differences in pronunciation. Others are local peculiarities in the stress or value given to certain sounds. In still others, the difference is largely a matter of voice quality and intonation. These differences in speech should be known and taken into account by the writer, but he or she need not actually indicate all of them in the script.

There is also a characteristic idiom indigenous to some regions, which is richly connotative and picturesque and which should be used by the writer. Obviously, it should not be assumed that every Texan greets friends by saying, "Howdy, pardner." Circumstances of the individual situation must determine the amount and kind of regional idiom to be used. Nevertheless, there are certain expressions in regional speech which are widely used and which are as valuable as pronunciation in giving the flavor of local speech.

In the following example, the writer used both spelling variations to indicate regional pronunciations of certain words and idiomatic expressions characteristic of the rural South to provide distinctive vocal patterns for each character and to set the scene in its geographic location.

MUSIC:     OPENING MELODY, SUGGESTING MORNING IN COUNTRY, FADING INTO:

SOUND:     THE SUBDUED SOUNDS OF DAYBREAK IN THE FLORIDA SCRUB.

              NOW A DISTANT COCK CROWS. PRESENTLY THE FAR OFF HOWLING OF A DOG. CLOSE AT HAND, THE SAD CALL OF MOURNING DOVES, DRAWN OUT, REPEATED, SUBSIDING RELUCTANTLY. (PAUSE) THEN THE SOUND OF WEARY FOOTFALLS MOUNTING STEEP STAIRS.

MAMA:     (A HINT OF PITY IN HER VOICE) Sleepin' and dreamin'...still full of their baby concerns. Hit ain't in my heart to waken 'em. Hit ain't in my heart to—Oh Lord, I'm fearful. I don't know iffen I'm actin' right or not, Lord.

SOUND:     THE MOURNING DOVES CALL SOFTLY AT THE WINDOW

MAMA:     Our father which art in heaven, Hallowed be they name. They kingdom come. They will be done on earth as it is in heaven (BREAKS OFF SOBBING)

JIM:     (STARTLED FROM SLEEP) Mamma! Mamma!

MAMA:     (REASSURINGLY) Nothin's wrong, Jim. Don't be scairt.

JIM:     Mamma, you ain't crying?

MAMA:     No, Jim.

JIM:     You're a-prayin'?

MAMA:     Yes, I were prayin. Hit'll be day soon. You better be risin' up. Your Uncle Holly'll be along directly.

JIM:     (WITH GROWING EXCITEMENT) Hit's really come. The day. The day we're going to Czardis in the wagon to see papa.

MAMA:     (DULLY) Hit's come, all right.

JIM:     Seems like I jest cain't believe yet we're goin'...

MAMA:     (CUTTING IN) There ain't time fur talk now, Jim. You best bestir yourself. And waken up Dan'l too.

SOUND:     RECEDING FOOTSTEPS ON FLOOR BOARDS

MAMA:     (VOICE MORE DISTANT—OFF-MIKE) Put on the clean things I washed fur you so you'll look decent and be a credit to your raisin'.

```
SOUND:     FOOTSTEPS DESCENDING STAIRS, THEN FADE-OUT

JIM:       Wake up, Dan'l Wake up!

DAN'L:     (WHIMPERING IN HIS SLEEP) Leave me be. Make 'em leave me be.

           Jim!...Jim!

JIM:       (PATIENT, KIND) Don't be feared, Dan'l. Ain't nobody a

           botherin' you.
```

*Source:* Edwin Granberry, "A Trip to Czardis," in Lass, McGill, and Axelrod, *Plays from Radio*, pp. 157–158. Reprinted by permission of CBS, Inc.

The writer must be cautious, however, not to allow the presence of distinctive vocal patterns to be construed as derogatory stereotyping of minority groups. Broadcasting depends upon the use of stereotypes. In most dramatic programs, very little time can be devoted to the development of characterization, particularly of secondary characters. The action of the plot must begin quickly to maintain audience attention. Lengthy character development interferes with that requirement, so characters are sketched quickly, using standardized stereotypes.

The practice is not inherently degrading to minorities, but in practice some stereotypical characterizations of members of minority groups have developed which are derogatory. We simply want to call attention to those differences that do exist in speech patterns because of geography or ethnicity and that are important, especially in radio, to the audience's understanding of characters, to the setting of a scene, and to vocal variety.

## CONCLUSION

There are times when the absence of a visual image can be a distinct advantage in broadcast communication. A few words, music, and sound effects can suggest a myriad of impressions, a whole world of make-believe. But the absence of the companion visual sense also puts a burden on the writer to provide frequent change in the sound patterns being transmitted.

This chapter discusses the special characteristics of sound that shape every aural communication—pitch, quality, volume, distance, acoustical setting, rhythm, and juxtaposition. The broadcast writer finds special problems and opportunities in sound using the three components of sound—effects, music, and voice.

Not only may sound be used as a medium by itself, but it also is half of any audiovisual presentation. We have concentrated here on the uses of sound when it is used alone, but these principles apply with little modification to audiovisual media as well.

**Exercises**

1. Listen to a radio dramatic program, with particular attention to its uses of sound effects. For each effect you hear:

   a. Name and describe what that effect is—fire crackling, siren, foghorn, teakettle whistling, machinery, and so on.

   b. What indication (clue) was given as to what the effect was; in other words, *how* do you know that the effect is what you named it?

   c. What purpose did that effect have? Did it heighten action, set a mood, set time or place, or what?

2. Similarly, in the same or a different program, listen for music cues.

   a. List all music cues; describe the kind of music.

   b. Note how long each cue lasted; indicate whether it was faded in, faded out or under, and so on; describe how it fit into the dialogue or narration.

   c. What purpose did each music cue serve?

   For both exercises 1 and 2, you may have to search to find radio dramatic programs actually on the air. Many public radio stations affiliated with National Public Radio carry the weekly series *NPR Playhouse*, which presents both original plays and adaptations of books and stage plays. Some commercial stations play recordings of old series. These recordings are also available on records and tape; check with your local recorded music store. If you are listening off the air, you may find it helpful to make your own recording, so you can go back over the material as you work on these exercises.

3. Choose a favorite short story and write for radio the first two scenes (or more if you wish). For this exercise, it is important that you:

   a. Choose the locations of your scenes, and decide how you will describe those scenes to your audience.

   b. Set time.

   c. Identify and describe the characters appearing in the scenes.

   d. Decide how to open the play; will you use narration to introduce the story? If so, how much?

   e. Determine how to provide the transition between the two scenes; will you use the preceding scenes to set up the following scene (as in the example in this chapter on the waterfront), or sound effects, or music, or narration, or a combination?

   Ideally, this assignment would combine considerations of the use of sound from this chapter with concepts of dramatic structure covered in

Chapter 16. If you have the opportunity, read that chapter as well before beginning this exercise.

4. You will need to select and record a television program for this exercise. Any program will do, but children's animated cartoon series are often the best examples. First, watch the program without sound. Then, listen to the program without looking at the video. Finally, watch in the normal fashion, with sound. Note what the sound contributes, particularly the music and sound effects.

**Note**

1. Albert Crews, *Professional Radio Writing* (Boston: Houghton Mifflin, 1946), pp. 64–65.

**Further Reading**

In addition to the titles listed in Chapter 4 for radio production, these texts deal with sound as it complements video writing and production.

Alkin, Glyn. *Sound Techniques for Video and TV*, 2nd ed. Stoneham, MA: Focal, 1989.
Mott, Robert L. *Sound Effects: Radio, TV, and Film*. Stoneham, MA: Focal, 1990.
Soifer, Rosanne. *Music in Video Production*. White Plains, NY: Knowledge Industry, 1991.

If you are interested in writing creatively for radio, you might seek out these collections of dramatic scripts. All are out of print but sometimes can be found in used-book stores.

Barnouw, Erik (ed.). *Radio Drama in Action*. New York: Rinehart, 1945.
Corwin, Norman. *Thirteen by Corwin*. New York: Henry Holt, 1942.
Lass, A. H., Earle L. McGill, and Donald Axelrod (eds.). *Plays From Radio*. Cambridge, MA: Houghton Mifflin, 1948.
Mackay, David. *Drama on the Air*. New York: Prentice-Hall, 1951.

A newer collection of radio scripts, this time emphasizing well-written news, documentary and interview programs as presented by National Public Radio, is

Stamberg, Susan. *Every Night at Five*. New York: Pantheon, 1982.

Finally, we recommend this title. It also is long out of print, but still one of the best references on the creative uses of sound. Portions of it formed the foundations for both this chapter and Chapter 3.

Crews, Albert. *Professional Radio Writing*. Boston: Houghton Mifflin, 1946.

# Handling Visuals

I n the forty-plus years since television became a major medium of communication, modern audiences have developed a quite sophisticated understanding of the rules and conventions of visualization. We are probably more aware of the visual conventions held by members of our culture than we are of literary ones. As a writer, you need to recognize, understand and appreciate these fundamentals of visual structure. With that familiarity, you will be able to write more precise and effective scripts for television and other audiovisual media.

When you finish this chapter, you will be able to

- recognize the psychological values and basic uses of different camera angles, distance and movement,

- understand the importance of the careful sequencing of camera shots,

- recognize the uses of common devices for scene transitions,

- consider the problems of matching pictures to narration,

- use these principles of visualization in your own scripts, and

- recognize and use these important terms and concepts:

camera distance: long, medium, closeup

camera movement: boom, dolly, pan, swish pan, tilt, truck, zoom

cutaway shot

digital video effects (DVE)

establishing shot

juxtaposition of shots

line of action

passing shot

reverse angle shot

scene and sequence

transitions: cut, match cut, jump cut; defocus; dissolve; fade; wipe

vertical camera angle: low, high, eye-level

We do not mean to suggest that the writer always controls the visualization of a program. In dramatic programs, for example, the director and editor usually will choose the precise camera angles, the sequences of shots, the frequency with which shots are changed, the type of change, and so on. In live programs also, the director will place the cameras, move them, and select the shots that will be seen on the air. In these kinds of programs writers are not required, or expected, or even encouraged to include visual directions.

On the other hand, in television journalism the writer is often also the reporter, the director (on location for a story), and the editor, and in smaller stations quite possibly the cameraperson as well. During the two to three stories a writer/reporter may put together in a normal day, it will be necessary at least to direct the camera operator to get the kind of shots necessary and then also to direct the editor on how those shots should be put together to provide visual continuity that supports and parallels the verbal story. Under those circumstances, understanding visual structure is critical.

Writers of television commercials similarly need a good basic knowledge in this area. Frequently the commercial will be written as a storyboard. Visual composition of the various shots that make up the sequence, if not the precise camera angle and distance, is important if the final product is to have the impact you intended when you began the assignment.

You will find as you read this chapter that you are already familiar with many of the ideas it contains. Over the years you have watched thousands of hours of television and film, looked at countless photos in newspapers, magazines, and books, and read comic strips. The principles presented in this chapter apply to all these media, and many of them you have already unconsciously absorbed. So read on and discover what you already know.


## VISUAL POINT OF VIEW

One fundamental principle of visualization is the relationship between audience and camera position. Simply put, there is a direct correlation between what the camera sees and what the viewer sees when watching the screen—the camera becomes the viewer's eyes.

People who have grown up in the age of movies and television often find it difficult to become interested in a live theater performance. The live play is likely to seem boring and slow to develop. In part that impression is due to the construction of a play. A theatrical drama, usually two to three hours long, can take longer to develop characters, mood, and plot nuances than does a 30- to 60-minute TV drama.

But in large part the feeling of frustration and boredom you may feel in the theater is because when you watch the theater presentation you have only one point of view—that from your own seat. What you are seeing will be a somewhat different angle or viewpoint from what the couple down in the front row is seeing and different again from the person in a seat in the balcony. For each of you, the point of view is slightly different, but most important, for each of you there is only one point of view.

Television and film, on the other hand, provide the viewer with multiple viewpoints. Each time the camera shot changes (or even within a single camera shot, if there is camera movement) the viewer is transported to a new viewpoint.

As we move from one camera position to the next, we experience the emotional and psychological payload each viewpoint gives us, and move on to the next. We absorb the story being told us by allowing the camera to be our eyes, and letting the rest of our being react to what the camera sees.

What are the effects of these maneuverings? How do camera positions affect us? In this chapter we consider five aspects of visual storytelling: vertical camera angles, camera to subject distances, camera movement, the juxtaposition and sequencing of shots, and transitions. These five provide a basic grammar sufficient for the beginning writer. In one final section we also discuss "Writing to Pictures," some considerations on how narrative should support the visual content of a news story, documentary or corporate video. When you are ready to go beyond these basics, you should turn to the literature of cinematography and television production.

# VERTICAL CAMERA ANGLES

The position of the camera in relation to the subject on the vertical axis is very important because it will determine to a large degree the emotional or psychological effect of the shot. There are three basic positions: the camera above the subject, below the subject or at eye level with it.

## Low Angle

People understood the power of low angles long before there were cameras. Architects built cathedrals as tall as possible and put the stained glass windows well above eye level for one purpose: to get people to look up at them. Sculptors, when designing statues of national heroes, put them on large pedestals for the same reason. The people who depict our religious, political and cultural heritage understand that in our culture we associate height and size with power. The taller something is, the more powerful it is. Conversely, the smaller, the less powerful.

Camera angles affect us the same way. When the camera is below the subject, that is a low angle shot. The camera will make whatever it is looking at seem big. If the camera is looking at a person, the person will look taller and larger than in real life—more powerful, possibly more dangerous. Since

**Figure 8.1.** Low angle shots.

the camera's point of view becomes the audience's point of view, from this low angle the audience feels small and perhaps helpless. Objects, too, look very large, even overwhelming, from this angle; see Figure 8.1.

A low camera angle also gives a general sense of dramatic intensity—an impression that momentous events are taking place. It could convey, for example, the importance of the signing of the Declaration of Independence, the power of a marching army, or the intensity of a man's mind. A low angle can also make a subject seem threatening; it is often used to build the stature of a villain or monster or to give a general sense of danger.

## High Angle

High angle shots are those where the camera is above the subject, looking down on it (Figure 8.2). The psychology behind the high angle shot is the reverse of the low angle shot. From the lofty heights of a cathedral window or a military hero placed high on his pedestal, we humans look small indeed. In the same way, when the camera is above the subject, it makes the subject look smaller. The high camera diminishes the subject in size. It takes a dominant position over the subject.

When we want to show weakness or vulnerability, therefore, a high angle is appropriate. During a dialogue between two leads in a drama, we would give the high camera angle to the weaker character, so we are looking down on that person, and the low angle to the stronger person, so we are looking

**Figure 8.2.** High angle shots.

up at that one. By visually reinforcing the psychological relationship between the two, we add depth to the meaning of the scene in a subtle but powerful way.

Of course, there are varying degrees of height we can take with a high angle shot. And each different height will change the meaning of the shot. Shots just slightly above eye level have more subtle effects, A slightly high angle is used in standard portrait photography because it is flattering to the subject, both physically and psychologically. It will make the subject look safe, nonthreatening, and friendly (Figure 8.2, top left).

As we raise the camera higher above the subject, we increase the drama and intensity of the effect. We are now looking down on the subject at a stronger angle. The subject will begin to look more vulnerable, even victimized. If we continue to raise the angle of the shot, the subject can look trapped, because of the extreme height in relation to the subject.

A high angle can also support a mood of compassion, of divine goodness looking down, say, on a young mother and her newborn child. This visual power gained by being above the subject can be any kind of power—benevolent, menacing, perhaps even detached and abstract. But being above a subject does give the camera/viewer power.

## Eye-Level Angle

The eye-level angle may serve either of two functions: It may provide a neutral narrative position, or it may support a high-impact, confrontational situation.

The narrative function is used more. Think of the millions of shots you have seen which have had no dramatic impact—the pictures you have looked at without emotion, just to get visual information. In most cases, these were eye-level shots. The camera position at eye level invites the viewer to "read" the shot, rather than to respond to it emotionally, as would be the case with either a high or low angle shot. It is the proper choice to deliver factual, nondramatic content (Figure 8.3).

Because the camera is at "normal" height, this angle feels the most comfortable and is the easiest for audience members to relate to. There is an equality between the viewer and the subject being viewed. We are literally "on the same level" with the subject, and it is thus appropriate to use this angle to convey an impression of honesty and frankness. The eye-level shot, for this reason, is often used for political advertising, in news broadcasts, and in commercials where the announcer needs to appear as honest and frank.

Take, for example, the sequence of shots in the Amtrak commercial in Chapter 5. The opening shot is a high angle of the announcer quite a distance away from the camera. He is very small in the frame, but as he walks toward us he gets larger. The camera moves toward him too, and gradually drops down in height. Finally the camera reaches eye level, and the announcer

**Figure 8.3.** Eye-level shots.

begins to speak. This opening, moving from a high angle far away to an eye-level close shot of the announcer, adds drama and intensity (as well as a mood of distance and nostalgia) to a shot which without the dramatic camera angle would be merely matter of fact and not as interesting.

But with just a little emphasis in the lighting, or a slight change in composition or in the subject's expression, the eye-level shot can take on a quite different emotional meaning. It can create an impression of intensity and tenseness that goes beyond honesty and frankness. This is the visual representation of confrontation, of the cliché phrase "eyeball-to-eyeball." In this context, the eye-level shot can convey dramatic intensity without distorting the visual information as much as an angled shot of the same subject.

Note, too, that being eye level to a person is very different from being eye level to an object. In that difference is a key to understanding the whole theory of camera angles. It is easy to understand the effect of eye-level shots when the subjects are people because when people are all standing, or sitting, they are naturally at eye-to-eye level. But telephones, as an example, are not normally found at that level. Our normal frame of reference is to be looking down at them. Our minds are used to seeing phones below eye level, so if you look at a telephone at eye level (straight across at it), the camera angle will not depict objectivity, as with a normal eye-level shot. Instead it will give power and weight to the phone, characteristics of a low angle shot.

We can set this theoretical discussion into a scene. Assume a plot situation in which the heroine has been knocked unconscious on the floor by an intruder. When she comes to, she struggles to reach the telephone on the coffee table—now at eye level. A shot of this scene will have the effect of showing the person as smaller and the phone as bigger and more important. As a consequence, all the impact of a low angle shot applies even though it is, strictly speaking, an eye-level shot (Figure 8.3, right).

Therefore, when we talk about the eye-level shot as being able to convey honesty, frankness and objectivity, we can't say that this is true in all cases. It applies only to people and subjects that are eye level in terms of our *normal frame of reference*, from roughly 4 to 6 feet in height.

To sum up, the camera angles on the vertical axis are of three basic types. The low angle shot, in general, confers power on the subject, the high angle shot conveys vulnerability, and the eye-level shot may convey either objectivity and honesty, or confrontation.

But as we shall repeat frequently throughout this chapter, it is a mistake to oversimplify. Camera angles alone do not give a shot its entire meaning.

## CAMERA DISTANCE

Another powerful, expressive device is the choice of camera distance—that is, the *apparent* distance between the camera (audience) and the subject. We emphasize the word *apparent*, because in reality what appears to be a close-up shot, of a football player in a game, for example, may be taken from a camera using a telephoto lens that is in reality some distance away.

The designations for camera distance in scripts are probably familiar to you. They include such basic terms as *long shot (LS), medium shot (MS),* and *closeup (CU),* and combinations—*extreme long shot (ELS), medium long shot (MLS), medium closeup (MCU),* and *extreme closeup (ECU).* But in practice it is difficult to set clear rules about the use of these terms to describe shots, because they are all relative.

For example, assume we have this series of three shots, which we label as a long shot, medium shot, and closeup, respectively (Figure 8.4). We decide to add another shot to the opening, which will be an even wider panorama. The new series is shown in Figure 8.5. In describing this new series, how shall we label the shots? Is the second shot still a long shot, even though it is not the longest shot? If so, what label do we give the first shot? We can call it an extreme long shot. The labels are arbitrary, but useful when production personnel must discuss the scene. Labels have meaning only in the context of the particular group of shots being considered.

**Figure 8.4.** Long shot. Medium shot. Closeup.

In the next sections we use the room pictured in Figure 8.6 to examine the different types of shots commonly used in writing for visual media.

## Long Shots

The overall picture will be called a long shot. It's also known as a *wide shot*, and sometimes an *establishing shot*. When it is referred to as an establishing shot, that means it is being used at the beginning of a scene to establish the scene and its location. The shot establishes the parameters within which the action of the scene will take place. It's an introduction (Figure 8.6).

When you see this long shot, you know immediately that there are two main characters in the scene. They are inside a room (where the decor, easily seen in an establishing shot, can make a significant expressive statement), and they are waiting for a phone call. The long shot can also establish the mood of the scene, by means of the lighting, the composition, and the blocking that is built into the shot. In short, when used as an establishing shot, a

**Figure 8.5.** Extreme long shot. Long shot. Medium shot. Closeup.

long shot will establish basic visual facts and relationships on which the rest of the scene is built.

But long shots can do more than establish. When they are used within a scene, not just at the beginning, they convey moods like loneliness, estrangement, and isolation. The farther away we are from someone or something, the less direct involvement we feel. We can reflect upon the subject matter and think about it without being asked to be involved with it. We are a safe distance away. These shots, in most contexts, are long shots (Figure 8.7).

Long shots frequently are also used to end scenes. Just as we draw away from something when our interest in it diminishes, the long shot pulls us away from the action of a scene when it is over, or nearly over. By doing so, the shot is telling us that we have seen all we are going to see of that situation. The long shot releases the visual tension of the scene and gives it a feeling of closure.

**Figure 8.6.** A long, wide, or establishing shot.

Long shots can, of course, be shot from high, low, or eye-level angles, and their meaning will change accordingly.

## Medium Shots

In our scene, a medium shot would be a shot of the two characters (a two shot), a shot of either character with the phone, or even a loose single shot of either of the characters. In general, medium shots of people are head and shoulder or waist-up shots (Figure 8.8).

Medium shots are used to deliver the bulk of the factual information that moves the story along. The emotional value of a medium shot is minimal, simply because the shot is neither very far away nor close to the subject. The camera is close enough to see significant details, but not so close as to produce emotional reactions from the viewer. This is the range at which we become aware of the subject's presence without becoming dramatically involved. Please note, as part of this discussion, that there is a range of medium shots—medium long, medium close—not just one length.

**Figure 8.7.** Long shots.

When the medium shot follows the long shot, it has the effect of narrowing the field of interest, focusing and heightening our attention to the subject on which the shot has narrowed.

When no other shot has been specifically indicated in a script, directors usually will choose medium shots.

**Figure 8.8.** Medium shots.

## Closeups

Closeups are the most penetrating, the most scrutinizing, and the most emphatic types of shot in visual stories. They get us the closest and most intimate looks at the subject matter.

In real life, getting close to something or someone can provoke intense reactions, from extreme pleasure to revulsion. Being very near heightens our reactions. As we move in close, we eliminate options; we eliminate chances for escape. We become involved, in a state of heightened awareness. Whatever we confront at this close range, we react to in a more intense way.

The closeup (sometimes also called a *tight shot*) creates this same reaction visually. The camera sees less of its surroundings than it does in a medium or long shot. The shot focuses on one subject. When it does that, its primary emotional effect is to convey intensity. As such, it becomes a very powerful tool in visual storytelling.

Possible closeups in our scene would be shots of the faces of either character, in which emotions might easily be read, or a shot of the phone, a character's hand picking up the phone or getting something out of a drawer in the table, some detail of the decor in the room—a portrait on the wall or a clock, emphasizing time. The specific closeups chosen from among these possibilities, of course, would be the ones that further the plot (Figure 8.9).

Closeups of people are commonly used to convey emotions and interior conflicts. Here is a situation frequently found in television news reporting: A reporter and cameraperson are covering a story in which a family's home has just been destroyed by fire. The camera opens with a wide shot showing the family with the charred remains of the house in the background, while the reporter asks the family: "What happened to your house?" The shot stays wide or medium while the basic facts of the story are presented. But when the reporter turns to questions that elicit the emotional responses of the victims—"What are you going to do now? How are you going to recover from the loss? What are your feelings?"—the camera shift to closeups—the faces of the victims, a doll clutched in the arms of a small child, and so on.

**Figure 8.9.** Closeups.

Closeups may also be used to channel the audience's attention to particular details that might be missed in a longer shot containing many different visual cues. This application, directing attention, is used in all types of productions but is particularly important in commercials and instructional scripts.

# CAMERA MOVEMENT

Our comments earlier regarding multiple points of view in a visual story referred primarily to the ability of film and video to provide rapid transitions from one camera position to another, an effect that is achieved in the editing process. It is also possible to change the viewing perspective *within* a single shot by moving the camera or zooming the lens. Several types of movement can be used. The most common are zooms and pans. Others include the dolly, the truck and the boom. Be careful, however, in writing these movements into a script. Too much camera movement will call attention to itself and distract from the message. Most changes in point of view should be accomplished in editing—cuts or dissolves from one camera position, distance and angle to another. The directors of live programs, where editing of course is not possible, may make greater use of camera movement but still will use cuts from one camera to another for most changes.

## Zooms

A *zoom* movement is accomplished by a special lens on a camera that permits changing the field of view continuously (either in, closer, or out, farther away) without losing focus during the movement.

A zoom-in has the effect of a change from a wide shot to a closeup, increasing the level of involvement and intensity. It literally pulls the audience into the scene. In addition, as the movement narrows the field of view, it directs the attention of the audience to those items which remain in view. There are now fewer items in the scene with which to deal, and these are seen in more detail; closer scrutiny is possible. And this focusing of attention is accomplished without losing the relationship between the larger scene and the detailed closeup, which might happen if, instead of a zoom, the sequence were to cut from long shot to closeup—that is, with a cut the audience might not be able to recall how the detail fits into the larger scene, but with a zoom the eye is drawn in a continuous motion from broader to narrower perspective.

A zoom-out provides the reverse. It establishes the detail first, then begins to reveal how that detail fits into a larger picture. And it pulls the audience away, psychologically, from the action, begins to disengage them emotionally, and sets the stage for the conclusion of the scene.

## Pans

A *pan* is accomplished by swinging the camera in an arc from its fixed position. The term is used for a horizontal sweep. A pan-type movement in the vertical plane is called a *tilt*.

A pan across an auditorium quickly establishes the size of the hall, the number of people present, and the level of movement or excitement involved. A pan may also follow a character across a room, or a car negotiating the twists of a mountain road. In the latter case the speed of the pan, which should match the speed of the car, imparts a sense of movement to the scene. If it's a fast-moving car, the need to hurry and the feeling of excitement are enhanced. In contrast, a slow-moving vehicle, and a slow pan, may suggest calm, deliberate, even reluctant movement.

Tilts can heighten the emotional impacts provided by the various vertical camera angles. From a neutral wide, eye-level shot, for example, a combination zoom-in and tilt up would dramatically increase the emotional level and the threat suggested by the subject of the shot.

Very rapid pans, called *swish pans*, which are so fast as to blur the action, accomplish a different purpose. They are transition devices, intended to separate two scenes or shots, yet at the same time maintain a relationship between them.

## Other Camera Movements

Several other types of camera movement can be used. We'll mention the three most common.

### Dolly

With this movement, the entire camera is moved closer to (*dolly in*) or back from (*dolly back*) the action. The word comes from the wheeled platform—a dolly—on which cameras are frequently mounted, but a hand-held camera walked into or back from a scene would provide the same effect. That is, it would provided it were held steady. The bobbing and jiggling of the hand-held camera, which originated with cinema vérité and early television news photography, now is used as a deliberate technique even when the camera can easily be kept steady. Audiences perceive a wobbly camera as adding "reality" or "immediacy" to a shot, but that's a stylistic consideration beyond the scope of this discussion.

A dolly has somewhat the same effect as a zoom, and has largely been replaced by the zoom, but they differ somewhat. The zoom makes a scene appear to move closer to the viewer. The dolly appears to move the viewer into the scene.

### Truck

This movement also involves the physical movement of the camera, horizontally and usually parallel to the action. It may, for example, be following a group of runners down a road, keeping a set distance and frame size by moving at the same speed as the runners. There is movement to the scene—action taking place—but a stable emotional relationship is maintained between the audience and that action.

### Boom

This is also called a *crane movement*. Many high angle shots are accomplished by placing the camera in a crane. When the crane is operated *during* the shot, the camera is physically moved in the vertical plane. As with the tilt, but even more emphatically, the emotional payload of the vertical camera angle may be manipulated by this movement.

## SEQUENCES OF SHOTS

So far we have discussed only individual shots. They are, of course, the essential building blocks of the video story, serving very much the same function that sentences do within a written essay or story. Each shot conveys a particular meaning and makes a specific, single statement. But a written story needs more than just a random series of sentences to be called a story. It needs organization. And so does a visual story. Individual shots must be put together in sequences that group the individual ideas into more complex patterns.

A sequence of shots is very much like a paragraph—it presents a series of statements which together make up a complete thought. The analogy between written paragraphs and visual scenes cannot be extended very far, however, because when you tell a story with pictures, the nuances, overtones, and implications of the actions you show are much more powerful, much deeper than they are with the written word.

Here are eight shots (Figure 8.10). Each has an individual meaning, and yet when they are placed together in order, each reinforces and adds meaning to the shot that comes next. To begin, the first man might strike us as a drug addict, just by the way he acts, and yet no direct statement was made to that effect. This perception is part of the rich visual subtext. The two people who enter the room might be there by accident. The gun on the table could be broken and not capable of firing. The room might remind us of another room we'd seen earlier in the story in which a person was killed, and so on.

The point is that with visual storytelling, the associations the members

**Figure 8.10.** Sequence of shots.
(1) Establishing shot: man looking out window of apartment; gun on table in foreground.
(2) Medium shot, low angle: two men burst into apartment.
(3) Closeup, low angle: man turns, shows surprise and fear.
(4) Closeup, high angle: gun on table; focuses attention, establishes gun as key element
in scene.

(5) Medium shot, low angle: men move toward camera.
(6) Medium shot, low angle: gun in foreground, man behind; he jumps forward.
(7) Closeup, low angle: man has gun, pointing.
(8) Medium shot: men are surprised, scared, move suddenly backward.

of the audience make as they follow the story are made quickly and cover a broad spectrum. Even visual information that is not consciously perceived by the viewer has an impact. The human eye makes hundreds of associations instantly each time a new image is shown. It picks up so much subtle information that if you were to try to use words to describe everything that *could* be happening in a sequence, it would take pages and pages.

Of course, as the writer of the script and the originator of its ideas, if you *need* to have some of these subsidiary ideas in your presentation, you will have to include them in the script, in character and setting descriptions.

## Juxtaposition of Shots

As an introduction to the grammar of visual sequences, you should understand two basic characteristics that affect the selection of shots to be placed next to each other.

First, everything in visual storytelling is relative. That is, the shot just before the one we are seeing has determined, to a great degree, our point of view for the one we are now seeing. And the shot we are now seeing will establish our point of view for the next one we see. We have already had one example of relativity regarding the distance of a camera shot. If we begin a scene with a long shot, then change our minds and precede that shot with an even longer one, the first long shot is not made any shorter in absolute terms, but it is shorter *relative* to the new, longer opening shot.

Second, visual storytelling makes extensive use of comparisons. Because one shot can quickly be cut next to another, the subject matter of the shots is quickly and easily compared. It is in that comparison that much of the meaning of the scene is derived.

One of the first persons to recognize these visual truths was the Russian filmmaker Lev Kuleshov. In a now classic demonstration, he created three film sequences. In the first, a shot of an actor's face preceded a shot of a plate of soup on a table; in the second, a shot of the actor was followed by a shot of a coffin in which lay a dead woman; and in the third, the face was juxtaposed to a shot of a little girl playing with a toy. The results were described by Kuleshov's associate, Vsevolod Pudovkin:

> When we showed the three combinations to an audience which had not been let into the secret the result was terrific. The public raved about the acting of the artist. They pointed out the heavy pensiveness of his mood over the forgotten soup, were touched and moved by the deep sorrow with which he looked on the dead woman, and admired the light, happy smile with which he surveyed the girl at play. But we knew that in all three cases the face was exactly the same.[1]

Kuleshov's demonstration established the fundamental principle of visual sequencing: The order in which you display pictures will directly affect the meaning those pictures will have for an audience.

The implications of Kuleshov's demonstration and other principles of film making that evolved from the early films by Pudovkin, Griffith, Eisenstein and others were set down in several books by Sergei Eisenstein. He developed a language that still forms the theoretical foundation for cinematic and video production. We recommend that you study his books if you intend to write extensively for visual media.

## Controlling Tension

Another consideration in the sequencing of shots is the control of the tension within the scene. Any good story, written or visual, builds and releases tension several times during the course of its telling. And the writers of expressive media which take place over a fixed time, such as a symphony, a ballet, a play, a movie or a television drama, are particularly concerned with tension.

As a general rule, the writer tries to make the flow of images reflect the natural tension points in the story. For example, a dramatic story about a celebrated jewel thief might have as its highest tension point his incredible break-in and theft of a highly guarded gem. The visual sequence should build to that point. If, on the other hand, the story is a news item about a convicted jewel thief, and the focus of the story is his release from jail, then that would be the point to which to build the tension. In either case, we look to the message of the story to suggest the proper point or points toward which to build the tension.

Generally speaking, closeups contain more tension than longer shots, and low angle shots contain more tension than high angle shots. Consequently it would seem that whenever you wanted to create tension, you would include closeups and lower angles, and when you wanted to release tension, you would change to longer and more neutral eye-level shots. This is generally correct, but with experience you will learn to sequence shots so that the energy associated with tension buildup and tension release will be transferred to specific ideas, regardless of the angles and distances of the shots.

## Building a Scene

Just as in a sentence, where the choice and order of words will determine the final character of the thought, the choice and sequence of the shots will determine the visual statement of the scene. There is no single right way to express an idea visually; there are many ways, each with its own subtle differences. For the sake of brevity, however, the following exercise explains some of the more obvious.

In this scene (Figure 8.11), the first idea we want to express is confrontation, the confrontation between the house and the man. The simplest form this scene can take is shown in the first three shots of this sequence.

### Shot 1

As a general rule, the opening shot in a scene will be an establishing long shot. It orients the viewer to the area in which the action will take place during that scene. In this case, we have chosen a very high angle. Why? It works with the long shot in establishing an opening position. Recall the feel-

**Figure 8.11.** Shots in a scene.
(1) Long shot, high angle: man in foreground, house on hill in background.
(2) Low angle: man looking at house.
(3) Medium shot, medium angle: house.

ing you got when you sat at the top of a children's slide at a playground, then slid down. That movement is similar to the relationship between the opening shot and the second shot in this sequence. We are propelled from a high, long shot (dissociation) into a low closeup (involvement in the action).

### Shot 2

The second shot is a low angle closeup. It is the opposite of the opening shot, and it maximizes the contrast between the idea of dissociation (shot 1) and the idea of involvement (shot 2). It is an emphasis shot. It doesn't further the action; the character doesn't do anything new. Instead, it emphasizes the personality of the main character and how he is reacting to his situation. Since the main idea we want to express in this sequence is that of confrontation, even though the second shot doesn't further the action, its characteristics—the low angle, and being in so close—support the idea of confrontation.

### Shot 3

The third shot follows logically from the second. It is a natural response to several issues the second shot raises. For example, the second shot asks the question, "What is this man looking at?" The third shot answers that question, and shows us that he is looking at the house. We have chosen an eye-level medium shot of the house to "describe" it for the audience. We might have used a low angle shot to present the house in a more dramatic, malevolent way. If the house were haunted, we would clearly emphasize the house by giving it the low angle. But in this situation such a shot would perhaps be excessive, overstated, too exaggerated.

Also, by giving our hero the "dramatic" shot in the sequence, we shift the emphasis slightly toward him and away from the house. As this shot flashes on the screen, the audience should feel a sense of resolution and of completion. With the introduction of the third shot, we have answered all the questions the first two shots asked and completed our first idea, that of confrontation. We have finished our first sequence. And we did it in a way that is formally correct.

What have we learned? We can say that it is acceptable to open a scene with a long shot, that generally each shot should offer a new bit of information, but that the information it offers does not have to further the action. It can instead be about a character's personality, the setting, or anything else that will enhance the story.

When a relationship is set up between two subjects, in this case the man and the house, cross-cutting between them will strengthen the relationship. It will also keep the relationship balanced.

Now, look at a different ordering of these same three shots (Figure 8.12).

**Figure 8.12.** Shots in a different order.
(1) Low angle: man looking at house.
(2) Long shot, high angle: man in foreground, house on hill in background.
(3) Medium shot, medium angle: house.

### Shot 1

The opening shot of a scene does not *have* to be a long shot. When we use a tight shot as the opening shot, the emphasis changes. The original sequence was organized to stress the idea of confrontation. This ordering, however, stresses suspense and mystery, and the opening shot is primarily responsible for this. By opening with the tight shot, we are immediately thrust into the action and our curiosity is high. Since we are deprived of the orienting, establishing shot, we immediately want to know, "What is going on?" The longer the shot is held, the more the suspense mounts.

### Shot 2

The long shot answers the question by showing us what he's looking at, and in so doing, breaks the initial suspense. But by showing us new information—he's standing by a car parked some distance from the house—new questions are raised—not so much about him, but about his purpose. We have shifted the suspense away from the man to the situation. So far this arrangement of shots is presenting the information in an interesting, balanced way.

### Shot 3

In this ordering, shot 3 does not fit well. Each shot should offer some new bit of information, and this shot does not. The sequence could end after shot 2. Not only has the information of the sequence been completed with the second shot, but by changing from closeup to wide shot, we have reduced the tension and signaled the end of the scene.

## Changing Scenes

When a change of direction or a new idea is introduced in a story, that is a transitional point. It is the appropriate place to start a new scene. That change of direction will be preceded by the release of tension (Figure 8.13).

**Figure 8.13.** Buildup of tension.

In the story we have been developing, the first scene contains the three shots of the man's confrontation with the house. Another scene begins with shot 4.

The number of shots in a scene can vary from two or three to at least ten, or possibly even more. There is no ideal number of shots, just as there is no ideal melody or ideal poem. Each sequence has to be tailor-made to express its particular message. What might take four or five pages to write might easily be said in a three-shot sequence. What might strike you as a particularly rich though brief written idea can be expanded into quite a long visual scene. However, if a scene runs fifteen or sixteen shots, say, without releasing tension, it probably has run too long.* Without the frequent building and releasing of tension, the audience will become bored. For a story to have life, it has to have pace (a concept we discussed at length in Chapter 6), and its pace is to a large degree created by the manipulation of tension and tension release. To control pace, control the speed and frequency of the changes in scenes.

The following group of scenes (Figure 8.14) illustrates the use of the concepts we have been discussing. It also introduces some new ones. We'll continue with the story we have begun; picking up the analysis with the fourth shot, which begins a new scene. This sequence of shots presents a new piece of information in the story—namely, "The man has a bomb in the trunk of his car." The scene will have to express the idea visually. It starts with a wide shot. Although it is really a medium shot, it is the widest shot in this scene

---

* We are using the terms *scene* and *sequence* somewhat interchangeably, but in a filmmaker's vocabulary a *scene* is a series of shots which the viewer perceives as taking place in the same location during a brief period of time, and a *sequence* is a larger unit consisting of a number of related scenes.

**Figure 8.14.**
(1) Long shot, high angle: man in foreground, house on hill in background.
(2) Low angle: man looking at house.
(3) Medium shot, medium angle: house.

(4) High angle, medium shot: man is getting something from back of car.
(5) Closeup, low angle: spy's face from trunk's point of view.
(6) Closeup, high angle: time bomb.

(7) Closeup, high angle: man sets his watch.
(8) Rear shot, long lens, low angle: man is framed by house in background; he walks
toward house.
(9) Low shot, low angle, wide-angle lens: man is silhouetted in doorway; he enters house.

and as such it helps separate this scene from shot 3, which concluded scene
1. Even more important in separating the scenes, however, is the camera
angle. In 3, we are looking straight on to the house, and in 4 we're clearly
looking down. Even though both shots are medium shots, they are completely different in point of view, and this shift signals the beginning of a new
sequence.

Shot 5 is a tight shot. We are developing the second sequence as we did
the first, by moving the camera closer, a standard approach. Shot 6 shows

  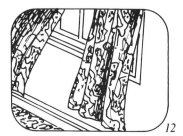

(10) Low angle, closeup: man looks around.
(11) Medium shot, high angle: chair.
(12) Medium shot, high angle: window with drapes blowing in the wind.

(13) Closeup, low angle: man spots something and is looking at it closely.
(14) Closeup, high angle: man holds book.
(15) High angle, over-the-shoulder shot: someone is watching our spy.

(16) Low angle closeup: he's watching intently.
(17) Medium shot, high angle: our spy continues to work.
(18) Extreme closeup, low angle: he's getting madder.

us what the man is working on—a time bomb. It's a tight shot, again from a high angle, and it simply extends the development started in 5 by moving the camera in even more. It focuses the attention of the audience on the bomb.

The scene ends here. The most important reason for ending at this point is that finally seeing the bomb—what the man was looking at—completes what the scene set out to say. It is also the third shot in the series, and three-shot patterns form natural, complete groups.

Shot 7 introduces a new idea, and confirms that shot 6 ended the previous sequence. It also heightens the suspense which this story is building by the sudden cut to a closeup (without an introductory wide shot) of the man's wristwatch. Although shot 7 introduces a new idea, it does not begin a new scene. Notice that shots 7 and 8 represent completely different ideas, each of which is expressed in a single shot. We call these *passing shots*—that is, they get us quickly through steps in the story we don't want to spend much time with. If we wanted to spend more time here and develop shots 7 and 8 into full scenes, we could. On the other hand, we could eliminate these shots and go directly to shot 9.

Shot 9 begins the third scene. When there are distinct differences between the last shot of a scene and the first shot of the new scene, it will be easy for the audience to follow the story. Compare shot 9 to shot 8. They are different, opposite in almost every way. Shot 8 calls for a telephoto lens, with its flattened perspective; shot 9 calls for a wide-angle lens that deepens perspective. In shot 8, the man is in the foreground, with the house in the background; in shot 9, the opposite is true. Shot 8 is outside the house; shot 9 is inside.

Pointing out obvious differences like these and suggesting you use the same techniques may seem to overstate the case, possibly even overstate the story. But when you consider that each of these images will be seen by the audience for only a very short time, their effect is much more subtle.

Shot 9, a wide shot, also orients the viewer to the new surroundings. Shot 10 then directs the attention to the man, who by now we may perceive as being a spy. We see that he is looking around. Notice that we have chosen a low-angle shot rather than an eye-level shot. It makes our spy look formidable and dangerous. However, there is an additional reason for this which we will deal with in a moment.

Shots 11 and 12 show us what he's looking at (the same relationship we had between shots 2 and 3, and shots 5 and 6). But we've included two shots here and not just one to get across the idea that he's looking around the whole room rather than just at one thing.

Shot 13 is an extremely tight shot, and now it shows the spy looking at something in particular, no longer just "looking around." What makes us feel that he is looking at something in particular, that somehow his situation has changed since we saw him in shot 10? Two things contribute to the change. First, his screen direction has changed. Originally he was looking off screen left; now he's looking off screen right. Second, he's looking down, as if he's seen something, rather than looking up as in shot 10. We've taken the basic idea of shot 10, and by changing both screen direction and camera distance, totally changed its meaning. Notice also that shot 13 is from a extremely low angle.

Shot 14 shows us what he's looking at. By now, you should have noticed the association that says if you use a shot showing someone looking at something, then you should include an accompanying shot showing what is being looked at. Shot 14 is also an extremely tight shot, so you can read the label "Top Secret" on the book. It also increases the tension.

Shot 15 begins the fourth scene, and introduces a new character. Once again, as the transition between scenes we have scene 3 ending with a tight shot, and scene 4 beginning with a wide shot, a standard transition. Notice that in the first shot of this scene, we immediately set up a visual relationship between the new character and the spy; the new character is larger than the spy, and thus more powerful and dangerous.

Up to this point in the story, we have reinforced the idea of the spy's powerful stature by showing him in low angle shots. Now we will switch the audience's association of power from the spy to the new character. We will show the new character with low angle shots and make him bigger in the frame than the spy. The spy will be shown from a high angle and behind, making him look weak. This shift may seem obvious to us, as we discuss it here, but during the actual viewing of these shots in the context of a story, the audience would feel the shift in power without consciously recognizing why. During this scene we build the tension by constantly moving in, cutting to progressively tighter shots of each character until we reach shot 18, where a confrontation is now inevitable.

We leave it to you to finish the storyboard of this plot.


## Horizontal Camera Angles

A selection of different camera angles in the horizontal plane does not carry the emotional implications of vertical angles. Horizontal camera angles are important only in maintaining sequence and consistency in visual point of view. They show relationships—relative positions—of the persons and objects in a scene.

Seldom are writers concerned with specific horizontal sequences, but you may be if you also work as a reporter or director in TV news. There you should be aware of these uses and cautions regarding horizontal shot combinations.


### Reverse Angle

This technique is most often seen in interviews. The main focus of attention is on the interviewee, while he or she answers a question. Then, when the reporter asks the next question, the camera angle shifts to the reverse angle, showing the reporter full-face. (Often these shots also show the second person in the scene, with the camera looking over the person's shoulder; consequently these shots are frequently called *over-the-shoulder shots*. See Figure 8.15)

The reverse angle is also used to give some feeling of size and shape to an event. At a political convention, the main focus would be on the speakers at the rostrum, but reverse angles shot from the rostrum toward the crowd would show the reactions of the audience to the speaker. Similarly, in a parade, shots of the spectators would be reverse angles. When a reverse angle

**Figure 8.15.** Reverse angles.

is used this way, to pick up images other than the main action in a scene, it is also called a *cutaway*.

### *Line of Action*

(Other terminology used to describe this rule is the *180° rule*, or *principal action axis*.) Generally speaking, all shots in a single scene should be taken from one side of a line drawn through the middle of the scene. Figure 8.6, seen from above, is diagrammed in Figure 8.16. The camera (or cameras, depending on whether this program is shot "live-style" with multiple cameras, or shot by one camera, recorded and the shots edited into a sequence) can be moved about to get a variety of angles, so long as it (they) stay on the same side of the line of action. Even reverse angles will have to be slightly less than 180° apart, so they don't cross this line. A direct cut to a shot taken from the opposite side of the line would confuse the audience, as the characters will suddenly seem to have reversed their positions in the scene.

Sometimes this rule can be broken. Professional football telecasts now use occasional shots taken from the opposite side of the field, but so far at least the announcers have been careful to explain that it is an opposite angle shot, or a graphic has appeared on the screen stating "Reverse Angle," so the audience will understand why the player who moments ago was running from right to left is now seen running from left to right. Also, as performers move about in a scene, the line shifts; camera shots can now move with the new line. Cutaways—to a picture on the wall, for example—also break the visual continuity of the scene and permit further shots to be taken from a different axis.

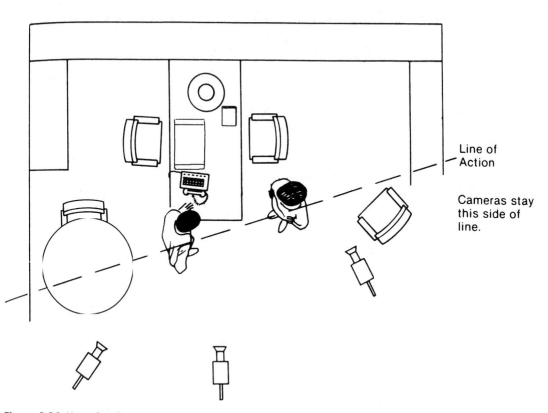

**Figure 8.16.** Line of action.

# TRANSITIONS

Another part of visual grammar is the means used to provide transitions between camera shots. In recent years the increasing sophistication of the switcher/fader units used in television have added all sorts of image splitting, wipes, page turning, spinning, and other tricks for the manipulation of transitions. We couldn't attempt to catalogue all of them here even if we wished to. But there are several standard transitions audiences have come to associate with certain meanings.

## Cut

This is the most used transition; a direct, immediate change from one camera position to another. Many films and video programs are put together using nothing but cuts. They are the simplest and least expensive transitions and are readily understood by audiences.

Most cuts are unobtrusive, natural transitions. They blend the two adjoining shots. These are *match cuts.* Another type of cut is the *jump cut.* Depending upon the circumstances, and on how careful directors are in using the terminology, you may receive instructions that say either: Don't use a jump cut under any circumstances, or: Use jump cuts to provide deliberately jarring transitions that throw the two shots into sharp contrast. For example, in recording a speech by a public official, and then editing that speech for broadcast, you have two quotes you wish to place back to back. If the two camera shots have been taken from the same distance and angle, and you splice them next to each other, you will have a jump cut. The speaker's head and face will not be in precise alignment in the two shots and will seem to jump unexplainedly between the two shots. You will need to insert some other material, at least briefly, between the two shots.

In a different situation, however, you may want to cut without explanation from one scene to something quite different. The unanticipated shift, although momentarily confusing to the audience, heightens curiosity.

## Dissolve

The dissolve is a slower, softer transition. It gradually blends two images by showing both shots simultaneously for a brief moment. While the first shot is fading out, the second one is getting stronger, until the first shot fades out completely. Dissolves allow more time for the audience to adjust and react to the transition, and they carry more significance to the audience than a cut. They also suggest that a relationship does exist between the two scenes. One common relationship might be that the two scenes are taking place simultaneously. Other relationships might be that a character remembers a former event, and the dissolve then is the "flashback" to the earlier time; or it may be a means of going into a person's mind for a "stream of consciousness" sequence.

## Fade

The *fade,* or *fade to black,* is an even more dramatic, stronger transition than a dissolve. During a fade, the scene gradually disappears into blackness, usually with an accompanying fading of the sound track. A fade-out or fade to black is used at the end of a scene to give a particularly "final" feeling. For a brief second, that audience is staring at a blank screen, hearing no sound, and feeling a definite sense of the story being stopped.

Because fade-outs produce this reaction, they are extraordinarily strong means of transition. They are most appropriately used to break the flow in a narrative or to string together several scenes that are to be seen as separate incidents. Often fades are used to indicate a major passage of time, change of place, or psychological shift in a character. The NBC network series *Law and Order* makes effective use of fades to black, ending many scenes in black and then inserting a white graphic title of the location and date of the upcoming scene before fading up from black to the new scene.

Fades and dissolves can vary in length, depending on the effect wanted. In a script the length will be written as a certain number of frames. Using the U.S. standard of 30 frames per second, a quick dissolve or fade would be about 10 frames (⅓ second), while a very slow fade or dissolve might last up to 120 frames (4 seconds).

Usually a fade to black in one scene is accompanied by a fade up from black to begin the next scene, but it is also permissible to cut to the next scene from black. (Video scripts use the terms "fade up" and "fade down," or just "fade"; film scripts use "fade in" and "fade out" to describe the same techniques.)

## Other Transitions

Of the many transition devices that can be used, four more deserve brief mention.

### Defocusing

The deliberate racking of a camera lens out of focus provides another way to change shots. Frequently the flashback and stream of consciousness transitions use a combination of dissolve and defocusing (or some other technique for blurring the image, such as smearing grease on the camera lens).

Defocus-refocus transitions can also be used for time or time and place changes. Defocus a scene on a street in a frontier village at noon, then refocus on the same scene with the lighting—the sun—at a different angle. It's now sunset; 6 hours have passed. Or defocus on the clock face of Big Ben with the hands at 10:30; refocus on a closeup of the hero's wristwatch at 5:00—a change in time and place.

### Swish Pan

We mentioned this camera technique earlier, in the discussion of camera movement. In order to prepare the audience for future action, the camera may at the end of a shot rapidly swish across the scene, so rapidly in fact that the movement is blurred. At the beginning of the next scene (say, for example, that an actor is leaving scene 1 and will next be seen entering a different location), a swish pan will end with the camera focused on the door through which the actor will now enter. In the editing, the two swish movements will be placed together to give a continuous blur. The emotional effect of the transition is that the actor has left scene 1 and arrived at scene 2 with the same sense of urgency, intensity, and purpose. If that is not the effect wanted, then use some other transition device.

### Wipe

A *wipe* is a transitional effect used often in television. It uses electronic techniques to accomplish the effects of either a cut or a dissolve, depending on the circumstances. When used within a scene, for example as a change of camera angle shot within a musical number, the wipe helps maintain the continuity wanted in that situation. It functions much like a cut, but not quite as abruptly. When used to conclude a scene, the wipe acts like a dissolve—one scene replaces another without any break in the continuity. There is an impression created that one scene has pushed the other off the screen, that the first scene may actually be continuing, even though we, the audience, cannot see it any longer. A wipe may move from left to right, right to left, top to bottom, or from the center out like the ripples on water caused by a thrown stone. The shapes of wipes are virtually endless, limited only by the complexity of the electronic switcher used to create them.

### Digital Video Effects

Very sophisticated electronic transition devices are available at the networks and at most production houses and stations. These devices, known as digital visual effects (DVE) generators, permit all sorts of split-screen and multiple-image effects, electronic focusing, color manipulation and wipes of many types. If you choose to use these effects in a script, make sure the DVE at the facility you are using can accommodate the effect you want, write DVE in the video column, and describe the effect to be generated. These techniques can be employed simply for their visual attention-getting capability, as in many commercials, or they can further the action of or add emotional force to a story. They function, however, only as variations on the basic transitional techniques we have discussed.

## WRITING TO PICTURES

When writing fictional programs for television, both the audio and video are completely under the control of the creative team. Experienced writers and directors will see that the narration and dialogue, and the pictures, support each other. Adjustments can be made during rehearsal if necessary to ensure that support. But the writing of narration to accompany informative content, such as the collected and edited video for a news story, a documentary or a corporate presentation, is quite a different task, particularly when the video is not under the writer-narrator's control. News and documentary producers talk of this task as the problem of writing to pictures. This can be a particularly troublesome concern for beginning writers.

In the simplest and broadest terms, the question is, What should be said to accompany pictures on the screen? Here is how one documentary producer approaches this question:

It is bad technique to describe in words exactly what is seen on the screen. . . . On the other hand, it is nearly as bad to refer to things that have nothing at all to do with what is on the screen. . . . If the picture is self-evident, no words are needed. But very frequently there are many things that the audience wants to know that are not clear from the visuals alone. *Where* is the scene; *who* are the people in it; *when* is it taking place; *how* does the technical process work? These are questions that commentary should answer, subject to one proviso. Does the audience need to know for the purpose of the film? It is possible to spoil a film by telling the audience too much. If they are likely to *want* to know all these things, well and good—if not, silence is golden.[2]

Using this broad principle, a reporter's narration, for example, should support the visuals in the story but not interfere with the powerful impact of the live or edited picture. If the story is coming live from the scene of a fire, the reporter need not say: "The flames are leaping high above the building. Fire crews are laying hoses and trying to get control of the situation." The picture shows the flames and firefighters (or should, if the camera crew is doing its job properly), and the phrase "trying to get control" is obvious and therefore meaningless. (On the other hand, if in an interview with a fire chief you learn that the fire is uncontrollable and they are going to have to allow it to burn itself out, that would be a fact worth reporting.)

As another example, consider a corporate program explaining a manufacturing process. Here there are more time and opportunity to match the narration with whatever video has been shot or to shoot and edit to match the script. If the narrator's script is written to say: "The key to this process is the smooth running operation of the eccentric cam which drives the shaft," then viewers need to see, at that point, the eccentric cam and its shaft, not some other part of the machinery, a wide shot of the factory, or even the talking head of the narrator. If the cam is hidden in the machinery, then perhaps an animated graphic will be needed to make the point visually.

Audio should support, amplify and expand upon the picture and add detail that cannot readily be seen. It should not be redundant, merely repeating what is visually obvious.

A related concern is whether narration is to be on- or off-camera. In several other chapters we have shown examples of news, documentary and corporate production that use both techniques, and we have considered the relative merits of each. The preceding examples, the reporter at the fire and the narration accompanying the eccentric cam, assumed that the narration was off-camera (also known as voice-over), at least at that point in the story. During other portions of the program, the narrator may be seen as he or she speaks. On-camera narration is also called a "talking head," and some producers use that term in a derogatory sense. (We consider that question again in Chapter 15.) But TV news departments want viewers to see their reporters at the scene of a story, so most stories include "stand-up" shots of the reporter speaking directly to the camera/viewer.

The important point is that in preparing scripts make sure it is clear from the context, or by writing specific instructions, whether on- or off-camera narration is intended and when shifts are to be made from one to the other.

## WRITING VISUAL CUES

As we have said, in real life most often the writer will not be expected to provide detailed camera directions, except perhaps in writing commercials (and drawing storyboards), and in preparing news stories in the field. But in the writing of assignments for critique in a class, you will have to give sufficient detail so that your instructor can visualize what you have in mind. To the extent that you will need detailed cues, you should use the terminology we have introduced in this chapter—high angle, long shot, dissolve, and so on—along with sufficient descriptive language to make your instructions clear.

A complete visual cue contains five parts:

1. Transition—cut, dissolve, fade, etc. If no transition is written, a cut is assumed.

2. Angle—high, eye level, low, etc. If no angle is designated, normal eye-level angle is assumed.

3. Distance—long shot, 2-shot, CU, etc.

4. Subject—what the camera is focused on.

5. Direction—what is happening in the scene, possibly including camera movement.

Simple examples include:

CUT TO CU GEORGE: GRIMACES

DISSOLVE TO MS GEORGE: PAN LEFT TO FOLLOW

Other cues, taken from scripts reproduced elsewhere in this text, include:

MEDIUM SHOT--BERNIE ON LEVEE (RIVER IN BACKGROUND)

FADE IN LS OF ROOM DARK WITH SHADOWS. BABY'S CRIB IN FOREGROUND. BACK OF ROCKER IN FRONT OF FIREPLACE IN BG. DOLLY IN SLOWLY FOR MCU OF BACK OF ROCKER.

```
CU--BABY--DAY

EXTERIOR: CLOSEUP ON GATE. ZOOM OUT AS GATE BEGINS TO
OPEN; CAMERA STARTS DOWN DRIVEWAY PAST SADDLE ROCK SIGN.
```

## CONCLUSION

Visual grammar is not a science; it is rather a codification of principles surrounding an art form. There are people who try to define the phenomena of visual communication in specific terms (part of the study of signs and symbols called *semiotics*). Our purpose has been much more general. We have presented some principles you can use to make simple visual statements. We have suggested how camera angles, camera distance, and camera movements can convey and reinforce certain emotional and intellectual messages. Audiences respond not only to the words and the aural tone of a message, they are deeply influenced by relationships, settings, needs, and behaviors they perceive visually.

Not only are audiences affected by single visual images or shots, but as we have also shown, they gather meaning from the juxtaposition of shots, the sequence in which shots are presented, and from the types of transitions used to separate scenes and sequences.

Using all these principles, you will have a basis on which to make artistic choices. These principles will help you intensify and sustain audience interest in your script when it finally makes it to the video screen. Understanding visual grammar and writing your requirements carefully and accurately into the script will also give you better control over the visual side of your script when it goes into production.

**Exercises**

1. Complete the story used to explain visual sequencing. Make up any ending you want, and take as many frames and scenes as you like to finish it, with each frame representing one camera shot. Describe each shot, as we did in the analysis, by writing under each storyboard frame the specific camera angle, camera distance, action taking place in the shot, and anything else you feel is necessary to explain what is happening. Also, explain *why* you have made the selection of shots as you have. Justify in the same way that we did the remaining shots in your story.

2. Write (draw) a television commercial in storyboard form, again with attention to visual shots and the development of the series of shots. For a commercial to be effective as well as visually interesting, you should incorporate into the commercial other principles from other chapters, if possible, such as persuasive motivation (Chapter 9), and suggestions on

the structure of commercial messages (Chapter 11). But the main thrust of this exercise should be the choice of camera angle, distance and possibly movement, and the juxtaposition of shots and transitions—the primary emphases of this chapter.

**Notes**

1. From V. I. Pudovkin, *Film Technique*, 1929. Quoted in Karel Reisz, *The Technique of Film Making*, 2d ed. (London: Focal Press, 1954), p. 31.
2. W. Hugh Baddeley, *The Technique of Documentary Film Production* (New York: Hastings House, 1963), p. 192. Excerpt reprinted by permission of Focal Press and the author.

**Further Reading**

From an extensive list of titles on video and film theory and technique we have selected the following as providing the best foundation or being the most directly useful. Some of the titles listed as references for video production (in Chapter 4) may also be useful in expanding your knowledge in this area.

Among the "original" sources of film theory are these reissued editions of Sergei Eisenstein's works:

Eisenstein, Sergei. *Film Form.* New York: Harcourt Brace Jovanovich, 1969.
———. *The Film Sense.* New York: Harcourt Brace Jovanovich, 1969.

and these early titles, no longer in print:

Kracauer, Siegfried. *Theory of Film.* New York: Oxford University Press, 1965.
Pudovkin, Vladimir I. *Film Technique.* 1929.

Other recommended titles on film, television or visual grammar in general are

Colby, Lewis, and Tom Greer. *The TV Director/Interpreter,* revised ed. Mamaroneck, NY: Hastings House, 1990.
Dondis, Donis A. *A Primer of Visual Literacy.* Cambridge, MA: MIT Press, 1973.
Morgan, John, and Peter Welton. *See What I Mean? An Introduction to Visual Communication,* 2nd ed. New York: Routledge, 1992.
Reisz, Karel, and Gavin Millar. *The Technique of Film Editing,* 2nd enlarged ed. Stoneham, MA: Focal, 1968.
Zettl, Herbert. *Sight, Sound, Motion: Applied Media Aesthetics,* 2nd ed. Belmont, CA: Wadsworth, 1990.

## PART 3

# Sponsors, Purposes, Audiences: The Business of Broadcasting

In Chapter 2 we outlined the various components of the communication process as they apply to broadcasting. We promised to return to two very important but sometimes neglected aspects of that process. The first of these is the role of purpose. Why do broadcast organizations, including stations, networks, advertising agencies and their client companies, and individuals, including individual audience members, spend money to put programs and announcements on the air? Obviously, writers must understand these purposes in order to write effectively for their employers and clients. The concepts related to purpose, including sponsorship, profit mak-

ing and persuasion, are considered in Chapter 9.

Those who pay to broadcast programs and announcements do so in order to reach and persuade audiences. So we need, also, to consider in some detail the role played by those who watch and listen. Definitions related to audiences, techniques of audience measurement, and viewer/listener gratifications are in Chapter 10. But the ideas presented in both chapters are very closely related.

If you, as a student, have had no professional experience in broadcasting, you will need to study these aspects of the process and their impact upon production and writing, in order to make sense of the sometimes confusing demands placed upon writers by the industry.

# Sponsors and Their Purposes: Persuasion

**W**riting for the broadcast media is not an activity in and of itself. Programs and announcements are placed on the air to accomplish the purposes of those who pay for that privilege. To write effective, successful scripts, you must understand why some individuals and corporations invest in the facilities of broadcasting—stations, cable franchises, etc.—and why other corporations are willing to pay to create programs and to insert advertisements on stations, networks and cable channels. You cannot afford to be ignorant of management and programming, because the content, sequence, form and style of your scripts are directly shaped by the commercial decisions made by advertisers, managers and programmers. What, then, are the purposes that dictate the actions of broadcasting's "originators"?

When you finish this chapter, you will be able to

- identify the organizations that operate and support the broadcast media and track the flow of financial support within the industry,

- appreciate the importance of profit making to those organizations,

- understand the importance of persuasion as a fundamental purpose behind the actions of broadcast media organizations,

- recognize persuasive appeals in broadcast copy,

- use those appeals in your own scripts, and

- recognize and use these important terms and concepts:

| | |
|---|---|
| advertiser | institutional advertising |
| availabilities | network |
| barter advertising | participation advertising |
| basic cable | persuasive appeals |
| cost-per-thousand (CPM) | premium-pay cable |

profitability

program advertising

public broadcasting

sponsors and sponsorship

spots

sustaining program

tiering

underwriting

The basic purposes served by a media system within a society may be found in detail in texts that discuss media and society. That discussion includes the relationship between media and government, between media and social institutions such as family, church, and school, and between media and individuals. These are important concepts for any professional in the industry, including writers, but they go far beyond our intent in this book. Some text recommendations in this area are included in the Further Reading section at the end of the chapter.

We can note, to begin our chapter, that these basic purposes will depend in large part on the social-governmental-economic system in which the media operate. In authoritarian societies, a government-controlled media system might use its persuasive power to convince audiences to support the state. In our democratic society, with its competitive, free-enterprise economic system, the relationships between those who use the system (by viewing and listening to programs) and those who pay for the system are quite complex. Without going into the details of programming strategy or sales practice, we'll try to make sense out of that complexity.

## SPONSORSHIP OF PROGRAMS

Up to this point we have used the term *originator* to refer to people and agencies involved in the preparation and distribution of messages. As we noted in Chapter 2, origination involves both the creative roles of writing, directing, producing and so on, and the financial support for those activities.

We now want to discuss the advertising-programming aspect of origination separately from the creative, and to do so, we introduce a new term, or rather we redefine an old term that has become badly misused. We will use the word *sponsor* to refer to individuals or, more commonly, organizations that have a financial interest in the content of broadcasting. Programming costs money, and the success of programming efforts depends on satisfying the suppliers of the money. In commercial broadcasting the money comes primarily from advertisers, but the relationships between program content and advertisers are complex, and we'll consider several variations. In public broadcasting, program underwriters, various levels of government, foundations and individual members and pledgees all contribute.

By this definition, stations, networks and cable system operators are also included as sponsors, because they are required to invest in some way in every program they distribute. Also included are those agencies which supply public service announcements and, in some circumstances, audiences themselves. Someone must pay, in some form—money, time, effort—for every bit of content that appears. Who, then, are the agencies making those payments? What do they want in return for their contributions? Here are the most common sponsors, but as the industry continues to change, new forms of sponsorship and additional purposes will undoubtedly appear.

## The Advertiser as Sponsor

Broadcasters tend to use the terms *sponsor* and *advertiser* interchangeably. We are attempting, however, to differentiate between the two. We want to use *advertiser* in its limited, but correct, definition to refer to that situation when a person or firm purchases time for placement of an advertising message. The advertiser is, of course, a sponsor, but advertisers are by no means the only sponsors.

The advertiser's financial stake is, first, the cost of airtime purchased for the presentation of a commercial. That purchase might be for only a single announcement, or for an extended campaign of spots on a number of different stations and programs, or the purchase of a block of time to present an

**Figure 9.1.** Copyright 1981 Ziggy and Friends, Inc. Dist. by Universal Press Syndicate. Reprinted with permission. All rights reserved.

entire program. In most cases, the advertiser also pays for the production (prerecording) of the commercial message (although often radio stations will produce simple commercials without additional charge). And the advertiser may pay an advertising agency to design the commercial and determine its best placement on the air. For a major advertiser, this combination of costs—airtime, production and research and media buying—can run to many millions of dollars a year.

The costs of advertising can be justified if the audience members who are exposed to that advertising can be persuaded to do what the advertiser wants done, which is usually the purchase of a product or service. So we might generalize that an advertiser's purpose is to increase or maintain sales. However, most commercials do not attempt to sell merchandise directly. Rather, they are intended to accomplish other, more indirect, purposes related to sales—such as getting the customer into the store or reminding him or her of the brand name of the product to be purchased. So we might more accurately say that broadcast advertising is intended to *help* in the sales of products or services. We'll have more on this point in later chapters.

Advertisers can have other purposes as well. For example, an electric power utility company that operates as a regulated monopoly in its community really does not have to sell its product. But it may wish to persuade its customers to modify their behavior in other ways. It may want to use its advertising to conduct a campaign on energy conservation or it may want to improve its public image in the community so that when it next asks for a rate increase, its customers will be sympathetic to that request. This type of advertising is known in the industry as *institutional advertising.*

Yet another slightly different purpose for paid advertising is represented by political campaigns. Their purposes are to obtain votes for a candidate or for or against a political proposition.

The relationship between advertisers and the stations and networks that carry their advertising can be very confusing. Creative advertising executives and media salespersons continue to find new ways to buy and sell advertising time, subject to changes in both regulation and the economic climate. We briefly consider three major ways that advertisers and media outlets work together, but variations abound.

### Program Advertising

Under this pattern a single advertiser purchases a block of time from a station or network for the presentation of a program, and includes within that program commercial messages advertising the product or products of that company. This was really the only method by which advertising was sold during the heyday of network radio in the 1930s and 1940s and the early period of television in the 1950s.

In program advertising the client is all important. Audience attraction, although important in exposing the commercial messages to large numbers of people, is secondary to satisfying the client. In early radio, instances existed where a program stayed on the air even with a small audience simply because the program's content satisfied the whims of its supporter, the client-advertiser.

Program advertising also makes it possible to integrate program and commercial content. In earlier times that integration was restricted by both regulation and industry practices, which limited the amount of program time that could be devoted to commercial material, but frequently the advertiser's name appeared as part of the program's title, and program talent delivered the commercials.

This traditional relationship between advertiser and program is seldom seen anymore on network schedules. There only a few program sponsors remain. One of them is Hallmark Cards, which still occasionally sponsors the *Hallmark Hall of Fame* series of prestigious dramas. But in other day-parts and on cable the practice flourishes. Some daytime soap operas are still sponsored by single companies. Fully paid religious programs are another example of program advertising.

A more recent form which is similar is the program-length commercial, also known as an "infomercial" and by other less flattering names. We discuss this form in parts of several later chapters. For many years this type of program was prohibited by the FCC, but the relaxation of commercial rules now permits this practice. Here, as in program advertising, an advertiser purchases a block of time, then proceeds to use the entire period for an extended pitch on behalf of a product or service, using talk-show or documentary techniques to sell the item to the audience. Kitchen appliances, money investment schemes and vacation travel packages are among the product categories that are sold using this approach.

Note, too, that portions of programs may also be sponsored, such as the weather segment in a newscast, or a quarter of a football game. There, however, the practice begins to merge into our next category, participation advertising.

### Participation Advertising

When television took over from radio as the dominant medium of home entertainment, and as the cost of producing programs increased substantially in the 1960s, advertisers became very nervous about spending large sums to sponsor program series, some of which turned out to be failures. They moved away from program advertising and toward what is now the most common practice on both television and radio—*participation advertising*.

With participation advertising, programs are designed not by advertisers, but by the stations or networks themselves (or by independent producers who sell their programs to the stations or networks). These programs contain short, blank periods of time that can be sold to advertisers for the insertion of commercial messages. These holes in the program's structure are known as *availabilities*. Other availabilities may be sold during periods between programs. The announcements that appear in the availabilities are called *spots* or *participations*. If an availability is not sold to an advertiser, the station will place a public service announcement (PSA) or a promotional announcement in that location. Individual participations are most commonly 30 seconds or 1 minute in length, sometimes less, but usually participations are clustered so that the total time block available may be up to 2 or 3 minutes.

Under this system an advertiser has no direct connection with the program in which its ad appears; it has purchased only the right to participate—only the length of time necessary to run the announcement. The emphasis for the writers of a new program, for example, which will be sold on a participating basis therefore must be on making that program as attractive as possible to audiences. If the station (or syndicator or network) believes the program can be successful in drawing audiences, the managers will place that program in the schedule. If the program draws audiences, its availabilities can then be sold to participating advertisers. But if, after a trial run, the program does not draw an audience of some size, advertisers will not "buy in," and soon the series will be canceled.

The writers of the commercials that appear in and adjacent to participating programs usually have no certain way of knowing which programs will surround their ads. They will write to attract and motivate a particular target audience group, but the placement of their ads will be made by others—advertising agency media buyers and station or network managers. Most times the target audience for the program—that is, the people attracted by its content—and the target audience for the commercial—that is, the people needed by the client in order to sell the product—will be the same, or close at least. But sometimes wild mismatches between program and advertiser target groups do occur.

### Barter Advertising

One additional practice that has become quite common in recent years in both broadcast and cable is that of *barter*, also known as *barter syndication*, because it is a means both of getting advertising into a station's schedule and of program syndication. Like regular syndication, a barter program is made available to a station by an outside producer, but unlike regular syndication, for which the station must pay a fee to purchase the rights to the series, these programs are made available at no cost to the station. In return, however, the producer-syndicator has kept some of the availabilities within the show and sold them to one or several clients. When the station gets the program, these commercials are already inserted in some of the available slots. While the station does not pay for the program, it also gets no revenue from the barter commercials inserted by the syndicator. Those built-in commercials are broadcast free by the station. That's the barter—program free to station in exchange for free advertising for the barter clients. The station makes its profit, if any, by selling additional availabilities left within the structure of the program. In principle, that's the way it works; in practice, the syndicators of some very popular programs require stations to pay some cash for the series as well as relinquish some of the availabilities to presold clients.

## The Station or Network as Sponsor

Each commercial broadcasting station and each programming network has a financial investment in almost every program they broadcast. They have to pay, in some way, for that content, with only a few exceptions. One exception, just described, is full program sponsorship. In that case, the advertiser pays a fee which covers both the costs of program production and the overhead charged by the station or network for its airtime.

Most of the time, however, the station or network must cover both the cost of production or other acquisition for each program as well as its general overhead—the costs of operating the transmitter, paying personnel, building rent, taxes and all the other costs of doing business. In return, of course, the station or network expects to recover those costs and add a measure of profit as well, by selling time for advertising messages in and adjacent to its programs.

The larger the audience for a program, the more the station or network may be able to charge advertisers of any type—program, participation, barter—to include their commercials. In most instances, then, the purpose of a commercial station or network can be easily stated: It is attempting to attract as large an audience as possible for each program, so that availabilities can be sold for the highest price.

There can be other purposes, however. One might be that of obtaining goodwill in the community. The station can accomplish that by showing programs that receive critical acclaim and are recognized by community leaders as having a socially significant impact. The station management can use these programs to strengthen the image of the station in the community. And having a strong image may lead indirectly to increased sales and profit.

Yet another purpose for the station might be to meet legal obligations imposed by the Federal Communications Commission. Recent changes in FCC rules have relaxed many of the requirements formerly imposed on stations. However, it is unlikely that the commission will eliminate all expectations for public service programming.

### Sustaining Programs

Some programs carried by commercial stations and networks do not contain advertising matter. These are called *sustaining programs*. There are several reasons why programs may be sustaining. First, the station may simply have been unsuccessful in obtaining participating advertisers. The program may be too new to have attracted an audience yet, and for the sales staff to have interested advertisers. Or the program may be in the wrong time slot to attract a sufficiently large audience to interest advertisers. Or the advertising rates and therefore the cost for reaching the audience may be too high, or some combination of these reasons.

A program may also be sustaining because it contains controversial material. Potential advertisers may be afraid that association with the program will result in negative publicity which would outweigh any positive exposure of their advertisement to an audience.

Finally, a program may be sustaining because the station or network feels that advertising would not be in keeping with the content of the program. Many public affairs programs are in this category, as are editorials, some commentary and cultural programs, and some religious programs.

Even for sustaining programs, the station's primary purpose usually is to attract the largest possible audience. Commercial stations and networks are generally reluctant to accept programs, either sustaining or commercial, that reach too small and narrow an audience, if for no other reason than that small audiences for one program will reduce the ratings for surrounding programs and for the overall schedule.

## Public Broadcasting

Thus far we have been discussing the programming and advertising practices of commercial stations. Programming on public stations presents a different situation because of their different regulatory status. Unlike their commercial counterparts, public stations are by definition noncommercial and nonprofit. They may not accept revenue from advertisers, and are therefore forced to get the funds to cover their programming and operating costs from other sources.

Most of their income comes from various levels of government— national, state, and local—and from private and corporate donations, including the funds solicited from individuals during auctions and pledge drives on the air. Public stations are also permitted to accept *underwriting*, in which commercial firms and individuals donate funds to cover the costs (only costs, not profit) of producing or acquiring programs. In return, the public station is permitted to acknowledge the underwriting gift on the air, but not to broadcast direct advertising messages from the underwriter. Note that in recent years the FCC rules that govern the definition of underwriting have been loosened, and these corporate identifications now come very close to looking like commercials.

Since the underwriter cannot present direct advertising on behalf of a product, we must conclude that the purpose in underwriting a program on a public station is that of collecting a measure of goodwill and improving public attitudes toward the company. It might be only coincidental, but during the late 1970s, when gasoline prices shot up very rapidly and the major petroleum companies were subject to a good deal of negative publicity, these companies began to underwrite quite a few public television series. In fact, so many programs were being underwritten by oil companies that one humorist suggested that the Public Broadcast Service (PBS) be renamed the Petroleum Broadcast Service.

Managers of public stations, like their commercial counterparts, may also look to maximum audience size as a possible purpose for choosing particular programs to broadcast. However, most of the managers (and governing boards) of public stations believe that their primary purpose is to provide alternatives to commercial programming. These alternatives, which include presentations for a wide range of minority audience groups, and instructional, educational and cultural programming, are likely to draw more specialized and smaller audiences than most commercial programs.

## The Public Service Agency as Sponsor

Some programs and announcements are broadcast on behalf of public service agencies—organizations like the Red Cross, the Boy Scouts, the Blood Bank, the local Council of Churches and so on. In these situations, the station broadcasts the message without any charge to the agency. The station pays the costs of the airtime involved, and may absorb production costs as well. As with sustaining programs, the station's purpose is that of building goodwill in its community.

On other occasions, the public service agency will produce an announcement, which it then delivers to the station for broadcast, or it will commit staff time and effort to the production of a program. The agency's purpose is similar to that of a commercial advertiser—to persuade audience members. That persuasion may take the form of an appeal for donations, or to encourage people to attend an event or to support a cause in some other way. Public service organizations may also sponsor programs to inform or enlighten the public or to raise cultural standards, although these are not common purposes.

## The Audience as Sponsor

Under the commercial system of broadcasting which has operated in the United States for the past fifty years, programs are brought to the audience "free of charge." There is no direct payment by the audience for the programming received. The audiences of commercial stations do, of course, pay for programming, but only indirectly, through purchases of products advertised. Most audience members are not even consciously aware of the fact that every time they buy soap, a new car or nearly any product, they are also paying for their radio and TV programming.

You are surely aware, however, that the practice of "free" broadcasting is being eroded by various situations in which audiences pay directly for the privilege of obtaining programs they wish to have. Pay services can be distributed in several ways, the most common of which are, of course, cable channels.

Yet another form of direct payment for programming takes place whenever you rent a movie or other program from your neighborhood video store. While that's not a broadcasting function as such, this form of audience involvement with programming has had a marked impact on the sizes of audiences available to watch traditional broadcast offerings.

In these cases, the audience members are, in a very real sense, the sponsors, since they pay directly to receive programming they want. And if, for example, a substantial number of people were to drop their subscriptions to Home Box Office, the producers and writers employed by that channel would quickly react to change its programming.

Note, however, that audience sponsorship differs from other types of sponsorship in that the audience's role comes *after* the planning, writing and production of the program, not before and during that production. With the exceptions of call-in programs that do permit audiences to interact with the presentation, audiences can only react to programs after they have been completed by making the decision on whether or not to tune in.

## MAKING A PROFIT

From this discussion and your own observations, you can safely conclude that one of the primary purposes behind the operation of American mass media systems, including broadcasting, is to make a profit. There are some exceptions. We've mentioned public broadcasting, and most larger cable systems have public-access channels that are also noncommercial and nonprofit. But these are just that—exceptions—and even they must operate in an environment where they compete with commercial outlets for audiences. For the most part, profit making, or at least the potential to make a profit, is what drives the system. Note, too, as we have discussed, that while consumers are increasingly being asked to pay directly for the programming they consume, the costs of most media programming are still covered by advertising revenues.

In many other countries of the world there is less emphasis upon the profit motive and upon advertising. Systems in some countries are owned by their national governments and are financed like any other branch of the government. The present (and some of the former) Communist governments use this approach, as do many Third World countries. Other broadcasting systems, including the BBC in Great Britain and the CBC in Canada, receive at least part of their operational funding from the government in the form of tax revenue. The government collects license fees from the owners of receiving sets and turns those funds over to the corporations that operate the broadcasting facilities and produce the programs.

But the trend throughout the world is toward advertiser-supported, profit-seeking electronic media—toward a system more like the U.S. model—either to replace existing models for financing media or to add competition within them. How does this system work?

## Broadcast Stations

Throughout their history broadcast radio and television stations have generally been profitable businesses. A few years ago some VHF network affiliates in major markets had profits as high as 20 to 30 percent per year, an excellent margin of profit for any investment. Independent TV stations, many of them in the UHF band, were slower to show profitability, although most of those are now also in the black.

The situation for radio stations has been a bit more difficult in recent years. Some major-market radio stations have been highly profitable, but even in the generally profitable period of the 1980s only about two-thirds of radio stations made profits, and the margins for radio were lower than for TV. Early 1990s numbers now show that more than half the commercial radio stations are losing money, and a number of AM radio stations have gone bankrupt and quit operating, something that would have been thought impossible just a few years ago. Both increased competition and a long-running economic recession are blamed for the poor showing, but despite this less favorable climate, the expectation of making a profit is still strong enough that there are willing buyers for most of the FM radio and TV stations that come on the market and numerous applications for new channels when those become available. Responding to this climate, the FCC has altered its rules on station ownership, and the industry is now in considerable flux.

For commercial stations, *profitability* can be simply stated as the ability to sell enough time to advertisers, at high enough rates, to have income greater than the costs of operation. (A second source of profit may come from selling a station to a new owner, and some entrepreneurs have done well at just that, but we'll ignore that one-time gain.)

The amount of time a station will be able to sell, and the rates it can charge to advertisers, depend on a number of factors, but in the simplest terms we can say that advertising rates depend on the number of listeners or viewers who are attracted to the programming offered. At the one extreme would be a small-market radio station with a very small audience. This station can charge only a few dollars for each commercial aired because the size of the audience is so small. At the other extreme would be the more than three-quarters of a million dollars charged for a 30-second spot in a Superbowl telecast. But many millions of viewers will view that spot—enough to make that price competitive with other announcements in other programs.

Consider the situations of two hypothetical radio stations. One station has recently changed its programming and has hit upon a very successful format. Audience sizes, as reported by Arbitron, have increased substantially, and advertisers, recognizing a good buy for their advertising dollars, have bought up much of the available time. The managers of this station will raise the rates they charge for advertising time. By doing so they will increase income, and increased income coupled with constant cost equals increased profit.

In contrast, the second station is not doing so well. For some reason —tough competition, poor promotion, poor programming, or whatever— audiences have been declining, and the number of advertisers and amount of time they have been buying have also been declining. The management of this station may do several things. It may cut costs to maintain profitability on reduced income. It may modify the format in an attempt to recapture lost audiences, or change format altogether and try to draw a totally different audience group. It will almost certainly have to reduce the rates charged for advertising.

The point at which a station reaches a balance among competing stations (and with other media, which also compete for advertising revenue) is roughly determined by a ratio known as the *cost-per-thousand (CPM)*. That is the cost to the advertiser to broadcast a commercial message to 1,000 individuals.*

The first of our two hypothetical radio stations will take advantage of its success—increased thousands of audience—and raise its rates, which were too low on a CPM basis, to the market average. The second station, to remain competitive, must do the reverse. As a consequence of its dwindling audience, it must lower rates to a CPM that also is competitive in the market.

The analysis is further complicated by the fact that most stations will have different sizes of audiences at different times of the day or week. These differences will be reflected in the rates. Radio stations that show only small variations in audience size may have only a single rate, but many stations have three or four rates for different day and time periods. A television station may change its rates hourly, or for each different program in its schedule, charging different rates for even small variations in audience size.

In summary, in order to sell time for commercials in a program, and in the breaks between programs, a station must be able to show potential advertisers that their announcements will be heard or seen by an audience. The more popular the program, which is the same thing as saying the more people in the audience, the more the station can charge advertisers for the

---

* Traditionally the CPM for radio stations has been based on the estimated number of *individuals* exposed to the advertiser's message. In television, CPMs were based on the number of *households* in which that commercial is estimated to have been seen. In recent years the TV industry has been shifting to a system that utilizes "people-meters" and measures individual viewing, but that shift is not yet complete. Later we will revise this generalized statement to consider the targeting of commercials to specific audience groups. Advertisers will pay higher CPMs to reach specific groups that are important for the sale of particular products.

spots they purchase. When income exceeds the cost of operation, the station is profitable—and that's the name of the game.

## Broadcast Networks

With few changes the preceding discussion of the operation of broadcast stations can be applied to networks as well. National radio networks began in the late 1920s and thrived into the 1950s, when television replaced radio as the dominant home entertainment medium. The "Big 3" radio network organizations—NBC, CBS and ABC—were also the leaders in early television, and these same corporations simply moved their well-established business practices to the newer medium. With the recent emergence of Fox, television now has four national commercial networks. Radio networks still exist; they are much more specialized in both content and target audiences than the TV networks.

Economic changes and the expansion of the number of choices for audiences, as noted above, are changing the business practices of networks as well. We can describe the role of a broadcast network in general terms as follows. The *network* consists of many stations (usually one station per market) that form together to carry common programming. Some of the programs are originated by the network; others are obtained by it from outside suppliers. (For programs it does not produce, the network leases the right to air the program from the producer, and for series, such leases usually permit two broadcasts of each episode.) Network programs, either produced or leased, are then fed via an electronic link (now usually by satellite) to the affiliated stations across the country.

The financial relationship between networks and their affiliates are complex, and in recent years, because of cable and other competition, this relationship has been subject to frequent negotiation and change. In general, affiliate stations receive network programming free of charge and some compensation from the network as well. They agree, in turn, to turn over substantial blocks of their time to the network. The network sells advertising to national clients in and adjacent to the network programs. These ads are seen throughout the country by audiences viewing the network program on all the affiliates that carry the program. The network makes its income from these national accounts. To be successful, it must be able to charge enough to cover the costs of program origination (production or purchase), distribution (satellite line charges) and whatever compensation may be passed on to the affiliates. Whatever remains is the network's profit.

Network shares of the total audience and network profitability have been declining. Consequently, these organizations have been cutting costs, reducing the number of employees, negotiating for cheaper programming and reducing affiliate compensation. In a substantial reversal of traditional practice, CBS recently even proposed that affiliates pay the network for programs received.

## Cable Franchises

The cable portion of the industry presents an equally complex picture. A local cable system, or franchise, is involved directly or indirectly in a multiplicity of financial arrangements with program suppliers, with advertisers, and often with its parent company, as most franchises are now held by large corporations known as MSOs (multiple-system-operators).

To market cable services to potential customers, the manager of a franchise selects from the dozens of potential services those which he or she believes to be the most attractive to subscribers. These programming services are then marketed in various packages to the subscribers. They are first offered a *basic service*, which contains mostly off-air stations, local origination channels and, possibly, a few specialty channels such as education or Spanish-language programming. Some national services which are in part advertiser-supported, such as Cable News Network (CNN) and the Weather Channel, may be included in this basic service, or they may be placed as part of a second-level offering, known as a second *tier*, available for an additional monthly fee.

Channels like Home Box Office, known as *premium-pay* channels, are included in higher tiers or priced individually. Several different tiers, or pricing packages, are usually offered, with different combinations of channels. In addition to channels which are paid for through monthly subscription, there is a trend toward cable marketing on a pay-per-view basis. Under this approach, subscribers pay (in addition to their basic fee) only for individual programs they want to watch.

The bulk of a franchise's income comes from subscription fees paid by those homes connected to the cable. Larger systems have local origination channels that operate for all practical purposes just like a local TV station but on cable. These channels originate or purchase their own programming, and they carry commercials for both local and national clients. The cable system gets the income.

As noted, cable systems also carry local broadcast TV channels, and cable viewers see the commercials that are aired by those stations, but cable operators have derived no income from that coverage. Carrying local broadcast stations has been a matter of considerable controversy between cable operators and local broadcasters. The 1992 act reregulating the cable industry requires cable operators to get permission from local broadcasters to carry their programming. That requirement will undoubtedly be challenged but, if it is upheld by the federal courts, it will change the revenue stream for both cable and local broadcasters in ways not yet understood.

## Cable Networks

There are many national cable networks, and proposals for new specialty networks keep surfacing. As with other forms of programming, the ability of a cable network to survive rests on its being attractive to sufficient numbers of viewers, but that is complicated by its being selected in the first place for a channel slot by franchise operators. As noted in the previous section, the operator will select those networks and other services believed to be most attractive to present and future subscribers, and many systems presently do not have the channel capacity to cover all the networks seeking exposure. That situation may change as technology promises to compress the frequency space needed for each channel. The industry now talks in terms of a potential for 500 or more channels.

Some cable networks carry advertising; they function in that respect partly like broadcast networks. Others are commercial-free, like Home Box Office. All obtain some revenue from the cable operators that choose to carry their service. They charge each cable system that carries the channel a fee per subscriber per month. Those that do not carry advertising depend entirely on that revenue source.

## PERSUASION: AN OVERRIDING PURPOSE

Recall, if you will, our reference in Chapter 2 to the Aristotelian position that all communication involves only three primary purposes—information, entertainment or persuasion. Although several of our chapters discuss informative and entertainment programming, it is our position that the basic purpose of almost all broadcast communication is in one way or another persuasive. Content is produced and presented with the intent, first, of attracting audiences. Then, if the channel is advertiser-supported, those audiences are subjected to a more direct form of persuasion—commercial announcements.

A news broadcast, for example, is a program in which the content is primarily information. Stations that air news—and note that not all choose to do so—have selected that form partly because of its value to the community but more because it is a program type that attracts generally good-sized audiences and can be profitable. The station wants to attract and hold an audience. (We do not intend to suggest that the station exercises directly persuasive intent in the form of news bias or editorial slant. That has happened on rare occasions, and with relaxed regulation may appear occasionally in the future, but most stations are careful to present news as objectively as possible.)

Advertisers who buy spots in news or any other programs do so to persuade the audience to purchase their products—or do whatever else the intent of that ad may be. And despite the value of the content of that news broadcast to the viewers, the station in all likelihood would remove that program from the air, or drastically revamp it, if the audience were to fall below a certain minimum size.

Similarly, a network television situation comedy may be seen as entertainment. Certainly audiences tune in to be entertained, or to receive some similar gratification. But just as with the news program, the network wants to persuade audiences to tune in, and any advertisers who purchase participations in the program want to persuade the viewers to their purposes. That program too will be removed if it fails to attract a substantial audience.

Even for noncommercial, nonprofit forms of broadcasting such as public television and radio, and cable systems with many channels of capacity, if programs are too esoteric and fail to draw at least reasonable-sized audiences, the pressures will mount to change programming, to reach more people and broader interests. The governments, foundations and individuals that supply the funds for the operation of these channels can be just as hardnosed about getting some results (audience) for the funds expended as any advertiser. If "Barbecueing with Ben" will draw a larger audience than the "Professional Women's Bowling Tour," and there isn't time for both, "Ben" will get the time.

The point we want to make is that originators that have spent money for programs and announcements expect something in return from the recipients of their messages. That something is some modification of attitude or behavior, or some action, such as the purchase of a product, a vote for a candidate or, at the very least, attention.

On the other hand, audiences are attracted to programs mainly because of the information and/or entertainment contained in them. There is a paradox here which you must recognize: The audience's reasons for choosing programs—to be informed or entertained—are frequently different from the sponsor's purpose. It will be your job as a writer to reconcile these different perceptions—to provide programs with sufficient interest to maintain interest and attention and to create advertisements that are persuasive but also sufficiently entertaining or informative that they do not drive audiences away from the programs that have attracted them. You must accomplish the purpose set forth by your employer—persuade an audience in some fashion, either to buy a product or at least to tune to and stay tuned to a program.

How do you go about that? In large part, you use well-recognized principles of persuasion.

## PERSUASIVE APPEALS

Persuasive, or motivational, appeals are deliberately manipulative. They are the means by which audience members are encouraged to act in accordance with the sponsor's goals. Most often that persuasion is exercised on behalf of commercial clients, inducing persons to purchase products or services, but it can also be employed to persuade on behalf of public service campaigns, to accept and act on an editorial opinion expressed by station management, to contribute to a religious organization or accept that organization's doctrine, to vote for a political candidate—any situation in which the sponsor's purpose is to elicit action from audience members.

From the substantial research that has been done and several of the volumes written on persuasive theory, we have constructed a list of persuasive appeals that can be applied to broadcast messages. When you start to write scripts of any type for your sponsors, it helps a great deal to understand these basic principles of persuasion. The typology we will use, listed alphabetically, contains the following headings:

1. Acquisition and saving
2. Adventure and change
3. Companionship and affiliation
4. Competition
5. Creativity
6. Curiosity
7. Fear
8. Guilt
9. Health and safety
10. Imitation and conformity
11. Independence and autonomy
12. Loyalty
    a. to family (love)
    b. to friends
    c. to social groups
    d. to nation (patriotism)
13. Personal enjoyment
    a. of comfort and luxury
    b. of beauty and order
    c. of pleasant sensations
    d. of recreation
14. Power and authority
15. Pride and vanity
16. Reverence or worship
    a. of leaders
    b. of traditions or institutions
    c. of the deity
17. Revulsion
18. Sexual attraction
19. Sympathy and generosity[1]

Lists of this sort are attempts to organize concepts that are really quite ephemeral and by their nature not subject to rigid organizational schemes. We think that having the list is nevertheless useful, especially for inexperienced writers, but keep these cautions in mind:

1. Appeals can be described in different terms—don't get stuck on the terminology. For example, appeals to health and safety and to fear are based on a primary motive of self-preservation. One, health and safety, approaches the idea positively; fear is a negative derivative.

2. Usually appeals do not operate individually, in isolation; instead, they are to be found in clusters. It is useful and almost unavoidable to use

natural clusters of appeals in a persuasive campaign. But be careful; while two or three appeals may be mutually supporting and add strength to the overall persuasive message, more than that number are likely to scatter the emphasis and weaken the effect.

3. Occasionally, two appeals will operate against one another. Adventure and fear, for example, may be self-canceling; our desire for adventure is overridden by fear of failure or of the unknown. Companionship and independence also may be seen as mutually contradictory; some people have a much greater need for one and others for the other.

4. Some appeals are more or less universal, but many of them have different strengths for different target audience groups. Those strengths are the result of previous experiences common to members of those groups. To take an obvious example, sexual attraction is not an appeal with strength for young children, because they simply have no experience with or understanding of sexual urges.

5. Similarly, there are obvious and easy connections between certain appeals and certain categories of advertised products. Writers frequently use these connections, often to excess. An advertising campaign which finds a new but legitimate connection between audience, appeal, and product will not only be successful; it will draw praise and awards for its creators.

6. Finally, most of our examples in the pages that follow are taken from advertising campaigns because those are the most obvious and the greatest users of persuasion. Keep in mind, however, that some programs have direct persuasive purposes as well, and that all broadcast content is persuasive at least to the extent that it attempts to keep audiences tuned in.

## Acquisition and Saving

The most obvious application of this appeal is connected with money and property—getting it, keeping it, and spending as little of it as possible to get the things we want. Every ad that says

```
On sale for this week only...

Twenty percent off the manufacturer's price...
```

or that in any way implies that the customer will make money or save money is aiming for this appeal.

One can save not only by spending less, but also by putting money aside. Banks and savings and loans use this appeal in almost all their ads:

```
Save with the highest money market rates and insured
safety at...
```

The appeal may also take the form of collecting. People like to collect a variety of things, from stamps, theater programs, and postcards to rare books and expensive art objects.

```
You'll want to have the entire set of these valuable col-
lector plates, so act now while they are still available.
```

This appeal is widespread among adults, and may be particularly strong for individuals or groups who have suffered financial setbacks at some point, but financial saving will have almost no value to children or others who have not had experience in managing money. On the other hand, children seem to be born collectors of all sorts of things, so acquisition in a nonmonetary sense can be a strong appeal for them.

## Adventure and Change

The thrill of excitement and the sense of the unusual and the unknown are present to at least a small degree in most people. But in general this appeal is likely to be stronger for younger groups than for older ones; for most people the appeal of adventure diminishes with age. It also takes different forms for males and females. The traditional outdoor adventure in the wilderness is still more male-oriented, probably due simply to childhood conditioning which perpetuates that stereotype, while the more glamorous, romantic adventure is more female-oriented.

In commercials, adventure can be inserted in the form of the setting—a glamorous resort, an ocean liner, an expensive restaurant—and/or in the activity—scuba diving, skiing, hang gliding, and so on. The product, whatever it may be, that is displayed in connection with that setting or activity takes on the aura of the adventure.

This appeal is also present whenever a "new" product is advertised. The emphasis on newness combines the appeals of change and curiosity.

## Companionship and Affiliation

Most of us prefer company in our activities, either with family or friends. We go to parties, join clubs, and do many other things to avoid loneliness. In our beliefs and opinions we also prefer to do what is socially or politically acceptable, what other people are doing, rather than chart an independent, and uncomfortable, course.

Whenever a group of people are together in an ad, this appeal is present, at least in moderate strength. It can be made stronger if the group members are obviously interacting and enjoying each other's presence. Companionship is a frequently used appeal in all sorts of beverage ads—coffee, soft drinks, beer—as more beverages are consumed in groups than by people alone.

## Competition

Competition, fighting and argument are nearly universal appeals. Small children fight over possession of a toy; adults take legal action when they feel wronged in some fashion; at the extreme, nations go to war. The appeal can be evident in intellectual forms—such as debate and verbal argument—or be more emotional and physical, involving anger and fighting.

A common application of this appeal is that of fighting back against forces which threaten us in some way. This appeal is easily combined with saving.

```
Fight back against high prices...buy our product on sale.
```

This appeal is also the basis for many consumerism campaigns. A very successful syndicated TV series appeared in the 1980s, hosted by consumer activist David Horowitz, and used both the appeal and the title *Fight Back*.

Competition has also been used extensively and effectively by the makers of athletic shoes. Nike, Reebok and others show their shoes being used by the winners of athletic competitions. Reebok built an extensive campaign around the decathlon competition between "Dan & Dave" as they prepared for the Olympics. When Dan didn't make the team, it had to do a quick turn-around and revise the approach to avoid advertising disaster.

Competition, again combined with savings, is also present in "comparison" ads in which the advertiser's product is compared with the competition.

```
Our product is better than...
```

```
Our remedy contains 25% more of the miracle ingredient...
```

## Creativity

This appeal may take various forms involving organizing or building and may include both physical creation—artwork or structures—and social creation—the organizing of people into athletic teams, political parties, business firms, and so on.

Creativity can be especially effective in public service campaigns. For example, a public service announcement on the formation of a new knitting club for senior citizens could apply the appeal in both senses: Join the club and help create a new social organization, and at the same time create articles by knitting them. That approach would also appeal to companionship; one can knit alone, of course, but by doing it as part of a club, companionship is added to the overall appeal.

There is a flip side to creativity or creation. That is destruction. We originally identified it as a separate appeal, but it is rarely applied. We mention it here as the negative counterpart of creativity, one that carries some dangers. Some years ago the owners of the Jack-in-the-Box restaurant chain decided to create a new image of their restaurants and target a more adult clientele. To dramatize the new image, they created a series of TV ads that showed the Jack-in-the-Box clown being blown up. On the positive side, the ads had a strong attention-getting device, the explosion, and the idea of change was forcefully expressed. On the other side, the campaign created unexpected and unwanted reactions in small children who were upset by the violence of the act and the loss of a friendly character to whom they had developed a loyalty.

Destruction can be used to precede the appeal to creation—destroy, then rebuild. It can be used, possibly in connection with competition, to demonstrate our ability to control the events in our lives and to show our superiority over the things we can destroy.

## Curiosity

Curiosity is nearly universal, but its form can vary widely depending on the individual or group of people involved. Children will tear apart toys to see what's inside. Adults will watch a parade to see a celebrity go by. Scientists and explorers are people who combine the appeals to curiosity and adventure.

In general we can say that people will be curious about topics, people, and situations of which they already have some prior knowledge, or where the writer of the program or announcement is able quickly, at the beginning of the broadcast, to make a connection in the audience's mind to the topic. If the listener's attention is caught, if he or she thinks: "This broadcast may be something I need to know about," then curiosity has been used effectively.

## Fear

This appeal has both positive and negative attributes. It may prevent us from doing things that bring danger, and it may also cause us to take actions to protect ourselves from that danger. Many ads for health care products and services appeal to fear. We will get sick, even die, if we don't take care of ourselves by using the sponsor's product or service. Or when we are sick, we should take the product in order to recover.

Similarly, products that emphasize personal protection—deadbolt locks on our doors or automobile tires which lessen the risks of skids and accidents in a storm—are using this appeal.

Physical injury or illness is not the only thing we fear. We may fear loss of a job, or property, or friends:

```
Use our deodorant (or mouthwash) or you will lose the
companionship and affection of friends....

Buy our insurance to protect your loved ones from the fear
of losing their home....
```

This last example points up another strong fear—fear of the unknown, of what we cannot anticipate or control in the future.

Fear would seem to be an almost universal appeal, but it is highly related to the action feared. Children who have not experienced ill health are not likely to respond to that form of the appeal, but children do have a strong fear of the dark and of the unknown. Coupling those fears with the appeals of adventure and curiosity can be a very effective way to capture children's attention to, say, an ad for a horror movie.

## Guilt

One of the most powerful social conditioners, at least in American society, is guilt. From early childhood our behavior is modified by parents, other relatives, friends, teachers and others who use guilt as their tool.

Advertisers also use this emotion for persuasive purposes. Guilt can be seen, along with sympathy, in appeals for charitable causes. It is used by life insurance companies in campaigns which suggest one has responsibility to loved ones even after death. Telephone companies have used guilt to remind us to call our parents long distance, and so on.

If the writer should choose to use guilt in a campaign to reach a particular target audience, it would be necessary to know what forms of guilt are likely to have been instilled into the members of that group. Different kinds have been implanted in each sex and in different social, racial and ethnic groups.

## Health and Safety

This appeal may be viewed as the opposite of fear, at least as far as fear relates to physical danger. Just as many health care products appeal to the fear of illness, they can also appeal to the positive attributes of well-being. Vitamin products and exercise clinics would be two obvious examples. So would a public service announcement urging participation in a marathon race. Companionship, health, and pride would be three appeals easily clustered together in that spot.

The health appeal can be made to most adults, but for older adults the negative approach, fear, may be more effective, as they are more likely to have experienced ill health and to be fearful of its consequences. It is difficult to make this appeal to young people who, if they think about it at all, seem to expect to live safely forever. Try, for example, to build a safety appeal into a public service campaign for bicycle safety for, say, sixth-grade children. It will be very difficult to find a way to use this appeal in such a campaign. If you should find a way to get those twelve-year-olds to practice bicycle safety, quite likely the appeals used will be different and much more indirect, involving, perhaps, imitation, or pride, or companionship.

## Imitation and Conformity

People tend to imitate others both consciously and unconsciously, and the appeal is evident in many types of persuasive copy. It can be seen in all the "keeping up with the Joneses" campaigns. It can also be seen in the latest fashions, styles, or fads in clothing, or activities in the social group to which the target audience aspires—a "get on the bandwagon" approach.

The appeal is often presented by a television personality or radio voice who is similar to the members of the target audience group. That person uses, enjoys, or gets some benefit from the advertised product and then, by direct statement or by implication, says to the audience: "You too can get the same benefit I am getting by using this product."

Imitation is used with many categories of products. Among the most obvious and frequent are cosmetic products—shampoos, shave cream, perfumes. All audience groups can be reached with this appeal, but one of the most susceptible groups is teenagers, who can rather easily be induced to participate in new fads and to purchase products that identify them as part of the crowd.

We also tend to imitate the actions, beliefs, attitudes, and opinions of people we admire and respect. This attribute can be very effective in political campaigns; an endorsement of a candidate or proposition by a respected figure can influence a good many votes from otherwise undecided persons. The endorsement of a product also can result in increased sales, especially if that product and its competitors are very similar in other ways. Examples abound, but change frequently. You may recall the series of ads for the American Express Card that featured people with well-known names but less well known faces, or the ads for Miller Lite beer that used a large number of ex-professional athletes whose names were well known to the target audiences of males.

Of course for the appeal to imitation to be effective, the audience must respond to the people shown on the screen or heard on the radio. For an endorsement to be effective, the person making the endorsement must be known to and respected by the target audience.

## Independence and Autonomy

In one sense, this appeal may be seen as an opposite of companionship. For example, when students are asked to recall commercials that use independence as an appeal, they frequently describe motorcycle ads in which a lone rider on a sleek, powerful machine rides off into the mountains, or the desert, or a futuristic landscape—a combination of independence and adventure as appeals. The same sense of individualism may be seen in an ad which features a lone mountain climber who drinks a thirst-quenching soda when he reaches the top of the peak. Independence, adventure, and imitation are all present in that situation.

Generalizing on the basis of these examples, the audiences to which independence is an appeal are more easily described in terms of their lifestyle than in demographic terms. The independent, individualistic, loner attitude is more psychological than demographic.

We should also point out the contrast between independence and imitation. They are not completely contradictory appeals, but they tend to operate as opposites. We will imitate others we admire, or are in our social group, but we do not want to be *forced* to imitate. Clothing, for example, must be in style, but also individual.

## Loyalty

This broad term is a general heading for several more specific and more readily identifiable subappeals.

### Loyalty to Family: Love

Obviously, this appeal is present in situations in which various family members are shown together in pleasant circumstances. It is extremely evident in all the commercial campaigns presented by life insurance companies; people buy life insurance to protect their families.

It also has been effectively used by AT&T to encourage people to contact other family members through long distance. "Reach out and touch someone . . ."

### Loyalty to Friends

This appeal is very similar to companionship. We are more willing to take action to help a friend than we will a stranger. Radio station disc jockey personalities frequently are seen as friends by the regular members of their audiences. They arouse a strong sense of loyalty in their listeners; then, when a product is "personally" recommended by that announcer, the audience responds favorably out of loyalty and possibly imitation as well.

### Loyalty to Social Groups

Such terms as "school spirit," "civic pride" and "club morale" indicate the types of loyalty included here. The appeal is frequently used for public service campaigns to support nonprofit civic organizations in their charitable efforts. The alumni organizations of schools and colleges appeal to this loyalty.

### Loyalty to Nation: Patriotism

This appeal evidences wide variation in its strength. Traditionally it has been strongest for older audiences, especially war veterans. During and following the Vietnam war, patriotism was decidedly out of favor, especially with younger groups, but the Persian Gulf war in 1991 brought a resurgence of patriotic feeling among almost all demographic groups. We see the appeal in campaigns to "buy American" and to support democratic traditions and institutions.

## Personal Enjoyment

In varying forms this appeal is present in a great deal of persuasive material. It is a universal appeal and a very strong one. Some of the forms in which it can be recognized are these:

### Enjoyment of Comfort and Luxury

This form is used in commercials for automobiles and furniture; used by airlines to push their service as being more comfortable than the smaller seats in the competitor's plane; used by hotels and resorts. Target audiences include both those groups who already are used to these comforts and those who may not yet have had the opportunity to experience the luxury, but who may reasonably be expected to have the opportunity later. The appeal can build an expectation: "When I'm able to do so I'm going to buy a Mercedes, or fly first class, or stay at the Ritz. . . ."

### Enjoyment of Beauty and Order

The term *aesthetics* is particularly appropriate here; it describes the enjoyment derived from the fine arts, from music, or from a drive through the beautiful foliage of a New England autumn. A commercial for a wine, with classical music playing in the background, makes use of this appeal, as does the classic Budweiser beer Christmas commercial which shows the Clydesdale team prancing through a pastoral winter snowscape.

The appeal does not have to be snobbish, as these examples might suggest. The design (beauty) of an automobile, along with its luxury, are as important in selling that car as are the appeals to economy and price.

Household cleansers, floor polishes, toilet bowl cleaners, and the like also make heavy use of this appeal in the form of cleanliness and sparkle.

### Enjoyment of Pleasant Sensations

This appeal is very similar to the other subcategories of personal enjoyment; all involve sensory gratification of some sort. But this category is related more emotionally to the senses—things that taste or smell good, or that are pleasant to the touch. Of course it is not possible to present these sensations in a broadcast, except for sounds and visual images. But it is possible to describe them, using forceful, descriptive words, and to cause audiences to recall similar sensory experiences they may have had.

Food products use this appeal extensively, as do other products that appeal to the senses—perfumes, deodorizers.

### Enjoyment of Recreation

We all enjoy the opportunity to engage in activities which are different from those assigned to us, either at work or school. Any product which is directly associated with recreation and fun will have the advantage of being seen from that pleasurable point of view. Recall the ad campaign by AMF products which showed their line of sporting goods coupled with the statement: "AMF makes weekends." Other products may not be directly associated with leisure, but if the writer can find a tie between them, the appeal can be used.

## Power and Authority

It is more difficult to recognize this appeal than most of the others we have listed. Usually individuals will not admit to seeking power over other persons, but they do. Why do men and women give up lucrative positions and spend millions of dollars to be elected to public office? At least part of the reason is because they will have power over others, and their principles and beliefs can be more easily made into policies and laws affecting others.

Because of the unwillingness of individuals to admit to seeking power, this appeal must be very carefully employed in persuasive copy. But it can be seen, along with loyalty and other appeals, in recruiting ads for the military services and in ads for various types of educational or self-advancement programs.

## Pride and Vanity

The appeal to pride can be extremely powerful. It can take several different forms: reputation, the estimate others give to an individual's worth; self-respect, the opinion one has (or wishes to have) of oneself; prestige, defined as reputation based on brilliance of achievement or character; and vanity, excessive pride or self-satisfaction. The differences are partly semantic; some of these terms are more positive in connotation than others.

People will put an incredible amount of effort into a job, or a volunteer activity, or into maintaining a home or other tasks if they perceive that the effort expended will raise their reputation. They may put in even more energy if the task is connected with their estimate of their own self-worth. The writer who wishes to persuade an audience on behalf of a product, or a service, or a cause, and who finds a means of connecting the audience's pride to that persuasive message, will be successful.

Earlier, in discussing the appeal of imitation, we referred to the cliché of "keeping up with the Joneses." That cliché is also tied very heavily to the appeal to pride and vanity.

```
If you want your lawn to look better than others on the
block, buy our lawnmower....

Be the first in your neighborhood to have this all-new
edition of our encyclopedia....
```

Many luxury products are sold on the basis of the vanity associated with the product (or self-esteem, or prestige; the term used depends a lot on one's attitude toward that appeal). Remember the ads for L'Oréal Hair Color which featured a young woman saying: "L'Oréal is a little more expensive, but then I'm worth it."

## Reverence or Worship

This appeal has at least three distinct forms:

### Hero Worship

Commercially the endorsement of products or positions by well-known personalities, which we discussed under imitation, might also be considered an application of hero worship or the personal awe important figures command. Frequently, well-known Hollywood or Broadway stars endorse political candidates or issues, even though they have no expert knowledge of the issue or candidate.

### Reverence for Traditions and Institutions

This form may be dramatically illustrated by the "baseball, hot dogs, apple pie, and Chevrolet" commercials of the late 1970s. In these ads the product, Chevrolet, was equated with three other American traditions. Hero worship and reverence for traditions are very similar to the appeal of loyalty and are frequently blended together.

### Reverence of the Deity

This form is not likely to be found in persuasive campaigns for commercial products, probably because of the danger of a backlash from the audience; that is, the audience might react negatively to an attempt to relate a product to the deity. But it is obviously the strongest appeal in all the persuasive religious programming that is broadcast. The Church of Jesus Christ of Latter-day Saints (Mormon), for example, airs very moving, emotional spots.

## Revulsion

Like fear, revulsion is a negative appeal. It can be used most effectively to get the audience to react against an activity or situation. Showing on television the slaughter of the cute, helpless baby harp seals in the Arctic led to a tremendous public outcry to stop that slaughter.

A public service announcement shown on television in New York City had as its purpose convincing people to clean up their household garbage and put it in metal garbage cans. The PSA showed closeup pictures of rats—crawling along telephone lines and down poles, and rummaging in garbage. The audience's revulsion at seeing the rats would then, presumably, motivate them to purchase garbage cans.

## Sexual Attraction

You were probably wondering when we were going to get to this one, because it is such an obvious and widely used appeal. It is also used in broadcasting for at least two somewhat different purposes. It can serve a structural purpose, that of attracting and holding audience attention in programs and commercials. Or, as a persuasive appeal, it can take the form of purchasing products because we believe that doing so will provide us with some sexual attraction to others. The distinction is a subtle one, and in practice both uses of sex attraction are often merged.

For example, a local boat dealer produces a TV spot featuring a boat with a bikini-clad local beauty contest winner reclining on the deck. Her presence visually catches the attention of males in the audience. The persuasive appeal added by her presence is indirect; it is the suggestion that if one buys the boat, girls who look like that (and who are clothed like that) will be available to the purchaser. That appeal can be made even more obvious if the girl is given a vocal part in the spot which says something with the effect of: "I really go for men who enjoy their pleasures . . . like this beautiful boat."

That example describes one obvious form of sexual attraction, that of physical appeal, but this is by no means the only form. The appeal may also be presented by any suggestion of romance and through music, most forms of which have sexual, romantic connotations. You should be aware, however, that in recent years there has been a good deal of negative criticism on the use of sex attraction in advertising. A number of campaigns have been criticized for what are seen to be exploitive uses of sex. Sex has also become a more sensitive topic since homosexuality has become more open; it is no longer safe to assume that sexual attraction always means heterosexual relationships.

### Sympathy and Generosity

These terms describe the emotional reactions of most people when they are confronted by situations, such as disasters or disease, which place other people in less fortunate circumstances.

This appeal is quite likely to be used in public service campaigns—for example, those which appeal for donations to support research and treatment for diseases, or for homeless and starving children, or for saving the whales, or dogs and cats, or for aid to the victims of floods, fires and earthquakes.

It may also be used in ads for commercial products that are themselves connected with unfortunate events—florists, funeral parlors, and the like.

Sympathy and generosity are frequently found in connection with the appeals to fear, guilt, and imitation. In order to evoke this appeal effectively in a target audience, the writer will need to make it possible for the members of the audience to see themselves in the situation of the less fortunate.

## CONCLUSION

In this chapter we have argued that all broadcast programming has some form of persuasion as its central purpose. Not everyone agrees with that point of view; many in the industry feel we are being unnecessarily harsh in ignoring entertainment and information as basic purposes. We will not belabor the point; you can make your own judgments, ultimately, on the matter. We will continue to point out, however, that the privately operated system in the United States is heavily dependent upon attracting audiences and to selling those audiences in some way—to advertisers or toward the purchase of subscriptions to cable channels, as just the most obvious purposes. And, as we have noted, many foreign systems have moved closer to the U.S. model of advertising support. Those that are still tightly controlled by governments are even more likely to use the broadcast media for persuasive—read, propaganda—purposes.

We also argued that writers who hope to prepare successful programs and announcements must look at success from the sponsor's point of view and, as a corollary, must have a clear understanding of who is paying for each program or announcement and what they hope to accomplish by their sponsorship.

Finally, we tried to explain the process of persuasion as it takes place in programs and, especially, in ads. In that discussion we have avoided judgmental or critical comments. There are critics who argue that the entire process of creating or stimulating wants and desires on the part of audiences and then showing how specific products can satisfy those wants—thereby leading to the purchase of those products—is somehow unfair. Other critics object to the process as being manipulative or underhanded. Advertisers should be more open; advertising messages should be straightforward and informational, they argue.

We want to avoid being drawn into these criticisms, either to attack or defend the process as it currently operates. Each individual writer is entitled to determine whether or not he or she can survive or is willing to be a part of "the system," or to what extent he or she wants to expend the effort and energy to attack, modify, or subvert the system. What we have done is to explain how that system works.

## Exercises

The exercises selected for this chapter are not directly related to writing. Rather, they are intended to heighten your awareness of broadcasting's business practices, including the roles of advertisers and sponsors and the importance of correctly assessing a sponsor's purpose. These exercises are best undertaken as group or class activities, where there is opportunity for discussion. Courses in electronic media sales and management also would provide excellent background.

1. View an assortment of television programs at different times and days and on different stations and cable channels, to get a variety of program types and sponsorship patterns. For each program attempt to determine

    a. Who was the sponsor for the program?

    b. What seems to be the sponsor's purpose?

    c. How did you arrive at the answers for (a) and (b)? Just from viewing, without any additional information, it is not always possible to make these judgments, especially distinguishing between participation and barter advertising, but the practice is valuable even if you are not correct in every instance. (This exercise may also be done with radio, but not as much variation exists in sponsorship patterns on radio stations.)

2. Assume you are writing a commercial for a product aimed at each of several different target audiences. First, select several fairly narrowly described target groups, such as white, middle-class male teenagers. Then, for each target group, consider

    a. What *authority figures* might you use in your ad to reach that target?

    b. What *specialized vocabulary* (slang) would you use?

    c. What *level of intensity* (hard sell, use and style of music, and so on) is likely to be most effective?

    d. What *persuasive appeals* (and what forms of those appeals) would you place in your campaign?

3. View a selection of television commercials and public service announcements (and/or listen to radio spots). What persuasive appeals do you detect in each ad? Which ads contain appeals that provide strong motivation to you personally? If the announcement does not contain strong appeals to you, do you think it has strong appeals for some other target group? For whom?

**Note**

1. The list of appeals, and the labels given to individual appeals, are adapted primarily from Douglas Ehninger, Alan H. Monroe, and Bruce E. Gronbeck, *Principles and Types of Speech Communication,* 11th ed. (Glenview, IL: Scott, Foresman, 1990), pp. 140ff.

**Further Reading**

One of the emphases of this chapter has been on the relationship between programming, selling and writing. If you lack background on the business practices of the electronic media industries, consider reading portions of some of these titles.

Baldwin, Thomas E., and D. Stevens McVoy. *Cable Communication,* 2nd ed. Englewood Cliffs, NJ: Prentice-Hall, 1988.

Blum, Richard A., and Richard D. Lindheim. *Primetime: Network Television Programming.* Stoneham, MA: Focal, 1987.

Carroll, Raymond L., and Donald M. Davis. *Electronic Media Programming.* New York: McGraw-Hill, 1993.

Eastman, Susan Tyler. *Broadcast/Cable Programming: Strategies & Practices,* 4th ed. Belmont, CA: Wadsworth, 1993.

Marcus, Norman. *Broadcast and Cable Management.* Englewood Cliffs, NJ: Prentice-Hall, 1986.

Pringle, Peter K., and others, *Electronic Media Management,* 2nd ed. Stoneham, MA: Focal, 1990.

Sherman, Barry. *Telecommunications Management.* New York: McGraw-Hill, 1987.

Warner, Charles, and Joseph Buchman. *Broadcast and Cable Selling,* updated 2nd ed. Belmont, CA: Wadsworth, 1993.

White, Barton C., and N. Doyle Satterthwaite. *But First These Messages . . . The Selling of Broadcast Advertising.* Needham Heights, MA: Allyn and Bacon, 1989.

These critical commentaries on industry practices, although some years old, are still worth your consideration.

Barnouw, Frik. *The Sponsor: Notes on a Modern Potentate.* New York: Oxford University Press, 1978.

Brown, Les. *Television: The Business Behind the Box.* New York: Harcourt Brace Jovanovich, 1971.

For further examination of persuasion, consult this title, a major reference on persuasion theory.

Maslow, Abraham H. *Toward a Psychology of Being,* 2nd ed. New York: Van Nostrand Reinhold, 1968.

These are widely used general texts in persuasion. They will also be helpful in supplying background on this area.

Bettinghaus, Erwin P. *Persuasive Communication*, 3rd ed. New York: Holt, Rinehart and Winston, 1980.

Bostrom, Robert. *Persuasion*. Englewood Cliffs, NJ: Prentice-Hall, 1983.

Pratkanis, Anthony, and Elliot Aronson. *Age of Propaganda: The Everyday Use and Abuse of Persuasion*. New York: W. H. Freeman, 1992.

Reardon, Kathleen Kelley. *Persuasion: Theory and Context*. Beverly Hills, CA: Sage, 1981.

Ross, Raymond S. *Understanding Persuasion*, 3rd ed. Englewood Cliffs, NJ: Prentice-Hall, 1990.

Simons, Herbert W. *Persuasion: Understanding, Practice, and Analysis*, 2nd ed. New York: McGraw-Hill, 1986.

A quite different approach to the analysis of persuasive messages from the traditional is presented in:

Toulmin, Stephen. *The Uses of Argument*. Cambridge: Cambridge University Press, 1958.

Finally, these are popularized discussions of persuasion. They were widely read and discussed when first published, are now somewhat dated, but are still worth reading.

Key, Wilson. *Subliminal Seduction*. New York: New American Library, 1974.

Packard, Vance. *The Hidden Persuaders*. New York: Pocket Books, 1957.

# CHAPTER 10

# Audiences and Their Expectations

I n the preceding chapter we viewed the communication process from the point of view of the originators of broadcast programs, particularly the noncreative but all-important financial supporters of the industry. As must have been obvious from that discussion, their goals cannot be met unless they effectively reach and persuade audiences. In this chapter, we consider the audience's perspective. Why do people choose television or radio in preference to other activities available to them, how do they choose among competing offerings, and how can writers use this knowledge to write more effective copy?

When you finish this chapter, you will be able to

- understand how the size and composition of potential, available and actual audiences affect programming and writing decisions,

- recognize target audiences for existing programs and advertisements and determine target groups for your own scripts,

- distinguish between quantitative and qualitative audience research and recognize the value of both in preparing copy,

- identify audience gratifications in existing programs and in program ideas you develop,

- analyze writing assignments using the concepts of (1) sponsorship, (2) purpose, (3) audience targeting and (4) gratifications, and

- recognize and use these important terms and concepts:

audiences: actual, available, potential, target

audience gratifications

coverage

day-part

demographics

drive time

empathy

narrowcasting

prime time

psychographics (lifestyle)

## POTENTIAL, AVAILABLE AND ACTUAL AUDIENCES

These three concepts of audience—potential, available and actual—help define the size, the composition and the behavior of television and radio audiences.

### Potential Audience

For all practical purposes, the total population of the country may be considered to be the potential audience for U.S. broadcasting. The 1 percent of the people who do not have access to television or radio are too small a group to be significant.

On the other hand, the potential audience for each station—that is, the audience which is able to pick up that station's signal—is different from that of every other station. Similarly, the potential audience for each broadcast program is different. Here are just a few examples of these widespread differences:

- In general, stations with *coverage* patterns covering a large area will have a greater potential audience than stations which are more restricted. Wide variations exist in the coverage area for radio stations, especially AM. Some AM stations operate with as few as 500 watts of power and reach out only a few miles from their transmitters. Others, which broadcast with maximum power (50,000 watts), can cover large regions, especially at night, when their skywaves are reflected off the ionosphere and are received hundreds of miles away. FM stations, on the other hand, are limited to line of sight between the transmitter and receivers, and that usually restricts these stations to a roughly circular coverage area of between 20 and 60 miles from the transmitter—depending upon the height of the antenna. Terrain features, such as mountain ranges and even large buildings in the path of the signal, also affect FM coverage.

  Television signals, like FM radio, are also line of sight between transmitter and receivers, and antenna height is the major factor in television coverage. Both propagation factors such as power and frequency, and geography, give each station a different coverage pattern, and thus at least a slightly different potential audience from every other station.

- Stations in large metropolitan areas have a much larger potential audience than stations in rural areas, even if their facilities are identical. There are simply more people within reach of the signal. The difference is recognized in the higher charges for advertising in metropolitan areas, the larger budget and larger staffs for most such stations, the generally larger margins of profit, and the higher prices paid to purchase urban stations.

- For cable, the concept of potential audience involves several levels of concern. First, only those homes that are passed by the cable system can be counted as potential audience for that system. Some communities are still without cable service; in others only the more densely populated, or more affluent, areas are wired.

    Then, the management of the system will decide which services to offer to subscribers. Those choices will be made based partly on the number of channels available on the system. Older systems tend to have fewer channels, thereby limiting the number of services that can be offered.

    Finally, each subscriber will decide which services (beyond the basic tier) he or she wishes to subscribe to and pay for. Only when a service is actually available at the TV set can that home legitimately be counted as part of the potential audience for that service.

- As with cable services, the potential audience for a network-distributed or syndicated program series depends on the number of stations that choose to offer it. Sometimes network affiliates choose not to air a controversial network offering, thereby reducing its potential audience. A large audience cannot be attracted to a program, no matter how well it is written or how important it may be, if it is not widely offered in the first place.

## Available and Actual Audiences

These audience groupings are smaller groups within the potential audience. The available audience are those who have ready access to the medium (TV or radio) at any particular time. The actual audience is, of course, those who are in fact listening or watching. While the potential audience is static, not changing significantly in size or composition, both the available and the actual audiences are dynamic. They change with time. Again, a few examples are sufficient to explain:

- The audience measurement (rating) services break down radio and TV schedules into *day-parts*, reflecting the changes in size and composition of the available audience through the day and week. The TV day-part from 4 to 6 P.M., for example, is known as "early fringe."

- The best-known day-part for television is *prime time*, those evening hours when the largest numbers of people not only are available to watch television but also do watch. Prime time represents the most valuable hours. The most expensive programs are placed in this time period, and the highest rates are charged for advertising.

- Radio has similar prime-time periods, known as *drive time*, when the largest number of people are in automobiles driving to or from work, and therefore somewhat of a captive audience for radio. At least that's true in most metropolitan areas. Drive time doesn't have much meaning in a rural community, where there is no commuter traffic.

- Programs aimed at children must be scheduled when they are available, not when they are at school, and preferably not when there is heavy competition from other members of the family for access to the TV set. Children's programming, therefore, shows up in the late afternoons on weekdays and early morning on weekends.

- In the summertime, TV programming reflects the fact that the available audiences are smaller. Many people have other activities—vacations, weekends at the beach or mountains, long evenings at the park—which take them out of the available, and thus also out of the actual, audience. Programming therefore is largely reruns or summer replacement series that are inexpensive to produce.

Remember too that the total actual audience in a market must be divided among all the stations in that market. There are millions of people in the potential audience in Los Angeles, for instance, but by the time the actual audience at any given hour is divided among a dozen or so television stations, 50 to 70 radio stations, plus cable and home VCRs, the actual audience for any one individual station may be quite small. Nevertheless, station owners, cable operators, and other entrepreneurs look at the potential audience in that market and are convinced they can capture at least their fair share of that potential.

## TARGET AUDIENCES

Target audiences are those groups which are identified *by the sponsor* of either a program or announcement as being the most important *in order to accomplish that sponsor's purpose.*

Most of the time, target audiences are described in *demographic* terms—by age, sex, race, education, income, place of residence, or other characteristics. Certain demographic groups will watch or listen to certain types of programs more than will others, or they will be the primary buyers of certain types of products. Occasionally, however, target audience groups are better described using nondemographic, behavior-oriented "lifestyle" characteristics.* The distinguishing characteristics of the potential buyers for small sail-

---

* The practice of describing audiences by behavioral indicators has gone by different names. Originally, the term *psychographics* was used. Then that word fell out of favor, and was replaced by *lifestyle*. Now, psychographics seems to be returning to the language.

boats, for instance, might be more accurately set forth in lifestyle terms—amount of leisure time, discretionary income, love of adventure—rather than by the more conventional demographic indicators.

We will present a few examples here in order to show the process used in defining target audiences. These are, however, generalized examples. In practice, both broadcasters and advertisers spend considerable sums on research aimed at identifying target groups.

## Target Audiences for Products

Advertisers were the first to recognize the importance of aiming messages at special groups. Usually, they aim for those target groups that are either most likely to purchase the product or service, or who will purchase the largest quantities of it.

### *Washing Detergents*

The makers of washing detergents want their commercials to be seen by and to influence the purchases of those people who buy the largest amounts of detergent. Who are they? Women, primarily between the ages of 20 and 35, who have families that include small children (who get dirty). You might go so far as to say those women who are least likely to send out their laundry. But those three demographic indicators—sex, age, and family size—are the most important.

To be sure, other groups of people also buy washing detergents—single people, older people, and so on—but they are likely to purchase smaller amounts as a group. The primary target is the group described, and the advertiser who wants to be successful in marketing a detergent must sell a large portion of it to that target. Secondary campaigns directed at smaller target groups can also be conducted if the budget permits.

### *Auto Stereo*

Similarly, let us assume that the makers of an aftermarket radio-tape-CD combination player for automobiles are preparing to introduce a new model that will sell for approximately $400. What group forms the largest potential buying group for this product? If there is any doubt, the manufacturer could—and very well might—conduct a preliminary study on potential target audiences before spending the money for a major advertising campaign. But a good guess for this product would be young men between the ages, say, of 17 and 30 who have enough money saved or borrowed to make this fairly significant purchase, who have a car and who like music.

Next, the advertiser and media buyer will have to consider how best to reach this target group—that is, they will have to find a program targeted for the same group. Marketing research will show them that these young men are heavy listeners of radio, and even more specifically of certain rock music radio formats. From those data, the writer can develop a successful ad campaign for the client.

## Target Audiences for Programs

As we have just seen, program producers also design programs, or whole formats, for specific audiences. The radio station with the rock format chose that programming specifically to draw the young male audience. Here are three more examples, these from television, of programs with specific targets.

### Meet the Press

The audience for this NBC network series is determined by the content and the style of the program. The content is purposely limited to important issues in politics, economics, and foreign affairs. The style is a straightforward interview with an expert in the subject matter. The target audience is men and women who have a serious interest in those topics, either as individuals or as managers and owners of businesses that might be affected. The target audience, then, might be described as both men and women with above-average education and income, therefore somewhat older, say 30 to 50 or even older. Equally important as the demographic description is the recognition that the audience is interested in the content and has the ability to follow the usually quite abstract interviews.

### Star Trek

Producers and programmers do not always accurately assess the target audiences for their programs in advance of broadcast. One example is the original *Star Trek* series. It was originally broadcast on the NBC network at 10 P.M., with only moderate success in drawing the adult audience available at that hour. After its network run, the series was released into syndication, where it has had phenomenal success in attracting young adult and teenage audiences in later afternoon time slots. What has turned out to be a primary audience for that series is not the same group originally targeted.

### A Prime-Time Sitcom

As a final example, you pick a half-hour situation comedy broadcast by one of the major networks in prime time. If we were to name any one particular series, there is some risk that it will no longer be in the prime time schedule by the time you read this, but it's a pretty safe bet that some sitcom series will remain in network schedules for years to come. It has become a very successful form in prime time.

As we have noted, the term prime time is itself an indicator of the nature of the target audience. The reason the period is called "prime" is because the largest and most demographically diverse audience group possible is available to watch television during those evening hours. The producers of this series and the network that is airing it want to capture as much of that available group as possible.

For the writer, the requirement to reach a large and diverse audience means that the level of language, the concepts of the plot, and the structure of the program must be understood by many different types of people—young and old, educated and uneducated. Under these circumstances, the appropriate writing style is to use simple language, plots, and characterization in order to ensure clarity and understanding for as many viewers as possible.

Please understand, however, that although prime-time network programs still are the most important group of programs from an economic standpoint, they represent a comparatively small portion of all programming. In general, the broadcasting industry is moving away from such broad-based programming and toward increased specificity in content and in audiences.

The trend toward specificity, or *narrowcasting* as it is called, can be seen in public broadcasting, in radio, and in cable. Public radio and television stations produce and broadcast a wide selection of programs intended for different minority audiences. Most commercial radio stations air a distinctive format of talk or music intended to reach a narrow segment of the total listening audience. As cable television and other new technologies of communication, satellite transmission, videotape, and so on expand throughout the country, the choices for audiences are becoming greater. Greater choice leads to more specific programming for increasingly narrow target groups. The writer who has a clear understanding of the target audience for whom a script is to be written, and of why that target has been chosen, is then in a position to make decisions on how to influence that audience's behavior.

## QUANTITATIVE AND QUALITATIVE MEASUREMENT

The entire economic structure of commercial broadcasting depends on quantitative audience measurement. Stations and networks set their advertising rates and make programming decisions based on the size and composition of their audiences as estimated by the rating surveys taken by measurement companies.

The data obtained from these surveys are voluminous, and are organized and analyzed in many ways. For each market and for each station in the market, information on the size and demographic composition of audiences is available. Trends can be shown by following similar data over the time span of several surveys. The viewing (or listening) habits of any particular age or sex group can be identified. The demographic breakdown of the audience attracted to a program, or to all programs of a particular type, can be charted and compared over time or in various sections of the country.

**Figure 10.1.** *Frank & Ernest* reprinted by permission of NEA, Inc.

Individual broadcast stations and networks collect this information for their own sales and programming purposes. A writer working for a station, network, or ad agency would have access to these data and should use them in designing programs and announcements to reach audiences of known composition.

Quantitative information is critical to programmers and sales managers, and it can be helpful to writers in knowing what the general relationships are between certain types of programs and audiences. But it doesn't help writers very much with the specific task of preparing a script for a new dramatic series or a public affairs program, or in developing any kind of a new program idea, because it doesn't give any indications of why individuals choose television or radio in general or why they choose particular programs and stations in preference to others. To get that information, we turn to qualitative research and, more specifically, to gratifications research.

## AUDIENCE GRATIFICATIONS

The broad area known as qualitative research includes several areas of study, including the effects of media upon individuals and groups, attitudes shown by persons toward the media and, of particular interest to us, the gratifications that audiences receive from their viewing and listening. Investigators in this field attempt to learn how media meet the basic psychological needs of individuals. What gratifications do people seek and receive when they choose to listen to radio or watch television? Research in this area began in the 1940s with studies of radio programs. By the late 1980s a substantial body of research studies on television gratifications had also been built up, research which comes from several countries—Great Britain, Scandinavia, Israel and the United States. The accumulated data from these numerous studies are now sufficient to show patterns in the uses that audiences make of

media. One of the leading researchers, Professor Jay G. Blumler, has identified three major orientations audiences take toward program content:

> First of all a *cognitive* orientation, whereby the audience member
> looks primarily for information about some feature of society and the
> wider world around him—as in "surveillance" sought from the news,
> information about party policies and other issues of the day from
> election broadcasts, or perhaps "reality exploration" as a use of
> many fictional series and serials scheduled on television and radio.
>
> Second, people want *diversion* of many kinds, including, for ex-
> ample, the relief from boredom and constraints of daily routines de-
> rived from chat shows, music, comedy, and other forms of light en-
> tertainment, as well as the excitement generated by adventure
> serials, quizzes, sports and competitive games, and even the horse-
> race appeal of following an election campaign.
>
> Third, uses and gratifications studies have often highlighted a sep-
> arate *personal identity* function, standing for ways of using media ma-
> terials to give added salience to something important in the audience
> member's own life or situation.[1]

By analyzing the conclusions of a number of qualitative studies, and by
modifying some previously devised lists, we have arrived at a list containing
eleven categories of gratification. It is our belief that the presence in a program of any of these characteristics represents an attraction, at least to some
audience groups. A popular program might have several gratifications, each
with moderate attraction strength for its target audience, or it might have
only one or two gratifications, but ones that are very strong in attracting that
group. These categories are:

1. *Tension.* The development of unresolved issues leading to a climax; various forms of conflict, both mental and physical.

2. *Action.* The presence of physical action and movement, including
   violence.

3. *Sex appeal.* Physical attractiveness; sexually suggestive situations and
   dialogue; plots using love as a theme; music, especially with love or sex
   in the lyrics.

4. *Comedy.* Humor, in a range of categories from very broad to sophisticated.

5. *Information.* The need or usefulness of knowing.

6. *Importance.* The relevance of information; the presence of authority, or
   of important personalities with recognized names; "bigness."

7. *Value.* Worthwhileness; ethical or moral values presented in program
   content and situations.

8. *Personalism.* The extent to which the audience can identify with characters, events, situations; includes empathy, sympathy, and nostalgia.

9. *Curiosity.* Our interest in other human beings particularly, but also curiosity about places, events, and so on.

10. *Realism.* The plausibility, believability, and reality of characters or situations.

11. *Novelty.* The presence of unusual characters, situations, presentations; freshness.[2]

The sequence into which these gratifications have been organized is a reflection of the three basic audience orientations identified by Blumler. The first four—tension, action, sex appeal and comedy—are most strongly found in programs that provide diversion for audiences. Information, importance, and value cluster together readily; programs in which they are found satisfy the cognitive orientation. Personalism, curiosity, and realism are related to the personal identity orientation, or at least more strongly related there than to the other orientations, in our view.

We make no claim that these are discrete categories. To the contrary, items on this list interact to a considerable degree. Some of these gratifications frequently cluster together and reinforce one another. You should also be aware of these further cautions:

1. Don't become bound by the labels given these categories. Each is identified by a single word or phrase with which we have tried to express the essential nature of the gratification, but each can be presented in a variety of ways and often is actually a cluster of related behaviors.

2. Understand that the concept of gratification is separate from that of content or program types. Quantitative research shows very easily the relationships between audiences and content (for examples, females in general watch situation comedies more than males). But, in examining gratifications, we are attempting to find factors that cut across program types and that may also separate popular from less popular programs within the same general type.

3. The list may not be complete. As research in this area continues, different factors emerge from studies that use different methodologies, different audiences and different content. Further studies may uncover new or modified categories of gratification. But based on present findings, this list, we believe, provides a reasonable explanation of the media choices audiences make.

4. You will also recognize some similarities between this list and the list of persuasive appeals presented in the preceding chapter. Sex appeal, for example, appears on both lists. There is a similarity in that both ap-

proaches deal with the relationship between content and audiences. However, two quite different perspectives are involved. Persuasive appeals are used by sponsors to influence audiences, to motivate and direct their behavior. Gratifications, on the other hand, are descriptions of the results of more or less freely made selections from among choices offered to audiences. They are the benefits the audience receives from the viewing experience.

5. There is also a relationship between program structure and gratifications. We believe that an individual's choice to tune to a particular program can be explained primarily by the gratifications he or she will receive, but a well-structured program will support those gratifications, whereas a poorly structured program will work against audience enjoyment. A program structured to provide above-average variety and fast pace will also be perceived as having tension and action, for example.

## Tension

The dictionary definitions of *tension* use such terms as mental or emotional strain, anxiety, suspense, and excitement. Another description would be "uncertainty about the outcome."

In dramatic programs, tension is present in the uncertainty over how the plot or plots are to be resolved. The well-written play is structured to provide climax, the heightening of uncertainty as the play progresses, until the final resolution at the end of the drama. Subsidiary climaxes are also provided at the end of each act, and in continuing series programs such as soap operas, a climax of uncertainty is reached at the end of each episode and not resolved until the following episode. We have discussed climax as a component of program structure; tension is highly related.

### Danger

One very powerful form of tension is found in physical danger. In dramatic thriller programs such as westerns, police or detective programs, or science fiction dramas, the uncertainty may be over the life or physical safety of the hero or some other characters, who may be in danger of being killed or of suffering some other terrible fate at the hands of a villain, or by the forces of nature—wild animals, a sudden blizzard.

A less physical but still very powerful form of danger is the fear of loss—loss of a job, loss of one's reputation, loss of a marriage, or loss of a girl- or boyfriend. Love plots are rooted in the uncertainty of the outcome, or at least uncertainty as to *how* the outcome will be resolved. Viewers of television soap operas will certainly recognize these forms of tension as prime appeals in those programs.

Danger can be present in nondramatic programs as well—for example, in adventure documentaries such as mountain climbing expeditions, and even in news broadcasts, as in the live, on-the-spot coverage of a hostage situation.

### Problem-Solving Tension

In dramatic programs this may involve "battles with one's conscience," in which the hero or heroine is forced to make an uncomfortable decision—which will hurt someone he or she loves or force an unpleasant outcome.

This form of tension also exists in game programs and quiz shows. Audiences are attracted at least in part because of their interest in finding out who will "win" the game. The gratification is further heightened if the program is structured so that the audience can play along. The tension is no longer just vicarious observation of the contest; now it is real. "Can I win the game before the on-screen contestant does, or before the solution is announced?"

In the short-lived dramatic series *Ellery Queen,* at a point about two-thirds of the way through the program, the detective, Queen, turned directly to the camera/audience, announced that he had sufficient clues to solve the crime and that the same clues had been presented to the viewer, and asked whether the viewers could identify the criminal. Although this program was unique in making that statement directly to the audience, most detective series provide indirect invitations to audiences to solve the problems presented on the screen; they keep the culprit unidentified until the climax of the show. But contrast *Ellery Queen* with *Columbo.* In *Columbo* the audience sees the crime in the opening moments and knows the criminal. Tension is replaced, at least in part, by personal involvement, as the audience follows Columbo through the process of identifying the culprit. The different plotting technique changes the gratifications that are present and in turn provides strength for different audience groups.

### Other Tensions

A panel discussion program in which the participants hold different, conflicting points of view provides tension through the conflict of ideas. Individuals in the audience will be interested in knowing which opinion will prevail: Will one participant be able to convince others to change or modify their opinions? Audience members can also test their own opinions against those held by the panel.

Uncertainty over the outcome is also one of the strongest gratifications for audiences of athletic contests. In most such broadcasts, uncertainty over which participant or team will win holds the audience to the end of the contest. But whenever the contest becomes lopsided, when one contestant is sufficiently far ahead that the outcome is no longer in doubt, tension is removed and the size of the watching audience declines sharply. Audience members find other programs to watch or other things to do.

By using a variety of examples to describe various forms of tension, we have tried to suggest that this gratification is present in many types of programs. It seems, also, that it is a gratification which can have strength for all types of audience groups—that it is not strongly differentiated by sex, age or other demographic characteristics. Quite probably tension is heightened by its interaction with realism and information (discussed separately below). Both network and syndicated schedules currently contain a number of "reality" programs, such as *Rescue 911, Cops* and *I Witness Video*, that effectively combine these gratifications. Some of these series use video of actual events obtained from TV news departments or amateur videographers; others create and dramatize situations but shoot them to look "real."

However, it seems to be possible to have too much tension and realism in a program. Probably you have watched programs in which the tension was so intense, in which you feared for the hero or heroine so much, that you were forced to leave the room until the scene was resolved. Even though audiences know intellectually that what they are watching is not real, the emotional tension can become so great that many people do have to remove themselves from the program until that tension is released.

The key to this gratification is that whatever the type of program or situation, if there is uncertainty, then there is tension, and for many audience groups at least, a positive attraction.

## Action

This gratification can be most quickly and easily described as a sense of movement or activity. Adventure programs are frequently listed in program logs as "action-adventure." Along with the uncertainty of the outcome, there is a great deal of movement—automobile chases, fights between cowboys and Indians, between police and criminals, between space warriors and robots, and so on.

Action can also be seen in variety programs in the movement of individual dancers or dance troupes on a stage; in news and documentary programs that report "real life" activities involving movement, and in game shows in which the contestants are involved with stunts.

The different types of action present in different types of athletic contests provide a clue to the strength of this gratification for different audiences. Broadcasts of sports events with a strong dose of physical contact, such as football, hockey, boxing and, to a lesser degree, basketball, attract a different (demographic) audience than broadcasts of noncontact sports, such as tennis, golf and baseball. The difference does not seem to be between team or nonteam sports but solely the amount of physical contact among participants, which we consider to be a form of action.

To some extent, the amount of action, or movement, that can be included in a program is a function of the budget and the production approach. Action-adventure programs are filmed or taped on location, where a large variety of different settings can be used. This variety of backgrounds in itself contributes to the feeling of movement in the program, in addition to the actual movement that takes place. In contrast, situation comedies are filmed or taped in a studio, frequently in front of a live audience. These programs must be contained within a few static sets. There is little opportunity for movement or action other than characters entering or leaving the scene. Consequently, action is minimal in such programs.

Action can be a gratification on radio as well as television; there it is the description or suggestion of movement in actors' lines or in narration which provides the appeal, as in the play-by-play account of a football game, for example.

Many programs—all types of adventure programs, both dramatic and documentary, and sporting events are examples—present both tension and action. But some programs present tension without much action—soap operas, for example—and other programs present action, or movement, without the necessary accompaniment of tension. We've seen an example in the athletic contest when the outcome is no longer in doubt. Tension is reduced, although not necessarily removed, but the same level of action continues until the game is over.

The only discernible relationship between this gratification and audience groups is a stronger positive attraction of men than women to physical activity. This tendency may be the result of conditioning and stereotyping— "Boys can climb trees, but girls can't"—but whatever its antecedents, it is an identifiable difference. The difference appears in early childhood. Boys watch action cartoons more frequently than girls. Action stays strong through early and middle adulthood, then falls off somewhat in older age, but remains stronger for men than for women throughout life.

The difference in the strength of gratification of the different types of sporting events—contact vs. noncontact sports—is at least in part due to other categories of gratification, but to the extent that there are differences in the type of action, it seems that contact sports appeal more strongly to lower education and income groups, and that noncontact sports have greater appeal for a more educated, higher income audience—again primarily men in both cases.

There may be an opposite pole to this gratification—quiet and calm. Certainly many programs do not contain action to any important degree, but whether the lack of action represents also a lack of gratification, or whether calm is in itself a positive gratification to some audience groups, there is no research to determine.

## Sex Appeal

This gratification should be familiar, and recognized, in one form or another by practically everyone except small children. It is presented in radio and television programs in a variety of ways, of which these are a few examples.

### Physical Attractiveness

The most obvious manifestation is the presence of "sexy" or physically attractive people on programs. The attribute does not have to be limited to physical features, however. Sex appeal may also be found in the personality of a performer who is not necessarily physically handsome. The important consideration is the degree of attractiveness and/or warmth of personality the person possesses.

Note also that sex appeal is not just a visual characteristic. It may be present in a person's voice, which, if it is warm, pleasant, friendly, and inviting, will contribute to the appeal.

The gratification is strong for both sexes; the individual providing the appeal may be either male or female. Blatantly obvious use of physical sex appeal, such as the costumes worn by female performers on the early editions of *Battle of the Network Stars* or on *Dukes of Hazzard*, led to strong criticism from feminist and religious groups and a consequent toning down of the more flagrant uses, or abuses, of this gratification at the network level. But costumes displaying skin (or muscle) continue to be a mainstay of some programs such as *American Gladiators, Paradise Beach,* and *Baywatch,* and commercials for products such as beer or diet soda. The success of cable channels showing R- and even X-rated films and music video channels also indicates that this is indeed a powerful attraction.

### Love Stories

Here we have the programs which dramatize "boy-meets-girl" situations, the love triangles common in soap-opera-type programs, and other romantic plots. Love stories are most commonly found in dramatic programs, but they can be found in other types of programs, such as game shows—a contestant is asked to tell how she first became acquainted with her husband, or he is asked to tell how she proposed.

### Talking about Sex

Included in this category are the sexually based conversations on *Love Connection* and similar shows, the selection of sexually related stories on *Hard Copy* and *A Current Affair* (programs which really talk much more about sex than they show), and the whole genre of radio call-in programs involving discussion of sexual attitudes and problems and making dates that fostered the name "topless radio." In recent years the FCC has cracked down on several radio stations and personalities that were stretching the limits of this content. Stations are now more cautious in their use of this gratification to attract audiences.

### *Music as Sex Appeal*

Many popular music selections, both current and older standards, have vocals that express love or deal with unrequited love. Even if the music is presented without vocals, listeners will fill in the lyrics in their own minds if they are familiar with the song. Old familiar music having a love theme has strong sex appeal value (along with nostalgia) for audiences of the age group who were in high school or college and "falling in love" at the time when the music was first popular. Some radio stations draw large audiences with these "oldies" formats.

Even without a direct love theme or lyrics, music has some sex appeal value; rhythms have a sexual connotation.

This gratification, as the examples suggest, is dependent upon both sex and age. It is practically nonexistent for young children (although even in children there is curiosity about sex without sexual drive). It is very strong for teenagers and young adults, then falls off in intensity slowly but steadily into old age.

Sex appeal is highly related to the gratification of personalism—that is, to the ability of audience members to identify with characters. This does not mean that performers need be of the same age as the audience to be attractive; many mature men are strongly drawn to programs featuring attractive younger women, for example. But in general the attraction is strongest for individuals to whom the audience can relate most easily.

The romantic story form of this gratification, as opposed to physical attractiveness or use of music, seems to be stronger for women generally than for men. However, the strength of soap-opera-type programs for women comes only partly from the sex appeal in the plots, and partly from other gratifications in these programs which also are strong for women.

In analyzing this gratification within a program, you should be aware that it can be present in a variety of forms, and have attraction for a variety of different audience groups. This brief overview barely scratches the surface of the possible manifestations of this powerful gratification.

## Comedy

One very effective force in attracting many audience groups is humor. Some programs offer comedy as their strongest gratification. In other programs the use of comedy is secondary, as in a serious dramatic program, when comic relief is used to relieve the tension of the drama.

Comedy can be a gratification only if it is recognized or perceived as such by the individual. We've all experienced situations at a party, or in reading the comic strips, where one person will find a joke outrageously funny and another one will say: "What's funny about that?" Even after an explanation, he or she may not appreciate the humor because that person's experience does not extend to the type of situation being made fun of. Political cartoons are especially susceptible to this problem. They cater to a minority audience that must be quite politically aware in order to see humor in the usually abstract illustrations.

The wide variety of comedy styles can be organized into several subcategories with the aid of another gratification—action—but in reality each use of humor in a program series is different from all others. These are but the broadest of categories.

### Broad Slapstick Comedy

This type is highly dependent on action and movement, and is strongly visual. Dialogue does not even have to be present, but when it is, it often involves the exchange of insults between characters. Characterizations are very broadly drawn. Older practitioners of this style were the Keystone Cops, Abbott and Costello, Soupy Sales and the Three Stooges—comics still seen on rerun children's programs. Newer examples would include some of Steve Martin's work, skits shown on *Saturday Night Live* and several of the children's programs aired by the networks on Saturday mornings.

### Situation Comedy

This of course, is one of the major programming forms of television, and in itself it exhibits a wide range of styles. The broader comedies—less realistic, with characterizations very broadly drawn and with lots of movement and visual humor—have appeal almost identical to slapstick comedy. Other scripts are more realistically drawn; the humor is more subtle and is more likely to be combined with human interest, tension, and personalism, as opposed to action and possible sex appeal. At the broader, more exaggerated end of the scale we might include *Gilligan's Island* and *Perfect Strangers*. At the other, more realistic end would be *Seinfeld* and *Murphy Brown*. Other series would range somewhere between these two poles.

### Gag Comedy

Standup comedy or gag comedy uses even less action and movement; no situations or locations are used. This style has been used for many years by Bob Hope in his TV specials. The *Tonight Show* monologue and similar routines by David Letterman, Arsenio Hall and other late-night hosts also fall into this category, as do the comedy showcase types of programs seen on some cable channels. Sometimes gag comedy involves characterizations. Minnie Pearl on *Grand Ol' Opry* and Grandpa Jones on *Hee-Haw* became famous playing country hayseed roles. Most often, however, the comic delivers this form of material "straight."

The emphasis is on the use of clever, laugh-provoking lines and the poking of fun at people, situations, events. The humor may be topical, aimed at politics and politicians, for example, and may involve a quite sophisticated satire; that is, it may require that the audience have a good background in the topic in order to recognize the people and situations being satirized. Then we have a situation similar to that of the political cartoon: The gratification will be limited to those people in the audience who understand.

We've already suggested the prime way that audiences relate to humor: It is funny only if you understand what's being made fun of. That means, for example, that children are likely to find humor primarily in the more visual, action-oriented, slapstick style and in broad situation comedy. Less sophisticated, lower socioeconomic, and less educated groups also respond more strongly to broader styles of comedy. Older audiences do not find any form to be strong, as a rule.

Although comedy is an important gratification in many programs, its presence is not always a strength. There are serious programs—news, documentary, religious, and others—in which the presence of comedy would be a serious breach of structural unity, and would weaken the other intended gratifications.

## Information

Information may be both content and gratification. Many programs—news broadcasts, public affairs programs, documentaries, and the like—provide content that is largely if not totally informative, and the popularity of these types of programs attests to the strength of information as a gratification. But other programs can also provide content which is perceived as informative, and which is gratifying to audiences.

Recall Blumler's cognitive orientation, which identifies two aspects of cognition as presented by programs: (1) surveillance, as in news broadcasts and other obviously "informative" programs, and (2) reality explorations, in which audiences may draw information from fictional programs as well.

### *Surveillance*

It is this gratification which we see most clearly when audiences tune in to news broadcasts, public affairs programs, and documentaries. Statements made by the respondents in one study showed that audiences tune to news programs for these purposes:

1. To follow what is going on in the world generally. "Watching the news keeps me in touch with the world." "I like to see how big issues are finally sorted out." "It tells me about the main events of the day."

2. To see the relationship between such events and the viewer's own personal circumstances. "I follow the news so I won't be caught unawares by price increases and that sort of thing."

3. To see the relationship between such events and the forming of judgments about the performance of powerholders in society. "Watching the news helps me to keep an eye on the mistakes people in authority make."

4. To help them make up their minds on current issues. "Television news helps me to make up my mind about things." "Television news provides food for thought."[3]

### Reality Exploration

Information is also present in many programs where we might overlook its presence, particularly in dramatic programs. These statements are responses to questions about listening to a radio serial drama:

"It sometimes helps me to understand what is happening in my own life."

"The people in [the program] sometimes have problems that are like my own."

"It deals with realistic problems without offending me."[4]

There is a strong relationship between the gratification of information in whatever form it is presented and that of importance (to be discussed next). In fact, we may say that information has strength as a gratification only to the extent that it is perceived to be important to and by each individual audience member. In a news broadcast, for example, for an item to have strong appeal it should deal with issues that may affect the audience members, or with persons or situations known to them.

A program about wheat farming may be of considerable interest to a person engaged in agriculture, but it offers no information of importance to the average city dweller, and consequently provides no degree of appeal for the urban listener. Similarly, we are likely to be interested in local news, which may contain names and places with which we are familiar, but will be less interested in happenings in other places unless we have been there or the newscaster points out at the beginning of the story how it may affect us.

As we have suggested, information is a highly selective gratification, but in general it is stronger for older audience groups, for males and for the more highly educated. Aware of these tendencies, broadcast programmers began a few years ago to take steps to attract younger audiences and more females, because the younger, female group is a much more important target audience for many products advertised on television. Among the more successful efforts at attracting this group have been newscasts that include more human interest and "how-to" features, often called "soft-news" stories, and even whole programs in that vein. These programs also avoid the negative, unhappy stories likely to be found in the major events taking place each day.

## Importance

LIke the situation with information, it is the individual's perception of importance that is critical to this gratification. In a public affairs discussion, the topic, say, of tax increases may have a very direct bearing on all the residents of a community, but unless each individual viewer understands how that topic may affect him or her, it has no strength. Importance can take several forms:

### Subject Matter Importance

This is the form of importance we have already linked with information. The link is strong and obvious in newscasts, in public affairs programs, and in religious programs. Audience members choose to tune to informative programming if they believe that the content of the program will be important to them in some way. That importance may be only that the person will be able to converse knowledgeably with co-workers about news events on the following day, but that gratification can be sufficient for individuals to tune in to certain programs.

### Authority or Star Quality

A second form of importance is the presence of authority or of a person who has "name value." Television and radio depend heavily on "stars" to attract audiences, a phenomenon that is also obvious in the motion picture industry. A script for a dramatic program might be extremely well acted by unknown performers, but audiences are not as likely to turn to it as they will to the same script with one or more well-known performers. New programs that feature unknown performers will use "guest stars" to attract audiences until the series is established, or if the program is a special, to help in the promotion for the show.

Using persons who are known and respected to endorse products is also an effective advertising technique. Sometimes the person presented as an authority on a topic or issue is legitimately qualified on that subject, but that is not a necessary qualification. Movie stars often are used to endorse political candidates or to speak on behalf of political propositions. They may have no qualifications to speak on the topic, but their name value is nevertheless important.

### Bigness

Finally, the mere present of "bigness"—of programs done on a large scale—can add some measure of gratification, especially for younger, less sophisticated and therefore more impressionable audiences. We include that as a form of importance. After all, if the producers are willing to spend all that money on the program, it must be important, right? Anyway, producers seem more than willing to include the cost of production in publicity releases about new programs, and their purpose in doing so is to impress the potential audience.

Importance will rarely be able to "carry" a program unaided. As a rule, it serves as a secondary gratification, reinforcing one or more other gratifications.

## Value

We have to be particularly cautious in defining and describing this gratification, and differentiating it from others. In one sense, all gratifications may be considered to be aspects of value. After all, what we have been saying all along is that people tune in to programs because they get some gratification from that activity. We might just replace the word *gratification* with *value*— saying that programs are chosen because audiences get value from so doing.

However, our definition is more narrow. *Value* in our view represents the "worthwhileness" audiences place on a program and its contents, especially when that quality has ethical, moral, or religious overtones.

This gratification is highly related to both information and importance. But value contains an emotional component that is not present in information or importance. It can be seen in audience responses to patriotism, to religion, or to the introduction in a program of babies, young children, elderly people or animals, all of which are representative of valuable attributes to some audience group.

A common comment made by individuals who view religious programs or who watch a Fourth of July special is that the program "makes them feel better" or makes them "proud." These comments indicate that the emotional stimulation provided by that program has been converted into a value by the individual. And that behavior points out a crucial aspect of this gratification. Even more than for information or importance, the strength of value as a gratification to an individual will be dependent on that person's perception of the program's content as providing value.

There are demographic relationships between certain groups and value, such as that between religion and older people, particularly women, and even more particularly older women who reside in certain geographic regions, or between older male war veterans and patriotism, or between women and the appeal of babies and small children, or between retired blue-collar workers and Democratic politics. But even more important than demographic generalization is each individual's perception of value. If audience members do not recognize that a program has value for them, then it does not (regardless of what the program's writer and producer may say in the publicity release).

## Personalism

We have chosen this term (used in several gratification studies) to label a broad-ranging gratification tied strongly to Blumler's description of the *personal identity orientation*. Other words used to describe the gratification are intimacy, or involvement, or identification or participation between audience and program content. In the theater yet another term is used—*empathy*—defined as the intellectual identification with or vicarious experiencing of the feelings, thoughts, or attitudes of another.

The gratification is present in many types of programs and is frequently found in conjunction with other appeals. Some of the forms in which it can be recognized include these:

### Personal Identification

This is evident in any program in which the audience can identify with the characters or plot situations, finding them believable, sympathetic, and, most important, real. A common comment that describes this appeal is: "I know how they feel: I've been through a similar situation myself."

Although identification is particularly strong in dramatic programs, the programs do not have to be fictional for this involvement to take place. One of the most successful television programs ever produced for targeting senior citizens was Lawrence Welk's musical program. Several strong gratifications were present (including nostalgia, which we'll discuss a bit further on), but particularly powerful was the feeling of many viewers that the performers on the program were just like family. These were friends that visited each week in the viewers' homes. Television fan magazines, and the articles about television stars that appear in other publications as well, feed off this gratification, along with those of importance and curiosity.

Viewers, especially men, also identify with sports teams, sometimes very strongly.

One may identify with locations as well as with persons. If you have been to a foreign city, and that city appears on the screen as the locale for a play, you are more likely to stay tuned to try to recognize the scenes, and vicariously, to relive memories of having been there. For athletic contests, having played the sport in high school or in college, or at least being familiar with the rules and therefore able to follow the progress of the contest more easily, makes enjoyment stronger. The networks have spent considerable effort and money to explain the rules and techniques of professional football to women in pregame and half-time shows. Their purpose, of course, is to get more women to watch, or at least to make them more sympathetic to their husbands' watching.

A more direct form of involvement is possible in programs that have audience feedback, such as telephone call-in talk programs. A few years ago some interesting experiments were conducted in two-way interactive cable programming. That form has pretty much died, at least temporarily, but we do see ads for "Interactive Network," which uses a device that allows viewers to "play" sports in competition with other viewers.

Some viewers identify with particular channels, especially on cable, where specialty programming has taken over complete channels. It is possible to identify with the Nashville Network if you are a country and western fan or similarly identify with the Court TV channel, the science fiction network, ESPN, and so on.

Under the heading of tension we mentioned that it may be possible to have too much tension, that the appeal may be so strong that individuals leave the room because of anxiety over the fate of a character. When that situation exists, it's a reflection of strong personalism as well. Of course we know the program is make-believe and prerecorded on a tape or film, but the empathy with the character has become so strong as to suspend disbelief.

### Fantasy

By this term we do not mean the use of supernatural or fantastic gimmicks as plot devices; we don't believe such devices have any particular appeal in themselves. But fantasy whereby individuals in an audience can imagine themselves in a role as depicted in a program can be a very strong gratification. We see it as an intense form of personal identification.

Some people who study audience motivations suggest that many people believe that their lives are different from what they really are—that they have fantasies about themselves being more powerful, more sexy or a better parent. Advertisers take advantage of this fantasy perception when they promote products that will make us more sexy (cosmetics, automobiles), a better parent (buying insurance protection for the family) and so on.

Children and teens are more likely to become caught up in this projection into media roles than are more mature adults. But who wouldn't like to have their fantasies come true, with no harm done?

Unfortunately, when carried to an extreme, fantasy has resulted in a few cases where mentally imbalanced individuals have opted to live out scenes from television, with terrible consequences. While these situations are rare, writers and producers should carefully consider that possibility when developing bizarre or life-threatening plots.

### Nostalgia

This aspect of personalism carries the connotation of favorable recollection of past events—situations in which audience members are reminded of their childhood, early school days, old friends and so on. The elements may appear in a television program that re-creates a past period of time. The long-running series *Happy Days* used this gratification effectively, as have *The Wonder Years* and *Brooklyn Bridge*. Quite a few radio stations have successfully built their formats around "golden oldies"—music from periods that will be recalled as pleasurable experiences from their youth by a target audience.

### Sympathy

There is a strong tie between personalism and human interest, as shown by the concept of sympathy. In addition to our interest in or curiosity about other people (or animals), there can be an emotional, sympathetic, feeling sorry for persons with troubles or who are less fortunate than ourselves. This combination of personal involvement and human interest can be a very strong gratification.

There are few obvious relationships between demographic audience groups and personalism. We have already mentioned the possibility that younger or less sophisticated groups may be more likely to fantasize their involvement with characters or situations. On the other hand, younger audiences do not have as many or as broad personal experiences to relate to their viewing or listening, and are not likely to find strength in nostalgia or sympathy.

Ethnicity may provide a strong tie to this gratification. Black audiences, for example, will watch programs that feature *believable* black performers, and so on.

## Curiosity

In some gratification studies, curiosity has been identified as a major audience orientation, given equal ranking with cognition, diversion, and personal identity. There is no question but that it is a very strong gratification in some program types, and reasonably strong in many others. To a large extent the gratification arises from our curiosity about and interest in people—in the way they behave, in their problems, and in the things that interest them. Therefore we have made human interest a major subcategory of curiosity.[5]

### Human Interest

This gratification is strongly tied to those of personalism and realism. We are especially interested in the activities and problems of people with whom we can identify. They don't have to be people like us—interest in celebrities, royalty, the wealthy negates such an assumption—but they do have to be "real," genuine people or, if in a fictional program, they must be believable characterizations. *Lifestyles of the Rich and Famous* has been successful in combining human interest and star-quality importance as primary gratifications.

*Love Connection* exemplifies another powerful combination, human interest and personal identification for young adults, along with a substantial dose of sex appeal.

Producers working for NBC on the presentation of the 1992 Olympic games were faced with the critical task of making the broadcast attractive to the broad audiences available in prime time. (If they had focused only on the actual contests, they would have limited their audience just to sports enthusiasts, an audience much too narrow to justify the advertising rates they needed to get to pay their costs and profit. As it was, they lost money anyway.) To attract this broader group of mostly women, the telecasts were filled with human interest stories about the athletes, the city of Barcelona and even the announcers describing the events. There was even a nightly music video.

The scriptwriter may strengthen human interest by

- Avoiding stiffness and formality in the style of presentation of an entertainer.

- Providing "stage business" for performers that is ordinary and normal routine. It makes the dramatic role human and believable if the leading character can't find a match to light his cigarette, or can't make his cigarette lighter work, or has difficulty tying his necktie, or bumps into a piece of furniture.

- Providing situations that are recognizable and commonplace. For example, in a comedy dramatic program, the plot may revolve around very common family situations—such as the problems arising when Junior brings home a report card showing a low grade in English, or the family turmoil created when the teenage daughter goes to her first formal dance, or the husband-wife differences with respect to plans for a family vacation. Situation comedies depend heavily on this aspect of human interest.

- Emphasizing the problems ordinary people face. We're not interested just in the fact that they have problems—all of us have problems—but in the way in which people react to problem situations. We like to know what things bother them, how they feel about things, and what they think. One early television (and before that, radio) series, *Queen for a Day*, awarded its daily prize to the contestant with the "worst" hard-luck story. Daytime talk programs—*Donahue*, *Oprah* and others—regularly pick topics and guests that fit this description.

Human interest is obviously a strong appeal in continuing serial drama programs, although some of these programs now tend to present characters and situations with more glamour than would be the case if human interest were the only appeal.

Television and radio news broadcasts have for years used the "human interest story" as a break from the straightforward, factual news story. Frequently this type of story is placed at the end of the newscast to conclude on an optimistic, lighthearted note and provide a bit of an emotional climax.

### *Intellectual Curiosity*

Although human interest forms a large portion of curiosity, it is not the only aspect that can be identified. We can be curious about places, about past or future time, about the operations of the world around us, and so on. The programs that most obviously cater to these forms of curiosity are travelogs; science information programs like *Cosmos, Nova, The Undersea World of Jacques Cousteau*; historical dramas like many of the series in *Masterpiece Theater*; and of course programs of formal education.

The kinds of programs we are describing contain large amounts of information, which is also a gratification, but they differ from other informative programs such as news and news commentary in that the information provided is not timely. They also differ in the sizes of the audiences they draw. The comparatively small audiences for programs which have intellectual curiosity as their primary gratification indicate that this gratification is not strong for most people.

Curiosity can be built into almost any form of broadcast message simply by withholding information the audience wants or expects to hear. In a drama, curiosity takes the form of building for climax; we stay tuned and watch to see how the plot is going to be resolved. In a commercial, a briefly stated problem is presented at the beginning of the ad, and then the product is introduced as the means of solving the problem. We become "hooked" by the problem and curious to find out how it will be resolved.

One well-known radio program series that very effectively uses curiosity as a primary appeal is *The Rest of the Story*, a series developed and presented by news personality Paul Harvey. Each broadcast in that series tells a little-known but interesting story about a famous person. The person's name is deliberately withheld until the end of the vignette. Audiences, with their curiosity aroused, stay tuned just to find out who the story is about. News headlines and "teasers" which hint at stories coming up later in the broadcast serve the same purpose.

## Realism

Of necessity we have mentioned realism several times already in connection with other gratifications. Realism, or the lack of it, is a consideration in every program and it clusters readily with both tension and information. The gratification, however, does not mean reality in a literal sense. Literal reality would deny appeal to any program that contains elements of fantasy—cartoon programs for children, broad farce situation comedies, and the long series of programs with supernatural gimmicks, such as *Superman, I Dream of Jeannie, Wonder Woman, Mork and Mindy, Bewitched, The Six-Million-Dollar Man, Gemini Man, Manimal.*

Rather, reality means that characters, events, behaviors must be believable or plausible in the perception of the individual audience member. We know that radio and television dramatic programs are fiction, and that the amount of literal reality, or fantasy, in a particular program can range over a wide scale. But in general we expect that the things that take place are things that reasonably "could happen," and that the characters who appear conform to our ideas of what those characters should be like in "real life."

If there is some sort of gimmick, it must be explained. Doogie Howser can be both a brilliant physician and a teenager because he was extremely precocious. *Quantum Leap* uses a complex premise, as does *Herman's Head*. We mentioned other examples in Chapter 6, when we discussed signatures in program openings. Often, the gimmick is explained in that type of opening. We will accept these unrealistic fictional situations so long as the rest of the dramatic action is realistic and so long as the behaviors of the characters are plausible.

Possibly the most frequent problem with the appeal of believability results from actions on the part of an actor that "don't fit" the character portrayed. Actions in any way out of the norm must be given sufficient motivation, in advance—and some actions simply "couldn't happen," regardless of the motivation. If the characters, the situations, and the actions of characters fall short of being plausible and believable, the overall attraction of the program will be damaged.

Our discussion has focused on realism (or its lack) in dramatic, fictional programs. We have assumed throughout that "real" programs, all types other than fiction, have this characteristic automatically, and that its presence is expected and normal. If for some reason implausible, unrealistic material should appear in a news documentary, for example, the combined effect of whatever other gratifications are present will be seriously weakened.

## Novelty

The effectiveness of a program is affected by the degree of freshness, newness, originality, and novelty it provides. This concept of "freshness" is one about which it is difficult to draw hard-and-fast conclusions. We all know of programs and program personalities that have been continually successful in attracting listeners over periods of many years. At the same time, every program has a tendency to wear out after a time—after the newness and freshness and novelty have worn off. Some highly successful programs have fallen off rapidly in listener attractiveness by the end of their third or fourth season of broadcasting. Further, some programs have skyrocketed into popularity within a period of a few months or even a few weeks, largely because they offered something new and quite different from other programs available to listeners.

One of the primary sources of fresh ideas, especially for prime-time series, is the originality and creativity provided by a program's producer. Susan Harris has a particular signature to her work, ranging from *Soap* to *Golden Girls*. The Stephen Cannell studios have developed a reputation for hour-long action dramas: *The A-Team, 21 Jump Street, Wiseguy, Renegade* and others. Another very creative producer is Steven Bochco, who conceived *Hill Street Blues* and *L.A. Law*. But being original and creative can also be risky. It is possible to be too far from the mainstream. Bochco was also the originator of one of the famous disasters in prime-time scheduling, *Cop Rock*.

In general, it seems safe to conclude that as the newness or freshness of a program wears off, the program will decline in attractiveness to viewers even though other gratifications remain unchanged. If the other gratifications are strong, the series may survive for some time, but programs that use novelty as their primary gratification usually don't last long.


## OTHER CONSIDERATIONS

Over time, we can expect to have to modify this list of gratifications. Programs will change; the tastes of audiences will also change; and new research will become available. Even now there are some appeal-audience relationships about which we have come to no firm conclusion.

For example, there seems to be a dimension of simplicity-complexity in viewing decisions. We discussed simplicity in the chapter on aural style, noting at that time that in order to capture large, broad audiences, prime-time television programs have to be kept simple in language and plot. We also noted that the trend toward narrow casting—more channels with more programs for more specialized audiences—will permit more complex programs. But this simplicity-complexity factor is not only structural; it behaves like a gratification as well. Some audience groups seem to be positively attracted to programs that are more complex and require more intellectual effort. Not surprisingly, these are groups with higher levels of education and socioeconomic status. The failure of "educational" television to live up to its promise of raising educational and cultural standards may very well lie in that program-audience relationship, the fact that those groups which watch educational programs are, generally, those who are already educated. They are the groups who are best able to organize and to appreciate receiving new knowledge. The less educated seek simpler fare that is more entertaining and requires less effort to process.

The examples given for each gratification are programs that, in our opinion, show the appeal strongly, but obviously not exclusively. Other programs, and new programs which will come on the air after this analysis has been written, may also exhibit certain gratifications to equal or greater degree. Two programs may seem to be very similar, but each will have its own unique mixture of gratifications. They will differ if ever so slightly in the gratifications presented, or in the forms in which they are presented, and therefore in the strengths of their overall appeal for different audiences.

That's the whole point of this analysis. We know that different groups respond differently to the various programs available to them, and this process of analysis gives a means of identifying, at least in part, why those differences exist.

The writer who chooses certain gratifications for inclusion in a program will not automatically be successful in gathering an audience for that program. There are too many variables, both in the writing of the script and in external programming factors, to even suggest that. Every season many programs on every station and every network fail to maintain audience interest and are removed from the air. If this analytical approach were a foolproof tool, that failure rate would be greatly reduced.

But a list of gratifications does have value for the writer. It is a method of approach the writer can employ to make programs more attractive to audiences. It is a particularly useful tool because it considers the consumer's interests. Writers who have been successful over a long period of time may not consciously go to a list and pick gratifications they want to use in a program. They have learned by trial and error what approaches are successful with various types of audiences. For the beginning writer, we have provided a substitute for that trial and error experience. An important question you should ask yourself when preparing a script for a program is this: What will there be in this program that will provide an attraction to my target audience? And you should be able to provide an answer.

## ANALYZING WRITING ASSIGNMENTS

In these two chapters of Part 3 we have considered the beginning and the end points of most communication models—origination and reception. First, we looked at relationships between the broadcast writer and those who pay for the programs and announcements that make up broadcast communication. Then, we turned to the important and active role that audiences play in the process. We believe that writers can ultimately be much more effective if they understand these larger parts of the process.

Our approach to the writing-programming-management relationship can be summarized with a sequence of four questions. These questions delineate a process writers need to learn in order to prepare effective copy. You should ask, and answer, these broad questions to clarify your understanding of what is expected of you whenever a piece of copy is to be written.

1. *Who is the sponsor for the program or announcement?* In most cases this question is easily answered. It is the organization that is *paying* for the material to be placed on the air. Remember that sometimes there are multiple sponsors, and recall, as well, that in a program which contains participation advertising, those advertisers are not the sponsors of the program. The program was selected *and paid for* by the individual station

or network, which makes that station or network its sponsor. In that case, advertisers are the second step in the process. They will buy participations only if that program is demonstrated to be a successful vehicle for reaching the target groups they need to accomplish their purposes.

2. *What is the sponsor's purpose?* The discussion in Chapter 9 includes most, but probably not all, of the reasons why programs and announcements are sponsored. Conspicuously absent from that discussion are information and entertainment as purposes. Those are, in our opinion, merely means to another goal. Most often that other goal is attracting a sufficiently sized audience so that participations may be sold at a profit.

3. *What target audience group (or possibly groups) must be reached in order to accomplish the sponsor's purpose?* Sometimes, when this question is not asked and answered in advance of production, a producer will create and air a program, then see what audience—if any—is drawn to it. But that is a very risky and expensive approach. A station or an advertiser, and the writers who work for them, will be better off by carefully delineating target groups in advance—that is, by identifying those people who are most important in accomplishing the sponsor's purpose.

4. *How can the individuals in the target audience be convinced that they should act in the manner desired by the sponsor?* What techniques can the writer employ to persuade audiences? What persuasive appeals can be worked into the script copy to accomplish the sponsor's purpose? Or if the program's primary content is information or entertainment, what gratifications will be used to attract and hold the attention of the target group?

Here are three typical situations. The decisions made in each case are, first, programming decisions. But judgments made by the program executives affect writers. They have to match the content of the programs and the audiences being targeted with effective copy. Test yourself by answering these questions as they apply in these three situations. Do you understand and agree with these analyses?

## Programming the 11 P.M. Slot

A Fox affiliate TV station is faced with the task of finding a new program for its 11 P.M. time period, Monday through Friday. The contract for the series currently in the slot is expiring and the program hasn't done very well in attracting audiences and advertisers anyway, so a change is obviously needed. There are any number of syndicated series that the station might select. Some may already be in its inventory; others it can purchase. The question is, what series would be the best?

*Who is the sponsor?* Although a number of participations will be sold in the program, the advertisers will not be the sponsors. The station is the sponsor. It will select the series and pay whatever costs are required.

*What is the sponsor's purpose?* The station's purpose is obviously to draw as large an audience as it can in that time period. If successful, it will be able to sell sufficient numbers of participations to advertisers at high enough rates to make back its cost for the series and a profit. The programming and sales staffs will work very closely together to select a series they feel has the best potential, balancing the costs against potential revenue.

*What target audience must be reached?* Although any of several possible target groups might be chosen, it seems a good choice would be young adults from 18 to 34, for several reasons. At 11 P.M. the large, diverse prime-time audience has dwindled. The remaining available audience is heavily skewed toward younger adults, as both children and older groups have retired. Several competitors are broadcasting local news programs at this time, a program type that tends to draw older audiences. Thus the availability of those groups is further reduced for this station. In addition, Fox programming in general is aimed at younger groups, so a young adult target should already be familiar with this station. It might as well take advantage of that predisposition.

*What gratifications will be most effective?* In this case, the program director will select the series not directly because of its gratifications, but because of its prior record in attracting audiences in similar programming situations. That record in drawing audiences in previous programming slots and markets was created, however, by the program's gratifications. It is assumed that the series selected will draw similar audiences in this new location. In the real case upon which this situation was based, the station chose *Married . . . With Children* for the time slot, and has been very successful with it.

## A Community Theater Promotion

A local radio station, in conjunction with a community theater group, agrees to air a series of 15-minute programs that will feature scenes from dramatic works. Some will be from plays the group will present during the coming season; others will be just good, strong dramatic material. There will be no commercial advertising involved, but plugs for the theater group will be a part of the overall program.

*Who is the sponsor?* Both the station and the theater group may be considered sponsors; both have made substantial commitments to the effort.

*What is the sponsor's purpose?* The station's purpose is goodwill. The theater group's purpose may be partly goodwill, but it also hopes to attract audiences to its productions with this promotion.

*What target audience must be reached?* The target audience for this program will be difficult to identify precisely. From the station's standpoint, it will be important to keep the audience it already has, which has been attracted by its regular programming, so we might say that the station wants to avoid alienating its already determined target. By accepting this program idea in the first place, the station's managers have implicitly assumed they will not materially damage their audience size or demographics. For the theater group, the target would be people who do not currently attend little theater presentations but who probably have had some prior experience with dramatic productions. The station's audience and the theater group's target must be pretty much the same; otherwise, it will be hard to reconcile the two. That is, if the station appeals to teenagers and the theater group wants to reach mature adults, the differences are too great for the program to be successful, regardless of how well written it is.

*What gratifications will be most effective?* That decision was made when the content and structure of the series were determined. Nearly any of our listed gratifications might be used. But the target audience finally selected should determine the relative emphasis placed on action, sex appeal or comedy, just as examples. A selection of "classic" plays would contain different gratifications and draw a different audience than would a series featuring scenes from light comedies or farces.

Here the writing task is to select appropriate plays, to translate portions of the stage dramas into radio scripts, and to include the necessary program openings and closings and promotions for the theater group—all, as noted, without alienating the radio station's audience.

## A Local Basketball Game Broadcast

The local high school basketball team has made it into the statewide finals being played in a city some distance away. A local pizzeria has agreed to sponsor in its entirety the radio broadcast of the game.

*Who is the sponsor?* This is program sponsorship; advertiser and sponsor are the same since the pizzeria is paying all the costs.

*What is the sponsor's purpose?* To increase sales for the restaurant, which may be accomplished both directly, by promoting specials and bringing the firm's name, location and product to the attention of a wider public, and indirectly, by gathering some goodwill through this community service broadcast.

*What target audience must be reached?* In this case we can identify two groups: First, people who eat pizza or who might be induced to try it. Second, those who have an interest in high school sports—students, their families and so on. Again, for the sponsor's campaign to be successful, the audience most likely to be interested in the program content (have strong gratifications) should be similar in composition to the target for the product. In this case, that seems likely. The commercials, when written, can emphasize product qualities, the sponsor's contribution to the community by bringing this significant event to the audience, or both.

*What gratifications will be most effective?* Here again the gratifications are inherent within the program's content. Tension, action and information are obviously powerful attractions.

A small amount of copy will need to be written to introduce the game, the announcers, and so on, but most of the actual broadcast will be done ad lib by the sports announcers. Given the situation and the target audience as analyzed, the primary writing task here is the commercials for the pizzeria.

## CONCLUSION

Throughout the chapters of this text you've seen us use the word *process* many times. We've particularly emphasized it in the two chapters of Part 1 and again in these two chapters of Part 3. We keep insisting that to be a successful writer, you must clearly understand what is to be accomplished by each writing task you are assigned. That understanding comes from a careful, systematic analysis of each new situation. That's what we mean by process. It is not possible to completely delineate the areas of program purpose, audience targeting, persuasive appeals or gratification. There are no absolute, final lists that can be developed. But you can use the analytical approach, which was introduced in those early chapters and refined in these, and the examples given, as guides in sharpening your ability to gather and analyze data and make judgments relating to every writing task, whether program or advertisement.

**Exercises**

1. Choose several different consumer products or services—a chain of fast food outlets, a savings and loan, a brand of automobile tires—or any item or organization with which you are familiar. Then analyze that product or service in terms of its target audience.

   a. What is the primary target group that *must* be reached in order for that product to be marketed successfully? How narrowly can you define the target? Is the target best defined using demographics or lifestyle characteristics, or some of each?

    b. Are there secondary groups of sufficient size that might be the targets of different campaigns for the same product? How would a company change its advertising approach to aim at those groups?

    c. How do you arrive at these judgments? For example, for a shaving cream, you would need to consider, among other questions: What groups use blade razors as opposed to electric shavers? Younger or older? Other differences? What are the differences between this shaving cream and its competitors? Price? Feel? Smell? Packaging?

You may not know the answers to some of the questions you raise; some form of research would be needed to answer them definitively. But if you are doing this exercise as a class activity, which we strongly recommend, any consensus arrived at by members of the class is likely to be pretty close to the truth.

2. Proceed through the same process of analysis as in the preceding exercise, but for a *new* product—something you invent or something just coming onto the market. At what audience would you aim your advertising? Why?

3. Look at a selection of television programs and/or listen to a variety of radio station formats. For each program, describe in detail and with as narrow a focus as possible the audience targeted. Then, if possible, verify your analysis. Talk to the programming staff at the station which broadcasts each program you analyzed, and find out how they describe the target. Be careful in making this analysis for programs with participating advertising. It is the sponsor's target audience in which you are interested, and that group may or may not be the same as any particular advertiser's target. Mismatches do occur, and you may be led astray by assuming that the target groups for products advertised are the same as the target for the program itself. While most of the time advertiser targets and program targets should be very close, sometimes advertisements are inserted into programs that are aimed at a different group.

4. Obviously the most important application of gratifications for writers is being able to write programs which contain the ones you choose to include, and which attract and hold the attention of your target audiences. But before you can do that, you need to develop some ability to recognize the types and strengths of gratifications in existing programs. The following exercises are directed toward that skill.

    a. View several different types of television programs—for example, a news broadcast, a drama, a game show. For each program, (1) Identify the primary target audience. Be as specific as possible; focus carefully on the one audience group most important to the sponsor. (2) List the gratifications you recognize as being present in the program. Describe for each the form of gratification—that is, for comedy, what type of comedy—and the way in which it was presented in the program. (3) Do you believe that the gratifications present were strong *for the target audience*? Explain why this program should be successful in capturing the target group, or why not.

b. Select two TV programs that are very similar in content and form— for example, two network evening news programs, or morning magazine programs, or soap operas, or situation comedies. (The exercise is even more meaningful if you can select two programs that are directly competitive, broadcast at the same time on two different channels.) (1) View both programs and, as in exercise 4a, list and describe the gratifications you recognize as being present. (2) Particularly important, attempt to discern any *differences* in the types and strengths of gratifications between the two programs. (3) How do you think these differences might affect the composition of the audiences drawn to each program? What differences would you expect to find in the audience groups that choose each program?

**Notes**

1. Jay G. Blumler, "The Role of Theory in Uses and Gratifications Studies," *Communication Research*, 6 (January 1979), p. 17.
2. This list and the labels given to its categories are derived largely from the work of Professor Harrison Summers, who taught at Ohio State University. Other and more recent studies, some of which use different labels for what seem to be very similar concepts, are given in the Further Reading section.
3. Adapted from Jay G. Blumler, J. R. Brown, and Denis McQuail, "The Social Origins of the Gratifications Associated with Television Viewing" (Mimeographed: Leeds, Eng.: Centre for Television Research, University of Leeds, November 1970), p. 52.
4. Ibid., p. 14.
5. See particularly Mervin D. Lynch, Brian D. Kent, and Richard P. Carlson, "The Meaning of Human Interest: Four Dimensions of Judgment," *Journalism Quarterly*, Winter 1967.

**Further Reading**

Just as the topics covered in Chapter 9 and this chapter are highly related, so do many of the readings listed there also have relevance here. In addition, here are several important discussions of audience behavior and gratifications. Some of the earlier-dated titles are no longer in print, but remain good references if you can locate them.

Ball-Rokeach, Sandra, and Muriel Cantor. *Media, Audience, and Social Structure*. Newbury Park, CA: Sage, 1986.

Barwise, Patrick, and Andrew Ehrenberg. *Television and Its Audience*. Newbury Park, CA: Sage, 1989.

Berman, Ronald. *How Television Sees Its Audience: A Look at the Looking Glass*. Newbury Park, CA: Sage, 1987.

Blumler, Jay G., and Elihu Katz (eds.). *The Uses of Mass Communications: Current Perspectives on Gratifications Research*. Newbury Park, CA: Sage, 1974.

Comstock, George. *Television in America*, 2nd ed. Newbury Park, CA: Sage, 1991.

Comstock, George, and others. *Television and Human Behavior*. Irvington, NY: Columbia University Press, 1978.

Frank, Ronald E., and Marshall G. Greenberg. *The Public's Use of Television*. Newbury Park, CA: Sage, 1980.

Rosengren, Karl Erik, Lawrence A. Wenner, and Philip Palmgreen. *Media Gratifications Research: Current Perspectives*. Newbury Park, CA: Sage, 1985.

These last texts contain excellent explanations of the processes used in quantitative measurement, gathering and analyzing audience rating data.

Beville, Hugh Malcolm, Jr. *Audience Ratings: Radio, Television, Cable*, revised student ed. Hillsdale, NJ: Erlbaum, 1988.

Fletcher, James A. (ed.). *Handbook of Radio and TV Broadcasting: Research Procedures in Audience, Program and Revenues*. New York: Van Nostrand Reinhold, 1981.

# Practice

In this part we examine in some detail the writing of broadcast announcements and the broad categories of programs that make up the bulk of most station schedules. One additional chapter considers writing for corporate and instructional programs, most of which are not actually broadcast, but which follow the same writing principles.

Not only do these genres represent the bulk of the content on station and network schedules, they are also the types beginning writers are most likely to encounter.

Before we consider the various types of programs, we do want to caution you about the use of generalized labels to describe television programs and radio formats. While it is useful to have shorthand labels to communicate within the industry, writers must be careful not to let labels obscure the basic principles of good writing. We have, for example, the term *soft news* to describe news programs and

stories that cover feature, nontimely items. The difference between soft news and traditional hard news, however, is not so much in the writing; it is in the different gratifications derived by audiences who watch the stories, and therefore in the different audience groups that will be attracted.

Similarly, *docudramas* are a cross between documentaries and dramas. They are based on real events and people, but they are fictionalized, re-created dramatizations, and their preparation follows the principles of dramatic writing.

Another term, *infomercial*, is a mixture of a commercial and a program. We consider infomercials in several different chapters since they contain both the persuasive appeals of a commercial and the length and structure of a program, as well as using news and documentary presentational techniques.

*Infotainment*, including "reality" programs such as *Inside Edition, Hard Copy*, and others, is a deliberate crossing of informational and entertainment gratifications; critics would say a deliberate "blurring." Another label is *dramady*, a mixture of (serious) drama and comedy but somewhat unrecognizable as a distinct form.

Another problem with program labels is that they don't all describe the same things; there is an "apples and oranges" problem. Some program labels describe the content of the program. News, music and public affairs programs are labeled this way. Other categories use terms descriptive of the structure or form in which the content is presented, such as drama, variety, or interview programs. Others may be labeled on the basis of their appeal—an adventure program, for example. Still others are described on the basis of their intended audience; children's programs or women's programs are examples of this practice.

Beware of program labels that inadequately describe the writing task. You should learn to examine each task on the basis of all four descriptors—content, form, appeal and intended audience.

Now, having provided those warnings, we will proceed to use typical and readily understood labels to title the chapters of Part 4.

# CHAPTER 11

# Commercials and Other Announcements

**I**n broadcasting, persuasion is accomplished primarily through the use of short materials—announcements. There are three basic types—the *commercial advertising announcement*, usually called a *commercial* or an *ad;* the *public service announcement,* or *PSA*; and the *promotional announcement*, or *promo*. The word *spot* is also used as a synonym for announcement—usually, but not always, to refer to commercials.

Another form of material we will consider is the editorial. Editorials are not really a form of announcement, as most people in the industry categorize content, but they are usually short, and their intent is basically persuasive, so they can be fitted within the approach of this chapter. In most of the chapter we will use the commercial announcement as our focus; separate sections will consider problems unique to PSAs, to promos, and to editorials.

When you finish this chapter you will be able to

- write effective commercials, PSAs, promos and editorials,

- organize announcements to attract attention and motivate action,

- apply principles of audience targeting to commercial writing,

- write announcements using different organizational patterns and visual/vocal styles, and

- recognize and use these important terms and concepts:

| | |
|---|---|
| attracting attention | editorial |
| climax/punchline | infomercial |
| commercial | pacing |
| comparison ads | positioning |
| demonstration ads | problem-solution ads |
| dialogue and multiple-<br>  announcer ads | product-as-star ads |

| | |
|---|---|
| promo | situation ads |
| public service announcement (PSA) | special effect ads |
| | spokesperson/testimonial ads |
| purpose and goal | |

## RESEARCHING A COMMERCIAL CAMPAIGN

Many millions of dollars are spent on radio, TV and cable advertising each year, and of course many other millions are spent in nonelectronic media as well. Why? There can be many reasons. Box 11.1 includes the most common ones. When you begin work on a client's campaign (either a real client or one provided for a course assignment), the list in Box 11.1 is a good starting place. It can help you identify clearly the specific reasons for that campaign.

These broad descriptions do not provide enough detail, of course, to conduct successful campaigns. Much more needs to be known about the client, the product or service to be advertised and the audience to which that advertising is directed. In addition to the huge sums spent to produce advertising messages and place them in the appropriate media, major corporations and their advertising agencies spend considerable amounts on research to find the most effective and efficient ways to influence consumer behavior. If at some future time you do work for a major agency or client, you may even commission special research for your client/product and on its customers.

Here we can only introduce you to the process of analyzing and writing advertising campaigns. We use a series of twelve questions. These are an expansion and slight modification of the set of four questions raised at the end of Chapter 10. This time we have phrased them to focus directly on advertisers and their interests. They are questions that you need to answer,

### Box 11.1 Why Advertisers Advertise

| | | |
|---|---|---|
| Sell products and/or services today. | Expand demographics. | Build company morale. |
| Build store traffic. | Move old inventory. | Start people talking. |
| Meet the competition. | Promote new store openings. | Target advertising better. |
| Build store image. | Increase name awareness. | |
| Create a new position. | Advertise location. | *Source:* Chris Lytle, "Why Some Ads Work and Others Bomb," *The Pulse of Radio*, July 30, 1990, p. 25. Reprinted with permission of *Radio Ink* magazine. |
| Educate consumers. | Build brand awareness. | |
| Promote new merchandise. | Promote regular price (or off-price) merchandise. | |
| Generate new customers. | | |
| Reinforce market position. | Support sales objectives. | |

or have answers supplied by your client, before you can write effective advertising copy. Our questions deal with purpose, target audiences, persuasive appeals and structure—all topics that have been introduced in earlier chapters.

We encourage you to review the appropriate sections of those chapters—on sponsors and their purposes, persuasive appeals and target audiences—in Chapters 9 and 10. Also review the discussion of audience attention in Chapter 6. For more detailed and alternative approaches, consult the items listed in the Further Reading section. Read ahead, also, to the final chapter, which considers some of the ethical problems raised by deliberate manipulations of the buying public.

*Purpose.* (1) What is the sponsor's long-range goal? (2) What is the specific purpose of this announcement? Does it differ from the long-range goal? How? (3) What other supporting materials are to be used in the campaign—other media, salespersons, point-of-purchase displays, special promotions?

*Target audiences.* (4) What audience group must the sponsor reach in order to accomplish the purpose intended? (5) Can that group be reached using the station/channel on which this ad is to be placed and at the time/day when it is to appear?

*Persuasive appeals.* (6) What appeals will be used to motivate the audience toward the action needed to accomplish the sponsor's purpose? (7) Are those appeals appropriate for the target audience? Do they relate directly to the specific purpose of the ad?

*Structure.* (8) What device will be used to attract the attention of the audience to the spot? (9) Are a limited number of concepts used so that the spot has a unified approach? (10) Will any form of structural variety be used? (11) What specialized pacing, or mood, if any, should be given to the spot? (12) Is any form of climax to be included?

## Purpose

The intent of the originators of all types of announcements is basically persuasive. For commercials, that's obvious. But the intent behind PSAs and promos is also persuasive, although in those cases it may not be so obvious. Many PSAs and promos are written in a factual style, rather than in persuasive language. For example, a PSA may say: "St. Michael's church will hold its annual bazaar and street dance next Sunday. . . ." A promo may announce: "The John Smith program is now heard at a new time on KXXX—Saturday mornings at ten o'clock."

The intent of both messages, although it is expressed in very low-key terms, is to persuade audience members, in the first instance to attend the function, in the second to tune in to the program. Varying degrees of intensity and styles of presentation may be used, but the sponsor's purpose remains the same—to get some form of action from the members of the audience.

Very early in the development of an ad campaign the writer must distinguish between the sponsor's long-range need, which we will call the *goal*, and the immediate and specific intent of the particular ad to be written, for which we will use the term *purpose*. For most commercial campaigns, the ultimate persuasive goal will be to sell a product or service, to create goodwill in the audience for the company, to get votes for a political candidate, or something similar that will benefit the advertiser. However, that goal may be quite different from the specific purpose of a particular commercial.

Here are some examples which show the process of analysis used to distinguish long-range goals from specific purposes.

### Selling Automobiles

Accomplishing the sponsor's goal for this product requires that the buyer come to the auto dealer's lot or showroom. Sales are completed by a salesperson at the dealership. Radio and TV ads, therefore, have as their specific purpose getting the potential buyer to the agency. The writer must use appeals that will motivate the listener or viewer to do that. Frequently used approaches include the appeal to curiosity: "New model, just arrived—come and see it and drive it." Or to savings: "Special price this weekend only, save hundreds of dollars." Or perhaps a mixture of curiosity, adventure, excitement, and sexual attraction: "Come to the big Ford carnival this weekend. See the flagpole sitter; ride the elephant; talk with Hollywood stars Jane Smith and Randy Brown; free soft drinks; see the show. . . ." Note that this approach doesn't even mention the product to be sold; it concentrates solely on getting the audience to the dealership using appeals that have nothing to do with automobiles.

Of course we are oversimplifying the complex persuasive process that leads a person to buy an automobile, and ignoring the many preconditions that must be present before individuals purchase autos or other major items, like having enough money or having an existing car that one is dissatisfied with. The critical point for the broadcast writer is that for this type of product, the broadcast ad cannot by itself close the sale and should not attempt to do so.

### Selling Collections of Recorded Music

In direct contrast to the preceding example, collections of recorded music are one type of merchandise that is sold successfully by direct appeal to audiences.

For your collection of the one hundred greatest hits by all-time favorite country singers, a collection that you

```
cannot get in the stores, send nineteen ninety-five, plus
three dollars and fifty cents postage and handling, to
post office box ...
```

You probably recognize the style of that announcement. Other products are sold by the same approach.

In this case, the general goal of the advertiser and the specific purpose of the announcement are identical—to sell the merchandise. All the appeals and motivations necessary to accomplish that sale must be present within the announcement itself. No other support or secondary action will take place.

Not only must the motivations be strong in the ad, but the action required must be easy to take and clearly stated. By the way, this type of selling has become much more successful now that credit cards are widely distributed and direct dial long distance telephoning using "800" numbers is common. The purchaser doesn't have to find a checkbook and then an envelope and a stamp. All he or she needs is to write down a phone number, call, and charge the purchase to a credit card.

### Selling Toothpaste

Grocery and drug items are sold using yet another marketing approach. Seldom does an individual make a special trip to a store to buy these items as a direct result of having seen or heard ads for them. (An exception might be something like a new cold remedy. A person really suffering from a cold might be persuaded to make a special trip for a new product that promised relief!)

Another factor that complicates the sale of grocery and drug items is brand awareness and brand loyalty. Advertisers are aware that some buyers change brands of common products for a variety of reasons—price, availability, competition from new brands, improved quality. At the same time, there are buyers who are loyal to brands they know and trust. Advertisers, therefore, are faced with a multifaceted task—continuing to remind loyal or previous customers about the product in the face of advertising by competitors, and at the same time trying to obtain new customers from those who have not yet established brand loyalty, or who might be pulled away from competing brands.

As with the automobile purchase, the final decision on which brand to purchase is made at the store, and that decision will be made sometime after exposure to the broadcast ad, a time period that may range from a few minutes to days or even weeks after the exposure. But contrary to the automobile situation, there usually is no salesperson present to "close" the sale in the grocery store. The customer alone will make the final decision on which brand of toothpaste to buy. In making that decision, the appeals of radio or television spots may be diluted or reinforced by a number of other factors such as price, or special displays at the point of purchase, or coupon offers, or competition. The advertiser, however, counts on at least some purchasing decisions being made as a result of the customer's having been recently exposed to broadcast ads for the product.

### Public Utility Company

In most communities, public utilities such as the local gas or power company are regulated monopolies. They do not have to advertise to sell their product. Any customer who wants electricity, for example, must deal with the local power company and pay the regulated rate. But these companies do advertise for purposes not related to direct sales. The goal may be to maintain (or improve) the image that company has among its customers, to negate or minimize the ill will that might otherwise be generated by the next rate increase. To accomplish that goal, the specific purpose of an ad campaign might be to show what a good neighbor the company is and how it contributes to and involves itself in community affairs.

Another purpose for utility companies which has become especially important in recent years is encouraging conservation, thereby reducing the amount of costly new construction needed to keep up with demand. Here the goal and the specific purpose are more directly related.

Yet another purpose for a utility company would be public safety, as in this announcement:

ANNCR:   (ECHO) Ben Franklin's historic kite flight...and you are there....

SOUND:   THUNDER

BEN:   (SINGING TO HIMSELF) I'm singing in the rain...just singing...

ANNCR:   Ben, this doesn't look very safe...I mean here you are flying that kite in a thunderstorm....

BEN:   Not to worry...not to worry.

ANNCR:   Shouldn't you also be in a wide open space...Away from trees and power poles....

BEN:   What's a power pole???

SOUND:   THUNDER—CRASHING ETC...

BEN:   Yeow....

ANNCR:   If only Ben had a copy of kite flight.... SMUD has copies to help kite flyers have more fun...They're free...call or drop in...SMUD wants to keep the fun in kite flight.

*Source:* Courtesy of Sacramento Municipal Utility District, Sacramento, CA.

### Political Advertising

The goals of political ads are easily stated—to elect candidates or to pass (or defeat) ballot propositions. Those goals are accomplished only at the ballot box on election day. Ads leading up to that point will try to influence the decisions of individual voters using indirect persuasive techniques. Detailed discussion of the types of persuasive manipulation used in political campaigns is beyond our capacity to cover in a few paragraphs, however.

Often, at the beginning of a campaign extensive polling of potential voters will be done to find out their positions and their preconceptions regarding a candidate or an issue. Working from that knowledge, political sponsors will use persuasive appeals important to the various voting groups who are not yet committed on the race or proposition, in an attempt to convince those voters that their own values are best preserved by voting in a particular way.

The political ad on this page uses people typical of the area in which the campaign was being conducted—two farmers and a senior citizen housewife; many voters in the district would be able to identify easily with these people. The ad touches on four issues important to those voters—stopping urban development, water, government waste, and government interference in individual activities. Finally, the appeals used—independence, authority, fear—are strong appeals in this predominantly rural agricultural area.

BERNIE RICHTER
TV Spot #2
"Testimonial"

| VIDEO | AUDIO |
|---|---|
| SLIDE—BERNIE IN FIELD W/FARMER | ANNCR: Bernie Richter <u>stopped</u> urban development of our agricultural land.... |
| FARMER ON TRACTOR<br>SUPER: BOB WALLACE FARMER—DURHAM | WALLACE: Since he's been our supervisor, none of our land zoned for farming's been subdivided.... |
| SLIDE—BERNIE TALKING TO GROUP | ANNCR: Richter's <u>leadership</u> removed one million dollars in waste disposal from property taxes.... |
| SENIOR LADY TAKING OUT GARBAGE<br>SUPER: JEANNE L. WHITE HOUSEWIFE BUTTE COUNTY | WHITE: I'm not paying for the disposal of someone else's garbage....I'm only paying for my own...and that makes sense.... |

| | |
|---|---|
| SLIDE—BERNIE IN FIELD WITH WATER | ANNCR: Richter <u>prevented</u> the export of our ground waters.... |
| YOUNG FARMER W/WIFE | JIM: Hundreds of wells would be pumping our |
| SUPER: JIM AND JOYCE MEAD ALMOND GROWERS—CHICO | water south if he hadn't stopped it during the drought.... |
| SLIDE—RICHTER FAMILY | ANNCR: Bernie Richter gets things done...re-elect Supervisor Richter. |
| SUPER: RE-ELECT RICHTER | |
| SUPER: PAID BY CITIZENS FOR RICHTER | |

*Source:* Courtesy of the writer, Frank LaRosa, and of Bernie Richter.

These examples have been chosen to suggest, first, that there is a common approach or method of analysis that can be used to determine both the general goal behind any sponsor's use of the broadcast media and the specific purpose to be accomplished by a particular ad or campaign, and second, that these goals/purpose combinations can vary widely with different products and situations.

Using this approach, you can make a similar analysis for each advertising campaign on which you work.

## Target Audience

In Chapter 10, we introduced several examples of target audiences for commercial products and PSAs—washing detergents, car stereos, a local theater group and a pizzeria. Here we reexamine the problems inherent in determining a target for the theater company, this time for a PSA campaign, and consider the target for a political campaign. Carefully review the analyses presented here and in Chapter 10. You should undertake a similar analysis for every client for whom you are asked to write commercials or PSAs.

### *PSA for a Local Amateur Theater Company*

The purpose of the campaign is to increase the size of the audiences attending performances by the company. We can assume that there is a small but loyal group of regular theatergoers who are familiar with this company, who know through nonbroadcast promotional means what plays are being presented and when. This group does not need PSAs to be induced to attend. A second group may be people who have had previous positive experiences when attending the theater and who might easily be motivated to attend, but who have gotten out of the habit for one reason or another, perhaps simply because they haven't been kept informed of what is available. For them, the approach used could be mostly informational, and this is the style usually employed by PSAs in campaigns of this sort.

But to increase theater attendance significantly in a community, new audience groups must be persuaded. The campaign is likely to require a considerable period of time to break down prejudices against attending live theater and to build up positive images in audience groups who have not had experience with the theater. Broadcast messages may not be able to accomplish this goal, or at least not alone.

### Campaign for a Candidate for a State Assembly Seat

Voter analysis in political campaigns has become a very sophisticated business, well beyond the few considerations we can suggest here. But here is a quick sketch of how a political analysis might be approached. We have chosen an assembly race, which is a partisan campaign, but one in which the election takes place within a reasonably confined geographic area. Since the voting group is defined geographically, one basic consideration would be to use media which match that geographic area. But most important would be to understand the existing political climate in the district, and to identify those groups of voters who might be persuaded to vote for the candidate.

Let's assume the district is balanced, with approximately equal numbers of Republican and Democrat voters, and that past elections have gone both ways. Our candidate in this election is the Republican.

One of the groups in the electorate will be strongly partisan Republicans. We should not take them totally for granted, but in all probability they will vote for our candidate, and it certainly will require very little effort to capture them. At the other extreme will be strongly partisan Democrats. Even if we campaign extensively (and expensively) to reach this group, there is little possibility of converting them to our cause. Better not waste a lot of effort and money on them.

The groups on which to concentrate, then, are voters who are not strongly partisan. In very general terms, these are likely to be younger voters and those who have recently moved into the area who do not have strong ties in the community. Our precampaign research should attempt to identify what issues and qualities these groups find important in a candidate. Then we should build the ad campaign around those concepts.

As with all our examples, this one is highly simplified, but it pictures the process of analysis that must be done before actual writing can begin on a successful ad. The writer needs to know what audience must be reached in order to accomplish the purpose intended. That audience should be defined as accurately as possible.

## Persuasive Appeals

We have already emphasized the importance of motivational appeals in persuasive copy. Briefly summarized, the target audience for any sponsor can be motivated to take action when it can be demonstrated to those individuals that taking that action will be in their own best interests. The copywriter's job is to provide these incentives, to motivate, to point out to the audience what the advantages are of doing what is suggested in the announcement.

Be careful not to dilute and weaken the effectiveness of the ad by using too many appeals. It does not follow that if one appeal is effective, six will be better. Concentrate on the one, two, possibly three appeals which are most appropriate to the target audience and the product, and which relate to each other as well.

The generalizations we made in Chapter 9 on the applicability of appeals to various demographic groups can be usefully applied to commercials, PSAs, and promos. However, in most campaigns those generalizations will need to be made much more specific. Survey research using samples from the targeted audience will attempt to determine attitudes and perceptions of the audience in detail, and how those attitudes and perceptions can be changed to meet the needs of the client. Here are two examples of how purpose, audience and appeals are considered in actual campaigns.

### A Public Service Campaign for Blood Pressure Testing

This campaign was directed specifically at the Mexican-American population in the Houston area. It was designed to make this population aware of the problem of high blood pressure and to encourage specific behavioral responses to that problem.

The analysis began with the findings of a community health survey which showed that only 15 percent of the Mexican-American population recognized high blood pressure as a primary risk factor in coronary artery disease. It also showed that only 35 percent of this group considered the physician the primary source of health care information. For 46 percent the primary source is the mass media—television, radio, newspapers, and magazines—and over 24 percent turn to television for health care information.

In the creation of the three television PSAs used in the campaign, two types of consultant groups were used—representatives from the target population and representatives of the mass media. In-depth discussions in Spanish were held with different groups of Mexican-Americans to discover what appeals would be relevant and involving and what kind of language should be used. From this input, a concept of the kinds of PSAs to use was formed.

Three different presentations were chosen: a street scene, a clinic, and a softball game. The street scene was a night sequence, and high blood pressure was presented as the silent killer lurking in the shadows. The camera took the role of the "killer" that stalked unsuspecting victims on the street. The spot's audio explained why one should be concerned with high blood pressure and what effects coronary artery disease could have on the family. The tone was mysterious and somewhat alarming. At the end of the spot—as in all of them—viewers were given a phone number to call for further information and were urged to have their blood pressure checked.

The clinic spot, targeted at women, emphasized that high blood pressure often has no symptoms, and opened with a visit of a woman to a fortuneteller to see what the future held for her. That visit resulted in another, this time a visit to a local clinic for a blood pressure checkup. The sequence was designed to familiarize viewers with the medical procedure and allay any apprehensions they might have.

The softball spot was designed to appeal to the men. This spot was very action-oriented and got right to the message that anyone—even youthful athletes—may be a victim of high blood pressure.[1]

### Selling Athletic Footwear

The term *positioning* is used to describe the process of developing a strategy for marketing a product. Advertising agencies for major brands work very diligently to find a niche for the product that sets it apart from its competition and to appeal to appropriate buying groups within the population. For example, a shampoo may claim it is the most effective dandruff fighter, it leaves hair the most manageable, or it provides the greatest sheen or the best body. Each style of automobile is designed, manufactured and marketed to appeal to a different group. That represents its position within the automobile industry. Once a position is established, then the advertiser and agency proceed to the next step, a marketing plan.

One very competitive area of retail merchandising in recent years has been athletic and leisure shoes. Several brands have fought to establish their positions and to claim segments of the market that are both large enough and affluent enough to purchase this product. Here's how AVIA Group International, makers of AVIA athletic shoes and apparel, went about developing one of its campaigns.

The quest began in 1988 when AVIA chose Borders Perrin and Norrander (BP&N), in Portland, Oregon, as its advertising agency. The agency talked with customers and retailers to determine what they thought of AVIA. BP&N senior vice president Michael Hoffman described the results of these talks.

> Serious athletes knew AVIA. Others weren't as familiar with the name. It was clear most AVIA customers already defined AVIA as for athletic use. We added the [word] "only" to punctuate the statement.[2]

In February 1989, AVIA debuted a complete new marketing package featuring "For Athletic Use Only." A not-so-subtle campaign in print and on television featured the athletic theme. Each ad featured a vice: smoking, drinking, being sedentary and eating junk foods. A television ad, opening with a shot of two cocktails, said, "If this is what an afternoon of mixed doubles means to you, AVIA doesn't want you to buy its tennis shoes."

These strong messages generated a great deal of attention from customers as well as the news media, but some of that attention was negative. The campaign was seen by some as too confrontational. So a search was begun for another approach. But senior staff at the agency and AVIA remained confident that the position of "For Athletic Use Only" was correct. The AVIA vice president of advertising, Pat Kipisz, remarked

> We spent time and effort redefining the AVIA customer, determining the demographics and psychographics of who buys our shoes. With FAUO we had something that was strategically sound. Finally, we asked again, why are we walking away from this position?[3]

The new campaign reflects the joy and passion that athletes feel toward sports. New ads focus on how the shoes should be used, rather than on how they should not be used. Radio ads are being used to target the core customer by taking advantage of radio's strength as

> a theater of the mind. We intend to leave our audience with the point that AVIA takes shoes and fitness very seriously, but we don't take ourselves too seriously. The new campaign has to pass the test of reaching our target customer and differentiating AVIA from other companies. Our search taught us that one campaign does that above all others: FOR ATHLETIC USE ONLY. Now we know the first answer was the right one for AVIA.[4]

Figure 11.1 is one of the spots used in the campaign.

## Structure

Structurally, announcements differ somewhat from other forms of broadcast content. They are the one short form of content that stands alone. Other short pieces of copy, such as individual news stories, are used as elements within longer programs, but announcements, even though they are usually placed within the structure of a program, are prepared and manipulated independently. The considerations of program structure discussed in Chapter 6 are important in the announcement, but not all of those considerations are as important as they are for longer materials.

### Attracting Attention

This is a crucial structural requirement for announcements. Audiences tend to look upon announcements as interruptions placed within or between the

B O R D E R S  P E R R I N  A N D  N O R R A N D E R  I N C.

RADIO COPY

| | | |
|---|---|---|
| DATE: | January 1991 | AS-PRODUCED |
| CLIENT: | Avia | |
| TITLE: | "NY Aerobics" | |
| LENGTH: | :60 | |

ANNCR:          To prove a little something about AVIA's popularity, we went to Times Square in New York City...

MAN #1:         AVIA, never heard of it.

WOMAN #1:       AVIA.  Isn't it water?  Natural spring water.

ANNCR:          It went...just like we expected...

MAN #2:         Bathroom tissue.  The two-ply kind they have out, the new kind.

WOMAN #2:       Something in the beauty line.  You know, maybe a shampoo, maybe a bath oil.  I don't know...

ANNCR:          Then we walked just a few blocks to New York's Vertical Club...and asked again.

WOMAN #3:       A-V-I-A.  Sure, common knowledge.

MAN #3:         Everybody who works out here knows AVIA.

WOMAN #4:       Not only have I heard of it, I live in them.

WOMAN #5:       I can't believe you're asking that question in a fitness center.

ANNCR:          The point?  That while we may not be known all over the place...we are known in all the right places.

WOMAN #6:       Everyone on the aerobics floor up there wears AVIAs.

ANNCR:          AVIA.  It means aerobic shoes...For Athletic Use...Only.

**Figure 11.1.** Courtesy of Borders Perrin and Norrander, Inc., Portland, OR.

programs they have chosen to view (or listen to) and enjoy. The announcements, in their view, are the price they know they must pay for enjoyment of the programs. They will tolerate the interruptions, but they don't have to pay attention to the announcements.

On the other hand, as we have seen, sponsors provide programs to attract audiences who will be exposed to the announcements. In the sponsor's view, the announcements are the more (commercially) important material. The commercial writer must recognize this difference in the expectations of audience and sponsor. Although the program material preceding an announcement will bring the audience to the moment at which the ad is aired, the writer of the announcement still must attract attention to the announcement itself.

The problem has been made worse in recent years by the widespread use of VCRs and remote controls. These devices permit persons to record programs and then zip through the commercials at high speed while viewing the recording. Even when a program is not prerecorded, the remote control allows viewers to turn down the sound or to quickly sample other channels during commercial breaks.

This increase in audience control—no longer do audiences sit passively through the commercials waiting for programming to resume—provides a real challenge for writers, directors and producers of commercials to find new ways to make ads look and sound different while maintaining the commercial's basic purpose—to sell the product. As we've noted elsewhere, some campaigns mix color and black-and-white images, whereas others feature sound effects with a visual of only printed words. We consider these and other techniques again later in this chapter.

Writers and producers who work in foreign markets have had to deal with this challenge for some time. In the United States, advertising is placed within the framework of a program, or in brief periods between programs. In contrast, many foreign broadcasting systems completely separate ads from programs. Several minutes of advertisements may be aired between programs. In that situation, even more than in the U.S. model, announcements must stand on their own. Structure, appeals and content must all contribute toward attracting audience attention, because there is no support from surrounding materials.

### Unity

In an announcement, the structural requirement for unity may be interpreted to mean that all the data appearing in the spot should relate directly to the specific purpose. Hence our insistence earlier that the writer must clearly understand that purpose. Unity is provided by limiting the number of ideas presented and the number of appeals. All the individual statements within the spot should develop and support, with variations and repetition, the specific persuasive purpose of the announcement.

For example, assume a new store has just opened in town. An obvious purpose of the inaugural ad campaign will be to get the audience familiar with the name of the store. Some other material will have to be present, of course, such as the nature of the business (is it a furniture store or a restaurant?) and why the audience should be interested in the store (good values, beautiful merchandise, spectacular view). But if name recognition is important—and it is certainly important for a new store—then the name should be repeated frequently in the ad, as in this radio spot.

```
ANNCR:     Are you tired of that same old pizza? Do they all taste alike,

           and look alike? Do your taste buds need an overhaul?

           Now...your problems are solved!

MUSIC:     FANFARE

ANNCR:     Now...there's Luigi's Pizza.

           Only the freshest, all natural ingredients are used at Luigi's

           Pizza.

           Three kinds of cheese on every pizza...at Luigi's Pizza.

           Dough made fresh, every day...at Luigi's Pizza.

           And three convenient locations...Franklin and Fruitridge in

           the South area, Folsom and Watt in the North area, and

           Eighteenth and K streets downtown.

           Luigi's Pizza. Give your taste buds a treat today!
```

### Variety

This can be provided in announcements in the same ways it is provided in longer program forms. (Review those portions of Chapters 6, 7 and 8 which discuss variety as a general structural principle, aural variety, and visual sequencing.) But when more variety and consequently complexity are added to a spot, cost in time and money is also added. Therefore many ads, especially low-cost ads prepared for local clients, and ads that must be produced quickly, use simple techniques with little variety.

In most spots, providing variety is not a crucial consideration, because they seldom exceed 60 seconds in length, which is within most people's attention span. Commercials aimed at children need to consider this requirement, of course, because of children's shorter attention span. Aural and pictorial variety also has to be considered in the longer ads that appear, usually on cable channels, and in infomercials, because they are in fact programs.

The announcements used as examples in this chapter demonstrate several ways of providing variety.

### Pacing

In longer forms of copy, this requirement is primarily a function of the number and length of program elements. In announcements, the term has a different meaning. It refers to the sense of speed or urgency (or lack of it) in the ad, and as such it becomes a contributor to the mood intended for the announcement.

An ad for a used car dealer, for example, may use a hurried, forcing style with a rapid breathless pace: "Hurry down today, while this fantastic sale is still on, and before all these terrific bargains are gone. . . ." In contrast, an ad for an expensive wine may want to set a much more leisurely, relaxed, slower-paced mood:

| VIDEO | AUDIO |
|---|---|
| RUSTIC CABIN, FIRE IN FIREPLACE, SNOWING OUTSIDE SEEN THROUGH WINDOW, LATE AFTERNOON DIM LIGHT | MUSIC: SOFT IN BG<br><br>MAN:    Our tenth anniversary. I want everything to be special this weekend, including the wine.<br><br>WOMAN: (HOLDING GLASS) This is a wonderful choice, John...so fruity and mellow. It's delicious.<br><br>MAN:    It's a new Chardonnay, from.... |

For each ad, the writer needs to make a decision about the pace and mood which are appropriate, and choose settings, voice, vocabulary, and style which establish and maintain that mood.

### Climax

The sense of climax in program-length materials is satisfied by a feeling of building up interest and anticipation as the program proceeds. It's part of the solution to the problem of maintaining audience interest over a period of time. In shorter announcements, that consideration is not as important. But climax serves another function in the announcement—that of leaving the audience with a bit of material to recall at the time and place where the product might be purchased. Recall our discussion about the lag between exposure to the advertising message and opportunity to purchase most products.

Climax, in this sense, takes the form of a tag or punchline to the announcement. Frequently it's some unanticipated or humorous twist to the situation. For example, look at Figure 11.2.

Now, after having answered the twelve questions asked at the beginning of the chapter, or having had them answered for you by a client, salesperson or account executive, you are ready to write the copy for the announcement.

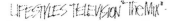

LIFESTYLES TELEVISION "The Mix".

SFX: Alarm Clock
(Woman comes out of bed.)

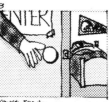

SFX: William Tell Overture
(Woman opens door to kids room.)
Woman: LET'S GO. EVERYBODY UP!

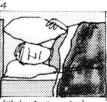

(older boy pulls pillow over head.)

(Daughter bangs on bathroom door.)
Daughter: LET ME IN!

(Woman combing hair in mirror.)
Woman: ALLEY, WAKE UP CHIP, WOULDJA?

(kid slams cymbals over brother's head.)
SFX: Crash!

(Woman tries to put on one earring with one hand and shoe with the other while she hops to keep her balance.)

(toast pops up burned.)

(kid eats chocolate cake for breakfast.)

(older brother chases kid carrying cymbals through kitchen.)

(Woman ties kid's shoe, notices he has two different shoes on.)
Anncr VO: NOTHING IS BETTER FOR

(Kids grab lunch, bags as they head out the door.)
AN IMPERFECT MORNING THAN THE
PERFECT MIX OF MUSIC.

(Woman sits down with coffee, turns on radio to relax for a moment.)
SFX: Mix Music Up

(Mom sees kid sitting under table, still eating cake.)

(Logo animates. The Mix, then 96 KYMX.)
ANNCR VO: THE MIX 96, KYMX.

**Figure 11.2.** Courtesy of Mering and Associates, Sacramento, CA.

## ORGANIZATION/SEQUENCE

All the questions asked earlier are important in the development of announcements, but two are also critical in the writing process itself. At the beginning of the announcement, there must be some device to attract attention and the action wanted from the audience must somehow be motivated.

### Attracting Attention

We've already discussed the structural importance of this step. Before there can be any hope of accomplishing the sponsor's purpose, you must have the attention of individuals in the audience. If those people turn their attention to other matters—pick up reading material, start talking with others in the room, run to the kitchen or bathroom, zip and zap with the remote control, whatever—the persuasive message will never be seen or heard.

A number of devices can be used to attract attention, and advertisers, ad agencies and writers have become very sophisticated in their techniques. Here are some suggestions. You undoubtedly will recognize some of these techniques in current campaigns. Note that with most of these approaches the secret is to find something unusual, something out of the norm in some way.

- *Changing images.* The rapid intercutting of images, the juxtaposition of seemingly unrelated pictures, and visuals that appear to be poorly shot can be effective.

  Many advertisers are out to confuse you and throw you off balance with film footage that wouldn't pass muster with a junior-high film club. You have to stare at the screen just to figure out what's going on—and that, of course, is part of the idea.[5]

  In one campaign for a computer company the ads were designed to look like "hazy, washed-out spots, people walk partially in and out of the camera frame, talking in computer jargon. But the confusion grabs attention, insists Jack Sansolo, vice-chairman of Hill, Holliday, Connors, Cosmopulos, the Boston ad agency that produced the spots." In other spots the viewer's eye isn't given quite enough time to fully process any scene, with the result that the viewer is challenged to pay attention in the attempt to bring order out of the chaotic montage.

  "Sudden changes in scene cause an involuntary increase in brain activity," explains Michael Rothschild, an associate professor of marketing at the University of Wisconsin, who works with the advertising industry. Rothschild has been wiring commercial-watchers up to devices that measure brain function. He's found that the ability to remember a commercial seems to increase with brain activity at viewing time. Pontiac has capitalized on this phenomenon with its . . . ads, in which a long shot is one and one-half seconds, and the shortest shots flash by in one-quarter of a second.

- *Other unusual or startling devices.* Begin with a shocking statement:

  ```
  Eight hundred American travelers will be killed on
  the nation's highways this weekend. Don't you be one
  of them. . . .
  ```

  Use unusual combinations of color or of no color. We are all so used to color in commercials that the use of black and white, especially if it is intended to suggest time past, is an effective contrast.
     Mixtures of animation and live action, or other forms of graphic manipulation, also attract attention.

- *Sound and sound effects.* Again, especially if they are unusual or possibly even discomforting, sounds can catch an audience.

  Neurophysiologist Eric Courchesne of the University of California at San Diego Medical School has been observing the powerful effects certain sounds have on human brain waves. His work isn't news to ad-makers, he insists. "Advertisers are using sounds to take advantage of the automatic systems built into the brain that force you to stop what you're doing and refocus on the screen. . . . You can't ignore these sounds." That's why ads are starting off with noises ranging from a baby crying (Advil) to a car horn (Hertz) to a factory whistle (Almond Joy). . . .

  Advertisers can even be downright merciless in their choice of sound. Ads for pain reliever Nuprin kick off by assaulting viewers with the whine of a dentist's drill, complete with a powerful flash of light from a dentist's examining light. Explains Harry Azorin, vice-president and group creative director with Grey Advertising: "We wanted to help the viewer recall a type of pain that we've all experienced."

- *Music.* Appropriately chosen music, such as a fanfare or a Christmas song, can attract attention. Frequently, a musical opening is continued behind the narration of an announcement. When it is used this way, it is called a *music bed,* and its function is primarily to maintain a mood for the ad. (Recall that section in Chapter 7.) Some radio stations as a matter of policy put a bed behind every spot, but too frequent use of music as background weakens its effectiveness for attention getting and mood setting. Use background music only when it provides a positive contribution to the spot and is not just there to "be there."

- *Unusual settings.* For TV, place the announcer and the product up in a hot-air balloon or at the whale tank at Marineland. For radio, simulate a similar situation setting by using narration, music and/or sound effects.

One of the great stories of radio is this one about humorist Stan Freberg, who was commissioned by the radio industry to write a "commercial" for radio that could be used to counter the competition from television advertising. Taking the role of a radio newscaster, Freberg announced that he was on location to report the event of the century . . . the creation of the world's largest cup of hot chocolate in Lake Michigan. Freberg explained in exciting detail how this monumental task would be accomplished through the assistance of the Royal Canadian Air Force.

The crews were ready. As Freberg shouted a step-by-step account over the roar of engines and horns, the whipped cream was sprayed from giant hoses with the appropriate squishing and whooshing noises. The moment of triumph had come. A squadron of helicopters hovered, ready to drop the jumbo cherry "bomb" dead center on the colossal confection. By now listeners could almost taste it. Amid a great whirring of helicopter blades, and the sound of guide cables whistling from the strain, the gigantic cherry dropped into place with a satisfying plop! Having created a picture only the imagination could create for the eye, Freberg issued a challenge from above the cheering crowd: "Now, you want to try that on television?"[6]

- *Humor.* Introduce a humorous statement or situation. Humor is very often used to attract attention but—as we have noted before—the target audience must identify with what's humorous in the situation. The power company's kite-flying ad used earlier in this chapter has humor. The long-running campaign for Energizer batteries, in which the bunny suddenly appears in what at first seems to be a straight ad for another product, effectively uses humor as well.

- *Drama.* Establish a dramatic situation in which characters interact. Frequently this device is used to set up a problem facing the characters. The interaction, possibly even conflict, thus established makes the viewer or listener want to stay tuned to see how the situation is resolved. The remainder of the ad is then used to solve the problem—with the aid of the sponsor's product, of course. The Perry Boys restaurant ad used as an example of layout form (in Chapter 5) uses both humor and drama to attract attention.

If a viewer has never seen an ad before, he or she may want to see it through—once. But the success of most ad campaigns depends on frequent exposure. Some campaigns rotate several different ads, often constructed in parallel fashion. The Energizer bunny is a good example of this technique as well, but it would be prohibitively expensive to create a new ad for each placement. An attention-getting device that will continue to work even after repeated exposure is a formidable creative challenge but a worthwhile goal.

## Motivating Action

The second necessary element in the successful announcement is to motivate action, and we've already discussed the persuasive tools which can be used to do that. At its simplest, the process of persuasion is one of convincing an individual listener or viewer that it is in his or her best interest to do what is proposed.

However, we do not want to overemphasize this motivational step and leave you with the inaccurate impression that every successful commercial must contain an expressed direct action on the part of the audience. Many ads, especially those for widely advertised national products, are quite indirect in their use of appeals to motivate. They often concentrate on a strong, frequently humorous, attention-getting device. There may be only one brief mention of the product, just to remind the audience of the name.

There will, however, be an association of that product with the people, activities, mood, or style presented in the ad, however brief, and that association ties together product and appeals. The physically attractive young men and women playing on the beach may not be seen drinking diet cola, and the sound track consisting of rock music may not even mention the product's name, but when the product logo appears at the conclusion of the spot, the product has been associated with sex appeal, companionship, and personal pleasure.

The success of having made that association will come when individuals who have seen the ad next decide to purchase soft drinks. They will choose this diet cola (or so the client and the ad agency hope) because its presence on the grocery shelf recalls in the memories of the individuals in the target group appeals that have some strength for them.

Note that we are now emphasizing individuals, whereas in the discussion of target audiences we were talking about demographic groups of people. While it is necessary sometimes to generalize about people, using demographic averages and the generalized and predictable behaviors of groups, in the final analysis it is individuals who buy (contribute, vote), and it is individuals who listen to radio and watch television. In writing announcements, talk to the individual.

The action step itself involves an important writing sequence, which can be explained as follows: First, make the persuasive appeals—show the audience members *why* they should take the action requested; show them the value in that action. Then, tell them *what* to do, specifically, to achieve that gain (and, of course, the sponsor's purpose as well): Go to the store, pick up the phone, mail a letter, go to the blood bank. Finally, tell them *how* to do it. Give the phone numbers, the addresses, the directions, the hours that the store is open; repeat the client's name; or provide whatever procedural information is important. Again, be specific.

Frequently the novice writer will get these steps out of sequence—for example, putting the information in *how* to order tickets to the play ahead of the material that provides the persuasive clincher to the audience. In that case, the listener will not pay attention to the what and how of accomplishing the sponsor's purpose, because he or she has not yet been convinced of the value of so doing. Later in the sequence, he or she may become convinced: "Hey that sounds like a great idea for something to do this weekend." But now it's too late to recall the details on how to take the action, because that information was not perceived as important moments earlier when it was presented out of sequence. That listener is now left with a frustration. There is something he or she has become convinced he or she would like to do, but now without the necessary information on where, when, how to do it.

## Organizing Strategies

As the preceding discussion has already indicated, you can use many different ways to organize the attention-getting material, the persuasive appeals, and other content within an announcement. Creative copywriters are constantly inventing new variations. Here are just a few of the techniques you may use. Even these suggestions are not mutually exclusive. Often combinations are used, such as testimonial and demonstration, or storytelling and problem solving.

### *Problem-Solution*

This method of sequencing is very common. First, set up a problem. Often the problem is developed in connection with the attention-getting device. An opening dramatic vignette, for example, sets up a conflict between two characters or expresses a problem that is for the moment without a solution. Later in this chapter we have reproduced two student-written radio spots for the fictitious Sun City Furniture store. Both of these spots use this approach.

Then, show how the problem can be solved by use of the sponsor's product. Sometimes the relationship is very direct and obvious: "Do you have dandruff? Then use (BRAND NAME) dandruff shampoo." Other times, the relationship is a bit more subtle: "Do you have a problem getting girls to pay attention to you? It may be dandruff in your hair. Use (BRAND NAME) shampoo." And in the final frame for television the young man is shown with a gorgeous head of hair and several attractive women hanging around him. The very obvious conclusion—it works, the product solved the problem!

You've undoubtedly seen a thousand variations of the problem faced by the couple in this ad for Formula 409 Spray (Figure 11.3). Note that this spot also exemplifies our next two categories. It is also a demonstration, as we see the product working, and the message is delivered within a story.

FOOTE, CONE & BELDING/HONIG

P.O. BOX 3183  SAN FRANCISCO, CALIF.

(415) 398-5200

Client:   THE CLOROX COMPANY
Product:  FORMULA 409 SPRAY
Title:    "THIRD STORY WALKUP, REV."
Commercial No.:  CXFS 4310
Date Approved:  8/20/84

 1. WOMAN: Oh, no!

 2. It's John and Mary!

 3. They're 30 minutes early. We've gotta clean this mess fast!

 4. MAN: Easy! We have 409.

 5. WOMAN: Here, I'll finish mopping -- you spray.

 6. (MUSIC UP)

 7. (MUSIC)

 8. ANNCR: (VO) 409's powerful grease-cutters dissolve greasy dirt

 9. fast.

 10. And 409 cuts easily through greasy grime on floors.

 11. (MUSIC RISES)

 12. Formula 409 -- starts to work

 13. before you start to wipe.

 14. MAN: There -- that's clean.

 15. (SFX: DOOR BELL)

 16. JOHN AND MARY: (VO) Are we early? MAN AND WOMAN: Oh, no...no!

**Figure 11.3.** Photoboard by Foote, Cone & Belding, San Francisco, CA. © The Clorox Company, 1984. Formula 409 and Clorox are registered trademarks of the Clorox Company.

### Demonstration

This approach to organizing a commercial, showing an advertised product in use, is primarily a television technique. It is possible for a creative writer to develop a radio situation in which a narrator or characters talk about and describe a product being used, but that's a difficult assignment. On television, however, audiences have come to expect demonstration. We watch the announcer-actor actually shampooing his or her hair; we see the coffee being brewed, poured, and drunk; and so on. Automobile ads, in particular, combine demonstration with the product-as-star approach.

### Situation—Telling a Story

This approach is also known as a "slice-of-life" spot. Here, a simple plot or story line is developed in which the product is involved. The opening of the story should catch the viewers' attention and involve them in the action. Characters that the target audience can relate to are introduced. Next, the product is brought into the plot, and finally the satisfied characters are shown using the product. They're pleased because the product contributed to their satisfaction. Frequently, this style is combined with problem-solution.

The storyboard used in Chapter 5 (Figure 5.10, for Stroh's Beer) is a situation spot.

### Spokespersons

Usually we think of a spokesperson for a product as being an individual who has a long-term relationship with the product. Candice Bergen has described herself on the air as the spokesperson for Sprint Long Distance. Bill Cosby does ads both for Jell-O and Kodak; Michael Jordan pitches for several products, including Nike; a number of different musicians and movie stars have been associated with various soft drinks. Spokespersons don't have to be live persons; the cartoon character Tony the Tiger is associated with Kellogg's Frosted Flakes and the Peanuts characters with Metropolitan Life Insurance. When a person or cartoon character or group is used to deliver commercials for a company or product over a period of time, then he, she or they become the "image" of that client in the minds of the audience.

But in reality anyone who delivers a commercial or is involved with a product, even briefly, becomes a spokesperson, at least for that moment. The most obvious and frequently used is to have an announcer deliver the client's message. If that announcer is recognized by the audience (as, for example, a popular radio disc jockey on that station), then that person is adding whatever credibility he or she has in the minds of the audience to the product by being its spokesperson. The owner or manager of a company may also appear as his or her own spokesperson.

Testimonials are a variant form of spokesperson spots. In this form a spokesperson does more than just talk about the product. He or she endorses it. The ad attempts to transfer to the product whatever importance or value that person carries in the minds of the target audience. Most testimonials can be classified into one of three variations:

1. The sales pitch is given by an expert. A person qualified as a wine expert or a restaurant owner, for example, talks about a wine, or an auto racing driver describes the handling and comfort of a new car, or endorses tires or a motor oil.

2. The pitch is given by a celebrity. In this case there is no obvious connection between the person providing the testimony and the product, but the implication is that the product must have value and importance because it is associated with a person who has these qualities. Of course the celebrity must be recognized as such by the target audience to whom the ad is pitched. Joe DiMaggio has done ads for Mr. Coffee. His was a good selection, since that client was targeting a mature audience, but he would not be a good choice for a younger target audience, who do not recognize his name, face, or notoriety.

3. The pitch is given by an "ordinary person." Here, the persuasive appeal is that of identification rather than importance. The members of the target audience identify with the person giving the testimony, who is "just an ordinary homemaker," or something similar. This form of testimonial is easily combined with the problem-solution approach. The "ordinary homemaker" is confronted with a problem, is asked to try the product, does so, and then testifies to the audience that the product solved the problem. How many headache remedy ads can you remember that have used this structure?

### The Product-as-Star

As the name for this approach suggests, the emphasis here is on the product, without other devices. The product—often food—is prominently, naturally, and appealingly displayed. This ad, "Rondo," produced by Foote, Cone & Belding for the California Raisin Advisory Board, is a good example. It won the 1983 CLIO award for Best Television Food Commercial (Figure 11.4).

### Comparisons

This approach compares the sponsor's product with competing brands. Not too many years ago it was considered bad practice to compare brands, or even to mention competitors. Then some products began to compare themselves to "Brand X," a thinly veiled reference to the major competing brand. Finally, direct references to competing brands began to be made and are now quite common. The writer using this approach needs to be careful. Don't just

# CALIFORNIA RAISIN ADVISORY BOARD
## "RONDO"

CLIENT: CALIFORNIA RAISIN ADVISORY BOARD
AGENCY: FOOTE, CONE & BELDING/HONIG

COMML NO. QCCI-2302
LENGTH: 30 SECONDS

Anncr—VO
Ahhh! The magic of raisins.
Singers

. . . You can turn a peanut butter
sandwich into something extra sweet
and chewy,

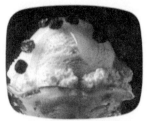

. . . You can make an ice cream sundae
lots more loveable and gooey.

. . . You can make an appetizer out
of creamy cheese and raisins spread
upon a stalk of celery.

. . . Raisins give a tangy taste to
almost anything you make

so let some raisins add a touch of
magic to your life.

. . . You can make a yogurt really
better

. . . or a toasted cheese with cheddar.

. . . You can make a barbeque

. . . or even Irish stew or French
ragout

. . . a picnic ham, a rack of lamb
. . . whatever turns you on

RAISINS ADD A TOUCH
OF MAGIC TO YOUR LIFE.

. . . 'cause raisins add a touch of
magic to your life.

**Figure 11.4.** Photoboard by Foote, Cone & Belding, San Francisco, CA. © California Raisin Advisory Board.

run down the competition; the audience may react negatively and begin to purchase the "underdog" competitor's product. Instead, emphasize the better qualities—ingredients, size, price—of your brand.

### Special Effects

The various types of special effects used in producing announcements do not in themselves really represent a separate genre. They are production techniques rather than strategies for organizing content, but effects are so important to the success of many ads that they deserve mention. They provide visual impressions—movement and color particularly—that can be very effective in attracting attention and in reinforcing emotional appeals.

Animation, including cartooning, has been used in commercials for some time. The computerized manipulation of images, in which a product spins, pops in and out of the frame, changes size or shape, or almost any other visual trick, is a more recent addition to the repertoire. It adds another whole realm of possibilities. Effects can also be combined with live action. We have chosen just one example, a "claymation" ad, again produced for the California Raisin Advisory Board by Foote, Cone & Belding—"What'd He Have for Breakfast?" (Figure 11.5). Note that this is also a storytelling spot; a sequence of action takes place. It is also one of a series of ads using the claymation technique, and like others in the series it uses a variation on a well known piece of music—"I Heard It Through the Grapevine." Claymation is a very slow and expensive technique; in order to show movement the clay characters must be manipulated between frames, and the spot filmed frame by frame. But this ad, and others in the campaign, were both critically acclaimed and successful.

If you choose to use any type of special effect, keep in mind that you are probably adding both considerable cost and time to the production of your spot. Only the more elaborately equipped production houses will have the equipment to handle sophisticated computer graphics, and only the largest advertising agencies (or special firms) can produce animation. You will need to work out your ideas with these specialists.

## Voices in Ads

We most commonly hear advertisements that use a single announcer's voice. These spots are fast and inexpensive to prepare. Even when recorded, they can be ready in a few minutes, and many are delivered live. When the voice is that of a recognized personality, whatever personal credibility that person has is carried over into the spot, and the announcement becomes a form of testimonial.

Unfortunately, single-voice spots are structurally weak, especially with regard to variety and in attracting attention. The use of more than one voice strengthens structure. At the same time, however, the use of multiple voices

RADIO ANNCR: Yep, it's a dull, boring morning.

(SFX: SQUEAKY DOOR) Sixty five degrees...

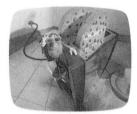

no wind...

low clouds.

Dull.
(RAISIN CHANGES STATION; MUSIC UP)
SINGERS: YEAH...

I HEARD IT THROUGH THE GRAPEVINE.

SINGERS: WHOO, HOO.

SINGER: RAISED IN THE CALIFORNIA SUNSHINE...

SINGERS: WHOO, HOO.

SINGER: WHOA MY.

SINGERS: DON'T YA KNOW I HEARD IT,

YEAH, I HEARD IT—YEAH 'CAUSE I HEARD IT...

THROUGH THE GRAPE VINE, YEAH!

SINGER: I HEARD...

SINGERS: HEARD, HEARD, HEARD IT.
(MAN WHISTLES)

PAPER BOY: Wow! What'd he have for breakfast?
(MUSIC & SINGERS OUT)

**Figure 11.5.** Photoboard by Foote, Cone & Belding, San Francisco, CA. © California Raisin Advisory Board. Lyrics based on ``I Heard It Through the Grapevine'' by Norman Whitfield and Barrett Strong. © 1966 by Jobete Music Co., Inc. Used by permission.

creates some problems for the writer. Here are some techniques, and some cautions, on using multiple voices in announcements.

### The Dialogue Announcement

The use of characters in a dramatic situation can provide high-interest material quickly, thus attracting attention. It is also effective in setting up the problem half of a problem-solution ad. However, it is difficult to deliver the solution or to motivate action believably by using dialogue. What would be considered by the audience as normal or believable dialogue doesn't usually have sufficient persuasive strength. On the other hand, lines of copy that do carry persuasive punch and deliver the sponsor's message won't sound "right" coming from the characters in the sketch.

The following student-written commercial for a fictional furniture store demonstrates the problem. When John begins to act as the salesman for the company, he loses his believability as a character.

CATHY:      Oh, John! I'm so happy that we've moved here for your new job and I can hardly wait to see our brand new apartment.

JOHN:       (WORRIED) Cathy, I think there's something that you should know!

CATHY:      What, John? Don't tell me you gave the cat away!

JOHN:       No, the cat's staying with Harold! Do you remember our old furniture?

CATHY:      Of course, John.

JOHN:       Well, Cathy, I sold every last piece of it last Saturday at our very own garage sale.

CATHY:      You mean that while I was visiting my mother...you were selling all of our furniture! I thought you were having a "wonderful" time at the neighbor's garage sale! John, what will we do?

JOHN:       We're going to buy all new furniture for our new apartment at Sun City Furniture, Cathy! Sun City Furniture has great looking furniture for every room in our apartment at prices we can afford. I've checked into it, Cathy, and we can have all new, modern furniture at a low monthly price at Sun City

MORE MORE MORE

Furniture. We can get a ten-piece bedroom set--frame, box springs, mattress, two end tables, two lamps, bedspread, dresser and mirror on sale this weekend for two-hundred, 99 dollars.

CATHY:    I think we've hit the jackpot, John! <u>Sun City Furniture,</u> here we come!

ANNCR:    That's right, folks. Come into <u>Sun City Furniture</u> located at 1000 Morse Avenue. Open ten to ten every day. Lots of free parking. You, too, can hit the jackpot!! At <u>Sun City Furniture!</u>

Although it is possible to write dialogue that is both believable and persuasive, generally the best solution is to use the dialogue to attract attention and set up the problem and then use an announcer to deliver the persuasive, motivating pitch. Here is a well-constructed example in which a student with the same assignment included the announcer as a participant in the drama.

YOUNG MAN:        Our first night in our own apartment! Here I come, honey.

<u>SOUND:</u>               <u>RUNNING ON FLOOR</u>

YOUNG WOMAN:      No, honey. Don't!

<u>SOUND:</u>               <u>CRASH</u>

YOUNG WOMAN:      Well you did it this time. What do we do now about a bed?

<u>SOUND:</u>               <u>CLICK, SCREECH ON RADIO TUNING TO STATION</u>

YOUNG MAN:        How'd the radio come on?

ANNCR:            (ON RADIO FILTER) We know that when you're starting out, furniture can be a problem.

YOUNG WOMAN:      You got that right.

ANNCR:            Come to the Sacramento grand opening of Sun City Furniture on Arden Way near Morse Avenue where overhead is low and the savings are passed on to you. Sun City Furniture where you get more for your furniture dollar. We will help you establish and keep a good credit rating. Need to get a good bed?

| | |
|---|---|
| YOUNG WOMAN: | Yes. |
| YOUNG MAN: | I'm going to the kitchen, honey. |
| ANNCR: | We've got a ten-piece bedroom set including frame, springs, mattress, two end tables, two table lamps, bedspread, dresser and mirror on sale for only two-hundred, 99 dollars, and this five-piece breakfast room set with four chairs and table on sale for just one-hundred, 49 dollars. |
| SOUND: | CRASH OF HEAVY OBJECT & GLASS BREAKING |
| YOUNG WOMAN: | Honey, what happened? |
| YOUNG MAN: | The table broke. |
| YOUNG WOMAN: | Sun City, you're just in time. |
| ANNCR: | That's Sun City Furniture on Arden near Morse. Plenty of free parking, open ten to ten every day. |
| YOUNG WOMAN: | Honey, we're going to Sun City Furniture before.... |
| SOUND: | CRASH |
| ANNCR: | That's Sun City Furniture on Arden Way near Morse Avenue. Where your credit is the least of your worries. |

Multivoice announcements do not have to use dialogue, however. Many use two announcers or other combinations of voices. Bob Elliott and Ray Goulding became famous in radio for humorous, bantering two-announcer ads. Some of the commercials reproduced elsewhere in this text have used more than one voice in varying structures.

### Infomercials

"We'll be right back, after thirty minutes from our sponsor" is the way one critic describes the *infomercial*. Another term used to describe the phenomenon is "sellovision." This type of long-form commercial, also known as a program-length ad, was prohibited for many years on broadcast stations and networks but developed on cable stations, where the FCC's rules were not applied. Now, after deregulation, they appear on broadcast stations as well. Since an infomercial is both a program and an ad, which raises ethical issues as well as writing and production considerations, we discuss this form in several different chapters. Infomercials are difficult to describe but not hard to recognize. One may look like a news documentary, a panel discussion program or a talk show with call-in audience participation, but as you watch or listen, you begin to realize that all the program content is supporting an advertising message. Is the program about buying and selling real estate— or is it about buying the host/sponsor's book on how to buy and sell real estate, his home-study course or his two-day seminar that's soon coming to your community?

Note that the home shopping channels are also direct sales presentations but not disguised as programs. The audiences for these channels tune in with the intent to shop and possibly buy.

From a writer's perspective, preparing infomercials combines all the techniques of writing persuasive copy with the structural concerns of full-length programs.

## PUBLIC SERVICE ANNOUNCEMENTS

Throughout this chapter we've attempted to emphasize the similarities between paid commercial announcements and public service announcements (PSAs). The sponsor's purposes are in both cases persuasive, although perhaps less obviously so with PSAs. Some action by the audience is wanted. Writers should approach PSAs with the same series of analytical questions described for commercials. The only difference that *should* exist, if PSAs are to be effective, is that the PSA is not paid for, whereas commercials are.

In practice, however, and precisely because they do not produce revenue, PSAs are the poor stepchildren of announcements. Usually they do not receive the same care in preparation or placement that commercials receive. Since they present a cost rather than income, they are likely to be written by inexperienced volunteers or interns. Usually only limited funds are avail-

## TANK McNAMARA®                             by Jeff Millar & Bill Hinds

**Figure 11.6.** Copyright 1992 Millar/Hinds. Dist. by Universal Press Syndicate. Reprinted by permission. All rights reserved.

able for production. The result often is a "noncompetitive" spot, without the structural or persuasive impact of commercial announcements.

Another problem arises in selecting those public service campaigns which will receive airtime. Each day stations, especially in major markets, receive dozens of news releases promoting all manner of events and items. Some of these are reviewed by the news department and may become the subject of a news story. Others are used in "community calendar" programs, which is the approach that many stations have taken to handle the tremendous volume of material. Only a few of these events or campaigns will be publicized by PSAs.

Some stations prefer to limit the number of public service campaigns in which they participate and instead concentrate on a few major projects of their own choice, in which they combine PSAs with news stories, documentaries, investigative reports and public affairs programs. The argument in favor of this approach is that it can make a larger, more measurable contribution to community welfare than a scattergun approach to public service. It also makes good publicity for the station.

When the public service directors or news directors of stations (whoever selects public service campaigns) make their selections, they will most likely use these considerations among their criteria:

1. Preference will be given to those campaigns which can be made to appeal to broad audience groups and particularly to the audiences which regularly listen to or watch that station.

2. Balance will be sought between national and local campaigns.

3. Preference will be given to campaigns which are well prepared, for which good scripts have been written and presented to the station (so time will not have to be taken by station personnel to write copy from press releases or rewrite badly prepared announcements).

4. Preference is often given to completely preproduced announcements, although some stations prefer to record their own announcements and use local talent.

Yet another problem with PSAs lies in the difficulty of finding persuasive appeals that will result in audience action. We all know we should contribute to charitable campaigns, give our time to the Boy Scouts, give blood at the blood bank, or take similar actions. But it's also very easy to find excuses and to postpone taking these actions. In order to contribute to the Cancer Society we have to find the checkbook, get an envelope and stamp, look up the address, and so on. Both the agency for which the PSA is written and the writer will need to work to make the action expected from the audience as clear and simple to execute as possible.

PSAs suffer from problems of ineffective placement as well as from poor preparation. Since no revenue is received from these announcements, they

**KTXL-TV40**

This pamphlet outlines the basic qualifications for public service time (free air time) donated by TV-40 as a part of its commitment to broadcasting different community interests and concerns, or promoting an event that benefits the entire community. Non-profit organizations in Amador, Yolo, Calaveras, Colusa, El Dorado, Nevada, Placer, Plumas, Sacramento, San Joaquin, Sierra, Solano, Stanislaus, Sutter, Toulumne and Yuba City counties are eligible, as well as state and national organizations.

**To qualify for consideration, TV-40 requires the following:**

1. A brochure or fact sheet outlining your background and aims as a non-profit, tax-exempt group whose goals are designed to benefit the local community, its interests, and promote the welfare of human beings in our society.

2. A copy of your official letterhead with a list of officers.

3. If soliciting funds, your Corporate Status Number (CSN).

**To qualify as a non-profit, tax-exempt organization you must:**

1. File an "Article of Incorporation" form with California's Secretary of State Office, Corporation Service.

2. File a "California State Exempt Status" form with the Franchise Tax Board.

3. File an "Exempt Status" form with the Internal Revenue Service.

**TV-40 has two different public service announcement formats:**

1. SHARED I.D. (0:06, 0:20)

   Called "Shared I.D." because TV-40 shares identification with the non-profit organization requesting public service time. Produced and scheduled at the discretion of TV-40.

2. PRE-PRODUCED TAPES (0:06, 0:10, 0:20, 0:30, 0:60)

   These are 1" and 2" videotapes provided by non-profit organizations requesting public service time.

   Logo, art work, slides (horizontal, 35mm, color) containing legible information (name of your organization, phone number with the area code) are also acceptable. All slides must be prepared by a professional photo finisher (check the Yellow Pages under "Photographers-Photographic" for commercial photo labs).

   NOTE: Request required for return of slides and tapes.

**Figure 11.7.** Published with permission of station KTXL-TV40, Sacramento, CA.

SAMPLE OF A TYPICAL PSA COPY SHEET
(Please submit on 8 1/2 x 11" letterhead)

START DATE:     January 1, 19XX      Contact: Mary Smith
Public Information Coord.

STOP DATE:     February 1, 19XX      Phone: (916) 444-LUNG

| VIDEO | AUDIO MESSAGE |
|---|---|
| (SLIDE/ART WORK/VIDEO TAPE) | (0:10, 0:20, 0:30, or 0:60) |
| )escription of slide and/or art work) | |
| | Reading time: 0:20 |
| **NOTE:** | GETTING TO KNOW YOUR LUNGS. |
| Since there is not enough scheduled air time in the day to use all of the public service announcements received by TV-40, requests for PSA's are, as a rule, accepted on a first-come, first-served basis and aired on a rotation schedule. | IS EASY. AFTER ALL, THEY'RE WITH YOU TWENTY-FOUR HOURS A DAY. AND YOU NEED THEM TO LIVE A LONG AND HEALTHY LIFE. NOW IS THE TIME TO DO SOMETHING ABOUT YOUR SMOKING HABIT. CALL THE AMERICAN LUNG ASSOCIATION FOR HELP. AND TAKE CARE OF YOUR LUNGS. THEY'RE ONLY HUMAN. |

Submit at least one month prior to scheduled date of event to:

Patricia Harris
Public Affairs Director
TV-40
P.O. Box 40
Sacramento, CA 95801

**Figure 11.7.** (continued)

usually are placed within or adjacent to less desirable programs, in the poorer time periods, and with no regard as to whether the target audience for the PSA may be present in the station's audience at that time. (To be fair, some stations do reserve a share of their prime-time availabilities for PSAs even though those spots could be sold, and some do consciously match up PSAs with appropriate audiences.)

If you have the task of seeking public service time on behalf of a community organization, find out in advance what requirements your local stations have. In major markets, stations will have guidelines prepared for you, similar to the one from KTXL-TV40 (Figure 11.7).

# PROMOS

The comments made in the preceding section about the writing and placement of PSAs are also applicable to promotional announcements. Some stations, however, now recognize that their own airtime is a valuable resource to be used in attracting larger audiences for programs and other station activities, and these stations are placing more emphasis on writing effective promos and putting them where they will be seen and heard by appropriate audiences.

Two general types of promos exist—those that promote events or activities that the station is involved with, including public service campaigns, and those that promote programs or station personalities. The following announcement is a particularly good example of the latter type, using clips from the program to support the narration.

| VIDEO | AUDIO |
|---|---|
| OCEAN; GENTLE WAVES | MUSIC: RELAXED MUTED |
| | ANNOUNCER: |
| | The open sea. (PAUSE) Free. (PAUSE) |
| | Boundless. (PAUSE) Its vast richness |
| | nurtures an amazing diversity of sea |
| | creatures whose very existence depends |
| | upon the delicate balance of nature...a |
| | balance which, more than once, has been |
| | threatened by mankind in its race to |
| | plunder the ocean's treasure. |
| WHALING SCENES; SLAUGHTER | From the days of the great whaling fleets |
| | that sailed off the coasts of North |
| | America and bloodied the waters from |
| | California to Hawaii with their |
| | slaughter...(PAUSE) |
| | MORE MORE MORE |

| | |
|---|---|
| OIL SUPERTANKERS;<br>DRILLING RIGS;<br>PRUDHOE BAY | To the multinational oil conglomerates with their supertankers and pipelines and floating production platforms that dot our coastlines and extend even to the stormy reaches of the North Sea... |
| DEAD FISH ON SHORE;<br>SLAUGHTER OF SEALS;<br>NOTICES OF POLLUTED<br>BEACHES, ETC. | The touch of man has more often than not been a blight rather than a blessing upon the oceans of the world and the creatures who dwell in them. |
| ACTION PICS: COUSTEAU AND<br>DOLPHINS | This Sunday, join us as we look at the plight of our world's oceans...and see how the work of one extraordinary man, Jacques Cousteau, may help to save those waters from devastation. |
| KEY: Our Fragile Seas (3)<br>Sunday--8:00 p.m. | Watch "Our Fragile Seas" Sunday night at 8, here on channel 3. |

*Source:* Courtesy of the writer, Joan Merriam.

One major problem that faces the promo writer is length. Often these announcements are no more than 10 or 20 seconds long, which provides little time to attract attention and to persuade.

## EDITORIALS

Editorials are the opinion statements of a station's owners and managers. We have placed them within this chapter because they share two characteristics with announcements. They are approximately the same length, in most cases from one to three minutes, and they have a persuasive intent, although as with PSAs and promos sometimes that persuasive thrust is rather low-key. Nevertheless, both structural considerations and persuasive appeals may, and should, be applied to editorials, just as they are to the various forms of announcements.

There is no requirement that stations air editorials, and some licensees choose not to. They may feel that to do so only angers and alienates audiences and/or commercial clients, or they may not want to spend staff time researching the issues to be discussed. Other licensees air so-called happiness editorials, commenting only on noncontroversial topics. Still others take the opportunity to comment on important issues seriously, do their research carefully, and treat their obligations to air opposing opinions with the same dedication.

For many years editorials came under a provision of the FCC regulations known as the Fairness Doctrine. That regulation set up some very careful guidelines dealing with controversial material, and it attempted to ensure that reply time would be made available to individuals or groups that disagreed with positions stated in station editorials. Although most Fairness Doctrine rules no longer apply, most stations that do editorialize continue to make reply time available for differing opinions.

Usually editorials are voiced by a senior member of the station's management, or by a spokesperson hired specifically to present editorials. And usually, even on television, they are delivered on camera and without accompanying visuals, although we see some of them now delivered from outside locations.

We have selected two editorials from Sacramento station KTXL (Figure 11.8). They are typical; each provides a brief background on the topic and each states a position. One, that on gun control, asks for a specific action on the part of audience members. The other attempts to influence government action by weight of the station's prestige and whatever other pressure may come from individuals who hear and agree with the opinion. Note also the nice play on words used in the editorial on the symphony musicians' controversy, using musical terms as part of the text.

# FINAL CONSIDERATIONS

## Product Identification

Names are important in announcements. The product name (or, if no product is involved, the sponsor's name) needs to be clearly and forcefully stated and tied in strongly with the product category it represents. It's not unusual, when asking students to describe favorite commercials, for them to be able to describe in detail an attractively produced mood piece or one which uses an unusual attention-getting device, but for which they cannot identify the product or sponsor. Winning awards for attractive commercial production may be great for the ego of the writer, but to the client, a more important consideration is selling the product.

If the product is already known to the target audience and the purpose of the ad is simply to remind the audience of the product, then only occasional mention of the name may be sufficient. Usually, however, the product or sponsor name should appear several times in the ad. And if the product

THE NATIONAL RIFLE ASSOCIATION, ONE OF THE MOST POWERFUL
LOBBYING GROUPS IN THE COUNTRY, IS PUSHING A BILL THROUGH
CONGRESS THAT WILL MAKE IT EASIER TO BUY GUNS ACROSS THE
COUNTRY...INCLUDING THE CRIMINAL'S WEAPON OF CHOICE, THE
HANDGUN.

THIS BILL, CALLED THE MC CLURE-VOLKMER GUN DECONTROL ACT,
WOULD MAKE IT SO MUCH EASIER FOR CRIMINALS TO GET GUNS,
THAT EVERY MAJOR LAW ENFORCEMENT GROUP IN THE COUNTRY IS
STRONGLY OPPOSED TO IT. ORDINARILY SUCH A DANGEROUS PIECE
OF LEGISLATION WOULD DIE FROM PUBLIC EXPOSURE.

BUT THE NRA IS TRYING TO AVOID PUBLIC DISCUSSION OF THIS
BILL. THEY USED SENATE RULES TO PUSH IT THROUGH THE SENATE
WITHOUT ANY PUBLIC HEARINGS. MANY SENATORS WHO VOTED FOR
THE BILL DIDN'T KNOW IT WAS OPPOSED BY LAW ENFORCEMENT
PEOPLE. NOW THE NRA IS TRYING THE SAME TRICK WITH THE HOUSE
OF REPRESENTATIVES.

IT IS IMPERATIVE THAT THIS BILL BE EXPOSED FOR WHAT IT IS...
A DANGEROUS PIECE OF LEGISLATION THAT MUST BE STOPPED. LET
YOUR REPRESENAVIVE KNOW NOW THAT YOU THINK THE MC CLURE-
VOLKMER BILL OR ANY LEGISLATION THAT MAKES IT EASIER FOR
CRIMINALS TO GET GUNS...IS A BAD IDEA.

-END-

**Figure 11.8.** Courtesy of KTXL TV-40, Sacramento, CA.

MAYOR'S SYMPHONY OFFER

M. MESSMER  NOV.85

(AIRS 15-18 Nov.)

IN AN ATTEMPT TO RESOLVE THE CONTINUING PAY DISPUTE
BETWEEN THE SACRAMENTO SYMPHONY ASSOCIATION AND THE
SYMPHONY MUSICIANS, SACRAMENTO'S MAYOR RUDIN OFFERED THE
ASSOCIATION TWENTY FIVE THOUSAND DOLLARS FROM THE CITY
TREASURY. WE APPLAUD THE MAYOR'S OFFER BUT CAN ONLY
CONSIDER IT AN OVERTURE.

FOR ONE THING, TWENTY-FIVE THOUSAND DOLLARS REPRESENTS LESS
THAN A DIME OF SUPPORT FROM EACH CITY RESIDENT. AND ITS A
ONE TIME OFFER. EVEN CITIES SMALLER THAN SACRAMENTO PROVIDE
MORE SUPPORT FOR THEIR SYMPHONIES THAN THAT. EVEN IF THE
COUNTY MATCHED THAT AMOUNT...AND IT SHOULD...WE'RE STILL
TALKING CHEAP.

SECONDLY, THE MAYOR'S OFFER HAD SOME STRINGS ATTACHED...SHE
WANTS TO PUT SOME POLITICIANS ON THE ASSOCIATION BOARD.
POLITICIANS AREN'T FAMOUS FOR THEIR HARMONY, SO WE DON'T
SEE HOW THIS SET OF STRINGS WILL CREATE BEAUTIFUL MUSIC.

SO, COME ON MAYOR. YOUR OFFER WAS A GOOD START...BUT WE'RE
NOT TALKING ABOUT DROPPING A DIME IN THE JUKEBOX. WE'RE
TALKING ABOUT GETTING THE SYMPHONY PLAYING AGAIN. PUT SOME
MORE MONEY ON THE TABLE...AND LETS START THE MUSIC.

-END-

**Figure 11.8.** (continued)

or sponsor is new in the community or to the target audience, then quite likely a major purpose of the ad will be name reinforcement, and frequent repetition of the name is called for.

## Repetition

We have mentioned repetition of product names, but other forms of repetition are also important in broadcast announcements. One of these is the repeated broadcast of the message. Once in a while a single exposure to a commercial will result in action by audience members; for example, you might know that you need a new set of tires for your car, you have the money to buy them and you know what brand you want. A single ad which says these tires are on sale at a 30 percent saving at your neighborhood tire store may be sufficient to get you to act.

But for most clients and products, frequent repetition is necessary, so that when customers are motivated to act there will be recognition and acceptance of that brand in their minds. Usually the writer has no direct control over this aspect of merchandising, but what the writer may be able to do is persuade the client to produce not just one ad, but a series—several ads which use similar themes and approaches, but with distinctive differences as well, so that the repeated broadcast of the sponsor's message will not be perceived as monotonous.

Another form of repetition is idea repetition within an announcement. We have cautioned against including too many different concepts within an ad and thereby weakening its impact. When the ideas have been chosen, and limited, the writer should strive to reinforce those ideas through repetition. If, for example, an ad is emphasizing a special preholiday sale with storewide reductions in prices, then the key words *sale, saving, price reduction*, and similar repetitions of the idea—not necessarily repetition of the same words, however—should be used throughout the announcement.

## Length and Timing

Most broadcast announcements are timed to precise lengths in order to fit openings between network programs or within prerecorded programs. The nominal lengths for most of these pieces of copy will be either 30 or 60 seconds; in practice, the actual recorded length is 1 or 2 seconds shorter than the nominal length, but no shorter than that. One of the first things you must know is the length of the copy you will be preparing.

Other lengths exist. An increasing number of 10- and 20-second spots are being created to provide greater flexibility in selling and placing ads into the 90-, 120- or 150-second openings between and within programs. Some advertisers have even created *split ads*—a commercial developed in two parts, with an ad for an unrelated product in the middle. The Energizer bunny campaign used split ads in its early stages; those were replaced with the parodies of ads for other products. Ads for headache medicines have also used the split ad to show before-and-after situations.

The only totally accurate way to ensure precise timing is, of course, to time the spot when it is recorded. But for those announcements which are not recorded in advance, or for approximate timing during production, these estimates may be used. Remember, that delivery speed and production techniques can affect the final timing; and for television, a continuous verbal narration may not be needed or appropriate: 25 words = 10 seconds, 45 words = 20 seconds, 65 words = 30 seconds, 125 words = 60 seconds.

These prerecorded, precisely timed lengths are supplemented by other, more relaxed practices. Many radio stations operate with casual formats, including ad lib commercials from disc jockey personalities that differ from standard lengths. Also, with the demise of the NAB codes of good practice which had established guidelines for maximum amounts of commercial time within a program, more flexible announcement schedules and longer announcements are appearing.

## CONCLUSION

The broadcast writer who is just beginning a career in the industry is quite likely to begin by writing promos and PSAs, perhaps also some commercials. Writing these kinds of copy may not seem to be a glamorous and exciting profession, but it is important writing. The industry depends on effective announcement writing for its economic success. The individual can look upon every new assignment as a creative challenge upon which to practice and improve his or her writing skills, for every assignment will be different.

The approach to writing announcements outlined in this chapter—analyzing purpose, target audience, persuasive appeals and structure and organizing the content of the announcement—provides a method by which the beginning writer can approach any assignment with confidence.

**Exercises**

1. Write a radio commercial. Since it is possible to write an announcement about almost anything and in almost any style, we have provided some restrictions to make the task more realistic. Choose a *product* from categoty I, a *presentational style* from category II, an *organizational scheme* from category III, and a *length* from category IV.

    I. Product

        a. A special Memorial Day holiday promotion for selected Stanley (brand) garden tools—shovels, hoes, pruning shears, garden sprayers, etc.—all are 30% off regular prices at "participating hardware stores."

    b. Another special holiday promotion, this one for Mother's Day, for Avon cosmetics. Selected fragrances of colognes for women in specially designed collector bottles are 30% off regular prices. Remember, Avon cosmetics are sold only by door-to-door salespersons—"Avon Calling."

    c. This company, called CONTEMPS, provides temporary help for businesses—secretaries, other clericals, accountants, security guards, custodians, etc. They've been around for a while and have a good reputation, but they are not well known. They seek to increase business by getting their name and what they do more widely known.

    d. This company is a high-volume discount stereo/TV/VCR/etc. store chain; the name is Rosenthal's. They have several outlets in your metropolitan area. They advertise regularly and heavily, with loss leaders and last year's models offered at ridiculously low prices. These are the ones they're pushing this week: Magnavox 13″ color TV with remote and 178-channel tuner—$179; Magnavox VCR with remote control and 4-event/1-year programming—$179; Sony 3-piece CD system with AM/FM stereo receiver, dual cassettes and graphic equalizer—$179; General Electric cordless telephone—$47.

II. Presentational style

    a. Straight one-voice announcer (male or female)

    b. Two announcer voices (male *and* female)

    c. Dramatic dialogue—at least in part

    d. Use music bed, with either (a) or (b)

III. Organizational scheme

    a. Problem-solution

    b. Testimonial

    c. Storytelling

    d. Comparison

IV. Length

    a. 20 seconds

    b. 30 seconds

    c. 60 seconds

If this is a class assignment, your instructor may select from each category; if not, you might draw the choices at random. If you draw, for example, D/C/A/B, you would write a 30-second spot using dramatic material in a problem-solution approach for the discount stereo store.

2. Write (draw) a storyboard for a 30-second TV spot. You could use an approach similar to the exercise above for radio, using either the same or different products and approaches, but we like to use as our product for this exercise a brand and blend of herbal tea, such as Celestial Seasonings' Red Zinger blend.

3. Write a one-minute radio public service announcement. The subject may be any actual (not fictitious) topic related to your university—which is your client. In choosing your topic, keep in mind that it should be an activity or event of sufficiently widespread community interest that it could legitimately reach its target audience on one or more radio stations in your community. (For example, an announcement aimed only at student interns in communication, or at students interested in a library orientation tour or a dormitory dance, would be too narrow to get radio coverage. On the other hand, a concert or concert series, an athletic event, guest speakers, or extension courses are appropriate topics for radio promotion.)

4. This exercise can be attached to any of the above as an additional part. For the announcement you have just written, write a paragraph of explanation on how you approached the task. Include at least:

   a. description of your target audience,

   b. why that target; the relationship that you see between the target and the product,

   c. what persuasive appeals you have attempted to work into the ad, and how you have worked them in,

   d. why you think these are appropriate appeals for the target.

5. From a local newspaper or other sources choose a topic for an editorial. If your source does not have enough background on the topic, do additional research on the issue until you can: (1) decide on the position you want to take, (2) choose a target audience, (3) select the arguments and the persuasive appeals appropriate to influence that TA, and (4) write the editorial.

6. Listen to (and, if possible, record) an editorial broadcast by a station in your community. Research and prepare a rebuttal opinion. (If you find this to be a topic on which you really do disagree with the station's

statement, you might proceed to place your statement on the air in opposition.)

**Notes**

1. K. Lee Herrick, Frank J. Weaver, and Amolie G. Ramirez, "A Successful Health Education Campaign Done with PSAs," *E&ITV*, June 1978, pp. 62–63.
2. Based on "AVIA Rallies Around Theme: For Athletic Use Only," written for in-house use by Sue Van Brocklin and Susan Thomas, Bowler and Associates Public Relations, Portland, OR.
3. Ibid.
4. Ibid.
5. Portions of this section were adapted from David H. Freedman, "Why You Watch Some Commercials—Whether You Mean to or Not," *TV Guide*, February 20, 1988, p. 5–7. Reprinted with permission from *TV Guide* magazine. Copyright © 1988 by News American Publications, Inc.
6. The Freberg spot was commissioned by the Radio Advertising Bureau.

**Further Reading**

Although one might expect to find a good many books that cover broadcast commercial writing, as there are for news and drama, such is not the case. We've selected some recent texts and arranged the titles in two groups. First, books that emphasize writing and production techniques, followed by a list of broader titles that discuss advertising strategies. Consult also the titles on persuasion in Chapter 9.

Baldwin, Huntley. *How to Create Effective TV Commercials*, 2nd ed. Chicago: Crain, 1988.

Book, Albert C., Norman D. Cary, and Stanley I. Tannenbaum. *The Radio and Television Commercial,* 2nd ed. Lincolnwood, IL: National Textbook, 1986.

Hagerman, William. *Broadcast Advertising Copywriting*. Stoneham, MA: Focal, 1989.

Meeske, Milan D., and R. C. Norris. *Copywriting for the Electronic Media: A Practical Guide*, 2nd ed. Belmont, CA: Wadsworth, 1992.

Orlik, Peter B. *Broadcast/Cable Copywriting*, 4th ed. Needham Heights, MA: Allyn & Bacon, 1990.

Schihl, Robert J. *Television Commercial Processes and Procedures*. Stoneham, MA: Focal, 1991.

White, Hooper. *How to Produce Effective TV Commercials*. Lincolnwood, IL: NTC Business Books, 1986.

For advertising in general and broadcast advertising more particularly, but not including writing or production:

Batra, Rajeev, and Rashi Glazer. *Cable TV Advertising*. Westport, CT: Greenwood/Quorum, 1989.

Diamond, Edwin, and Stephen Bates. *The Spot: The Rise of Political Advertising on Television*, 3rd ed. Cambridge, MA: MIT Press, 1992.

Fletcher, Alan D., and Thomas A. Bowers. *Fundamentals of Advertising Research*, 4th ed. Belmont, CA: Wadsworth, 1991.

Jewler, A. Jerome. *Creative Strategy in Advertising*, 4th ed. Belmont, CA: Wadsworth, 1992.

Jones, Kensinger, and Thomas F. Baldwin. *Cable Advertising: New Ways to New Business*. Englewood Cliffs, NJ: Prentice-Hall, 1986.

Moriarty, Sandra E. *Creative Advertising: Theory and Practice*, 2nd ed. Englewood Cliffs, NJ: Prentice-Hall, 1991.

Norris, James. *Advertising*, 4th ed. Englewood Cliffs, NJ: Prentice-Hall, 1990.

Ogilvy, David. *Ogilvy on Advertising*. New York: Crown, 1983.

Patti, Charles, and Sandra Moriarty. *The Making of Effective Advertising*. Englewood Cliffs, NJ: Prentice-Hall, 1990.

Ziegler, Sherilyn K., and Herbert H. Howard. *Broadcast Advertising*, 3rd ed. Ames: Iowa State University Press, 1991.

# CHAPTER 12

# News

I t must be obvious to even the most casual observer that news broadcasts are an important part of the schedules of almost all television stations and of many radio stations. This category of programming in turn represents a wide range of subforms; many styles of presentation and types of content are involved. In addition, our perceptions of what is news change over time and are different for different audience groups.

For the writer, news represents a major career opportunity, usually combined with the task of gathering information, or reporting.

In just one chapter we can hardly hope to present all the considerations involved in the presentation of news stories. We concentrate on the general process by which news personnel, including writers, select the stories to be included in a newscast and on the techniques they employ to ready those stories for the air. As examples, we focus on four types of content: the breaking disaster story, the investigative report, the soft-news feature story and the news commentary.

When you finish this chapter, you will be able to

- recognize criteria used to choose and rank news stories for broadcast,

- use those criteria to select the important facts and statements to be included in stories you write,

- recognize and use the basic forms of television news presentation, including live presentation and recorded packages,

- organize news content into producible scripts, including leads and using various story structures, and

- recognize and use these important terms and concepts:

| | |
|---|---|
| cut sheet | lead-in |
| graphics and fonts | leads: straight, throwaway, feature, umbrella |
| impact | natural (raw) sound |

outcue                          shot sheet

package                         sound bite

personalization                 soft news/hard news

prominence                      standup

proximity                       timeliness

reporter involvement            voice-over

rewrite

## MANAGEMENT DECISIONS

The production and presentation of broadcast news, particularly television news, are highly competitive. Each station and, at the national level, each network wants to be there first with a major story. This competitiveness puts great pressure not only on news directors and assignment editors particularly but also on reporters, editors, anchors and all newsroom personnel. Judgment is critical, especially knowing where and when to put one's resources. It takes experience—sometimes years of experience—to become comfortable in reacting when news happens.

To begin at the beginning, first, station management decides whether or not to put news in the station's schedule. Then, there are determinations on what kinds of news, how much, and whether to originate one's own newscasts or purchase news material from networks and/or syndicators. After these long-range decisions are made, news personnel are faced with the task, on a daily or even hourly basis, of selecting stories from among all those that might be aired at that time.

### News and Gratifications

The primary audience gratifications associated with news on either television or radio are those we previously identified in Chapter 10 as information (particularly its surveillance function), importance and value. Included in these broad definitions is the need for safety. People also seek news to assure themselves that the world is safe or to ascertain when safety is threatened, as during the Persian Gulf War and natural disasters like Hurricane Andrew in 1992.

Other gratifications can be present as well. Frequently news exhibits some of the gratifications normally associated with entertainment programming. In fact, a number of critics have argued that news (especially on television) is simply another form of entertainment. They have used as their arguments the facts that some stations: (1) choose attractive reporters and anchors in preference to seeking the best journalist for the job (sex appeal gratification); (2) select stories with strong visual content, and stress the involvement of the reporter in each story, as in the "Eyewitness" news style (action gratification); (3) look for stories with strong elements of controversy (tension gratification); and (4) choose stories with sensational, often sexual themes (sex appeal gratification again). To the extent that a station deliberately makes those choices, it legitimately may be accused of choosing entertainment-oriented gratifications over information-oriented gratifications in its attempt to attract different and possibly larger audience groups to the newscast.

Similarly, the gratifications of personalism, curiosity (especially human interest), and novelty may be found in soft news or lifestyle stories. In fact, it is the very presence of these appeals which distinguishes these types of stories from the traditional hard-news story.

## Scheduling News

Television stations, as a rule, have fixed time periods set aside for news broadcasts. Radio stations can be somewhat more flexible, but most of them also program news in predetermined amounts at predetermined times. The writer must realize that under these generally inflexible schedules, even the most complex stories must be handled within a fixed story length. On busy news days, when there are many important, complex stories, some major items may be left out or treated as mere headlines. On a slow news day, the news producer will have the option of treating major stories in greater depth or of adding less important stories, ones that on busier days would not even be considered.

When important events do occur—the outbreak of war, the assassination of a president, or something of that significance—networks and stations will interrupt their fixed schedules or change the established format of a news program. For example, the ABC late-night news program *Nightline* usually broadcasts for a half-hour, limiting its scope to one topic covered in depth, but when a major story breaks, the program is extended beyond its normal length. Cable News Network, because of its all-news orientation, can also be more flexible than the traditional networks. When the Persian Gulf war erupted in early 1991, all the networks interrupted regular programming, but CNN was able to stay with that story longer than the others.

Other examples of flexibility exist. Public TV and radio stations also preempt regular programs to carry important congressional investigations or continuing news stories. The confirmation hearings for Clarence Thomas to the Supreme Court quickly preempted other programs on national media when Anita Hill's charges were being investigated. These examples, and others, suggest to us that the changes in the electronic media that have increased the number of options available to audiences, such as increased cable penetration, are also changing the previously inflexible news practices of regular broadcast stations. Nevertheless, most news stories must still be written to fit precise lengths and be ready for broadcast at preset times.

## CRITERIA FOR SELECTING STORIES

After all the management and programming decisions have been made which establish the style and quantity of news a station will present come the daily decisions as to which and how many stories will be presented on each newscast, from among those available at the time. On any given day there will be more stories available than there is time in the newscast. This is the gatekeeping function; not all stories will get through the gate. News directors and assignment editors use the following criteria to select among the stories available at any one time. You will recognize similarities between this list and our generalized descriptions of audience gratifications in Chapter 10.

### Audience

We have emphasized the concept of target audience at numerous points throughout this book; its importance cannot be overemphasized. A story needs to have relevance to its audience. A story involving a rock music star should get heavier attention on a radio station which plays rock music than on a TV newscast which attracts a broader, more general audience. A story on possible cutbacks in social security programs should be prominent on stations in Sunbelt cities where many retired persons live, but it would merit less attention in a small college town where the bulk of the population is much younger.

### Timeliness

How important is the story *now*? A story is never as important later as when it first breaks. Tomorrow, different events will capture the audience's attention, and today's events, by definition, are no longer as newsworthy.

Many stories, however, continue over several days, even longer. The space shuttle blows up today; tomorrow I want to know why. The news writer-reporter assigned to the story revises and updates the content for each newscast, and places the newest material in the lead each time, to emphasize the timeliness of the story. Also, on stories that are likely to continue for a period of time, the writer may be asked to prepare a background story—a longer, more analytical piece that places the details of the story in context and more fully explains their significance to the audience.

Some stories do not have an obvious time element. This is particularly true of investigative pieces. On a particular day the story is ready, and the assignment editor decides to present it in the newscast. The writer should try to find an angle that gives the story some timeliness—some explanation in the lead as to why this story should be of interest to the audience at this time. If no time element can be found, it may not have been a good piece to work on in the first place.

## Impact

The criterion of impact is highly related to the two that follow. The proximity of a story and the extent to which it can be personalized strongly affect its impact upon an audience. And that's the definition of impact. How much are *individual persons* in the audience affected, how many are affected, how direct is the effect and how immediate is it?

A change in the income tax laws reducing the allowable deductions for dependents will have immediate effects on many people, but a change in the oil and gas depletion allowance will have a direct effect on only a few investors—that is, until it is pointed out that a longer-range result of that change may increase the price all of us have to pay for gasoline. The writer working on that story would improve its impact by emphasizing the price aspect.

Similarly, a story on a cold spell in November would not have much impact on people in northern and eastern states where such weather is common at that time of year, but a story describing cold weather in Florida in November would have impact not only in Florida itself, but also upon those residents of colder states who come to Florida to escape cold winters. And the story could be given national impact if that cold weather were to destroy the Florida citrus crop and thereby lead to increased prices for orange juice throughout the country.

## Proximity

People are interested in stories that take place close at hand, or in which some local angle can be developed. This criterion ties in closely with impact, because local stories are more likely to have an effect on local audiences.

A classic example involves two train wrecks. One is a local wreck in which a single car is struck by a train, killing two local youths. The second wreck is in India. A train trestle collapses, and several hundred persons are killed in the disaster. If you have time for only one story, which would you use? Of course there is no right answer, because all the criteria need to be weighed in making the choice. Were the teenagers well-known local personalities, high school football stars, for example? That would give added prominence to the local story.

## Personalization

Strictly speaking, the personalization of stories is not a criterion to be used in selecting stories. It is, rather, an approach to the writing of a story. Some stories are more easily written in personal terms than others, and to the extent that a story can be personalized for the target audience, it will be more interesting for that audience. Editors look for stories with this in mind.

A story may be personalized for an audience by describing a location that is well known to area residents, or highlighting local people who are involved in the story (even though it may take place elsewhere), or through emotional ties such as religion or economic interests. Personalization also includes telling a story in terms of individual persons who are involved, rather than in the abstract.

For example, a story on farm price supports originating with the Department of Agriculture in Washington can be presented by highlighting their effect on an individual dairy farmer in your own town. Similarly, a story on changes in state benefits for the elderly and handicapped might feature brief interviews with the residents of a local nursing home.

As we noted earlier, personalization may also be considered an aspect of impact. What will be the impact on *individual persons* in the audience?

## Prominence

Names are important in news. Of course, the names must be those which are recognizable, prominent, or important to the audience. Individuals and families that are regularly in the news, such as entertainment personalities or political figures, have a prominence that leads to more intense news coverage than would otherwise be appropriate. Accusations of rape and sexual abuse are important news items but comparatively common. They become major stories, however, when the accused is a Kennedy, even a comparatively unknown Kennedy, as happened in Florida in 1991, or when a nominee is being considered for the Supreme Court.

## Conflict

In Chapter 10 we considered various conflicts under the gratification heading called tension. We do not want to imply that people get pleasure from the forms of conflict that appear in many news stories, such as war or political conflict or social upheaval. But audiences will stay tuned to stories about such topics so long as the outcome is in doubt.

Conflict is a component of most news. It may be person against person, nation against nation, persons against nature, persons against a political, or economic, or social system, or many other confrontations.

## Novelty

This characteristic we also considered as an audience gratification. The obvious manifestation of this criterion is the classic cliché "if a dog bites a man, that is not news, but if a man bites a dog, that's news." The unusual, the unexpected, and the bizarre increase the news value of a story. In soft-news stories some of the other criteria for news value may be missing or weak, such as a lack of timeliness. The compensating criterion in many such situations is novelty.

In each station, whoever makes the broadcast-by-broadcast judgments on which stories to include, and how much coverage to give each story, will make those judgments by assigning some relative weight to each of these criteria. The experienced newsperson does so without formal evaluation of each story, but nevertheless uses this process.

These various criteria, which may also be viewed as just another way of describing audience gratifications, carry different weight for different target groups. We've already described how the traditional and impersonal presentation of hard news was not attractive to female and younger audience groups and led to the soft-news program, which emphasized impact and personalization.

Note that we've changed our wording here slightly. In Chapter 10 we used *personalism* to describe a cluster of behaviors in which individuals identify with characters, events, locations, and so on. Personalization as a news technique is highly related but not exactly the same. Personalizing a news story can heighten a viewer's sense of involvement and in that way increase the strength of that gratification, but that effect is primarily upon the group that can identify with persons in the story. Other groups will not have that sense of identity, but can still follow the story better than if it were abstract.

Impact and personalization continue to be important as stations try to broaden their audience base for news. To that end, many stations now employ consumer advocate reporters, health reporters, science reporters and others who specialize in content areas that audiences find useful. A current phrase, used by some stations as a promotional slogan, is "News You Can Use." A question worth asking is, How does each story affect potential viewers in your viewing area?

## WRITING THE NEWS STORY

Recall for a moment the basic differences between print and broadcast (discussed at length in the concluding section of Chapter 2). The reader of a newspaper story can stop reading at any point at which a sufficient amount of detail has been obtained, can pick up at midstory later, can review at any point, can go at any speed, and generally is in control of the way in which the story is received and processed.

In contrast, the broadcast story is totally organized at its source. The audience member must be able to process the story through his or her ear, eye, and brain as presented by the newscast. There is no opportunity to ask for a repeat or clarification. The story must be understood the first time through, and the sequence and speed with which the facts and ideas in the story are presented must be such that the audience can process them as they come. Too many facts, names, or numbers presented too fast, or an abrupt shift in ideas without warning will cause the audience to fall behind, and once that happens it's impossible to catch up on that story.

Traditionally the print news story has been written using what is known as inverted pyramid organization. The lead is followed by the remaining facts in the descending order of their importance as determined by the reporter and editor. This sequence permits the reader to stop at any point in the story whenever she or he feels enough detail has been read. It also permits the compositor of the newspaper to delete paragraphs in reverse order, from the end of the story, if necessary, to fit the space available.

Providing facts in descending order of importance leads to a writing style that skips back and forth among various aspects of the story. In print, that's not a problem. A reader can see the various transition points marked by paragraphs, but a listener would have trouble with this structure at the points where the story shifts. For that reason, this print style is not usually a successful approach to writing the broadcast story.

Instead, the broadcast writer assumes that if the story has a good lead and is well written, the listeners will remain attentive for a certain period of time—the length of the story. The writer can present the important facts in logical sequence and spaced appropriately throughout the length (time) of the story.

## Story Length

Time is the main constraint that broadcast news writers must deal with. First there is the overall time of the newscast. A half-hour program has about 22 minutes of news content; the rest is divided between opening and closing signatures and commercials. The 22 minutes is, in turn, divided into segments, to allow for commercial breaks. Individual stories may get an allotment of 45 to 90 seconds, depending on the importance of the story, the type of story, its position in the newscast and the number of important competing stories that day. In longer newscasts, longer stories may be used. We do see a trend toward somewhat longer stories, up to perhaps 3 minutes, as stations program longer blocks of time with news.

Another constraint is audience attention. It is more difficult to maintain attention throughout longer stories.

### Caution: Don't Crowd

Often beginning writers feel a compulsion to cram as many facts as possible into the story, especially when they realize that they have only 20, 30 or 60 seconds to tell the story. But be careful. Too many facts, presented too fast, will simply overwhelm the listener. The most important or most interesting material must be selected and spaced throughout the story using some repetition—not of the same words, but of major ideas. On the other hand, don't waste precious seconds with material that has little importance or relevance to the story, or especially to the audience's interest in the story. With practice you will soon get a feel for the middle ground between too much compression and needless repetition.

## Story Structure

Like most written material, the broadcast news story has three parts. It begins with a *lead,* which is the attention-getting device. That is followed by the body of the story. Then it concludes with some sort of wrap-up, or as one reporter describes it, the story's "punctuation." Most stories don't end with formal conclusions or summaries, but the last sentence in the story should sum up, or anticipate future developments in the story, or in some way give a sense of closure. Don't end abruptly with new material or an incomplete explanation.

## News Leads and Lead-Ins

The lead is the first sentence, or possibly two sentences, of the story as narrated by the anchor or reporter. It gives the audience a reason to listen. It explains why that story will be important or interesting to them. Obviously, as we have been saying throughout the previous discussion of gratifications and of the criteria for selecting news stories, the writer will need to know something about the audience for whom the story is intended in order to determine what those most important or interesting facts may be.

Textbooks used for courses in print journalism have traditionally emphasized the *comprehensive* lead—that is, a lead which contains the who, what, where, when, why, and how of a story, or at least most of those six elements. But for broadcasting, including all these elements in the lead would overwhelm the listener. Individual listeners simply cannot process so much information that fast by ear, especially at the beginning of the story when the person hasn't yet come to understand what the story is about or decided if it is sufficiently important to warrant attention. Instead the writer should determine which two or three elements are the most important in each individual story. That decision will depend in turn on the content of the story and the style in which it is to be developed.

*Who.* If the story features prominent names, the "who" should be in the lead, but an unknown name in the lead does not attract sufficient audience interest.

*What.* Usually what happened will be included in the lead, but if the "what" is complex and cannot be simplified without distortion or confusion, another approach should be used.

*When.* Since broadcast media are immediate, it is assumed that stories are current, and the precise time of a story is not often significant in the lead. It may be significant, however, if the story has an unusual time frame or if it is a major story that is just breaking. Only a word or two is needed to express time—today, this morning, last night—so this element usually can be included without cluttering.

Feature stories, which are not timely, can often ignore this element except that you probably wouldn't do a Christmas story in the middle of summer, and, if you did, it would only be because there was a twist in the "when" of the story.

*Where.* The location where the story takes place may or may not be important in attracting audience attention. If the president makes a major statement about the state of the economy, most people won't care (in the lead) whether he spoke from an Iowa farming convention or from Washington. Residents of Iowa, however, who would be familiar with the location of the speech, would be an exception. In Iowa, put the location in the lead because it adds proximity and personalization for those listeners.

On the other hand, the location of a major plane crash would be important to everyone, if for no other reason than to allow them to determine that it happened, or did not happen, where they have family or friends.

*Why and How.* These elements of a story usually require a more lengthy explanation than can be accomplished in a lead sentence, and therefore they should not be included in the lead.

### Lead-Ins

It is common practice, especially in television, to use one or two *anchor* announcers who provide continuity to the broadcast. Many of the stories in the cast are introduced by the anchor, with the rest of the story delivered by a reporter. In these situations the story has both a lead-in presented by the anchor and the reporter's narration which opens with a lead. The writer (often also the reporter) has to decide what material goes into each. Often the lead-in sets the background of a continuing story, provides transition between two stories, or simply provides an attention-getting throwaway lead-in as a tease to hold the audience for the story.

```
State authorities have broken up what they say is a
fraudulent smog-check ring that sold thousands of phony
smog certificates to motorists all over northern Califor-
nia. Call Three reporter Mike Luery tells us tonight...the
phony documents were selling for roughly ten times their
normal value...because the promoters never inspected the
cars in question.
```

```
Polls show that most Californians favor some form of con-
trol on foreign investment. People fear the state is being
bought up, mainly by Japan. But foreign investors have
made it clear California may lose valuable business if the
investment climate isn't right. In the conclusion to "yen
for Sacramento"...Channel Three's Tom DuHain looks at part
of that controversy. But he begins with a look at Japanese
ventures outside the Sacramento area.
```

```
It could be a late night on Capitol Hill. At this hour the
House is debating a budget package tentatively approved
today by a joint conference committee. Mary Jones has the
story.
```

The practice works well when the respective jobs performed by anchor and reporter are understood by the writers involved, but remember that the reporter will also begin the recorded story with a lead sentence. Be sure that the same information is not merely repeated in both lead-in and lead.

## Types of Leads

There are many ways to approach a lead sentence, but in general they can be grouped under four basic types—the straight lead, the throwaway lead, the feature lead and the umbrella lead.

### The Straight Lead

The straight, or direct, lead is a straightforward statement of fact, using those facts most likely to catch the attention of the listener. It is the most common form of lead:

```
Fire swept through the gambling casino of a luxury hotel
in San Juan, Puerto Rico, earlier today, killing at least
fifty people, most of them Americans.
```

```
The Miami Dolphins made it five wins in a row earlier to-
day with a 36 to 28 victory over the Cardinals in Phoenix.
```

```
The Clinton administration has unveiled a twelve billion
dollar plan to clean up the nation's waterways, but it
has drawn immediate criticism from Republican leaders in
Congress.
```

### The Throwaway Lead

Sometimes also called a *delayed* lead, or a *setup* lead, the throwaway lead is a pure tease for the audience. It tells little about the facts of the story, but introduces a provocative statement or question, to which the audience responds: "I wonder what that's all about?" and stays tuned.

The throwaway lead is effective if the story is complex and a straight lead would be confusing, or might misrepresent the facts of the story, or would have to be too long in order to introduce the story correctly.

Things continue to be a bit shaky along the coast of northern California. [Lead for a story about a minor earthquake that did no damage.]

There's bad news and good news from the Magic Kingdom tonight. [Lead for a story about employees going on strike at Disneyland and the park remaining open anyway.]

In the long continuing state college professors' strike, both sides have agreed to disagree. [The story was that an impasse had been reached, had been formally declared, and that under the rules for negotiation a neutral mediator would now be brought in—all much too complicated to include in a straight lead!]

The throwaway lead is a good change of pace in the newscast, but be careful not to overdo it.

### The Feature Lead

The feature lead is very similar to the throwaway lead; its primary purpose is to attract attention rather than deliver information. It is, as the name suggests, used with soft-news, feature stories. It is also called a *soft* lead.

Can you imagine a baby horse that lives in a house, sleeps in a playpen, and watches television?

Whoever said children should be seen and not heard didn't work in television.

### The Umbrella Lead

The umbrella lead is used to tie multiple stories together, if the stories have something in common. It is more likely to be used as a lead-in by an anchor, with different reporters covering each story, as in these examples:

Tornadoes touched down in three midwestern states this afternoon. Damage was extensive, but no injuries were reported. We have reports from Chicago and St. Louis.

The presidential campaign found both President Bush and Governor Clinton out on the trail. Jane Jones covers the

Clinton campaign from Los Angeles, and Robert Wilson is
with the Bush forces in South Carolina.

The economy sent a series of confusing signals out yesterday as to the direction it may be heading. The stock
market had its biggest advance in more than two months.
Gold and silver prices plummeted. And overseas the dollar
dropped against most foreign currencies. We have three
reports, beginning with Bill Smith on Wall Street.

Leads of whatever type must be kept brief and uncluttered. Don't include in the lead such things as these:

- Addresses. The general "where" can be amplified with a more specific address in the body of the story, if it is useful to the story.

- Ages. The precise ages of persons involved in the story are not that important; if age is important, a general term—"elderly man," "two small children"—will keep the lead from sounding like an obituary.

- Statements that don't actually lead into the story: "The City Council held its regular weekly meeting last night at City Hall." There has to be a reason why you are going to talk about the meeting; tell us, in the lead, what it is.

## Organizing the Body of the Story

The lead will be followed by the *body* of the story. The writer will have to look at the total collection of facts and opinions that make up the story, decide which will be used in the broadcast, and then find some sequential pattern in which to present these items. Any logical arrangement that will present the story clearly and accurately, within the time allotted, will do. There are some commonly used approaches, and we've provided examples of three, but many stories cannot be fitted into any one pattern.

### Chronological Sequence

This structure is the easiest and best for stories in which there is a sequence of events. It is expecially common for crime, disaster, accident, and similar stories. The following story has a long lead, which brings the continuing story up to date. Otherwise it follows a chronological approach.

| | |
|---|---|
| ANCHOR<br>KEY: SNIPER PIC | A little less than a day after the terror began...San Francisco police today burst into a room at the top of a 16 story skyscraper and captured a sniper who fired more than 40 bullets into the Market Street area and held a secretary hostage.<br><br>The 55-year-old woman was released unhurt. |
| SNIPER MINI<br>SUPER:<br>SAN FRANCISCO | This was the scene yesterday afternoon, when the unidentified gunman began spraying gunfire into the business district.<br><br>One man was wounded.<br><br>After that, police cordoned off a 20 block area and the stalemate began.<br><br>The sniper identified himself as Chief Cherokee of the Sla Woo, which he claims is a terrorist group, and he demanded money for rehabilitation of San Francisco ghettos. |
| BACK TO PIC | Then, just after 4 this afternoon, police decided to rush into his barricaded room and found him asleep.<br><br>He was captured with no struggle.<br><br>Tentatively, the gunman has been identified as Chico Cochran.<br><br>A police investigation of the incident is continuing. |

*Source:* Courtesy of KCRA, Sacramento, CA.

The audience will be helped through a complicated series of chronological events by frequent use of time-oriented transition words. In the story above, *then, after that, today, yesterday,* and *less than a day after* are all used. Other similar words—*next, while, first, finally, last night, now, meanwhile*—also help. (Reread the news story in Chapter 3, which was also chosen to emphasize time transitions and chronological sequence.)

### Effect-and-Cause Sequence

We are used to hearing that phrase in the opposite order—cause and effect—but the news story is most likely an effect, a happening, whatever gives the story its timeliness, and so that comes first in the sequence. Then the writer can go back to explain the cause, what led up to the action, and give meaning to the effect. Frequently used transition words are *since, because* and *for.*

In this story the *effect* is the results of a study just released.

| | |
|---|---|
| ANCHOR | The results are in from a nationwide study on people working with video display terminals. A group of clerical workers calling itself "Nine to Five Working Women" studied three thousand people, some of them here in San Francisco. Michael Brown reports that the study found that spending long hours in front of a VDT may be bad for your health. |
| BROWN (VTR) IN OFFICE w/VDTs | The three year study has some video terminal workers wondering, wondering if the stress, headaches, blurred vision, even psoriasis some of them suffer isn't caused by the machine. It questions whether radiation levels are too high, if the cautions like shields and screen filters too few. But a disturbing find concerns pregnant women who work at display terminals. They found companies around the country where as many |

MORE MORE MORE

as half the pregnant women working at terminals seemed to have miscarriages or malformed children. And one of those companies was here in San Francisco. It's the airlines reservations office where Carol Blank works. In the survey, half the pregnant women there suffered adverse outcomes. Carol says she has had a miscarriage and a prematurely born child who died, and thinks it's because she works at a display terminal.

CAROL BLANK SOUND BITE

(We don't know if it's radiation or if it's pulses or if it's the fact that we're so heavily monitored because our computer equipment is so sophisticated. We're constantly under stress because of the monitoring type situation with our productivity.)

BROWN

Carol said the airlines modified her work space to make it safer. Mildred Jones with the Berkeley labor group called the VDT coalition says cases like Carol's are a warning to industry.

MILDRED JONES SOUND BITE

(What that tells us is that there is a problem there, and we don't know what's causing it. We don't know if it's the VDT or if it's unrelated to the VDT, but we know research is needed.)

BROWN V/O

Pete Peterson represents an electronics industry group.

MORE MORE MORE

| | |
|---|---|
| PETE PETERSON SOUND BITE | (No, working with the equipment isn't going to cause that, that incident, in our opinion and in the opinion of research scientists.) |
| BROWN | Meanwhile studies go on, suspicions go on, but everyone agrees that it's time to find out for sure. |

### Action-Reaction Sequence

This approach is similar to effect and cause. It is often used with issue-oriented stories in which there is more than one point of view. One person or agency takes an action, which is reported in the story, and then followed by the reactions—comments, responses, counteractions—of other persons or agencies. This story has an action-reaction component in the statements from the two attorneys. It also has a complicated time frame that stretches back several years. The reporter-writer had to work a number of elements together carefully.

| | |
|---|---|
| ANCHOR | Back in 1982 a boy and a girl were hit by a car in Oakland. Both were badly injured. One is now permanently disabled. The driver who hit them had no insurance so a lawsuit was filed against the city. Tonight Ben Williams reports on how that case was settled and why some city officials are not happy about it. |
| BEN W/SUSAN in YARD | Susan Smith is eleven now. The accident that left her paralyzed from the waist down happened when she was five. She and her eighteen year old cousin were both struck by an uninsured driver while crossing an Oakland street. This month she was awarded two million dollars put into an annuity to last her lifetime. Her mother says the accident is so far behind her now she's no longer bitter. |

MORE MORE MORE

| | |
|---|---|
| SOUND BITE MOTHER | OUTCUE: "...live with it so long." |
| BEN AT SITE OF ACCIDENT | The case is unusual because the driver that hit Susan and her cousin was uninsured and so poor that the family lawyer went after the city of Oakland. The little girl and her companion were in this crosswalk. It was ten o'clock at night and dark. When they got about here they were both struck by a speeding truck. The little girl was knocked sixty feet. The attorney contended that the intersection was improperly lighted and that three streets intersecting with an 84 foot long crosswalk without proper traffic controls, he said, is a danger trap for pedestrians. |
| SOUND BITE ATTORNEY | OUTCUE: "...far more responsible than the truck driver." |
| BEN | Oakland's attorney says the city should be only partially to blame for the layout of the street and the ruling that forces the city to pay big settlements simply because it has a lot of taxpayers' money, is wrong. |
| SOUND BITE CITY ATTY | OUTCUE: "...when it is in fact only one or two percent liable." |
| BEN W/SUSAN | Susan is a straight A student who already has plans for her life. |
| SOUND BITE SUSAN | OUTCUE: "...when I grow up." |
| BEN: STANDUP | I'm Ben Williams for Channel 5 Eyewitness News. |

When using an action-reaction approach to a story, you can help guide the audience through the transitions with words and phrases like *however, on the other hand, in contrast, but.* But be careful not to bounce back and forth between the various sides of the controversy, as newspapers will do when they use the inverted pyramid approach. Instead, cover the statements, arguments, positions of one side with as much detail as the story requires (or time permits); then use a transition to move to the other side.

## Rewrites

We have concentrated so far on the original or first-time writing of stories, but the broadcast writer will spend a great deal of time rewriting. There are two types of rewrites. First, modifying a story to give it a local slant, shortening it, changing its style to fit your station, or just reworking it into good aural style. Often these rewrites will be taken from network, wire service or syndicated material or from a newspaper. Second, freshening an earlier story for a later broadcast. If new information has been gathered, that should of course be added, probably in the lead as that heightens timeliness. Part of the writer-reporter's job is to try to find new material. Call the hospital, the police department, or any agency or person associated with the story. Even if no new material can be found, a fresh approach should be written.

Here are two versions of a story—when it first was put on the air and a rewrite for a later cast:

```
ANCHOR              Officials in Greece say a Swissair DC-8 jetliner
KEY: JETLINER    with 154 people aboard caught fire after skidding to a
                 halt on a rainswept runway at Athens International
                 Airport.
                    Preliminary reports indicate at least seven people
                 are dead.
                    A number of others were hurt as flames engulfed the
                 plane within seconds of touchdown.
                    Witnesses say flames shot from the plane's
                 undercarriage as it attempted to brake to a stop,
                 finally halting at the end of the runway.
                             MORE MORE MORE
```

Most of the 142 passengers and twelve crew members managed to escape by sliding down emergency chutes.

The DC-8 was on a flight from Switzerland to the Far East with a stop in Athens.

The airport has now been closed and flights diverted elsewhere.

ANCHOR
KEY: JETLINER

Authorities in Greece now say at least eight people died when fire gutted a Swissair DC-8 just moments after it landed in a rainstorm at Athens International Airport.

Two other passengers are in serious condition and not expected to live. Many others were hurt and at least twenty people are unaccounted for.

However, officials believe they may have wandered away on their own accord.

Witnesses say the plane's undercarriage burst into flames as it tried to brake on the slippery runway, and once it stopped smoke and fire swept into the plane.

Fortunately, most of the 154 passengers and crew, including one hundred doctors headed for a medical meeting in China, managed to flee down emergency chutes.

*Source:* Courtesy of KCRA, Sacramento, CA.

You must be careful, however, when rewriting for updates of a story, to include some of the basic information that made it a story in the first place. You cannot automatically assume that all the persons in the audience will have heard an earlier version and are familiar with the story. On the other hand, you probably will not have time for a complete recap, and those in the audience who have heard the story will not want all the details over again. There's a delicate balance between too little and too much recapitulation.

## THE BUILDING BLOCKS OF TELEVISION NEWS

The language of news—that is, the basic principles of aural style—is the same for television and radio. Going beyond the basics, however, we now address the differences.

One difference is that in a visual medium the availability of pictures, or the lack thereof, may influence the selection of stories. A story of minor news value may get heavier emphasis than justifiable because the news crew got "good footage." The opposite is also true. A major story that has little pictorial content may be dropped from the TV newscast or given brief treatment just because it is not visual.

Another obvious difference is that both aural and visual techniques must be selected for telling the story. In Chapter 8 we considered the importance of matching verbal and visual elements under the heading of "Writing to Pictures." We expand upon that discussion with a brief examination of both audio and video structural options, but if you plan to work seriously in TV news, you will need to refer to some of the TV news-gathering and editing texts listed in the Further Reading section for more detail on this topic.

Both circumstances and resources affect the decisions on what structural techniques to use in presenting a given story. Each day news producers and assignment editors allot news personnel and equipment—reporters, camerapersons, remote units—to cover several stories they have selected to be included in the day's schedule. Other unanticipated stories may break and have to be dealt with. The pressures of dealing with all the day's stories affect how much time is available to get any one story ready for the air. Other considerations include what visuals, if any, are available and if so, what kind. Each story is unique in some way, but in the final analysis only a limited number of different techniques are available from which the writer-reporter can select those used to build a story.

It may help your understanding of this part of the newswriting process if you answer these questions as you assemble the parts of each story you write. They are the answers that directors and producers of newscasts need to know if they are to get the story and program on the air without errors.

*Audio:* Who is talking? Where is the sound coming from? Is it live or recorded? (And for television: Is the person delivering the sound/voice seen or not?)

*Video:* What are we seeing? Where is it coming from? Is it live or recorded?

Some portions of every newscast are aired live. The audio of some stories is delivered live by anchors and reporters. In some circumstances the video is also live. Other stories, or parts of stories, have been prerecorded onto videotape. These are sequences of pictures, with or without sound, that have been selected by the reporter, writer and/or editor and edited into a *package*.

So a first decision is will the story—sound, pictures or both—be live, tape or some combination? Many stories are combinations, but in this section we try to consider live and recorded techniques separately as much as possible.

## Live News

First we consider four "live" options.

### Anchor Live, On-Camera

In most newscasts a few stories are delivered by the anchor (or anchors) without any form of visual support. These are the less important, shorter stories and perhaps late-breaking items for which no visual material is available. For all purposes these are radio stories—read by a "talking head." We see and hear the anchor throughout.

Anchors are assumed to be live, so that a direction to that effect need not be written into the script. In the absence of other instructions, anchors are also assumed to be reading the story on-camera; for example, KCRA, Sacramento, uses the word TALENT in the video column:

| | |
|---|---|
| TALENT-DAVE | For the second time this year...a new condor egg has arrived at the Los Angeles zoo. Zookeepers spotted the new egg yesterday morning, via closed-circuit TV.<br><br>It was removed within ten minutes and placed in an incubator. And in about ten days, zoo officials will know if the condor egg is fertile. The latest egg raises hopes that some of the endangered birds could be released back into their natural habitat late this year or early next.<br><br>There are only forty of the enormous vultures left on earth...all in captivity. |

*Source:* Courtesy of KCRA, Sacramento, CA.

### Reporter Live, On-Camera

Often a reporter will deliver a late-breaking story or update a continuing story live, on-camera, without any form of visual support. Visuals would be preferred, of course, but they may not be available. Alternatively, the reporter may be at a remote location—outside the courtroom, for example, and waiting for the verdict of a major trial, with location thus adding some visual interest. The story is fed back to the studio by microwave (or satellite, if it's a major story worth the cost of the satellite feed). Whenever a reporter is seen on-camera from a remote location, the segment is called a *standup*. The whole story might be done that way, but usually the standup is the opening, followed by a recorded package.

Occasionally a reporter will deliver a live, on-camera story from the studio. Using the reporter in this way adds variety to the newscast and presumably some credibility to the story. It also ties up a reporter when perhaps the anchor could deliver the story just as well. A recent variation places the reporter in the newsroom, where he or she is presumably working diligently on the story and has broken away from the investigation just long enough to provide a live update and perhaps answer a question or two posed by the anchor. (We talk later about reporter involvement; this technique is part of that concept.)

Another variation shows the anchor in the studio and the reporter live on location simultaneously by using some form of split screen or box. The anchor converses with and asks questions of the reporter; the audience is "let in on" this display of news gathering.

Both these techniques—anchor live on-camera and reporter live on-camera—are frequently used to introduce a story, with the remainder to be a recorded package. In this case the sequence often is anchor live, reporter live, then package. The following example follows that pattern; after the reporter begins the story on-camera, he continues to narrate live over the video package.

| | |
|---|---|
| ANCHOR | This afternoon violence erupted for the first time on the picket lines outside the Greyhound bus terminal in downtown Chicago. Our John Jones was there and he's here now to give this report. |
| JONES IN STUDIO | That's right, Stan. What had been a peaceful demonstration by striking Greyhound workers turned violent today when a group of nonstriking supervisors attempted to cross the picket lines. |
| TAKE VCR w/NAT SD | Several minor injuries were reported, but no one was hurt severely enough to require.... |

### Anchor with Key

Whenever possible, some form of graphic will be used with even the simplest, shortest stories. The narration is still live by the anchor, but a drawing or picture, often with caption, is inserted into the background over the shoulder of the anchor. When a new story is started, a new graphic is put up to help signal the transition. Different stations use different terminology in the script to indicate when this device is to be inserted on the screen; *key* is one such designation.

| ANCHOR | Headline News, I'm Bob Loeser. Israeli |
|---|---|
| KEY: LEBANON HOSTAGES | officials say they are willing to talk with |
| | kidnappers in Lebanon, but Jerusalem says it |
| | will not knuckle under to any ultimatums.... |

### Live Narration, Off-Camera

Instead of an on-camera talking head, with this technique the narration is delivered over some form of visual. The narrator is not seen. The script designation is VOICE-OVER, or V/O. These are common forms of video for which live voice-overs are frequent accompaniment.

- Location video. Location shots that parallel a reporter's live narration may themselves be either live or prerecorded. Live location video might be, for example, the scene of a fire. The reporter, not seen, describes what has taken place and what is currently happening. At any moment, the production technique could shift to the reporter on-camera, perhaps as he interviews participants or delivers a standup closing.

  The other option would be for the reporter to deliver live narration over a previously recorded video package, as with the Greyhound strike story. However, if the video has been prerecorded, the narration usually will be as well, a technique we consider next.

• Still full-screen graphics. The graphics may include maps, charts, outlines, diagrams or photos. Here are excerpts from two stories that use full-screen graphics, a diagram of a pyramid and a set of outline points:

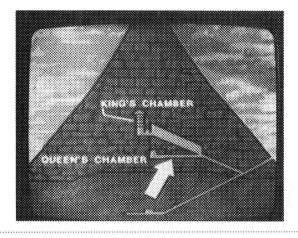

| | |
|---|---|
| ANCHOR (V/O)<br>FULL-SCREEN DIAGRAM | ...their discovery, a hidden cavity filled with sand, possibly an architectural feature to prevent earthquake damage. The Japanese followed with more advanced equipment.... |

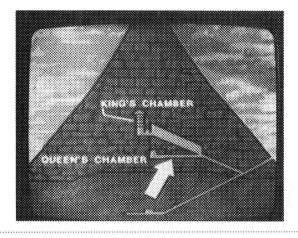

| | |
|---|---|
| ANCHOR<br>OUTLINE: FULL-SCREEN | The changes include streamlining licensing procedures, faster processing of export license applications, and fewer trade regulations with |

MORE MORE MORE

```
Western Europe, Japan, and China—steps U.S.

manufacturers have been urging for some years.

But, the Commerce Department proposals may not

resolve all of the problems....
```

In these examples the script is clear that these are full-screen visuals. Be sure you indicate when the visual is to be removed; a common way is to put ANCHOR into the script, meaning the video should return to the anchor at that point.

- A slide with a picture of the narrator-reporter. In wartime or during other fast-moving international crises, there may not be time to establish a visual connection with a reporter in a foreign city, but a telephone contact can be made and live audio fed directly to the audience. The video is a still picture of the reporter, perhaps embellished with the reporter's name, location from where the report is coming, and station or network logo.

As noted, in these situations sound is provided by the live narration voice-over, but for location video packages there may also be natural sound, recorded and run in the background under the narration.

## Recorded News

We turn now to the several options for video and audio material that can be prerecorded, then selected and edited into various packages. Since the structure of the package and its assembly are done independently and in advance of the newscast, the program script will not contain either video or audio details of the content appearing in the package. The video sequence is assembled from *shot sheets*. These pages simply catalogue the various shots that the camera operator recorded on the original tape. From them the reporter and editor select and sequence those shots that best tell the story. Shot sheets are a temporary tool used only in preparing the package. Sample shot sheets for a package are reproduced in Chapter 14, as part of a documentary script.

Nevertheless, control room personnel need some information about the package in order to insert it into the program at the proper time. The items they need are included in a *cut sheet* which then is bound into the program script:

1. Notation of the proper time to take the package. Often, the anchor will have a line like "Mark Jones has the story," but in the video script all that's needed is the word TAKE, followed by indication of the video source.

2. The video source. The technical director needs to know on what video playback unit the package has been set up, so the cue may be TAKE VCR #1, TAKE SONY, or similar. In the Greyhound story it's TAKE VCR w/NAT SD. In that example, while the reporter continues to narrate live from the story script, the video package is running with natural sound in the background.

3. Any identifying graphics. These include reporter's name, names of soundbite interview sources, locations, etc., that will be inserted by the chyron operator. These are FONT inserts; we discuss them in more detail in a moment.

4. The length of the package and its outcue.

A cut sheet for a package is also reproduced in Chapter 14.
Within the package, the following are commonly used elements.

### The Reporter's Standup

We mentioned this technique earlier, as a live option. It used to be that most of these bits were prerecorded and included as the first shots within a package, but more often now, as stations use microwave trucks for remote feeds, the opening standup is live, followed by a recorded package. In either case, the reporter is seen, on-camera, on location, delivering at least a part of the story. Preferably the standup is not the full story but is accompanied by some other form of visual. The reporter may be seen at the beginning, as a bridge between two other visual sections, and/or at the end of the story. The British have another name for this technique, which may be more descriptive: They call it a "piece to camera."

Seeing the reporter on location where the story is taking place provides another benefit that has nothing to do with the actual delivery of information to audiences. It increases *reporter involvement*. News directors and consultants believe that having the audience see the reporter involved in the process of gathering information adds credibility to the report. For this reason, many stations have a policy that some part of every location story show the reporter in a standup.

Several techniques can be used. On a story about a drought and its effect on farmland, the reporter would stand in the middle of a field and dribble the parched earth through his or her fingers. If the story involves a press conference, the camera will cut away from the speaker to show a quick shot of the reporter in the audience taking notes on the speech or asking a question. At the very least the reporter will deliver the standup in front of a building associated with the story, perhaps the state capitol or a courthouse.

### Location Video

Using tape footage in a story involves, first of all, sending a crew out to shoot the footage. Most stations make this commitment willingly as part of their news programming budget, but only major stories will justify the cost in time and money. An assignment editor earns his or her salary by making these judgments daily.

Two steps are involved in preparing a tape story—collecting the footage and then editing that footage and writing an accompanying narration.

When collecting footage on location, keep these guidelines in mind.

1. Get enough material. Beginning reporters and writers often make this mistake and find, when it comes time to edit the package, that they don't have enough good footage to cover the narration, or the right kind. They find they have to jam the facts together or leave out important material in order to keep up with the visuals.

   One news producer suggests at least 20 seconds on each single shot, to allow for selection in editing. Most stations expect to shoot about three to four times as much material as is used in the final story.

2. Look for visuals that will tell the story without a lot of narration. In some stories, that's easy. Rushing flood water, raging fires, the pomp of a military parade, a somber funeral—all can carry a story for a substantial period without explanation. At other times it's more difficult. Look for movement, conflict, personalization and the visual representation of the other criteria we gave for good stories.

3. Get the transitory material first. Your editing job will be easier if you can shoot the story in roughly the same order as it will be presented on the screen, but more important, shoot events *as they happen*, because you cannot recapture those visuals.

4. You will need a variety of shots—establishing, cover shots, "people" shots that add human focus to the story, and cutaways and closeups which will add drama and variety to the final story. Selecting footage to fill these requirements will be much easier if you have decided, at least tentatively, on an organizing scheme for the story before you arrive on location, and have discussed that approach with your cameraperson.

5. In addition to the visual footage, get natural sound if possible.

### Reporter's Narration

The reporter narrates (voice-over) the location video, but not live. This time she or he has prerecorded it to work with the video sequence. For this step in the process consider these guidelines:

1. Whenever visual materials are *not* on the screen, during a talking head or standup segment, the narration can be written as a radio story, in whatever language and verbal pattern seems most logical.

2. When visuals are present, the narration and the pictures must "fit." The narration must relate to what the audience is seeing. It should introduce,

explain, amplify and provide transitions—in short, provide the viewer with facts that cannot be seen. It should not repeat what the viewer can see.

For example, assume a story about the president leaving Washington for a vacation in California. We have footage of his getting in the helicopter, waving to the people on the White House lawn and flying off. The narration should *not* say, "And the President and Mrs. Clinton got in the helicopter and took off for California," because we see that; it's clear visually. The narration also should *not* say, "In his remarks to the group assembled on the White House lawn the President stated his firm belief . . ." You don't have footage of his remarks. *Showing* him climbing into the helicopter and waving while at the same time *saying* that he spoke to the group does not match.

You might, however, use this narration over the same footage: "The president will be in California for ten days on what he describes as a working vacation. During that time he will have to decide on whether or not to veto the farm bill, which Congress . . ." That commentary amplifies and projects the story forward, just as the helicopter is moving forward.

Review also the section on "Writing to Pictures" in Chapter 8.

3. Select a strong visual sequence, using the principles of visual continuity and juxtaposition described in Chapter 8. Usually that means beginning with an establishing shot, using medium shots for most of the factual presentation, with closeups to show emotional responses where appropriate. Your visual sequence must, of course, support the basic organizational scheme you have chosen—chronological, action-reaction, or whatever.

### Sound Bites

Sound bites are the actual recorded comments of participants in the story, of observers or experts. Other sounds gathered on location, such as the gunfire of a battle, a band in a parade or sirens are *natural* or *raw* sound.

The advantages of sound bites are obvious. They add credibility, impact and personalization to a story. These are the real people who are involved with the story. An eyewitness can describe what it was like to see the bank robbery and be threatened with a gun. An expert can provide information on the cause of a fire or speculate knowledgeably on the impact of a new government policy—information and opinions beyond the level of expertise of the reporter. The proponents and opponents of a new garbage dump site can themselves make the most effective statements on their beliefs as they argue for their positions.

Structurally, too, the sound bite adds variety to the story. In a short story, that may not be an important consideration, but in a longer piece, the use of voices and pictures other than the reporter's helps maintain audience attention.

There is no ideal length for a sound bite. In a short story, there may not be time for more than one bite of just a few seconds. In longer stories, more and longer bites can be accommodated. The trend in recent years has been toward shorter bites. One media researcher timed the average length of bites in 1968 at 42.3 seconds and in 1988 at 9.8 seconds.[1] We believe bites have been shortened too much and that many reporters are "bite happy," inserting brief lines that do not move the story forward. Anything less than about 10 seconds, unless it is very dramatic, is disruptive rather than illuminating. The reporter can use the time more efficiently by summarizing what would be in a brief bite. We think the quote should be long enough for the audience to grasp that someone other than the reporter is speaking, what is being said, and how it ties to the rest of the story.

An exception would be a *series* of brief reactions to a situation by several different persons—responses, for example, to the question: "What did you think of the Supreme Court's action?" or: "When the engine fell off the wing of the plane, how did you react?" This technique assembles several short responses into a montage. It can show the variety of reactions in a situation, or it might show a unanimity of response, depending on what you get in the responses and how the tape is edited.

A long sound bite, on the other hand, takes control of the story away from the reporter, and is likely to be an inefficient use of the time involved. Eyewitnesses or experts who are not used to speaking for broadcast media are likely to express themselves in fragmented or convoluted statements that are hard for an audience to follow, and to take considerable time to make a point. If aired in their entirety, these statements will slow the story unnecessarily. Better use two or three separate short quotes than one long, rambling statement. Choose those bites which add information and credibility to the story, and put them in logical places in the development where they can also provide variety.

A fully written out, word-for-word sound bite seldom appears in a script. It's unnecessary because the writer-reporter and the story editor have already selected the bite in the editing room, extracted it from the raw tape, and put it on the story tape that will roll during the newscast. What is needed, if the narration following the bite will be live, is an *outcue*—the last few words of the bite. Then the narrator and director will know when to move to the next segment or story. In our chapter on script mechanics (Chapter 5) we showed typical layouts for media news sound bites in Figures 5.3 and 5.4. The TV news story in that chapter, Figure 5.8, also used several sound bites as part of its package. That script was reassembled from computer storage; it reprints only parts of the various bites as used in the story.

Contrary to standard practice, in some of the scripts used in this chapter we have written out the wording of each bite so you can follow the content of the story. The two scripts used earlier as examples of effect-and-cause and action-reaction stories were rebuilt from recordings of the stories. For one of them, the story on video display terminals, we printed the complete sound bites; for the other, the Oakland accident story, only the outcues are shown.

The stories on rice burning and the California drought in a later section show complete cues which, we repeat, is not the normal practice.

Note that in these examples the source for the bite was not specifically identified by the reporter. That task was accomplished visually, by placing the person's name and title on the screen using a character generator. For radio, of course, identification of the source of a bite must be done verbally by the reporter, usually in the lines preceding the bite or sometimes immediately following the bite. In television, you have the choice of using visual (character generator) or verbal identification or both.

As sources for bites, seek out individuals who can contribute some unique perspective to the story and select bites that really add to the audience's understanding.

Finally, in leading into the sound bite, avoid the all too common scripting error of a "parroted" or "echo chamber" repetition, where both the reporter and the bite repeat the same facts.

| REPORTER | He said he would avoid calling out the National Guard until all other solutions had been exhausted. |
| GOVERNOR (SOUND BITE) | I will avoid calling out the National Guard until all other solutions are exhausted.... |

### Natural Sound

Usually location video is shot with an open microphone. Fire sirens, people yelling and flames crackling are all part of a fire scene. Natural sound can be eliminated in editing; the edited video is placed in the package without sound, and the reporter narrates over the silent footage. Usually, however, natural sound is left in the package, as it adds presence to the story. Occasionally, if there is strong visual material and equally powerful sound, a package can open "cold" with video and natural sound and run for several seconds before the reporter's narration begins. Some stations have a policy to include natural sound as background in packages unless the script indicates otherwise. A simple cue can indicate if natural sound is to be included, as in the Greyhound bus strike story used earlier.

Other sounds not captured on the location video can be added during the editing process, a technique known as "sweetening." But adding anything not present during the original taping brings up ethical questions. To what extent, if at all, and for what purpose, should the reporter augment the story?

### Graphics and Fonts

The same selection of maps, charts, still pictures, etc., that was mentioned earlier to support live narration can also be put on tape and edited into the package. Obviously they are used if, in the reporter's opinion, they contribute to the audience's understanding of the story.

Graphics which identify—the reporter's name, names and titles of sound bite interviewees, visual identification of locations, for instance—are added to the package as it is aired. These items are inserted with a device known as a *character generator* (or, in many stations, as a *chyron*, after the brand name of a commonly used generator). The exact names or other words to be inserted are written into the script at the point they are to be inserted. Stations use CHYRON, FONT, SUPER or CG in the script to identify these inserts. This is a typical example:

| CITY HALL | It was yesterday, when the Mayor reported on |
|---|---|
| FONT: (4) JANE HANSON | how city agencies were doing, that the subject |
| | of drug testing among municipal workers came |
| | up. |

These instructions show that the report is coming from a camera shooting a standup of the reporter at city hall. The reporter's name is to be shown as a lower screen insert, as that is standard practice in the absence of other instructions.

## Package Stories

Every story is unique in some way, and so is its script. For our examples in this chapter, plus the story reproduced in Chapter 5 as an example of script mechanics, we've tried to present you with a reasonable selection of story structures. To conclude this discussion of building stories, here are two more stories, each containing a package with a sound bite. You should by now recognize the more common bits of "control" language: VO, SOT, CG (for character generator), OUT Q, VTR, DVE (for digital visual effect).

| | |
|---|---|
| TALENT=KELLY | In Sacramento today...Environmentalists are kicking off a campaign aimed at a gradual phaseout of the burning of rice fields in the valley. |
| VTR=RICE BURN | (\*\*\*VO\*\*\*) |
| CG=11-THIS MORNING/ SACRAMENTO | A coalition calling itself "Californians United against Rice Burning" presented examples of rice burning pollution at a McKinley Park news conference. State air quality officials say that rice field burning is one of the big contributors to the Central Valley's air pollution problem. The environmentalists now want something done about it. |
| @__:20____ | (\*\*\*SOT\*\*\*) |
| RUNS=:21 | |
| CG=RON MAYER NATIONAL TOXICS | (Within the rice burning industry there are hardliners and there are moderates. The hardliners don't think rice burning is a problem. Well, the citizens do feel it's a problem, so we're going to work for a solution at the local level. We're also working with groups in Yuba and Sutter counties, and we're |

looking for regulations to phase out the
burning there as well.)

@__:37
OUT Q=as well
TALENT=SAME

The group plans to take legal action as well
as work for rice burning regulations. They
plan to sue officials who allow rice field
burning. They say that the majority of members
of the Sacramento Valley Air Basin Control
Council are either rice growers, or in the
agriculture industry. They want that changed
as well.

TALENT=CAROL
CG=02-[CAROL BLAND

Governor Wilson said today he is prepared to
declare a state of drought emergency. Such a
declaration would give him broad powers to
force water conservation by suspending
statutes, regulations and contracts.

VTR=DROUGHT

(***VO***)

CG=02-[STATE CAPITOL

The governor told a capitol news conference
that although the water situation is
critical...there is no need to panic.

@__:07

(***SOT***)
(Our first priority, in law and logic, must be
to provide water for human consumption: water
for drinking, for bathing, for safety and
sanitation. Even under a worst-case scenario,

```
                          we will provide the water required for human

                          health and safety.)
RUNS=:15

OUT Q=HUMAN HEALTH
     AND SAFETY


                          (***VO***)

                          The Governor rejected the notion that water

                          for city dwellers should be taken from

                          agriculture. He said that would be too hard on

                          California's economy. The governor is urging

                          local governments and agencies to step up

                          efforts at conserving water voluntarily.
VTR RUNS :45
```

*Source:* Courtesy of KCRA, Sacramento, CA.

## POINT OF VIEW

The actual writing of almost any form of copy begins by identifying a point of view, but this concern is particularly important in the preparation of news stories and documentaries. We began the discussion in Chapter 1; reread that introductory discussion to refresh your memory on it. We bring it up again in Chapter 14, on documentaries; you might jump ahead to that section as well. Please understand that a point of view is not the same as taking an editorial position, espousing one side of a controversy, or making evaluative comments on a statement made by a source. Quite the contrary. It is an important responsibility to maintain as much objectivity as possible as the story is being developed.*

Consider these situations. The first, about land zoning, was also used in Chapter 1.

* An extended discussion of the issue of objectivity—to what extent it is possible or desirable to be objective—would quickly lead us far afield of our primary purpose. We consider some aspects of the problem in Chapter 17. Some forms of writing commonly associated with news are not intended to be objective. By definition, editorials (considered in the previous chapter) and news commentary (discussed later in this chapter) are opinions. Here we'll simply say that in regular news stories professionals and audiences alike expect reporters to deal with the content in a fair and balanced way.

- You're doing a story about land rezoning. Last night the city council accepted the planning department's recommendations for major rezoning of a large block of land. As noted in the previous discussion, you can simply summarize the report and the council's action. If you have only a brief time to prepare and a short slot in the newscast, that's probably all you can do. If you have more time, you can also approach the story by looking at its implications on community development or from the gain or loss on the part of various groups. You might organize the story to emphasize the *process* of zoning and rezoning, focusing on the roles of the various government bodies involved—planning commission, board of supervisors, citizens' advisory groups. The argument on rezoning a particular piece of land can then be treated as a case study of how the process works. Or the same topic might be approached as a controversy, viewed in the form of the opposing forces—status quo versus development—with the governmental bodies caught in the middle trying to find a compromise acceptable to both sides.

- Your story is to report on a federal project which intends to spend millions of dollars to repair river levees. If there is serious concern that water control projects have been neglected and that neglect poses a threat to public safety through possible breaks in levees, then that's probably the point of view to take on that story. Point up the dangers, seek out the ways danger can be reduced, tell people how to protect themselves from the floods that may come with the spring runoff. If the danger is not acute (but you decide to do the program anyway), the focus might be on possible squabbling between various government agencies over who has the responsibility for water control, cutbacks in government programs that have lessened preventive maintenance, and so on.

- The topic is breast cancer. You've been assigned to prepare a series of reports to bring viewers up to date on this serious medical problem. You might take a clinical approach. What are the most recent research findings and newly accepted medical techniques for prevention, detection, and control? Or it might concentrate on how women who have had breast cancer have coped with surgery, chemotherapy, and so on. Also, we've recently learned that breast cancer is not just a woman's disease; men are increasingly afflicted. That program, which contradicts the conventional perception, would attract a good deal of audience interest.

If the report is to be organized into a series—three- and five-part series are common—then there will need to be an overall point of view for the series as well as one for each individual program. The zoning story, for example, could easily be structured into three parts—one concentrating on the developers' position, one on a citizens' group trying to slow or stop development, and one on the planning commission as the battleground.

In the next section we consider four broad kinds of stories. As you read through the examples in those sections, identify the point of view used by the writer and think about other points of view that might be taken.

# TYPES OF STORIES

At this point we can no longer continue to generalize about the structure of individual stories. We will now consider four kinds of stories—the "breaking" disaster story, the investigative report, the "soft news" feature story, and the news commentary. These four provide a reasonable range among the many possible types.

## The Disaster Story

Accidents and disasters of various kinds make up a large share of "breaking" stories—auto, bus, truck, plane and train crashes, fires, earthquakes, hurricanes. Most are unforeseen events, and all too frequently they involve the loss of human lives. The reporter-writer cannot even begin to prepare this type of story in advance, and with the possible exception of fires and storms, won't usually get to the scene until the event has concluded.* The story will have to be reconstructed from the accounts of survivors, witnesses and professional persons—doctors, police, fire personnel, others—who are at the scene.

The most important information to be gathered and worked into the story can be grouped under the traditional six categories:

*Who:* Number of people involved? Anyone important or prominent? Other identifications: names and roles of people who are providing information.

*What:* Nature and magnitude of event, subsequent events, extent of death and injury, and so on.

*When:* The chronology of events and following activities.

*Where:* Get the exact location, but repeat the location using landmarks familiar to your audience, if possible.

---

* For a particularly gripping account of on-the-spot disaster reporting, read Dan Rather's description of his experience in covering hurricane Carla from Galveston, Texas, in 1961. It's in his book *The Camera Never Blinks*. Another classic example is the 1937 radio account of the explosion and crash of the dirigible *Hindenburg*.

*Why:* If there is a cause that can be verified, state it—but be cautious, for example, in attributing cause in an auto accident until the appropriate authorities so state.

*How:* In this type of story, how is mostly a description of the progress of the event. The hotel fire started in a conference room and spread between floors and walls undetected, then shot up a stairwell and erupted on several floors simultaneously, and so on.

If the story is a major one, numerous chances exist for follow-ups—the continuing condition of injured survivors, statements by authorities including condolences to victims, relief to the stricken area, promises of future aid to prevent future catastrophes and so on.

The following script from an actual disaster shows how the content of the story was organized. It also shows how many of the building blocks of a TV story are displayed in a script. There are several reports from different locations and a mix of live reporting and prerecorded packages.

```
ANCHOR: STAN                    Topping our news tonight at

                                five...Twelve people have been

                                hospitalized in the town of Gilroy just

                                South of San Francisco after a major

                                earthquake rocked the area.

                                The tremor...which registered six point

                                two on the Richter scale...was centered

                                just East of San Jose.

                                It was felt as far away as Carson City,

                                Nevada.

                                The quake jarred houses from their

                                foundations...and sent skyscrapers in

                                San Francisco swaying.

WIPE TO SONY                    In San Jose...a shopping center there

RUNS  :21                       sustained major damage.

  FONT: SAN JOSE (3)            Elsewhere in the city...flames broke out
```

LIVECOPTER IN MON

LIVECOPTER FULL

   FONT: LIVECOPTER

   FONT: ROY STEARNS

TAKE VTR    2

   RUNS:   :46

   FONT: SAN JOSE (3)

   FONT: LEE SUESS
        Dep. Fire Chief

FONT: LEE KING
      Pet Store Owner

ANCHOR: SUSAN

---

sporadically after the tremor was reported.

Residents also report damage to buildings in Morgan Hill...which is about twelve miles Southeast of San Jose.

Channel 3's Roy Stearns has been on the scene for us....

...He's aboard livecopter three right now...Roy, what can you tell us...

SOUND FULL

OUTCUE: damage was much less than it could have been.

SOT FULL

SOT ENDS: little bit saved.

Not too far away in the San Francisco Bay area...the quake was felt as a rolling motion that lasted about 25 seconds.

Thousands of people were in high rise offices at the time...and they got quite a scare.

Channel 3's John Gibson was among those shaken by the big tremor.

| | |
|---|---|
| TAKE VTR   <u>1</u> | SOT FULL |
|   RUNS:   <u>120</u> | |
|   TOP FONT: (3) SAN<br>        FRANCISCO | |
|   FONT: JOHN GIBSON | TAPE ENDS ON CUE: for Channel 3 Reports. |
| ANCHOR: STAN | It's miraculous with an earthquake of |
| | this size...that there have been no |
| | deaths and no serious injuries. |
| | But several people have sustained minor |
| | injuries...and there has been damage. |
| 2 SHOT | Channel 3's Mike Boyd is standing by |
| LIVECAM IN MON | live at the Office of Emergency Services |
| | in Sacramento with an overview. |
| TAKE SACRAMENTO LIVECAM | SOUND FULL |
|   FONT: LIVECAM | |
| | OUTCUE: the quake struck at 1:15 this |
|   FONT: MIKE BOYD | afternoon. |
| TAKE VTR   <u>2</u> | BOYD: VOICEOVER |
|   RUNS:   <u>60</u> | |
|   TOP FONT: (3) SACRAMENTO<br>  DEPT. OF WATER RESOURCES | |
|   FONT: (3) OFFICE OF<br>  EMERGENCY SERVICES | |
| TAKE LIVECAM FULL | Boyd introduces OES spokesman. |
|   FONT: MIKE BOYD | |
|   FONT: LIVECAM | |
|   FONT: AL LOCKHART<br>      OES Asst. Director | |
| 2 SHOT | Boyd wraps up...tosses to studio. |
| LIVECAM IN MON | |

*Source:* Courtesy of KCRA, Sacramento, CA.

The story begins with an opening summary delivered by the male news anchor (STAN). He opens on-camera and continues as a voice-over for the first videotape package. The writer called for the effect of wiping that segment onto the screen. As soon as the tape is rolling, a graphic is inserted. KCRA uses the word FONT to identify graphics. This one is a visual identification of the location and the station's logo (SAN JOSE 3). The anchor continues narrating for the 21 seconds that the tape runs and then cues the next segment.

Segment 2 is live aboard the KCRA helicopter. The transition is accomplished by first showing the helicopter shot in a video monitor on the set with the anchor, who turns and talks to the monitor. When the reporter answers, the helicopter feed full-screen (FULL) is punched up. Full-level sound is also called for as the reporter in the helicopter begins his report. During the report, which is live and obviously not scripted, two FONTS are inserted—LIVECOPTER and the reporter's name. To know when to return from the live report, an outcue ("damage was much less than it could have been") has been prearranged and included in the script. (If there is no time to arrange an outcue, the reporter will simply have to say something like, "Back to you, Stan." We hear that a lot on live remotes using microwave or satellite feeds.)

The third segment is the second videotape package, this one with sound (SOT). It begins directly—no bridge from the anchor. It runs 46 seconds, comes from San Jose again (identified by a graphic, SAN JOSE 3), and includes two sound bites. Both persons in the bites are identified by graphics giving their names and positions. The outcue is in the script: "little bit saved."

Now the female coanchor (SUSAN) picks up the story and leads into the next tape package, from San Francisco, lasting 120 seconds. A FONT variation is used; now the station logo and location are in a top-screen title, the reporter's name in the normal, lower-screen position. Again, an outcue is given.

Back to the male anchor (STAN). He provides a bridge and then the same form of transition as was used to introduce the helicopter report. He turns to the on-set monitor, which shows a LIVECAM shot from the Office of Emergency Services.

The LIVECAM and its sound come up. Two FONTS identify it and the reporter, who delivers the live report, with a prearranged outcue. Since the same reporter had previously recorded a package, the live story serves as an intro to that package, which is run as silent tape with the reporter's live voice-over. The two locations used in the package are identified by top-screen graphics. At the conclusion of the 60-second package, back to LIVECAM for a live interview, including three FONT inserts to identify the LIVECAM, the reporter again and the interviewee.

The reporter finishes with a live stand-up, then "tosses" the story back to the anchors (2 SHOT) in the studio. There might be a final question-response with the reporter still seen in the monitor on the set, a thank-you, and the story closes.

We have used the term *breaking* story to contrast this type of story with other types that can be prepared on a schedule determined by the journalist. Accidents and disasters, which come without warning, make up one major category of breaking stories, but many breaking stories are developed out of scheduled events. The governor may schedule a press conference, for example, and the station can assign a reporter to cover it, but the story can't be written until after the meeting is over. It's still a breaking story, the result of an event, and it may have to be written in a hurry to meet a deadline. Parades, conventions, sporting events, and demonstrations are other scheduled events that lead to breaking stories.

## The Investigative Report

Investigative reports are prepared on a scheduled basis. They do not depend on an event or outside trigger mechanism except that, for example, the death of a group of destitute transients in a flophouse hotel fire might call the attention of an assignment editor to the possibility of doing a series of reports on the plight of the elderly poor.

A problem with the investigative report, which we have already touched upon, is its possible lack of timeliness. If the report can be timed to correspond to a breaking story, then the problem is solved. To use some of our earlier examples, a series of reports on the rezoning of residential and agricultural land might be timed to coincide with the release of a major study on urban planning. Or the story can be prepared and released when some aspect can be highlighted that gives it timeliness, such as a story on individual retirement accounts released shortly before April 15, the income tax deadline, or a story on water control projects that coincides with the annual runoff from snow melt.

Sometimes other criteria will have to substitute for timeliness. A series of reports on breast cancer may use impact and possibly personalization as its raison d'être.

Once the topic has been chosen, the research begins. Quite possibly both library research and interviews with experts will be used. Some of the interview material may later appear in the report as actualities. The research will help determine the scope of the topic, identify the most important material, and locate the best "experts." If the topic concerns an issue about which there are different opinions, the question of how to present those viewpoints fairly also will have to be dealt with.

The type of story that we have been describing may appear under various labels. In addition to investigative report, it may be called a special report, or minidocumentary. The script of the program on AIDS in the chapter on documentaries (Chapter 14) is very much like an investigative report. But although there is a great deal of similarity between investigative news reports and documentaries, and frequently the same topics and even the same raw camera footage are used for both, we prefer to use the term documentary to describe a somewhat different approach to story development, and we develop the difference in Chapter 14.

## The Soft-News Feature Story

We have used three terms to describe this type of story—*soft news, lifestyle* and *feature*. All three terms are interchangeable, although *feature* seems to be more common in radio and the others in television. There is nothing inherently different in the construction of this type of story. They use standups, packages, sound bites, and so on, just as in any other structure. The difference is primarily in the gratifications that are emphasized. Personalism, curiosity and novelty are likely to be stronger in this type of story.

The subject matter may aim at specific groups. A story on a new type of shoe for joggers that cuts down on sore feet would be of interest really only to joggers; it would be difficult to find a point of view to that story which would give it appeal to a broader audience. (The placement of that story would be an important consideration—on a cable channel that attracts the appropriate target audience, perhaps, but not likely on the 6 o'clock news.)

Timeliness is not an important consideration, although such stories may well be timely. A story of a man who carves statues with a chain saw will be just as interesting to an audience one week as the next, unless of course the statues he makes are all of Santa Claus. Then there would be an appropriate time for the story.

Here is how one such story was prepared. Professor Richard Goedkoop of La Salle University shadowed feature reporter Wendall Woodbury of WGAL-TV, Lancaster, Pennsylvania, as he prepared this story. We have substantially edited his much longer account.

> The story was to focus on the return of a 132-year-old statue of Robert Fulton to the Fulton Opera House (one of the oldest theatres in the country) in Lancaster, Pennsylvania. Until two years earlier, the seven-foot statue was on display in an outdoor alcove of the theatre some 20 feet above the marquee. Since 1854 the wooden statue, sculpted by Philadelphian Hugh Cannon, had suffered damage from the elements and had endured 25 coats of paint. It had been taken to the laboratories of the Winterthur Museum in Wilmington, Delaware and remained there for two years of study and restoration. It was now returning and would be put on display in the theatre's lobby.
>
> Wendall's coverage of this story had begun two years earlier when he had reported on the statue's departure. By replaying the videotape in the newsroom, he was able to refresh his memory on the story and also located footage that could be edited into the day's report. After this, he spent some time at his desk preparing questions for the curator and Fulton employees, as well as making a rough outline of how he saw the story taking shape.

At 10:30, Wendall, [photographer] Larry Poole and I left for the story site. Along the way, we discussed the ideas he had in mind for the story as well as some of the questions he intended to ask the Winterthur conservator. Wendall told me that he had a tentative line for a "standup" he planned on giving outside the theatre: "After 130 years of watching the traffic on Price Street—he's going inside to watch some shows."

Once we had arrived at the theatre, we discovered that the moving van had just arrived from Winterthur and the refurbished statue was going to be unloaded. Larry parked and got his camera ready for action as quickly as possible.

Some shots, like the unloading of the statue from the truck, could only be taken once. Closeups, reaction shots, cutaways, interview segments, numerous takes of the statue from various angles—all had to be gotten right.

Of course, this did not mean that all of the footage collected by the team was a spontaneous "mirroring" of the reality/event that occurred at the theatre. At several points during the two taped interviews, the subjects were asked by Wendall to repeat key phrases that they had spoken.

In addition, a number of the more visual shots (toasting of champagne glasses, closeups of the curator making final adjustments on the statue, features of the statue itself) were planned, posed and repeated so that they would be sure to have them available in good measure for editing and use as B-roll for some of the story's narration. From time to time, Wendall did make suggestions to Larry about shots he thought he needed. But the communication between this reporter/photographer team was so good that Larry was often setting up the shot before Wendall had spoken about it.

Once back at the station and after lunch, the editing process began. Larry was able to log the videotape for Wendall before being asked to work on another task by the assignment editor. Meanwhile, Wendall was writing the main segments of his script, using his cassette recorder, notebook and typewriter all in tandem while paying close attention to the visuals he knew had been taped. There were many details about the statue and its restoration that he felt guilty about leaving out of the piece but he was too constrained by the nature of television news and his assigned "1:45–2:00" to do much else.

The completed story on Robert Fulton's return to the theatre named for him was finished about 45 minutes before it was needed on the 7:00 p.m. newscast, and ran 1:53 in length. Its "coming" was announced at the end of the 6:00 p.m. newscast and teased twice within the program in which it aired. It was recycled for the noon newscast the following Monday. In many ways it was a microcosm of local television news itself. One part information and one part entertainment, both tightly edited, packaged and promoted to meet the needs of the newscast and the organization that produced it.[2]

## News Commentaries

The most obvious difference between news commentary and other types of news writing is the shift from objectivity (or at least the attempt to remain objective in presenting a story) to a subjective and more personal point of view. This two-part commentary, broadcast over two consecutive days, exemplifies that difference. It was written and presented by news anchor Dick Cable on KXTV, Sacramento, California. It is part of a regular feature called "Cable's Comments."

| | |
|---|---|
| CROSS TO CABLE | Tomorrow is one of those "Theme Days" and Dick Cable is ready to get on the backwagon. |
| | * * * * * * * * * * * * * * * * |
| TAKE CABLE | Tomorrow is the "Great American Smokeout" ...promoted by the American Cancer Society and its local units all across the country. |
| | The object is to motivate and support smokers to quit for the day and consider the dangers involved in smoking...and if the motivation and the message is strong enough...to get you to stop smoking forever. |
| | I'm impressed that each year the smokeout has been conducted...many smokers have tried to quit...and a few of them have been able to kick the habit. |
| Key: Comment | The day will mean little or nothing to you if you don't quit...It may only aggravate you that that bunch of holier-than-thou goodie-two-shoes are bugging you again. |
| | I've bugged you before...and I intend to do it again. |
| | MORE MORE MORE |

A friend of my teenage daughter smokes...and my daughter expressed concern that her friend was smoking more and more. Why does she smoke? I asked. "She says it calms her nerves," came my daughter's reply.

I understand that process well...as a one-time three-pack-a-day smoker, I know all about smokers' nerves. An addicted smoker gets nervous for the same reason a heroin addict gets nervous...because his body is craving a fix. A shot of heroin calms the heroin addict...a cigarette calms the smoker. It is not the nerves being soothed...it is the addiction.

Key: Comment

When I gave up cigarettes...my skin turned a sickish green, I broke out in cold sweats, my hands shook, my voice trembled and I suffered from stomach cramps. Those were cigarette nerves...and somehow I finally had found the guts to cure them rather than appease them by lighting up again.

We're all going to die. I'm not trying to prevent death...but I hope to live until I die.

The leading risks from smoking are heart disease, stroke, emphysema, and lung cancer. With the exception of a massive fatal heart attack...death from these causes is a slow and ever-worsening torture.

The emphysemic slowly strangles...it can take years. Lung cancer is shorter...perhaps six months, but a year or more is possible...and the pain beggars description.

Key: Comment

Only 9 percent of lung cancer patients live five or more years after diagnosis. 83 percent of lung cancers in men are caused by smoking.

MORE MORE MORE

Give the American cancer society a call...they've got lots of help and ideas and support for you if you want to finally kick the habit.

That's Cable's comment.

CROSS TO CABLE

Speaking of the great American smokeout...some viewers have taken umbrage over an analogy made by Dick Cable in his comment last night.

\* \* \* \* \* \* \* \* \* \* \* \* \* \* \* \*

TAKE CABLE

Yes...but rather than apologizing, I'm going to turn the screw a little tighter.

Talk about smoker's nerves. I must have rubbed quite a few of them raw. The switchboard logged a good number of calls from viewers who said..."How dare he equate cigarette smoking with heroin addiction? We don't go out robbing and killing to feed our habit."

Key: Comment

Actually, I didn't equate cigarette smokers with heroin addicts...but I did make a statement about addiction. When a smoker's nicotine blood-level begins to decline in the interval between cigarettes...he or she begins to feel fidgety, nervous...and reaches for another smoke. The cigarette relieves that nervousness...and reinforces the habit. That is very much like heroin addiction. When the level of morphine in the body declines...the addict becomes increasingly agitated and is only relieved by another dose.

The important thing to understand is that almost all smokers are...in a true medical sense...addicted to nicotine in much the same way that heroin addicts are to their drug.

MORE MORE MORE

Key: Comment

Some of the callers who said "How dare you" to me noted that unlike heroin addicts, they do not rob or kill others nor prostitute themselves to feed their nicotine habit. I suggest to you there's only one reason why that might be true. Cigarettes are <u>cheap</u>. If heroin was 50 cents a hit, heroin addicts wouldn't be a crime problem either. Conversely, if cigarettes were $100 a pack, thousands of you would be transformed into thieves and prostitutes.

Let me tell you something else too. Cigarettes, in and of themselves, are more dangerous to your health than heroin, in and of itself.

Heroin addicts die only rarely from the drug itself. It is <u>not</u> poisonous!

They usually die from impurities used to cut the street heroin...from dirty needles, malnutrition or from being killed during a holdup or by a pusher who didn't get his money on time.

Key: Comment

A lit cigarette, on the other hand, is loaded with poisons, poisonous gases and carcinogenic agents. Nicotine itself is one of the most potent poisons on earth. I've heard it said that a single drop in a bucket of water is enough to kill a horse.

Besides tar and nicotine, cigarette smoke contains hydrogen cyanide, volatile hydrocarbons and carbon monoxide.

Smoking is not only addictive...it also poisons its addicts.

That's Cable's comment.

*Source:* Courtesy of KXTV, Sacramento, CA.

Analysis of these commentaries shows both similarities with an ˉˉˉˉˉˉˉ ences from other types of stories. They have impact, timeliness, personalization, conflict—all strong criteria for any news story. They are also personal—use the pronoun *I* and make personal references to the reporter's own family and friends. An objective story on the same topic might give information on the success of similar smokeout days in past years, how many people might be expected to quit this year, and what arrangements were being made by the local Cancer Society chapter. These commentaries go much beyond that; they have a strong and subjective point of view.

We said early in the chapter that we would not attempt to cover all types of stories. There is no way we could. But most stories will fit reasonably well into these basic patterns. Sports stories, for example, represent a change in content, but not in approach. The most common sports story is a breaking story after a scheduled game. Other sports stories will be investigative, feature, or commentary.

The one major category that does differ is the reporting of weather. To be successful as a weather reporter or writer requires some expert knowledge of meteorology. It also seems to require a heightened sense of showmanship, as this is the one type of news story most often presented ad lib, without script, and that often attracts the more outrageous presentational styles.

## CONCLUSION

It would be superficial in the extreme to summarize what is already a very brief summary of the process of gathering, organizing, and writing news for broadcast. Several excellent texts delineate the various steps in much greater detail, and we have listed them in the Further Reading section. We will, however, leave you with these four questions, which you can use as a test of your ability to write a good news story:

1. Is the story *clear*?

2. Is the story *concise*?

We have seen that under most circumstances broadcast stories will not exceed 90 seconds, and may be considerably shorter. In order to be both clear and concise, the writer must understand the details of the story and be able to identify those which are most significant to the target audience.

3. Is the story *correct*?

There is an expectation on the part of the audience, one shared by any professional journalist, that a story *is* correct. There have been occasions when news has been deliberately slanted by a reporter or by a manager or station owner, but fortunately these have been rare. What is no longer rare is the accusation, or a perception of slanting or bias. Any conscientious professional journalist will try to present every story in an impartial, balanced fashion, although he or she may not succeed to everyone's satisfaction in every case.

4. Is the story *complete*?

Under the time constraints that broadcast journalists face, it's almost impossible to present as much detail as one would like. The story is never really completely told. But within those constraints the audience should feel that sufficient detail has been provided, even if the story is little more than a headline. Review *who, what, when, where, why* and *how*. Which of these are absolutely necessary to communicate the essence of the story to the audience?

Judge your stories by these catchwords: *clear? concise? correct? complete?*

**Exercises**

1. Repeat Exercise 3 in Chapter 3. Rewrite a major news story from a newspaper account as a 90-second radio story. Place particular emphasis on building a strong lead, a logical organizational pattern for the body of the story and aural style.

2. Using a newspaper as your first source, *plus at least one other non-newspaper source,* write a 60- to 90-second news story for radio. The story should be "hard" timely news, *not* a feature. It may help to think of the relationship of the two sources in one of three ways: (1) The newspaper had the original story; your second source will *update* it for later broadcast. (2) The newspaper story was based on state or national material, originating elsewhere; your second source will give the story a *local slant.* (3) The newspaper left unanswered some questions which your target audience would want to know; your second source will *clarify* or *expand* on these points.

3. Write a 90-second news story for television, based on original research. The story should be a true news story, not a feature, which means that it should have significance *now.* However, that significance can come in either of two ways: You can cover a breaking story—event, press conference—or you can develop the timeliness into the story. You are encouraged to consider, but not required, to use sound bites. Of course, since this is a TV story, you will have to indicate what visual material is to be seen throughout. (You may assume your camera crew was able to shoot whatever you want.)

4. Do Exercise 2 for television, and/or 3 for radio.

5. Write a soft-news story for a television station in your market, on one of the following:

   a. The anniversary of a local landmark—a bridge, statue, building, or similar.

   b. A unique fundraising event held by a local charity.

   c. An out-of-the-way place to spend an unusual weekend or vacation.

   d. A new arrival at the local zoo.

6. Write a news commentary for radio on one of the following (but make the general topic specific to your community):

   a. Sex education programs in the local public schools.

   b. Remembering the significance of Memorial Day.

   c. Support for (or opposition to) gun control legislation.

   d. The importance of voting in an upcoming local election.

7. Record the competing television news programs of local stations or of networks, that is, broadcasts aired at approximately the same time. Compare. Consider (1) the choices of lead story; (2) the length, resources used and point of view when the same story is covered; (3) differences in the choice of stories, the personnel used or the overall newscast that provide different gratifications or varying strengths of gratifications, and thus attract different audience groups. This exercise can be merged with the exercise suggested in Chapter 1, which considered point of view as just one part of this broader analysis.

**Notes**

1. Quoted in Richard Rose, "American Culture Dying Bite by Bite," *San Francisco Chronicle Datebook,* June 24, 1990.
2. Revised from Richard Goedkoop, "Anatomy of a Feature Report," *BEA Feedback,* Fall 1988, pp. 11–16. Reprinted by permission of Broadcast Education Association.

**Further Reading**

A great many books have been written about several subfields of journalism. There are texts for broadcast news writing (often combined with news production), reporting (for both print and broadcast), news writing in general (meaning primarily for print), journalism ethics, news management, biographies, personal accounts by news personalities and critical works. We have space to list only a few titles in a few of these categories. Consult also the Further Reading lists at the ends of the chapters on production, talk programs, documentaries and legal and ethical concerns for other worthwhile texts.

We begin with the most directly related titles, those that emphasize broadcast news writing:

Block, Mervin. *Rewriting Network News.* Chicago: Bonus, 1990.

———. *Writing Broadcast News: Shorter, Sharper, Stronger.* Chicago: Bonus, 1987.

Boyd, Andrew. *Broadcast Journalism: Techniques of Radio and TV News,* rev. ed. Oxford, UK: Heinemann, 1990.

Cohler, David Keith. *Broadcast Newswriting.* Englewood Cliffs, NJ: Prentice-Hall, 1990.

Gibson, Martin. *Editing in the Electronic Era*, 3rd ed. Ames: Iowa State University Press, 1991.

Hausman, Carl. *Crafting the News for Electronic Media: Writing, Reporting, and Production.* Belmont, CA: Wadsworth, 1992.

Hewitt, John. *Airwords: Writing for Broadcast News.* Mountain View, CA: Mayfield, 1988.

Mayeux, Peter E. *Broadcast News: Writing and Reporting.* Madison, WI: Brown and Benchmark, 1991.

Musberger, Robert B. *Electronic News Gathering: A Guide to ENG.* Stoneham, MA: Focal, 1991.

Shook, Fred, and Dan Lattimore. *The Broadcast News Process,* 4th ed. Englewood, CO: Morton, 1992.

Stephens, Mitchell. *Broadcast News,* 3rd ed. Ft. Worth, TX: Harcourt Brace Jovanovich, 1993.

Weaver, J. Clark. *Broadcast Newswriting as Process.* White Plains, NY: Longman, 1984.

Yoakam, Richard D., and Charles F. Cremer. *ENG: Television News and the New Technology,* 2nd ed. New York: McGraw-Hill, 1989.

Yorke, Ivor. *The Technique of Television News,* 2nd ed. Stoneham, MA: Focal, 1987.

———. *Basic TV Reporting.* Stoneham, MA: Focal, 1990.

Other useful texts, but ones that focus on the more general process of gathering the news, include

Gibson, Roy. *Radio and Television Reporting.* Boston: Allyn & Bacon, 1990.

Goald, Robert S. *Behind the Scenes at the Local News.* Washington: RTNDA, 1992.

Goedkoop, Richard J. *Inside Local Television News.* Salem, WI: Sheffield, 1988.

Kessler, Lauren, and Duncan McDonald. *Uncovering the News: A Journalist's Search for Information.* Belmont, CA: Wadsworth, 1987.

Lewis, Carolyn Diana. *Reporting for Television.* New York: Columbia University Press, 1984.

In the chapter we mentioned Dan Rather's personal reminiscence:

Rather, Dan, and Mickey Herskowitz. *The Camera Never Blinks: Adventures of a TV Journalist.* New York: Ballantine, 1987.

Many other well-known air personalities have also authored accounts of their careers and of their perceptions of broadcast journalism. Here are just a few of those titles.

Chancellor, John, and Walter Mears. *The News Business.* New York: Harper & Row, 1983.

Donaldson, Sam. *Hold On, Mr. President.* New York: Fawcett, 1988.

Ellerbee, Linda. *And So It Goes: Adventures in Television.* New York: Berkley, 1987.

———. *Move Over: Adventures in the Real World.* New York: Putnam, 1991.

Schorr, Daniel. *Clearing the Air.* Boston: Houghton Mifflin, 1977.

Finally this title, which although written more than forty years ago is not considered old. It is, rather, a classic in the field.

White, Paul W. *News on the Air.* New York: Harcourt, Brace, 1947.

# CHAPTER 13

# Talk, Interview and Discussion Programs

**T**alk programs take a variety of forms and make up large parts of the schedules of many radio and television stations. The best known on television are the network morning shows, the daytime syndicated series like *Geraldo, Donahue*, and *Oprah*, and the late-night series—*Arsenio Hall, Late Night with David Letterman*, and *The Tonight Show*, among others. Many others may also be found on cable channels and local TV stations. On radio both locally produced and syndicated programs abound; *Rush Limbaugh* may be the best known. Often programs are developed around a single category of discussion—political and social issues, personal finances, home repair, medical questions or sports. Other programs are open-ended; call in and talk about anything you want to.

When you finish this chapter, you will be able to

- research and prepare interview and discussion programs for broadcast, including
    determining purpose
    analyzing target audiences
    choosing topics and guests
    preparing interview questions
    structuring the program, and

- recognize and use these important terms and concepts:

| | |
|---|---|
| audience participation | magazine talk programs |
| audience surrogate | program scope |
| call screener | qualifying guests |
| closed-end questions | selecting topics and guests |
| conversation | semi-script |
| double and compound questions | talking heads |
| live-to-tape production | |

Talk programs and the talk segments that make up portions of other programs are not easily categorized. There are many forms. But we can divide them on the basis of the number of persons participating in the talk, as that has some bearing on the structural strength of the presentation. Using that approach, there are three categories—the straight talk, or monologue; two-person talks, including interviews and conversations; and discussions, which involve more than two people.

One-person talks include lectures, political speeches, sermons and monologues. In general, because there is little variety possible, or change of pace, these are weak materials. Television producers refer to one-person talks, usually derogatorily, as "talking heads." The managers of political campaigns, for example, are aware of this weakness and seldom purchase time for speeches by candidates to further their campaigns. Instead they have developed a variety of alternatives, some of which we consider later in the chapter. Even the comedy monologues popular on late-night talk shows last only 3 to 4 minutes so as not to bore the audience.

Two-person talks are usually in the form of interviews, although we'll discuss the "conversation" as a variation. Structurally they are better than single talking heads, but audience attention is still difficult to maintain for long periods.

Discussion programs, forums and other talks involving more than two people provide more variety, but still have little structural strength. Maintaining audience attention is a real challenge for writers and producers of talk material, and for that reason talk, interview and discussion segments often are combined into more complex programs. In this chapter we spend most of our time on methods of strengthening the structure of interviews and discussion programs.

In Chapter 1 we divided the preparation of any kind of program into four steps: research, writing, production and postproduction. For talk programs those tasks may be amplified as:

1. *Research.* What topic or topics will be discussed on the program or series? Will guests be used? If so, what guests will be selected? Gather background material on the topic and the guests.

2. *Writing.* Organize the background material into questions or other notes to be used by interviewers or moderators; sequence the material into a logical progression that can be followed by listeners.

3. *Production and postproduction.* The entire production process is approached quite differently depending on whether the program will be presented live or prerecorded. Some talk programs are aired live. Many more are "live-to-tape"; the production is handled as if it were a live show, with no or very little editing and postproduction. In these situations the program is recorded only for the convenience of delaying it to a later airtime or of marketing the program via syndication. Other pro-

grams are prerecorded in segments, which allows the different segments to be separately produced and edited in postproduction. This approach allows for greater variety and can result in a structurally stronger program—but at added cost and with longer delays.

# RESEARCH

The research step can be further divided into determining the purpose of the program, analyzing the target audience, selecting the topic and guests and gathering material on both.

## Determining Purpose

By now you should be familiar with the reasons why sponsors choose to produce and broadcast programs of any type. And you should also be aware that the discussion of purpose includes an examination of point of view, a concept we have examined in several chapters. Point of view is what gives each different series its own character and it involves considerations both of structure and format and of gratifications.

If the program includes interviews, for example, what kind of interviews? An interview with movie star Elizabeth Taylor, for instance, could focus on her career and personal life, or on her role as a spokesperson for AIDS research and education. There are as many variations as there are programs. Consider what topics and questions would be the most appropriate to ask her if, for example, she were being interviewed on *The Today Show*, *Donahue*, *Meet the Press* or *Late Night*. A clear understanding of the purpose and point of view that your program intends to take is an important early step.

During this early stage of preparation you should also consider the weight to be given to all three of the Aristotelian purposes for communicating—persuasion, information and entertainment—for all are used in talk programs in varying degrees and combinations.

Persuasion is most evident in religious programs. A preacher's sermon is most definitely a persuasive talk.

We've already noted that political campaign managers some years ago all but abandoned broadcast talks by candidates because of the structural weakness of that form of presentation. Instead, they have used short announcements, identical in structure and approach to ads for consumer products. In the 1992 presidential campaigns we saw a return to some forms of talk programming, but using several new approaches, particularly appearances by candidates on regularly scheduled talk programs and the use of infomercials. Other forms of political talk include press conferences, call-in programs with some form of audience participation, and debates.

Persuasion may also be the reason behind the appearance on an interview program of the local chapter president of the Red Cross, who wants to encourage participation in Red Cross activities and stimulate donations to the organization, or of a school superintendent, who might use a weekly talk show to convince parents that closing a local school really was necessary to save money, or for many similar situations. Frequently people who hold strong opinions on an issue will agree to appear in a discussion or interview program in the hope of persuading the audience to that point of view, even though the program itself does not have persuasion as its purpose.

Information and entertainment are often mixed in talk programs. It may help to think of these kinds of programs along a scale from the more serious (informative), such as *This Week with David Brinkley* and *Meet the Press*, to the more humorous (entertaining) *Late Night* and *Evening at the Improv*. Somewhere in the middle of the scale will be programs like *Donahue*, *Oprah* and *Geraldo* or similar programs that replace them. Their topics and guests provide a mix of information and entertainment and a good mix of gratifications—information, value, curiosity, human interest, personalism, and so on.

Further complicating this mixture of information and entertainment is the fact that talk segments appear in programs that contain other types of material as well. *Late Night*, *The Tonight Show*, *Arsenio Hall* and others like them are really variety programs. They mix monologues and interview segments with humorous and dramatic sketches, and with music—trying to maintain a balance among different content segments that will give the program a unique identity and strong gratifications that will keep an audience tuned in.

For example, it took the producers for the original Letterman program a while to find the appropriate niche for that show. A *Newsweek* feature article on the *Late Night* show describes the evolution of the program this way:

> What they have done . . . is energize the talk-show format by melting it down and recasting it in Letterman's own odd image. The first step was to take comedy and information, two commodities that coexist uneasily in many talk shows, and shift the balance firmly to comedy. That didn't happen quickly. At first *Late Night* tended to book serious guests . . . and Letterman often found himself constrained to be a serious host. "It just didn't work," he says. "I'm not really comfortable as an interviewer, because that's not what I am." Today . . . "the priority is on comedy," says producer Barry Sand. "If we have a serious guest, it's somebody Dave can be funny off. If it's a funny guest, it's somebody Dave can help to be funnier. . . . The idea of it is that if you've learned anything from the show when you go to sleep, we really made a terrible mistake."[1]

As this example shows, the form of the program, including topics and guests, will be determined by the audience that is being targeted. Letterman's change of network and change to an earlier time period, which will result in a different available audience and direct competition with *The Tonight Show*, will force some changes in the content and structure of his program.

## Analyzing the Target Audience

Analysis of the target audience for talk programs is not substantially different from analysis for any other type of program or announcement. The researcher should be able to answer these four questions regarding the audiences for the program being prepared:

1. What is the sponsor's target audience?

2. How can the target audience be attracted to the program?

3. What does the target audience already know about the topic and guest?

4. What does the audience want to learn from the expert(s) who are appearing on the program?

### What Is the Sponsor's Target Audience?

As part of the general discussion of target audiences (Chapter 10), we looked at the target audience for *Meet the Press*. A similar analysis can be made for any talk program. The Letterman staff describes its audience as "hip and ironic, at once silly and knowing," and young.

In general, the more serious topics appeal to more highly educated and probably older audiences. Lighter topics—celebrity and feature interviews, for example—are more successful in attracting younger and less educated groups.

### How Can the Target Audience Be Attracted to the Program?

The targeted audience will stay tuned only if they quickly perceive that their interests are being served. Thus it is important that the opening material in the program or segment quickly catch their interest and show its value. Consider three different types of interview questions: those that elicit opinions, provide unusual features, and highlight celebrities. These are not all the forms of interviews that exist, but they are the most common.

*Opinion Interviews.* The person appearing on an opinion interview is an expert in some area or has some unique perspective or position. The intent is to draw out information and opinions related to the interviewee's expertise and transmit that material to the audience. The strongest gratifications are information and importance as that importance relates both to the topic and the guest.

Alternatively, the opinion interview can take the form of "person in the street" interviews, in which a cross section of "ordinary people" are asked their opinions on some topic that may range from something humorous to a serious question of community or world affairs. Since these people are not experts with knowledge to impart, the strongest gratification is human interest, rather than information.

***Feature Interviews.***   In this form, the person being interviewed is not well known, but has done something or been somewhere unusual or interesting. Perhaps he has just returned from a world trouble spot, maybe she rents out the wild animals used in making jungle films. The feature must be organized so it gets quickly to the unusual characteristic which makes that person interesting, because the audience will not be particularly attracted until the novelty is introduced. That gratification, novelty, along with curiosity and human interest are the strongest; information is probably present as well.

***Celebrity Interviews.***   Most often celebrity interviews emphasize the personality of the guests who appear, because it is the audience's curiosity that provides the major gratification. Other gratifications would be personalism, human interest and big-name importance.

Some programs, however, emphasize the role of the host as much as or more than that of the guest. *Firing Line*, produced and hosted by William Buckley, is perhaps the best example. Buckley is a superb practitioner of an interview style in which the focus of attention is maintained much more strongly on the interviewer than on the interviewee. Usually interviews should focus on the opinions and information imparted by the guest, but with Buckley's approach the guests are secondary, and are chosen because they will provide a foil for the host, who has the more important role in the program and whose opinions are given the greater exposure.

Similarly, on his radio show, Rush Limbaugh takes phone calls from listeners, but he seldom gives the listeners much time, nor treats their ideas seriously. They are instead fodder for his comments. Listeners don't tune in to hear what the callers have to say but what Limbaugh says.

In summary, be careful how you design your program and what topics and guests you select. If the topics and guests are selected without careful planning, then the audience may not be the one you set out to attract.

### What Does the Target Audience Already Know about the Topic and Guest?

It may be difficult to get a precise answer to this question, but general knowledge of the target group will help, and whatever assumptions have to be made can be refined over the span of time during which the program series is broadcast, and by independent research if necessary. On *Meet the Press*, for example, the questions asked of the guests reflect the assumption that the audience has a good general knowledge of national and international political and economic issues. Knowledge of basic geography, the fundamental differences among various political ideologies, and the forms of government currently operating in major countries are assumed, and questions which cover those points are not asked.

By way of contrast, assume that a typical *Meet the Press* guest, the administrative head of the European Economic Community, were to be the guest on a similarly structured interview program, but one for which the target audience is high school students. The questions would have to be quite different, starting at a more fundamental level and covering such items as geography and the forms of government in the EEC countries.

Also part of this question is the audience's knowledge of the guest(s) and their understanding of how the guest's expertise and background relate to the topic. An interview with the president of the United States will require little if any explanation. Neither would an interview with the chairman of the Joint Chiefs of Staff—so long as the topic of the interview was military matters, on which he is an immediately recognized expert. But if the chairman of the Joint Chiefs of Staff were to be interviewed on, say, the growing of orchids, the program would have to provide some explanation to the audience as to why this person was being interviewed as an expert on that topic, because the relationship is not likely to be one of which people are aware.

A similar approach will be necessary for all topics and guests. The program writer should determine in advance how likely it is that the guest is known and recognized by the audience, and how much prior knowledge of the topic the audience may be assumed to have.

### What Does the Audience Want to Learn from the Expert(s) Who Are Appearing on the Program?

This question comes back to fundamental considerations of purpose and gratifications, and the very first question audiences continue to ask—Why should I watch (or listen); what's in it for me? A great many programs, particularly local public affairs programs, fail to attract or hold any substantial audience simply because they fail to make any connection early in the broadcast between the topic and the audience.

We use the word *learn* in this question in a very broad sense. In most informative interviews we do assume that some learning—or at least the transmission of information to the audience—takes place. More formal instructional programs, such as an interview with the head of a company or with an academic expert, have as a purpose learning in a more strict sense. In persuasive political or religious talk programs, the learning would be acceptance of the point being made by the program.

Recall that *Meet the Press* contains two purposes. The sponsor's purpose will be to attract a target audience of some size and demographic composition in order to expose them to advertising messages. But the structure, form, and content of the show are a genuine attempt to convey opinions and information on topics about which the audience has concerns.

We can summarize by emphasizing that the writers and interviewers or moderators of talk programs are acting as *surrogate* for the audience. Their jobs are to prepare and to ask the questions that elicit the information which audience members would themselves ask if they were in a position to do so. And in order to be an effective surrogate, writers need a clear picture of who the audience members are, what their background and prior knowledge are, and what they might want to learn from the program. Hence our insistence on the careful analysis of audience.

## Choosing the Topic and Guests

This might seem to be the place to begin preparation of a talk program rather than being the third step in the research task, but what we have tried to suggest by the preceding discussion is that good choices of topic and guests, and a good sequence of interview questions or discussion topics, cannot be made until the preliminary questions of purpose and audience have been determined. (Of course, on many programs, especially those that are episodes of continuing series, the purpose and audience decisions for the series have long since been made, and the researcher-writer does begin at this point—choosing topics and guests for each individual broadcast.)

The questions here are very straightforward. *Why* this topic (at this time)? And *why* this guest or guests? The answers should be easy to state. If there is any difficulty in answering them, the topic or guest is probably not appropriate for this program at this time. If a lengthy introduction must be given to explain the topic to the audience, probably the wrong topic was chosen. If long biographies of the guests have to be delivered to show their relationship to the topic, probably the wrong guests were chosen.

Let's follow these research steps through with an example fairly typical of a local public affairs discussion program. (We carry this example throughout the chapter and build a program around this situation.)

The program you research/write/produce is a weekly series, a half-hour in length, broadcast late Sunday afternoon. The topics are chosen by the station's programming staff, and usually involve local issues. Frequently the topics arise from discussion with civic officials. This week the city council voted to place before the local voters at an upcoming election a bond issue to build a new centralized sewer system. The program director has decided that the sewer topic would be appropriate for your program.

*Your purpose?* The accepted purpose of this program series, and of all individual programs in the series, is strictly informative. No editorial positions are taken. Advocates for or against various issues do appear regularly, but the station carefully chooses its participants to obtain balance in every program.

*Your target audience?* Since the program has been on for a while (and, we will assume, has been reasonably successful in attracting a regular following), you should have no difficulty describing the audience you regularly reach. We will assume these people are a high education/income group and politically aware. They vote regularly, and they influence others. They are opinion leaders. If the city hopes to pass the sewer bond, these are the individuals who will have to be convinced to vote for the bond, and to persuade friends and associates to do so as well. But remember, this program is not intended to be politically persuasive.

*How can the target audience be attracted to the program*? What are the gratifications for them? Snce this is an ongoing series, the attractions and gratifications for your regular audience have been built up over a period of time. They will include importance, information, value, possibly human interest, maybe tension. (It is at this point that you should speak out if you feel this topic is inappropriate to the overall concept of the program. We'll assume the general topic—the sewer bond—is acceptable to you.) Your regular audience may be expected to at least tune in at the start, and so long as this program does not deviate too far from the regular pattern, you can expect to hold them through the broadcast because the gratifications they generally obtain will stay consistent in this program.

If you should want to try to attract additional audience, other than the regular target group, it will require additional promotional efforts—announcements on your station, a press release, word of mouth and so on. You would do that only if the topic was of such importance that you wanted to make the extra effort (or if the station had made a decision to provide extra promotion for this series).

*What does the target audience already know about the topic?* Well, since the city council just voted to place the bond issue on the ballot, we can assume the audience doesn't know much about the ramifications. But there must have been something in the past that caused the council to act. Maybe the old sewer system is inadequate in size and is restricting future development in the community, or perhaps it has broken down frequently, causing unpleasant smells and potential health hazards. Rarely does an issue of sufficient importance to become a topic of a program appear suddenly. There's usually some background, and this particular target audience may be assumed to have some background on most community issues.

*What do the audience members want to know*? As we have said repeatedly, they want to know how the topic will affect them. In this case, what the implications are for them of passing or defeating the bond issue. They will want to know what the project will cost in fees or taxes, what the benefits would be, what will happen to the community if the issue doesn't pass, and so on. We'll develop this point when we look at the sequencing of the specific subtopics within the program.

*What is the topic and who are the guests*? The general topic has already been chosen, but the specific subtopics to be covered and the proper people to cover them must now be determined. One choice would be to assemble a group of engineers who could speak knowledgeably about capacity, flow rates, direction and size of connectors, and so on. But it should be obvious from the decisions already made that that approach is neither consistent with our purpose nor appropriate to the target audience. (Amazingly, however, a good many producers of local public affairs programs fall into precisely this trap when they do not adequately analyze purpose and audience.)

We may want the city engineer as one guest on the program, but not to discuss technical matters. She or he can discuss how badly the city streets will be disrupted, and for how long—issues of vital importance to the target audience. And the engineer can talk in general terms about the size and complexity of the proposed new sewer plant—again not from a technical standpoint, but only to satisfy a general curiosity in the audience.

Another possible guest panelist would be a member of the city council, who could give background to the issue and explain why the council voted as it did. If the council vote was split and there was considerable dissension, then both positions on the council's action probably should be covered by inviting an advocate on the opposing side as well. And even if the council was unanimous in its position, there may be other opposition in the community that should be heard if you want to maintain balance on a controversial issue. You are not forced to air opposing positions on the same program, but doing so provides tension, which is a gratification for some audiences, and you should at least recognize the ethical question of providing balance on a controversial issue.

(For many years you would have had to consider the FCC's Fairness Doctrine rules as well. At this writing, those rules have been eliminated, and there seems little likelihood they will be reinstated, but some form of regulatory "fair play" may be enacted at any time, especially if broadcasters begin to air programs taking strong positions on only one side of controversial topics.)

A local businessperson, speaking on behalf of the Chamber of Commerce, could be another panelist. He or she could speak to the implications of the sewer for future community growth. Any number of possible panelists might be chosen, but each choice should be tested for his or her value to the program, using the question: What information does this person have that the audience would want to know?

We'll choose these four for the program:

Mary Smith, city councilwoman. She voted for the bond issue, but with some reluctance. She is known to be very fair, quite articulate, and capable of seeing both sides of an issue.

Paul Jones, vice president of the Chamber of Commerce. Strongly in favor personally, and represents the Chamber, which has pushed for a new sewer.

Fred White, longtime resident and major landowner in the city. Well respected, conservative, opposed to the bond issue.

Joe Brown, city engineer. Knowledgeable on technical matters, and on why the project will cost what the bond issue is being asked to cover. A possible problem may exist here: He might feel intimidated by the more political types on the panel, but people who know him are certain that won't be the case. However, that's the kind of caution producer-writers must take into account in putting a panel together.

The choice of four panelists is arbitrary, but that seems a sufficient number to get the major points of view. Having any more people would cut down the amount of time each would have to articulate his or her concerns, and increase the risk that someone might be squeezed out of the discussion.

We've used a panel discussion program for this example, but the process applies to any talk-type program—just substitute the word *interviewee* or *speaker* for *panelist* and recognize that there would be fewer people involved as participants in an interview or a straight talk program.

# PRODUCTION

We'll continue the example above; but now we are ready to consider the next stage in the preparation process. Normally, that would be the writing, but we need to jump ahead, to determine at this point whether our program or segment will be prerecorded, with some opportunity for postproduction editing, or presented live. The writing and sequencing of interview and discussion questions will be approached differently depending on whether the program is live or whether it is prerecorded and its content can be rearranged and compressed before it is aired. Reread the section on "Factors Affecting Scripting," in Chapter 4, to refresh your memory on this matter.

Live, unedited programs require that particularly careful attention be paid to the sequence of questions or topics discussed, to make sure that the audience (and, for that matter, the participants) can follow the flow of the content. The producers of some interview programs take pride in announcing that the program is "spontaneous and unrehearsed." By so doing they are assuming that the live approach increases the excitement, the immediacy, and the credibility of the program. It's also cheaper and faster to produce a live show. On the other hand, editing of one form or another is frequently done either to conserve broadcast time or to improve the structure of the program.

For the researcher-writer, the significant difference between edited and live programs is the development of the *sequence* of material in the program, and the phrasing of the questions to be asked. If the raw material of an interview is to be lifted out, edited, and placed back into a news or documentary program, the sequence in which the original questions are asked is not critical, or if questions are not clearly stated or understood by an interviewee upon first being asked, they can be rephrased and asked again. These options are not possible in the live broadcast. The sequence and wording of the questions must be clear to both the interviewee and the audience the first time.

That is not to say that sequence and wording are not important when the program is to be edited. The less time spent conducting any interview— live or edited—and the less time spent in searching for the right questions and answers in the editing room, the less costly the project will be and the earlier the program can get on the air. An experienced writer-interviewer will conduct an interview as if it were live whenever possible, just to cut down on the amount of editing needed later. A few extra minutes spent in research and preparation may save several extra hours in editing.

## SCRIPTING TALK PROGRAMS

Very seldom will a completely scripted interview or panel program be presented, and then only if the material is so complex and the explanations so important that even a slight miswording would have serious consequences. One possible example might be an interview with a government official who may be quoted, and who might insist on a complete script for absolute accuracy in phrasing. Sermons, political talks, lectures, and other "straight" talks are usually scripted, but because these programs are structurally very weak, the writer must pay particular attention to aural style to maintain audience interest.

In general, however, the disadvantages of completely scripting far outweigh any possible advantages. Many nonprofessionals cannot read well from a script. The result will sound forced, artificial, and lacking in spontaneity. On television, the use of a script is almost always a disadvantage (except possibly when written out on a prompting device), because it is difficult to hide a script from the audience, and the lack of contact with the audience will be resented.

At the other extreme from the completely scripted talk program are interview and discussion programs done completely ad lib, without any form of script. Conducting successful ad lib interviews or panels requires a very experienced interviewer or moderator with considerable poise and the ability to organize material on the spot. Most hosts are not able to do this for an entire program, and expect to have at least an outline to follow.

The middle ground, then, between the completely scripted and the completely ad lib program is the *semi-scripted*, or *outlined*, interview or discussion. This approach provides written questions for the interviewer or moderator, but leaves the answers or comments to be given ad lib by the interviewee or panelists. This approach controls the organization and progress of the program while still preserving a degree of spontaneity. The semi-script is the most common written preparation. It will include:

1. A completely scripted opening.

2. A sequence of questions to be asked of the guest or guests. If the program is live, there will be both major questions and some less important throwaway or *pad* questions. These pad questions will be used if the guests' answers are short and they are needed to make the program come out on time, but if the guests' responses to the questions are more lengthy,

and the program is in danger of running over its allotted time, these pad questions can be discarded without destroying the continuity of the topic.

3. A completely scripted close. For a live program, this close will have some final adjustments for timing that can be made in order to end precisely on time. Review the section in Chapter 6 on how this can be accomplished.

## The Program Opening

As for all types of programs, the critical functions are attracting attention and identifying the program and its participants. Another necessary function of a talk program is to establish the scope of the program.

### *Attracting Attention*

This task can be difficult. The strongest material generally available is a statement which provides information to the audience members on the importance of the topic to them and gives the unique qualifications of the guests to speak on that topic. Think again of what gratifications you are trying to provide. You can also use the criteria for selecting news stories (Chapter 12) as a checklist.

For television, if the budget permits, some unusual video material shot on location will be stronger than just graphics (the printed titles) and the faces of participants. Sometimes programs begin with a cold opening—some startling statement or area of controversy or pictorial material with strong movement or action at the very beginning to catch attention.

### *Identification*

The program should be identified—both the series title (if it is part of a series) and the specific topic of the broadcast. The host-moderator should be identified and, of course, the guests. Not only are the guests identified, but they are also *qualified*—that is, there is some statement of the reason why they have been chosen to be there. We mentioned this consideration earlier, at the point where guests are chosen. It comes up again here, because qualifications must be included in the script itself. The extent to which the guests will have to be qualified will depend upon several things, including the topic, the audience's familiarity with the topic, and how closely the guests may be connected with the topic in the minds of the audience.

As noted in that earlier discussion, the president of the United States, to take an extreme example, would not need to be qualified on any topic. The only introductory statement necessary would be: "Our guest is ———, president of the United States."

In contrast, not many people would recognize the U.S. ambassador to

Poland. A program on current unrest in Poland would require something like this:

```
"Our guest today is ——, current ambassador to Poland.
Mr. —— was appointed to the post two years ago, after
having served twenty years in the diplomatic corps. He has
served in Poland twice previously and is fluent in the
Polish language."
```

That brief statement gives the audience enough information to realize that he really is an expert on the topic, without going into unnecessary detail. Additional information on his current job as ambassador or his previous tours of duty in Poland and his job at those times can be brought out during the program, if important.

### Setting the Scope of the Program

In previous sections we've emphasized how important it is for the researcher-writer to understand the purpose of the program. It's also important that the audience know early in the program what is going to take place. (In an on-going series with a loyal, continuing audience this can be accomplished very quickly; in a one-time or less familiar program series, it may take longer.)

We can make the point by using again the example of the president of the United States. Talking to him about almost any topic would be of interest to some audience, but an interview on his personal life as president—what it's like to have that job, what the responsibilities are, what he misses from the time before he became president—is much different in scope from an interview on foreign policy decisions, or on economic matters, or on his decision to run (or not run) for a second term. The audience has a right to know what topic is to be covered, and the approach to that topic, and it has a right to expect that the questioning will stay within that framework.

The opening for a talk program should be completely scripted, even if the body of the program will be in semi-script form. Here is an opening for the sewer bond public affairs program we began to develop earlier in the chapter:

| VIDEO | AUDIO |
|---|---|
| SIGNATURE | MUSIC: SIGNATURE |
| GRAPHIC: TITLE | V/O: This is "City Scene," a weekly examination of the problems and issues faced by the citizens and the government of Fair River. Here is your host: Janet Williams. |

MS: HOST

KEY: Janet Williams

Good afternoon, and thank you for joining me on "City Scene." Each week we try to bring to your attention a topic which will affect all of us who live here in Fair River, and this week's topic will certainly do that for many months, even years, to come.

Earlier this week our city council voted to place on November's election ballot a bond issue in the amount of five million dollars for the replacement and improvement of the city sewer system. If that bond issue is passed by the voters, practically every street in the city will be torn up at some time in the next five years, and every property taxpayer will see an increase in taxes to pay for the new system. In return, we will have a sewer which will permit, perhaps even encourage, new residential and industrial growth, and which should not break down--as did the present sewer line on Power Station Road last month.

But the immediate controversy surrounds the bond issue. Already people are choosing sides-- supporting or arguing against passage of that ballot measure. Our guests today will discuss both the implications of the bond issue and of the system which would be installed should the revenue measure be approved by the voters. They are:

MS: GUEST #1

KEY: Mary Smith

Mary Smith, member of the city council. Mary was elected to the council last year from the South

MORE MORE MORE

district. Her campaign argued for fiscal restraint and a go-slow attitude on new city growth. Tuesday night she voted for the sewer bond issue, but only after considerable hesitation. We'll ask her to explain the nature of her hesitation, and her decision.

MS: GUEST #2
KEY: Fred White

Fred White. Mr. White's family have been residents of Fair River since before the turn of the century. He was born here and has lived in his present home on East Third Street since the 1940s. Fred owns property in the business district and throughout the community. He is opposed to the council's action and the bond issue.

MS: GUEST #3
KEY: Paul Jones

Paul Jones. Paul is the owner of Jones Hardware on Main Street. He is also vice president of the Chamber of Commerce. The Chamber took a position in favor of a new sewer system more than a year ago, arguing that civic growth was being stifled by the present inadequate system. Paul chaired the Chamber's committee on the sewer problem, and will head another Chamber committee to support the bond issue.

MS: GUEST #4
KEY: Joe Brown

Joe Brown. City Engineer. It has been Joe's responsibility to determine the overall scope and size of a new system, to estimate its cost, and therefore the size of the bond issue required to finance it. Joe has been the city engineer for just about five years, having come to Fair River from Albany.

This opening is simple and inexpensive. It's typical of many locally produced public affairs programs, but it's not strong structurally. There's very little attention-getting material. If time and money permitted, other devices could be used, such as these:

- Open with the videotape of a news story tied to the topic—tape of the sewer break last month, and the cleanup work done by city crews with a voice-over narration tying that to the topic.

- Show tape of the city council meeting, a condensed montage of the arguments and the vote of the council members.

- Begin the program with the discussion already in progress; after a couple of minutes the moderator interrupts to introduce the program title and the participants, and tie down the topic, which by that time should be evident. This approach is tricky; it requires a lot of skill on the part of the moderator, and even with the best planning the "cold" opening may not contain high-interest material.

- If you can prerecord and have at least a little time to edit, take one strong statement from each guest out of the body of the program which typifies that person's position and repeat those statements back to back in a short cold open.

If any of these openings or similar attention-getting devices are used, they should be used regularly and made part of the format for the continuing series. If the program is not part of a series, then use whatever opening device seems most appropriate to the topic, and that time and money will permit.

## Structural Requirements

Talk programs, at least in their simpler, purer forms, have difficulty meeting the requirements of strong structure, and for this reason alone they also have difficulty attracting large audiences. As we noted at the beginning of this chapter, network and syndicated talk programs, having recognized this problem, are seldom seen as pure talks or interviews or panels. Go back to the structural analysis of *This Week with David Brinkley* (Chapter 6). There are six different major segments within the hour-long program, and some of those are further divided by topic.

Other programs worthy of detailed structural analysis are the three network morning programs: *Today*, *Good Morning America* and *This Morning*. These programs, and others like them that consist of independent segments of talk (and sometimes other material), are known as magazine programs. The reason for the label is obvious; like a magazine, they cover a range of topics which the producers believe will be interesting to the targeted audience groups. The segmented structure is partly to maintain audience attention by providing frequent change and thus variety and partly to allow audience members to flow in and out of the programs easily. Magazine programs are often scheduled during day-parts when there is considerable audience turnover. For these morning programs it is particularly important that persons be able to enter and leave the audience easily and frequently, as these persons are busy getting ready to go to work or getting children ready for school. This structure permits listeners to catch segments of the program and then turn to other tasks. Late-night talk programs are similarly segmented; the audience decreases after each different guest or act as viewers turn off the set and go to bed.

We use the word "listeners" advisedly when talking about these programs, for these audiences are as likely to just listen as to view the content as they go about other tasks. Most of the segments, therefore, do not rely on strong visual content to capture audience attention. For the most part the flow of the conversation (or music) can be followed without watching.

### Unity

We just discussed this concept, but under a different name—setting the scope of the topic of the program. If the program's researcher-writer has carefully considered the topic and the audience's interest in it, then unity should follow. But if the topic has not been clearly defined, and the guests have not been carefully chosen on the basis of what they can contribute to the topic, the likelihood of having a wandering, disjointed interview or discussion is increased. If an interview with the president, for example, contains random questions on foreign policy, economics, politics, and family matters, it lacks unity. The problem could have been avoided easily simply by defining the topic and the target audience's interests before beginning to prepare questions.

This is the least difficult structural principle to manage in talk programs. Even *This Week with David Brinkley*, which may discuss several topics, can cluster them under the single heading, "implications of important public issues that came up this week."

### Variety

The requirement of variety is difficult to satisfy in any type of talk program. In a straight talk, with just one person's talking head on the screen, it's nearly impossible. An interview is a bit better; there are two people to be seen and heard. *This Week with David Brinkley*, as we have seen, uses not only multiple interviewers but also different segments with different guests and some segments with no guests, just the regular panel in a discussion format. *Nightline* also uses several different presentational techniques to improve variety.

### Pace

The programs we have just mentioned use their frequent changes in the methods of presenting material to provide a sense of pace as well as variety. With an unstructured and unedited live talk show, it's very difficult to control pace. Whatever control exists depends on the talents of the interviewer or moderator, who must know when and how to break into long, monotonous speeches in order to keep the program moving. Programs of the *Donahue* style also use audience participation (studio audiences and/or telephone call in) to provide pace and variety.

### Climax

This requirement also is difficult in a live, uncontrolled program. It is best managed by the structure and sequence of the questions and subtopics asked by the interviewer or moderator. To attract audience attention at the beginning of the program, some high-interest questions should be asked early. But additional important or provocative material should be held to-

**What I like about 'Nightline' is that after a program they do a panel discussion to see if they did it right.**

**Figure 13.1.** Reprinted by permission of Richard Guindon.

ward the end of the program so that the audience will leave with a feeling of climax.

Magazine programs can save the more important guests, or the more provocative topics, to the end of the program and provide teases to hold the audience. (As noted above, the networks' morning magazine programs work differently; audiences get smaller during the course of the program as more people leave their homes for work or other reasons. The stronger segments are presented early in the show. Late-night programs do the same; the more important guests are on early, when the audiences are largest.)

## Preparing Questions

If all of the preceding sections about choosing the topic and relating it to the audience have been carefully considered, then the preparation of the actual questions to be used for the interview or discussion will be easier. Each question should meet these simple tests:

Does the question fit the topic and scope of the program?

Does it provide material the audience wants to know?

Does it follow logically from the preceding question (or has adequate transition been provided so that both audience and guest(s) realize a change in subtopic has taken place)?

Is it appropriate for the expertise of the interviewee (guest)?

### *Sequencing Questions*

The important considerations in sequencing or ordering questions are these:

1. Begin with the known; that is, begin with questions that are the direct, logical result of matters which are (or what you can assume should be) known by the target audience.

2. Continue with questions in logical progression. Each new question should *seem* at least to flow out of the preceding response. In order to do this well, you will need to research the topic and the guest's likely responses carefully in advance, and possibly ask the guest some key questions before the actual interview or discussion begins in order to know where he or she stands on specific points.

3. When you must change a topic—the previous one has been covered to the extent you feel it warrants—then use adequate warning in the way of transition words and phrases so that both guest and audience are aware of the change which is coming.

4. Use strong, important questions early—to attract and hold attention—and at the end—for climax and to leave the audience members with something to remember after the program is over.

### *Phrasing Questions*

Although it is usually possible to find exceptions to almost any rule, here are some guidelines to use in the phrasing of individual questions.

1. Keep questions short, simple, and conversational. The focus of attention should be the guest, not the host. Long, involved questions place that attention in the wrong place, and make it more difficult for both guest and audience to follow the sequence.

**Poor:** What is your response to the allegations made by some practicing defense lawyers that the administration's position on this case is a disregard of personal rights?

The qualifying phrases are intended to restrict the question to a narrow response, but instead they only confuse.

**Better:** How will the outcome of this case affect personal rights?

A frequent phrase used as a crutch by beginners is the line "Can you tell us . . ." as in this question asked of an automobile executive:

**Poor:** Can you tell us about some of the new innovations you see in future Chrysler automobiles?

Ask the question directly:

**Better:** What are some of the innovations planned for future Chrysler automobiles?

2. Avoid double questions. They are confusing to both guest and audience. If the point to be made is sufficiently important, ask both questions but separately.

**Poor:** What was the cause of death of both victims, and when did the murders take place?

**Better:** (Ask the questions separately.)

**Poor:** (Question to an unsuccessful candidate for a local government appointment): Do you feel the candidates were being evaluated on their

qualifications, or that there was an ethnic factor
involved?

**Better:**  Do you think race was involved in the decision?

3. A variation on this weakness is the compound question. This form is frequently heard at press conferences. There is a reason for using it in that setting; the questioner may not get the opportunity to ask another as the rotation moves around the room. But in a broadcast sequence it's not a good technique because it's difficult for both the audience and respondent to remember all the parts to the question.

**Poor:**  What are your opinions on the proposed legislation, and if
you are in favor of it, why, and if not, what should be
done?

**Better:**  Are you in favor of the proposed legislation?
(Then, depending on the response, use either of the following:)
What are the benefits?
How should the proposal be changed?

4. As a general rule, avoid asking closed-end questions—that is, questions that can be answered with just a yes or no. Experienced interviewees, such as political figures, won't respond with yes-no answers, but less experienced persons who might be nervous at being interviewed (or who don't really want to be interviewed) may answer simply yes or no if the question permits them to do so. A good habit to develop is to ask questions using *why*, *what*, or *how* as the operative words, rather than *do*, *will*, or *are*.

An exception to this rule would occur when you want to determine the interviewee's position on a topic, as the basis for the further line of questioning, or to hone in on a specific detail. (That's the case in item 3; the questioning proceeds after we find out quickly whether the guest is in favor of the legislation or not.) Another exception might be for timing; use a brief closed-end question to wrap up and get the interview out on time.

5. Don't ask questions that assume an answer. If you have done your research well, you are likely to have an idea of what the guest's response will be, but don't assume that answer in your question. Let the guest present his or her own position.

**Poor:**  Is it true you made thirty-five dollars an hour at your
last job, and now you're looking for comparable work?

**Better:**  What wage did you make at your last job?
What kind of job and wage are you looking for now?

6. Similarly, don't word questions that lead a guest and force her or him to agree. Loaded questions can be embarrassing, and they do nothing to move the interview forward.

**Poor:** Isn't it true that this team has the highest average salaries in the league?
And yet isn't the team batting average this season the lowest?

If you know that the team has the highest salaries and the poorest average, then simply state that and move on to the more important point:

**Better:** What are you going to do to get better run production from these highly paid players?

If you aren't sure of the facts, then a series of questions may be needed:

**Better:** What is the team's salary average?
How does this compare with the league average?
And how does the team batting average compare with the rest of the league?
What will you do in the off-season to bring these two statistics more into line?

7. Don't take an accusatory approach in your questions. There are situations in recorded, edited documentary programs like *Sixty Minutes*, where an accomplished interviewer like Mike Wallace can ask some pretty strong questions. In these cases, if he gets a refusal to answer, the program will be restructured and new material added to fill up the time, something you cannot do in a live show if the guest refuses to continue the conversation.

In all cases, the interviewee has the option of not answering the question if he or she feels it is unfair or misleading, so if you really want information, and if you really want your audience to learn something from the answers provided by the guest, you must be sufficiently neutral so that the interviewee doesn't refuse to respond.

You may think that forcing the interviewee into a statement of "No comment" shows your toughness as an investigative reporter, and that you finally found something the interviewee is trying to hide. In fact, you have just terminated the audience's opportunity to gain any information from the interview.

8. Phrase your questions as questions, not statements.

**Poor:** (Asked of a political candidate): Critics would charge that by spend-

ing this much in the campaign, if you win, you'll have a
lot of debts to pay.

**Better:**  (Make statement above but follow with): How do you answer that
criticism?
(Or): By borrowing that much money to finance your campaign, what political debts will you then have to pay?

9. Finally, and we noted this at the beginning of this section, ask questions that are within the scope of the knowledge or expertise of the guest;
don't ask him or her to speculate on matters outside that area. For example,
this question was asked of Harold Washington during his campaign for mayor
of Chicago:

**Poor:**  Why did Jane Byrne cancel her write-in campaign?

He won't know, and it's unfair to ask why another candidate canceled. If you
want an answer to that question, you'll have to ask Jane Byrne. But it would
be appropriate to ask this:

**Better:**  What effect will the cancellation of Jane Byrne's campaign
have on your candidacy?

In the continuing preparation of our sewer bond program we're now
ready to construct some questions for the body of the program. We'll begin
with one question directed toward each guest, then work the remainder of
the program from a list.

1. (For Mary Smith): Despite the rather serious sewer break last month, it
   seems that this issue hit the city council without much warning, and that
   the council made a hasty decision to go for a bond issue. How much prior
   consideration of the issue did you have? (This isn't a major question, but
   it's a good warm-up and establishes the process by which the council
   acted.)

2. (For Joe Brown): What process led to this particular choice of system,
   in terms of size and cost? (Follow up, if he doesn't cover it.) What are
   the major features of the proposed new system?

3. (For Paul Jones): You personally, and the Chamber of Commerce, have
   been vocal in support of a new sewer system. Why do you feel we can't
   just maintain or make minimum improvements on the present system
   and save millions of taxpayer dollars?

4. (For Fred White): It seems, from these statements, that we really do need
   a new sewer system. Why are you opposed? (We'll assume, for the remainder of the sequence of questions in the program, that this opposition

is not to a new sewer system as such, but only to the bond issue as a means of financing it. His position is that property owners will have to pay all the costs, and that a better way would be to charge actual sewer users, including tenants.)

Additional questions (not necessarily to be asked in this sequence):

5. What other methods of financing the project were considered by the council?
   Why were these other methods rejected?
   What is it that makes the council think this is the best system?

6. Why is it necessary to have a project this large? Couldn't a less expensive approach be taken that is smaller in scope? Why not?

7. The council's action only placed the issue on the ballot. The people of Fair River will make the final decision on whether or not to go ahead. What seems to be the present public attitude?
   What plans are underway to convince people to vote for the issue?
   Is there any organized opposition? If so, what form will the opposition take?
   What arguments will they make?

8. If the bond issue passes, what happens then?
   When will construction begin?
   How long will it last?
   How will the construction affect the citizens of Fair River?

9. What will be the financial impact on the average citizen if the bond issue passes?
   Will it have a greater impact on certain groups or individuals? Which ones?
   Why? Is that fair?

10. What happens if the citizens reject the bond issue?

The moderator will hope that after the opening round of questions addressed to each individual there will be a continuing interchange of opinions and conversation among all the parties. But if that interchange does not develop, the follow-up questions can be directed as well:

| #5 | Primarily for Councilwoman Smith, but possibly for Mr. Jones |
|---|---|
| #6 | For Mr. Brown and Mr. Jones |
| #7 | For Mr. Jones on the favorable side; Mr. White for the opposition |

#8          For Mr. Brown

#9, #10     For anyone

## The Program Closing

The closing of interview and discussion programs will include most of the following:

### Timing Adjustments

If the program were to be prerecorded and then edited, the final timing would be done as part of the editing. For a live show, some adjustments for timing will have to be built into the closing—material that can be left out or included as necessary. Most of the remaining functions can also be manipulated to assist the program's timing.

### Sense of Closure

You've probably encountered programs in which the host says: "Well, I see we've run out of time. Goodbye." The audience is left without a sense of closure, which is an uncomfortable feeling. The program should have a solid closing, including thank-yous to the guest(s) and possibly a summary of the topic discussed and the major points made.

### Identification

Some audience members will have tuned in during the show. They need identification of the program title, and of the guest(s), which they did not get from the opening. The closing for *City Scene*, shown below, does that in a very quick and easy but effective manner.

### Promotion

Subsequent broadcasts in the series may be promoted as part of the closing. Usually the topic and guests for the next broadcast can be announced:

```
Tune in next week when our guest will be Ethel Watkins.
She will discuss what effect the current oil glut will
have on the prices you pay for gasoline, home heating, and
electricity.
```

Some programs make a point of not naming guests in advance, but on being flexible to interview whoever is currently in the news. In those cases the promotional announcement has to be more general, but it is also weaker.

Here is the closing for the sewer bond program. Like the opening, it is very simple and very brief. The closing signature can be constructed to provide some time adjustment, and a bit more time can be manipulated in the closing statements themselves. As written it lasts 0:40, and the major timing adjustments will have to be made in the body of the program to leave between 0:30 and 0:45 for the close.

| | |
|---|---|
| MS: HOST | Thank you. For the next few months, at least until the November election, you're going to hear a great deal about the Fair River sewer project—its scope, its cost, its method of financing, alternatives. This program has provided a beginning for the continuing discussion of that issue. Our thanks to our panelists: |
| CAMERA PANS PANEL | Mary Smith, |
| | Joe Brown, |
| | Paul Jones, and |
| | Fred White |
| MS: HOST | for their contribution to the discussion. Next week on "City Scene," another topic of current interest and importance to <u>you</u>—the community of Fair River. I'm Janet Williams. Thank you for joining us. Good afternoon. |
| LOGO | <u>MUSIC: SIGNATURE—START AT 28:30, UP TO END</u> |

# PRESENTING INTERVIEW AND DISCUSSION PROGRAMS

The actual presentation of interview or discussion programs is not a writing task as such, and we won't take much space here to discuss this aspect of preparation. But it's not unusual for the roles of writer and host/interviewer or moderator to be combined, and it is helpful for the writer to understand the tasks the host must perform. Here are some guidelines for conducting interviews, and a few additional comments on panel discussions. Again, we are assuming live, nonrecorded, or at least unedited, programs.

## Conducting Interviews

1. Have the opening and closing of the program prepared in advance, including whatever materials are to be used for the timing adjustment.

2. Have a sequence of questions worked out in advance. As a general rule, follow that sequence, which should provide a logical approach to the topic. If the guest begins to freeze and to provide stiff, short, unresponsive answers, shift to material with which the guest is more comfortable, or about which he or she is more enthusiastic.

3. Allow some time before going on the air for warmup with the guest. It helps to put the guest at ease, and it gives you some indication of how responsive she or he is going to be to the questions asked. You may be able to avoid the kind of problems mentioned above.

4. Keep the focus of attention during the interview on the guest. The reason for talking with that person in the first place is because she or he has some content the audience wants to hear. Your role as the interviewer is to draw out that content. You are the voice of the audience members, acting on their behalf. See that the questions used are short, simple, and conversational.

    You may on occasion be stuck with an interviewee who is not very articulate, and who does not provide much material for you to work with. Some interviewers who face this situation frequently, such as sports interviewers, have developed a habit of asking lengthy questions that are really statements of opinion by the interviewer, followed by the question: "Isn't that true?" This approach places the focus of attention on the interviewer—the wrong place. A better approach is to have a longer list of questions ready than you would normally expect to use. If you have an inarticulate interviewee who provides very short answers, you will still have enough material to cover.

5. Listen to the answers given by the guest, and modify the wording of the following question so that it appears to come spontaneously from the preceding answer. If the sequence was well worked out in advance, this should not be difficult to do. Also, by listening to the answers, you can avoid the embarrassing situation of asking a question that has just been answered. If the answer to a question is given before you get a chance to ask it, then just skip over it. But in order to know that, you must listen to the response being given.

6. Don't repeat, or parrot, a response. The audience heard the answer the first time. This needless repetition indicates only one thing, that the interviewer wasn't ready to ask the next question and was caught without anything to say. If the proper preparation of a sequence of questions has been done in advance, this embarrassing situation won't happen.

Note that most often two-person talks are interviews, and that's why we have spent most of our time on this form. Occasionally, though, two people will engage in a "conversation," a subtle but important difference. Here the two individuals are equally knowledgeable (or nearly so) on the topic; they have mutual respect for each other's opinions. They just talk to each other, and we listen in. An orchestra conductor may talk with the composer of a work, and we listen to their prerecorded conversation during the intermission of the concert, just before the work is to be performed. Or a former secretary of state talks with the current occupant of that post. Siskel and Ebert review new films using this technique. Questions can be used, but they aren't necessary as long as both participants are knowledgeable on the topic and articulate.

## Moderating Discussion Programs

Moderating a panel discussion program differs from conducting an interview in several significant ways.

1. In the interview there are usually only two participants—interviewer and interviewee (although, as in *Meet the Press*, some programs assign the role of interviewer to several people asking questions in turn). The panel will have more than one guest. In the interview, the two-person structure results in a fairly direct question and answer pattern, whereas in the panel there may be several answers to the moderator's question, possibly answers to answers, and even possibly questions asked by persons other than the moderator. The pattern of discussion is therefore much more free-flowing in the panel than in the interview.

2. Having more than one respondent in the panel permits the introduction of varying points of view relating to the topic. (It would be a poorly structured panel program if all participants held the same position; there is nothing more boring than to hear one panelist state a position and then have three other panelists all say: "I agree.") Structurally, diversity of opinion provides variety; it also provides tension, which is a strong gratification for some audiences. Diversity of opinion in the interview can be accomplished only if two or more interviews are conducted separately and then intercut in the editing process.

3. Whereas an interviewer is an important participant in the conversation with the interviewee, asking questions as a surrogate for the audience, the moderator of a panel discussion program plays a much less prominent role. If the various participants are interacting as expected, then the panel moderator can be—and should be—almost invisible. His or her role is to keep the discussion on the topic; to bring it back if it begins to stray into unimportant details, repetition or personal bickering between panelists; to

avoid having the program monopolized by one or two panelists; and to bring it out on time.

An outline should be prepared for the moderator, something like the questions we prepared for the sewer bond program, but as long as the program stays basically on its topic, and as long as all the participants are involved, the moderator should not attempt to force a rigid sequence of questions or topics on the guests. An inexperienced moderator working with a rigid outline sometimes will try too hard to shape the discussion to that outline, and arbitrarily cut off a lively and interesting conversation in which the audience has become intently involved.

4. The panel discussion has the potential at least to be structurally stronger than a straight talk or an interview program. We've already mentioned that a well-chosen group of panelists will provide variety, not only in points of view but also visually and vocally. That variety contributes to pace, and to the possibility that the discussion will build to some sort of climax.

## Hosting Call-in Programs

We've already mentioned the talk programs that feature audience participation as a smaller or larger part of their structure. Television programs in the *Donahue* style use a studio audience that can ask the invited panelists questions and make comments. They also take telephone calls. Whole radio formats have developed around telephone call-in programs on various topics. This form of interactive media, in which the audience really gets to participate, has had a big impact on radio, and its importance is growing in television as well.

Often these programs are oriented to a specific subject matter, such as finance, medicine, car repair or sex, and the host or hostess is chosen for expertise in that area. Other times the programs are free of topic restrictions; callers are encouraged to discuss whatever is on their minds, or in a warm-up at the beginning of the program the host may pick a "topic of the day" from the current news or suggest some stories as possible starters.

When the program's format changes topics regularly—daily or even from hour to hour—then often the regular host will be supported by one or more guests who are expert in each topic. In radio, these guests can be present in the studio or participate by a telephone remote. (For television, a remote video connection can be arranged for guests, but the costs are high; only the networks can afford to use these hookups regularly.) When guests are used, the program will probably begin as an interview and then open out to include the phone-in questions from the listening audience. Another variation has been the "dating emporium," in which persons calling in describe themselves and try to link up with other callers for a date.

In preparation, the host will have collected background stories on the daily topic or current news to start the discussion and to fill slow spots. If a guest is used, his or her qualifications will have been researched. If the topic is open-ended and no guest is used, the host will prepare a series of questions and present those to the audience at the beginning of the program, to provoke call-in responses. But most of the actual time on the air is done ad lib. To be successful, the host should be practiced in listening and conversational technique and be able to think and respond quickly.

One position often filled by student interns or entry-level elmployees is the "call screener" for call-in shows. This person receives the incoming telephone calls, talks with the callers to make sure their comments are appropriate to the topic being discussed and that they're not just "kooks" who want to get on the air, and selects those calls that will be aired. The success of this type of program depends primarily on the host, but a large part of his or her ability to keep the show flowing smoothly and to avoid having to deal abruptly with divisive or contentious callers depends in turn on the screener's ability to choose good calls.

# CONCLUSION

Talk-type programs are efficient ways of attracting audiences and imparting information. That is not to say that they attract large audiences—they don't, but in relation to cost, which is almost always very low, they are efficient ways to fill large quantities of broadcast time. In one form or another you can expect these programs to remain in existence—and the beginning writer may expect to be asked to prepare them.

What particular forms of talk programs will be most prominent in years to come is a matter of speculation. Almost certainly, interviews and panels will continue to be popular. Quite likely the upsurge in audience participation conversations that has begun on radio will become an even more prevalent program type on both broadcast and cable TV. Technical, economic and regulatory changes in the media all will affect program types.

The approach to the preparation of these programs, however, should remain essentially the same. Preparation begins with research into the interests of the audience, the background of the topic, and the expertise and opinions of the program guests. The information gained from that research is then committed to paper, most often in the form of a semi-script, which controls the organization and structure of the program for the interviewer-moderator-host, but leaves the responses from interviewee-guests ad lib. Next the program is produced, and finally aired, either as an unedited live or live-to-tape program, or in edited form in which the talk materials are woven into a documentary or news program or condensed for a more tightly organized and structured presentation.

**Exercises**

1. Assume you are a reporter for a local news–talk radio station. Your assignment editor has given you the assignment of interviewing a local

person (one who was prominent in a story in the morning newspaper) for a follow-up story that will appear in your afternoon drive-time news today.

a. Choose a story and person who was prominent in that story from today's paper.

b. Then prepare: (1) a lead for the story, which will conclude with this line: "A short while ago we talked with ———, and recorded the following interview"; (2) a series of six to eight questions you want to ask in order to bring the story up to date. Often these questions and answers will be edited before they are aired, but some stations do broadcast live "newsmaker" segments using almost exactly the format described here. We will assume this will be live, so you should consider the *sequence* of the questions, as well as the content and phrasing of each individual question.

2. You have been assigned as researcher-writer for a television network interview program, a half-hour in length (similar to *Meet the Press*). The guest each week is a major figure in politics, economics, or other national or international topic of importance.

   Your assignment is, first, to select the guest for this week's program, and then to prepare for the program:

a. A *scripted* opening that identifies the program and the participants, introduces the topic, and attracts audience attention.

b. A series of questions to be asked of the guest. This is a *live* program, so the sequence is important, as are the presence of "pad" questions the interviewer can use to adjust the timing. You will need 9 to 10 major questions, plus some secondary or sequencing questions and pads.

c. A *scripted* close that ends the program appropriately, and that also contains material which can be used to make final timing adjustments.

3. Record on audiotape a radio or TV interview of approximately 5 to 8 minutes (from a network program like *Nightline, Good Morning America, The Tonight Show,* or a locally produced equivalent). Copy the questions asked in the interview. Analyze the sequence of the questions and their wording using criteria presented in this chapter. Reorganize the sequence if you think it can be improved, and add questions that would improve the flow of the interview. Rephrase any questions that are poorly worded. Explain your changes.

---

**Note**

1. "A Fine Madness at the Midnight Hour," *Newsweek,* February 3, 1986, pp. 46–53.

**Further
Reading**

For this chapter we have concentrated on titles that cover aspects of interviewing. As we have said, interviews are used in several ways—as the content for talk programs, as the raw material for actualities in news and documentary programs, and simply as a means of gathering information. These titles deal primarily with the last of these areas, as do several of the reporting texts listed in the previous chapter.

Biagi, Shirley. *Interviews That Work: A Practical Guide for Journalists*, 2nd ed. Belmont, CA: Wadsworth, 1992.

Cohen, Akiba A. *The Television News Interview*. Newbury Park, CA: Sage, 1987.

Stewart, Charles J., and William B. Cash, Jr. *Interviewing: Principles and Practices*, 5th ed. Dubuque, IA: Brown, 1988.

Wilson, Gerald L., and H. Lloyd Goodall. *Interviewing in Context*. New York: McGraw-Hill, 1991.

This next one is very broad, covering many topics in addition to factual interviews, such as employment interviews, counseling, and so on. Still, it contains good ideas.

Sincoff, Michael Z., and Robert S. Goyer. *Interviewing*. New York: Macmillan, 1984.

An alternative point of view is presented by these final titles. They consider interviewing from the perspective of interviewees. They discuss ways to prepare for interviews and press conferences, both for promotion of ideas or products and as damage control when countering a hostile press. They are highly recommended, to see how the other side views the interview process.

Hannaford, Peter. *Talking Back to the Media*. New York: Facts on File, 1986.

Hilton, Jack, and Mary Knoblauch. *On Television: A Survival Guide for Media Interviews*. New York: AMACOM Division of American Management Associations, 1980.

# CHAPTER 14

# Documentary Programs

A precise definition of the term "documentary" is impossible. Different practitioners use the word differently. There is a professional understanding between them about its meaning, but that meaning may vary according to context. In addition, documentary techniques are subject to continuous evolution. . . . At one extreme, documentaries border on current affairs programmes; at the other, on drama.[1]

The above statement is taken from the British Broadcasting Company's Television Training Manual on documentaries. We share its point of view. Attempting to define or describe what is or is not a documentary is a difficult task; there is no universal agreement. The term came originally from the French *documentaire,* and was first used by John Grierson in the 1920s. He described it as "the creative interpretation of actuality."

Others have given the documentary a very limited definition: "an authoritative, journalistic look at the important public-affairs issues of our time."[2] A contrasting, broader view sees the form as encompassing a "personal and idiosyncratic vision of virtually anything with general significance."[3] There are also humorous definitions: "A film without a plot, without a love story, and without anticipation of a profit."[4]

You do not need a precise definition, however, to prepare programs that fall at least loosely within this category. Our approach is to describe a group of characteristics which, taken as a whole, give the documentary its unique character and to contrast the documentary with other forms of presentation with which it shares some of these characteristics.

When you finish this chapter you will be able to

- distinguish between documentaries and other presentational forms,

- recognize, prepare, and use shot sheets,

- write concepts, treatments and other script materials for documentaries, emphasizing the distinctive presentational techniques of that genre, and

> • recognize and use these important terms and concepts:
>
> | | |
> |---|---|
> | audience involvement | re-creation (dramatization) of material |
> | concept | slice of life documentary |
> | docudrama | sound-on-tape (SOT) list |
> | editorial bias | treatment |
> | logging | using actualities |
> | minimizing narration | |

We can continue our consideration of what a documentary is by first looking at what it is not. For example, although documentaries frequently depend on the elaboration of abstract points of view, as in presenting a topic on foreign policy, they are not talk programs. Documentary as a technique requires that the program use locations, not just people talking in a studio.

Neither is the documentary a drama. A popular term in the broadcasting industry is *docudrama*, used to label what used to be called historical dramas. Evidently the prefix *docu-* lends some suggestion of historical accuracy the earlier label did not provide. But these programs are not documentaries; they are dramas, and should conform to the requirements for dramatic development. Both in television (the so-called reality programs like *Hard Copy* and *Inside Edition*) and in film (*JFK,* for example) there now appears another confusing form: programs that combine actuality footage of news events with re-created, dramatized scenes. Often the distinction between what was real and what re-created is deliberately blurred, leading to a serious ethical question.

The documentary is also not an overt expression of an editorial position, although a well-written documentary may lead members of the audience to take a position on the issue being considered.

**Figure 14.1.** *Shoe*—reprinted by permission: Tribune Media Services.

Finally, the documentary is not news, although here the difference is often not clear. The distinction, which we will develop in greater detail, is simply one of degree. The documentary relies heavily, even exclusively, on the actual places and people involved in the story. It attempts to involve the audience in the story. The news story, in contrast, depends more on the presence of a reporter to explain the story to the audience.

# CHARACTERISTICS OF THE DOCUMENTARY

We can suggest three characteristics which are found in well-written and -produced documentaries. None of these is unique to the documentary, but taken together they do set this genre apart from other types of content and forms of presentation.

First, there will be a distinct point of view. Second, the documentary makes a deliberate attempt to involve its audience in its presentation. Third, the true documentary, by definition, documents; it does not re-create or fictionalize its topic.

## Point of View

We have argued that effective writing of most broadcast materials requires a point of view in order to maintain unity and to shape the content for the target audience. On this ground, the documentary is no exception. Take, for example, this situation: You have been asked to write a television documentary for your station based on the premiere of a new musical work that will be performed by the community symphony. You might take a common journalistic approach—record the performance, get interviews with music critics after the performance on their impressions, possibly even add comments by "ordinary" persons who attended the performance, and then edit that material into a composite, interspersing sections of the music with the previously recorded comments.

Another point of view might be to follow the conductor's involvement with the work. In this case the conductor might become the narrator and the catalyst for the entire presentation. He explains why and how the work was chosen, how he studies the score and prepares himself for the presentation, what he hopes to emphasize in the presentation. Next you record rehearsals, as the conductor molds the orchestra to get the sound he wants. Finally you record the performance itself. The final, edited television presentation follows this chronological approach, concluding with the performance, or a portion of it if time does not permit presenting the entire work.

Yet another point of view, if there were enough preparation time available to take this approach, would be to follow the composer through the steps of composing this new work, then observe his reactions during rehearsals, note the last-minute modifications made in the work as the result of conversations between conductor and composer, and then present the performance, with occasional visual cutaways to the composer to observe his reactions to his own work and to the audience for their reactions as well.

Still other approaches might be considered. There are only two real limitations on the writer when it comes to choosing a point of view—the amount of time available to complete the production, and the budget.

From the above you can infer that point of view means looking at a topic from someone's perspective. That person might be one of the participants—the conductor or the composer in our example above. Or it might be the reporter's point of view. Any good reporter will recognize that he or she invariably takes a point of view on every story. The process of selecting material to be included (or left out), of deciding the relative importance (length of time on the screen) of various parts of the story, and of what comes first and what later—all these decisions are influenced by the point of view the writer-reporter brings to the story.

But our concern here is not with subtle or subconscious decisions in regard to reporting or editing the material; it is rather with the deliberate choice to use the reporter's perspective, which is assumed to be as objective and "neutral" as possible, as the point of view of the presentation.

Multiple points of view are also possible. Some very interesting programs have been developed by examining a topic through the eyes of different persons who are affected in different ways.

## Audience Involvement

We first considered audience involvement in Chapter 10. It is part of the broad and powerful gratification we labeled personalism.

Compare, once again, the documentary with news and with drama. Personalism may be present in some degree in a news story, to the extent that audiences can identify with persons, places, and events in the story, but that gratification is not usually emphasized. The strongest gratifications in most news stories are those of information, importance, and value. A well-written drama, in contrast, makes us care about the characters. We expect to become emotionally involved in the outcome, to have empathy for the characters, to cheer or to boo the outcome.

Here the documentary more closely approximates drama than news. The content of the documentary will contain information, and have importance and value for its target audience, but now added to those gratifications, deliberately, is the emotional strength of personalism. The audience should be drawn into the topic, and invited to participate in whatever process or activity is taking place, even though it must be a vicarious participation.

*TV Guide* magazine once asked several of the best-known producers of television programs what forms of the documentary the American public watched and why. Their answers reveal the importance of audience involvement:

> Reuven Frank, at that time executive vice-president of NBC News: "Drama. You cannot interest people unless you tell stories. Usually in a good story there's a protagonist, a conflict, and a resolution."

> Burton Benjamin, documentary producer for CBS: "Plot values give you the highest ratings."

> Bob Drew, president of Bob Drew and Associates, Inc., an independent documentary production company: "Nothing can compete with dramatic logic. Reality films must have similar ingredients to those in fiction—a protagonist, a dramatic conflict."[5]

Involvement is accomplished by exposing viewers to the real people, places, and events involved in the topic, permitting them to hear the voices of the actual participants and the actual sounds of the location, and to see the actual conditions in which the participants are involved.

Suppose you were given an assignment to cover the plight of the elderly urban poor in your community. These are people who are forced to live in substandard flophouse hotels and who, your research shows, are exploited by the managers of those hotels. It would be possible to cover at least part of the content by means of an interview with a local housing official, who reports that there are $x$ thousands of elderly poor in the community, that there are only $y$ thousand housing units, and that $z$ thousand of those units are substandard.

A different technique would be to follow several of these elderly poor people through some of the activities of a typical day—trying to cash a Social Security check or to find a decent meal at a reasonable price, climbing the stairs to a filthy room because the elevator in the hotel has broken down, lying in bed and seeing the rats crawl up the wall. The interview, with the statistics and the official's presence, is simple to do and authoritative. But it carries none of the dramatic value or emotional weight of experiencing through the camera's eye the struggle of one handicapped person up a stairway or the sight of one rat running up a wall.

## A Documentary Documents

At first glance, that heading may seem redundant. But it makes a difference in the preparation whether the material used in the program is real—the actual people, places, and events—or whether the actions of the program have been re-created.

The point is simply that *a true documentary cannot be scripted in advance of its shooting.* In this sense, the documentary is similar to news. The story has to come back from its location, and the tape footage has to be viewed and a selection of shots made before the final sequence can be determined and the final narration written. In many programs, no script, in any formal sense, is ever prepared. Instead, writers and producers will put the completed program together from a variety of shot sheets and other notes.

In contrast, any program content that is to be re-created, or staged, and therefore to some degree fictionalized, can be and should be written *in advance* of shooting. A complete script will be needed to describe to actors and crew what is to be performed for the camera. That is why we have insisted that the re-creation of situations, as in a docudrama, is not truly documentary, and should follow the guidelines for dramatic development. After all, in those situations both picture and sound are under the complete control of the writer and the director. By this assertion we do not mean to suggest that the writer's role is any less important or creative when crafting a documentary than with any other type of program, only that the sequence in which the various production tasks are performed will differ.

# COMMON DOCUMENTARY TYPES

We do not have the space, nor is this introductory text the proper place, to consider all the forms a documentary might take. But we can consider, briefly, five types we believe will give the beginning writer a better grasp of the requirements of writing these programs. These are the documentary based on public affairs issues, the documentation of a creative effort, the event or process documentary, the nature documentary and the "slice of life" documentary. The terms are largely our own; other authors use different labels.

Another variation is the re-creation of a historical event or period using old photographs, music appropriate to the period and commentary by historians. *The Civil War,* which was first broadcast on public TV stations in 1990, is an outstanding example of this form. The producer of this series collected and used hundreds of still photographs from the war; narrators read letters and selections from the diaries of soldiers and members of their families; and music and sound effects were inserted. In addition, present-day sources were used, notably interviews with historians who have researched the period. These contemporary interviews are not in the strict sense a documentary technique.

## The Public Affairs Issue Documentary

This is perhaps the best-known type. These programs examine topics of public concern—hunger, poverty, war, and other social and political issues. Issue-oriented documentary programs presented by the television networks are sometimes able to stir up sufficient public concern and pressure to help solve the problems documented.

One of the most famous examples of a public affairs documentary, presented by CBS in 1960, was "Harvest of Shame." It presented the problems of America's migrant workers, and showed in graphic detail the miserable conditions in which many of these workers lived.

> Using the photographic record of environment and the direct interview, the *CBS Reports* unit (led by producer David Lowe and with [Edward R.] Murrow as narrator) followed the path of the migrants as they traveled the harvesting route in ramshackle caravans from their Florida shacks. The cameras recorded their squalor and the deadly and hopeless monotony of their labors. In disturbing interviews we listened to mothers forced to leave children alone in rat-infested hovels because they could not afford the pennies to send them to a day-care center; or parents unable to provide milk for their infants more than once a week. As the film progressed, we were offered a devastating visual contrast between the shacks occupied by migrants and the comfortable, clean stables nearby. We saw scenes of cattle cars stopping at regular four-hour intervals in order to water and exercise the cattle, contiguous with scenes of the pitiful migrants riding buses and overloaded trucks for ten uninterrupted hours at a stretch.[6]

The program triggered tremendous resentment on the part of major agricultural interests. Its producers were accused of being blatantly editorial. But it aroused sufficient public indignation to enact some protections for migrant workers.

At the local level, some individual stations are equally forceful in exposing social ills, but a great many stations are reluctant to present documentaries on major issues. The programs are expensive to produce, tying up news crews and editing facilities which might instead be used for straight news programming. Documentaries do not draw large audiences even when presented in prime time, nor do they easily attract sponsors. And they are controversial, and who wants willingly to antagonize leading members of the community or potential advertisers? At least those are the arguments frequently used to excuse the relative paucity of local public affairs documentaries. You may judge for yourself if they are legitimate.

Some stations have found an interesting way to reduce the costs of documentary production and to increase viewership by first producing a series of investigative news reports on a topic and airing them within the local newscast. Then, if the topic does generate viewer interest and public reaction, the story will be reworked as a longer documentary. The revised version can include the reactions of public officials to the original stories, but it will also include repeats of much of the raw material from the original.

With this approach, using the same topic for both a news series and a documentary, and using the same content only slightly repackaged, the distinctions between news and documentary become blurred. Such is the case with the script on young people and AIDS reproduced later in this chapter. The staff at the station, Sacramento's KOVR, prepared both a series that was shown within its news programs and a self-contained program. The script is from the first of the news stories. The topic is certainly important enough to justify this effort; it is also sufficiently sensitive to require careful presentation.

## Documenting a Creative Effort

This type of documentary exposes its audience to the process of creation, often of some sort of artistic work. It might document the making of a sculpture, following the sculptor from the choice of material, through the various steps in designing and executing the work, to its final placement. Or it might follow an orchestra conductor through the steps of preparing a new work— a topic we brought up when considering point of view. Or it might follow the process of the creation of a film.

One very successful such effort was "The Making of *Thriller*," which documents the production of Michael Jackson's video "Thriller." No script remains for this documentary effort, but the producer's point of view and organizational plan are clear from these comments:

> I didn't just want to come out of the project with a bunch of documentary footage. . . . I wanted to establish just how extraordinary this whole undertaking was, with all the incredible talent and energy involved. To me, "Thriller" is more like an art-film than a music video—it really is a mini-movie, with all the special effects and makeup, right down to the "scary music."
>
> Whereas a normal music video will be shot in one or two days, they were shooting for nine days in the various locations around East Los Angeles, and because we were there all the time, not just during the actual shoot, but also at pre-production meetings, rehearsals, post-production, etc., we were shooting for a total of 14 days straight. . . .
>
> We started off by dividing the entire project into separate chapters, each with its own title like "The Fans" or "Graveyard" or "Metamorphosis." So first you meet some of the fans who've found out about the location shoots and have turned up just to get a glimpse of Michael. And you also see Richard Baker, the special effects wizard, work his magic on Michael and the zombie extras. . . .
>
> Along with the behind-the-scenes views and the actual footage are various intercut references and portions of other clips to help shape it and put it in perspective.[7]

## Documenting an Event or Process

This form of documentary may itself be considered on several levels, based on the amount of creativity and artistic freedom allowed its writers and producers.

At its least creative level it represents merely the recording of a process or event, such as a manufacturing sequence—how the doors are bolted onto an automobile—or documentation of the firing of a rocket motor, or observing from a single fixed camera position a parade going by.

Taken a step more creatively, that basic documentation can be edited and provided with a narration, to be used in a training tape for workers or in a promotional piece for a company. This sort of presentation, which is often called a "sponsored" film (or tape), is in part the subject of the following chapter on writing for corporate/instructional productions.

But when writers and producers are allowed the creative freedom to employ all the principles of structure and style, and to emphasize audience gratifications as well, documentation can be turned into a much more interesting sort of program. Documentaries of this sort might present a parade, or a circus, a political convention, or even an entire political campaign. Other topics might be the progress of an athletic team throughout a game or a season, or the documentation of the preparation and launching of a spacecraft.

## The Nature Documentary

This form should require no introduction to anyone who has watched television at all. Historically, the popularization of documentaries about natural phenomena probably dates back to Walt Disney's "Beaver Valley" and several other similar films. Those of you now in college have grown up with *Wild Kingdom*, National Geographic specials, *Nova*, and of course, the several series featuring Jacques Cousteau. We have reproduced an excerpt from a Cousteau program script later in this chapter.

## The Slice of Life Documentary

This variation can easily be combined with other forms. It can also be a very powerful and effective approach in its own right. Here the writer-producer chooses to document a "chunk" of human existence. The content is most often combined with a video style that eliminates the subject's awareness of the camera by using hidden or "candid" cameras. This technique, which in some of its variations is also known as the *vérité documentary*, seeks to break down the aesthetic distance between the subject and the viewer and thereby heighten viewer involvement.

Often the central focus will be on a location, a particular site from which it is possible to observe the behaviors of persons who happen to be in or passing through that place. This approach was used in "Terminus," a documentary film produced for the British Transportation Commission, as described by its producer:

The first germ of the idea came from John Maddison of the Central Office of Information, who said to me one day, "Why don't you make a documentary of a night at King's Cross Station?" It was, of course, an interesting subject but seemed likely to prove depressing on the screen. After all, King's Cross was old, inadequate and due for re-building. So I did nothing about it. . . .

Some time later I was looking at some candid-camera material showing the handling of parcels at King's Cross—film taken as time-and-motion study to help us analyse parcel and luggage handling, in relation to the layout and general efficiency of the station. In these pictures members of the general public were seen, as well as railway staff. We were fascinated by the material. Quite apart from its purpose as a study of procedure, the actions of the people—quite oblivious of being shot—were extraordinarily interesting. . . .

There the idea rested perhaps a couple of years. Then John Schlesinger came to me to make a film. We discussed various ideas and then he said he would like to make a film of a day in the life of a railway station. Someone mentioned Waterloo. Waterloo has two important advantages. It's modern and light enough for unlit candid-camera shooting. . . .

How would it relate to British Transport's policy? Two things, it seemed to me, might be put over in such a film: that British Railways still have a vital national job to do and if you sit at a London terminus throughout a day, you see enough vital things happening to prove it; and secondly the film could show the staff were human, warm-hearted people, trying to do a good job.

Both these things seemed very much worth saying.[8]

## WRITING DOCUMENTARIES

We have already explained that in the true documentary, in contrast to programs which are re-creations, the sequences cannot be scripted in detail in advance; they can be only loosely planned. The precise shots will have to be left to the judgment of the director and cameraperson on location. In such a situation, if the final program is to have any similarity to the one originally conceived by its author, the preliminary steps in production must be all the more carefully worked out.

### Concept

The task of writing a documentary begins with an idea of your own, or with an assignment from a supervisor. That idea or assignment is the essence of the *concept*. A concept statement serves the same purpose for a documentary that it does for a drama; it allows the originator to communicate the program idea to others who will be involved with the program. The producers' statements for both "Terminus" and "The Making of *Thriller*" which we quoted earlier are concept statements, although in both cases they were written after the production (and we edited them heavily).

The next steps in the process are the same as those for the development of any other type of program. The purpose will have to be accurately assessed, and the target audience identified. The method of delivery, a step we have not considered in previous chapters, will need to be considered. Broadcast is no longer the only alternative. This production might be for example, a "sponsored" presentation, prepared on behalf of a corporate client for training or promotional purposes and shown on a closed-circuit video system. Or it might be produced for possible sale in videocassette form, as was "The Making of *Thriller*." Or it might be aired in the traditional manner, by a station or network.

## Treatment

The answers to these considerations, plus the determination of the point of view, lead to the *treatment*, which is very much the same as the treatment for a dramatic program—a narrative description of the proposed program. In addition to describing the subject matter, the treatment should indicate style and method of presentation. How much of the verbal description will be provided by spoken actualities, and how much by commentary? Will music be used; if so, how? What will be the mood?

The treatment should be carefully written and agreed to by all the key members of the production team, as well as by the sponsor, to avoid misunderstandings later in the production. Without a detailed treatment, the crew that goes out to shoot the raw footage from which the final program will be edited has no guide to follow. They might shoot the wrong stuff, or at the very least they might shoot much more material than will be needed, thereby complicating and slowing the editing process and costing additional money. A good treatment will prevent those complications.

One way to approach the treatment is to suggest a series of impressions, as in this description from "Terminus."

> Flying high above London and the Thames. The House of Parliament on our left.
> Insistent notes of the harpsichord suggest the time, 8 A.M.
> We are now hovering over Waterloo, featuring the enormous acre of glass that covers it.
> Titles—Terminus, etc., etc.

Various angles on the glass roof under titles.

From the mount of the station—trains are running both ways.

Inside, the rush to the city is beginning.

The signal box—the dots of the indicator run towards the station. Intent old faces. Silence. "Give me #23, George." Levers are pulled. Kettles steam with the House of Parliament in the background. Harpsichord.

The business train from Guildford rattles past the box—swift pan to a cat looking down from the internal telephone exchange in the signal box.

The men in the business train pack up newspapers, take down their umbrellas, bowlers, brief cases—"See you on the 5.45" etc., and join the march.

Outside the station, the cars and their executive occupants drive away—The Lion and the insignias of War and Peace over the archway gaze down at them.

Public gazing at train arrival board. The destinations change like magic. A special notice indicates the arrival of boat train from Southampton. Australian line.

On 11—the people who are meeting the train gather. Curiosity at whom they are meeting. The Salvation Army man—elderly foreign-looking woman—a young girl with a bunch of flowers.

Bill, the porter, sits on some scales. He whistles, the pointer on the scales registers the rhythm.

The officials of Crooks, Dawson's, Poly Tours join the group.

Black Homburg, and top hat—the insignia of the Station Master. Phone conversation about delay of boat train.

On 11—they wait. Their voices perhaps tell us whom they are meeting. A married sister, a prodigal son returning after ten years, a comrade from the Salvation Army. An ambulance at the ready on the concourse—Nurse in evidence.[9]

The treatment should not be carved in stone, however. It will evolve and expand as additional research proceeds on the topic, and as the camera crew finds and shoots new and interesting material. You might begin the preparation of a documentary on the elderly urban poor with the assumption based on your early research that all the flophouse hotel managers in the city treat their tenants poorly, charge high rates for poorly furnished and maintained rooms, and so on. And then you discover one hotel which is clean, and where the staff is helpful and supportive of the tenants. To be accurate and fair, this hotel should also be featured in the final production. It also will make a good contrast, and provide variety in what otherwise might be a pretty depressing exposition.

Be alert for new and powerful visual opportunities, and be flexible.

## Notes and Scripts

Once there is film or tape, the next task is editing. One of the first steps in this process is reviewing the video and cataloging all the various shots available, which is called *logging*. The list of shots is called a *shot sheet*. The sheet gives a brief description, often only a word or two, of each camera shot. Sometimes those shots that contain important sound, such as a sound bite, an interview or even good background sound, are kept separately as a *sound-on-tape (SOT) list*. On the sheet the location on the reel and the length of each shot are noted, so that any item can be retrieved easily if it is chosen for the final edited program. Sometimes running times are used; more likely this notation will be the counter number on the VTR or an electronically inserted time code.

For the programs on young people and AIDS, KOVR's producer prepared separate sheets for each interview or location. We show only the first page or so from a taping session and an interview with a young man (John) who has the disease (Figure 14.2). Similar sheets were constructed from interviews with medical experts and social workers. Asterisks mark the producer's feeling that these were particularly good visuals or strong statements.

*John Coleman  #1*

| | |
|---|---|
| Top of tape | toys around apartment/incense |
| 1632 | John in kitchen |
| 1759 | coffee maker |
| 1818 | did you want chocolate almond or vanilla? (nat sot) |
| 2001 | grinding coffee (John) nat sot |
| 2142 | water for coffee (nat sot) |
| 2319 | making coffee (soft focus) |
| 2451 | answering door for nurse |
| 2756 | needles on table |
| 2809 | John sits down at table |
| 2524 | nurses full |
| * 2939 | John talking (nat sot) |

**Figure 14.2.** Courtesy of KOVR, Sacramento, CA.

Interview

3357    I do this for an hour a day 5 days a week . . . in all 3 hrs a day.

*** 3443    ". . . It's not a lot of time but doesn't include time I spend thinking about it. I have this in my arm all the time & it's a definite reminder I'm not living a normal life anymore."

*** 3848    "I do about an hour of the drip . . . DHPG 3-4 hrs . . . alot of time thinking about it. It's not a normal life."

**** 3935    I can take walks visit w/friends watch TV a lot of things I can't do I'm not going to run marathon anytime soon. Things that cause me stress I can't do—which means I can't work. Big thing."

** 4023    "A year ago I was taking classes at CSUS, working, tutoring things have slowed down markedly."

4148    working on computer

** 4237    Dan 2    what about prospects of employment?
       A    pretty slim you're seeing me good but . . . not so good a while back."

4359    2    How did you find out?

4414    rest every block—you have pneumonia & they diagnosed me April 13th—I have CMV in eyes.

4451    Right now I'm stabilized been good 2 months now.

**Figure 14.2.** (continued)

When the stories for the AIDS series went on the air, each was a completely preproduced package, requiring only an anchor lead-in and lead-out. These packages had been prepared totally from the shot sheets. Scripts were written only after the fact for the station files (which KOVR labels as "backup"). Figure 14.3 shows the script for the first segment in the series, including the anchor lead-in, the story proper and the lead-out. Also, for each story appearing in its newscasts, KOVR requires that a *cut sheet* be prepared. This page, Figure 14.4, contains the slug, the story length, the outcue, and any graphics that are to be inserted by the chyron operator. In this story there were two inserts, one to identify the AIDS victim and another to identify the medical expert.

```
DAN SAYS                          The percentage of young people getting

                                  AIDS is growing at an alarming rate.

                                      They're contracting the virus most

                                  likely in their teens and getting full

                                  blown AIDS by the time they're thirty.

                                      I spent the afternoon with a young man

                                  who now has AIDS and assumes he got it in

                                  high school.

                                      * * * * * * * * * * * * * * * *

TAKE ENG "AIDS PART ONE"          SOT FULL

TAPE #2 IN: 1353                      (NAT SOT/John "This is what I do

(JOHN PUMPING I-V)                everyday so I won't go blind.")

                                      John Coleman just turned 27 and he has

                                  AIDS. He's part of a growing group of young

                                  men and women being infected with the

                                  virus.

TAPE #2 IN: 4728                  (SOT/John "You become infected and you just

(JOHN INTVW)                      don't know it. Then ten years down the

                                  road...you're sick.")

TAKE ARTWORK/GRAPHIC                  Research shows that statewide...about 17

WITH NUMBERS                      percent of all new AIDS cases are people
                                  MORE MORE MORE
```

**Figure 14.3.** Courtesy of KOVR, Sacramento, CA.

between the ages of 20 and 29. In Sacramento County...that figure swells to an alarming 22 per cent.

TAKE TAPE #1/SAC AIDS FOUNDATION/PATTY BLOMBERG

(SOT/Patty Blomberg "Twenty two per cent is a higher number than anywhere else in California and the U.S. That's alarming.")

TAPE #2 (JOHN)
IN: 4617

(SOT/John "I can assume I was infected in high school...when I was a teen if you consider the incubation rate. The illness came over a period of a month. It was nothing I expected.")

SHOTS OF KIDS IN SCHOOL

When you're young...you just don't think it can happen to you. But AIDS is happening to our young people. And kids need to know about its dangers and consequences.

TAKE ARTWORK AND LIST/HIGH RISK

You're high risk for the virus if you're a gay male...an I-V drug user...or have two or more lovers a year.

TAKE ARTWORK/HOW AIDS IS TRANSMITTED/LIST

AIDS is transmitted through the exchange of blood...semen or vaginal secretions. You can also get it by having oral or anal sex...sharing needles...even ones used for steroids or ear piercing or by pen or pencil tattoos.

TAPE #2 "JOHN" IN: 4814

(SOT/John "The information wasn't there before. Teenagers who become infected now have no excuse. It's a luxury I didn't have.")

SHOTS OF KIDS

The AIDS virus can take as long as 10 or 11 years to incubate. That means the new
MORE MORE MORE

**Figure 14.3.** (continued)

wave of young people getting sick was infected in their teens. Kids aren't getting the word about AIDS.

TAKE TAPE/DR. FLYNN #1
IN: 1324

(SOT/Dr. Flynn "There are some very good teachers out there...some are committed to saving the lives of these teenagers...but it's spotty. There's no plan at each school district. It's hit and miss.")

TAKE/DR. FLYNN W JOHN
TAPE #2 IN: 526
TAPE/DR. FLYNN IN OFFICE
#1 IN: 63

Dr. Neil Flynn calls himself something of a crusader. He's one of Sacramento's leading AIDS doctors and is committed to fighting the virus. He sees patients at the U-C Davis Medical Center AIDS Clinic. It was one of the first in the country when he helped set it up 12 years ago.

John Coleman is one of his patients.

(NAT SOT "...no skin lesions?")

TAPE/JOHN W DR. FLYNN IN
OFFICE #2 IN: 1122

I spent the afternoon with John to better understand how AIDS has changed his life. John keeps a positive attitude but one thing is for sure. His life is now very different.

TAPE #1/JOHN IN: 3935

(SOT/John "I can take walks...visit with friends...watch TV. But there are a lot of things I can't do. I'm not going to run a marathon anytime soon. Things that cause me stress I can't do...which means I can't work. That's a big thing.")

MORE MORE MORE

**Figure 14.3.** (continued)

TAPE #1 JOHN & NURSE           A home nurse visits John at least once a
IN: 2348                       week to draw blood samples and check his
                               medication. He takes six different kinds
                               daily.

DRAWING BLOOD                  (Nat SOT "It's drawing good...I'm amazed.")

                               John hooks up to an I-V for daily
                               treatments of one of his medications which
JOHN WITH I-V                  keeps him from going blind.

                               He's talking with us in this special
                               report to help get the word out to young
                               people.

JOHN TAPE #3                   (SOT/John "It's a real good example of what
                               you do has consequences. It's important to
                               communicate that...especially to kids.")

JOHN TAPE #3 W DAN             There's another dimension of AIDS John
                               has to live with which raises a very big
                               question.

JOHN TAPE #2 IN: 5130         (SOT/Dan Q. "Do you suspect you infected
DAN QUESTION                   others?")
SAME TAPE JOHN FULL WITH       (SOT/John A. "Probably. It's not something
ANSWER                         I want to think about to be truthful.")

                                * * * * * * * * * * * * * * * *

LIVE DAN SAYS                  Tomorrow night...what your kids are
                               learning in school about AIDS.

YRON FULL SCREEN:              If you'd like this brochure about
AIDS BROCHURE                  AIDS...please write KOVR-TV...2713...KOVR
KOVR TV                        Drive...West Sacramento...95605.
2713 KOVR DRIVE               This brochure was prepared by Channel 13
WEST SAC., CA 95605           and the Sierra Foundation.

**Figure 14.3.** (continued)

# Cut Sheet

| Running Time | Video | Audio | "Out Cue" or Chyron |
|---|---|---|---|
| TOP | ENG | SOT | |
| @ :10 | | | CHYRON:  JOHN COLEMAN |
| | | | HAS AIDS |
| @ :47 | | | CHYRON:  DR. NEIL FLYNN |
| | | | UCD MED CENTER |
| | | | |
| | | | |
| | | | |
| | | | |
| | | | |
| | | | |
| | | | |
| | | | |
| | | | |

**TRT**

3:41

**Out Cue** to be truthful."

**Last Video**

**Figure 14.4.** Courtesy of KOVR, Sacramento, CA.

Our second example is a portion of the script of "Dolphins" from the *Cousteau Odyssey* series (Figure 14.5). This is a different type of documentary, a nature production. It was shot entirely on location, mostly aboard Cousteau's ship *Calypso*. The sequence of production, however, was as we have described it. After the concept and treatment had been worked out, video was shot, including sync sound in both English and French. During the editing process, as the video sequences were selected, the script was written for the narration needed to tie the video sequences together.

Narration, music, and possibly some sound effects were added in post-production. Rod Serling is the primary narrator; only his voice is heard. In addition to being seen and heard at various places in the video, interacting with his crew and the dolphins, Cousteau also appears as a narrator (script page 4A). We discussed this dual-narrator technique in Chapter 7.

This very detailed script, cleanly reproduced by the Cousteau Society, was undoubtedly prepared after the production was complete.

## ADDITIONAL CONSIDERATIONS

In preparing the final production the writer should consider all the requirements of an effective presentation—purpose, gratifications, structure, aural style—in short, all the principles of good writing. In particular, however, the writer should use techniques that are the logical extensions of the unique characteristics of the documentary—extensive use of actuality material and a minimal dependence on narration. In addition, the writer should be careful about editorializing and about re-creating material.

### Use Actualities

Audience involvement, which we seek in the documentary, comes from being able to experience as closely as possible the situations in which the participants are found. For the viewers, that vicarious experience is transmitted through the video screen by the use of actualities. Sound bites, which are the actual words of participants, are better than the words of the reporter-announcer in this regard, but they are still not as powerful as the actions and natural sounds of the documented activity.

Here the documentary again contrasts with the writing of news. The most efficient method of news exposition—that is, the method that provides the clearest statement of the news story in the briefest period of time—is

METROMEDIA PRODUCERS CORPORATION
8544 SUNSET BOULEVARD
HOLLYWOOD, CALIFORNIA 90069
TEL: 213-652-7075

DATE February 9, 1972    PAGE   1.

PRODUCTION   Dolphins

PRODUCTION NO.

PREPARED BY

ROUGH:     REVISED:  FINAL: XX

| V I D E O | A U D I O |
|---|---|
| | PROLOGUE |
| DOLPHIN IN LAGOON (DOLLY) SWIMS UNDER DIVING BOARD | JEAN (SYNC)<br>Over here, Dolly. Come on.<br><br>SERLING<br>Free to join its own kind, this dolphin has chosen human companionship.<br><br>JEAN (SYNC)<br>Come on, now.  Tell me, are you a good girl?<br><br>DOLPHIN (SYNC)<br>That's right. |
| CLOSE-JEAN | JEAN (SYNC)<br>Good girl, come on. |
| CLOSE-DOLLY | DOLPHIN (SYNC)<br>Okay... |
| INTERCUT JEAN-DOLLY | JEAN (SYNC)<br>Are you a pretty girl?  Pretty girl?<br><br>DOLPHIN (SYNC)<br>Awww....<br><br>JEAN (SYNC)<br>(laughs)<br>Well, I don't know what that was for.<br><br>DIP FOR:<br><br>SERLING |
| DOLPHIN MAKES SOUNDS | Between Jean Asbury of Florida and this dolphin that came to visit and out of affection stayed -- there is kinship, and communication. |

MPC Form 313 (12-68)

**Figure 14.5.** Copyright © 1972 The Cousteau Society, Inc., a nonprofit, membership-supported organization located at 870 Greenbrier Circle, Suite 402, Chesapeake, VA 23320. Annual dues are $20 for an Individual Membership and $28 for a Family Membership.

**METROMEDIA PRODUCERS CORPORATION**
8544 SUNSET BOULEVARD
HOLLYWOOD, CALIFORNIA 90069
TEL: 213-652-7075

DATE                                              PAGE  2
PRODUCTION
PRODUCTION NO.
PREPARED BY
ROUGH:        REVISED:        FINAL:

| V I D E O | A U D I O |
|---|---|
| DOLLY KISSES JEAN | **JEAN (SYNC)**<br>Give me another kiss, Dolly?  Give your mommy<br>another kiss?<br>(DOLPHIN KISSES HER)<br>Ohhh, beautiful.  Juicy, but beautiful.<br>(Jean applauds)  You're a good girl!<br><br>**DOLPHIN (SYNC)**<br>Thank you, thank you. |
| DOLLY PLAYS COY.  DUCKS<br>UNDER WATER | |
| | **SERLING** |
| DOLPHIN FOLLOWS ZODIAC,<br>LEAPS IN RESPONSE TO<br>HAND SIGNALS | We are familiar with the trained dolphin --<br><br>those put on display -- taught to mimic |
| DOLPHIN BODY SURFS | the human voice -- and to respond to man's |
| LAST LEAP | signals, and applause.  (BEAT)  But there |
| U/W WILD DOLPHIN SWIM | are great herds of dolphins still living in |
| U/W OBSERVATION PORT<br>AND SWIMMING DOLPHINS | freedom.  (BEAT)  Too swift to be easily<br><br>observed, little is known about the dolphin in<br><br>the wild.  This air-breathing mammal was once |
| T/S DOLPHIN SWIM | an earth-bound animal -- but sixty million<br><br>years ago he fled the confines of land for the<br><br>wide waters of open seas -- and became the<br><br>legendary friends of Gods, men and children. |

MPC Form 313 (12-68)

**Figure 14.5.** (continued)

| VIDEO | AUDIO |
|---|---|
| | **METROMEDIA PRODUCERS CORPORATION** 8544 SUNSET BOULEVARD HOLLYWOOD CALIFORNIA 90069 TEL: 213-652-7075 — DATE / PRODUCTION / PRODUCTION NO. / PREPARED BY / ROUGH: REVISED: FINAL: — PAGE 3 |

| VIDEO | AUDIO |
|---|---|
| U/W DOLPHIN SWIM | SERLING (CONTINUED) Now, in the dolphin's natural domain, Captain Cousteau, and divers of Calypso would explore the continuing relationship between man and dolphin -- a relationship that has inspired philosophers and poets from the beginning of recorded time.  END OF PROLOGUE |

MPC Form 313 (12-68)

**Figure 14.5.** (continued)

| V I D E O | A U D I O |
|---|---|
| | **METROMEDIA PRODUCERS CORPORATION**<br>8544 SUNSET BOULEVARD<br>HOLLYWOOD, CALIFORNIA 90069<br>TEL: 213-652-7075 |

DATE          PAGE 4
PRODUCTION
PRODUCTION NO.
PREPARED BY
ROUGH:     REVISED:     FINAL:

| V I D E O | A U D I O |
|---|---|
| | <u>ACT ONE</u> |
| |        SERLING |
| CALYPSO-GIBRALTAR | In pursuit of dolphins -- Calypso cruises the waters of the Strait of Gibraltar, off the coast of Spain. |
| |        COUSTEAU (FRENCH SYNC)<br>Bon, vous tournez la?  Hein?  Bon. |
| |        SIROT (FRENCH SYNC)<br>Oui. |
| SOUND |        COUSTEAU (FRENCH SYNC)<br>Alors, Philippe, nous approchons! |
| JYC-PILOT HOUSE | DIP FOR:<br>       SERLING<br>As they approach a dolphin herd, Captain Cousteau alerts the crew to prepare for filming. |
| PUSH IN-DISTANT HERD | (MUSIC AND EFFECTS IN THE CLEAR) |
| JYC AND FALCO | |
| |        COUSTEAU (FRENCH SYNC)<br>Well, listen, I think it's time to go. |
| |        FALCO (FRENCH SYNC)<br>Yes. |

MPC Form 313 (12-68)

**Figure 14.5.** (continued)

---

**METROMEDIA PRODUCERS CORPORATION**
8544 SUNSET BOULEVARD
HOLLYWOOD, CALIFORNIA 90069
TEL. 213-652-7075

DATE                                          PAGE    4A
PRODUCTION
PRODUCTION NO.
PREPARED BY
ROUGH:          REVISED:          FINAL:

---

| V I D E O | A U D I O |
|---|---|
| | COUSTEAU (FRENCH SYNC) |
| | Go to the bow and I shall stay in contact with you. |
| | DIP FOR: |
| | SERLING |
| | Cousteau and diving supervisor, Albert Falco, |
| | also plan to collect a dolphin, for study |
| | at sea. |
| DOLPHINS-JYC LOOKS | |
| | COUSTEAU |
| | Filming free dolphins is a challenge. They are too |
| | swift for divers to approach them.  They never |
| DOLPHINS SWIM - "TALK" | stay behind or alongside a ship -- but they are |
| | attracted to the bow as to a magnet.  To Calypso, |
| EXTENSION OF CALYPSO | we have attached an extension with an underwater |
| | camera -- aimed backward -- toward the |
| | nose of the ship.   (BEAT) We hope the extension |
| | camera will reveal dolphins swimming head on  -- |
| PUSH IN ON EXTENSION | never before achieved on film. |
| | Meanwhile, frolicking hitchhikers come from all |
| | directions, but the main herd continues to outrun |
| | the ship, its underwater camera boom, and all othe |
| CREW OBSERVE DOLPHINS | protruding contraptions. |

MPC Form 313 (12-68)

**Figure 14.5.** (continued)

| VIDEO | AUDIO |
|---|---|
| | **METROMEDIA PRODUCERS CORPORATION**<br>8544 SUNSET BOULEVARD<br>HOLLYWOOD, CALIFORNIA 90069<br>TEL: 213-652-7075       DATE     PAGE   5<br>PRODUCTION<br>PRODUCTION NO.<br>PREPARED BY<br>ROUGH:     REVISED:     FINAL: |
| CU-JYC. REVEAL SIROT<br>JYC MOVES TO TV ROOM | <center>COUSTEAU (FRENCH SYNC)</center>Ah oui, oui les voila qui arrivent je les vois. Ah oui, y en a d'autres qui arrivent je les vois. Vous les apercevez sur l' ecran? |
| JYC AND OMER VIEW | <center>OMER (FRENCH SYNC)</center>No, not yet Captain.<br><br>DIP FOR:<br><br><center>SERLING</center>As skipper Philippe Sirot pursues them, Cousteau<br><br>fears that the new extension camera might<br><br>frighten the dolphins away. (BEAT)<br><br><center>COUSTEAU (FRENCH SYNC)</center>Well, I am going to go and see.<br><br><center>OMER (FRENCH SYNC)</center>Well, well magnificent.<br><br><center>COUSTEAU (FRENCH SYNC)</center>I am coming.<br><br>DIP FOR:<br><br><center>SERLING</center>But the system devised by underwater cameraman<br><br>Yves Omer works! Now, for the first time,<br><br>front view shots of dolphins swimming freely<br><br>toward camera! |

MPC Form 313 (12-68)

**Figure 14.5.** (continued)

through narration. However, in order to provide variety and maintain audience interest, writers and producers will insert brief actualities within the narrated story. (This technique is developed at some length in Chapter 12.)

The documentary, in contrast, uses extended actualities, a much higher proportion of actuality in relation to the amount of description, narration, and commentary. Ideally, a documentary would be constructed totally from actualities. All the visual sequences would be "documentation," the actual scenes at the actual locations. And the sound track would be made up entirely of the actual voices of the people involved and the actual sound effects present at the scene. In practice, however, some supplemental visual material and some narrative commentary are usually required.

The contrast between news and documentary might be summarized this way: In news the actualities support the spoken narrative story, while in the well-written documentary the narrative supports the actualities.

## Minimize Narration

We've already touched on minimizing narration in the preceding section. Whenever possible, use actualities; they are more powerful than the commentary provided by a narrator. But commentary is often needed *to amplify and clarify the picture*. Review the discussion on "Writing to Pictures" in Chapter 8. There we quoted Hugh Baddeley, who described the production of "Terminus" in his book *The Technique of Documentary Film Production*. His comments are worth remembering, with some modification of his final line, that "silence is golden." We enthusiastically agree that the use of narration should be limited, but some form of sound is necessary. Audiences expect to hear something on the audio track continuously and become edgy—convinced that the transmission is faulty—if sound disappears for more than just a few seconds. If the actuality sound is not appropriate or available, and if narration is not needed, then consider music, or an "independent" sound track. The latter technique is described by the producer of "Terminus":

> There are times when the words can be quite independent of the visuals. In "Terminus," for instance, we made candid recordings in the booking office so that we could hear passengers asking for tickets to various destinations and the ticket clerk's replies. These words we placed over the visuals showing quite different station activities— we retained a perfectly free relationship between sound and picture—and of commentary, in the conventional sense, there is none.[10]

Music, too, can be effective not only in filling gaps in the audio, but in making a positive emotional contribution to the program. The best would be original music, such as the very powerful score by Virgil Thomson for Pere Lorentz's *The Plow That Broke the Plains*, which is now an American classic in its own right. That approach, of course, is very expensive, but an effective musical background can also be culled from recorded music libraries. Or, if the style is appropriate, you may be able to get a local folk music group to perform standard, noncopyright selections which you can use.

When narration is used, the most common approach is that of voice-over narration, in which an off-screen voice reads the commentary. Other techniques are available, however. The narrator might assume the role of a guide or questioner. He or she is then seen on-screen frequently, making comments and asking questions. In that role, the narrator becomes a surrogate for the viewers as they are guided through the content of the presentation.

Another technique uses an on-camera expert who speaks directly to the audience. News documentaries frequently place the reporter in that role. Another variation combines off-camera narration with an on-camera expert to provide a two-voice narration, as in the Cousteau script. It's a technique that is strong in audience involvement.

Yet another variation is that of the overhead conversation. The viewers "listen in" while two experts, or an expert and a subordinate, discuss a process or problem. This approach closely approximates the actuality, and is also good in maintaining audience involvement, if it can be written to appear natural.

## Don't Preach

On this point we have often been misunderstood. There is considerable and legitimate disagreement among critics, producers and writing instructors on the editorial position to be expressed within a public affairs documentary. Many people feel that such documentaries should take a stand on whatever topic is presented. They argue that if there is a social wrong to be exposed, the station or network should perform that task. Others take a more neutral position; they feel that controversial topics should be examined from different perspectives. We have no quarrel with any of the various positions that might be taken. These are legitimate management decisions. Station and network managers, including perhaps producers and writers, will decide what topics should be addressed and how strong a position should be taken on any particular topic.

Fairness is an important consideration, although, as we have noted previously, it is no longer mandated by the FCC. But that is not the point we want to make. The point we do want to make is that if a public affairs documentary is well written and presented, it need not push an obvious editorial position. Frequently, in doing the research on a topic and in preparing the treatment for the program, you will find that there is a social injustice involved, and you will want to bring that injustice to light in the program. But don't *tell* the audience what the problem is, and don't *tell* people what they should feel or believe with regard to the issue: *Show* them. *Document* the problem, and *document* proposed solutions.

To return to our program on the elderly poor as an example, you may find that these people really are receiving poor treatment at the hands of their landlords. Don't preach. Don't point out the obvious. And don't tell audience members how terrible the situation is, or what they should be feeling. Frequently there is a backlash in such an approach; audiences resent being talked to in that way. Instead, take advantage of the documentary's ability to involve the audience. Follow some of these elderly people through their activities, as described earlier.

Let the actualities speak for themselves. If the scenes you show have been wellchosen, and if the viewers really do have the feeling of being involved in the plight of these unfortunate people, the audience will come willingly to the conclusion you want. Then, in a brief summary to the program, the narrator can channel that emotional reaction and suggest ways in which viewers can make their concerns felt—letters or calls to government agencies, contributions, or whatever is appropriate.

## Re-creation: An Ethical Problem

In shooting and editing the documentation—that is, the raw material for the documentary—we have emphasized the value of using real experiences the audience can respond to in emotional terms. But suppose a particular sequence is not available on film or tape. Perhaps the camera was not there when the event took place, or through an error the footage is unusable. To what extent is it legitimate to re-create a visual sequence?

In the docudrama, or any other historical re-creation by whatever name it is called, the entire program is re-created, dramatized, even though it may be based on carefully researched information. Critics sometimes complain that these programs are not sufficiently accurate historically, but audiences generally understand that these are dramatizations and accept them as such.

On the other hand, the audience watching a documentary will assume that the material is real. To what extent in that situation is re-creation acceptable? In "Terminus," the producer used a combination of ordinary people and "planted" actors

> who could be brought in to act the more complex parts, and give point and emphasis to the more difficult sequences. . . .
> They each had a part to play, among the ordinary passengers. One was a man who was late and just missed his train—both morning and evening—and retired frustrated to the bar. Then the little lost girl was "planted," although the later tears were genuine enough. The whole thing proved rather much for her. Among the other "planted" actors were, of course, the prisoners on their way to Dartmoor—we shouldn't have been allowed to film real prisoners and reveal their identify.[11]

Another producer was making a program on the blooming of the California desert in the spring, with "flowers blossoming, lizards blinking awake. But the lizards were not cooperative, so [he] stuck them in the refrigerator; when it came time to film, they warmed up appropriately on camera."[12]

Any re-creation involves some dramatization, or perhaps better stated, fictionalization. So what is an acceptable level of fictionalization? When is that level exceeded? When does the staging of an event become distortion? If a simulation or re-creation does take place, is it faithful to the original situation? Or was it staged to support a predetermined editorial position?

We're very good at asking the questions; answering them is another matter. These are ethical judgments. They all touch on the very sensitive issue of editorial discretion. And the answer will have to be: It depends.

In the creative documentary on the musical premiere, there would be little problem in asking the symphony conductor to re-create a scene in which he works out passages of the music on the piano. It is less clear, however, in the public affairs documentary. Is it appropriate to re-create the scene of a handicapped senior citizen struggling up a flophouse stairway? Visually, it's a powerful image, and probably it's faithful to the overall point of view of the documentary. But is it honest?

If the topic of the documentary is controversial, as we have made our program on the elderly poor, then there are likely to be attacks by those holding another opinion on the accuracy and honesty of the presentation. It will do your credibility no good if they are able to prove that you faked even one scene. Be careful.

If the issue is legitimate, and if you approach the documentation with an open mind and not a closed editorial policy, you should be able to document fairly. But if you assume that these hotel managers rent filthy rooms and don't clean up their hotels, and then you can't find the filth and have to scatter a can of garbage down the hall, you have not treated the topic fairly.

A directly parallel situation exists with regard to editing the material to be shown in the documentary. Take care to edit fairly, to show a balanced view of what you saw when you were collecting the visual material in the first place. In recent years, we have seen a number of cases in which documentary producers and the stations and networks that have aired their programs have been sued for libel, or have been the subject of congressional investigation, as a result of charges of biased editing, of taking statements or scenes out of context. It goes beyond the scope of this text to comment on these charges. Nor can we provide any advice that would protect the writer-producer against similar accusations in the future. If the program investigates a controversial issue, if there is a social wrong to be righted, you may expect attack. Your defense will be the truth, both in the presentation itself and in the process by which you developed the program.*

* One of the disquieting grounds which the Supreme Court now permits claimants in a libel suit to use as part of their suit is to inquire into the "state of mind" of the program's writers and producers, to see if "actual malice" might have been present in the process of writing and editing the program. We expand on this matter in Chapter 17, but for a concise review, we recommend Sydney Head and Christopher Sterling, *Broadcasting in America*, 6th ed. (Boston: Houghton Mifflin, 1990), pp. 466–468.

# RADIO DOCUMENTARIES

Thus far our examples have referred exclusively to visual documentation, using film or videotape to collect the images out of which the video documentary is made. The form can be presented on radio as well, but it's not easy to do. If we attempt to apply to radio all the characteristics we set forth as distinguishing the documentary form, then very few radio programs will qualify. Some of these characteristics are very hard to build into a radio program.

It's much more difficult, for example, to get audience involvement in a problem or process when audiences cannot see what's going on. The sounds of an activity without the accompanying visuals do not effectively or accurately place the audience into the situation. Only if audience members have had some prior experience in similar situations will they be able to develop mental images of what is going on, and even then their mental view will be conditioned by their prior experiences and will not likely be accurate in reproducing the image you want to portray in your program.

In describing our program on the elderly urban poor, we have used visual images—struggling up a stairway, rats on the walls. The sounds of these activities are not helpful. The voices of the people who suffer these conditions would help; they can describe their problems and frustrations. But now you're putting together a news interview program, something that is no longer really a documentary.

A radio documentary on the development of a new symphonic work should be possible, since the topic is aural to begin with, but we'll miss those wonderful images of seeing the composer react to the first performance of his work. We'll have to be content with asking him his reactions afterward. A radio documentary on the preparation of a new ballet, to choose a parallel topic, would be very difficult, and you would probably have to revert to interview and discussion.

Effective radio programs on documentary topics almost always require a considerable amount of narration, another characteristic we tried to avoid in the TV documentary. Narration is necessary to give accurate descriptions, to introduce, and to bridge between whatever sound documentation is to be used.

So although radio programs can be developed in many of the same content areas we have described for the TV documentary, and although they can be equally effective, they must use different techniques in order to be successful. The differences diminish the distinctive qualities of the documentary. Many radio stations that advertise documentaries on local issues are really producing extended news stories or some cross between news and a public affairs interview/discussion program.

The one organization that consistently comes the closest to meeting all the characteristics of the documentary on radio is National Public Radio. The quality of the writing and editing on its *Morning Edition* and *All Things Con-*

*sidered* programs is excellent. The verbal descriptions of locations, events and people provide strong images for listeners. The script uses an extensive but very descriptive opening narration to set its locale and the topic, and then—to a greater extent than most radio stories—it allows the actual voices of participants to carry the remainder of the story.

# CONCLUSION

We began this chapter with two brief quotes that set forth contrasting views of what should constitute a documentary. On the one side is a view that documentaries should be limited to "authoritative, journalistic" presentations. The other view is that documentaries can encompass the "more personal and idiosyncratic vision of virtually anything with general significance." Those two quotes come from a pertinent and provocative article entitled "The Last, Best Hope for the TV Documentary" by Philip Weiss.[13]

Weiss is concerned about the future of the genre. He even uses the terms *suffering* and *dying* to describe the plight of the documentary form. Although documentaries are still fairly commonly found on public television and some cable networks, they have largely disappeared as independent programs from prime-time and network schedules. And when the networks do take the risk of presenting a prime-time documentary on a major social issue, audiences are small. Even *The Civil War* was seen by comparatively small audiences because it was broadcast on public stations, although it should be noted that it has picked up additional viewers through videotape sales and rentals and its use in schools. We also exclude the very popular *60 Minutes* and its counterparts on the other networks. Although the segments that appear in these programs are often referred to as "minidocumentaries" and use documentary techniques in part, they rely more heavily on news, interview and other talk-program techniques.

And yet, documentary writers and producers know that no more powerful form exists with which to arouse public opinion and promote social change. They continue to seek ways to attract audiences to their ideas, and in so doing some producers have expanded the traditional, journalistic approach to the more encompassing and more dramatic, and thus have brought on the controversy over what is a proper form for the genre or proper topics to be presented.

While there are few separate social issue documentaries being produced and aired at the network level, there are other outlets. Documentary techniques are used in many short pieces aired within local newscasts. We cite the AIDS program from this chapter as an example.

Cable access channels also provide a very available outlet for independent documentary productions. In those cases, production funding usually will have to come from other sources. Corporate production, the topic of our next chapter, is yet another outlet for the documentary writer-producer.

MAPLE SUGARING

NOAH ADAMS        At just about the right time, at the time it really
                  needs to, spring begins to come to New England. The
                  snow still falls, but it's softer and wetter. The sun
                  is up earlier and stays later. The frozen ground gets
                  muddy. The nights are still cold and crisp, below
                  freezing, but daytime temperatures climb into the
                  forties and the low fifties. On the snow-covered
                  hillsides, deep inside the sugar maple trees, the sap
                  begins to flow. The sap of a sugar maple contains about
                  1 or 2 percent sugar. If you drill a hole into the
                  tree, the sap drips out. If you collect the sap and
                  boil it down, you've got maple syrup. Boil it some
                  more, you've got sugar. It takes about thirty-five
                  gallons of sap to make one gallon of syrup. It works
                  out just about like this: Each spring one sugar maple
                  tree will produce enough sap to make one gallon of
                  maple syrup.

                      In late February, in the Connecticut River valley of
                  Vermont and New Hampshire, the farmers get ready for
                  their first crop of the year. Donald Crane of
                  Washington, New Hampshire, likes to tap a couple of
                  trees early, as a test. Then each day he checks the
                  buckets. A couple of weeks back, in March, Art Silver-
                  man stopped by the Crane farm to see how the 1978 sea-
                  son was going to be, to see if the sap was flowing yet.
                                    MORE MORE MORE

**Figure 14.6.** From *Every Night at Five: Susan Stamberg's* All Things Considered *Book.*
Copyright © 1982 by National Public Radio. Reprinted by permission of Pantheon Books, a
Division of Random House, Inc.

| SFX | CREAKING/GROANING/SAP DRIPPING BEATS |
|---|---|
| SILVERMAN | Where're the buckets that you have up now? |
| CRANE | They're right here beside the road. You didn't notice them? |
| SILVERMAN | No. |
| CRANE | You're not very observant. |
| SFX | WALKING/SNOW CRUNCHING |
| SILVERMAN | Let's concentrate on not falling down and not stepping in anything. |
| CRANE | Well, it's a good idea to look down because you have two things in sugarin' that bother your footin'. One's ice. The other's mud. |
| SILVERMAN | And if you have a few oxen there might be a few other things? |
| CRANE | Well, that's why a farmer never looks up. |
| SFX | BUCKET SOUNDS/WALKING |
| CRANE | I tapped this tree three days ago. See that little icicle right there? That means the tree's willing, but it can't do it. And this one over here is just as dry as can be. You see, this tap is a little more to the west; that one is a little more to the southeast, and it apparently just hasn't got warm enough right here yet. Those trees are froze clear through, you know. So it takes a little time to get 'em loosened up. |
| SFX | TAPPING SOUNDS/CLANKING BUCKET HANDLES |
| ADAMS | For those who are involved in the sugaring, the beginning of spring means about six weeks of hard work for everyone in the family. Someone has to cut the firewood. Someone has to haul the sap buckets. And |

MORE MORE MORE

**Figure 14.6.** (continued)

there's another problem: Almost every day is laundry day.

FIRST WOMAN       Because maple sap is very sticky, and when it's boiling away it seems like it's a rather nice pretty cloud of white steam coming off the evaporator, and it's very tempting to lean over and kind of smell that steam coming off the evaporator.

SECOND WOMAN      But, unless you want to look like a candy-coated apple, you don't do it.

FIRST WOMAN       You don't do it. Nope.

SECOND WOMAN      No.

FIRST WOMAN       No. Because that steam is very sticky. It's pretty and it smells really nice, but it gets on everything-- everything! Everything you own smells like maple syrup after a while.

SECOND WOMAN      Right.

FIRST WOMAN       And it takes so long. The amount of time that they spend preparing the maple syrup doesn't include the hours that those of us who don't tap and collect and boil spend supporting the people that actually do those things. By "supporting" I don't mean just feeding them, but I mean washing their clothes, getting their meals, picking them up, driving them home to sleep for four hours before getting up and driving them back up to the sugar house so that they can boil some more. Dealing with meals for lots and lots of people.

SECOND WOMAN      Hearty meals that are going to be served to all of the people who come help. Instead of pay.

FIRST WOMAN       Regular meals.

**Figure 14.6.** (continued)

| | |
|---|---|
| SECOND WOMAN | Regular. |
| REPORTER | That's a lot of work. Is it worth it? Do they make much money? |
| FIRST WOMAN | Not at all. |
| SECOND WOMAN | No. |
| FIRST WOMAN | They wouldn't do it if they really had to make a living at it, because they wouldn't be able to. Takes too much time. It's a passion, and that's the only reason they're doing it. Something happens when you start tapping a tree and you see little stuff dripping out of it, drip-drip-drip, and then a few days later you pour it out of a can. There's just some magical thing that happens, and they all get addicted. |
| SECOND WOMAN | In the springtime, when the trees start to operate, you want to be in on it. You want to watch spring start up right from the beginning. You want to watch the sap starting to run. And during sugaring season, you're just so intimately involved with the coming of spring, it's like you breathe the coming of spring. |
| REPORTER | You forget everything else? |
| FIRST WOMAN | Yeah. You don't even worry about mud season anymore. |
| SFX | MUSIC/TAPPING/WHISTLING |
| TEACHER | Can you get maple syrup out of any other tree except a maple tree? |
| CHILDREN | No! No! No! |
| FIRST CHILD | You can get it out of an oak tree. |
| SECOND CHILD | You can only get oak out of oak trees. Eric's being ridiculous. |

**Figure 14.6.** (continued)

1. Prepare a concept statement for one of the following:

   a. A documentary on a creative effort

   b. A nature documentary based on a location (such as a forest or a swamp) or on an animal or plant (unique local butterflies, an endangered plant species, or something similar)

   Choose a real topic with which you are already somewhat familiar or can readily get information, to ease the burden of research.

2. Prepare a three-part minidocumentary series or "special report" on a topic of your choice, but one that might legitimately be found on the late-night news broadcast of a local TV station. Each segment should be planned for about 4 minutes of airtime. One segment (probably the first, but not necessarily) should be a detailed treatment. The other two may be more loosely outlined. For the detailed segment:

   a. Follow the appropriate format for television news scriptwriting.

   b. Make sure there is ample visual description. What are we supposed to be seeing at all times?

   c. If sound bite interviews are used, the questions or the leads to the answer (if the actual question is not to be heard) should be written out completely. (The sound bite itself need not be written word for word, but give a suggestion of what is expected in the answer, and the out-cue. You will have to anticipate much of this, since you wouldn't know for certain what would be said until you actually went on location.)

   d. Pay particular attention to the sequential development of the material, and to the use of appropriate and adequate transitions, so the audience will know at all times where the story is leading.

   For the other segments:

   a. Write out the open and the close completely.

   b. Provide a sequential outline for the remainder of the segment, indicating each major content point to be made, and a general description of the visual material you would try to collect to support each point.

   Overall, make sure there is an obvious and logical division of the topic into the three segments; at the same time, each segment will stand on its own. Keep in mind that the less narration, the better. Let the real scenes and people tell the story as much as possible. But be careful to provide sufficient narration so that the audience can follow the progress of the story.

## Notes

1. Gordon Croton, *From Script to Screen: Documentaries,* 2d ed. (Borehamwood, Hertfordshire, UK: BBC Television Training, 1989), p. 35.
2. Philip Weiss, "The Last, Best Hope for the TV Documentary," *Channels of Communication,* November–December 1983, p. 86.
3. Ibid.
4. Dudley Moore, presenting the awards for documentary film production at the 1983 Academy Awards show.
5. Edith Efron, "The Great Television Myth," *TV Guide,* May 6, 1967, p. 9.
6. A. William Bluem, *Documentary in American Television* (New York: Hastings House, 1965), p. 104.
7. Iain Blair, "The Making of *Thriller,*" *On Location,* February 1984, pp. 124–125.
8. W. Hugh Baddeley, *The Technique of Documentary Film Production* (New York: Hastings House, 1963), p. 24. Excerpts reprinted by permission of Focal Press and the author.
9. Ibid., pp. 24–25.
10. Ibid., p. 197.
11. Ibid., p. 27.
12. Weiss, "The Last, Best Hope for the TV Documentary," p. 85.
13. Ibid.

## Further Reading

There are only a few recent titles that deal primarily or exclusively with video documentaries. Most general production and news production texts contain sections on documentary production. Earlier references, some still very useful, focused on the film documentary, and of course many of those techniques can be transferred to television. Hugh Baddeley's text quoted in the chapter is one such example.

Baddeley, W. Hugh. *The Technique of Documentary Film Production,* 4th edition. Stoneham, MA: Focal, 1975.

Bluem, A. William. *Documentary in American Television.* New York: Hastings House, 1965.

Croton, Gordon. *From Script to Screen: Documentaries,* 2nd ed. Borehamwood, Hertfordshire, UK: BBC Television Training Manuals, 1989.

Ellis, Jack C. *The Documentary Idea: A Critical History of English-Language Documentary Film and Video.* Englewood Cliffs, NJ: Prentice Hall, 1989.

Hewitt, Don. *60 Minutes: Minute by Minute.* New York: Random House, 1985.

Rabiger, Michael. *Directing the Documentary.* Stoneham, MA: Focal, 1987.

Wolverton, Mike. *Reality in Reels: How to Make Documentaries for Video/Radio/Film.* Houston, Gulf, 1983.

For radio, the book from which we took the "Maple Sugaring" script is the only source of scripts that approach documentary style.

Stamberg, Susan. *Every Night at Five: Susan Stamberg's* All Things Considered *Book.* New York: Pantheon, 1982.

# Corporate/Instructional Programs

**I**n this chapter we describe scripts for corporate clients (for example, employee training, promotion or sales) and for instruction. We have abbreviated the two most common descriptive terms of such scripts, *corporate* and *instructional,* into C/I. Other labels used for this form are "institutional," "industrial," or, simply, "nonbroadcast."

Throughout the earlier chapters, we have emphasized basic principles that underlie all good writing for electronic media. We believe it is both possible and legitimate to generalize on considerations of style, structure and gratifications, among other things, because there are certain constants in the communication process when radio and television are used as the media for the delivery of the message.

For the most part, those basic principles also apply to the preparation of C/I presentations, and any or all of the forms of presentation—news, talk, drama, documentary—discussed in other chapters can be applied to C/I scripts. But there is one crucial difference. Corporate/instructional programs generally are *not* presented to audiences through broadcast. Instead, the content is most often delivered by some form of closed-circuit system. Under those circumstances the audience's involvement with the presentation may be changed substantially, and if it is, so are the writer's concerns. The focus of this chapter, then, differs from previous ones in that we concentrate on how the writer is affected by differences in the delivery of C/I programming.

When you finish this chapter, you will be able to

- sense the broad scope of C/I presentations and the opportunities they present for writers,

- understand how nonbroadcast delivery affects the structure and content of C/I writing,

- rephrase basic research questions for C/I presentations and apply the modified questions to C/I scripts,

- write treatments and scripts for C/I clients, and

- recognize and use these important terms and concepts:

audience interaction

closed-circuit (nonbroadcast)
   delivery

forced exposure

multimedia instruction

purpose: needs assessment,
   learning objectives

video news release (VNR)

telecourse

# TYPES OF C/I PROGRAMS

Within the two broad categories—corporate and instructional—we describe a number of programs with different purposes, different content, different means of presentation in different settings and for different target audiences. From this admittedly incomplete collection we hope to provide you with a sense of the tremendous variety of C/I programming while showing how the basic principles of research and preparation apply to them all. The actual scripts, or portions of them, are reproduced for some of these programs.

*Sales and sales promotion:* Since television and television commercials are so much a part of everyone's daily life, it's no surprise that companies have extended the use of video to assist with product sales in other ways. One common use is point-of-purchase sales, where videotapes are shown on small automatic players within a store. Often the tape is seen by only one customer at a time and is set up so that the customer can start the playback. The manufacturer of the product and the store have designed the video to assist a salesperson in explaining the product and its features and in making a sale.

You've undoubtedly seen some of these—for skis, perhaps, or kitchen appliances. We'll refer to a video we saw that advertises a riding lawnmower. Similar playback arrangements are used at conventions and conferences. A playback unit in the booth on the exhibit floor attracts individuals so that the staff in the booth can follow up with a sale.

The distinction between sales and promotion videos is often pretty slight. Promotional programs are frequently produced to support sales campaigns, but they use less obvious, low-key techniques. Our three examples might be placed in either category.

"Learning," a promotion for the Apple Computers educational marketing division. It focuses on applications for computers in elementary and secondary classrooms.

"San Francisco Is . . . ," a production for the San Francisco Convention and Visitors Bureau. This tape uses lush photography, striking color, and fast-cut images to build the desire to travel to and experience San Francisco.

"Saddle Rock Ranch," a video to promote a horse breeding farm. The target group was horse owners who might want and who could afford to have their mares bred at this farm.

*Attitude change:* One video we saw that neatly describes this category was produced for orthodontists. Children may hate going to the dentist, especially to one who puts braces and rubber bands all over their mouths. So maybe a video would be a good way to give children a more positive feeling about the experience? This tape was shown to children visiting an orthodontist's office for the first time. It explains the importance of having good, straight teeth and how an orthodontist can straighten them. But, as we'll see, it wasn't totally successful.

*Employee training:* We were particularly struck by an approach used by General Foods Corporation for training lift truck operators. Its producers explain the problem they faced:

> The level of training and on-the-job efficiency of more than 600 lift truck operators is of vital importance to General Foods. The company sells over seven billion packages of product in this country each year, and it's the job of the lift truck operators to load and unload that mountain of product onto and off of the fleets of trucks and railroad cars that keep it all moving through the distribution pipeline.

Management wanted a training program for these employees. The solution, which we will talk about at various points in the chapter, was to produce two 30-minute programs that covered "safety, sanitation, preventive maintenance, loading and unloading methodology, and dunnage requirements— in a format that GF management certainly never expected, but was delighted with once it saw the results."

A game show format was chosen for the programs, which were titled "Highstacks I" and "Highstacks II."

> As the familiar game show format unwinds on the screen, [the viewers] become personally involved in the questions and answers that encompass between 60 and 70 instructional points important to lift truck operators. And while the contestants on the screen move through the game show's familiar series of main rounds, lightning rounds, bonus rounds and commercials, the lift truck operator audience moves along with them, laughing at their foibles, exalting in their correct answers, groaning at their apparent shortcomings, and learning all the way.

That, of course, is the point. They're learning. The game show format is functioning as an instructional and motivational device to make learning easier and more attractive—creating an environment in which new employees can acquire needed information in an interesting, nonthreatening way, and experienced operators can learn the errors of their ways without criticism.[1]

*Individual education:* The King Accelerated Schools produce and market video courses designed to prepare pilots and aircraft mechanics to pass FAA exams. Each course contains 10 to 14 hours of video, plus supporting printed materials—notebooks, forms, exam questions, etc. These videos are marketed through ads in magazines. You can watch the videos in your own home when and as often as you like. The company has successfully tapped into a highly motivated target audience—pilots, potential pilots and others interested in private flying. The audience is also sufficiently upscale to afford individual tapes at $24 and courses at $129.

*Interactive instruction:* This area is the newest and most exciting subfield in writing and producing C/I materials. Schools at all levels from kindergarten to postgraduate are purchasing and producing many programs (using that term now in both its audiovisual and computer senses) that direct students through individualized self-paced learning, using a variety of devices—videotape, videodisc, slide-tape, audiocassette, and CD-ROM players and personal computers. In recognition of the many possible devices that may be included as parts of interactive systems, the area is increasingly being described by the term *multimedia* production or instruction.

For example, many classrooms now have videodisc players. These units can store thousands of individual video frames on each disc and display them on command on a TV screen, as either still frames or motion video. One company which operates in this field, the Pioneer Electronic Corporation, markets a system that combines a personal computer, videodisc player, monitor and software with a barcode reader. Its system (LaserDisc) is not only interactive, but individually so. Each student works through a lesson independently. Access to material is determined by the student's responses to preceding material. Here the media writing task is only part of the overall instructional and computer software design.

*The video news release (VNR):* A cross between a C/I presentation and a news story, these videos are produced by (or for) corporations for distribution to local TV news departments. Here's how one corporate producer, working for the 3M Company, describes her first experience with VNRs:

I first heard the term video news release (VNR) about four years ago when a fellow producer and I were asked to put one together in less than 24 hours.

The 1987 America's Cup yacht races were underway, and our company, 3M, was supplying a new type of hull coating to the American team. It was a great story, and everyone wanted to cover it. However, because the races were in Freemantle, Australia, not everyone had the resources to do so. It turned out to be a perfect public relations opportunity.

Using beautiful footage shot for us by an Australian crew, we put together a VNR about the American yacht's "new secret weapon," the 3M hull coating. Not only did we get a lot of publicity when we released the VNR, but also nearly every time reporters mentioned the races over the next few weeks, they mentioned our product.

Since then, 3M has become fond of VNRs. Our department, Audio-Visual Communications, has produced many for our internal clients, and it's a practice that we'll most likely continue as long as there are television newscasts.[2]

The attractiveness of VNRs, especially to smaller and poorer news operations, is that they are already produced, are often very slickly done, and are free. That's one less story that the local news crew has to prepare. However, there are some ethical considerations. Is the story really news, or just free hype for the company? We consider that issue in a later chapter. Note, too, that VNRs are prepared for broadcast use. Throughout this chapter we emphasize the implications of nonbroadcast delivery, so VNRs are in that sense an exception to our exception.

## IMPLICATIONS OF NONBROADCAST DELIVERY

As we have noted, many C/I presentations are not delivered to their audiences by broadcast. Most often the delivery system will be some sort of closed-circuit system, and frequently it will be a playback device that is actually present in the same room with the audience. When that situation exists, two of the fundamental characteristics of broadcast communication are no longer operative: (1) *Repetition is possible*. No longer does the content pass by the audience only once, without provision for repetition. (2) It is now possible to have *immediate feedback* from the audience to the source of the message, and therefore also possible to modify the message in some ways during its delivery. This possibility is not always taken advantage of, but often it is there.

Contrast these altered characteristics with those originally postulated for broadcast delivery (Chapter 2), where the presentation must be linear, with speed and sequence totally controlled from the source. Now the audience can interact with the presentation. A videotape can be stopped and started, either at preplanned pauses to allow for group discussion, or just because the audience members decide to stop it.

Control of the flow of the presentation by the recipients may also make it possible to use a combination of "live" presenters along with the mediated material, and/or to integrate printed materials with the electronic delivery. This presentation can also be designed to branch in different ways to meet the needs and interests of very small groups of people, even of individuals, in the target audience.

The use of a nonbroadcast delivery system also modifies the program-audience relationship in two additional ways that are critical for the writer. It creates the possibility of *forced exposure* of the audience to the program, and that, in turn, may affect the *gratifications* audience members receive from their exposure.*

## Forced Exposure

In the early chapters we placed considerable emphasis on the necessity of using style, structure and gratifications that will attract and hold audiences, because the audience members always have the option of doing something else—changing the channel or finding some other activity—if the program is not interesting. Several of the examples we are developing in this chapter are ones in which the audience members do *not* have that choice. The lift truck operators, for example, must watch "Highstacks" as part of the requirements for the job. Their viewing is forced, and at least some pressure exists to watch and learn.

In another forced-viewing situation, this author and his children were on our first visit to the orthodontist when we saw the tape mentioned earlier. The doctor's assistant turned on the VCR, and we were instructed to sit in the waiting room and watch the videotape before the dentist would appear. Neither the content nor the style of the presentation was appropriate for us, and so we sat there but didn't pay much attention. In this particular case the doctor's staff should not have used the tape. The content and presentational style were aimed at a younger target group, and for us the result was attitude change all right, but negative.

In contrast, the producers of "Highstacks" knew that even though one may be forced to sit in a room and be exposed to a presentation, it does not necessarily follow that individuals will be attentive and actually learn anything. So they included strong gratifications for their target group. In summary, even when viewing is forced, the presentation will not accomplish its purpose unless there are some gratifications for each individual to get from the experience.

---

* Of course, not all instructional materials are delivered by closed-circuit systems or in interactive formats. Corporate and instructional productions also appear from time to time on broadcast and cable channels, and when broadcast delivery is used these presentations are subject to all the principles and limitations that affect all the other types of content delivered by that means and that we considered in earlier chapters.

## Gratifications

The relative strengths of the gratifications received from the reception of corporate/instructional presentations are likely to differ considerably from those obtained from broadcast presentations. We emphasize the word *relative* because we believe that the overall list of gratifications does in fact remain the same, but the stronger gratifications in free-choice broadcast viewing, such as action, tension, sex appeal, comedy, and personalization, are not likely to be the stronger gratifications in forced-viewing situations. There value, importance, and information are likely to be stronger.

Consider, for example, the gratifications received by viewers of a broadcast college telecourse. Such presentations were fairly common on broadcast station schedules in the 1960s. Not many such series remain because more flexible and less expensive alternative delivery systems are available, but some colleges still produce their own courses, and others lease them from national syndicators. The series then are aired on local stations or cable systems. Viewers can watch at home, and if they enroll, pay the necessary fees and complete assignments and exams, they will receive college credit just as for any other course.

The enrolled viewers watch the programs as part of the requirements to receive college credit. They may have chosen the course solely to satisfy college requirements and get credit; they may not have any particular interest in the subject matter. For this group the expected gratifications are value and importance, *but those gratifications are achieved externally to the broadcast,* in the form of the credit, the degree, or the boost in salary from an employer as a result of having completed the course. These individuals will do whatever is necessary to get the credit, including watching the presentations if they have to. But if they can find a way to get the credit without watching, say, by reading the text and taking exams, they may choose that option. They have no commitment to the programs themselves.

Others will choose to watch the presentations (for this is a free-choice viewing situation) because they do get gratifications from the content, or possibly from the style of the programs. Information will be the primary gratification for this group. Value and importance may also be present, in the form of valuable or important content. If the script is well written, it might also include personalism in the form of an articulate, interesting instructor, and possibly comedy if the instructor presents the content in a witty manner. Curiosity and novelty may be present as well.

The tape on lift truck safety poses yet another problem in gratification. We have already established that this is a forced-viewing situation—a requirement of the job. The company wants to increase the level of training and on-the-job efficiency of its employees. But the employees may not be similarly motivated; they may feel that they already know how to do their jobs well enough. Writing and producing a program that contains gratifications for this audience, who may enter the viewing situation a bit hostile to the presentation, or at least unenthusiastic, will be a formidable challenge.

Research has shown, however, that a good way to overcome hostility and any implied threat to any employee from the instruction is to use an interactive format in which the audience members are encouraged to respond actively to the presentation. You already know how that was accomplished.

# PLANNING AND WRITING C/I PROGRAMS

We pointed out in other chapters that the broadcast writer is quite likely to leave the creative process before production takes place, having turned over the script to experts in other aspects of the production. The writer who is involved in corporate/instructional production, in contrast, may very well be involved in: (1) planning, including the writing of the script; (2) production, quite possibly as the director; (3) presentation, for the writer might also be the instructor for a course; and (4) two forms of evaluation, both the pretest of the message before it is delivered to its target audience and postpresentation evaluation, which assesses whether the program did in fact accomplish its purpose. We'll consider only the first of these four tasks, planning and writing. But you should develop skills in production, presentation, and evaluation as well if you are to work professionally in this area.

The planning function can be further divided into five steps: (1) defining purpose, (2) describing the target audience, (3) selecting the medium to be used for delivery, (4) organizing the content, and (5) selecting techniques for the presentation. The first two we've considered before with other types of content. The third we've not had to take into account previously, since up to now the only medium we've considered has been broadcast. The final two steps also differ from broadcast in part because of the different preconditions that may be set up by the first three steps.

## Defining Purpose

In two previous chapters we've worked through the process of identifying purpose. We began in Chapter 9 with a generalized discussion; then in Chapter 11, when considering announcements, we cautioned you to distinguish carefully both the long-range goals and specific purposes of your clients. A similar caution is appropriate here. Make sure your purpose is clearly stated and understood by all parties—client, producer, and, of course, you the writer.

The people who design educational marketing campaigns for Apple have as their long-range goal selling more Macintosh computers to schools. When they decided to produce "Learning," they probably asked themselves these questions and considered these factors:

Who makes the recommendations and decisions regarding purchasing of such as items as classroom computers? How can we build more supportive attitudes and greater acceptance of computers in the classroom within these groups that will ultimately result in purchases of our product?

Budgeting and purchasing decisions are made by school boards and by superintendents and other top administrators in larger districts where they are delegated that authority. These persons, in turn, receive recommendations from principals, teachers and curriculum specialists. Parents and students may also influence decisions, especially if they are aware of the value of computers from having units at home.

The best way to build support is through demonstration—document existing situations where computers in schools are having a substantial impact on learning.

Such a brief purpose statement gives all the participants in the production process a place to begin, and it controls the development of the script. As creative ideas begin to flow from writers and producers, the ideas should be checked to see that they adhere to the central theme.

Educational planners who are preparing more formal instructional programs often divide the purpose step into the *needs assessment* and the *learning objectives*. Their approach is worth consideration.

### Needs Assessment

As an example, let's go back to the lift truck operators. Assume there have been a number of minor accidents in the company warehouses. Management is concerned about employee safety and the costs to the company of disposing of damaged products. There is pressure to find a solution. From management's point of view, one logical way to attack the problem might be to authorize the preparation of an audiovisual presentation to be shown to employees. One can imagine a manager saying:

> After all, we have the video production folks down there and that's why we set up the unit in the first place—to help solve personnel problems. I'll bet they're just itching to produce a program. Give them the job and let them take care of the problem.

In this case the program worked, and very well, but in other circumstances the problem might not be solvable using an audiovisual presentation. There might be a morale problem. Warehouse supervisors might be treating employees unfairly, keeping them tense and edgy, which leads to a high accident rate. Or perhaps the warehouse is poorly lit, the products poorly stacked, or the aisles too narrow. There could be many possible causes.

We have taken minor liberties with the "Highstacks" story here and extended it far beyond its original scope, but to make a point. It may seem hard to believe that a client corporation would not know precisely the nature of a problem existing within the organization, but sometimes management's perceptions of a situation are not accurate, and the actual causes of a problem are not those the media production team is being asked to correct. If you are confronted with that kind of situation, it will require diplomacy and tact to insist to management that adequate research be done on the causes of the problem before any decision is made to use media to tackle the solution.

### Learning Objectives

Lists of learning objectives may be presented in a variety of forms. Frequently they are stated as *behavioral* objectives, in terms like these: "The learner will list from memory the six steps..." or "The learner will assemble the parts...."

We prefer instead this list, which was developed by our colleague at CSU, Sacramento, Patrick Marsh. He has identified nine categories of purpose, which he calls *strategies*.

To *inform*.... provides the receiver with new information in an effort to enable the receiver *to recognize* it. Recognition implies the ability to discriminate an item from other items in a set. Given several instances or items, an informed person would recognize or identify the appropriate one.

To *stimulate*.... attempts to elicit or prompt the receiver to recognize intuitive knowledge which may be fanciful or even false; the effort is *to elevate* implicit thoughts from the experience level to the explicit level.

To *interpret*.... attempts to create a context which enables the receiver *to retrieve* tacit knowledge... in essence, [tacit] means that we know more than we are able to tell. Interpretation enables the receiver to retrieve and then to communicate what was originally unaccessible and uncommunicable knowledge.

To *instruct*.... guides the receiver in the acquisition of knowledge, attitudes, or skills which may be performed by recall or demonstrated at will. Since the tactics of such guidance are differentiated, three sub-types of instruction are defined: To instruct (*details*) involves forming associations; to instruct (*concepts*) involves forming classifications; to instruct (*relationships*) involves forming relationships.

To *solve*.... guides the receiver through a selected process in an effort to identify a solution which reduces the gap between the desired state and the actual state of affairs. This strategy seeks to prevent further complaint or search after the "solution" is identified.

To *persuade (to promote)*. The strategies "to persuade" and "to promote" are similar with only one essential difference. In the strategy "to persuade," the source makes plausible intellectual and/or emotional appeals in an effort *to change* selected attitudes, beliefs, or values already held by the receiver. The change can be in either strength, direction, or both. The best evidence of change is the unsolicited change in behaviors related to the changed beliefs, attitudes, or values. The strategy "to promote" differs only in that it seeks *to mobilize* the changed attitudes, beliefs, or values to achieve a specific, desired action. Evidence of the desired action's performance is the criterion.

To *argue*. In [this strategy] which is defined here more narrowly than in popular usage, the source submits a reasoned case in support or in refutation of a particular proposition in an effort *to test* the case's adequacy against the receiver's most critical response. Successful argument means that the receiver has been unable to debilitate the source's case. The crucial difference between the strategies "to argue" and "to persuade" lie in their differing goals and methods. Persuasion attempts *to change* the receiver; argument attempts *to test* the case. Persuasion uses all available appeals; argument employs only reasoned discourse.

To *entertain*. . . . attempts *to hold* the attention or interest of the receiver in an effort *to divert or amuse*. Literally, to entertain means "to hold between," which connotes tension and suspense. The most general categories of amusement are probably inspiration, portrayal, and down-play. Evidence of having entertained takes various forms depending upon the category involved.

To *transform*. . . . guides the receiver through processes intended to cause the receiver *to reframe* his or her perceptions of the self and the situation or context so that his or her everyday activities in life reflect the reframed perceptions . . . its accomplishment is typically characterized by behavior changes on several dimensions.[3]

Use this set of objectives, or any other similar list, to test yourself. Can you clearly identify the intended outcomes of the program you are about to write? Which of these does the client wish the program to accomplish?

This very brief introduction to the complex issues raised in needs assessment and learning objectives is barely enough to begin. If you are to write instructional programs, we urge you to read some of the works on instructional planning cited in the Further Reading section.

## Describing the Target Audience

Any well-written program has a clearly defined target audience. We've discussed that concept in several previous chapters and already in this one. The difference between most C/I programs and broadcast programs in this regard is that the target for the C/I program is even more specific than for the most narrowly targeted broadcast. It might be just the nursing staff at one hospital, or a crew that performs only one assembly function on an automobile, or the lift truck operators. In these cases the audience is completely preidentified, and the time and place at which it will be exposed to the message can also be preselected.

The audience for the point-of-purchase sales presentation on the riding lawnmower is somewhat broader, although still not as broad as it would be if the client had decided instead to produce an ad for broadcast or cable TV. In this case, the manufacturer of the lawnmower has decided to produce a videotape extolling the virtues of this machine and to place copies of the tape, along with a player, in the showrooms of major garden supply dealers.

The client would be wise to choose those dealerships where nearby residents are likely to have large pieces of property. Those are the customers who are more likely to want a mower one rides like a small tractor, which is a large and expensive piece of equipment. The audience would be men (probably) who have come into the dealership. They might have been attracted to the showroom to see this product by a broadcast commercial, a newspaper ad, or some other means, or they may have come to buy some other product. But for whatever reason they have come, once inside the store they become the target audience for this presentation.

Narrowly selected target audiences are an advantage for the writer in that they make it much easier to tailor both content and approach to a specific group. However, the cost of a presentation goes up as the audience is narrowed. That is, when the fixed cost of production is divided by smaller audiences and fewer presentations, the cost per viewer is increased. At some point it becomes uneconomical to produce for a very small audience and necessary to generalize the presentation to a wider, less specific group.

The Apple video may seem to contradict this instruction. In our analysis in the preceding section, we identified several different potential target groups. Fortunately, they are all groups with a common interest—improving the learning of their students. A presentation that shows how computers contribute to that improvement can be effective with all these groups. Now, for this presentation we have defined a purpose and target audiences, and in the process we've also begun to form a broadly stated concept for the tape.

The orthodontist's videotape provides another example. We've already identified the problem. The presentation featured a actor in his midtwenties who played the role of a bumbling, comic "tooth fairy," an approach that was obviously intended for very young, unsophisticated children. For an audience of older children and adults it was very condescending. Since children's levels of interest, attention span, and ability to understand complex material change very rapidly, the orthodontist really needed a whole series of presentations, each one geared to a different age.

A highly specialized audience, but one that is easily identified, is targeted for the videotape for the horse breeding farm. It was intended to be shown only to the owners of mares who would be willing to pay substantial fees to have those mares bred to the sires owned by the farm. It was shown, by invitation only, at several shows and sales of high-priced thoroughbreds.

What is critical from the writer's standpoint is that a careful assessment be made of the target group. Not only must it be accurately identified, but a determination must be made on what content is relevant to those people (which is the area of gratifications) and how that content can be presented in an authentic manner.

If the targeted group is company employees, gathering the information to determine gratifications and to provide for authenticity in the presentation should not be difficult. You can get background information from personnel records, and arrangements can be made to observe the group or even meet with representatives from it if that would be helpful.

In the case of the lift truck operators, the program producers studied the educational levels and at-home TV viewing habits of the target group. They found that these employees frequently watch game shows at home on their own time. They enjoy the fast action, the rapid-fire give and take, and the excitement of tension-building situations in which a lot is riding on fast and accurate decisions.

With that information in hand, the possibility of using a game show format began to be considered. But the producers found that using such a format had both advantages and problems:

> On the one hand, it meant that a training program presented as a game show would be readily accepted by the target audience. On the other hand, it meant that, to be believable, the show would have to be authentic—not just a simulation of a game show, but as close to the real thing as possible. It would have to look, sound, feel, and above all, play like a real broadcast TV game.[4]

## Selecting the Medium

Frequently the corporate writer/producer, as opposed to the broadcast writer, will have the opportunity to choose the medium of delivery of the message. The writer who works for a radio or television station or an ad agency knows that his or her work will have to conform to the conventions established for those media, such as standard lengths for programs and announcements, the need to leave places in programs to insert announcements, and so on. In contrast, the corporate writer often will have the opportunity to suggest and possibly even to decide what delivery system will be used, and can ignore some of broadcasting's conventions.

The choice of delivery system will depend on at least four factors: the budget available for the production, the amount of time available to complete the production, the complexity and form of the concepts to be presented, and the circumstances under which the program will be shown to its audience.

### Budget

In some situations, programs will be produced "in house" by a media department of a corporation. An in-house department will probably have a fixed operational budget for all its activities, some fraction of which will be made available for each individual production. The allocation for your project often will be less than you would like to have, but if you approach management with a well-prepared proposal, with clear objectives and a well-thought-out budget, and if management understands that a successful outcome depends on a well-produced program, then you may be able to spend what you need.

Other corporations "contract out" their media presentations to companies that specialize in such production. Contract production involves careful negotiation, so that both parties know precisely what is to be produced, and at what price. That price will include not only all the direct costs of production but also overhead and profit for the contractor.

### Time

Allow sufficient time for proper planning and production, and then allow extra time for the inevitable problems that will arise and eat into your timetable. You may have scheduled an interview with the company president, for example, parts of which you intend to use as the basis for the narration of a program. But when the day arrives, the president has to cancel: He must go out of town for an important meeting. Or shooting is completed and you are ready to do the postproduction editing and a critical piece of equipment fails. Those things happen. The well-prepared writer-producer will have built a cushion into the schedule.

When a presentation must be done on a short schedule, then it will have to be done more simply. The result may not be as eye-catching or as effective as you would like, but if you must meet a deadline, meet it with the best presentation you can.

### Complexity of Content

If the information to be conveyed consists primarily of words, then a sound-only medium (audiotape) may be the most efficient. Even if there is some visual material to be presented, the low cost of preparation and presentation may still suggest audiotape, supplemented with some sort of printed handout.*

If a substantial amount of visual material must be presented, but the use of motion is not important to the learning, then slide-tape has traditionally been the preferred medium. However, there is a trend away from the use of

---

* We are not considering corporate or instructional presentations which use no audiovisual support at all, or nonmediated support such as chalkboards, display charts, and overhead projectors. Those types of presentations are not within our scope.

slide-tape presentations. They are being replaced with videotape even in those situations where the only visuals are still photos, because videotape eliminates some of the problems commonly associated with slide presentations, such as having slides stick in the projector or difficulties in synchronizing audiotape sound tracks with the slides. The use of videotape also permits the writer-producer to introduce special effects not possible with slides.

When the content of the presentation requires motion, then the choices are reduced to only two—videotape or film. A few corporate/instructional productions are still shot on motion picture film, and some producers still believe that film provides a final product with higher visual quality, more suitable if the presentation must be projected for large audiences. But for our purposes it makes little difference to the writer whether the program is shot on film or on video. Both approaches will require that the raw visual material be edited before the final production can be presented. About the only significant difference is that it takes longer to process film for editing, while videotape is ready to edit as soon as the electronic image is put on tape.

### *Circumstances of Presentation*

You will need to consider here how the presentation is best delivered to its audience or audiences. How easy must it be to operate? How many times will the presentation be shown? How frequently? How disastrous will it be if it doesn't come on at the precise time scheduled? What would happen if a slide were to jam in the projector? In short, how bulletproof must the presentation be?

## Organizing the Content

Now that you have defined purpose, described the target audience, and chosen the medium of presentation, you can begin to shape the content into specific form. You will be faced with questions like these: Will it be presented in a series of lessons to be broadcast so many a week over an entire semester, as is our telecourse? Will it be a single, one-shot presentation? If not, what sort of segmentation should be used? If the program is to be presented to groups, what activities should be planned to take place during breaks in the presentation? Should the audience be required to answer study questions, participate in group discussions, or take exams?

### *Audience Interaction*

One key consideration in the organization is the amount of interaction wanted or expected from members of the audience. We know from research studies that learners who are required to respond immediately after material has been presented are much better able to understand and retain that material than they are when no response is required. A program that encourages active responses from viewers draws them into a dialogue. It provides them with a chance to check and clarify their understanding of the information. They gain a sense of achievement because of their progress.

In addition, interaction is important for the producer-writer. It provides information on the effectiveness of the program, and points out difficulties learners may have with the content.

One study on video training programs found some additional benefits from programs that emphasize interactive instruction:

> The ... process is viewed by employees (trainees) to be a less authoritarian or hierarchical form of training and corporate communications than traditional linear means. Some users feel that interactive video is an important step in eradicating the invisible barrier that often hampers information exchange and learning. . . .
>
> No longer must employees wait for classroom training sessions (which are conducted sporadically) to clarify key information. . . .
>
> It was found that the privacy and concentration required in using the video technology produces a worker who is more independent, and "work-involved" in his or her actual work environment.
>
> Because interactive video emphasizes personal involvement, independent problem-solving, and self-initiated information retrieval, communications managers believe this training technology has cultivated a more mature employee who requires little supervision. It is clear that the technology's capacity to allow user control over the training and communications processes has functioned to nurture such positive employee attitudes as increased confidence and creativity.
>
> What is most surprising ... is the lack of data to confirm the feelings of depersonalization or other negative reactions because of an automated training process. The concerns that the technological intrusion into the workplace might cause isolation and other undesirable effects are based primarily on opinions and assumptions of those who have considered, yet have not actually used or tested, interactive training. Actual users report increased training satisfaction and improved job effectiveness among employees.[5]

Yet another benefit from an interactive presentation is that individuals can make mistakes without exposing their errors to other students or instructors—without, in effect, showing how "dumb" they are. They are able to work through the material without threat.

In general, the more complex the material to be learned, the more important it is that the audience become involved with the presentation and interact with it. If we were to construct a hierarchy of levels of interaction, at the one extreme would be presentations with no provision for interaction on the part of the audience, such as a telecourse, or any other "broadcast" program that calls for no active feedback from the recipients and proceeds linearly at a speed determined by the source.

The next level of interaction provides opportunity for the audience, either groups or individuals, to start and stop the presentation at will, and to back up for review by starting and stopping a videotape recorder or similar device. This is not a very high level of interaction, but at least it places some control in the hands of the recipients, not solely with the source. (If an individual should happen to have a VCR at home, he or she can easily convert a broadcast program with no built-in interaction, such as the broadcast telecourse, into this next level simply by recording the broadcasts for later review, then starting and stopping as he or she wishes.)

Another level of interaction would be introduced by using printed materials in conjunction with the mediated presentation—discussion guides, outlines, study questions, quizzes.

Yet another form of interaction takes place when an instructor or discussion leader is present along with the audiovisual presentation. Here the question becomes, which is the primary and which the secondary source of the instruction? Is the presentation to be made primarily by a "live" instructor, supplemented by audiovisual demonstration, or is the presentation made primarily by the videotape, and the "live" individual used as a discussion leader or to respond to questions? Either approach may be correct, given the specific circumstances. Primary emphasis on the mediated presentation will provide consistency and uniformity to the presentation, which may be important if that presentation has to be given frequently to different audiences. But a greater degree of flexibility is provided by giving the major instructional role to the "live" instructor.

At the top of our hierarchy a variety of learning materials can be integrated into the sort of individualized, interactive instructional system that we briefly described earlier, one that combines several types of computer-driven devices and that is responsive to the learning style and speed of individual students.

## Selecting Techniques for Presentation

When planning has been completed and it is time to begin actual writing on the script, the techniques available to the corporate/instructional writer are basically the same as those used in broadcast, although cost constraints and time considerations often force the use of the simpler forms of presentation. On the audio side, they range from single-voice narration through the use of music, sound effects, and multiple voices to full dramatic presentation. Visual techniques range similarly.

Recall that within each program or segment, the basic principles of program structure still apply. There should be unity, which should not be difficult to accomplish if purpose and objectives are clearly understood. There

should be variety, which may be more difficult to achieve. If ᴏ
eration, then costly techniques like location shooting, large amou...
production editing, or multiperson casts may not be possible.

Pacing, the idea of having program elements that will change frequently
to reattract audience attention, remains an important consideration, especially in linear, noninteractive presentations. But as we have shown, many
corporate/instructional presentations are broken up by nonmedia activities,
and therefore pacing is somewhat easier to accomplish.

Even climax should be considered. The audience members are more
likely to remember or to be persuaded by the material they receive near the
end of the program. So build the development of the content to conclude
with the most important points.

### Talking Heads

"Talking heads" is the simplest and least expensive visual technique: having
a person narrate, lecture, or explain on-camera. Interviews and panel discussions also fall into this category, except that more than one head is involved.
Writers and producers have mixed feelings about the use of heads, as is
shown by this comment:

> The face shot, or "big talking head," has been the bane of in-house,
> closed-circuit television. It smacks of low-budget production, ab-
> sence of visual material, and a real lack of creativity and imagination.
> We have all lost sleep over finding cutaways to hide a droning voice—
> talking away, paragraph after paragraph, in front of the camera.
>
> Admittedly, head shots do not make maximum use of the full po-
> tential of the television medium. But even as I hear the echoes of my
> supervisor's voice saying, "I don't want to see one talking head in
> this videotape," I still believe that talking heads have a deserved
> place on the screen. Creative things can be done with them to help
> them add an important dimension to the videotape program.
>
> We must remember that, for certain professions, there is a great
> advantage in using well-known, credible authority figures on camera
> when gathering testimonial footage or presenting lectures. At times,
> nothing is more important than letting practitioners talk directly to
> other practitioners.[6]

If you choose to or are forced to use talking heads for the bulk of your
presentation, consider these suggestions for minimizing the structural weaknesses that technique presents:

1. At the very least, make sure your talking head is articulate, or if you must
   use a poor speaker, pair that person with a second voice who is articulate, and use a two-narrator approach.

2. Get a presenter who is credible, one who is perceived as an authority by the audience. Audience members will be more likely to suffer the talking head if it is an individual who has recognized expertise in the content.

3. Try to place the talent "on location" rather than just in a studio. Use a location in an office, a shop, or outside the plant if appropriate. Or consider an atypical location such as driving to the factory, or at the talent's home doing some task not directly related to the content of the program, but which shows the talent in a comfortable, favorable situation.

4. Shoot silent footage on location, then use a professional voice to do nonsync voice-over commentary. Or use two voices, the expert and the professional narrator, as in the scripts for the *Cousteau Odyssey* programs (Figures 7.1 and 14.5).

5. Use actuality inserts as in a news broadcast. Select only the most succinct statements using the talking head of the authority, with most of the content paraphrased and delivered by a narrator.

6. Use role playing by actors; dramatize the situation.

7. Juxtapose different points of view. Intercut between different individuals and locations to avoid long sections of material from one source.

### *Other Techniques*

Any of the forms of presentation discussed in other chapters can under some circumstances be effectively used for C/I presentations. The production techniques used for news, for example, are used in preparing video news releases and in the regular newscasts that many corporations produce to be seen by their employees on in-house cable systems. Interviews, demonstrations, documentaries and role-playing dramas can also be used effectively in C/I production. Note the wide range of techniques used by the examples that we've been following.

The script for "Learning" evolves as a series of six minidocumentaries showing computers (Macintoshes, of course) being used in various classrooms, plus, for contrast, a reappearing sequence of vignettes in which one skeptical teacher gradually learns how to use a computer. The use of separate sequences gives different audience groups (those interested in different grade levels or subjects) better opportunity to relate to at least one segment. It also provides structural strength—variety and pace. There is no overall narration; portions of the exposition are divided among the teachers in each of the various segments. They, and the skeptical teacher, talk directly to the camera/audience but in very brief statements. Although each sequence was carefully staged, all were shot in documentary style, as if they were unrehearsed. The script describes what the scene should contain, but the final version was put together in the editing room. Although Apple computers are seen throughout, Apple is never mentioned, and at the end of the presentation only the Apple logo appears briefly on screen.

Figure 15.1 is the script for the first two documentary sequences and the first two vignettes with the skeptical teacher.

## Learning

**A vision video for Apple K-12 marketing**

**Final Version 2/15/91**

Writers:   Keith Yamashita, Doris Mitsch,
           Mark Krigbaum

Eclipse Productions, Inc.
Walnut Creek.CA

**Figure 15.1.** Courtesy of Apple K-12 marketing division.

*Black screen, school noises over. Schoolyard sounds, etc. Music in background. School bell rings. Schoolyard sounds stop. Fade in title:*

**Learning**

*Stephen Mitchell, an eleventh-grade history teacher, is a veteran who's been teaching for twenty five years. He's seen everything, and was, at least at first, skeptical of computers. He teaches at a tough, urban school.*

Mitchell (start with voice over (VO) and dissolve to face):
Twenty five years ago, I became a teacher because I believed that young people are this country's greatest asset. I chose teaching because I *knew* I could make a difference.

Maybe that sounds idealistic. But I still believe it.

*(Reminiscing, a bit)*

Back then, it was just me, a textbook, and a piece of chalk. And I did pretty well with that, you know.

*Tight shots of memorabilia from his early teaching career—a yearbook showing Mr. Mitchell in the teacher section, old textbooks, old photos of classrooms, yearly pictures of his students, and so on.*

Mitchell (VO):
Then the administration came to me and said, Mitchell, we're going to give you a computer for your classroom.

(pause)

I told them I didn't want one.

*Continue cuts of memorabilia. End with a shot of a plaque: "Stephen Mitchell—Teacher of the Year—Irving High School—1980*

I couldn't think of anything I needed a computer for.

**Learning**        **Final (vrs. 11)**        **Page 2**

**Figure 15.1.** (continued)

*Fade in to title:*

**Making connections.**

*Tight shot of Sheri Morgenstern speaking directly to the camera.*

Morgenstern:
Sometimes I worry that I'm boring them. I mean, it can be hard to get kids to care about physics!

*Tight shot of Student speaking directly to the camera.*

1st Student: (totally resistant)
What does physics have to do with anything?!!

*Cut directly to a full screen shot of video disk playback from the Visual Almanac, Point of View is the driver.– John F. Kennedy addresses Congress (May 1961) he pledges that America will put an astronaut on the moon before the end of the decade. (Don't show that it is Macintosh controlled yet)*

JFK:
"No single space project ... will be more impressive to mankind ... none will be so difficult or expensive to accomplish ... it is a heavy burden "

*Cut to a different Student*

2nd Student:
Physics is just a lot of useless math and formulas.

*Cut to Close up of the TV monitor. In live-action, we see the Apollo Mission's lunar lander module lifting off from the surface of the moon. Pull out to show that the image is being controlled by a Macintosh. Dissolve to a different Macintosh screen, the program is Physics Interactive. It is modeling the Apollo's Lunar Module as it attempts lift-off from the Lunar surface. The craft seems to lift slightly then drops back to the surface.*

*Cut to two students in a very lively "discussion", as they work on the Physics Interactive modeling program. Consider using the 1st Student from the opening of the scene as one of the team members.*

Student (agitated):
It's not working! What's wrong? (turns to classmate)

Learning          Final (vrs. 11)          Page 3

**Figure 15.1.** (continued)

Classmate (puzzled ):
I think it's too much mass for the force. Maybe the payload's too heavy.

*Cut to Sheri Morgenstern (the physics teacher) is at the front of the class, talking to the students. Andrew Dubberly a Civics instructor is sitting nearby listening.*

Morgenstern :(sync)
OK, for both classes: physics and civics. Let's talk about your team projects. You need to show how physics affected the course of history—or you can do it the other way around, and trace an historical event that led to an advancement in science.

Dubberly: Either way, it's important that you include both the science and history in your project.

*Cutback to the video disk image full screen. JFK concludes his speech to congress.*

JFK:
"In the eyes of the world, we will be judged, in our ability to provide leadership to the free world. It is for this reason, that we accept the challenge of landing an astronauton the moon and returning safely before the end of this decade." (this is not actual text)

*As the video clip of JFK's speech plays we dissolve to a close up of a student listening intently. We recognize this student as the 2nd Student from the opening of the scene. The one who said that Physics was just formulas and "stuff".*

Dubberly: (VO lead)
I teach civics. She teaches physics. This year we thought we'd do something *completely* different. And while at first you might not think the two subjects have a lot in common, you might be surprised...

Morgenstern:
We have some really bright students here, and we wanted to find a way to challenge them. We wanted to make the subjects more dynamic.

Dubberly (VO):
*This*approach allows us to do things we could only dream of before. We can take an important event in our nation's history and show the effect it had on economics, international politics, science, the arts—our students quickly discover how interconnected the events of our lives really are.

*Dissolve to a tight CU of the Lunar Lander simulation on the Mac - the LM has achieved lift off. We see it mid flight and hear a voice lead from our 1st student as he watches.*

**Learning**          **Final (vrs. 11)**

**Figure 15.1.** (continued)

500

First Student: (VO lead)
No way! How did you get it to work?

*He is standing behind the student who is working on the successful simulation. His other team member walks into frame. They are very interested in this because this guy has succeeded and they want to know how.*

Classmate: (matter of factly )
Did you check the formula? Are you using earth mass or lunar mass? *(looks them in the eye—slight smirk—obviously he is a better student)*

*1st team looks at each other with a "boy-are-we-stupid" blank stare, kind of look.*

*Quick cut to curser scanning planetary mass values in a chart. Cuts to the gravitation formula being called up from the interactive physics worksheet. CU of the lunar mass value being changed in the formula.*

*Blast-off! The little lunar lander simulation lifts off on the interactive physics program. A quick cut of the team reacting to their success.*

Morgenstern (VO):
I love physics. And now my students can see it the way I see it. Physics is more than just a list of equations. It's about powerful things, like putting an astronaut on the moon.

Dubberly:
And history isn't just names and dates. It's about struggle and sacrifice, events of national pride and difficult decisions. This is an interdisciplinary approach. And frankly, more interesting.

*(pause)*

*(VO over kids clustered around computer. Show tight shot of screen. We see a series of dissolves between important events : the atomic bomb, a black and white television image of civil rights actions, JFK once more, and the first step out onto the surface of the Moon )*

Morgenstern(with confidence):
And they're getting it. No—they get it.

**Learning**           Final (vrs. 11)

**Figure 15.1.** (continued)

**Mitchell mini-vignette—Part I**

*This next scene is a part of a longer story that is told throughout this video. It tracks Mr. Mitchell's first experiences with his Macintosh. It is intended to show Mitchell's transformation from a computer skeptic to a teacher who finds creative and appropriate uses for computers in his classroom.*

*It could be shot in black and white with minimal (or no voice overs), just sound and music.*

*In extreme close-up a finger comes into frame and turns on the power. Tight shot of Macintosh screen (perhaps Macintosh LC). Show smiling Macintosh icon. Cut to a shot of Mitchell—with a skeptical look on his face, half surprised and half intrigued.*

*End on shot of Mitchell speaking into LC microphone. "Uh, hello... This is Stephen Mitchell." He looks at the microphone as if he expects a response.*

*Fade to black.*

Learning          Final (vrs. 11)          Page 6

**Figure 15.1.** (continued)

Fade in title:

**Getting through.**

*Michelle Mills is a second-grade teacher. This vignette is set in her reading class. The reading class is no more than 15 students. The 15 are split into 2 groups — one group reads while the other does desk work. We hope to include one or two kids that have disabilities (obvious physical disabilities) in this scene. Mills teaches in an Urban school and her students come from a wide variety of backgrounds. (For those filmmakers who are wondering about the small class size — reading is typically taught this way. Mill's class might be 30 or more kids, but she will have 1/2 come early and 1/2 come late so they can work with a more manageable size — per Jenny House.)*

*The camera glides past students in a reading group. They are listening (or follow along) as one student reads out loud. (The book she is reading is one of the titles available on Discus books).*

Student: (*reading*)
Peter looked at the garden. "I want to eat those carrots," he thought. He remembered mother's warning. "Don't go near the garden," she said. (*She begins to struggle with one of the words. As she tries to sound it out, we hear the teacher off screen helping her figure it out.*)

*The sync sound audio of the student and teacher segue into the teacher's Voice Over comments.*

Mills (*VO, reflective, contemplative. Less like she is talking to us, and more that we are hearing her thoughts*):
I think one of the biggest misconceptions is that all kids are created equal...It's just not true... Some are very quick...

*Camera moves about the reading group. It settles briefly on individual students as they listen or read.*

Some are slower. Each of them learn in different ways. What works well for one student might not work at all for another.

*We cut to a close up of a Macintosh screen. We see Peter rabbit once again as he ponders his dilemma. Small hands move the mouse. In tight close up we see a section of text as it is high-lighted. The student listens intently as the words from the story are played back on the Mac.*

**Figure 15.1.** (continued)

**Mills:**

Some of my students have special needs. I know, for instance, that every year I'll have one or two students with learning disabilities ... and I have a growing number of students that speak English as a second language.

*Cut to a tight close up of the screen. One of the words is high-lighted and the mouse is double clicked. The word "garden" is translated into Spanish.*

**Mills:**

Here's my challenge. I want to create a classroom where each of my students can learn—and succeed. But it's more complicated than it sounds. Every student has a particular learning style...auditory, visual, tactile...if I can find ways to involve all their senses, I have a much better chance of getting through.

*As she speaks we dissolve into a group of kids working on a mix of computers (a few Apple IIe's, a GS, and an LC. They're using the computers to write Big Books—their own stories and illustrations.*

*The action is quick paced as they type in giant font and paste up pictures. The printer (an ImageWriter) is constantly buzzing back and forth across the page. Music comes up briefly.*

*We cut to one of the students reading her own Big Book to the class.*

**Student:**(*reading confidently from her own book*)

My brother's name is Ben. He plays football and swimming. He is very tall and gives me rides on his shoulders. (*points to a picture she drew*) Here's Ben, and that's me right down here ...

**Mills:** (*Voice over*)

So how do you know when you're making a difference?

I *know* I am making a difference. Sometimes it's obvious...and sometimes, it's not anything dramatic...it might be a small victory...when a student tries something new, like writing a story for the first time.

But each small victory is a step toward a much bigger success. When I see something like that, that's when I know I've found the right approach. That I'm really getting through.

**Figure 15.1.** (continued)

**Mitchell mini-vignette—Part II**

*Continuation of Mitchell scenario:*

*Two part scene:*

*Cut to a close up of a locker door, it is open and the books have been thrown in. A foot attempts to kick the door closed but it takes two or three tries. We cut to an extreme long shot of a heavily back lit hallway as the tall silhouette of a student walks toward the exit. He bounces a basketball every couple of steps creating an echoing sound through the empty building. Mitchell sits at his desk working on his Macintosh. The screen lights his face.*

*Jump cut to closer shot of Mitchell. Then to a shot of the Mac.*

*He is changing the tab on a WriteNow file. As he does, the sound of "click -click- click" gives the process an almost tactile feeling. He seems intrigued as the paragraph titled "Lesson Plan" indents automatically to the tab's dotted line. He changes the setting again, its obvious that he is "playing" with the software -- he finds this simple function amusing. And he's learning a lot.*

In "San Francisco Is . . . " the producer, Eclipse Productions, described its task this way:

> The real challenge for this project was to take landmarks which are familiar to everyone, and show them in a way that was completely new and exciting. The answer was to make the viewer part of the scene, to keep things moving and changing, and to surprise the audience with a number of unusual approaches.
>
> The film begins as if the viewer is about to watch "just another travelogue," but suddenly it stops, rewinds and changes mood—creating a truly unusual and unique look at one of the world's most favorite cities.[7]

Figure 15.2 presents the script for the opening sections.

# SAN FRANCISCO IS...

## SAN FRANCISCO
## CONVENTION & VISITORS BUREAU

FINAL SCRIPT

Mark Krigbaum / Rod Gross
Eclipse Productions, Inc.

January 21, 1991

**Figure 15.2.** Courtesy of the San Francisco Convention and Visitors Bureau.

| VISUAL | AUDIO |
|---|---|
| ELEGANT BLUE GLEAMING LETTERS APPEAR ON SCREEN RIGHT. THE TALL LETTERS FILL MOST OF THE SCREEN AS THEY PASS RIGHT TO LEFT. | MUSIC UP FULL -- ADVENTUROUS, EXCITING JAZZ/ROCK FUSION. |
| AS THE FIRST 2 LETTERS BECOME RECOGNIZABLE, AND BEFORE WE CAN MAKE OUT THE ACTUAL WORD, WE FLASH CUT TO AN ACTION SHOT. | MUSIC ACCENTS PUNCTUATES THE INTERCUT ACTION SHOTS. |
| THE FLASH CUT IS FOLLOWED BY A CONTINUATION OF THE REVEALING TITLE, FOLLOWED AGAIN BY ANOTHER ACTION FLASH CUT , FOLLOWED BY THE NEXT PART OF THE PHRASE, ETC... | |
| AS THE TITLE CONTINUES WE RECOGNIZE WHAT IS BEING SPELLED OUT: | |

*SanFranciscoIs...*

| VISUAL | AUDIO |
|---|---|
| THE TITLE CLEARS THE FRAME AS IT CONTINUES TO MOVE TO SCREEN LEFT. AS THE LAST LETTER CLEARS OUR FIRST GRAPHIC BULLET CUTS INTO VIEW: | THE MUSIC TRANSITIONS INTO THE SOUND OF A JET AIRLINER COMING IN FOR A LANDING. |

*SanFranciscoIs...*
*Accessible*

| VISUAL | AUDIO |
|---|---|
| CUT TO: 747 TAIL FINS CROSSING, BAGGAGE TAGS, TAXIS, BUSES, MORE PLANES, FACES, ARRIVAL/DEPARTURE MARQUEES AND TOTE BOARDS SHOWING ARRIVALS. | THE JET'S ROAR COMES UP FULL THEN QUICKLY TRANSITIONS INTO ROCK 'N ROLL  MORE JET ENGINES ARE HEARD ON THE TRACK AND ALMOST SOUND LIKE ACCOMPANIMENT TO THE GUITAR. |

*SAN FRANCISCOIS_*     Final Script     Page 2

**Figure 15.2.** (continued)

| VISUAL | AUDIO |
|---|---|
| | **NARRATOR:** (BIG) |
| FLIGHTS ARRIVE FROM ALL OVER THE WORLD, THINGS ARE BUSY, EFFICIENT AND DOWN RIGHT EXCITING. | FROM THE FOUR CORNERS OF THE WORLD -- SAN FRANCISCO IS SERVED... |
| THE VISUALS CONTINUE FOR A FEW SECONDS, EVEN THOUGH THE NARRATOR HAS STOPPED. | (NARRATOR STOPS SUDDENLY AND TALKS DIRECTLY TO THE DIRECTOR IN THE CONTROL BOOTH) |
| CUT TO NARRATOR IN THE RECORDING BOOTH. AS THE CAMERA ROAMS AROUND THE BOOTH, WE SEE HE IS WEARING HEADPHONES AND IS DRESSED VERY CASUALLY. | "A LITTLE SOMETHING LIKE THAT? IS THAT WHAT YOU HAD IN MIND?" (THE MUSIC SUDDENLY STOPS COLD AS THE TAPE "STOP" BUTTON IS HIT) |
| | **DIRECTOR:** (WE HEAR HIM RESPONDING THROUGH THE "TALK-BACK") |
| CLOSE UP OF TALK BACK BUTTON. | "I LOVE IT , DENNY, BUT IT'S NOT RIGHT FOR THIS MOVIE. I NEED |
| DIRECTOR - CONTROL ROOM. | SOMETHING THAT'S EASIER. THE IDEA IS IT'S EASY TO GET INTO |
| MICHAEL, THE ENGINEER, FIDDLES WITH BUTTONS AND KNOBS. | TOWN AND ONCE YOU'RE HERE... YOU'RE GONNA LOVE IT." |
| NARRATOR IN BOOTH. | **NARRATOR:** "OK...LET ME BACK OFF AND TRY SOMETHING. MICHAEL ROLL IT." |
| CUT TO - OUR FILM FOOTAGE RUNNING RAPIDLY IN REVERSE TO THE POINT WHERE WE FIRST HEARD THE NARRATOR BEGIN. | |

*SAN FRANCISCOS*      Final Script

**Figure 15.2.** (continued)

| VISUAL | AUDIO |
|---|---|
| THE PROGRAM "RESUMES" PLAYING. | (THE MUSIC RESUMES) |
| | **NARRATOR:** (CONVERSATIONAL, FRIENDLY) |
| SF AIRPORT - PEOPLE ARRIVING, GOING PLACES. | FROM THE FOUR CORNERS OF THE WORLD -- SAN FRANCISCO IS SERVED BY OVER TWELVE HUNDRED NATIONAL AND INTERNATIONAL FLIGHTS EACH DAY ... A DESTINATION WHICH IS UNIQUE... BEAUTIFUL ...AND ORIGINAL ... (CASUAL, ADLIB ASIDE, SNEAK IT IN) *IT'S A GREAT PLACE, YOU'RE GONNA LOVE IT.* |
| SCENIC SHOTS OF THE CITY. | |
| PUTS HAND OVER MIC - LOOKS AT CAMERA. | |
| QUICK FADE OUT THEN POP ON THE NEXT TITLE: | (MUSIC UP AND OUT) |

## *INVITING*

| | |
|---|---|
| THROUGH THE EYES AND EARS OF THE CAMERA, WE EXPERIENCE THE SIGHTS AND SOUNDS, THE IMPRESSIONS AND FEELINGS OF SAN FRANCISCO.<br>--A WAVE CRASHES ON THE ROCKY COAST<br>-- A HILLTOP VIEW OF AQUATIC PARK AND ALCATRAZ<br>-- A JAPANESE HOSTESS IN A BEAUTIFUL KIMONO SMILES, BOWING LOW<br>-- SAIL BOATS CUT THROUGH THE BAY<br>-- A SMILING FISHERMAN SHOWS US HIS CATCH | THE MUSIC TRANSITIONS INTO A BROAD, SWEEPING, SENSUAL PIECE. |

*SAN FRANCISCO'S...*          Final Script

**Figure 15.2.** (continued)

| VISUAL | AUDIO |
|---|---|
| -- A STREET PERFORMER WINKS AT THE CAMERA AND CONTINUES THE SHOW<br>-- CHILLED NAPA VALLEY WHITE WINE IS POURED INTO TWO GLASSES<br>-- A FRIENDLY DOORMAN EXCHANGES GREETINGS WITH US<br>-- GHIRARDELLI SQUARE AT NIGHT<br>-- FRENCH BREAD FRESH OUT OF THE OVEN<br>-- CABLE CARS ON NOB HILL<br>-- THE GOLDEN GATE BRIDGE AT SUNSET<br>-- AND A COUPLE EMBRACES AS THEY WATCH A SUNSET. | |
| FADE OUT THEN QUICKLY UP ON THE NEXT TITLE: | |

## *INTERNATIONAL*

| VISUAL | AUDIO |
|---|---|
| WE FADE UP ON A JAPANESE MAN IN HIS MID-THIRTIES. HE IS IN FRONT OF A GOLD DOMED, RUSSIAN ORTHODOX TEMPLE AND HE IS TALKING DIRECTLY TO US -- IN JAPANESE. | *ENGLISH SUBTITLES:*<br><br>*"SAN FRANCISCO IS...RUSSIAN ARCHITECTURE, IRISH COFFEE AND ONE MORE THING...* |
| HE HOLDS UP A ROUND, CIRCULAR TYPE OF BREAD. | *...BAGELS!!* |
| HISPANIC MAN AT THE JAPANESE TEA GARDENS | *"FOR A MARVELOUS NIGHT ON THE TOWN, START WITH A SUSHI BAR"* |
| 50 YEAR OLD RUSSIAN WOMEN IN FRONT OF CHINESE RESTAURANT. | *"SHOULD I BUY A GIFT FOR MY DAUGHTER, OR EAT DIM SUM ON GRANT STREET??*<br><br>*DIM SUM!!"* |

**Figure 15.2.** (continued)

"Saddle Rock Ranch," as we noted earlier, is a video made for a very exclusive target audience. Only one copy was made, and it was shown to only one potential client at a time, at horse shows. But it wasn't an expensive production. The audio is primarily single-voice narration, supplemented by occasional use of effects and natural sound. It depends on its strong visual impact—lush scenery, beautiful animals and documentary approach. It also depends on having carefully identified the appropriate target audience and on being able to reach it. Figure 15.3 shows the marked-up version of the script used by the production staff to assemble the final edit.

"Weather" is one of the series of instructional tapes produced and sold by King Schools for airplane pilot certification. Production is very simple. The video for this example consists of stock footage (hurricane, clouds) and computer-generated graphic diagrams. The audio track is voice-over narration. Production is primarily postproduction—editing the various individual video shots into a sequence and adding the narration. Since the production follows such a simple and regular pattern, the script need not be very complicated, and it's not. Figure 15.4 is a portion of this script.

"A Cool Cure for the Summertime Blues" is the script for a video news release produced by the 3M Company. The only obvious connection to 3M in the script is in the suggested tag, to be delivered live by a local announcer, but the company's name is seen visually in some of the shots of the luges in action. The audio consists of voice-over narration and sound bites; the video is mostly shots of luges, with a suggested graphic to be inserted at the end to promote the tryout tour. (See Figure 15.5.)

The actual scripts for "Highstacks" are too long to reproduce here (54 pages for each of the two programs), but this further description by the producer gives the flavor of the shows:

> [The programs utilize] the classic elements of the game show format to provide maximum instructional and motivational effectiveness. "Main" rounds were used to disseminate large blocks of general information, e.g., how to load a railroad car. "Lightning" rounds were used to introduce such specific information as the seven steps necessary for the correct opening of the door of a railroad car, and to reinforce other general information. "Bonus" rounds served to weave in such warehouse mottos and instructional concepts as "Work Smarter, Not Harder," and such basic principles of warehouse operation as "Inspect, Correct, or Reject."
>
> Regular game show viewers also expect several commercial breaks in a 30-minute show, so these were included. They provide information on lift truck safety, maintenance, and sanitation. In addition, they also give the show the pacing needed. . . .
>
> The set is a colorful re-creation of a General Foods warehouse, complete with light-up lift trucks and a background of assorted General Foods product cartons. . . .

(text continues on page 521)

**Double Vision**                                    READING TIME: 2:55

DATE 12/28/82 _____        ORiginal          PAGE 1 ___ OF 5

CLIENT SADDLE ROCK RANCH ____   JOB # _____   WRITER BENVENUTI _____

| ① VIDEO | AUDIO |
|---|---|
| EXT. Up on close up gate; zoom out as gate begins to open, and we start down driveway past SR sign. | 1   ① Music — Ambient sounds |
| ② C.U. sign | 2   (sound of horse whinnying) |
| ③ Full shot of mountain — pull back — [6 sec] truck passes by. [4 sec] | 3            NARRATOR |
| | ℗ ② 2½                    ③ 6 |
| | 4   WELCOME TO THE SADDLE ROCK RANCH. / WE'RE LOCATED IN |
| | 5   SONOMA, CALIFORNIA, IN THE HEART OF THE BEAUTIFUL |
| | 6   WINE COUNTRY'S VALLEY OF THE MOON. . . . 4 — APPROXIMATELY |
| | 7   ONE HOUR'S DRIVE NORTH OF SAN FRANCISCO. |
| ④ 8 secs shots of Nadom, either in paddock or inside arena. | ④ 8  ℗ 8   THE SADDLE ROCK RANCH — HOME OF CHAMPION S.R. NADOM — |
| | 9   IS PRESENTLY OFFERING BREEDING SERVICES FOR A LIMITED |
| | 10  NUMBER OF APPROVED MARES. |
| Truck unloading a mare. show usual procedure. | ⑤ 3½  Ⓣ 11  OUR SERVICES INCLUDE EVERYTHING that WE PROVIDE OUR OWN |
| ⑤ C.U. on feet or head. Zoom out ⑥ Activity | 12  MARES — ⑥ CLEANLINESS, SAFETY, COMFORT, AND PERSONALIZED |
| | 13  CARE BY A HIGHLY QUALIFIED STAFF. |
| Medium and close ups of groom receiving & leading mare toward barn. ⑦ Ms Groom & mare ⑧ Leading toward Barn | ⑦ 4  Ⓣ 14  WHEN YOUR MARE ARRIVES AT THE RANCH, SHE'LL BE ASSIGNED |
| | ⑧ 4  15  TO A GROOM / WHO WILL BE RESPONSIBLE FOR HER WELL BEING |
| | 16  THROUGHOUT HER STAY. |

**Figure 15.3.** Courtesy of the writer, Jeanne Benvenuti.

# Double Vision

DATE 12/28/82                                          PAGE **2** OF **5**

CLIENT SADDLE ROCK RANCH          JOB # _____  WRITER BENVENUTI

| VIDEO | | AUDIO |
|---|---|---|
| ① 5½ sec total<br>INT. Shot from aisle of barn toward door in which groom is entering with mare. On one side of aisle is person rebedding a stall. As groom & mare pass, there is brief exchange. *Then narrator speaks, they continue*<br>② Shot of open stall. groom leading horse into ~~stall~~ *picture &*<br>*places in stall* | 1<br><br>Ⓣ2<br><br>3 | ①<br>SHE'LL BE SURROUNDED BY ALL THE COMFORTS OF HOME. |
| | Ⓣ4 | ②<br>A SPACIOUS 12 by 16 STALL, WITH AUTOMATIC WATERING AND |
| | 5 | FLY CONTROL./ (THE STALLS ARE CLEANED AND REBEDDED |
| | 6 | DAILY.) |
| ⟨?⟩<br>Cut to another horse feeding ④then to CU of hands stirring grain. | ③6<br>Ⓣ7 | ③6<br>LIKE ALL THE OTHER HORSES ON THE RANCH, SHE'LL |
| | 8 | RECEIVE HER DAILY NUTRITIONAL REQUIREMENTS. NO SHORT |
| | 9 | ④4 *The highest quality alfalfa,and*<br>CUTS./GRAINS SPECIALLY MILLED FOR SADDLE ROCK ~~AND THE~~ *Ranch.* |
| | 10 | ~~HIGHEST QUALITY ALFALFA.~~ |
| ⑤ Over shoulder from ¾ angle. close enough to see screen. 3 sec zoom. Person walks in Operator looks up & takes sheet. | ⑤ 7½<br>Ⓣ11 | ⑤ 7½<br>TO ENSURE THAT YOUR MARE'S INDIVIDUAL NEEDS ARE MET, |
| | 12 | WE ENTER ALL PERTINENT DATA INTO THE RANCH'S COMPUTER |
| | 13 | SYSTEM IMMEDIATELY UPON HER ARRIVAL. |
| Lab person looking at printout.<br>*Zoom ...* | Ⓟ14 | ⑥4½<br>DETAILED PRINTOUTS ARE MADE AVAILABLE TO THOSE INVOLVED |
| | 15 | IN ANY ASPECT OF HER CARE. |
| | 16 | |

**Figure 15.3.** (continued)

# Double Vision

DATE 12/28/82                                    PAGE 3 OF 5

CLIENT SADDLE ROCK RANCH      JOB # _____      WRITER BENVENUTI

| VIDEO | AUDIO |
|---|---|
| ① someone looking at workboard. Overshoulder. | ① 3-½ (T)1 YOUR MARE'S WORK PROGRAM WILL BE TAILORED TO HER |
| | 2 REQUIREMENTS. |
| show as mentioned: 100' outside work ring, inside arena covered bullpen. different mares. ② ④ (T)3 | ② ① 5 3 OUR EXERCISE FACILITIES INCLUDE THIS 100 FOOT |
| | 4 OUTSIDE WORKING RING. . . . [AN 80 BY 200 20 INDOOR ARENA . . ] |
| | ④5 (P)5 . . AND A COVERED BULLPEN. |
| ⑤ mare being bathed. If possible, show same mare at hot walker. Start in close & pull out. (T)6 X | ⑤ 4½ 6 HER WORKOUT COMPLETED, SHE'LL BE RETURNED TO THE |
| | 7 COMFORT OF HER STALL AFTER A SOOTHING BATH . . . |
| ⑥ Walker | ⑥ 4 (T)8 AND A COOLING OFF ON OUR COVERED HOT WALKER. / |
| ⑦ wide shot of mares in grassy paddock | ⑦ & ⑧ 10 (P)9 ON NONWORK DAYS, WEATHER PERMITTING, MARES AT SADDLE |
| ⑧ CU one of mares | 10 ROCK HAVE THE OPPORTUNITY TO STRETCH THEIR LEGS IN |
| Zoom in on CU OF Fencing(?) | 11 ONE OF OUR GRASSY PADDOCKS.  TO FURTHER ENSURE THEIR |
| | 12 SAFETY, THE RANCH IS DOUBLE-FENCED. / |
| ⑨ Mare being groomed, original mare, if possible. ⑩ close up of hands grooming. grooms voice | ⑨ 10 Cu (T)13 AND, OF COURSE, EACH MARE ON THE RANCH IS TREATED /TO X |
| | 14 A DAILY GROOMING. (Sound of groom talking to mare; |
| | 15 as well as ambient sounds of other horses in barn |
| | 16 talking to each other) // |

**Figure 15.3.** (continued)

# Double Vision

DATE 12/28/82            PAGE 4 OF 5

CLIENT SADDLE ROCK RANCH     JOB #          WRITER BENVENUTI

| VIDEO | | AUDIO |
|---|---|---|
| Health barn, breeding area. May need to start with outside wide shot of barn and then shot of people activity inside. need to show its cleanliness if can. | ① ⓟ1 | ① 6½ THE SAME PERSONALIZED CARE IS PROVIDED IN OUR |
| | 2 | BREEDING AREAS, WITH AN EMPHASIS ON SAFETY, |
| | 3 | CLEANLINESS AND EFFICIENCY. ② 3 TWO MEMBERS OF OUR |
| ② staff working in lab or in breeding area. | 4 | BREEDING STAFF HAVE DEGREES IN ANIMAL HUSBANDRY. |
| Mare in stall with light overhead. Pan right | ⓟ5 | ③ 4 AS AN ENCOURAGEMENT TO EARLY BREEDING, MARES ARE |
| | 6 | PLACED UNDER 16 HOURS OF LIGHT DAILY. |
| teasing of mare by stallion Pan left & mike | ⓟ7 | ④ 5 playout IN OUR CONCERN FOR SAFETY, THE MOST UP-TO-DATE |
| | 8 | EQUIPMENT IS USED FOR TEASING. // |
| ⑤ mock artificial insemination procedure | ⓟ9 | ⑤ 1c WHEN THE ARTIFICIAL INSEMINATION METHOD IS CHOSEN, |
| | 10 | EFFICIENCY BECOMES ONE OF THE KEY FACTORS. OUR |
| | 11 | LABORATORY AND INSEMINATION STOCKS ARE IMMEDIATELY |
| ⑥ person evaluating semen in the lab. | ⓟ12 | ADJACENT TO THE STALLION COLLECTION AREA, / ⑥ 5 AND THE |
| | 13 | LABORATORY IS FULLY EQUIPPED FOR EFFICIENT SEMEN |
| | 14 | EVALUATION. |
| ⑦ wide shot ⑧ cu t/equipment staff person using ultra sound on mare | ⓟ15 | ⑦ 7 TO ALLOW YOUR MARE TO RETURN HOME AS SOON AS POSSIBLE, |
| | 16 | |

**Figure 15.3.** (continued)

# Double Vision

DATE 12/28/82                                   PAGE 5 OF 5

CLIENT SADDLE ROCK RANCH         JOB # _____         WRITER BENVENUTI

| VIDEO | | AUDIO |
|---|---|---|
| | 1 | SADDLE ROCK /*CU* USES ULTRA SOUND AS AN AID IN EARLY |
| | 2 | PREGNANCY DETECTION. // |
| ① shot of foaling stall with mare inside. ② cut to same type of shot viewed in TV monitor. over shoulder of observer. | Ⓟ3 | ① 4 LOCATED ALSO IN THE HEALTH BARN ARE FOALING STALLS. |
| | 4 | ② 4  *Continually*   *Closed Circuit* THESE ARE MONITORED ~~CONTINUALLY~~ ON ~~REMOTE~~ T.V. /: |
| ③ shot of mare in isolation stall | Ⓟ5 | ③ 3½ AND IF THE NEED SHOULD ARISE, ISOLATION STALLS ARE |
| | 6 | ALSO AVAILABLE. |
| series of cuts for reviewing types of services rendered (horse being **fed**, being groomed, being exercised) *Review shots* | Ⓟ7 | YES, AT SADDLE ROCK RANCH YOU CAN REST ASSURED THAT |
| | 8 | *OUR* YOUR MARE WILL BE TREATED JUST LIKE /OWN. ASK OUR |
| | 9 | ＊CLIENTS. |
| ④ *or coming out of barn,* original mare being led toward truck; other trucks in background. | Ⓟ10 | ④ 3 AND WHEN IT'S TIME FOR YOUR MARE TO RETURN HOME? |
| | 11 | 4 IF NEEDED, WE CAN ARRANGE TRANSPORTATION BY THE |
| | 12 | MOST MODERN EQUIPMENT. / |
| ⑤ shot of truck leaving down driveway | Ⓟ13 | ⑤ 3 THANK YOU FOR VISITING US *AT SADDLE ROCK.* / |
| ⑥ *cut* pan to fillies in field to right of driveway (facing toward gate) Freeze frame, bring up logo. go to black. | Ⓟ14 | ⑥ 5 WE HOPE THAT NEXT YEAR YOUR MARES HAVE FILLIES AS |
| | 15 | FINE LOOKING AS THESE. |
| | 16 | |

**Figure 15.3.** (continued)

# WEATHER

*VIDEO – Hurricane*

[51] *Graphic (W1)* ————————

[52] *Graphic (W2)* ————————

☐ *Graphic (W56)* ————————

*Graphic (W3)*
*Graphic (W4)*
*Graphic (W5)*
*Graphic (W6)*
*Graphic (W8)*

*Video – Clouds*    **?**
*(Graphic)*

☐ *Graphic (W54)* ————————
*· Modify*

July 16, 1990  3:45 pm

## AIR MASSES

STANDARD TEMPERATURE AND PRESSURE FOR SEA LEVEL - are 15° C and 29.92" Hg. (59° F and 1013.2 millibars).          (1386)

EVERY PHYSICAL PROCESS OF WEATHER - is accompanied by, or is the result of, a heat exchange.          (1381)

VARIATIONS IN ALTIMETER SETTINGS - between weather reporting points are caused by unequal heating of the Earth's surface.     (1382)

DIFFERENCES IN DIRECTION BETWEEN WINDS ALOFT AND ON THE GROUND - are caused by friction between the wind and the surface.          (1396)

THE BOUNDARY BETWEEN TWO DIFFERENT AIR MASSES - is referred to as a front.     (1422)

ONE WEATHER PHENOMENON WHICH WILL ALWAYS OCCUR WHEN FLYING ACROSS A FRONT - is a change in the wind direction. (1424)

ONE OF THE MOST EASILY RECOGNIZED DISCONTINUITIES - across a front is temperature.          (1423)

## CLOUDS

CLOUDS ARE DIVIDED INTO FOUR FAMILIES - according to their height range.          (1417)

THE SUFFIX "NIMBUS" USED WHEN NAMING CLOUDS - means a rain cloud.          (1416)

## MOISTURE

THE AMOUNT OF WATER VAPOR WHICH AIR CAN HOLD - largely depends on the air temperature.          (1399)

MOISTURE IS ADDED TO UNSATURATED AIR BY - evaporation and sublimation.     (1401)

DEWPOINT - is the temperature to which air must be cooled to become saturated.     (1398)

CLOUDS, FOG, OR DEW - will always form when water vapor condenses. (Not necessarily when relative humidity equals 100 percent.)     (1400)

**Figure 15.4.** Courtesy of King Schools, Inc.

IF THE TEMPERATURE/DEWPOINT SPREAD IS SMALL AND DECREASING - and the temperature is 62° F, fog or low clouds are likely to develop. (1446)

Graphic (W9)

CG: ~~~~ 4.4

YOU CAN CALCULATE THE ALTITUDE OF THE BASE OF CUMULUS CLOUDS - by dividing the temperature/dewpoint spread by 4.4 and multiplying by 1000.

Graphic (W10)

change numbers in graphic

EXAMPLE - Surface air temperature is 82° F and the dewpoint is 38° F. What altitude above the surface would you expect the base of cumuliform clouds? (1411)

CG

82° F - 38° F = 44° F

44° F ÷ 4.4 = 10, x 1,000 = 10,000 feet AGL

Graphic (W11)

change numbers in graphic

EXAMPLE - Temperature is 70° F, dewpoint is 48° F, surface elevation is 1,000 feet MSL. What is the cloud height? (1410)

Graphic (W12)

change numbers in graphic CG

70° F - 48° F = 22° F

22° F ÷ 4.4 = 5, x 1,000 = 5,000 feet AGL

1,000 feet + 5,000 feet = 6,000 feet MSL

To find the MSL altitude of the clouds add the surface elevation to the cloud height.

## STABILITY

Graphic (W19)

TO DETERMINE THE STABILITY OF THE ATMOSPHERE - compare the actual lapse rate with the standard lapse rate. (1404)

Graphic (W58)

MOIST, STABLE AIR FLOWING UPSLOPE - can be expected to produce stratus type clouds. (1407)

STABLE AIR - is characterized by stratiform clouds, steady vs. showery precipitation, and smooth air (little or no turbulence). (1406,1415,1425)

Graphic

WARMING FROM BELOW - would decrease the stability of an air mass. (1405)

THE DEVELOPMENT OF THERMALS - depends upon solar heating. (1395)

UNSTABLE AIR IS CHARACTERIZED BY - turbulence and good surface visibility. (1414)

A MOIST, UNSTABLE AIRMASS IS CHARACTERIZED BY - cumuliform clouds and showery precipitation. (1413)

**Figure 15.4.** (continued)

☐ Graphic (W59) ———— IF AN UNSTABLE AIRMASS IS FORCED UP-
WARD - expect it to produce clouds with considerable vertical development and associated turbulence.                                    (1408)

TOWERING CUMULUS CLOUDS - would indicate convective turbulence.                 (1421)

### ICING

VIDEO — Rain (in flight)

ONE IN-FLIGHT CONDITION NECESSARY FOR
STRUCTURAL ICING TO FORM - is visible moisture.                                       (1431)

☐ Graphic (W45) ————

THE HIGHEST ACCUMULATION RATE OF
AIRCRAFT STRUCTURAL ICE - is most likely in
freezing rain.                              (1432)

ICE PELLETS AT THE SURFACE - is evidence of
freezing rain at a higher altitude.         (1403)

**Figure 15.4.** (continued)

A COOL CURE FOR THE SUMMERTIME BLUES

| VIDEO | AUDIO |
|---|---|
| Person in starting gate Sliding down luge track (Lake Placid, NY) | NARRATOR: Looking for a cure for those summertime blues? How about a winter sport? How about THIS winter sport? It's called luge. And it combines speed, precision and driving skill in rides up to 80 miles an hour. |
| Ron Rossi U.S. Luge Association | RON ROSSI, SOT: "It's very similar to a roller coaster ride— except you're the one that's driving the roller coaster." |
| Sled on track | NARRATOR: Luge isn't very well known in this country, although it's popular in Europe. But the |

MORE MORE MORE

**Figure 15.5.** Script by Elizabeth Fuller. Reprinted by permission of 3M.

| | |
|---|---|
| Summer luge event (Minneapolis, 1989) | United States Luge Team is working to change all that. They're taking their sleds on the road this summer—literally—in search of new talent. The team is holding luge clinics on city streets around the country, inviting kids ages 12 to 18 to come try luge sleds on wheels. |
| Dan in starting gate | Two years ago, Dan Dellenbach didn't know any more about luge than most of us. Then he saw the wheeled luge tryouts on TV at his home in Salt Lake City. Now he's a member of the U.S. Junior Development team, working to become part of the senior team that goes to the Olympics. |
| Dan Dellenbach Luge Team Candidate | DAN DELLENBACH, SOT: "There's no way I could have guessed it. I didn't know anything about the sport. I would never have guessed I'd be here." |
| Summer clinic | NARRATOR: It can happen. So if you know a teenager looking to cure those summertime blues—or a taste of Olympic gold—encourage them to give it a try. |
| Dan | DAN DELLENBACH: "Well, it just, it was different from anything you've ever felt, because when you get up on the walls, it feels like your guts are going up." |

**Figure 15.5.** (continued)

FADE TO BLACK

CG OVER BACKGROUND:

<u>3M Luge Challenge</u>
San Francisco
  July 6-7
Los Angeles
  July 12-14
Salt Lake City
  July 20-21
Minneapolis/St. Paul
  August 10-11
Chicago
  August 17-18
Pittsburgh
  August 24-25
<u>U.S. Luge Association</u>
(518) 523-2071
or
(518) 523-1512

SUGGESTED TAG:

The 3M Luge Challenge will be in these six cities this summer. For more information, or if you'd like to sign up, call the United States Luge Association at (518) 523-2071 or (518) 523-1512.

**Figure 15.5.** (continued)

The first contestant in this head-to-head confrontation of lift truck logic is Big Moose Wheeler from Fork Worth, Texas, "a man who can pull-pack 27 cartons of Log Cabin Syrup on a slipsheet of Kleenex"—an impressive accomplishment among warehousemen. His opponent is Gnat Stacker the Third, from Cargo, North Dakota, "a clamp truck operator who can't get a grip on himself.". . .

Moose and Gnat match wits from behind their lift truck podiums while show host Bill O. Lading, "the man with a warehouse of knowledge," quizzes them on categories selected by the show's glamorous hostess, Honeycomb Dunnage.

Throughout the game, Moose and Gnat are challenged to look for mistakes being made by the lift truck operators who appear on the chromakey pickup screen. When he spots one, the contestant is to honk the horn on his podium. He who honks first gets a chance to identify the mistake, describe the proper procedure, and score points to win the game and go on to play the exciting "10,000 bonus" round where he can pick up some really "sweet" prizes—10,000 marshmallows.

According to the manager of General Foods' Video and Graphic Communications Department, William Hoppe, the programs are an overwhelming success:

What we saw in the game show and what attracted us to use it for this program, is its tremendous potential for conveying a large number of individual pieces of information in a relatively short period of time. The professional game show format has developed the art of pacing into a science to achieve a maximum of audience attention, suspense, entertainment, and involvement. That's what we were after.[8]

## CONCLUSION

The actual writing of C/I scripts does not differ significantly from broadcast. Even the differences in purpose and audiences between broadcast and C/I programs are diminishing. The fields are moving closer together in a number of ways. Corporate promotional tapes are frequently shown on cable channels. Sponsored programs such as travelogues or fashion shows may be aired by broadcast stations (now that FCC rules on program-length commercials have been lifted). Corporate public relations departments regularly produce and distribute video news releases to broadcast stations. We've already discussed the training tape in the form of a game show, and we recently read of a program produced for the purpose of aiding the moves of corporate employees who were being transferred to other cities. It was structured in the form of a rock music video.

The planning process for this genre, however, is often different from broadcast because of the use of closed-circuit delivery, and that in turn changes the relationship between content and audience.

Writing scripts for C/I presentations provides one more type of content on which you can practice all the principles of good media writing. This is also one area that continues to expand as a career field, in contrast to the somewhat static number of writing positions in radio and TV stations and networks. And it is one in which the beginner has some opportunity to break in. You might begin by assisting a professor in your department to prepare a short tape for classroom use (in fact, we have included just such an exercise). Or you might become an intern at the university media center and have the opportunity to plan and write instructional programs for any of a number of purposes.

If you are interested in this area as a career, it will require some expertise in four disciplines: in educational pedagogy, that is, the study of teaching and learning; in the content area to be presented; in media writing itself; and in computer program design. In the first edition of this text we listed only the first three of these disciplines, but as we hope we have made clear throughout this chapter, the concepts of instructional media are more and more linked with computers. Computers are used both to control the access to and use of media for instruction and as devices to present instruction, including graphics, animation, and so forth.

**Exercises**

1. For a course you are taking this term, or one you have taken recently and are still familiar with, plan and script a mediated module for teaching a portion of one class, final length to be between 10 and 15 minutes. Your purpose and target audience are defined in this situation, but all the other planning steps outlined in this chapter you will have to decide. For example, the 10 to 15 minutes does not necessarily mean a videotape that length. Instructor-student interaction and student responses to the mediated material, if appropriate, can be included within that length.

2. Arrange to visit a commercial production agency or the in-house media production department of a local business—manufacturing, hospital, retail chain, or whatever organization in your community has such a department. Find out what C/I productions are currently in progress, and at what stage of development. If possible, view some completed projects. Check the steps the agency uses to design productions against those described in this chapter. Write a report on your observations, or make a class presentation.

3. Find out if your university (or another in your area) is currently offering a telecourse. If so, observe the presentations for one week. What forms of presentation are used—talking head, interview, discussion, demonstration, documentary, other? At what level audience do the programs seem to be aimed—introductory, advanced, graduate? Are the presentational techniques appropriate for that audience? Will the programs hold their interest? Are there gratifications in the presentations, or will the students have to seek their rewards outside of the programs? Explain in a written report or class presentation.

**Notes**

1. Bob Shewchuk, "Edutainment Pays Off with Game Show Antics," *Video Systems*, July 1982, p. 60. Reprinted with permission.
2. Elizabeth Fuller, "25 Helpful Tips for Producing Usable Video News Releases," *AV Video*, May 1991, p. 22. Published by Knowledge Industry Publications, Inc.
3. Patrick O. Marsh, *Messages That Work: A Guide to Communication Design* (Englewood Cliffs, NJ: Educational Technology Publications, 1983), pp. 9–10. Reprinted with permission.
4. Nat Skyer, "The Training Game: How General Foods Made Two Programs with Help from Production Companies," *E&ITV*, May 1982, p. 38. Copyright 1982 by C.S. Tepfer Publishing Company, Inc. Reprinted by permission.
5. Linda Hershberger, "How Interactive Training Affects Corporations," *E&ITV*, January 1984, pp. 64–65. Copyright 1984 by C.S. Tepfer Publishing Company, Inc. Reprinted by permission.
6. James Onder, "Techniques to Use with the Talking Head," *E&ITV*, February 1980, p. 44. Copyright 1980 by C.S. Tepfer Publishing Company, Inc. Reprinted by permission.
7. Press release, Eclipse Productions, Walnut Creek, CA, May 1991. Reprinted by permission of the San Francisco Convention and Visitors Bureau.
8. Skyer, "The Training Game," pp. 38–39. Copyright 1982 by C.S. Tepfer Publishing Company, Inc. Reprinted by permission.

**Further Reading**

These first titles emphasize instructional and message design, in contrast to the second group, which is more directly related to scriptwriting and production of C/I materials.

Baird, Lloyd S., Craig Eric Schneier, and Dugan Laird (eds.). *The Training and Development Source Book*. Amherst, MA: Human Resource Development, 1983.

Cartwright, Steve R. *Secrets of Successful Video Training: The Training with Video Casebook*. White Plains, NY: Knowledge Industries, 1990.

Hudspeth, DeLayne R., and Ronald G. Brey. *Instructional Telecommunications: Principles and Applications*. Westport, CT: Praeger, 1985.

Marsh, Patrick O. *Messages That Work: A Guide to Communications Design*. Englewood Cliffs, NJ: Educational Technology, 1983.

Solomon, Douglas S. *Message Design: A Manual on Formation Evaluation*. Norwood, NJ: Ablex, 1983.

As suggested in this chapter, writing and producing C/I scripts does differ in some respects from writing for regular broadcast programs. The titles listed here have been chosen because they emphasize those differences; however, the texts on audio and video production listed for Chapter 4 can also be helpful in developing your skills as a writer or producer in this area.

DiZazzo, Ray. *Corporate Scriptwriting: A Professional's Guide*. Stoneham, MA: Focal, 1992.

DiZazzo, Ray. *Corporate Television: A Producer's Handbook*. Stoneham, MA: Focal, 1989.

Eustace, Grant. *Writing for Corporate Videos*. Stoneham, MA: Focal, 1990.

Gayeski, Diane. *Corporate and Instructional Video*. Englewood Cliffs, NJ: Prentice-Hall, 1991.

Hausman, Carl. *Institutional Video: Planning, Budgeting, Production and Evaluation*. Belmont, CA: Wadsworth, 1991.

Morley, John. *Scriptwriting for High-Impact Videos*. Belmont, CA: Wadsworth, 1992.

Richardson, Alan (ed.). *Corporate and Organizational Video*. New York: McGraw-Hill, 1992.

# Dramatic Programs

Writing full dramatic programs is not one of the forms of broadcast writing that young and inexperienced writers are likely to be asked to do, nor does this area even employ very many experienced writers. The cost of dramatic production is high, and for that reason if for no other, dramas are produced primarily for broadcast and cable networks, outlets that ensure the programs will be shown to very large audiences, and thus keep the costs per viewer within reason. Writing for the network soap operas, for example, is limited to a handful of thoroughly experienced writers under contract. And the writers for prime-time series are usually chosen from a small group of individuals known to the show's producers. Only a few TV series will even consider scripts submitted by free-lance or unknown authors.

Nevertheless, we include a chapter on this form because drama can be a very effective presentational technique for other types of material. Dramatic principles and short dramatic scenes can be used in commercials, in vignettes that might appear in religious programs, in so-called reality programs (which are actually mostly staged dramas), in role-playing scenes as part of a corporate training tape, and many other places. If you hope to develop a career writing dramatic scripts, don't let these comments deter you. Television drama is not going to go away, and writers, even though small in number, will still be needed to develop the ideas and prepare the scripts for these programs. Become proficient at other forms of writing and practice dramatic writing whenever the opportunity arises, but understand that it takes time and experience to "pay your dues" in this field.

When you finish this chapter, you will be able to

- recognize the common stages of dramatic script development—concept, treatment and final script—and plan your scripts using those stages,

- apply principles of program structure to dramatic scripting,

- develop settings, plots and characters,

- construct appropriate scene headings and directions, write dialogue and prepare scripts in correct form, and

- recognize and use these important terms and concepts:

| | |
|---|---|
| characters | foreshadowing |
| climax | intercutting |
| complication | master-scene scripting |
| concept | plot and subplot |
| crisis | reversal |
| denouement | scene headings |
| directions, business | setting |
| epilogue | stereotype |
| exposition | treatment |
| flashback | visualization |

The historical development of the conventions of Western drama goes back at least to the fifth century B.C., to the early Greek dramatists and to the first recognized dramatic critic, Aristotle. Centuries later, the dramatists and critics of the Italian and French Renaissance revived, then revised, the early theories to form the basis of dramatic construction as we know it today. In the last hundred years those conventions, originally developed for the stage, have been further modified and applied to three new media of communication—to film, then to radio, and most recently to television. The critics, teachers, and writers who have worked in each of these media have in turn added significantly to the body of works and of critical comment available for study.

For film, we have already mentioned the important contributions of such early practitioners as Eisenstein, Pudovkin, and Griffith. Their pioneering techniques form the foundation of film theory, which has carried over largely intact to television. Similarly, the innovations of Norman Corwin, and of Arch Oboler, among others, are important works to study for the radio writer, as are the radio dramas of Orson Welles, who wrote, produced, and performed in the most celebrated radio broadcast ever aired, the 1938 Mystery Theater adaptation of *War of the Worlds*.

The forty or so years of television drama represent only a tiny fraction of the time span of dramatic history, but there are critics who believe we have already passed the Golden Age of TV drama. These critics remember fondly the period when television drama was presented live, and they point to plays like *Requiem for a Heavyweight* by Rod Serling, *Marty* by Paddy Chayefsky, or *Judgment at Nuremburg* by Abby Mann as the "classics" of the genre.

It's a matter of opinion as to whether the quality of television drama is as high now as it was in the 1960s. Certainly there is a wider range of program subtypes, and production is more sophisticated than those early, live (before videotape) presentations. But, as we have noted, most of television's dramatic principles have been borrowed from film or radio, and we suggest you study critical works, production manuals and collections of plays for all three media to get a well-rounded sense of the complexities of writing for any of them. We include some works from each category in the Further Reading Section.

In case there is any question, we are using the term *drama* to refer to any form of fiction writing. Some authors and critics tend to use that word to describe primarily the hour-long or feature-length "serious" drama, and use other terms, such as dramady, sitcom, and so on, to describe other genres. The crucial difference that we want to emphasize, however, is that for any type of fictional script, total control of the final presentation is in the hands of the creative team: writer, director, editor. In contrast to other forms of production, news or documentary, for example, where the reporter and editor must work with images captured at the scene of the story, the fiction story allows (cost permitting) the writer and director full freedom to create the precise scene and activity they want.

In this chapter we do not focus on any particular form of drama but on the various steps in the preparation of dramatic scripts in general. Most of the chapter considers television, but we have reserved one section to consider the unique challenges radio provides. To begin, recognize that the evolution of a dramatic script from the first germ of an idea through to the finished production is a single, ongoing process. There are, nevertheless, two intermediate stages which are generally recognized in the industry as important points in the marketing of scripts—the *concept* and the *treatment*—so we'll divide the process into three steps: concept, treatment, and finished script. Understand too that there are very few absolutes in this business. If you look, you can find exceptions to just about any rule or principle. But in general, it works this way.

## CONCEPT

The story line for a drama, be it a feature-length film or the introduction to a commercial, begins as an idea, a single thought:

> A story idea can be derived from any personal experience or observation, any music, poetry, or book that moved you, a newspaper article that intrigued you, any source under the sun that sparked your imagination. However, the selection of the story idea must be more rational. First and foremost, it must have a hook—a unique

premise that will grip the audience immediately. If the hook is strong, the story has a much better chance of eventually reaching the screen.[1]

This *idea* will next be expanded into a *premise,* or *concept,* or *approach*— all these terms are used to describe the same thing. Major characters will be identified and described, the point of view will be determined. The central conflict will be sketched out, and the resolution of the story will be decided.

Consider at this point the type of material you wish to present. Although television has presented a tremendous range of material, including big spectacles with "a cast of thousands," the TV screen is best suited for more intimately scaled productions. The medium is also well suited for the dramatic development of "ordinary" stories. One of the best-known television dramatists of the 1960s, Paddy Chayefsky, describes the contrast between writing for the stage, the movies, and television in this way, in an introduction to the published version of his teleplays *Marty* and *The Mother*:

[These teleplays] both deal with the world of the mundane, the ordinary, and the untheatrical. The main characters are typical, rather than exceptional; the situations are easily identifiable by the audience; and the relationships are as common as people. The essence of these two shows lies in their literal reality. I tried to write the dialogue as if it had been wire-tapped. I tried to envision the scenes as if a camera had been focused upon the unsuspecting characters and had caught them in an untouched moment of life.

This sort of meticulous literalness is something that can be done in no other medium. On the stage, reality is a highly synthesized thing. The closest thing to reality I ever saw on the stage was in *Death of a Salesman,* but even this extraordinary play involved a suicide and an incident in which the son discovers his father in a hotel room with a woman other than his mother. These are excellent dramatic incidents, but they are not everyday occurrences in the life of the lower middle class. In writing the stage play, it is necessary to contrive exciting moments of theater. You may write about ordinary people, but the audience sees them in unordinary and untypical circumstances. . . .

In television, however, the same insights into a character or into a social milieu can be made with the most identifiable characters and the most commonplace situations. I set out in *Marty* to write a love story, the most ordinary love story in the world. I didn't want my hero to be handsome, and I didn't want the girl to be pretty. I wanted to write a love story the way it would literally have happened to the kind of people I know. I was, in fact, determined to shatter the shallow and destructive illusions—prospered by cheap fiction and bad movies—that love is simply a matter of physical attraction, that virility is manifested by a throbbing phallus, and that regular orgasms are all that's needed to make a woman happy. These values are dominant in our way of life and need to be examined for what they are.[2]

That description, although written after the production, exemplifies much of what is included in the concept of a teleplay. The following excerpts are from the proposal submitted to the networks by Gene Roddenberry, creator of *Star Trek*. He outlined his concept for that series using these descriptions. Trekkies will note that some changes had been made by the time the series made it to the TV screen.

**STAR TREK**
**Created by**
**Gene**
**Roddenberry**

STAR TREK will be a television "first" . . . A one-hour science-fiction series with continuing characters.
Combining the most varied in drama-action-adventure with complete production practicality. And with almost limitless story potential.
STAR TREK keeps all of Science Fiction's variety and excitement, but still stays within a mass audience frame of reference. . . .
By avoiding "way-out" fantasy and cerebral science theorem and instead concentrating on problem and peril met by our very human and very identifiable continuing characters. Fully one-third of the most successful of all Science Fiction is in this "practical" category. Tales of exotic "methane atmosphere worlds with six-head monsters" are rare among the Science Fiction classics. The best and most popular feature highly dramatic variations on recognizable things and themes. But even within these limits, there are myriad stories, both bizarre and shocking, plus a few monsters legitimus. Space is a place of infinite variety and danger.
Or to put Star Trek into the language of television . . .
 The format is "Wagon Train to the Stars"—built around characters who travel to other worlds and meet the jeopardy and adventure which become our stories.
 The time could be 1995 or even 2995—close enough to our times for our continuing cast to be people like us, but far enough into the future for galaxy travel to be fully established.
The Star Trek key is the bold establishing of . . .
 GALAXY TRAVEL FULLY PERFECTED. April and his crew, unlike our limited astronauts of today, are in charge of their own destiny, must find their own answers to the jeopardies they meet on far-off worlds. The perfected spaceship concept allows us to move efficiently from story to story, freeing the audience from tiresome details of technology and hardware. Our aim is drama and adventure.
 THE USS ENTERPRISE. A permanent set, also provides us with a familiar week-to-week locale. There is even a suggestion of current

naval terminology and custom which helps link our own "today" with Star Trek's "tomorrow."

As with "Gunsmoke," 's Dodge City, "Kildare" 's Blair General Hospital, our Cruiser is a complete and highly varied community; we can, at any time, take our camera down a passageway and find a guest star (scientist, specialist, ordinary airman, passenger or stowaway) who can propel us into a new story.

THE SIMILAR WORLDS CONCEPT. Just as the laws of matter and energy make probable the other planets of Earth composition and atmosphere, certain chemical and organic laws make equally probable wide evolution into humanlike creatures and civilizations with points of similarity to our own.

All of which gives extraordinary story latitude—ranging from worlds which parallel our own yesterday, our present, to our breathtaking distant future.

PRINCIPAL CHARACTER. Robert T. April. The "Skipper," about thirty-four, Academy graduate, rank of Captain. Clearly the leading man and central character. This role, built about an unusual combination of colorful strengths and flaws, is designated for an actor of top repute and ability. A shorthand sketch of Robert April might be: "A space-age Captain Horatio Hornblower," constantly on trial with himself, lean and capable both mentally and physically.

Captain April will be the focus of many stories—in still others he may lead us into the introduction of a guest star around whom that episode centers.

A strong, complex personality, he is capable of action and decision which can verge on the heroic—and at the same time lives a continual battle with the self-doubt and the loneliness of a command.

As with such men in the past (Drake, Cooke, Bougainville, and Scott), April's primary weakness is a predilection to action over administration, a temptation to take the greatest risks onto himself. But, unlike most early explorers, he has an almost compulsive compassion for the rights and plights of others, alien as well as human.

Other cast regulars are a variety of excitingly different types: "NUMBER ONE," a glacierlike, efficient female who serves as ship's Executive Officer; JOSE "JOE" TYLER, the brilliant but sometimes immature Navigator; MR. SPOCK, with a red-hued satanic look and surprisingly gentle manners; PHILIP "BONES" BOYCE, M.D., ship's doctor and worldly cynic; and uncomfortably lovely J. M. COLT, the Captain's Yeoman.[3]

Generally, the concept statement will be written in narrative form. Depending upon the length and complexity of the final program or series, it might vary in length from a few sentences to several pages.

# TREATMENT

Sometimes an established author will sell a script on the concept alone. More probably, one more stage of development will be needed to get the idea into sufficient detail for presentation to a buyer. That would be the *treatment*. This is a scene-by-scene description of the drama. Length will be about 3 to 15 pages, in narrative form, as is this first part of a treatment for a one-hour teleplay written by a student.

**Script Treatment for GAMBLERS by Dennis Rasmussen**

Prologue:

A train pulls up to the AMTRAK Train Depot in Sacramento. Out front of the station a car pulls up and stops. A man and wife, Brad and Nancy Millar, get out with their bags. Another woman, the driver, also gets out, helps the couple with their bags and wishes them well—and good luck—on their trip. Says to win big in Reno. She hugs and kisses both man and wife and gets back into her car. She says this little trip will be good for both of them, considering . . . alluding to some problems in their marriage.

The couple goes into the depot. He says he must make a phone call before they board the train; she protests, says it is about to leave; he says he'll hurry. In his absence she goes to the candy counter to buy some gum. She sees someone familiar—a man who politely nods, pats his breast, and taking care to be private, opens his coat just enough to reveal a gun. He buttons his coat, nods and leaves. She acknowledges the gun with a nod.

Brad is at the phone booth talking to someone in a desperate manner. He explains he will have the money by Monday. He has a system and is sure he'll win. He knows it's his final, desperate chance to save his company from going bankrupt. He has taken all his savings and will bet it all in order to win big. Brad Millar is in a huge financial mess and this is his last hope. He hears the "final boarding" announcement, goes back to his wife, and they hurriedly go out to the train.

We see a sign which reads "Reno Gamblers' Express" as the couple board the train. They are the last ones on and the brakeman signals to the conductor. The train pulls out of the station.

Act One:

Aboard the train the couple is in a coach car. He is full of hope and anticipation and she is too, but for a very different reason. She is sitting by the window looking out. In a brief conversation he suggests they go up to the lounge car for a drink. They get up and go. Transition to exterior of train crossing river.

Inside the lounge car they order drinks and find a seat. They begin playing a two-handed game of poker as the man from the candy counter scene comes in. He says, in mock surprise, he didn't know she was on the train. Nancy, quite uncomfortable, introduces the stranger to her husband as Mr. Marvin Karr, an associate of her employer, whom she met once before. He explains he is going to Reno on business. Brad invites him to sit down and join their little poker game. Nancy doesn't like it but cannot say anything. They play with nickles and dimes but soon Karr talks them into playing with "real money."

In a series of shots, the game progresses, intercut with scenes of the train moving higher and higher into the Sierras. In time we see it is Nancy who is the big winner in their little three-handed game.

Karr is a poor loser and excuses himself. There's an expression of worry on Nancy's face but Brad can't see it. He says her good luck is an omen; that they are bound to win in Reno. She is pessimistic and says it is HE who must get lucky. In an ironic comment she says, "Reno can kill you." The train winds its way through the mountains—[4]

In order to write a satisfactory treatment, like the one above for *Gamblers,* you have to consider in careful detail these four aspects of the script's development: *structure, settings, plot* and *characters.* They interact, of course, especially the relationship between plot and characters, but we'll try to consider each separately.

## Structure

Earlier in the text we devoted an entire chapter (Chapter 6) to program structure. For dramatic programs, those principles should be applied at the treatment stage.

### Unity

The concept of dramatic unity has been recognized by successful playwrights, and by critics, for centuries.

From Aristotle:

> The structural unity of the parts [of a play] is such that if any one of them is displaced or removed, the whole will be disjointed and disturbed. For a thing whose presence or absence makes no visible difference is not an organic part of the whole.

From Voltaire:

> Ask anyone who has crowded too many events into his play what the reason for the fault is. If he is honest he will tell you he lacked the inventive genius to fill his play with a single action.

And from veteran Hollywood screenwriter Alfred Brenner:

> A single action means there is one main plot, one protagonist, one central conflict, one central emotional line, and one climax, which is the focal point of both the plot and the struggle of the main character.
>
> Thus each incident the writer selects must move the protagonist a step further toward his goal. All other incidents, no matter how exciting or dramatic, must be dispensed with.
>
> In the same way, each of the characters is there only to advance the main character's story. There should be no others. Moreover, *that story will be told largely from the protagonist's point of view.*[5]

This is not to say that a television drama may not have secondary plots moved forward by secondary characters, but when there are secondary themes, they should be connected back to the main plot at or before the climax. Note, too, that shorter programs have little time for secondary development. We consider secondary themes again when we discuss plotting.

### Variety

Variety must be accomplished *within* the framework of unity. Plot, characters and settings may all be used to create variety. We've just mentioned the idea of subplots. Where there is time and opportunity for them to be developed, they add variety. Another form of plot variety is provided in programs that feature multiple, independent plots. Soap operas do this; several story lines that do not intersect are presented in parallel fashion. *The Love Boat* and *Hill Street Blues* made good use of this technique; more recently, *L.A. Law* and *Going to Extremes* have also used it.

Character variety is provided by making sure that each character is seen by the audience as a unique individual. In each scene different combinations of characters are presented, thereby setting up different interactions among the characters. Even if all your characters come from the same ethnic, economic, sex, age and social groups, each should be differentiated in some way—appearance, voice, mannerisms, for example.

Settings also add variety. The number and types of settings for television dramas are dictated by the type of program. A fast-action police drama is not likely to be convincing if it doesn't use a lot of different locations, and both interiors and exteriors. The writer of a historical drama will have to be particularly careful to describe scenes that are authentic to the period and the action, and then the set designer will have to ensure accuracy in their reproduction. On the other hand, a soap opera or situation comedy may very well be confined to a series of interior sets in a studio. Audiences have come to accept that limitation in programs in which settings are not usually critical to the development of the plot.

When cost or other factors prohibit frequent setting changes, it becomes even more important to move characters in and out of scenes quickly to provide the necessary variety to maintain audience attention.

## Pace

The number of program elements and the frequency with which they change dictate the pace of any program. (You might pause here and review the discussion of program elements in Chapter 6.) In a drama especially, the frequency of element change—that is, the pace—also contributes a great deal to the mood of the program. Audiences expect a police drama, for example, to move at a rapid pace (even though in real life police officers report that they seldom encounter the types of situations or act with the urgency suggested by these dramas). On the other hand, even though soap operas have picked up the pace of their action in recent years, the public perception of these programs is still that they move more slowly than life. Long program elements and even longer scenes are the primary cause of that perception.*

## Climax

The climax is the resolution of the plot and normally the final scene in a theatrical play. In a television play, however, the conclusion of the drama and the conclusion of the program are not the same. If they were, where would the sponsor put those final commercials? And don't forget the closing credits—and the trailer for next week's episode!

The common convention used to accommodate closing program elements is to include an *epilogue*. Final commercials come immediately following the climax, while audience attention is still high. The writer tries to hold the audience by providing one final scene after the commercials. In dramatic theory, the scene or action that follows the climax is the *denouement*, the untying of the knot the complications have formed. It restores order and provides an ending that seems necessary and probable.

For the television drama, this epilogue will be a scene in which the detective explains how he figured out who the murderer was, or in which the major characters express their relief at the outcome of the action. If the epilogues for a series are well written, the audience will hang around just to see what the author has thought up this time. Good epilogues, however, are a real challenge for the writer, and are not done well on many programs. The

---

* Recall, from Chapter 6 also, that a program element is not necessarily the same as a scene. Several characters may move in and out of a single scene. Each time a major character enters or leaves, and causes the audience members' attention to be drawn again to the screen, a new element is begun—within that scene. Neither are program elements and camera shots synonymous. The camera may view a scene, and a program element within the scene, from a number of different angles, all of which help direct the audience's understanding of the action, but do not contribute sufficient attention-getting force to be classified as new elements.

epilogue, if one is present, is then followed by the program closing—a trailer that previews the next episode, credits, and the production company logo.

One other aspect of climax to be considered in any dramatic program that contains commercials is providing secondary climaxes at those breaks to carry audiences through to the next act. The writer should provide high-interest material immediately preceding each break—an unresolved bit of conflict between characters, a misunderstanding, or an explanation left incomplete—something to keep the audience interested.

### Strong Start

The structural requirement of a strong start has been brought up in a number of places previously. You must interest viewers as quickly as possible, because they don't have to stay tuned, and if you don't get their attention, they won't. For this reason, many dramatic programs use a *cold opening*, beginning with the opening scene of the play before any titles, credits, or commercials.

But whether the drama opens cold and is followed by the program opening, or the program opening precedes the drama, the drama itself must still capture audience interest in its opening scene. It does that by establishing the premise quickly, by introducing major characters and quickly arousing our curiosity about them and their problem, and by setting the mood of the drama, whether that be comedy or menace.

## Settings

The dramatic actions that form the plot must take place somewhere—in a setting of some sort. In a well-constructed drama, each location is chosen to further, or at least support, the action or mood. In preparing the treatment for your script, choose your locations carefully and describe them accurately. If you leave the decisions to the program's director or set director, the choices may not reflect accurately the locations you had in mind.

The setting should be appropriate to the action and dialogue that take place there, whether it be a restaurant, an apartment, a car, or in the bleachers at a ballpark. Logically two characters at the ballpark might discuss the game, or baseball in general. They might also talk about a third friend who couldn't come to the game with them. They might discuss other things of mutual interest that could as easily take place in other settings. But the ball game has brought them together; it provided the catalyst for any number of changes in the conversation.

On the other hand, it would be less likely that two characters would choose a ballpark in which to get together to plan a bank robbery. They could too easily be overheard.

Sometimes, however, a twist in the setting for a piece of plot action will do just that—use an incongruous location. A "bad guy" who is being trailed by the police goes to the ballpark to meet his accomplices, using the crowd as a means of protection and deception. It's difficult to present "rules" about dramatic development, for a creative writer can add to the strength of a plot and heighten tension by occasionally doing precisely the opposite of what would be expected.

We've already noted that program type tends to dictate the number and type of sets. A police drama will have a much different feel if it uses many action scenes—car chases and other activity on the streets—than if it is confined to sets inside a station house. Cost is also a factor. The police drama that requires location shooting is obviously expensive to produce. A situation comedy confined to only a few sets in a single studio costs much less. Look at well-known situation comedies, and note that *Cheers*, for example, takes place mostly in the bar, with usually only one secondary setting.

Most television programs use fully realistic settings, either on location or in a studio. If the setting is the livingroom of a house, all the details of an appropriately decorated livingroom will be there. A good deal of information about the characters, the plot, and the mood of the drama can be transmitted to the audience by the composition, lighting, and color used in the setting. This information will be subconsciously processed by the viewers, quite apart from and before any action or dialogue takes place.

A few programs use *suggestive* settings. In a suggestive setting, a livingroom might be indicated by a table containing a bouquet, a couple of chairs, and a lamp—set in limbo with no walls, doors, or windows to be seen. The decision to use a suggestive set may be dictated by cost, or by time (too little to prepare a realistic set), or by other considerations. Be careful, however. That decision should also consider the audience for whom the drama is targeted. An audience that is not familiar with the use of suggestive settings may not be comfortable viewing a play staged in that manner and may tune away.

## Plot

The difference between a plot and a story, according to novelist E. M. Forster, is that a story is

> a narrative of events arranged in their time sequence. A plot is also a narrative of events, the emphasis falling on causality.
>
> "The king died and then the queen died" is a story. "The king died and then the queen died of grief" is a plot.
>
> Or again, "The queen died, no one knew why until it was discovered that it was through grief at the death of the king." This is a plot with a mystery in it, a form capable of high development.[6]

Constructing the scenes and actions that are the plot of a play is one of the most difficult tasks for most beginning writers. As you become more experienced, you will find your own best technique for developing sequences, and will intuitively recognize patterns of development that work. But until you reach that point, we suggest you use this series of steps to develop the plot.

First, write the treatment of your *climax*. After all, it was the climactic idea, the outcome, that prompted your script from the very beginning, and that idea should have been stated as part of the concept. Now develop it into a full scene. The climax usually will be the next-to-last scene in the teleplay. For structural reasons, the final scene is usually an *epilogue*, separated from the climax by the closing commercials. Don't worry about that scene yet.

The climax is the scene in which the uncertainty developed in the play is finally resolved. It is the culmination of the plot. If your basic story idea was sound and its expansion into the concept was faithful to that original idea, then the climactic action is already determined. Either the cavalry will arrive and rescue the hero and heroine from the Indians, or it won't. The pursuing suitor will get the girl, or he won't. The money will arrive in time to avert bankruptcy, or it won't. And so on.

Next, move to the other end of the story—the opening scene. This scene, of necessity, will introduce characters and place them in some sort of physical location, or setting. It begins what is called by drama theorists the process of *exposition*. It should also establish the dramatic problem that ultimately will have to be resolved by introducing the first *complication*.

One common technique used in drama since the ancient Greeks is to open "in the middle of things." An event is already in progress in which the major characters, or at least some of them, are involved. Establish quickly why this particular point in time, this location, and this action have meaning for these people.

Remember that one of the critical differences between television and radio drama, as opposed to the theater or movies, is that the audience can easily tune away from an uninteresting play. The opening scene must attract attention, so there is likely to be more action and less dialogue and character development in the opening scene of a teleplay than in a staged production or film.

Now, develop the remaining scenes that will connect the opening to the climax, and build the tension and uncertainty over the outcome. Again using the terminology of dramatic theory, there will be further *complications*, forces introduced into the play that will affect the course of the action. These complications will lead to *crises*, clashes of interest that build in intensity toward the final crisis, the *climax*. Complications also result in *reversals*, in which the protagonist is embarked on a course of action that seems to lead to a solution, only to have a sudden change of direction lead instead to possible disaster.

The number of scenes you need will depend on the overall length of the play, but again recall that structurally there will need to be frequent changes to maintain audience attention. Seldom should a scene exceed 3 minutes in length, and on the average should not exceed 1½ minutes. Here the teleplay is much different from the theater, where scenes can be many times that length.

Most plots are presented in linear, chronological order. However, that does not mean the plot must proceed in "real time," as the Greeks believed. Modern audiences are perfectly willing to accept time lapses, even very long ones—years, or even generations—between scenes or acts. Whatever the time lapse between scenes, however, each scene is presumed to take place after the preceding one and somehow to be the result of the actions in that preceding scene.

There are exceptions. *Flashbacks* to an earlier time are a legitimate plotting technique, often used to explain the motivation for a character's behavior. They need to be clearly identified to the audience, however.

One important aspect of plotting is the concept of *foreshadowing*, described by one author this way: "A startling idea must not be sprung upon an audience wholly unprepared to accept it." A further description of foreshadowing is this now classic line: "If you are going to sink the ship in the last act, you must first let the audience know that the vessel is leaky, and then later inform them that a storm is approaching."

Foreshadowing applies not only to the actions of the plot, but equally to the motivations of the characters. Characters must behave in a consistent fashion. If the outcome of the plot is dependent upon a change in behavior on the part of a major character, that change must be forewarned.

Two other aspects of plotting that we earlier mentioned in discussing structural variety are the *intercutting* between independent plots and the use of subplots. Intercutting between plots helps maintain audience attention. Frequently in soap operas a climax in a plot is followed by a commercial break. After the break a second plot begins. This is purely an editing technique; in *The Love Boat*, for example, not only were three plots being developed in parallel fashion, but each script was written by a different author.

Subplots are also important if, as we have noted, time permits. A complex main plot may need the full program time for development and drive out any secondary development, but even sitcoms often use subplots. Writer Gary Provost describes the relationship between sitcom plots and subplots this way:

> If you watch TV situation comedies, you will see that each show always has an A and a B story, which you can look at as plot and subplot. When the scripts are well written, there will be a connection between the stories. In the A story, maybe Golden Girl #1 is trying to get rid of a persistent suitor. This is usually played with humor and a certain amount of poignance. In the B story, usually played only with humor, maybe Golden Girl #2 is being tormented by telemarketers, and she develops elaborate fibs to explain why she can't buy aluminum siding, subscribe to magazines, or donate to the Esophagitis foundation. Two stories, but both deal with the ways in

which we reject people or, perhaps more specifically, the lies we tell to avoid hurting other people's feelings.

So a subplot is not chosen at random. It has some connection to the main plot. That connection might be in the form of a repetition, a contrast or a parallel plot—it could manifest itself as a continuing dream that a character has, a persistent memory, a romance, a major ambition, a pressing project. The subplot could be anything as long as it somehow resonates with the main plot or, to change the imagery, sheds some new light on the main plot.[7]

## Characters

The plot of a television drama can be moved along from opening scene to climax only through the actions, reactions and interactions of characters. Contrast this method of development with many works in print that are primarily descriptive or narrative, forms of exposition that are not generally effective on television because they do not provide opportunities for change and for the refocusing of audience attention.

We've examined a number of books by fiction writers, both broadcast and print, who describe their writing techniques. There seems to be a very pronounced difference of opinion on how best to develop characters and to relate them to plot. The differences carry over, also, to the writing of dialogue, which we consider later. Some authors argue that

the characters are not preconceived. They evolve as the plot evolves, out of the main incidents of the story. They grow and change in accordance with the demands of the plot. At the same time, however, the characters affect and change the plot. . . . There is a constant interaction between the development of the characters and the development of the plot.[8]

Other playwrights counsel the beginning writer to develop each major character thoroughly at the treatment stage:

Know your principal characters as you know yourself. Study your characters as if you were a psychologist—and good writers are, by nature, fairly good psychologists. Know their occupations, motivations, habits, fears, joys, prejudices, vices, how they walk and dress and talk.[9]

This approach is often used by authors who write novels. They will develop elaborate biographies for their characters, describing in detail physical attributes and family history, as well as the characteristics mentioned above. Using this approach of giving your characters a past that suggests their lives will help the beginning writer to make characters seem more lifelike, avoiding the wooden, one-dimensional characters found in poorly written scripts. It will also make it easier for you to provide consistency in the behavior of characters as they evolve during the play.

In television, characters are revealed to the audience through a combination of appearance, behavior, and speech. Appearance includes physical characteristics, clothing, and other physical objects with which a character is associated, such as the car the person drives. Behavior includes the patterns or habits the character displays, and the body language. Speech—including vocabulary and dialect—will be considered in more detail in the final phase of script development, when we talk about dialogue. However, you should remember that what a character does *not* say can be just as revealing as what he or she does say.

A frustration for many playwrights and a topic of considerable criticism is the limited amount of time available in most television dramas for the development of interesting and rounded characters. Successful characters will be those about whom the audience really cares, those the author makes believable. Yet the time constraints of the medium and the necessity to get the program off to a strong start in order to hold audience attention work against detailed character development.

If the program is part of a series, especially a long, ongoing series such as soap operas, *M\*A\*S\*H* or *Murder, She Wrote*, then there is opportunity for incremental character development. The audience builds its affinity for, or antagonism toward, a character over time. Hawkeye Pierce and Jessica Fletcher are fully developed individual characters, but that complexity did not become evident in the first episode of the series. Fortunately for those programs, the characters were sufficiently interesting from the start to attract audiences. Many programs that fail after just a few episodes do so because the characters held no interest for audiences.

Try to avoid the use of stereotypes in establishing character. For secondary characters who appear only briefly, or for other situations in which only limited character development is possible, it is an easy out to resort to recognizable "standard" character types—the absent-minded professor, the jock, the blonde bimbo, and so on. These cliché characters have been so overused that they no longer hold the attention of audiences, if they ever did.

Even more important, don't perpetuate demeaning racial and sexual stereotypes—the female office worker who always has a dominant male boss, the black or Latin domestic servant. Give each character a unique identity even if that identity must be briefly sketched. It takes a bit more work, but it's worth it.

All these suggestions regarding character are part of this critical rule:

Audiences must *identify* with the characters, they must *worry* about what's happening to them, they must *love* and *hate* the characters, they must be *entertained* by them. . . .

Your audience must take sides in the conflict raging between your characters. The audience must be partisan. Their sympathies must be roused and sustained. Detachment on a spectator's part must be avoided at all costs. A disinterested audience is an uninterested audience.[10]

A character can be developed only in part through the writer's script. After the part has been written into the script, the casting director will choose a performer to play the role. That choice further defines the character. Then, to a major extent, the character will be brought to life by that performer. Nevertheless, the more accurately the writer describes the character, and the more precisely the written dialogue fits the character, then the more precisely will the portrayal match the intent of the writer's script.

Finally, and we mentioned this once before, the number of characters in the drama should be limited. Television is an intimate medium, most effective presenting small-scale situations involving only a few characters. Of course, over time—as, for example, over many episodes of a continuing series—the total number of different characters can be increased.

## A Script Development Checklist

At this point your treatment ought to be complete. Many authors believe that at this point the hardest task has been accomplished. The characters and their motivations, the basic actions and settings, the sequence of events, and the structural form are all in place. Before we leave the treatment, however, let's review some of the considerations of its development, using these questions:

1. Is each character an individual, not a stereotype, and has sufficient development been given to each character for the audience to recognize that individuality?

2. Is there proper and adequate motivation for the actions?

3. Is there adequate foreshadowing? Has the audience been forewarned that things may turn out as they do?

4. Do subsequent actions logically follow from previous actions?

5. Do the behaviors and attitudes of characters remain consistent throughout? If there is change, is there explanation of and motivation for the change?

6. Does each scene contribute to the action and move the plot forward toward its climax?

7. Is the setting of every scene adequately described? Is it appropriate to the action? Better yet, does it contribute positively to the pace and the mood of the drama?

8. Does the structure of the drama meet the demands of the program format, and does it support the audience's expectations of unity, variety, pace, strong start and climax?

Although your play will be well developed at this stage, it is still a treatment. There will still be time to fix details if it is discovered later that they won't work. Be patient in putting together the final script. As one producer put it: "There's nothing worse than having the *structure* of this 'house' (story) we're building creak and crumble as we take up residence." You should try to make your treatment as polished as you can, but don't worry about every detail at this point.

# FINAL SCRIPT

Three more steps need to be taken to complete your script. Some aspects of *visualization* should be detailed, beyond the description of settings as provided in the treatment. *Dialogue*, the actual spoken lines of the characters, has to be written. And the final draft should be typed in an appropriate form.

## Visualization

In the script treatment you will have described the various settings in which the action takes place. Now, in the completed script, those descriptions are made specific, as scene headings and directions.

*Scene headings* may be of two categories: (1) master scenes, which are general descriptions; (2) shots, within the master scene, which give more specific detail such as angles, inserts, point of view, and similar. Normally you will write what is called a master-scene script, one that uses only master-scene headings; specific camera shots will be added in a later version known as the shooting script. Occasionally you will want to include specific shots when a precise angle or point of view is important to the story, but most often these details are left to the discretion of the program's director and added in that later version.

A scene heading usually includes

- Indication of interior or exterior location—INT. or EXT.

- Time of day (often just DAY or NIGHT is enough, but be more specific if need be).

- Camera angle and/or distance, if necessary in a master-scene version; required in a shooting script.

- What the camera sees. Remember what the camera sees is what the audience sees.

Here are a few of the scene headings used in "Silk Stalkings," a portion of which was reproduced as Figure 5.9.

```
40   EXT. ROXANNE DOCKWEILER'S HOUSE-DAY
43   INT. ELECTRONICS COMPANY-DAY
48   ANGLE-RITA
```

Scene headings are followed by *directions*. Directions, also called the "business" of a scene, and often flagged within the script as BIZ, expand upon the treatment and explain in detail the action of the scene. They are also used to describe the behavior of characters, their idiosyncracies and so on. If a character is supposed to show nervousness in a scene, for example, you might write a direction to tap a pencil on the desk or nervously and continuously flick the ash from a cigarette. Again, from "Silk Stalkings":

```
40   EXT. ROXANNE DOCKWEILER'S HOUSE-DAY

     The use of the word "house" is an affectation. What
     this is is a concrete fortress designed in the twen-
     ties by Senator Dockweiler. There are enough European
     doodads stolen from the great castles of Europe to
     qualify this house as an historical monument. Three
     acres and a mega-yacht go with the package. Peter
     drives up the open drive in a police black and white,
     stops and gets out . . . walks up to the front door,
     rings the bell which SOUNDS like the noon tolling of
     Big Ben. After a beat, the door opens and a very old,
     very starched English butler is standing there. His
     name is FREDERICK.
```

Since this is the establishing shot for a new location, a complete description is needed, but as noted in Chapter 5, Stephen Cannell sometimes puts more "description" in the description than the production crew really needs. You might at this point want to review the descriptions and uses of various shots, discussed in Chapter 8.

```
43   INT. ELECTRONICS COMPANY-DAY

     A man with his back to Rita is going through the
     files. He turns with a slip of paper in his hand,
     moves to Rita. He is a German merchant named KLAUS
     REINAGER.
```

This scene opens in the middle of the action. The reason for Rita's presence in this location has been forewarned, and only a brief scene is needed

to supply information. The action described is followed by dialogue, and then
a brief bit of final description as Rita leaves.

```
48    ANGLE—RITA

      She goes to the note and looks at it without touching
      it. It reads:
```

Scenes 44 through 50 are quick scenes, mostly single camera shots, without dialogue. They move the plot forward simply through action—Rita's discovery of Butch Lonigan's corpse. That discovery provides the necessary
climax as we come to the end of Act 2 of this four-act play.


## Dialogue

Without doubt, the most difficult aspect of fiction writing for either television
or radio is constructing dialogue. It is difficult to teach, difficult to learn and
even difficult to describe. Yet dialogue is the single most important way that
audiences learn to understand characters. In television, performers can be
identified by physical means—dress and behavior—but the character, the
role, is given depth and emotion and made into someone the audience cares
about primarily through dialogue.

We suggest you begin by reviewing two earlier chapters, those on aural
style (Chapter 3) and on sound (Chapter 7), especially the section on voice
as a component of sound in Chapter 7.

Two other suggestions are frequently made to beginning writers to prepare them for constructing dialogue. The first stems from the earlier advice
to create a complete biography and environment for each of your characters:

> The more you know the character in your play, the easier it is for
> the character to help *write his own dialogue.* . . . See him in your
> mind's eye as he appears in the drama. Know what he looks like, how
> he moves, what he thinks. Imagine the sound of the character's voice,
> the timber, the inflection. Now put him into a dramatic situation and
> *let him talk. Aloud. Through you.*[11]

Second, listen carefully to the voices of people in all types of conversations, and use what you hear as the pattern for your dialogue. If you have
trouble remembering what you hear, you may want to use a tape recorder
to capture vocal styles for future study, if it can be used without disrupting
or changing the normal progress of conversation.

But be careful. Script dialogue should *seem* to sound like actual conversation, but in fact actual conversation rambles a lot and is wasteful of time.
The dialogue for your radio or television drama must move along more rapidly—to keep the listeners interested and to move the plot forward.

You can make constructed dialogue seem natural, however, by using the limited vocabulary most of us use in everyday speech and using the vocabulary expected from the type of character you have created. You should also make frequent use of sentence fragments, pauses, and interruptions, as these, too, are common in normal conversations. Here, excerpted from author and teacher Richard Blum's *Television Writing: From Concept to Contract*, is a checklist of the most common problems in writing dialogue for television:

*1. Too Head-On.* This is dialogue that is much too literal and embarrassingly obvious. It sounds very contrived. For example:

```
MARIAN comes in the door and STEVE smiles.

                STEVE
        Marian, I'm so glad to see
        you. I love you so much.
        I've been waiting to see you
        for so long.
```

That kind of dialogue is pretty embarrassing. No subtlety at all. It would be more effective if he were too overtaken to speak. Or, he might grab her close and say nothing. Then, after a *Beat*, he might say:

```
                STEVE
        Y'know, I can't stand to
        see you.
```

And they hug.

*2. Too Choppy.* This is dialogue that is staccato. Filled with one liners. . . .

```
                MARSHALL
        I'm hungry.

                SANDY
        Me too.

                MARSHALL
        Let's go out to eat.

                SANDY
        O.K.

                MARSHALL
        Is the deli o.k.?

                SANDY
        Yes, it's o.k.
```

One solution to the problem is providing credible motivaton for dialogue. The characters need a motivation and intention for speaking. They need a pre-established pattern of thought and behavior. Marshall, for example, might be checking out the refrigerator through an earlier piece of action, then:

<pre>
                    MARSHALL
          Hey, there's nothing in the
          fridge. Wanna go out for a
          bite?

                    SANDY
          Mm. I'm famished.

                    MARSHALL
          How does the deli sound?

                    SANDY
          Like chicken soup in heaven.
</pre>

And they get ready to go.

*3. Too Repetitious.* Dialogue becomes repetitious when a character repeats himself or herself in a number of different ways. The character offers redundant information, or repetitive phrases:

<pre>
                    RONNIE
          I had such a good time on the
          trip. It was one of the best
          trips I ever had.

                    ARNIE
          I'm glad you enjoyed the trip.

                    RONNIE
          It was so good to be away. It
          was a terrific trip.
</pre>

If the problem of repetition is examined, it might stem from one or two problems: the writer doesn't know what the character should say next, so relies on earlier dialogue; the writer is afraid the audience won't "get" a specific point unless the character emphasizes it in dialogue. One solution to redundancy in dialogue is to go back into the script and clearly motivate each speech—or delete the speech altogether. This is how the dialogue above might be handled in revision:

```
                    ARNIE
         You must have had some time.
         I never saw you so excited
         about anything.

                    RONNIE
         It was fantastic. I'm just
         sorry it's over.
```

*4. Too Long.* Dialogue that is too long reads like an editorial speech or a philosophical diatribe. It creates static action in the script and often includes related problems of redundancy and preachiness. Let's examine this speech:

```
                    RITA
                  (to Anne)
         They fired you because you're
         a woman, not for any other reason.
         If you were a man you would have
         been promoted. Don't let them do
         that to you. Go back and fight for
         what you believe in. They wouldn't
         get away with that on me, I can
         assure you that. I remember when
         I was growing up, my mother always
         told me to look out for bigots
         like that. You've got to stand up
         and let them know you're not going
         to take that kind of treatment.
```

The speech tends to dominate visual action and incorporates too many different thoughts, without essential breaks for transitions or reactions. It would be helpful to intersperse reactions and stage directions at the end of each major unit of thought. That makes the speech seem less formidable, and its impact more immediate. Here's what it might look like:

```
                    RITA
                  (to Anne)
         They fired you because you're
         a woman, not for any other reason.
         If you were a man you would have
         been promoted.
```

Anne tries not to pay attention. She's in no mood for Rita's harangue.

> RITA (cont'g)
> Don't let them do that to you.
> Go back and fight for what you
> believe in.

Anne says nothing. Rita sees she's getting nowhere,
crosses over to her friend and speaks softly but
urgently.

> RITA (cont'g)
> I was always warned to look out
> for bigots like that. You've got
> to stand up and let them know you're
> not going to take that kind of treat-
> ment.

A BEAT, then Anne turns to look at her friend. The
conviction is sinking in.

The idea is to integrate reactions and dialogue in a long pattern of
speech, and to trim the "excesses" wherever possible. Long
speeches are not always a problem. It might be possible, for example,
that Rita blurts out her dialogue in anger and frustration. That reaction might be dramatically imperative and germane to the character's state-of-being. If so, the speech can stand on its own merits.

*5. Too Similar.* Sometimes characters sound the same; their dialogue
patterns are indistinguishable from each other. Once that happens
the character individuality has been lost. Can you distinguish between these two characters:

> MARILYN
> Hey, did you see the race?

> EDDIE
> Yeah, I saw the race. They
> were fast, weren't they?

> MARILYN
> Yeah, they were fast. Did
> ya win?

> EDDIE
> Nah, not when I needed it.

The characters sound precisely the same, and they're redundant on
top of it. One way to counter the problem is to provide some psychological richness to the scene. The characters need to be re-
examined in terms of motivations, intentions, and sense of urgency.

Psychological dimensions might provide a greater dimensional canvas for the creation of dialogue. Since Marilyn and Eddie are two different human beings, their inner thoughts and attitudes might be expressed in totally different dialogue structure. Here's how the scene might play:

>                    MARILYN
>                 (tentatively)
>             You saw the race?

Eddie shrugs off the question.

>                     EDDIE
>             Sure. They were fast, Ran
>             neck and neck--

>                    MARILYN
>                 (interrupting)
>             Never mind that. Did you
>             win? Eddie?

No response. Then:

>                     EDDIE
>             Not this time. Not when I
>             needed it.

When creating dialogue remember that your characters are unique human beings, with ability to interact at the highest levels of subtlety and complexity. One producer told me he covers the names of characters during the first pass at a script, to see if they're drawn dimensionally. If he can't distinguish between the blocks of dialogue, he discards the script as "characterless."

6. *Too Stilted.* This is dialogue that sounds as if it came from a history book, a poem, a newspaper, a grammar text, but not from a person. This is an example of stilted dialogue:

>                     ALLEN
>             It is my responsibility to
>             provide you with my interpre-
>             tation of the event. You are
>             the only person that might
>             accept that perspective. You
>             must hear me out.

Unless Allen has a particularly pedantic problem it would be more effective for him to colloquialize and get to the bottom line quickly:

                          ALLEN
                 You gotta listen to me!

And that says it all. . . .

*7. Too Preachy.* This is a problem related to being "head on," "redundant," "too long," and "too stilted." The character tends to
sound very formal, and espouses thematic ideas or philosophical
notions. He or she becomes an ideological mouthpiece for the writer
rather than a dimensional being. This speech, for example, borders
on the preachy side:

                          MARK
                 Do you see what happens when
                 criminals run free? They belong
                 in jail or they threaten the
                 very fibre of society. This sort
                 of thing would never happen if
                 we had stronger lawmakers and
                 laws.

If a character must speak with strong convictions, it doesn't have
to sound like an editorial. Mark can get the same point across by
growling:

                          MARK
                 The creep belongs in a cage for
                 everyone's protection. I don't
                 care <u>what</u> the law says.

*8. Too Introspective.* This problem deals specifically with the character who is alone, and speaks out loud. This cliché is typical:

                          JUDY
                     (to herself)
                 Oh, how I long to be with
                 him now.

That's enough to make any writer cringe. How often does a person
actually talk to himself or herself? Not very. And when we do, it's not
in complete, logical sentences. . . .

*9. Too Inconsistent.* This means a character is saying something that
doesn't "fit" the personality already created. The dialogue is incongruous with character. In some cases, that inconsistency is due to

lack of proper transitions in the scene. This is an example of erratic
dialogue or attitudes that change too quickly to be believed.

```
                    DEBBIE
          I wish you would both listen
          to me.

                    HOWIE
          No! David and I have better
          things to do.

                    DEBBIE
          I'm telling you this for your
          own good--

                    HOWIE
          O.k., we'll do it.
```

The thought transitions are simply too quick to be credible. It might
work better if the proper actions and reactions are built into the
scene through suggested transitions. This is one way of handling that
problem:

```
                    DEBBIE
          I wish you would both listen
          to me.

                    HOWIE
          No!
```

He glances up at his sister, and sees the hurt in her
eyes. Then, softer, he tries to explain.

```
                    HOWIE (cont'g)
          David and I have important things
          to do...
```

That obviously has no impact. She tries to control the
urgency in her voice.

```
                    DEBBIE
          I'm telling you this for your
          own good--
```

A long BEAT, then Howie turns away, heading toward the
couch. He mulls it over. Finally:

```
                    HOWIE
          O.k., we'll do it.
```

Debbie breathes a sigh of relief.

Sometimes the problem of inconsistent dialogue can be helped by analyzing the character's inner drives and attitudes on a moment-to-moment basis in the scene. The solution might simply lie in the need for more transitional time; or there might be a need for more thorough character development in the script.

*10. Too Unbelievable.* This is a catch-all category that implies a character doesn't sound real—for any number of reasons. A writer can test the credibility of dialogue by speaking it aloud, seeing if it rings true. It should sound like a real person responding to the immediate circumstances we've just seen. If there is a problem, try this exercise: put the same characters into a different conflict situation. That kind of written exercise provides a direct conflict of wills, with totally opposing intentions. The two characters might thrash out the conflict in two or three pages. One may give in, one may walk out, both may compromise; the outcome is strictly up to you. However, the dialogue and reactions must integrate, the motivations and behavior must be logical and consistent. Once you know how the individual characters interact, the integrity of the character is assured. The original dialogue can be tested against your heightened insight into motivations, intentions, and attitudes.[12]

## Format

After you have written and checked the dialogue for naturalness and consistency with the character, then the lines are inserted in the script as shown in the excerpt from "Silk Stalkings" in Chapter 5. Fiction scripts are typed into a very precise layout form. All the elements of a dramatic script—scene headings, directions, dialogue and other production instructions—are placed in specific alignments, as members of a production crew expect to find the items they are responsible for in a specific position on the pages. In Chapter 5 we gave you a simplified set of instructions for setting up this form, but if you plan to write drama for television, you should get, read and keep for reference detailed instructions. The references cited there are repeated in the Further Reading section.

Here are the opening scenes of "Gamblers," which we saw earlier in its treatment stage. Compare that narrative with this master-scene script.

GAMBLERS

Prologue

FADE IN:

1  EXTERIOR. SACRAMENTO AMTRAK RAILROAD STATION, DAY                          1

A passenger train pulls into the station. A crowd of travellers
are waiting on the platform as the train comes to a stop. Crowd
and train noises.

2  SAME, BUT IN FRONT OF STATION                                             2

A car pulls up in front of the depot and quickly a couple jump
out. They are Brad and Nancy Millar. Another woman, the driver,
also gets out and helps the couple with their bags. This is Jil
Raymond, their best friend. Brad Millar is in a mood of high
expectation but Nancy, by contrast, is quieter and in a mood
which, to Jil, appears to reflect the strain of the Millars'
marriage. It is not working well.

                          JIL
                     (cheerfully)
          Good luck, you two. Wish I was going too.

                     (motherly aside to Nancy)
          Give it a chance, honey, this should do both
          of you some good.

                         NANCY
                     (sarcastically)
          Well, for one of us anyway.

She looks over to Brad who is closing the trunk.

                          JIL
                   (hugging them both)
          Hurry or you'll miss the train.

                     (getting back into her car.)
          Win big in Reno. Bye.

Nancy and Brad wave thank-yous to their friend as she drives off.
Quickly they go into the depot.

3  INTERIOR OF TRAIN DEPOT                                                   3

A crowd of travellers hurry here and there in the busy depot. We
hear the announcement: "All passengers Eastbound to Colfax,
Truckee and Reno, now boarding at Gate 5." Brad looks at his watch
as they stop in the middle of the depot.

                         BRAD
          We still have a few minutes. Here...
                   (hands her a checkbook)
          You get the tickets. I have to make a phone call.

                                              (CONTINUED)

3 CONTINUED:

NANCY
(protesting)
The train is about to leave!

BRAD
I won't be a minute.

He goes off and leaves her to buy the tickets. She heads for the ticket counter.

4  AT A PHONE BOOTH IN THE DEPOT                        4

Brad puts in a coin, dials and waits a moment.

5  Nancy is seen buying tickets. When she's finished she gathers up    5
her bag and purse and starts to walk toward the waiting area. She looks up to see someone familiar—someone she expected to see. He is a big, muscular, slimy man who gives her a half smile and a nod. He is well dressed and gestures to his breast, giving something under his coat a careful pat. She returns his half smile and nod, then turns away. We hear the announcement: "Passengers Eastbound...last call." She anxiously looks through the crowd for Brad.

6  AT THE PHONE BOOTH                              6

Brad is finishing up his conversation.

BRAD
If I come up with the money by Monday we
won't have to go bankrupt.... I know that,
but it's my only chance.... What other options
do I have?.... Yeah, and if I can win, maybe I
can buy myself back into this marriage, too.

He looks across the depot to see Nancy impatiently waiting.

The train is about to leave... Bye.

He hangs up the phone, picks up his bag and hurriedly walks over to his wife. They quickly go out to the train.

7  EXTERIOR, AT THE TRAIN PLATFORM                    7

Brad and Nancy are the last to board the train, which carries a sign: "RENO GAMBLER'S EXPRESS." The brakeman makes a signal and the train pulls out of the station.

FADE OUT.

*Source:* Courtesy of the writer, Dennis Rasmussen.

# RADIO DRAMA

It's difficult to find complete dramatic programs on radio these days. A few commercial stations still replay old series, but just about the only new material is on public radio. Some stations affiliated with National Public Radio air *NPR Playhouse*, a series that highlights programs originated by various member stations. Dramatic material appears in other formats, however. Several companies market short comedy vignettes for use as inserts in station formats, and, of course, even though they are brief, dramatic sketches are used as parts of many radio commercials.

## Plot

Full-length radio dramas have essentially the same constraints as those for television. The time frame—30 minutes, an hour, or whatever—limits the number of complications that can be developed. But in contrast to TV, the number of scenes, and the number of characters involved, can easily be increased. It costs very little more to add scenes and locations, just a few words in the dialogue and perhaps a sound effect. New characters are also added easily. The actors already in the studio can change their voices to create a line or two for an added character.

But be careful. Just because location changes and new characters are easy to create, that doesn't mean you should create them. Don't add without purpose; that just adds clutter and reduces the audience's understanding of the plot development. But scenes you might leave out of a TV drama because they would be too costly to set up and shoot for just a few seconds on-screen may be added in radio.

## Characters

In Chapter 7 we spent some time discussing vocal techniques used to develop radio characters. It goes without saying that the only ways to give a radio character a personality, and to differentiate one character from another, are through words, dialect, inflection, and pauses and hesitations in vocal delivery. Listen to people's speech patterns and copy those patterns you want when writing radio characters.

## Settings

The beginning writer preparing a dramatic program for radio sometimes overlooks the fact that the requirement to have a setting for each scene applies to this medium just as much as it does for TV. One of the strengths of radio drama, however, is that the script dialogue and effects need only provide a brief sketch of a locale. Details will be provided for each member of the audience by his or her own imagination.

## Structure

The structural requirements for radio drama are no different from those for television. Audience responses to both forms are the same. If you succeed in attracting attention with a strong opening; provide unity, variety, and a sense of pace throughout; and build to climaxes before commercial breaks and at the end, you should be able to hold an audience throughout.

## Dialogue

Radio dialogue differs from television dialogue in one important way: Television dialogue should not describe what is obvious to the audience visually; radio must use dialogue (or narration, which is often a weaker alternative) to accomplish this.

Here are two brief bits of dialogue used to set up the problem in a problem-solution commercial. In the first example, a few key words and phrases provide all the description of both location and characters that is needed. The target audience, which is the same group as the characters in the dialogue, will be able to supply mental images from their own experience to fill in details from this description:

```
MARY:      Steve, when are we going to get some decent furniture in this
           apartment? I'm ashamed to invite friends over because all we
           have are these old broken, hand-me-downs from your parents.
STEVE:     I'm sorry, honey, but we both know it's hard to afford new
           furniture when you're newly married. Just as soon as I get a
           raise at work....(FADE)
```

In addition to the topic of the conversation, furniture, the keys are *apartment*, which sets location, and *parents* and *newly married*, which establish the age and relationship of the characters. In contrast, this dialogue was another student's attempt to set up the same situation:

```
MARY:      Steve, we need new furniture.
STEVE:     Why, what's wrong with what we have?
MARY:      Well, the sofa and the chairs don't match; the lamp shades are
           filthy; and the mattress on the bed is all lumpy....
```

Any dialogue will give the listeners some information, but this one isn't very helpful. The location could be anywhere from a small apartment to a mansion; the characters could be newly married to elderly; and the furniture might be broken hand-me-downs, or expensive items just slightly used by a very fussy couple. Even the relationship between Mary and Steve is not clear.

One additional way in which radio dialogue differs from television is in the frequent use of names. Since characters cannot be seen, the audience needs to be reminded frequently which characters are present, and who is speaking to whom. Don't use names in every bit of dialogue, but do use them more frequently than you would in normal conversation, or for TV.

## Format

The correct format for general radio production, including drama, was given in Chapter 5. Review those guidelines and examples in preparation for writing dramatic radio scripts.

# CONCLUSION

If it is your ambition to be rich and famous as a television writer, you will probably have to make your success as a dramatic writer. The odds are not in your favor, however. Only a fraction of the ideas, concepts, treatments, and scripts written with the hope of being sold are in fact accepted. Even fewer are actually produced and broadcast. Cynics would argue that an even smaller fraction of what is broadcast is worth airing, and that the number of worthwhile dramas which appear on television is indeed few. The countering argument is that network television audiences are so large that even an occasional worthwhile production will be seen by millions more than will the best and longest-running theatrical productions.

Although the chances of being successful as a dramatic writer for television are slim, the rewards are substantial for those who do succeed in getting an original series onto a network, or who get a contract to write a serial drama, a miniseries, or an original play.

If you are to succeed you should study drama—its history, its theory, and all its forms. Attend the theater, study films, watch television, and if you can find it, listen to radio drama as well. Watch people; make note of interesting characters you may want to use later in your plays. Become a careful observer of the actions of individuals, and of their interactions with others. Catalogue interesting places that would strengthen the action in a drama. Carry a recorder, or take notes when you think of an idea.

And write. It is possible, sometimes, to get a job writing commercials or PSAs without any significant prior experience. And it is even possible to land a position as a newswriter without specific broadcast writing experience, by relying on expert knowledge of a topic area or by having had experience in print journalism. But we have never known of a successful dramatic writer who did not put in considerable time and effort practicing on every opportunity that came along—commercials, corporate scripts, comedy vignettes, whatever.

You might become another Henry Slesar. In the early 1970s, he was the head writer for not just one, but two successful television serial dramas, *The Edge of Night* and *Somerset*. He originated 10 new half-hour shows a week, 520 programs a year, and he had a gross annual income estimated at $350,000, out of which he paid an agent, subwriters, a secretary "and a murderous tax bill."

Before he became "the writer with the largest audience in America," he wrote 4 novels, had 700-odd short stories published, wrote screenplays, and contributed articles to *Playboy*. "One of his greatest thrills was discovering at age 8 he could mesmerize the kids on the block with his ghost stories. When he first began selling science-fiction and mystery stories, it was 'like tasting blood—unimaginable that people would pay for doing what I so enjoyed.' "[13]

**Exercises**

1. a. Do a structural analysis of a TV dramatic program following the instructions in Exercises 1 and 2, Chapter 6.

   b. Then, comment on the other aspects of dramatic construction by answering the questions in the script development checklist in this chapter.

2. Write a concept statement for one of the following:

   a. A daytime TV soap opera.

   b. A situation comedy that features a supernatural gimmick.

   c. A one-time special historical drama featuring an important person in the history of your community.

3. Using a favorite short story as your plot, rewrite enough of it to get the first two (at least) scenes for a radio drama. Consider especially these matters:

   a. How will you introduce the story, and its characters, and set the first scene?

   b. What characterizations are the performers to give to the roles they play? What dialects, if any, or other vocal techniques should they use?

   c. How is the transition from scene 1 to scene 2 accomplished? How is the second location (and/or time) distinguished for the listener? What transition device is used?

**Notes**

1. Richard A. Blum, *Television Writing: From Concept to Contract*, rev. ed. (Boston: Focal Press, 1984), p. 78. Reprinted by permission of the publisher and the author.
2. Paddy Chayefsky, *Television Plays* (New York: Simon & Schuster, 1955), pp. 173–174. Copyright © 1955 by Paddy Chayefsky, renewed © 1983 by Susan Chayefsky. Reprinted by permission of Susan Chayefsky.
3. Stephen E. Whitfield and Gene Roddenberry, *The Making of Star Trek* (New York: Ballantine Books, 1968), pp. 22–30. Reprinted by permission.
4. Courtesy of the writer, Dennis Rasmussen.
5. Alfred Brenner, *The TV Scriptwriter's Handbook* (Cincinnati: Writer's Digest Books, 1989), pp. 80, 81.
6. Ibid., pp. 59–60.
7. Gary Provost, "Plot Partners," *Writer's Digest*, October 1992, pp. 24–25. Reprinted by permission of the author.
8. Brenner, *The TV Scriptwriter's Handbook*, p. 72.
9. Constance Nash and Virginia Oakley, *The Television Writer's Handbook* (New York: Barnes and Noble Books, 1978), p. 7.
10. Coles Trapnell, *Teleplay: An Introduction to Television Writing* (San Francisco: Chandler, 1966), p. 23.
11. Michelle Cousin, *Writing a Television Play* (Boston: The Writer, Inc., 1975), p. 79.
12. Excerpted from Blum, *Television Writing: From Concept to Contract*, rev. ed., pp. 102–111. Reprinted by permission of the publisher and the author.
13. Albert J. Zuckerman, "The Writer with the Largest Audience in America," *TV Guide*, December 11, 1971, pp. 16–19.

**Further Reading**

Although it may seem surprising for a field in which there are limited professional opportunities, there are a great many books that deal with aspects of fiction writing for film and television. Many inexperienced writers want to try selling their script ideas, and so there is a market for books they think will help them accomplish that goal. Check the ads in *Writer's Digest* magazine or a catalog for a mail order house such as Script City to see some of the variety available. We've selected a representative group, all of which we think are useful. Note that some of these titles are phrased to suggest they cover all writing for television; they are, however, limited to fiction writing.

Armer, Alan A. *Writing the Screenplay: TV and Film*. Belmont, CA: Wadsworth, 1988.

Berman, Robert A. *Fade In: The Screenwriting Process*. Stoneham, MA: Focal, 1988.

Blum, Richard A. *Television Writing: From Concept to Contract*, 2nd ed. Stoneham, MA: Focal, 1984. A new, expanded edition tentatively titled *Television and Screen Writing*, 3rd ed., will be published by Butterworth-Focal Press in 1994.

Dancyger, Ken, and Jeff Rush. *Alternative Scriptwriting: Writing Beyond the Rules*. Stoneham, MA: Focal, 1991.

DiMaggio, Madeline. *Writing for Television*. Englewood Cliffs, NJ: Prentice-Hall, 1990.

Mehring, Margaret. *The Screenplay: A Blend of Film Form and Content*. Stoneham, MA: Focal, 1989.

Paice, Eric. *The Way to Write for Television*. London: Elm Tree, 1987.

Perret, Gene. *Comedy Writing Step by Step: How to Write and Sell Your Sense of Humor*, 2nd ed. Hollywood, CA: Samuel French, 1990.

Perret, Gene. *Comedy Writing Workbook*. San Bernardino, CA: Borgo, 1990.

Phillips, William H. *Writing Short Scripts*. Syracuse, NY: Syracuse University Press, 1991.

Portnoy, Kenneth. *Screen Adaptation: A Scriptwriting Handbook*. Stoneham, MA: Focal, 1991.

Rouverol, Jean. *Writing for Daytime Drama*. Stoneham, MA: Focal, 1992.

Seger, Linda. *Creating Unforgettable Characters*. New York: Henry Holt, 1990.

Straczynski, Michael. *The Even More Complete Book of Scriptwriting*. Cincinnati, OH: Writer's Digest Books, 1992.

Swain, Dwight. *Creating Characters: How to Build Story People*. Cincinnati, OH: Writer's Digest Books, 1990.

Scripts from a wide range of television drama series can be purchased from several suppliers for study. You can get a catalog from Script City [8033 Sunset Blvd., Suite 1500, Hollywood, CA 90046; phone (213) 871-0707] or Hollywood Scripts [5514 Satsuma Ave., North Hollywood, CA 91601; phone (818) 980-3545]. In a library or used book store you might find these collections of classic plays from the early days of live television.

Chayefsky, Paddy. *Television Plays*. New York: Simon & Schuster, 1955.

Serling, Rod. *Patterns*. New York: Bantam Books, 1957.

Vidal, Gore (ed.). *Best Television Plays*. New York: Ballantine Books, 1956.

Frequently a book will be published that describes the development of a particularly popular TV series. We quoted from the description of *Star Trek*:

Whitfield, Stephen E., and Gene Roddenberry. *The Making of Star Trek*. New York: Ballantine, 1968.

Others include

Alley, Robert S., and Irby B. Brown. *Murphy Brown: Anatomy of a Sitcom*. New York: Delacorte, 1990.

Altman, Mark. *Twin Peaks: Behind-the-Scenes*. Las Vegas: Movie Pub. Services, 1991.

Gross, Edward. *The Wonder Years: Growing Up in the Sixties*. Las Vegas: Movie Pub. Services, 1990.

Thompson, Robert J. *Adventures on Prime Time: The Television Programs of Stephen J. Cannell*. Westport, CT: Praeger, 1990.

We promised to repeat the references from Chapter 5 on the layout of film scripts and teleplays. Those include this brief version from the Writers Guild of America:

Coopersmith, Jerome. *Professional Writer's Teleplay/Screnplay Format*, rev. ed. New York: Writers Guild of America, East, Inc., 1983. [Available directly from the Guild, 555 W. 57th Street, New York, NY 10019. Write or phone (212) 767-7800 for current prices and ordering information. Price is around $4.50.]

and these much more detailed versions, in two volumes:

Cole, Hillis R., Jr., and Judith H. Haag. *The Complete Guide to Standard Script Formats—Part I: The Screenplay*. North Hollywood, CA: CMC, 1989.

Haag, Judith H. *The Complete Guide to Standard Script Formats—Part II: Taped Formats for Television*. North Hollywood, CA: CMC, 1988.

The authors of these two volumes distinguish between "filmed" one-camera production (covered in volume 1) and "taped" multiple-camera production used in sitcom and variety show production (in volume 2). These books are not available through regular book outlets. Address inquiries to the publisher: CMC Publishing, 11642 Otsego Street, North Hollywood, CA 91601 or to Script City, 8033 Sunset Blvd., Suite 1500, Hollywood, CA 90046. Another reference is:

Lee, Robert, and Robert Misiorowski, *Script Models: A Handbook for the Media Writer.* Mamaroneck, NY: Hastings House, 1978.

Finally, for radio drama:

Ash, William. *The Way to Write: Radio Drama.* London: Elm Tree, 1985.

## PART 5

# Entering the Industry

I n general, instead of providing a specific chapter on entering the broadcast industry as a writer, we have preferred to make comments throughout this text. In the introductory chapters, we brought up the writer's place in the creative process, including the strong probability that writers work as part of a team and in a corporate environment. In Part 3 we emphasized the importance of understanding the part that sponsorship plays in programming and how that in turn affects creativity, including writing and production. Other chapters have considered other aspects of the preparation expected of you, if you are to enter and be successful in this field.

This final chapter adds one more group of questions you should address. If you decide to enter the profession, you will be faced with legal and ethical questions from time to time. As you read these comments, test your own feelings about the issues raised, and consider how comfortable you are in dealing with these questions.

# CHAPTER 17

# Legal and Ethical Considerations for the Broadcast Writer

**O**ur book thus far has been designed to sharpen your talents and provide you with the tools to enter the electronic media industries in some type of writing capacity. We would be remiss, however, if we did not include some discussion of legal and ethical questions. This brief chapter cannot substitute for the much more detailed examinations of these issues found in specialized texts and courses on media law and ethics and should not be thought of as a definitive review, but we pose questions regarding some of the topics that writers will most likely face.

When you finish this chapter, you will be able to

- understand, in broad terms, the protections of free speech and press provided by the First Amendment,

- recognize the importance of seeking competent legal advice when writing in sensitive areas, particularly content that may touch on obscenity or indecency, libel, commercial speech or copyright questions,

- consider and discuss ethical practices regarding news writing and judgments, advertising practices and entertainment programming, and

- recognize and use these important terms, concepts and issues:

| | |
|---|---|
| actual malice | Federal Trade Commission |
| advertorial, infomercial | First Amendment |
| commercial speech | invasion of privacy |
| conflict of interest | misappropriation |
| copyright | obscenity and indecency |
| defamation: libel, slander | program-length ad |
| the dilemma of objectivity | reasonable person test |
| fair use | violence on television |
| Fairness Doctrine | withholding information |

## THE FIRST AMENDMENT

Any discussion of legal concerns and constraints facing writers—for any medium—almost has to begin with an understanding of the all-important position of the U.S. Constitution. Under our form of government all governmental powers and all regulations which are imposed upon us must have a basis within the Constitution. The Constitution (as interpreted by the Supreme Court) grants only limited powers to the government. Especially important for writers is the First Amendment, which further spells out the protection of speech and of the press:

> Congress shall make no law respecting an establishment of religion, or prohibiting the free exercise thereof; or abridging the freedom of speech, or of the press; or the right of the people peaceably to assemble, and to petition the Government for a redress of grievances.

The key phrases for writers are obvious and their wording is simple and brief: *Congress shall make no law . . . abridging the freedom of speech, or of the press*. The interpretation of those phrases, however, has been the subject of many cases at law, and casebooks, and provides a good living for many communications lawyers.

Note, first, that the amendment places its restraint upon Congress (later, through the extension of the Fourteenth Amendment, that restraint was placed upon state and local governments as well). In practice we tend to interpret these phrases inaccurately. We think of the amendment as conferring freedoms upon speakers and writers, but it does not. It acts negatively in that it prevents various organizations of government from enacting laws that abridge speech and press. That inaccuracy often leads in practice to a misunderstanding of how the First Amendment operates to protect speech and the press.

Misunderstanding also happens when writers assume that all speech is protected by the First Amendment. Although the protections are broad, they are subject to interpretation, notably by the Supreme Court, and to the balancing of speech/press issues against other freedoms protected by other portions of the Constitution.

Ralph L. Holsinger, in his text, *Media Law*, summarizes the Supreme Court's application of First Amendment theory. In those parts of his summary which have particular importance to broadcast writers, Holsinger finds that the Court has

- Come very close to giving absolute protection to speech directed at influencing governmental policy. This includes peaceful action, such as picketing, demonstrating, and even burning the U.S. flag.

- Held that public officials and public figures cannot win a libel suit against the media unless they can offer clear and convincing proof they were victims of a false and defamatory assertion of fact.

- Extended First Amendment protection to truthful advertising for legal products or services. The government can regulate such advertising only if it can prove that regulation is necessary to further an overriding public interest and does not encroach on otherwise protected speech.

- Held that, because broadcasters must be licensed by the government in order to obtain access to the people's airwaves, they have a lesser degree of First Amendment freedom than do owners of print media.

- Held that there is no First Amendment protection for obscene materials, so-called fighting words, false and misleading advertising, advertising for illegal products or services, and language that directly incites illegal acts. However, the Court acts on the assumption that communications directed at the general public are protected by the First Amendment. If the government attempts to punish or suppress such communications, it carries the burden of proving that it has the authority to do so, that its interest in doing so is greater than the public's right to know, and that its proposed action will sweep no more broadly than necessary to protect its asserted interest.[1]

In the next section, we highlight a few of the areas in which a writer's freedom is subject to restraint.

# LEGAL RESTRAINTS

You should include for reference one or more textbooks on media law in your personal library. We've listed a few in the Further Reading section at the end of this chapter. Of course, if you are writing professionally on topics that may be sensitive, you should consult lawyers who specialize in communications law. Many larger firms—stations, networks, advertising agencies and others—have a communications attorney on staff or on retainer. Here are just a few of the areas in which freedom of expression is not absolute and in which broadcast writers should seek accurate, up-to-date legal advice.

## Obscenity and Indecency

Regulation of materials which may be obscene or indecent represents a confusing and complex territory. At first glance, the federal regulations on this point seem very clear. Broadcasting "obscene, indecent, or profane language" is specifically prohibited. But then comes the problem of definition. Obscenity, indecency, and the related terms profanity and pornography have been subject to different definitions over time, in different jurisdictions, and for different media. The restrictions placed on print media or motion pictures (or, for that matter, cable, which in this area is regulated much more like print) are quite different and looser than those imposed on broadcast TV and radio.

One of the key cases in this area is the Pacifica Foundation case (*Federal Communications Commission v. Pacifica Foundation*, 1978). Acting in response to a complaint from a listener, the FCC reprimanded the Pacifica station in New York, WBAI, for its broadcast of George Carlin's "seven dirty words" comedy monologue. In its review of the case, the Supreme Court ruled, first, that the monologue was not obscene but was indecent, thus upholding the FCC's reprimand. But in its opinion, the Court put considerable emphasis on the fact that the monologue had been aired during the daytime, when children were likely to be in the audience. By that emphasis, the Court seemed to suggest that indecent material might be broadcast at times when children are not likely to be listening or viewing. Such a position gives broadcasters and their audiences wider choices of content and provides a more "free speech" interpretation of the law. Responding to the Court's decision, the commission has at times supported a late-night "window" for indecent material. At other times it has changed its position and forbade such programming at any hour. Other federal courts have also entered the controversy, which remains unresolved.

In other cases the FCC has taken action against sexually explicit language in radio morning programs and against the broadcast of music containing sexual language. Although the issue remains in flux and the positions of the FCC and of the courts are subject to change, we can summarize the concerns this way. Broadcasters are unwilling to risk substantial fines and even possible loss of license by airing material that stands any chance of being found obscene. Most of them are equally unwilling to air indecent material, especially when children might be in the audience. Thus, with only few exceptions, by cautious self-regulation on the part of its licensees and the threat of FCC action in an area with ill-defined parameters, the broadcast media avoid these materials.

## Libel

The broad legal term in this area is defamation, and the legal concept is the protection of reputation. A related term is *slander*, referring to defamation from spoken commentary; broadcast defamation, however, generally falls under libel laws. A person who feels that his or her reputation has been damaged by a publication (including broadcast) may file a suit to recover damages from the perceived libel, which may be a news story, a documentary, or other item, even an advertisement, in which that person is named. Whether or not a court will find in the person's favor depends on a number of factors. (Sometimes threats to file libel actions are made in an attempt to intimidate the publisher and ward off the publication of a story that might be embarrassing to a prominent individual.)

The potential for a libel action arises in nearly any story in which an individual is named and some possibly negative statement is made about that person. Most often the individuals will be in the news because they hold a public position or are otherwise well known. As noted earlier, in order to win an award, these public officials and public figures (and those terms have been defined by libel case law) must offer convincing proof that they were victims of a false and defamatory assertion of fact in the published (broadcast) item. Note the use of *false* in the preceding sentence. Publication of the truth has long been held as sufficient defense against a libel action, but what about the inadvertent publication of inaccurate material? In the key case, *New York Times v. Sullivan*, 1964, the Court opinion stated:

> A rule compelling the critic of official conduct to guarantee the truth of all his factual assertions—and to do so on pain of libel judgments virtually unlimited in amount—leads to . . . "self-censorship."

Thus the Court, concerned that the media would not fully investigate and publish wrongdoing for fear of libel actions over minor inaccuracies, imposed an additional safeguard for the media. To obtain a libel award, a public official or public person must prove that

> the statement was made with "actual malice"—that is, with knowledge that it was false or with reckless disregard of whether it was false or not.[2]

Subsequent to *Sullivan* the courts have added other provisions, making it somewhat easier for plaintiffs to prove actual malice, but that concept remains the key defense to libel actions involving public officials and figures.

## Commercial Speech

The phrase *commercial speech* is the legal term used to describe advertising. Earlier we noted that the Court has extended First Amendment protection to truthful advertising for legal products, except when the government can demonstrate an overriding public interest in regulating. For broadcasters, the significant exception is that of cigarette advertising. Here is a legal (but regulated) product, the advertising for which is permitted in other media but not on radio and television stations. The regulators' argument is that public health concerns override any First Amendment protections the advertising might otherwise enjoy. Strangely, this particular restraint has never been directly tested in the Supreme Court, but restrictions on other advertising have been upheld when similar arguments have been presented.

Liquor advertising represents another area of concern. In general, advertising of hard liquor or other ads that may seem to promote the use of hard liquor are not aired. But this restriction is self-regulatory; broadcasters and the liquor industry have agreed on the ban, perhaps anticipating a prohibition that might be enacted should the two industries change their policies. On the other hand, "soft liquor"—beer and wine—are heavily advertised on radio and television. Advertising these products has been criticized, including their blatant use of sexual imagery and their possible promotion of unsafe drinking and driving practices. Both broadcasters and liquor companies are aware of the potential of restrictive regulation, and ad campaigns are carefully designed to preserve the very profitable advertising practice.

Deceptive or false or misleading advertising comes under the jurisdiction of the Federal Trade Commission (FTC). The role of this commission, and the funds available for it to carry out its mission of consumer protection (among others) have been subject to a good deal of partisan politics. Even in the best of circumstances the commission could not be expected to monitor and evaluate every advertising campaign, but it does a credible job of reviewing the claims of national advertisers. If you are writing commercials, you should recall the FTC's basic policy statement, known as the "reasonable person" test:

> The Commission will find an act or practice deceptive if there is a misrepresentation, omission, or other practice that misleads the consumer acting reasonably in the circumstances, to the consumer's detriment.[3]

You should also become familiar with other cases in which advertisers' claims have been found deceptive. One area, for example, in which the FTC has been active recently has been the labeling of food products—questioning the use of such words as *light* and *healthy* and claims of low fat and low cholesterol.

## Copyright

The Constitution (Article 1, Section 8) gives the power to Congress "to promote the progress of science and the useful arts, by securing for limited times to authors and inventors the exclusive right to their respective writings and discoveries." Implementation of this broad power currently rests in the Copyright Act of 1976, with later amendments. Broadcast writers should study the act and leading cases in which the courts have interpreted its provisions.

Briefly stated, the act gives the creators of written, musical and artistic works the opportunity to copyright that material and thus retain control over the subsequent use of that work by others, either to deny its use or to get some compensation for the use. Broadcasting stations, for example, pay substantial fees for permission to play copyrighted music on the air. The range of items that may be copyrighted is very broad, but there are limitations on some important categories. News cannot be copyrighted, nor the facts of history, nor events in an individual's life. But a station's newscast or a drama based on historical facts or a person's life may be copyrighted. A professional football game is not copyrighted, but the TV network broadcast of it is, and the network will bring legal action for compensation against persons who inappropriately use the accounts in that telecast.

Some exemptions exist; several criteria have evolved under the general heading of *fair use*, which allow limited use of copyrighted works without permission. In addition, stations and networks regularly exchange permission to use each others' accounts of events. If you find yourself writing and reporting for a news department, study carefully the provisions of fair use and know what agreements your station may have with other news-gathering organizations for the use of copyrighted accounts.

Become familiar, also, with the legal basis of a related topic known as *misappropriation*. Holsinger describes the concern this way:

> Every reporter borrows from the work of other reporters. Reporters working on newspapers in areas served by more than one paper are asked by their editors to follow up on stories clipped from competing publications. Reporters from broadcast stations find story ideas by reading the newspapers. A news feature may begin in one newspaper and then make its way, in altered form, through several others, and, perhaps, into the wire services, and end as a special on the evening television news. It's part of the game, and as long as a reporter doesn't take too much, too often, all is well. But . . . courts have penalized the systematic taking of news, even when it is not covered by copyright. . . . Courts call such a systematic taking of another's work "misappropriation." . . . Implicit in [their] decisions is the assumption that information is property. Thus the law of misappropriation is broader in scope than copyright law, which focuses on protection for the manner in which information is presented while offering little or no protection for the information itself.[4]

Of particular concern to broadcasters is the unauthorized use of video shot on location by news organizations for their own use and then transmitted back to the home station or network or distributed to affiliates using a satellite feed. Those pictures, of a hurricane's destruction or of a major sporting event, as examples, can be picked up from the satellite transmission by other stations, and if it's a major story, there is a tremendous temptation to use the pictures, even without an agreement for their use or compensation. Stations that have intercepted and used material this way argue that since they are news, the pictures are not and cannot be copyrighted, or if the transmission is copyrighted, they argue fair use. However, the legal counsel for the Radio-Television News Directors Association cautions against the practice, commenting in this instance especially on sports feeds:

Statutory authority for "fair use" of copyrighted material, including sports programming, is a point in its favor, especially where an extraordinarily newsworthy sporting event is involved. But there is case precedent declining to recognize "fair use" of ordinary sports highlights. Further, the conclusion that any given use is a "fair use" under copyright law is made chronically doubtful by the balancing test that courts use in case-by-case determinations.[5]

Until you have had considerable experience in this area, do not use more than incidental material or conceptual ideas from other sources without permission or before checking carefully with management and legal counsel.

## ETHICAL CONCERNS

As a professional writer you may be faced with ethical issues and decisions in nearly any task that you are assigned. You can be sure that some situations will call for such judgments. Some of these occasions will be directly related to your professional duties. Others may involve relationships with colleagues. Each situation will be unique in some way.

These are the situations in which one makes a moral judgment about what's the right course of action in a given set of circumstances. Although many ethical topics are similar to legal ones, these situations are not those for which one can be fined or sent to jail or for which stations might lose their licenses. (An employee might be fired or otherwise reprimanded by an employer, however, for a poor call on an ethical matter.) We cannot, nor would we wish to, supply you with fixed rules that would replace your own process of making ethical judgments. Even the various codes of ethical practice provided by major news organizations and associations provide only broad guidelines. Here we raise a few questions and encourage you to think about and discuss those questions with the help of texts, codes, and other materials that take up these considerations in more detail. We organize our discussion around the three main areas of broadcast programming: news, advertising and entertainment. Ethical questions arise in all three.

### Ethics and News

Questions that have at least some ethical component arise whenever new judgments are made. We've selected several commonly used headings under which many judgments may be categorized, but this list is far from exhaustive, and examples or cases may contain issues involving more than one category.

### Maintaining Objectivity

The very process of having to make daily, even hourly, news judgments leads, in one sense, to this form of ethical issue. There are rare, and fortunately only rare, instances in which management deliberately attempts to control or slant the presentation of news. But choices have to be made. Among all the stories in today's news, which ones will be aired and which will not? We listed some criteria for making those decisions in our chapter on news, but honest, ethical individuals can still differ in their applications of those criteria.

After the initial decision on whether or not a particular story should be aired at all, there are further choices. Which story will be placed in the lead position? Which stories in television will be assigned a camera and have visual support, and which will be read by the anchor without supporting video? Stories must be organized so the audience can follow and understand their content. To do that, the writer-reporter must select a perspective or, as we discussed the concept in several chapters, a point of view that will best provide that structure. Does the point of view distort or bias the story in some way? Finally, given the time constraints of telling any story, what facts within the story will be included and what left out? Consider this situation:

> A few weeks ago, NBC's *Today* show aired a program on shoddy products and their manufacturers, a program put together by a local affiliate in Chicago. But by the time the program went out over the NBC network, a significant change had been made—the name of one of the manufacturers, General Electric, had been deleted.
>
> General Electric owns NBC.
>
> It was not the first GE embarrassment as a news owner. Shortly after GE bought NBC in 1986, a corporate official said employees of NBC should start their own political action committee to influence congressional legislation in favor of company projects. His memo said failure to do so would raise questions about an employee's "dedication to the company." The new corporate leader had to be reminded that it might cost them ratings—and therefore millions of dollars—if NBC anchor Tom Brokaw were known to be a lobbyist for GE-favored candidates. News persons were exempted from lobbying for GE.
>
> Nevertheless, months later, when GE sold its familiar home appliance division to a foreign firm and thus lost the basis for decades of advertising of GE as a friendly home presence, this major American transaction was reported by ABC and CBS, but not by NBC.
>
> More and more major media companies around the world belong to large national and multinational corporations. Episodes like the

GE case raise the social specter of the heavy hand of the owning corporation reaching deep into the news process and producing self-serving propaganda instead of professional, reliable news.[6]

Granted that the producers of a broadcast have the right to select what goes in that broadcast, nevertheless we think ethical questions are raised, as did the author of this article, media critic Ben Bagdikian, when omissions are made such as those described. Among the questions to be raised are: Was the omission accidental or deliberate? Was it the result of conscious application of legitimate news criteria?

All these decisions affect the objectivity with which the story is finally presented—or at least the perception of objectivity as seen by the viewers of the newscast. Peter Sandman and his colleagues, in their text *Media: An Introductory Analysis of American Mass Communications*, called this problem the "dilemma of objectivity":

It can be argued that objectivity is a false god. All too often, objectivity means writing in such a way that the reader or viewer cannot tell where the reporter's sympathies lie. If the reporter does in fact have sympathies and those sympathies are in fact influencing the story, this simply makes the prejudice less obvious. Reporters who talk to representatives of both sides in a controversy, who quote and attribute every judgment they use, who start the story with who/what/where/when and only then go to why, are protecting themselves from criticism. The story may be no less misleading for all its objectivity, but it is safer. . . .

Suppose a reporter is somehow successful in keeping his or her values from influencing the story. Is this necessarily good? What is the value of having humane and concerned journalists if they hide their humanity and concern when they set out to cover the news? Was objectivity a good thing in the 1950s, when it forced the media to be "fair" to the incredibly unfair allegations of Senator Joseph McCarthy? Ultimately, why should a conservative reporter be "fair" to the scourge of Communism? Why should a radical reporter be "fair" to the capitalist Establishment?

On the other hand, the notion of objectivity does impose a useful discipline on journalists. Even if it is unattainable and sometimes a bit hypocritical, objectivity as a goal reminds reporters that they are paid to tell us about events, not about their own feelings; that they are obliged to talk to all sides in a dispute before writing their story; that they should resort to volatile language sparingly and only where it is justified. Objectivity is journalism's cautious response to its own power. In limiting the reporter's freedom to guide the audience, objectivity also limits the reporter's freedom to misguide the audience.[7]

Objectivity incorporates the concept of balance. What obligations do program producers have to provide balanced coverage? For many years the FCC enforced a regulation known as the Fairness Doctrine. This doctrine applied only to "controversial issues of public importance" and required stations, when they aired such issues, to provide balance among the two or more different opinions on the issue. (Contrary to common belief, it did not require "equal time" for the different sides, and the balance could be provided within a single broadcast or over a series of programs. Equal time is still a requirement for broadcasts by political candidates, although that rule has been weakened by the many exceptions to it now permitted.)

Under intense lobbying from broadcasters, who argued that the Fairness Doctrine imposed upon them restrictions of free speech that were not imposed on other media, the FCC has rescinded the rule. Broadcasters also argued that the wide variety of choices available to viewers and listeners would ensure that balance occurred within the marketplace, if not within individual programs or on individual stations. You may make your own evaluation as to the legitimacy of that argument in your own community.

### Seeking the Truth

Highly related to the consideration of objectivity is the commonly expressed journalistic goal of seeking and communicating the truth. But what is truth? Are truth and objectivity different terms for the same concept? And how, if at all, in any given situation can a reporter know that the story being presented is the truth?

Further considerations implied by these questions include a reporter's faith in the honesty of sources and in his or her own ability to observe events accurately and then condense those events into the limited number of words, or words and pictures, that can be presented in a brief span of time within the deadlines for their preparation.

### Deception

Deception is also highly related to objectivity and truth. In fact, it may be seen as simply a negative phrasing of seeking the truth. It is *not* telling the truth: distorting, lying, selectively editing video to prove a point of view, or staging a scene for video recording. This last example has become an all too frequent activity in the recent rash of "reality" TV programs. Sometimes the program's producers will specify that scenes are staged, "dramatized" or "re-created" to approximate the original event. They may have a narrator give that announcement at the beginning of the program, or they may include a graphic on the screen to that effect. But we've seen a number of instances in which that explanation is so fleeting that it is very easy for viewers to miss it, and in some cases there has been no announcement whatsoever that what is being seen is a fictional reconstruction. In the chapter on documentary writing we considered additional instances in which this issue can arise.

Another form of deception involves whether reporters are obligated to identify themselves:

> Doing so naturally puts people on their guard; often you'd get a better story without your press card. Nonetheless, it is generally accepted that sources have a right to know that they are talking to a reporter.
>
> But there are plenty of exceptions. A restaurant critic does not announce his or her identity before sitting down to eat. The temptation to the staff to provide special service and unusual dishes would be too great, and the journalistic goal would be defeated. Similarly, a consumer reporter would have a tough time making an accurate appraisal of an auto repair service if the mechanics knew a story was in the works. Most journalists accept this sort of deception because the reporter is simply doing what ordinary citizens do— eating in a restaurant or getting a car fixed and then evaluating the service received.[8]

Consider also the problem reporters face in presenting stories that may be only seconds in length. Broadcast news stories are usually brief and simple. When does a brief story become oversimplified to the point that viewers don't have enough information to understand or make judgments? That's an inadvertent deception but deception nonetheless. How much time will each story get in the newscast, and will that time be enough to tell the story accurately?

### Invasion of Privacy

When, in their attempts to get a story, do reporters invade the privacy of individuals? In answering this question and related ones, we need to make distinctions in the first place between those instances in which the inquiry into the behavior of individuals may or may not be legal and, second, if legal, in which the inquiry breaks ethical codes. Note, too, that journalists usually draw distinctions between situations involving "public" persons such as politicians or other well-known personalities and "ordinary" persons who are not normally in the media's spotlight but have been thrust there by the circumstances of a news event. Journalists in general are more willing to pursue their inquiries into the lives of public persons.

Although this area of journalistic behavior can encompass a wide range of situations, consider these two examples, the first dealing with public figures and the second with a family that except for tragic circumstances would not have been in the news.

In each presidential election, some questions of personal character are sure to arise. The media feel it is their obligation to provide voters with a detailed profile of each candidate, including the candidate's personal behavior. In the months prior to the 1988 election, for example, the front-running Democratic candidate for the presidency was Gary Hart. *The Miami Herald*, checking rumors that Hart was a womanizer, staked out Hart's apartment and then reported

> Hart had put himself in a compromising position with a woman friend ... thus legitimizing inquiries into the former U.S. senator's fitness for national office. Although Hart retaliated by accusing the *Herald* of untruthful and biased reporting, his popularity plummeted, and he soon withdrew from the Democratic race. The debate that followed concerning the *Herald's* news-gathering techniques and whether Hart's personal life was legitimate news was almost as intense as the controversy about the candidate himself.[9]

In the 1992 election, questions arose again, first about an alleged affair between Bill Clinton and an associate. Later in the campaign allegations surfaced that George Bush had also had an extramarital relationship. For whatever reasons these stories did not have as strong an impact on the campaign as 4 years earlier, but the ethical question remains: Where is the dividing line between legitimate news inquiry into the "character" of a public, especially elected, official and invasion of privacy?

The second example considers privacy in a different kind of story, one in which quite ordinary individuals are suddenly and unfeelingly thrust into a media spotlight. Consider these comments by Michael J. Arlen, longtime television critic for *The New Yorker* magazine. They are the opening paragraphs of his essay "The Interview."

> A few weeks ago, viewers of New York's WCBS regular Saturday-evening news broadcast were shown a fairly long film report of a fire in a Harlem tenement, which early that morning had killed a six-month-old Puerto Rican baby and had destroyed a good part of the building. It was a depressing and grief-stricken scene. The dead child's parents, who had been out at the time of the fire, were very young and very distraught. The child's baby sitter was also on hand: a frightened, tearstained, Puerto Rican girl of sixteen, who unfortunately had left the apartment for a few key minutes in order to buy some diapers for the baby. "This is a story of human lives and tragedy," intoned the WCBS reporter, Lucille Rich. A microphone was thrust at the young babysitter, who muttered wretchedly, "I went to take out the baby and I get to the kitchen, but I can't see nothing, so I can't take out the baby . . ." Then the baby's mother was produced, or, rather, discovered, sitting stunned in her sister's apartment in the same building. A microphone was thrust at the eighteen-year-old mother and she was asked, "Do you feel any animosity toward the young babysitter?" The young girl, barely in control of her feelings, stumbled through an awkward reply: "Well, I don't know, I don't know how to say it. I don't feel it right now. In a way, I don't know if . . ."

At the end, she simply said, "It doesn't matter, right?" Finally, Miss Rich went to interview the family that lived on the floor below, whose small apartment had also been ruined. "And now that you see all this mess, with your apartment ruined, how does that make you *feel*?" the reporter asked a woman in the family. "Bad," said the woman. Miss Rich then summed up the experience for the benefit of the audience: "In the midst of grief and pain, one looks for answers, but answers to the whys and ifs and onlys don't come easily. Maybe time is there to help heal the hurt . . . Lucille Rich, Channel 2 News."

When I called WCBS a few days later to ask for a transcript of what had seemed like an astonishingly jarring set of interviews, the news director expressed regret at the quality of media intrusion that had been visited upon those distraught people in the fire-torn tenement. "It should never have happened," he said, which seemed a decent attitude for a news director to take, even though one knows that should an airliner crash tomorrow near a Trappist monastery not even the brothers' celebrated vows of silence would protect them from the bombardment of inane and often unanswerable questions which is by now an accepted convention of television's crisis-oriented news coverage. Even so, it was not merely the issue of invasion of privacy which made me prick up my ears at the WCBS Harlem-fire story, for that is both a larger issue and one which is as deep and tangled as the country's psychology itself. Rather, it was the story as an *interview*; for this was an unusually bad series of interviews and it made me wonder, generally, about the role of interviewing on television.

To take an obvious example (which occurred twice in Miss Rich's questions): Why is it that, time after time, almost as if it were an inevitable—a magical—question, TV reporters at crucial moments must extend their microphones toward a subject and ask, "How do you feel?" Whether the interviewee is an astronaut returned from walking on the moon or a politician who has won or lost an election or someone in the middle of a personal tragedy, the question, or one of its equivalents, is so frequently asked by television reporters as to have become a commonplace. "Well, Luis, how does it feel?" a microphone-thruster asked the Red Sox pitcher after a recent World Series victory. Another reporter went further: "I bet victory can't feel much better than that now, can it?" Or "Tell me what you felt when you saw your new face," as a local-news reporter asked a patient in a story on plastic surgery.[10]

In the remainder of that essay Arlen argues that, although it is understood that TV interviewers in those kinds of situations are trying to capture a moment or show the feel of a situation, they more often both trivialize the situation and exhibit an unconscious hostility to the persons involved.

### Withholding Information

Of equal magnitude to the questions about accurately and ethically reporting stories are questions about when to withhold a story or information within a story. Journalists are regularly faced with situations in which sources do not wish to be identified. Also, they may be given information which provides "background" to an ongoing story but on the condition that this information remain confidential and not be used.

Journalists respect those confidences—usually—or they soon will lose their access to sources. In occasional, unusual situations reporters have broken promises of confidentiality. In other cases, even when pressured by courts in judicial proceedings, reporters have gone to jail rather than reveal the names of sources who have given them information under promise of confidentiality. (Some journalists refuse to accept information on "background" and thus avoid having to make decisions on each case as to whether they should honor requests for confidentiality.)

Perhaps, while following leads in a story, a reporter will uncover information that is pertinent to the story but that will be damaging to otherwise innocent persons. Perhaps the story comes from a usually reliable source but cannot otherwise be verified and, if reported, might also damage individuals. Where is the balance between good, responsible reporting and getting out the story in advance of the competition? Or between withholding information because it is not totally verified and possibly preventing a crime?

Reporting on matters involving national security, especially during wartime, brings special responsibilities. This topic was heatedly discussed when the Department of Defense placed severe restrictions on journalists during the Persian Gulf war. Then the question was finding a proper balance between the public's interest in details of the war and preventing the release of information that might endanger ongoing operations.

The reverse side of the issue of withholding information is that of releasing self-serving information under the guise of news. In Chapter 15 we discussed and printed the script of a video news release (VNR), a form of corporate advertising and public relations which has become quite popular. Of course, television news departments are not obligated to air VNRs sent to them, but the temptation to broadcast these slickly produced—and free— stories is very strong, especially in small markets where the stations have small and overworked staffs. What ethical questions are raised by airing these stories that promote the corporations that produce them?

### Loyalty

Our discussion in the previous section, about promises to sources, might also be considered under the heading of loyalty. Another form of loyalty often considered in ethics texts is loyalty to one's profession, in this context to journalism. It takes the form of maintaining high professional standards. Yet another would be loyalty to one's employer. In one of the best short compendiums of media ethics, *Media Ethics: Issues and Cases*, by Philip Patterson and Lee Wilkins, the authors frame that question this way:

> The late twentieth century has added one more complication. Most journalists work for a corporation. Most journalists believe they owe at least some loyalty to their corporate employers. However, such loyalty is tenuous because it seldom involves a face-to-face relationship. Modern corporations are often willing to demand employee loyalty but are much less willing to tell employees their loyalties or responsibilities. Yet it is this concept of mutually understood promises that is essential to corporate loyalty, where the fear is that allegiance to the organization will promote the interest of the organization over that of the individual or the community.
>
> Loyalty to a media corporation means that the organization's goals and needs should be subject to examination by the employee as well as the employer and that there can be worthy, less worthy, and unworthy organizational aims. Scrutiny of these aims can lead to civil disobedience (when the organization is a government) or whistleblowing in the private sector. Journalists use such motivations in getting a story, but they also should be willing to apply them to the organizations for which they work.[11]

### Conflicts of Interest

Another broadly ranging category of ethical issues is conflicts of interest. Should a financial reporter, who regularly interviews stockbrokers and managers of financial institutions and who thereby learns of pending deals prior to their becoming common knowledge, abstain from personal financial actions based on that knowledge?

How should a TV station handle a situation in which its news anchor is married to a political candidate?

Should a female television news anchor participate (on her own time) in a pro-life demonstration and, having done so, should she be fired by her station for conduct that (in the station's view) was damaging to the journalistic credibility of the station?

All three of these very abbreviated situations are based on real events. None is easy to call, but in the case of the financial reporter, the conflict of interest between reportorial duty and personal gain is pretty obvious. Most critics and managers would agree that a reporter who learns inside information should not profit from that knowledge. In that situation there is a legal as well as ethical question. The reporter would probably be prosecuted for misappropriation of information.

In the case of the anchor married to a candidate, the New York station involved was very careful not to give the anchor any campaign stories to report on. And the news anchor who demonstrated in front of the abortion clinic was dismissed. In that case, the station argued that its credibility could not be restored any other way and used provisions in its contract with the woman to terminate her employment. The larger issues raised by the conflict between her personal right to demonstrate on behalf of causes she believes in and the station's position were left unresolved.

The question involving General Electric and NBC, mentioned earlier as a problem in objectivity, also carries a question of conflict of interest.

## Ethics and Advertising

The majority of ethical dilemmas facing broadcast writers probably are related to the gathering and reporting of news, and so we have spent the major portion of this section in that area. Ethical issues also arise when dealing with advertising and with entertainment programming.

A few media critics take an extreme position regarding advertising. They argue that advertising is unethical simply because it attempts to change a person's attitude or behavior; they see any form of persuasion as being unethical. Given the fact that media are paid for largely through advertising, this position doesn't get much attention in the industry. But note that there is a slow but evident trend toward the consumers of media paying directly for their programming: premium cable channels, pay-per-view, sales and rentals of home videos, and so forth.

Advertising dollars that are available are being spread through an ever-enlarging range of media. The results? The sales managers at many stations (and the networks) are willing to accept and often actively promote advertising practices that earlier would not have been considered, and the dividing line between honest advocacy and deception becomes an increasingly difficult one to draw.

We've already mentioned the legal concerns; deceptive advertising is subject to penalties imposed by the Federal Trade Commission. But the line between advertising and program content is getting very fuzzy and deliberately so, as advertisers seek new ways to attract and hold audience attention. In previous chapters we've described the long-form commercial that goes by the names of *infomercial* or *program-length ad*. These programs-ads were for many years prohibited by FCC regulations on broadcast channels, although permitted on cable. Deregulation now permits these complete programs that look like news, documentary, talk, or interview programs, but that are in their entirety a pitch for "micro-diet," "Juicemaster," "wealth-without risk," or other kitchen products, real estate sales schemes, travel packages, and so on.

We've also considered the *video news release*. VNRs are, first, a form of promotion for the companies that produce and distribute them. Since the companies do not pay to have them placed on the air, they technically aren't advertising, but they have an effect much like that of advertising. Finally, they really aren't news, but as we have noted, they are slickly produced and add breadth and interest to a local station's newscast.

Another form is the *advertorial*, a coined word merging *advertisement* and *editorial* which describes an advertising message disguised to look like program content. (In this context *editorial* refers to all nonadvertising material in a publication or broadcast, not just the expressions of opinion by management, as we frequently use that term.) Advertorials are common in print media—special sections in magazines, for example, that look just like the publication's regular articles. But they have their manifestations in broadcast as well. We recently saw a series of 90-second vignettes in a local TV newscast running over several days that described innovative medical practices. At first glance these seemed to be legitimate news stories. They were produced in that fashion, but then we noticed that each vignette came from the same hospital, whose name was prominently displayed, and each featured a staff doctor at that hospital. When we checked with the station, we found that, yes, these were paid commercial inserts.

Any of these terms may be used to describe a paid ad that contains "informational content," as one salesperson cautiously described it. In some sense every ad contains information, but what she was unwilling to admit was that these ads go beyond just providing information. They are structured to look like news stories or other programs, and when they appear they are very difficult to recognize as commercials.

All these practices are legal, now that previous regulations have been removed. An ethical question of deception remains, however, when listeners and viewers cannot distinguish between the content of programs and the persuasion of advertisements.

Another problem area in the relationship between editorial content and advertising arises when advertisers use their financial clout to kill editorial content to which they object. The problem is often discussed with regard to the print media, where major advertisers in a magazine, for example, are able to kill articles that might be unfavorable to that company or industry. A parallel problem exists in broadcasting. In some situations advertisers cannot be found for programs that deal with controversial issues, or, on occasion, advertisers will pull out of sponsorship of a program when the content and approach become known. As with the magazine advertiser, they may do so because they feel the program will be unfavorable to them. Or, regardless of the specific content, they may feel that the program is too controversial and that any benefits of advertising will be outweighed by negative publicity. In earlier times, when television advertising was a seller's market, stations and networks could often find replacement advertisers willing to risk their ads on controversial programs. Now that's not so easy to do, and broadcasters are cautious about presenting programs with content that may alienate advertisers.

Finally, even within ads that obviously are ads, what are the legitimate limits, for example, of using sex appeal as an attention-getting device? When does the use of scantily clad women (or men) in a beer commercial step over the line and become sexual exploitation? Here, too, there are ethical questions.

## Ethics and Entertainment Programming

A quick glance at the daily listings for TV broadcast stations and cable channels is all that's needed to confirm that the bulk of programming time is devoted to satisfying the public's demand for entertainment. What ethical issues arise in this context? Here are just three of many possibilities: depictions of violence, especially the effects of violence on children; stereotyping; and the blending of entertainment and news. Each of these areas merits lengthy and detailed consideration, but here we can only sketch an outline of the issues.

### Violence

Many studies have attempted to analyze the relationship between violence as viewed on TV and violence in society, especially as TV violence may affect children's behavior. Most researchers now seem to agree that TV violence does have societal implications, although some broadcasters and regulators continue to deny or ignore that evidence or, at least, to deny any responsibility for violence in society.

In a striking bit of incongruity, we have heard network executives extol the values of television to advertisers—noting how persuasive well-written ad copy can be in manipulating consumer behavior. Then, in nearly the next breath, these same executives deny that their medium could possibly change social norms, particularly the society's drift toward violence.

Equally incongruous is the position taken by former FCC chairman Mark Fowler, as noted by Patterson and Wilkins:

> Former FCC commissioner Mark Fowler once stated that television was simply an appliance and had no more social responsibility than a toaster. However, Fowler appears to have been wrong in one important aspect: the maker of a toaster can be held responsible when the product it produces is defective—i.e., burned toast—while the same standard does not apply to "defective" television programming.
>
> Should the sender of a mass-mediated message have the same legal or moral responsibility to the consumers of the message as the manufacturer of a household appliance has to the users of its product? And if a media message is defective, causing harm to its listeners, readers, or viewers, can a resulting liability suit enable the consumer to recover damages, as would be the case if a defective appliance caused a house fire?[12]

What makes this problem particularly difficult is that violent programming contains strong gratifications for many audience groups. Programs containing violence receive high ratings. Is that fact simply the result of years of conditioning? Would a reduction in violent programming result over the long term in both lowering the attractiveness of those programs and reducing the level of violence in society? What network will take the lead and risk audience share by eliminating programs containing scenes of violence?

### Stereotyping

We've shared our concern of stereotyping in earlier chapters. Stereotyping is the result of the oversimplification of characters, and some of it is inevitable as writers compress reality into 30- or 60-minute programs. But well-written material need not perpetuate demeaning racial, sexual, age or other stereotypes. The controversy will continue as writers and producers seek the proper balance between the electronic media as conveyors of art and/or of reality.

**Figure 17.1.** Copyright 1982 Ziggy and Friends, Inc. Dist. by Universal Press Syndicate. Reprinted with permission. All rights reserved.

### Mixing Entertainment and News

We've also brought up before the issue of mixing entertainment and news. In one form it involves news producers and staff who are more concerned about the appearance of the news program, and the attractiveness of reporters and anchors, than they are with the accurate depiction of news stories. In another form it involves the many "reality" programs that are in fact fictional or contrived but that are structured to appear to be news or documentary. Audiences, especially those made up of younger people who do not have wide experience, are likely to be unable to distinguish between fiction and reality.

## CONCLUSION

By now, you must surely recognize that if you write for any medium, you will from time to time be faced with situations that call for legal and/or for ethical decisions. Unless you have also trained in communications law, get professional advice in the former situations. In the latter, you can and should when possible discuss the implications of your decisions, but ethical judgments are often personal decisions. We have only hinted at some of the issues. You will need to develop for yourself a method of analyzing situations and applying the principles you adopt.

The various ethical codes prepared by professional organizations in communications can be useful as guides, but they cannot serve as a replacement for your own principles. We have reproduced two brief codes for your reference: the "Code of Broadcast News Ethics" of the Radio-Television News Directors Association (Appendix A) and the "Statement of Principles of Radio and Television Broadcasting," issued by the board of directors of the National Association of Broadcasters (Appendix B). Other useful items are the "Code of Professional Standards" of the Public Relations Society of America, the "Code of Ethics" of the International Association of Business Communicators, and the "Code of Ethics" of the Society of Professional Journalists.

The television networks have their own codes guiding program production and selection and advertising, as do many individual stations, both radio and TV. Some years ago, in an attempt to provide some standards that might be accepted by the industry as a whole, the National Association of Broadcasters produced two codes of good practice (one for radio, the other for TV) that described, in broad terms, appropriate and inappropriate practices for both program content and advertisements. But these codes and the substantial body of specific application that developed from them were struck down by a federal judge as being a restraint of trade, even though they were voluntary. The present value of those codes is primarily historical.

Having used this discussion and other more complete sources to develop your own principles, you are then left with this final question: Can I work, with my principles, within the media system?

If you watch television news stories with the suspicion that more has been left out of the story than put in, or that the reporter is telling the story from a biased viewpoint, and if you can't overcome those feelings, then you'd better not plan on becoming a TV newswriter. Similarly, if you have serious misgivings about the role of advertising in society, if you feel that advertising creates false wants and hopes and fuels the American business enterprise at the expense of the consumer, and if you can't overcome those feelings, then you need to recognize now that you won't make a good commercial copywriter.

Some individuals do plan on careers in broadcasting precisely because they want to reform the media—to do the job better, and more honestly, than those who are now doing it. If you are in that category, we don't want to diminish your desire to make broadcasting better. But recognize, please, that reform is a very difficult and often lonely task and that most of the time your result will be frustration—not change. You stand a better chance of personal success as a writer if you don't choose to fight the system.

Fortunately, the hard questions don't come up very often, but when they do, each writer will have to decide where his or her values lie and whether they will be compromised in a particular situation. If you are to be a broadcast writer, recognize now that you will have to establish standards, and you will have to live with them throughout your career.

**Exercises**

The exercises suggested here do not bear directly on writing. They are aimed instead at the broader perspective of preparing for a career in the industry, and how you might fare in that activity.

1. Arrange an interview with a broadcast writer—someone whose job is like one of those described in Chapter 1. The focus of your interview should be to verify the assertions we have made about writing careers, or to modify those statements for your own time and place. Ask your interviewee:

   a. What other tasks are performed besides writing; how is a typical day divided among the various jobs to be performed?

   b. What types of research are performed; how important is research to the overall job?

   c. How much control does the writer have over the final product, be that program or announcement?

   d. What background—experience, college courses, etc.—does the interviewee have for the job? What other skills or knowledge does he or she think are important by way of preparation?

   e. What bothers him, or her, most about the job? What ethical problems
      have had to be faced, and with what results?

   Also ask about working conditions and about any problems with sexual
   or ethnic bias (if appropriate). Try to get a sense of how, in this interviewee's opinion at least, one should prepare to be a broadcast writer.

2. Investigate professional organizations in your community or nearby that
   deal with matters of interest to media writers. Among the national organizations which have chapters in many major cities are: International
   Association of Business Communicators (IABC), International Television
   Association (ITVA), Radio/Television News Directors Association
   (RTNDA), Sigma Delta Chi. There may also be local clubs which include
   advertising and public relations writers among their members. Most such
   clubs welcome students and sponsor activities that help student members to enter the profession. Specifically, you should:

   a. Establish a list of appropriate organizations.

   b. Arrange to attend a meeting of each club or invite a representative
      from each club to speak to your class.

   c. Consider joining the club, if its goals are compatible with your own
      and its members are supportive of the direction in which you wish to
      take your career.

3. Use the sections in this chapter on ethical questions, and additional readings, to organize a class discussion on one or possibly several related
   issues. The discussion might be organized as a formal debate between
   different class members taking different positions on the issue, or as an
   interview with a guest. Invite someone who writes for a station, agency,
   or network, or who, as a manager, must make frequent judgments—for
   example on the content of news stories (an assignment editor), or on the
   selection of program series to make up a station's schedule (a program
   director).

**Notes**

1. Condensed from Ralph L. Holsinger, *Media Law*, 2d ed. (New York: McGraw-Hill, 1991), pp. 32–33. Reprinted by permission of McGraw-Hill, Inc.
2. As cited in Holsinger, *Media Law*, 2d ed., p. 112.
3. Ibid., p. 520.
4. Ibid., pp. 585–586. Reprinted by permission of McGraw-Hill, Inc.
5. J. Laurent Scharff, RTNDA General Counsel, in *Legal Notes*, an occasional publi-cation for members of the Radio-Television News Directors Association, May 1992.
6. Ben H. Bagdikian, "Journalism's Sins of Omission," *Sacramento Bee*, January 24, 1990. Copyright 1990 by Ben H. Bagdikian.
7. Peter M. Sandman, David M. Rubin, and David B. Sachsman, *Media: An Introductory*

*Analysis of American Mass Communications*, 3d ed. (Englewood Cliffs, NJ: Prentice-Hall, 1982), pp. 83–84. © 1982. Reprinted by permission.

8. Ibid., p. 88. Reprinted by permission.

9. Louis A. Day, *Ethics in Media Communications: Cases and Controversies* (Belmont, CA: Wadsworth, 1991), p. 98.

10. Michael J. Arlen, *The View From Highway 1* (New York: Farrar, Straus and Giroux, 1976), pp. 37–39. Adapted from "The Interview" from *The View from Highway 1*, by Michael J. Arlen. Copyright 1974, 1975, 1976 by Michael J. Arlen. Originally appeared in *The New Yorker*. Reprinted by permission of Farrar, Straus and Giroux, Inc.

11. Philip Patterson and Lee Wilkins, *Media Ethics: Issues and Cases* (Dubuque, IA: Wm. C. Brown, 1991), p. 84.

12. Ibid., p. 203.

**Further Reading**

We've included titles under three categories: (1) those that deal with legal and regulatory issues, including both general texts in media law, and some that cover specific subheads; (2) those that discuss ethical problems and cases; and (3) some other useful readings that don't quite fit those headings.

For legal and regulatory background, consult

Bensman, Marvin. *Broadcast/Cable Regulation*. Lanham, MD: University Press of America, 1990.

Campbell, Douglas S. *The Supreme Court and the Mass Media: Selected Cases, Summaries, and Analyses*. Westport, CT: Praeger, 1990.

Carter, T. Barton, and others. *The First Amendment and the Fifth Estate*, 2d ed. Westbury, NY: Foundation Press, 1989.

Francois, William E. *Mass Media Law and Regulation*, 5th ed. Ames: Iowa State University Press, 1990.

Franklin, Marc A., and David A. Anderson. *Cases and Materials on Mass Media Law*. Westbury, NY: Foundation Press, 1990.

Holsinger, Ralph L. *Media Law*, 2d ed. New York: McGraw-Hill, 1991.

Lively, Donald E. *Modern Communications Law*. Westport, CT: Praeger, 1991.

Overbeck, Wayne, and Rick D. Pullen. *Major Principles of Media Law*. Ft. Worth, TX: Harcourt Brace Jovanovich (published in a new edition each year).

Pember, Don. *Mass Media Law*, 5th ed. Madison, WI: Brown and Benchmark, 1990.

Ray, William B. *FCC: The Ups and Downs of Radio-TV Regulation*. Ames: Iowa State University Press, 1990.

Watkins, John J. *Mass Media and Law*. Englewood Cliffs, NJ: Prentice-Hall, 1990.

Zelezny, John D. *Communications Law: Liberties, Restraints, and the Modern Media*. Belmont, CA: Wadsworth, 1993.

These books cover more specific legal topics.

Hopkins, W. Wat. *Actual Malice: Twenty-Five Years after Times v. Sullivan*. Westport, CT: Praeger, 1989.

Labunski, Richard. *Libel and the First Amendment: Legal History and Practice in Print and Broadcasting*. New Brunswick, NJ: Transaction, 1989.

Weil, Ben H., and Barbara Polansky (eds.). *Modern Copyright Fundamentals*. Medford, NJ: Learned Information, 1989.

Wright, R. George. *The Future of Free Speech Law.* Westport, CT: Quorum, 1990.

Since ethics is one of the major branches of philosophy, a logical place to begin any extended review would be with the original works of ethical philosophers. Texts for courses in ethics also provide extended and comparative discussions of the several systems of ethical reasoning that philosophers have developed to guide behavior. Consider these excellent overviews:

Bok, Sissela. *Lying: Moral Choice in Public and Private Life.* New York: Pantheon, 1978.
———. *Secrets: On the Ethics of Concealment and Revelation.* New York: Vintage, 1984.

More directly related to your immediate study are these titles, which apply ethical principles to media situations, including news writing and reporting.

Christians, Clifford G., Kim B. Rotzoll, and Mark Fackler. *Media Ethics: Cases and Moral Reasoning,* 3d ed. White Plains, NY: Longman, 1991.
Day, Louis A. *Ethics in Media Communications: Cases and Controversies.* Belmont, CA: Wadsworth, 1991.
Fink, Conrad C. *Media Ethics: In the Newsroom and Beyond.* New York: McGraw-Hill, 1988.
Goodwin, H. Eugene. *Groping for Ethics in Journalism,* 2d ed. Ames: Iowa State University Press, 1987.
Hausman, Carl. *Crisis of Conscience: Perspectives on Journalism Ethics.* New York: HarperCollins, 1991.
Hulting, John L. *The Messenger's Motives: Ethical Problems of the News Media,* 2d ed. Englewood Cliffs, NJ: Prentice-Hall, 1985.
Matelski, Marilyn J. *TV News Ethics.* Washington: RTNDA, 1991.
Olen, Jeffrey. *Ethics in Journalism.* Englewood Cliffs, NJ: Prentice-Hall, 1988.
Patterson, Philip, and Lee Wilkins. *Media Ethics: Issues & Cases.* Madison, WI: Brown and Benchmark, 1991.
Rivers, William L., and Cleve Mathews. *Ethics for the Media.* Englewood Cliffs, NJ: Prentice-Hall, 1988.
Swain, Bruce M. *Reporters' Ethics.* Ames: Iowa State University Press, 1978.

Some of the titles in this final group are now out of print. However, they all provide important and timeless insights into the issues that media professionals face.

Bagdikian, Ben. *The Media Monopoly,* 4th ed. Boston: Beacon, 1993.
The Commission on Freedom of the Press, *A Free and Responsible Press.* Chicago: University of Chicago Press, 1947.
Friendly, Fred W. *Due to Circumstances Beyond Our Control.* New York: Random House/ Vintage, 1967.
———. *The Good Guys, the Bad Buys, and the First Amendment: Free Speech vs. Fairness in Broadcasting.* New York: Random House, 1976.
Seibert, Fred S., Theodore Peterson, and Wilbur Schramm. *Four Theories of the Press.* Champaign: University of Illinois Press, 1956.

# Radio-Television News Directors Association
# Code of Broadcast News Ethics

The responsibility of radio and television journalists is to gather and report information of importance and interest to the public accurately, honestly and impartially.

The members of the Radio-Television News Directors Association accept these standards and will:

1. Strive to present the source or nature of broadcast news material in a way that is balanced, accurate and fair.

   a. They will evaluate information solely on its merits as news, rejecting sensationalism or misleading emphasis in any form.

   b. They will guard against using audio or video material in a way that deceives the audience.

   c. They will not mislead the public by presenting as spontaneous news any material which is staged or rehearsed.

   d. They will identify people by race, creed, nationality or prior status only when it is relevant.

   e. They will clearly label opinion and commentary.

   f. They will promptly acknowledge and correct errors.

2. Strive to conduct themselves in a manner that protects them from conflicts of interest, real or perceived. They will decline gifts or favors which would influence or appear to influence their judgments.

3. Respect the dignity, privacy and well-being of people with whom they deal.

4. Recognize the need to protect confidential sources. They will promise confidentiality only with the intention of keeping that promise.

5. Respect everyone's right to a fair trial.

6. Broadcast the private transmissions of other broadcasters only with permission.

7. Actively encourage observance of this Code by all journalists, whether members of the Radio-Television News Directors Association or not.

Reprinted by permission of the Radio-Television News Directors Association.

# Statement of Principles of Radio
# and Television Broadcasting Issued
# by the Board of Directors of NAB

## Preface

The following Statement of Principles of radio and television broadcasting is being adopted by the Board of Directors of the National Association of Broadcasters on behalf of the Association and the commercial radio and television stations it represents.

America's free over-the-air radio and television broadcasters have a long and proud tradition of universal, local broadcast service to the American people. These broadcasters, large and small, representing diverse localities and perspectives, have strived to present programming of the highest quality to their local communities pursuant to standards of excellence and responsibility. They have done so and continue to do so out of respect for their status as daily guests in the homes and lives of a majority of Americans and with a sense of pride in their profession, in their product and in their public service.

The Board issues this statement of principles to record and reflect what it believes to be the generally accepted standards of America's radio and television broadcasters. The Board feels that such a statement will be particularly useful at this time, given public concern about certain serious societal problems, notably violence and drug abuse.

The Board believes that broadcasters will continue to earn public trust and confidence by following the same principles that have served them well for so long. Many broadcasters now have written standards of their own. All have their own programming policies. NAB would hope that all broadcasters would set down in writing their general programming principles and policies, as the Board hereby sets down the following principles.

## Principles Concerning Program Content

### Responsibly Exercised Artistic Freedom

The challenge to the broadcaster often is to determine how suitably to present the complexities of human behavior without compromising or reducing the range of subject matter, artistic expression or dramatic presentation desired by the broadcaster and its audiences. For television and for radio, this requires exeptional awareness of considerations peculiar to each medium and of the composition and preferences of particular communities and audiences.

Each broadcaster should exercise responsible and careful judgment in the selection of material for broadcast. At the same time each broadcast licensee must be vigilant in exercising and defending its rights to program according to its own judgments and to the programming choices of its audiences. This often may include the presentation of sensitive or controversial material.

In selecting program subjects and themes of particular sensitivity, great care should be paid to treatment and presentation, so as to avoid presentations purely for the purpose of sensationalism or to appeal to prurient interests or morbid curiosity.

In scheduling programs of particular sensitivity, broadcasters should take account of the composition and the listening or viewing habits of their specific audiences. Scheduling generally should consider audience execations and composition in various time periods.

### Responsibility in Children's Programming

Programs designed primarily for children should take into account the range of interests and needs of children from informational material to a wide variety of entertainment material. Children's programs should attempt to contribute to the sound, balanced development of children and to help them achieve a sense of the world at large.

## Special Program Principles

### 1. Violence

Violence, physical or psychological, should only be portrayed in a responsible manner and should not be used exploitatively. Where consistent with the creative intent, programs involving violence should present the consequences of violence to its victims and perpetrators.

Presentation of the details of violence should avoid the excessive, the gratuitous and the instructional. The use of violence for its own sake and the detailed dwelling upon brutality or physical agony, by sight or by sound, should be avoided.

Particular care should be exercised where children are involved in the depiction of violent behavior.

### 2. Drugs and Substance Abuse

The use of illegal drugs or other substance abuse should not be encouraged or shown as socially desirable.

Portrayal of drug or substance abuse should be reasonably related to plot, theme or character development. Where consistent with the creative intent, the adverse consequences of drug or substance abuse should be depicted.

Glamorization of drug use and substance abuse should be avoided.

### 3. Sexually Oriented Material

In evaluating programming dealing with human sexuality, broadcasters should consider the composition and expectations of the audience likely to be viewing or listening to their stations and/or to a particular program, the context in which sensitive material is presented and its scheduling.

Creativity and diversity in programming that deals with human sexuality should be encouraged. Programming that purely panders to prurient or morbid interests should be avoided.

Where significant child audiences can be expected, particular care should be exercised when addressing sexual themes.

Obscenity is not constitutionally protected speech and is at all times unacceptable for broadcast.

All programming decisions should take into account current federal requirements limiting the broadcast of indecent matter.

### Endnote

This statement of principles is of necessity general and advisory rather than specific and restrictive. There will be no interpretation or enforcement of these principles by NAB or others. They are not intended to establish new criteria for programming decisions, but rather to reflect generally accepted practices of America's radio and television programmers. They similarly are not in any way intended to inhibit creativity in or programming of controversial, diverse or sensitive subjects.

Specific standards and their application and interpretation remain within the sole discretion of the individual television or radio licensee. Both NAB and the stations it represents respect and defend the individual broadcaster's First Amendment rights to select and present programming according to its individual assessment of the desires and expectations of its audiences and of the public interest.

July 9, 1990

# INDEX